August 18, 1997 Purchased by VERLE Williams at GRAbiL, In Antique MALL.

John E Peterson
Doris M. Peterson

August 18, 1997 Purchased by VERLE Williams at GRAbiL, In Antique MALL.

CARROLL COUNTY INDIANA RURAL ORGANIZATIONS

1828 - 1979

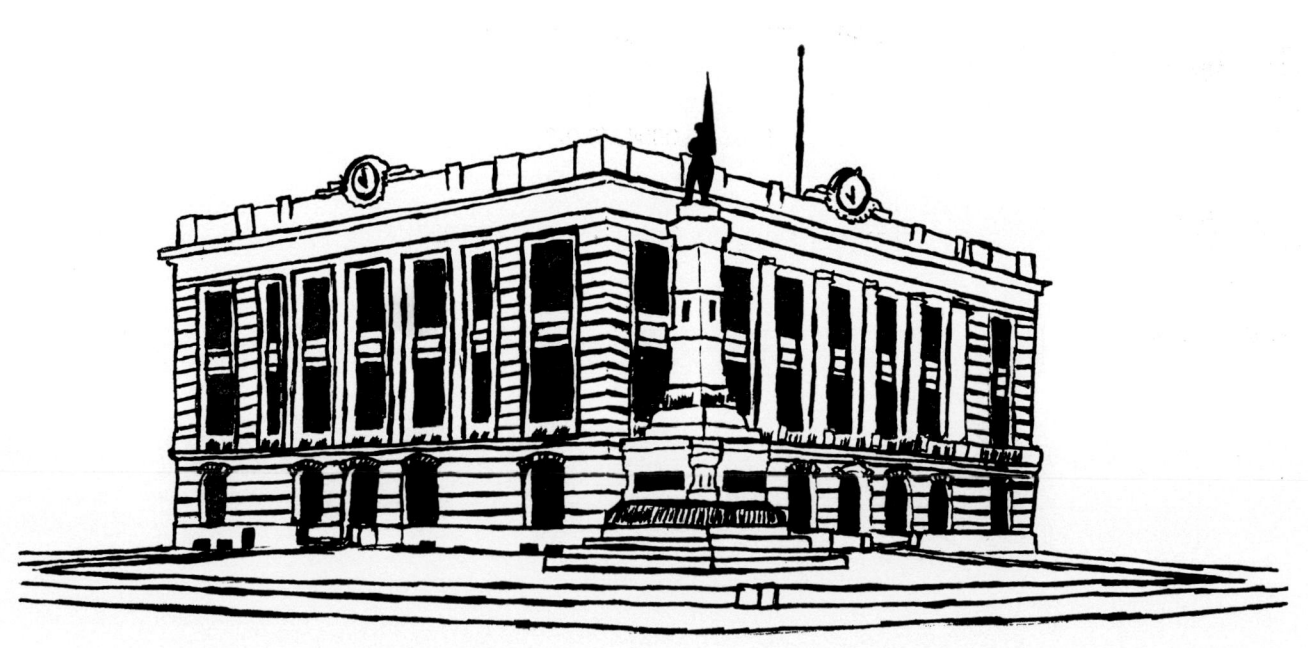

VOLUME I HISTORY

John C. and Doris M. Peterson

Copyright 1980 John C. and Doris M. Peterson

ISBN 0-9604376-0-6

Library of Congress Cat. Card No. 80-82231

Published By
John C. & Doris M. Peterson
R. 1, Box 25, Delphi, IN 46923

CONTENTS

Dedication iv

Preface v

Illustrations .... vi, vii

Acknowledgments .... viii, ix

Abbreviations x

Bibliography xi

Map of Carroll County xii

Chapter I   General Information *(INTERURBAN PAGE 10)* 1-34

Chapter II   The Early Years 35-62

Chapter III   Grange 63-70

Chapter IV   Extension Service 71-93

Chapter V   Extension Homemakers 94-110

Chapter VI   4-H and FFA 111-149

Chapter VII   Farm Bureau 150-199

Chapter VIII   Farm Bureau Cooperative Association 200-239

Chapter IX   Rural Youth 240-258

Chapter X   REMC 259-299

Chapter XI   Other Organizations and Events 300-348

Index of Names 349-379

General Index 380-389

iii

DEDICATION

This book is dedicated to the hundreds of people who have given unselfishly of their time and talent to help make Carroll County a better place in which to live. It is written for their grandchildren so that they may better understand and appreciate the many things that they take for granted.

PREFACE

If you want to find out how little you know about your community, try writing a book about it. As residents of this county and active members of several organizations during about one third of the time since the county was created, we were amazed to find so much information available about things that have happened during that time. Limited time has not permitted the collection of all available information and limited space has not permitted the recording of all the information that we found. Information about many worthwhile organizations has been omitted. We hope that this book does inspire others to record information while it is still available.

Much of the information on the early history of the county was taken from other histories of Carroll County including those written by Helm, Odell, Stewart, Stuart, Mayhill and others. These books are listed in the bibliography, and reprints of several are available at the Carroll County Historical Society Museum in the Courthouse. Other information was secured from newspapers available since 1850, magazines, books, minutes and other records of organizations, and from people who have been involved. Carroll County Farm News, printed from October 1941 to December 1978, was a most valuable source of information.

We have tried to limit this book to the story of rural organizations in Carroll County. Even in this field there has been so much activity that we have had to omit much important information. We have included more detail about some activities than would be justified by their importance. Two reasons for this are: These detailed reports are a representative sample of what happened in other situations, the second (and probably more important) reason was that the information was available.

We had planned to include biographical sketches of people in Carroll County who have been active in rural organizations. Time and space did not permit using the information in this book so we are planning a second volume for the biographical sketches.

In the early efforts to build local farm organizations, one of the most difficult jobs was to find local people who could conduct meetings and lead the new organization. In many cases that leadership was found among the people who had learned the technique in their church activities. There is no way to measure the value of the contribution which the churches have made in the growth and development of farm organizations. We have included very little information about churches, not because of the lack of importance, but because there is so much information available that it would be a subject for an entire book.

There are several cases in which two or more people have the same name and in other cases a person may be listed by two or more different names. Since, in many instances, we had no way of knowing the correct name, we listed them as we found them. In some instances changes have been made to correct minor grammatical or other errors in quotations from newspapers. Credit for some photographs is given. Others were taken by the authors or the photographer is unknown.

Because different chapters of the book were completed and given to the printer earlier than others, some portions of the book has more updated information than others.

Every article has been checked by people familiar with the subject, but there may still be errors. We would appreciate it if errors were reported to us so that corrections may be made for future use.

Many people are concerned about the centralization of power in government and in organizations. A study of history shows that the concentration of power in the hands of a few people leads to corruption and eventually to the downfall of a government or an organization.

It is our hope that this book will help encourage people to take a more active part in local government and local organizations so that both might continue to serve them for a longer period of time.

Doris M. Peterson

John C. Peterson

ILLUSTRATIONS AND PICTURES

Page

Page	Description
xii	Map of Carroll County Indiana 1979
5	Burnett's Creek Arch
6	Marker, Burnett's Creek Arch
6	Mentzer Tavern
8	Pittsburg in 1885
10	Interurban station, Delphi
13	Covered Bridge near Cutler 1950
14	First automobile in Delphi 1899
17	View looking south from the Courthouse in Delphi
18	Second Courthouse in Carroll County
18	Laying corner stone for Courthouse in Delphi 1916
19	Third Courthouse in Carroll County
19	Courthouse Bell
20	Carroll County Jail built in 1873
22	Reception for Esther Gregg 1958
22	Statue at Entrance to Camp Tecumseh
23	Log cabin being built at Camp Tecumseh 1979
29	Out of the Wastebasket
36	First Mill in Carroll County
37	Adams Mill near Cutler 1978
39	Harry Baum, Horseshoer
41	Grain threshing separator built in 1918
43	Street Fair in Delphi 1908
45	Letterhead of Carroll County Fair Association 1924
50	Farmers and Mail Boxes 1900
53	Telephone operators at Delphi 1960
54	Telephone operators at Flora Telephone Exchange
55	New dial telephone system at Telephone Exchange
56	Office of Yeoman Telephone Company built in 1955
63	Grange Emblem
68	Tipwa Grange Float 1955
70	Tipwa Grange officers 1979
79	Ralph Maggart, County Agent
80	Ralph Maggart, Howard McCarty, Harold Berry, Dale Kasten, Charles McCoy, County Agents
81	Steve Nichols, County Agent
81	Cora Zell St. Amand and Jeanne Muller, Home Demonstration Agents
81	Members of Home Economics Club entertaining
82	June Lowther, Elaine Kull Liley and Norma Sullivan, Home Demonstration Agents
83	Reneé Krieg and Bruce Ragan, Youth Agents
83	Carroll County Extension Staff 1979
83	County Extension Executive Committee 1950
84	Meat Caravan 1952
86	Farmers getting record books checked 1952
87	Officers of Farm Management Association 1951
88	Purdue Ag Alumni Association officers 1951
94	Extension Homemakers Emblem
96	County Home Economics Club officers 1950
96	County Extension Homemakers officers 1979-80
99	Carroll County Chorus members and friends ready for trip to Washington, D.C. 1950
100	Variety Show Acts 1950
101	Location of Extension Homemaker Clubs
108	Modern Homemakers Club members 1948
111	4-H Emblem
117	Tug of War across Deer Creek 1931
119	Exhibit Association members 1978-79
121	Black Lamb sold at 4-H Auction 1979
122	Grand Champion Steer at 4-H Fair 1945
123	4-H Commercial Beef Feeder banquet 1954
123	Pork Chop Barbecue for Carcass Evaluation Contest members 1979
124	4-H Electric Project winners 1951 and 1954
125	4-H REMC Electric Award winners 1956, 1957, 1959 and 1965
126	4-H Fire Prevention winners 1957
128	4-H Farm Bureau Achievement delegates to Chicago 1949
129	4-H Farm Bureau Achievement delegates 1950 and 1951
131	County delegates to 4-H Junior Leader Training Conference 1951
133	County 4-H Achievement Program at REMC 1952
135	Clyde DuVall Family
136	4-H Junior Leader officers 1954
137	Rotary 4-H Leaders Training School 1979
137	Winning Share the Fun act 1979
138	County 4-H Leaders 1978
139	4-H Foods, Plant Science and Forestry, Woodworking, Junior Clothing and Achievement Award winners 1979
140	Grand Champion Barrow, Wether Lamb, Crafts, Gardening, and Showmanship Award winners 1979
141	4-H Fair Dress Revue, Child Development and Home Furnishings winners 1979
142	FFA Emblem
145	Delphi FFA members and load of fertilizer 1949
150	Indiana Farm Bureau Emblem
151	Arthur E. Arnott
162	Members of Hoosier Farmer Northwest Expedition 1951
164	Farm Leaders 1920
166	Township Farm Bureau Roll Call Captains 1952
167	Entertainers for Farm Bureau Victory Supper 1950
169	Pet and Hobby Clubs from Clay, Jackson and Monroe Townships 1950, 1951
170	Madison, Deer Creek and Burlington Township Pet and Hobby Clubs 1951 and 1952
171	Group from county S & E Conference 1952
171	District Tax School at Delphi 1950
172	District Tax School at Delphi 1950
172	District Farm Bureau Meeting 1952
173	Township Farm Bureau S & E Directors 1949
173	Nominating Committee meeting for Farm Bureau 1952
173	Directors of County Farm Bureau 1979
173	Officers of County Farm Bureau 1952
173	Past Officers of County Farm Bureau 1952
175	Thirty Year Farm Bureau members 1949
176	Danny and His Dainty Dollies 1951
177	Carrollton Township Farm Bureau meetings 1951
178	Play "A Typical Farm Bureau Family" 1950
178	Monroe Township Farm Bureau Quartet 1933
179	Carroll County Entertainers 1951, 1956, 1950
180	Carroll County Entertainers 1950 and 1951
181	Carroll County Farm Bureau Band 1940
182	Farm Bureau Public Speaking contests for women 1951 and 1952
186	Public Relations Committee of County Farm Bureau 1961
190-191-192	Farm Bureau Insurance Agents
192	Farm Bureau Insurance Employees at Delphi 1979
193	Employees at Delphi and Flora 1980 and 1979

vi

Page	Description
193	Secretary of Carroll County Farm Bureau 1941 to 1946
193	Farm Bureau Building at Delphi 1980
194	Jesse Hoover family 1951
194	Farm Bureau Secretaries 1949 and 1950
200	Farm Bureau Co-op Emblem
214	William F. and Paulita Justice 1979
214	Arthur R. Mullin
217	Wm. Lee Henderson, first manager of CCFBCA
218	County Farm Bureau Co-op Association 1963 and 1938
219	Co-op tractor 1949
219	Wayne Hiatt, Hatchery Manager 1937
220	Employees of CCFBCA Fred Kuszmaul, Fred Gerard, Agnes Reed and Ralph Hanna
221	Employees of CCFBCA John DeLaCroix, and Morris Skiles
222	CCFBCA Bulk Oil Plant at Camden 1930-1976
223	Petroleum Department Employees 1980
223	Fertilizer Department officials and employees 1949
224	Myron Beesley and Jay L. Small, CCFBCA Managers
224	Camden Plant Food and Fertilizer Plant employees 1980
225	CCFBCA Fertilizer Plant at Camden and Big "A" 1980
226	CCFBCA Lumber Yard and Woodworking Plant at Yeoman
227	Volunteers to help at Fertilizer Plant at Indianapolis 1943
227	CCFBCA Feed Mill at Camden 1945
228	CCFBCA Elevator at Bringhurst 1979
228	CCFBCA Employees at Bringhurst Elevator 1980
229	Richard L. Denhart, Manager of CCFBCA
229	Aerial View of Central Carroll Facilities 1977
230	Manager and Employees at Central Carroll 1980
231	Members of Tour to Farm Bureau Enterprises in Indianapolis 1946
234	Directors of CCFBCA 1980
234	Captain Stubby and Buccaneers 1950
240	Indiana Rural Youth Emblem
240	First Rural Youth Training School in 1933
243	Rural Youth Training School in 1935
247	Rural Youth Officers for 1950
247	Rural Youth float at Delphi 1950
247	Rural Youth Members Entertain at Farm Bureau Meetings 1951
248	Rural Youth Officers 1952
248	Rural Youth Members who helped at Fish Fry 1952
248	Recently Married Rural Youth Couples 1952
249	Rural Youth Members at Purdue 1954
249	Shirley Eis at Rural Youth Talk Fest 1954
249	Rural Youth Officers 1955
250	Rural Youth Officers 1956
250	Rural Youth Quartet 1956
250	Rural Youth at County Fair 1959
251	Rural Youth Officers 1977
252	Irene Vaughan with Snake Necklace on Trip to Florida 1946
253	Ken and Julie Pyle 1952
254	Rural Youth Variety Show Entertainers 1952
255	Rural Youth Variety Show Entertainers 1952
256	Rural Youth Chorus to Seattle, Washington 1952
257	Kay and Charles T. Black at Rural Youth Reunion 1951
257	Ren Groninger Family at Rural Youth Reunion 1951
260	Carroll County Electric Light Company at Delphi 1898
267	First REMC Pole set 1937
272	REMC Managers, Clarence Darragh, R. E. Thomson and Robert Clawson
272	Lewis N. Mullin, REMC Attorney
273	REMC Employees
274	REMC Employees
275	REMC Office Building
276	Plaque in REMC Building 1951
277	REMC Storage Buildings
281	REMC Trucks 1941
282	Melody Men 1950
283	REMC Directors 1954
291	Welding School at REMC 1952
293	Willie Wiredhand
295	Incorporators of Carroll County REMC Still Living in 1979
296	Directors of REMC in 1979
297	New REMC Directors and Retiring Directors 1980
301	Artificial Breeders Association Directors 1953
301	Artificial Breeders Association Officers 1954
303	Susan Mann and Dr. Earl Butz at Pork Festival 1979
303	J. R. Rinehart, Winner of Hog Calling Contest at Pork Festival 1979
304	Employees of Federal Land Bank at Flora 1979
306	Employees of Production Credit Association at Delphi 1980
306	Employees of FmHA at Delphi 1980
308	Employees of ASCS at Delphi 1980
308	ASCS Committee for 1980
309	Community Committee Members of ASCS 1979
311	Soil Conservation District Supervisors 1950
311	Essay Contest Winners 1952
312	Mauri Williamson Speaker at CCSWCD Meeting 1979
313	Goodyear Award Winners 1950
314	Employees of CCSWCD 1978
315	Soil and Water Conservation District Supervisors 1978
317	Wabash and Erie Canal Emblem
325	Mr. and Mrs. Miles T. Martin hosts for Farm Progress Show 1954
329	Hathaway Family Singers 1978
332	Old Settlers 1955
333	Indiana Sesquicentennial Emblem 1966
333	Pat Wagner, Queen for Sesquicentennial 1966
333	Beth Barnard at Sesquicentennial 1966
334	Raymond Romein, Mrs. Reuben Smith and Mrs. Faye Wise 1966
335	Flora Centennial 1972 Emblem
336	Flora Historic Marker 1972
337	American Revolution Bicentennial Emblem 1976
338	Burlington Sesquicentennial Emblem 1978
340	Tourists on Carrollton Bridge 1921
341	Burnett's Creek Arch
342	Historical Society Officers and Directors 1979
343	Spinning at Old Settlers 1974
344	Clifford Kurtz in Cherokee Indian Costume 1976
345	Camden Library Employees and Board Members at Camden Historic Marker 1977

ACKNOWLEDGMENTS

There is no way that we can give adequate recognition to the hundreds of people who helped collect material for this book during the last four years. Officers, directors, employees and members of many organizations helped get the information and check the manuscript for errors.

Robert Brookbank, president of the Carroll County Historical Society, furnished several pictures and made prints for other pictures. Some pictures were from plates made by Andrew W. Wolever and now owned by William H. Bradshaw.

Officials in the Courthouse helped find information in the various offices.

Librarians and school officials in the county helped locate information.

Al Moss and the staff of the Carroll County Comet helped with publicity, furnished several pictures and let us use files of old papers.

Thomas Meek of Fort Wayne provided information about the Wabash and Erie Canal.

Charles Dillon, secretary of the Indiana State Grange and Robert G. Proctor, secretary of the National Grange furnished information about the Grange.

Howard Dieslin, Paul Crooks, Charles Gosney, Raleigh Fossbrink, Janice Breiner, Howard Crussel, Mauri Williamson, J. C. Bottum and others at Purdue provided information.

Bill Hadley sent reports about Tax and Legislative activities of the IFB. Judy Carley and Mary Glick checked the records at the state FB office for information about winners of FB contests. Gene Wilson sent information from early issues of the Hoosier Farmer. Herb Kinnear wrote a feature story for Hoosier Farmer.

Miss Catherine Horton, Marshall Lawrence and others furnished information about the FB Co-op Association.

Kenneth Murray and Bernard Dauby furnished information about PMA.

We thank Richard B. Cross and his crew at Oxford, Indiana for printing the book for us and we also thank the many people who ordered a book before it was published.

The following list of more than 300 people were among those who furnished information:

Mrs. Edith Aldrich, Mrs. Lenore Allen, Mrs. Hanna Appleton, Loren Ayres, Meredith Ayres, Mrs. Laura Baker, Mrs. Hilda Baum, Mrs. Ethel Benner, Myron Beesley, Enos Berkshire, Harold Berry, Tony Berto, Wilbur Bitler, Mr. and Mrs. Charles T. Black, Kim Black, Mrs. Fannie Blue, Mrs. Wm. Bordner, Miss Hilda Bowen, Mr. and Mrs. Leo Bowman, Margaret Bowman, Mr. and Mrs. Robert G. Bradshaw, Mrs. Marion Briggs, Mr. and Mrs. Robert Brookbank, Mr. and Mrs. Ross D. Brower, Ted L. Brown, Mrs. Donnabelle Brown, Mrs. Josephine Brown, Mrs. Lucille Brown, Mrs. Mabel Buck, Mr. and Mrs. Albert Burkle, Mr. and Mrs. Elwood Burkle, Mr. and Mrs. John Burkle, Mr. and Mrs. Alfred Burton, Charles Burton, Louis Brubaker, Mr. and Mrs. Cleon Carter, Mrs. Marjorie Shonk Clauer, Mr .and Mrs. Mahlon Clawson, Robert Clawson, Mr. and Mrs. Clarence Cleaver, Mr. and Mrs. George W. Collins, Mrs. Dale Craig, Mr. and Mrs. Leo Craig, Mr. and Mrs. Byram Crosby, Mrs. Patricia Maggart Crow, Lee Crowel, Mrs. Lucile Crowel, Mrs. Clarence Darragh, Lewis Deardorff, Mrs. Robert Deel, John DeLaCroix, John Dempsey, Richard Denhart, Mrs. Roberta Denk, Miss Irene DeWinton, Mr. and Mrs. John T. Downham, Mrs. Hazel Draper, Mr. and Mrs. Robert Duff, Mr. and Mrs. William Duff, Mrs. Mary DuVall, Norman Ebrite, Mr. and Mrs. Glenn Eikenberry, Wayne Eikenberry, Don Elliott, Viola Emrick, Mr. and Mrs. Melvin Fisher, Charles M. Flora, Mr. and Mrs. Lee Flora, Mrs. Helen Forgey, Tom C. Fouts, Mrs. Clarence Frey, Jerry Frey, Lewis Funkhouser, Richard Funkhouser, Mark Garrison, Mrs. Phyllis Garrison, Charles Geheb, C. E. Gerard, Mrs. Fred Gerard, Mrs. Orpha Goslee, Dan Gottschalk, Mr. and Mrs. Dick Grantham, Mrs. Roy Gregg, Mrs. Dale Griffey, Michael C. Griffcy, Gordon Groninger, Ren C. Groninger, Mike Guckien, Mr. and Mrs. Charles Hanna, Mrs. Marie Hanrahan, Mr. and Mrs. Charles Harter, Mrs. Orville Hathaway, Don Henderson, Mr. and Mrs. Joe Henderson, Mr. and Mrs. Wayne Hiatt, Mrs. Mary Hildebran, James Hodges, A. L. Hodgson, Mrs. Martha E. Hoffman, Mrs. Alice Holtman, Mr. and Mrs. Burton D. Honan, Mrs. Charles Hoover, Mr. and Mrs. Jesse Hoover, Ted Howard, Mrs. Francis Humbarger, Donald E. Huff, Herb Isaacs, Mr. and Mrs. Gene Jennings, Mrs. Evelyn Jervis, Mr. and Mrs. Carl Johnson, John T. Johnson, Mrs. Pauline Fouts Jones, Mr. and Mrs. Virgil Joyce, William F. Justice, Dale Kasten, Mr. and Mrs. Bill Kearns, John Kennard, Mr. and Mrs. James Kremer, Mrs. Lois Lane, Wayne Landes, Marshall Lawrence, Richard Leiter, Mrs. Elaine Kull Liley, Mrs. Pat Lohrman, Mrs. Lucy Long, Mrs. Ethel Lybrook, Mrs. Virginia Lyons, Miss Margaret Mabbitt, Mrs. Nellie MaCurdy, Richard G. Marsh, Mr. and

Mrs. Miles T. Martin, Roger Mayhill, Tom Mayhill, Mrs. Teresa Maxwell, Mrs. Carl Mays, Mr. and Mrs. Fred McCain, John McCain, Mr. and Mrs. Richard McCain, Donna McCarty, Mr. and Mrs. John McCormick, Dennis McCouch, Mark McCracken, Art McDowell, Mrs. Reneé Krieg McKee, Mr. and Mrs. Charles Meade Sr., Mrs. Magdalene Mears, Cleo Metzger, Mrs. Esther Million, Herbert Million, Mrs. June Million, Mrs. LaVaune Million, Mr. and Mrs. Dean Mills, Mr. and Mrs. Robert Mills, Steve Mills, Mrs. Phyllis Moore, Miss Louise Morrow, Al Moss, Jack Moss, Arthur Mullin, Mr. and Mrs. Estal Mullin, Mr. and Mrs. Lewis Mullin, Mrs. Charles Mummert, Mrs. Elsie Myers, Steve Nichols, Mr. and Mrs. Raymond Nicoll, Dennis Noble, Ray Orr, Mr. and Mrs. Dean Overholser, Robert Pearson, Charles E. Peek, David L. Peterson, Mr. and Mrs. Joseph E. Peterson, Mrs. Norma Peterson, W. O. Pettiner, Mrs. Robert L. Plank, Mrs. Truman Plank, Mr. and Mrs. Mark Porter, Earl Powell, Mrs. Mary M. Thompson Powers, Richard Pulley, Mrs. Lucile Quinn, Bruce Ragan, Mrs. Sherrie Randle, Mrs. Lois Reagon, Mrs. Agnes Reed, Bennie Redding, Mr. and Mrs. Forrest Redding, Robert Reiff, Mr. and Mrs. Lee Reppert, Mrs. James Riley Sr., Mrs. Ralph Rinehart, Mr. and Mrs. Walter Ringer, Charles Ritzler, Mrs. Darilee Robbins, Mrs. Marjorie Shanks Roberson, Ray Robertson, Mr. and Mrs. Eldon Robeson, Leroy Robeson Sr., Mr. and Mrs. Leroy Robeson Jr., Miss Pauline Robeson, Mr. and Mrs. Sylvester Robinson, Mrs. Fred Rodkey, Mrs. Carolyn Schiele, Mr. and Mrs. Fritz G. Schnepf Sr., Mr. and Mrs. Robert Schock, Joe Scott, Mr. and Mrs. Claude Sheets, Mrs. Mary Sheets, Mrs. Mary Sheldon, Mr. and Mrs. Arthur Shonk, Mr. and Mrs. Ora Shirar, Marilyn Shultheis, Mrs. Ted Sidenbender, Mrs. Donnabelle Sieber, Mrs. Clara Sims, Mr. and Mrs. Keith Sink, Albert Smith, Mrs. Betty Smith, Mrs. Betty Lou Smith, Mrs. Cathy Smith, Fred Craven Smith, Garnette Smith, Herb Smith, Mrs. Louise Smith, Reuben L. Smith, Wm. B. Smith, Mr. and Mrs. Junior Snider, Mr. and Mrs. John Snoeberger, Roy Snoeberger, Mr. and Mrs. Fred Stewart, Mr. and Mrs. Max Sullivan, Mr. and Mrs. Ralph Sullivan, Mrs. Mary Mason Thomas, Mr. and Mrs. Harold Thompson, Mrs. Thelma Trent, Mrs. Ralph Tyler, Mrs. Lee Voorhees, John Walker, Suzannah Walker, Mrs. Betty Ward, W. S. Weaver, Arthur Weddell, Terry Weigle, Larry Welborn, Mr. and Mrs. James White, Herschel Whitham, Bob Williams, Don Willy, Mrs. Harry Wilson, Homer Wilson, Mr. and Mrs. Robert C. Wingard, Mrs. Opal Wise, John Witter, Mrs. Opal Wood, Robert Wood, Ernie Wyant, Charles Yeager, James York, B. Jesse Zook and Orton Zook.

ABBREVIATIONS

AAA—Agricultural Adjustment Act or Administration
ACP—Agricultural Conservation Program
ACWW—Associated Country Women of the World
AFB—Air Force Base
AFBF—American Farm Bureau Federation
AIC—American Institute of Cooperation
AMPI—Associated Milk Producers, Inc.
APC—Area Plan Commission
ASC—Agricultural Stabilization Committee
ASCS—Agricultural Stabilization and Conservation Service
BZA—Board of Zoning Appeals
CCFB—Carroll County Farm Bureau
CCFBCA—Carroll County Farm Bureau Cooperative Association
CCREMC—Carroll County Rural Electric Membership Corporation
CCRY—Carroll County Rural Youth
CCSCD—Carroll County Soil Conservation District
CCSWCD—Carroll County Soil and Water Conservation District
CFC—Cooperative Finance Corporation
CF Industries—Central Farmers Industries
CIMCO-44—County Improvement Membership Committee of 44
CPPC—County Pork Producers Council
CWS—Cooperative Wholesale Society
EFNEP—Expanded Food and Nutrition Program
EH—Extension Homemakers
EMT—Emergency Medical Technician
EPA—Environmental Protection Agency
EWA—Emergency War Agent
FACTS—Fast Agricultural Communication Terminal System
FB—Farm Bureau
FBCA—Farm Bureau Cooperative Association
FCA—Farm Credit Administration
FFA—Future Farmers of America
FFR—Farmers Forage Research Inc.
FHA—Future Homemakers of America
FLBA—Federal Land Bank Association
FWA—Farmers and World Affairs

FmHA—Farmers Home Administration
GLF—Grange League Federation
HDA—Home Demonstration Agent
IFB—Indiana Farm Bureau
IFBCA—Indiana Farm Bureau Cooperative Association
IFYE—International Farm Youth Exchange
IFYE—International 4-H Youth Exchange
IRY—Indiana Rural Youth
JP—Justice of the Peace
KKK—Ku Klux Klan
KWH—Kilowatt Hours
NFLA—National Farm Loan Association
NFO—National Farmers Organization
NIPSCO—Northern Indiana Public Service Company
NRECA—National Rural Electric Cooperative Association
PCA—Production Credit Association
PCA—Producers Commission Association
P & C Family Foods—Producer and Consumer Family Foods
PMA—Producers Marketing Association
PTO—Power Take Off
PWA—Public Works Administration
REA—Rural Electrification Administration
REAP—Rural Environmental Assistance Program
REC—Rural Electric Cooperatives
REMC—Rural Electric Membership Corporation
RFD—Rural Free Delivery
RPS—Registered Professional Sanitarian
RY—Rural Youth
SCD—Soil Conservation District
SCS—Soil Conservation Service
S & E—Social and Educational
SWCD—Soil and Water Conservation District
SWCS—Soil and Water Conservation Service
TRAP—Total Registration of All Property
USDA—United States Department of Agriculture
USSCS—United States Soil Conservation Service
WPA—Works Progress Administration
WVPA—Wabash Valley Power Association
YMCA—Young Men's Christian Association

BIBLIOGRAPHY

NEWSPAPERS

Camden Record 1880-1946
Carroll County Comet since 1974
Carroll County Farm News, October 1941 to December 1978
Delphi Citizen and preceding papers until 1966
Delphi Journal 1850-1966
Delphi Journal Citizen 1967-1974
Hoosier Democrat 1897-1974

BOOKS

Brooks, John, Telephone, The First Hundred Years 1976
Burlington, Our Town Then and Now 1978
Colby, Edna Moore, Hoosier Farmers In a New Day 1968
Cooper, Donald H., Rural Electric Facts 1970
DeLong, George, Canalling on the Wabash and Erie 1832-75, 1970
Flora, Indiana Centennial 1972
Gardiner, Charles M., The Grange—Friend of the Farmer 1867-1947, 1947
Gerard, C. E. and Griffey, Michael G., Carroll County Sesquicentennial Publication 1977
Gray, Ralph D., Alloys and Automobiles 1979
Groninger, Addie McCain, History of Rockcreek Township 1916
Haywood, Homer and Brown, Walter, As We Remember It 1976
Helm, T. B., History of Carroll County Indiana 1882
Hoag, W. Gifford, The Farm Credit System 1976
Hull, I. Harvey, Built of Men 1952
Jacobs, Leonard J., Corn Huskers Battle of the Bangboards 1975
Kile, Orville Merton, The Farm Bureau Through Three Decades 1948
Latta, W. C., Outline History of Indiana Agriculture 1938
Mather, J. Warren, Supply Operations of Major Regional Cooperatives 1977
Mayhill, Dora Thomas, Old Wabash and Erie Canal in Carroll County and Pre-Canal History of the Wabash River 1953
Mayhill, Dora Thomas, Postal and Allied History of Carroll County Indiana 1954
Needler, Louis Leroy, From 80 Years Ago 'Til Now 1975
Odell, John C., History of Carroll County Indiana 1916
Phillips, Clifton J., Indiana in Transition 1968
Robinson, W. L., The Grange First Century of Service and Evolution 1867-1967, 1967
Smith, Clarence Beaman and Wilson, Meredith Chester, Agricultural Extension System 1930
Stewart, James Hervey, Recollections of the Early Settlement of Carroll County Indiana 1872
Stokes, W. N. Jr., Credit to Farmers 1973
Stuart, Benj. F., History of the Wabash and Valley 1924
Thompson, Dave O. Sr., Fifty Years of Cooperative Extension Service in Indiana 1962
Turner, Paul, They Did It In Indiana 1947
Van Buskirk, V. Friederika, The Wabash-Erie Canal 1832-1876, 1965

MISCELLANEOUS

Carroll County Farm Bureau, Minutes, Annual Reports, News Letters
Carroll County Farm Bureau Cooperative Association, Minutes, Annual Reports
Carroll County Historical Society, Minutes, News Letters
Carroll County REMC, Minutes, Reports, Kilowatt Ours Since 1948
Carroll County Rural Youth, Minutes, Reports, Scrapbooks
Carroll County, State and National Grange, Minutes and Reports
Extension Service, Annual Reports, 4-H Reports, Extension Homemaker Reports
Indiana Farm Bureau, Annual Reports, Handbooks for Officers, Hoosier Farmer since 1919
Indiana Farmers Guide
Indiana Statewide REC, Indiana Rural News since 1952
Prairie Farmer
Purdue University, Bulletins, Reports
USDA, Bulletins, Reports, Yearbooks of Agriculture

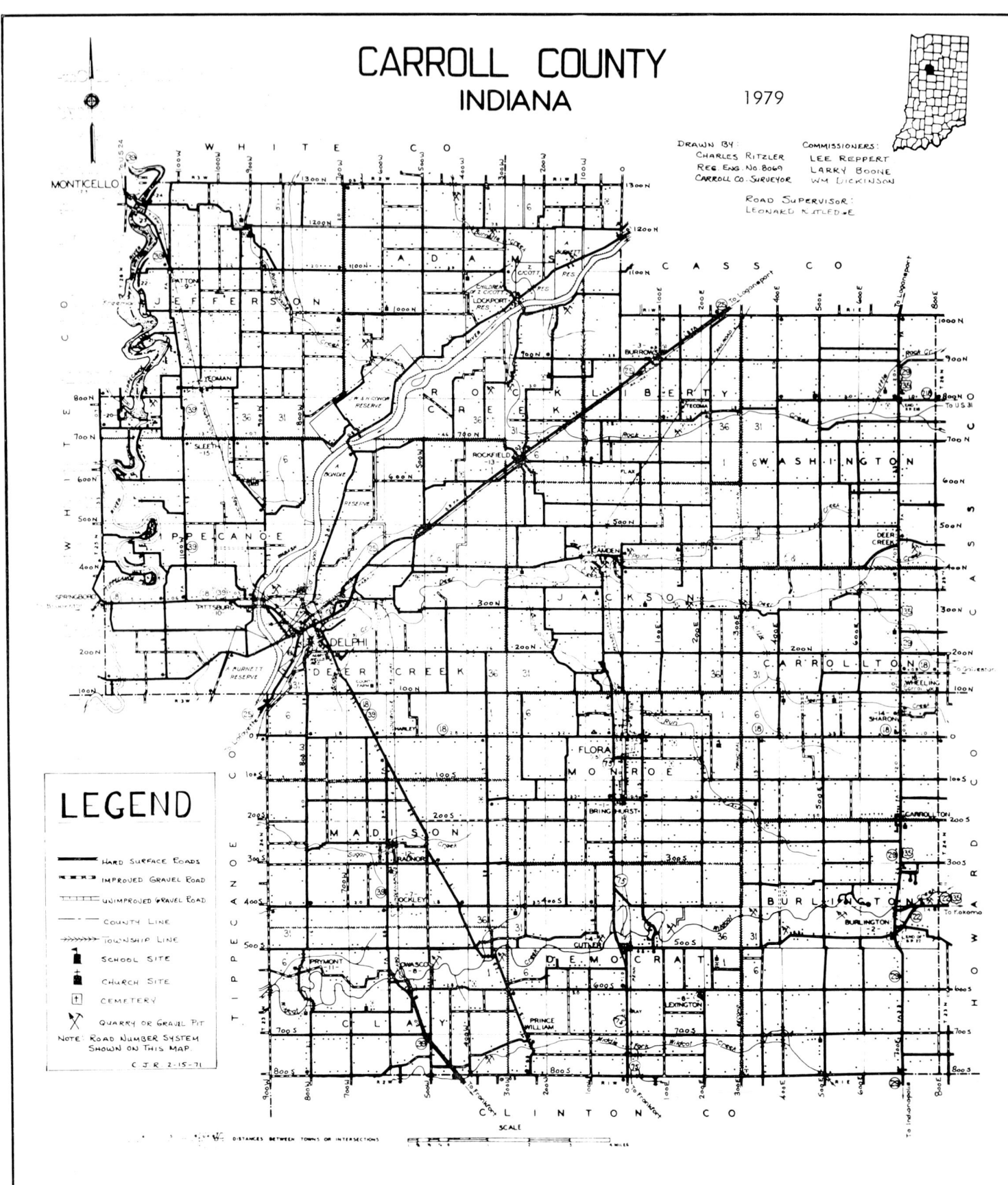

CHAPTER I

GENERAL INFORMATION

This chapter presents general information about Carroll County. The rest of the book gives information about some of the rural organizations that have been involved in the history and development of the county.

LOCATION

Carroll County is located in North Central Indiana about 70 miles north of Indianapolis, 125 miles southeast of Chicago, and about 20 miles northeast of Purdue University in West Lafayette, Indiana.

It is surrounded by five counties, each of which has a city larger than any in Carroll County. These cities, which tend to be the trading center for areas in the county close to them are: Lafayette in Tippecanoe County, Monticello in White, Logansport in Cass, Kokomo in Howard and Frankfort in Clinton.

Interstate 65 is located about 10 miles west, U.S. 31 about 13 miles east and U.S. 24 is about two miles north of Carroll County. Traffic on these main roads go near but not through the county.

ELEVATION

The lowest point in the county is along the Wabash River near the Tippecanoe County line and is about 520 feet above sea level. The highest point is 820 feet, and is located south of Burlington near where State Road 29 crosses the County line.

POPULATION

The first census in Carroll County in 1830 reported a population of 1611 people. In 1840 there were 7819 and by 1850 there were more than 11,000 people. Population reached a peak of 20,021 in 1890, and then declined for several years and reached a low of 15,049 in 1930. It slowly increased again and reached 17,734 reported by the most recent census in 1970. Of this number, 4217 were listed as Rural Farm and 2687 were noted as living in Delphi. The remaining 10,830 were listed as Rural Non-Farm, which included all towns of less than 2500 population. The largest of these was Flora with a population of 1877.

About 13% of the adults in the county who work are employed in agriculture.

The census reported that 36.8% of the people who work at jobs other than agriculture are employed outside the county. The state average is 16.9%.

Of the 10,050 people in Carroll County who are 25 years of age or over, more than half have completed high school and about 6% have completed four or more years of college. The median number of school years completed is 12.2. These figures are about the same as the state average.

NATURAL RESOURCES

Water

A good supply of water is available from the Wabash and Tippecanoe Rivers and the smaller streams including Wild Cat, Deer Creek and Rock Creek and their tributaries. There are about 150 miles of open streams and channels in the county with a combined surface area of about 1500 acres.

The largest body of water is Lake Freeman in the Tippecanoe River valley. It was created by the Oakdale Dam a third of a mile long, completed in 1925. The lake covers 2800 acres, and was the largest artificial lake in Indiana at the time it was built. In the fall of 1924, it was generally agreed that the lake would be called Lake Delphi, but in April 1925, the State Conservation Commission officially named it Lake Freeman.

The Soil and Water Conservation Service of the USDA has listed at least 12 potential water impounding sites ranging in size from 20 to 500 acres of surface water. There are nearly 100 privately owned ponds of less than six acres in size.

In addition to surface water resources, abundant supplies of ground water can be obtained from sand and gravel deposits in the ancient Teays bedrock valley which passes through the county northwest of the Wabash River. Sand and gravel deposits of variable thickness and the shallow bedrock supply adequate water for the city and towns, and for household and farm needs throughout the county. Most wells are less than 200 feet deep.

Stone and Gravel

A good supply of gravel is available in many parts

of the county and is used for building roads and making concrete. Most of the area is underlaid with limestone bedrock at varying depths.

The processing of limestone near Delphi started on a small commercial scale about 1840, and grew into one of the largest industries in the community. The Delphi Lime Company was organized in 1870, and operated several kilns near Delphi for burning limestone. One kiln continued to operate until 1917. The lime they processed was of high quality, and was widely known as Delphi Lime.

A stone quarry near Delphi has been in operation since 1944 in a reef of high magnesium and calcium limestone. The business was started by the Stuntz Yeoman Company, and the name was later changed to Delphi Limestone Company. Some minor zinc deposits have been found during mining of limestone.

The Indiana Geological Survey, Bloomington, recently discovered a unique and valuable mineral resource in Carroll County. It was a reef of high calcium limestone located southeast of Camden in Jackson and Carrollton Townships.

In 1978 the Medusa Aggregates Company of Cleveland, Ohio, and the Marblehead Lime Company of Chicago signed leases with the owners of nearly 400 acres of land in this area, and proceeded with plans for re-zoning the land and securing permits and approval from various agencies. Each company plans to begin mining operations in a few years, and produce special limestone products which can be made only from this kind of high calcium limestone. The companies plan to invest about $25 million in the projects.

Gas and Oil

There were several gas wells in the southeast part of the county. There were nine near Delphi, but none produced much gas. Several oil wells have been drilled, but none have produced enough oil to be of commerical value.

Land

Carroll County has 239,300 acres of land. In 1976 cropland accounted for 74.8%, grassland 11.0%, woodland 6.6% and other uses 7.6%. The other uses included urban areas, roads, farmsteads, recreation land and water areas.

When the early settlers arrived, most of the land was in timber. This provided a valuable source of building material and fuel for the settlers. Most of the level land has been cleared for agricultural uses, and most of the remaining trees are on the steep slopes along the stream valleys. The process of clearing land is continuing. In 1958, 9.9% of the land was in timber; and in 1975 only 6.6% was woodland.

Excess seasonal ground water was the number one problem on about two thirds of the land in the county. Most of this problem has been solved by a combination of open ditches and tile drainage.

Crops and Livestock

About half of the land in the county can be used for continuous production of row crops. The principal crops produced are corn, soybeans, wheat and hay. The largest crop is corn, and much of it is fed to hogs, cattle and poultry.

Carroll County has more hogs than any other county in Indiana, and ranks 19th in counties in the U.S. It has a higher density of hogs per square mile than any except one other county in the U.S. Carroll County ranks fifth in Indiana in poultry production.

Corn not fed on the farm is sold through one of the many local elevators, or through one of the two grain terminals in the area, The Andersons near Delphi and Indiana Grain just north of the County near Logansport, both built in 1975. Most of the grain handled by these terminals is exported.

INDIAN RESERVES

When the Government of the United States signed treaties with Indian tribes in which the Indians agreed to give up their right to certain tracts of land, there were some who wished to remain. Some of them were given tracts of land upon which they could live, and which they or their heirs could not sell without permission of the President of the U.S. These tracts of land were surveyed by measuring a distance from the river, then along a line nearly parallel to the river until enough land was included, then back to the river along a line parallel to the first line.

When the land in Indiana was surveyed using ranges, townships and sections, these reserves were not included in the survey. When the houses in the county were numbered by the Rural Electric Membership Corporation, lines were drawn on the map dividing the area into sections as it would be if surveyed. The same method was used in numbering the county highways, but deeds to the land still describe the land as surveyed for the Indian reserves.

Bondie's Reserve

By the provisions of a treaty concluded October 6, 1818 at St. Mary's, Ohio, between the Indians and Commissioners appointed by the United States Government, two sections of land along the Wabash River were granted to the children of Antoine Bondie, a French trader who married the daughter of a Potawatami Indian chief. This land is located in the northwest corner of Deer Creek Township along the Wabash River near the Carrollton bridge, and is shown on the map as Bondie's Reserve. The Patent Deed for this land, issued June 26, 1823 was signed by James Monroe, President of the U.S. Monique Bondie, daughter of Antoine Bondie married Jacob Mitty, a French trader. They and their children and others of the tribe lived on the reservation.

In 1839, John E. Hunt, who at that time owned part of the Reserve, had three-fourths of it surveyed and subdivided into 15 lots. This was known as Hunt's Survey of Bondie's Reserve, and this survey is still referred to in deeds for the land.

Other Reserves

By the terms of the Treaty of the Wabash concluded October 16, 1826 and ratified February 7, 1827 the Potawatomi Tribe of Indians ceded to the U.S. the right to a large tract of land on the north side of the Wabash River. The Government of the U.S. agreed to pay the tribe certain annuities, to build for them a mill, and furnish them a miller and blacksmith, etc.

The U.S. also agreed to grant tracts of land to certain persons. Abraham Burnett was given three sections of land. Two are located in the southeast corner of Tippecanoe Township, and one is located east of Lockport.

Zachariah Cicott, who was married to an Indian woman, was given one section of land which includes the present location of Lockport. Their three children, Baptiste, Sophia, and Emelie Cicott were each given one-half section of land down the river from that given Zachariah.

James, Henry, and William Conner were each given one section of land north of the river near the Carrollton bridge, and located in Adams, Jefferson and Tippecanoe Townships. The Conner boys were white, but had been raised by the Indians. They served as interpreters when the U.S. Government made treaties with the Indians.

TOWNSHIPS

Carroll County has 14 townships. In May 1828, the county was divided into three townships: Tippecanoe, Deer Creek and Rock Creek. Jackson was formed in 1830, Clay and Adams in 1831, Burlington 1832, Carrollton, Democrat and Washington in 1835, Jefferson 1836, Madison 1837, Monroe 1840, and Liberty in 1937.

TOWNS

The development and changes in the kind of roads and transportation have played an important part in the location of towns.

The first towns in Carroll County were located along the rivers and streams. Since there were no roads, the rivers provided the best means of transportation. The smaller streams were used as sources of water power to operate mills for sawing lumber and grinding grain.

Delphi was established along the banks of Deer Creek in 1828. The same year construction began on the Michigan Road, one of the first state roads in Indiana. It crossed the eastern edge of the county and connected Madison on the Ohio River with Michigan City. It is now State Road 29. Burlington was laid out along this road and Wild Cat Creek, in 1828. Other communities such as Carrollton, Sharon, Wheeling and West Sonora (now Deer Creek) located along the old Michigan Road.

Incorporated Towns

Delphi was established in 1828 and first incorporated in 1835. Burlington was laid out in 1828 and incorporated in 1967. Camden was laid out in 1832 and incorporated in 1908. Flora was platted in 1872 and incorporated in 1896. Yeoman was platted in 1880 and incorporated in 1925.

Other Towns

New towns were located along the railroads. Rockfield developed in 1856 and Burrows in 1865. Flora and Cutler located along the railroad in 1872 and Bringhurst in 1875. Yeoman located along the Monon Railroad in 1880, Radnor in 1883 and Owasco and Ockley in 1884.

Since the county was formed in 1828, thirty six platted town sites have been recorded in the Courthouse. Many of them, especially the canal towns and the mill towns along the streams have ceased to exist.

These towns and their location are listed in "Postal and Allied History of Carroll County" by Dora Thomas Mayhill. The book also lists 10 crossroads settlements and 21 unplatted post office sites.

TRANSPORTATION

WABASH RIVER

With no roads except Indian trails, the early settlers used the rivers for much of their transportation needs. Beginning about 1636 the river was used by Jesuit missionaries and French traders. An interesting story about the Wabash River was written by Mrs. L. H. Smith, and published in the Indianapolis Sunday Star and in the Delphi Journal on January 13, 1938.

"The Wabash River, which today apparently means little to the residents in its vicinity, except for its scenic beauty, its fishing and musselling in summer, and a high water menace at times, once had the distinction of being a part of the great line of communication between Canada and the military post at Fort Vincennes and the Mississippi River.

"Many interesting stories are told of the early efforts to navigate the upper Wabash beyond Pittsburg, which was generally considered to be at the head of navigation. However, many attempts were made by energetic citizens of Logansport and Peru to prove that they were at the head of navigation. It is said that the city of Peru once offered 15 barrels of whiskey to the owner of the first boat to successfully make the trip to their town.

Feat Accomplished

"This was finally accomplished during the "June freshet" of 1835, when the little steamer Science made the trip from Lafayette to Godfrey's Indian village beyond Peru. Many people of Lafayette, Delphi and Logansport made this pioneer trip. The steamer had trouble at the rapids above Logansport and had to return to that city for the night. After unloading over 200 barrels of salt and flour, the passengers walked past the rapids and the journey was continued. On the return trip they encountered the fighting Irish at Peru, who threatened to sink the steamer. The captain ordered the crew to push off at once, leaving some of the passengers at Peru.

"A sad attempt to make the trip from Lafayette to Logansport had been made a year earlier by Capt. Towe in his steamer, the Republican. All went well until the steamer passed Delphi, where several passengers joined the people from Lafayette for an excursion on the first steamer to navigate the upper waters of the Wabash. At Tipton's Port they stuck fast on a sandbar, but were finally able to proceed, with the aid of the passengers, who helped to lift and pull the boat.

Detained by Rapids

"They reached Georgetown, but the rapids above that place detained them several days until the water fell in the river and the boat was prevented from ascending or returning down the river. After four days the steamer was abandoned by all except the captain and crew. Two or three weeks later the steamer was hauled into Logansport by 12 teams of oxen, arriving on July 4, 1834. Soon after that the boat bilged, leaving Capt. Towe the honor of commanding the first steamer to visit Logansport.

"The last efforts to navigate the upper river, which is considered by the War Department to be navigable to Wabash, Indiana, was made during the high water in 1837, 100 years ago last month (December). At that time the Queen of the West reached Peru and returned to Logansport with a lone fiddler, an editor, several politicians and 500 bushels of corn on board. The same day the Mascotte left Logansport for its return trip through Delphi.

Aided by Canal

"But the Wabash river gained its greatest importance after the building of the Wabash and Erie canal from Toledo, Ohio, to Terre Haute, and the Ohio river. Pittsburg, Indiana became one of the busiest towns on the river, rivaling Lafayette and Logansport. It was at the head of steamboat navigation, yet it derived more benefit from rafts and flat boats. The dam furnished power for three sawmills, four grain elevators, one grist mill, a woolen mill, chair factory and organ factory. The town had large stores, cooper shops, harness shops, cabinet shops, shoe shops, blacksmith shops, wagon factory, large warehouses and the largest tannery in the state. The trade extended from Frankfort to Rensselaer. Great loads of wool were brought from all parts of the country and were exchanged for yarn and woolen goods.

"Pittsburg held its own better than most canal towns when the Wabash railroad was put through Delphi in 1856. Then the canal ceased to function, but when the dam was dynamited on February 9, 1881, the town died a natural death, and the businessmen lost thousands of dollars. Pittsburg is today, a quiet village on the banks of the Wabash where Indianapolis fishermen stop for bait on their way to Lake Freeman and Lake Shaffer, farther north on the Tippecanoe river.

"The only remainders of this past and energetic civilization are a few crumbling and decaying landmarks, a score of faded photographs, shrouded in the childhood memories and the youthful reminiscences of the older inhabitants, who are likewise rapidly passing away as time marches ruthlessly on."

WABASH AND ERIE CANAL

On March 2, 1827 the U.S. Congress made the first of three grants of land to the State of Indiana for the purpose of building a canal along the Wabash River. The grant included every alternate section of the public land in a strip five miles wide along each side of the canal, except Indian reservations and section No. 16 reserved for schools. This amounted to about 3000 acres per mile of canal.

Work was started near Fort Wayne on February 22, 1832 and was completed to Logansport in 1838, to Georgetown in 1840, to Lafayette in 1841, and to Evansville in 1853, a total of 21 years for construction. The total cost was 15 million dollars. Part of the money was paid by the State of Indiana, some from the sale of canal land, and some from revenue collected for use of the canal as sections of it were completed. Most of the money was obtained by the sale of bonds guaranteed by the State of Indiana. A majority of these bonds were purchased by the Rothchilds of London.

The length of the canal was 375 miles in Indiana and 84 in Ohio, making a total of 459 miles. This was the second longest canal in the world. The longest was the Grand Canal in China.

Men did most of the work in building the canal. Trees were cut and a strip of land from 90 to 180 feet wide was cleared. Horses and oxen were used to drag out the trees. One-horse carts were used to haul part of the dirt from the canal bed to the towpath along the side. The job was finished by men with wheelbarrows. The completed canal was at least 40 feet wide at the top and 26 at the bottom, and at least four feet deep with banks two feet above the water line. The channel was wider and deeper wherever it could be done without extra expense. The towpath was covered with gravel and the canal was lined with clay to help hold the water in the canal. The clay was leveled and made more waterproof by dragging brush in the canal bed.

Most of the workers were Irish. As a result of malaria, whiskey, and fights, a worker died for each six feet of canal built, and many of them were buried in the towpath.

Aqueducts and Arches

The builders of the canal were authorized by the state to use any timber they needed. They used timber to build aqueducts for the canal to cross Deer Creek, Crooked Creek, Rattlesnake in Carroll County, and the Eel River at Logansport.

Two large stone arches were built to cross Cottonwood Creek and Burnett's Creek. The arch at Burnett's Creek, one-fourth mile east of Lockport is 120 feet long, 20 feet wide at the bottom, and 10 feet high. The stones were hauled by ox team from the quarry at Kenneth, near Georgetown. Some stones were 12 feet long, two feet thick and several feet wide. Large black walnut logs were laid in the creek as a foundation for the stone, and they are still in good condition. The arch was used for the canal, the towpath, and a road. It is still in good condition, and is used as a bridge for a road across Burnett's Creek.

Bridges and Locks

Between Logansport and Delphi, a distance of 25 miles, there were 12 locks and 16 overhead bridges. The bridges were 18 feet high and 12 feet wide. Two locks were located at Barnesville, and the name was changed to Lockport. The stone walls for one set of

Burnett's Creek Arch east of Lockport.

Marker erected by "CIMCO-44" at site of Burnett's Creek Arch.

locks are still located near the Burnett's Creek arch east of Lockport. These locks had stone walls 116 feet long, six feet thick, and 18 feet deep. The chamber in the locks was 15 feet wide and 90 feet long between the gates at each end and had a lift of 10 feet. The length and width were the same dimensions as those of the New York, Ohio and Pennsylvania locks so that the same boats could be used in the entire canal system.

Carrollton Bridge

This information about the Carrollton Bridge is from an article written by William C. Smith, President of the Carroll County Historical Society, in the Delphi Journal September 1, 1927.

During 1838 and 1839 a wooden covered bridge was built across the Wabash River where the canal crossed the river at the town of Carrollton, and was called the Carrollton Bridge. A ferry boat was used to cross the river at this point before the bridge was built. This was claimed to be the first permanent bridge across the Wabash River in Indiana. The north abutment of the bridge was a part of the canal lock on the north bank of the river.

A tramroad built along the lower side of the bridge was used by the horses and mules to pull the canal boats across the river. Sometimes they were pulled into the river and drowned when the current in the river was swift during floods.

At the insistent demand of the citizens of Logansport, a part of the covered bridge was built as a draw bridge so that steamboats might go up the river to Logansport. Only one steamboat used the draw bridge to go up the river, and it was wrecked near Logansport and did not return.

A storm on July 4, 1873 destroyed the covered bridge, and it was replaced by an iron bridge with five spans. In 1879 the four north spans of the bridge were swept away by an ice gorge. The iron was recovered, and the bridge rebuilt. It was used until replaced by the present concrete bridge which was dedicated on Sunday, September 4, 1927. About 3000 people attended the ceremony which included talks by Indiana Governor Ed Jackson, and Ben F. Stewart, a Carroll County Historian.

The Mentzer Tavern

The Mentzer Tavern located on the east side of the road at the north end of the Carrollton bridge was one of many taverns located along the canal to provide food and lodging for passengers and crews on canal boats. Water from a nearby spring was piped to the tavern and added to the variety of liquid refreshments available for customers. The building was built in 1840 by George Friday and Ignatious Mentzer and was used as a cooper shop and later converted into a tavern. After the tavern went out of business the building was used for several years as a residence. The building located on land owned by the Grantham family was torn down between 1915 and 1920 and part of the lumber used to build a corn crib across the road. Some of the lumber was used to panel a family room in the Richard Grantham home, and some was also used to panel an office in the Ralph Sullivan home.

Report of Chief Engineer

In 1847 Jesse L. Williams, Chief Engineer of the Wabash and Erie Canal made a report to the Indiana House of Representatives. The report listed the current condition and recommendations for repair on locks, flood gates, culverts, arches, aqueducts, bridges, dams and other structures along the canal. He reported that the covered bridge across the Wabash at

Mentzer Tavern

Carrollton was in good condition. Five piers were built with stone from the Georgetown Quarry. The length of the six spans of the bridge were listed. One was 105 feet, three were 94 feet each, one was 70 feet, and the other was 43 feet and it was built as a draw bridge.

The Dam near Pittsburg was listed as being built with timber cribs filled with stone resting on the rock bottom in the river. The abutments were built of timber, and both were listed as needing to be replaced during the next two years. Mr. Williams had served as engineer in charge of building the dam.

The report listed a dam built across Deer Creek between the canal and the river, 170 feet long and 10 feet above the low water level, formed of cribs of stone resting on a foundation of brush and trees on the mud bottom in the creek. A towing path bridge was a wooden structure about 10 feet wide resting on one stone pier in the strongest current and three timber bents.

A bridge over the canal just before it entered the Wabash River north of Delphi was used to change the towing path from the north to the south side of the canal.

Most of the structures along the canal were built of wood, and many of them had to be replaced about every five years.

Pittsburg Dam

The longest dam in Indiana, 590 feet long and 12 feet high from low water level, was built in 1838 across the Wabash River just north of Pittsburg to raise the water enough for the boats to cross the river at Carrollton and go through Delphi. Logansport and Peru objected to the dam because it prevented steam boats from coming up the river to them. A lock near the east end of the dam was built in 1841 for steamboats using the river. No steamboats were allowed on the canal because they caused damage to the canal banks.

Boats on Canal

Boats used on the canal were 10 to 15 feet wide and from 40 to 100 feet long and used a towline about 250 feet long. Freight boats were pulled by three mules hitched single file and traveled about two or three MPH. Some freight boats hauled an extra team of mules on the boat. Freight hauled included the many products produced on the farm, and everything needed to supply people living in the Wabash Valley.

The canal connected with other canals, so it was possible for passengers to go to Cincinnati or New York City by boat.

Line boats hauled passengers and traveled about the same speed as freight boats. They served no meals, and had no accommodations for sleeping.

Packet boats were "First Class" transportation and cost about five cents per mile which was one or two cents more than "Tourist Class" on the line boats. A Packet boat carried about 50 passengers and traveled from five to nine miles per hour. They were pulled by three horses, and teams were changed about every 25 miles. Regular meals were served three times a day, and bunks were provided for sleeping at night.

Meals were served at regular times, and some people would get on the boat at mealtime, eat all they could while the boat traveled one mile, and then pay their five cents and get off. This practice became so common that the boats charged a minimum of 15 to 25 cents for a ride.

Some boats carried mail, so it was a bright spot in the day in a canal town when a boat arrived with a load of passengers and the mail.

Boats were able to use the canal from about March 1 to November 1 each year. Some companies operated stage coaches along the route to take care of their passengers in the winter.

When two boats met, it was the rule that the boat going upstream had the right-of-way. The boat coming down stream was supposed to move to the other side of the canal and stop so that the other boat could pass over its tow rope. However the matter was usually settled by the boat with the toughest crew having the right-of-way. Crew members were hired for their fighting ability, more than for what they might know about operating a boat.

The canal was also used to transport logs. The logs were fastened together like a raft, and after going through locks were connected to others, sometimes making a raft 300 feet long.

Maintaining Canal

Maintaining the canal was a problem. It would freeze over in the winter, and the spring floods would cause damage that had to be repaired before it could be used again.

"Towpath Walkers" each walked and inspected about 10 miles of canal per day. They checked bridges and locks for needed repairs, and carried straw to mix with the clay if they found a leak in the canal bank. If the leak was too bad for them to fix, they sent a messenger on horseback to get a wrecking crew who came as fast as they could with a boat which carried clay, straw, stakes, ropes, pile planking, picks and shovels.

Revenue

Most of the revenue for operating the canal came from toll charges for boats. The cost of shipping freight the entire length of the canal from Toledo, Ohio to Evansville, Indiana was $5 per ton. Another source of money was a charge for use of water power at $30 per horsepower per year. The canal supplied water power for 11 flour mills, 11 saw mills, three paper mills, 10 oil mills, four grain elevators, one woolen mill, a chair factory and an organ factory.

While the canal was being built, extra revenue was used to finish building the canal, instead of paying interest on the bonds. In 1835-36 the State Legislature authorized the building of more canals and railroads that would have cost about $30,000,000. The state was not able to meet these obligations, and in 1847 the canal was turned over to the bond holders.

The End of the Canal

The high cost of maintaining the canal, along with the loss of business to the Wabash Railroad built in 1856, made it unprofitable to operate the canal. During 1874, total receipts were $274,000 and expenses were $436,500 and it was abandoned that year. The last boat through Delphi on the canal was in 1874. While crossing Deer Creek, the bridge collapsed and mules and the colored driver were drowned. When the bodies were recovered they were all buried in the same grave. Sections of the canal were sold, and parts of the canal were used for local traffic for a few years.

On March 29, 1875 the part of the canal between Lafayette and Ohio was sold for $85,500. The State of Indiana lost all the money they had invested in the canal and the bondholders lost more than 50% of their investment.

The dam at Pittsburg continued to supply power for industries at Pittsburg, and two paper factories in Delphi.

On February 9, 1881 the dam was dynamited, probably by farmers upstream who objected to having their land flooded, and the great canal era ended.

The canal played a most important role in the growth and development of the Wabash Valley. The lower cost of transportation on the canal reduced the cost of some supplies by one half, and doubled the sale price of some farm produce. During the 47 years, from the time the first grant was made in 1827 until the last boat in 1874, the population of the Wabash Valley increased from 250,000 to about 1,750,000 people.

RAILROADS

Wabash

The Lake Erie, Wabash and St. Louis Railroad Company, organized in 1852, built a line along the valley of the Wabash River from Toledo to Lafayette. Work was started in 1853. The section through Carroll County was built in 1856, with the first train through the county in June, 1856. It became one of the busiest railroads in Indiana and was one of the major factors in killing the Wabash and Erie Canal. The name of the railroad was changed to Wabash,

Wolever Photo

Pittsburg in 1885. Buildings along the river housed several industries using water power from the dam north of town until it was blown up in 1881. The bridge across the river, built in 1869, was the first iron bridge built in Carroll County. The bridge was replaced in 1935 by the State Highway bridge about two blocks downstream.

St. Louis and Pacific, and was generally known as the Wabash. It is now a branch of the Norfolk and Western.

Penn Central

The first effort to get a railroad in Carroll County was in the fall of 1851. Several meetings were held at Delphi, Pittsburg, and Camden to try to get the Richmond and Newcastle Railroad to build a line from Logansport through the county. They decided on a line to Camden, and in 1852 built the bridges and roadbed, but abandoned the project before it was completed. The Logansport, Camden and Frankfort Railroad, which later became the Logansport, Crawfordsville and South Western, was organized in the spring of 1869. It took over the partially completed road bed and right-of-way from Logansport to Camden, and built a line through the county in 1872. It was known as the Vandalia Line. The name was changed to Pittsburg, Chicago, Cincinnati and St. Louis Railroad, then changed to the Pennsylvania Railroad, and is now Penn Central. For several years there were eight passenger trains daily.

Passenger trains were discontinued, with the last passenger train going north through the county on Friday, May 23, 1958.

The Vandalia Railroad built the first depot in Flora, on the west side of the tracks between Walnut and Main Streets. In 1908 the Pennsylvania Railroad built a new depot at a cost of $10,000. It was located on the east side of the track between Main and Columbia Streets. It was badly damaged by a train wreck in 1910.

In 1969 the town of Flora purchased the ground where the railroad station stood and made it into a parking lot. The depot was moved to State Road 75 where it is now used as a Laundromat.

The depot at Camden was moved and converted into a Dentist Office by Dr. B. C. Kerkhove. He sold it to Dr. Dianella Lawson in 1979.

Monon

The Indianapolis, Delphi, and Chicago Railroad Company began about 1871 to build a line through Carroll County. Progress was slow, and by 1878, trains were operating between Delphi and Rensselaer. In 1881 the railroad was purchased by the Chicago and Indianapolis Air Line Company. The line was completed and the first trains went completely through the county on January 9, 1882. This is the line now known as the Monon Railroad.

According to an article written by L. K. Runyon in the Delphi Journal July 23, 1936, the name Monon is of Indian origin and means "Swift Running." The following information about the building of the Monon railroad is from the same article:

"The New Albany & Salem Railroad, now a part of the Monon Route, received its charter to operate as a railroad in the state of Indiana in the year 1847, with James Brooks as president.

"Actual construction was started during the early part of 1848 at New Albany. Coming north to Salem personal hardships and uncertain financing were ever present, and the work was done entirely by 'hand power,' reaching Salem, a distance of thirty-five miles in January, 1851.

"The first engine which was put into service in the year 1849 was purchased at a cost of $7500. This engine was a crude wood-burning affair, weighing less than 16 tons, with a tank capacity of 1500 gallons of 'hand pumped' water, and carried around 80 pounds of steam pressure.

"Wood for this engine was purchased from farmers living along the right-of-way at the low rate of 75 cents per cord. One cord of wood provided power for an average run of 30 miles.

"This engine, in active service, averaged a speed of twenty miles per hour over an unballasted track constructed of oak stringers mounted on small cross ties, spaced at three and four foot intervals, upon the level ground. Flat strap iron mounted upon the wooden stringers completed the outfit. Many times during a single trip the engine crew was forced to dismount and renail the stray ends which caused no end of trouble and embarrassing delays.

"The conveniences of the first passenger coach were somewhat meager compared to our present day modern air conditioned coaches. The early coaches were uncomfortably small, with wooden seats arranged on each side of the car, which accommodated about fifty passengers.

"For night travel there was an oil burning lamp, suspended from the ceiling about the center of the car. Stoves of the caboose type were placed at each end of the car, which provided heat during the winter months.

"A charter amendment was secured by the New Albany & Salem railroad in February, 1848, for an extension through Orleans, Bedford, Bloomington, and unnamed points northward.

"With work progressing slowly the rails finally reached Bloomington during the latter part of 1853, and passed beyond to Gosport.

"The Crawfordsville & Wabash railroad was absorbed within a few weeks of its completion in June, 1852, by an exchange of stock, which brought rails from Crawfordsville to Lafayette.

"That section of the road from Michigan City south to Lafayette was completed in 1853. This left a remaining portion of unfinished trackage between Gosport and Crawfordsville, a distance of 56 miles. This part was finished in June, 1854, and the first passenger train left Michigan City early in the morning of July 3, 1854, enroute to its southern terminal of New Albany, arriving at that point that same evening.

"This train was in all evidence the first to run from one end of the state to the other. This route later provided equipment for Civil War troop trains. It is to be remembered that President Lincoln's funeral train moved over this railroad from Lafayette to Michigan City, en route from Indianapolis to Chicago, May 1, 1865.

"As time progressed a change of name was effected from the name New Albany and Salem railroad, to the Louisville, New Albany, and Chicago railroad. A complete reorganization of this line followed in January, 1873. An addition to the property was made May 5, 1881, at which time they acquired the Chicago & Indianapolis air line railroad, which was completed between Indianapolis and Hammond, with trackage right into the heart of Chicago.

"Still another reorganization occurred March 31, 1897, when the name was changed to its present name, the Chicago, Indianapolis and Louisville railroad.

"This property now embraced the Louisville, New Albany & Chicago; the West Baden and French Lick Springs; the Lafayette and Monon; and the Chicago & Indianapolis Terminal Company.

"Many hardships and shaky financing were encountered in the early days of construction of what is now known as the Monon route. The early organizers were no less than financial 'Wizards.'

"Passenger fares were placed at five cents per mile, in comparison to our present day rate of two cents per mile. Passenger train speeds in the olden days averaged about 20 miles an hour, while today we speed along at 80 miles per hour in perfect safety.

"The Monon route may well be claimed as Indiana's own railroad. It extends from Louisville north to Michigan City, thence from Indianapolis to Chicago, crossing its own line at Monon. There is also that portion extending from Wallace Junction westward to Vigo, serving many coal fields.

"They also pass through the center of the Indiana Limestone District, with the network of tracks serving the majority of the quarries and mills. It transports quarried stone destined to all parts of the United States.

"Indiana Limestone is nationally known for its architectural qualities. More buildings throughout the United States are built with Indiana Limestone than any other stone.

"Incidentally this Hoosier railroad has two passenger trains named 'The Hoosier,' plying between Indianapolis and Chicago."

Old timers report that sometimes the flat strap iron used as track would come loose from the wooden stringers and the loose end would go up through the floor of the car and anything else that might be in the way, including baggage and people. These were known as "Snake Heads" because of their resemblance to a snake as they came through the floor.

INTERURBANS

Indiana's network of interurban lines began in 1895 with 305 miles of track, and reached a peak in 1925 with 2485 miles of track. Indianapolis was the hub of the network which extended to the neighboring states. Lines were owned by several different companies, but they were connected so that a person could travel to many places by interurbans.

The Indianapolis Traction Terminal, later the Indianapolis Bus Station, located one half block from the State Capital Building was built in 1904. It was the largest terminal of its kind in the world.

The Fort Wayne and Wabash Valley Traction Company, reorganized in 1911 as the Fort Wayne and Northern Indiana Traction Company, operated an interurban line along the Wabash River between Fort Wayne and Lafayette. Cars went through Delphi, Rockfield and Burrows from July 1907 to May 21, 1932. For many years there were 12 cars each way daily, and they made regular stops at all towns and would stop for passengers anywhere along the route. This made convenient transportation and many stu-

Wolever Photo

An interurban at the station on South Washington Street in Delphi. The line through Carroll County operated from July 1907 to May 21, 1932.

dents rode to school on the interurban, and others depended on it to get to their work.

The interurban line had stations in many towns where they would pick up milk, cream, eggs and other farm produce and haul it to market. Some lines had special cars to haul livestock.

An interurban route was planned from Delphi through Flora to Burlington. Another route along the Michigan Road from Logansport to Burlington was considered but neither was built.

As better roads were built and more automobiles were available, the interurban went out of business. An old timer reported that a hearing was held at Indianapolis when an interurban company requested permission to discontinue a line. A large crowd was present to protest at the hearing. A survey revealed that they all came to the meeting by auto instead of by interurban.

PLANK TOLL ROADS

In 1849 the Delphi and Frankfort Plank Road Company was organized and built a plank road between the two towns. The road bed was graded and wooden stringers laid and thick plank, eight feet long, spiked to them. It took about four years to complete the road, and for a number of years it was a grand thoroughfare. A toll gate was located south of Delphi near the present intersection of State Road 39 and County highway 200 N.

In 1851 another company was organized and built a plank road from the Courthouse in Delphi, west on Franklin St. and across the canal to what was known as the South Road, and is now county road 850 West. It followed that road to the Wabash River where a ferry was constructed to Pittsburg. This gave warehouses in Delphi and Pittsburg better access to the canal, and it became a heavily traveled highway. When the Wabash Railroad was built in 1856, it provided the warehouses a good connection with the railroad.

After a few years, both plank roads wore out and were discontinued as toll roads. It's hard to imagine a road much worse than a plank road with part of the planks rotted out. In 1881 the plank road to Frankfort was replaced with a gravel road.

GRAVEL ROADS

This created a demand for better roads, and in 1877 the State Legislature passed the first law permitting county commissioners to build and repair roads. Most of the gravel roads in Carroll County were built under provision of the "three mile gravel road act of 1908."

STATE HIGHWAYS

One of the first state highways in Indiana was the Wabash Highway, established by an act of the Legislature in 1826. It was created to promote the development of the country along the Wabash River, and extended from Terre Haute by way of Lafayette and Delphi to the mouth of the Salamonie River. By another act of the Legislature in 1828 it was extended to Fort Wayne and the Ohio line. In Carroll County it went from Delphi on what is now the Carrollton Road to the Wabash River. The old road went straight ahead where the present road now turns about one half mile south of the Carrollton bridge. From there it followed the south bank of the Wabash River to the "Old Trading Post," now French Post Park and on to a ford at Logansport where it crossed the river.

Another early state highway was the Michigan Road, now State Road 29 which was established by the Legislature in 1828. The state completed the road in 1837 and it was turned over to the counties to be kept in repair. In 1867 Carroll County granted by a franchise to the Logansport and Burlington Turnpike Company, the right to operate a Toll Road on the 18 miles between Burlington and the Cass-Carroll County line. The company operated the road for nearly twenty years, but let it get out of repair and almost impassable. People refused to pay toll, and the county again took over the road. In 1886 the county sold bonds for $25,000 and graveled the road through the county.

The following is part of an article from the Indianapolis News, July 27, 1904, which gives an interesting report on the Michigan Road.

"For several years after the state was admitted to the Union, the Potawatomi Indians continued to inhabit and own the country between the Wabash River and Lake Michigan. They had to be dealt with in the settlement and civilization of the country. - - -

"As navigable streams were comparatively few and railroads were not yet introduced, road building seemed to be the only resort for domestic transportation. One of the earliest projects of this kind was a wagon road from Lake Michigan across Indiana to the Ohio River. - - Such a work was thought worthy of national and state aid, and it received both. - - -

Indiana Owned Right-of-Way

"The first step in the undertaking was to secure the right-of-way from the Indians. In 1826, Congress authorized the negotiation of a treaty with them for this purpose. It was concluded on October 16 of that year. The commissioners on the part of the U.S. were James B. Ray, General John Tipton of Indiana and General Lewis Cass of Michigan. The latter gave his name to Cass County, Gen. Tipton, who performed many important public services and served several years in the U.S. Senate, gave his name to the county and town of that name. By the treaty of 1826, the Indians ceded to the U.S. 'a strip of land commencing at Lake Michigan and running thence to the Wabash River one hundred feet wide for a road and also one section of good land contiguous to said road for each mile of the same, and also for each mile of a road from the termination thereof through Indianapolis to some convenient point on the Ohio River.' - - -

Price of the Land

"This magnificent cession of land amounted to 171,414 acres. The Indians were to receive from the government $2000 in silver annually for 22 years; a government blacksmith and shop; a grist mill on the Tippecanoe River with a miller and 160 bushels of salt annually. The next year, 1827, Congress passed 'An act to authorize the State of Indiana to locate and make a road therein named.' On January 24, 1828, the Legislature passed 'an act to provide for surveying and making the road from Lake Michigan to Indianapolis' and appointed three commissioners to take charge of the work. - - -

The Michigan Road

"The road as surveyed began at Trail Creek on Lake Michigan running thence an easterly course to the southern bend of the St. Joseph River, which it crossed, thence south to the Wabash River, thence to Indianapolis, thence to Greensburg and thence to Madison. - - - As most of the country was dense forest the work was difficult. Trees had to be cut down, trimmed and rolled to one side, underbrush cut and much grubbing done. The roadway was to be 100 feet wide, leaving no stumps more than one foot above the level of the ground. It was to be grubbed 30 feet wide in the center of the road. Travelers were expected to get over or around the stumps the best way they could. In swamps or low ground, trees were rolled in, making a corduroy road. This was not a boulevard, but it was the beginning of a road that was destined in time to be very useful.

Lands Sold at Auction

"As the work progressed, the lands granted for it were sold at public auction. By the Act of Congress, authorizing the work, none of the land was to be sold for less than $1.25 an acre. - - - People were afraid of the Indians and the sales were not as successful as had been hoped. Up to the close of October, 1832, there had been sold 58,432 acres for $90,141.00. Later sales realized higher prices and some of the lands in the central and southern portions of the state brought as high as $5.00 an acre. Of the original land grant of 171,414 acres, all but 1840 acres had been sold by 1836. The money realized had gone into the construction of the road.

"During 1830-1831-1832, the Legislature passed several acts approving the reports of the commissioners and providing for opening different sections of the road. By February 1832, it had been opened from Indianapolis to Madison southward and as far north as Logansport. - - -

Road Completed in 1834

"By 1834 the road was practically completed and nominally opened though improvements on it continued for 2 or 3 years longer. In 1835, the commissioners reported that 'the uncommon immigration toward the north' had kept the road constantly in need of repair. Work on it ceased in 1837, and from that time it was turned over to local authorities to be kept in repair. When finally opened, it was 254 miles long, and, owing to the land grants, it was made without cost to the state. The reports of the State Auditor from 1829 to 1841, show gross expenditures on account of the road of $242,000.00 and receipts $241,331.00. It is doubtful if any state enterprise would be as honestly or economically managed nowadays (1904). That was the day of small salaries and grafts had not yet been invented.

D. D. Pratt's Opinion

"Although the road was completed its whole length in 1834, it was a very rough road and barely fit for travel. For several years after that it was full of stumps and almost impassable in places. The Hon. D. D. Pratt of Logansport, (afterward U.S. Senator), had traveled over the road on horseback and in all sorts of conveyances as a pioneer lawyer. In a paper he wrote in 1876:— 'Indiana in the past was regarded as the headquarters of profanity, which for variety and strength of expression had been equaled nowhere except perhaps in the Southwest. For the widespread evil and wickedness, I think the roads of the state, more than any other single cause, were responsible. I have seen men stand mute with rage, violently gesticulating, because they could not on the spur of the moment find cusswords sufficiently strong to express their feelings. There are people (1876) respectable, gray-headed men, from whose mouths a stream of profanity will issue in a continuous current for five minutes, more or less, if you but mention the Michigan Road. Between Logansport and Indianapolis the driver of a four-horse team with a loaded wagon would frequently stop for the night in sight of his starting point that morning.'

"The road was in no condition for autos but there were no autos in those days and the pioneers made the best of such roads as they had. Those who travel over the Michigan Road today should give a grateful thought to the pioneers who laid it out through the wilderness."

A note added by Mrs. Hazel F. Wiley on July 11, 1972 said: "One corduroy section was south of the town of Deer Creek. Sycamore trees were used in that low spot. These trees sprouted and there are still trees on each side of the road. At the south end of these rows of trees is this sign:

Sycamore Row

"This row of sycamores sprouted from freshly cut logs used in the 1830's to corduroy a swampy section of the historic Michigan Road, the first state road in Indiana running from Madison to Michigan City."

ROADS AND BRIDGES

There are 100 miles of two-lane State Highway in the county. Three State Roads: 22, 75, and 218 end in the county, and four: 18, 25, 29 and 39 (which is also U.S. 421) go through the county. There are about 28 bridges in the county on State Highways.

There are 160 miles of high quality black top, 430 miles of a single seal, and 260 miles of gravel roads, making a total of 850 miles of roads in the County Highway system. The county roads have about 120 bridges, many of which need to be repaired. More than one half are one-lane, and nearly half have a load limit of ten tons or less.

There are two covered bridges, both built in 1872, the Lancaster bridge over Wild Cat on road 500 West is open for light traffic. A covered bridge across Wild Cat north of Cutler near the Adams Mill is closed for everything except foot traffic.

COMING OF THE AUTO

The first automobile seen in this part of Indiana was on July 4, 1894 when Elwood Haynes drove his car on Pumpkinville Pike near Kokomo at a speed of six to eight MPH.

The Haynes "Horseless Carriage" was one of the first built in the U.S. with a gasoline engine. It used a one horse power engine with two forward speeds and no reverse. In low gear it would go up a 4% incline, and in high gear it would go up to 8 MPH on level ground. The engine would run either direction, so it was possible, but not very convenient, to run the car backwards. It made 56 miles per gallon and at that time gasoline cost six cents per gallon. A Chicago newspaper sponsored a contest for a better name for "Horseless Carriage." The name "Motorcycle" was picked as the winner, but it was soon discarded in favor of "Automobile" or "Car."

The first auto race in the U.S. was sponsored by the newspaper and held on November 28, 1895. Six vehicles entered but only two finished the race from Chicago to Evanston and back.

The auto manufacturers who got together for the race organized the American Automobile league on November 1, 1895. This later became the National Association of Automobile Manufacturers.

Henry Ford built his first car May 13, 1896.

The first Auto Show was held in 1900 in New York City with 70 different makes on display.

In 1901 the Indianapolis Auto Trade Association held the first auto show in Indianapolis.

In 1902 the Hoosier Motor Club was formed by motorists "Who banded together for mutual protection against irate owners of horse-drawn vehicles." The Delphi Journal for April 2, 1903 reported that Louis Niewerth, engineer at the Delphi City Water Plant owned the first automobile in Delphi. It was a Stanley Steamer with a six horse power steam engine, using gasoline for fuel.

James Shirk, a banker had a Marmon automobile in 1904.

1905 was the first year a registration number was required on each car. A number was assigned for the car, and the owner had to make his own plate.

In 1905 the speed limit set for autos in Indiana was eight MPH in business districts, 15 MPH in other parts of cities and towns, and 20 MPH in rural areas.

The Hoosier Democrat, May 25, 1907 reported 12 automobiles in Flora. They were owned by Van C. Blue, Gertha Voorhees, Edward Voorhees, Eugene Furnas, E. G. Kitzmiller, Ward B. Hinder, Ross R.

The covered bridge across Wild Cat near Cutler in 1950. Since then it has been closed and has been badly damaged by vandals. The only other remaining covered bridge in Carroll County is the Lancaster bridge built the same year, 1872, across Wild Cat about six miles downstream in Clay township. It was open for light traffic in 1979.

The first automobile in Delphi was in 1899. It was owned by Clyne Brothers of Logansport, Indiana.

Penn II, Edward Hedderich, Lee Hedderich, Frank Bingaman and John Brown.

An article in the Delphi Journal, April 22, 1909 stated: "Warning to owners of automobiles: The statutes of Indiana limit the speed of automobiles to eight miles per hour on the business and populous streets. This law will be enforced in Delphi after each owner has been served with a notice."

In 1909 two marathon auto races were held in Lake County, and the same year a 2½ mile track was built at the Indianapolis Motor Speedway. The first auto race was held there on August 19, 1909. Races were held there in September and December 1909. A race was held in May 1910 with 30,000 people present. Races were also held in July and September that year.

On May 30, 1911 the first annual 500 mile race was held at Indianapolis. The race was won at a terrific speed of 74 MPH. This has become an Indiana institution for which Indiana is known all over the world.

In 1916 the U.S. Congress appropriated the first money for rural roads, and in 1917 the Indiana State Highway Commission was created in order to use the federal money in Indiana.

In 1926 there were 3624 automobiles in Carroll County. This was more than in any neighboring county with similar population. The number of passenger cars registered in Carroll County in 1978 was 9671.

AIRPLANES

The first airplane seen in Carroll County was on September 15, 1915 when a plane circled over Delphi five times during a county meeting of the Odd Fellows.

On October 1, 1918 the first airplane flew over Flora and landed in a field east of town.

Two public airports are located in the county and several airports are located near the county.

The Hoosier Democrat for July 12, 1919 reported: "The Wabash Training and Transportation Company came to Flora Tuesday with a Canadian Curtis Aeroplane and throughout the day was kept busy taking passengers into the air to get a birdseye view of the town and countryside some 1800 to 2600 feet below. Mrs. Raymond DeVinney was the first passenger to take a ride from Spitler's field with aviator Henry Fawcett. Thirteen made the trip at a price of $15 for fifteen minutes."

The following is a report from the Flora Centennial Souvenir Booklet, published in 1972:

Lee O. Eikenberry

"Lee O. Eikenberry, a pioneer in the air industry in the United States first was bit by the air bug in 1911 when he saw Lincoln Beechy fly from the Logansport fair grounds. He was using a Curtiss Pusher.

"The winter of 1916 while in Miami, Florida, Glen Curtiss came down from New York State with three of his latest training planes. He used a sand field right where the Miami International Airport is located today. His instructors were charging $600 to solo a student. Lee didn't have that kind of money, so all he could do was watch them fly, and dream about flying someday. World War I came along a few months later, and he was paid for learning. So in 15 short years after the Wright Brothers made their first flight, Lee was in the air flying Curtiss J-N-4D's which were nicknamed Jenny's.

"He was with an artillery unit the first six months in the Army and then transferred to Kelly Field in Texas. Early in the war he saw the first parachute jump ever made from an airplane. It was over Kelly Field by Vernon Castle of the famous dance team of Vernon and Irene Castle.

"In 1919 he was discharged from the Army and immediately signed on with the Kokomo Aviation Company which had purchased 16 carloads of war surplus Curtiss Jenny's to use for barnstorming and resale.

"In 1920 he purchased his own Curtiss airplane and brought it to Flora, thus becoming the first airplane owner in Carroll County. He landed in Spitler's Field near the school house, and through the generosity and civic mindedness of the late Bill and Harry Spitler, Flora and Carroll County were furnished a landing field free of charge for the next 21 years. It was known as the closest-to-town airport in this part of the country. You could land near the school house and be less than a city block from downtown.

"He operated Curtiss Jenny's out of Spitler's Field for several years, doing passenger carrying, and flying wing walkers and chute jumpers at county fairs in Indiana, Ohio and Kentucky. In the early days in hot weather, many times it took him one solid hour to climb 5,000 feet, with a chute jumper.

"In 1927 the Flora Aviation Corporation was organized. Dr. John Flora was president; Clayton Ayres, vice-president; Lynn Ledman, secretary and treasurer; and Lee Eikenberry was the chief pilot. They taught students, did passenger carrying and charter flights, and were dealers for Eaglerock and Waco airplanes.

"Two of the more famous pilots Lee trained were Vic Pixey of North Judson, who became chief test pilot for Republic Thunderbolt during World War II and Eddie Hudson of North Judson who, in 1967, had been with North American Aviation in California for 30 years.

"Lee was fortunate to stack up some firsts during his 32 years and 15,000 hours of flying. In 1919 he was on the first air mail flight in Indiana. In 1920 he won the cross country trip out of Indiana. He flew a Jenny to Florida to fly at the State Fair. In 1928 he flew the first retractable landing gear job in the U.S. and in 1932 he flew the first two-control plane in the U.S.

"Lee retired in 1949 with many fine memories of his flying experiences.

"On October 1, 1966 Lee was the keynote speaker at the dedication of the Flora Municipal Airport.

"Lee passed away November 17, 1970 at his residence in Flora.

"The town of Flora is very honored to have been the home of this great pioneer in the air industry."

This is another report from the Flora Centennial Souvenir Booklet published in 1972.

Flora Municipal Airport

"A Municipal Airport for the Town of Flora came under consideration by the Town Board of Trustees in the early spring of 1966 when they entered into a contract with Irvin Calhoun to purchase acreage for the site. An agreement had been made between the town board and the local flying club that if the land was purchased, the flying club would provide money to grade, seed, fence, install boundary markers and other necessary equipment to have the airport accepted and approved by the Indiana State Aeronautics Commission.

"Local merchants and businessmen were solicited by the flying club, and members of the club dug into their own pockets to raise a total of $4000 for the development.

"The site was then purchased by the town of Flora and work was begun to prepare the airport for use. The airport was opened for public use on July 4, 1966.

"The official dedication was held in October of 1966 with an invocation by Rev. Milton Craig, pastor of the First Christian Church, followed by a talk by Leland Eikenberry, a pioneer of aviation in this area. A guest speaker from Bunker Hill AFB (now Grissom AFB) was also present.

"Runway lights were added to the field in 1967 and flashing strobe Runway End Identification Lights were installed in 1970, making the airport useable at night as well as the daylight hours.

"At present five planes are based at Flora Municipal Airport, and itinerant traffic is increasing each year.

"Many people in the community have been taught to fly by Keith Sisson and have earned their private pilot license through his efforts. Elaine Smith is the only woman to receive her private license from this airport."

Delphi Municipal Airport

The Delphi City Council met Monday evening, May 19, 1969 and accepted a donation of 18.8 acres of land to be used for a Municipal Airport. The land given by Wayne Pearson and Louis Brubaker was located two miles south of Delphi on the south side of the County Base Line Road and one-quarter mile west of County Road 800 West, known as the Dayton Road.

The City Council approved the use of $15,000 from a Capital Improvement Fund created from cigarette tax revenue collected by the state and given to cities for such purposes. The Delphi Chamber of Commerce also donated $10,000 for the airport. This was probably the largest project ever undertaken in the community without the use of local tax money.

For several weeks during August 1969, many local Delphi area people furnished labor and equipment to prepare the landing strip for the airport. They moved more than 55,000 cubic yards of dirt and applied more than 4,000 cubic yards of gravel for the runway. Among those who helped were: Eric McCormick, John McCormick, Norman Peterson, Mike Clawson, Bill Duff, Lee Flora, Tom Flora, Bill Pearson, Jim White, Edgar Fountain, Tom Fountain, Joe Fountain, Harold Shanks, Mike Shanks, Fred Wise, Keith Wagoner, Donald Brubaker, Louis Brubaker, Jim Brubaker, Wayne Pearson, Ralph Wise, James Lloyd, Woodrow Whiteman, Jerry Wagner, Jack Cohee, Paul Sutherlin, Ed Stuntz, Lee Sterrett, Bill Shanks, Ralph Furr, Fred Arihood, Dave Abel, Steve Brubaker, Wayne Zinn, Ed Waymire, Cliff Baldwin, Don Brosman, Bill Dyer, Bob Gray, Laddie Daye, Russell Cable, Kenneth Flora, ABC Inc., Alloy Crafts Company and Jackson-Lee Inc.

In October, 1969 Smith Construction Company of Flora applied about 2500 yards of asphaltic concrete to make a runway 2900 feet long and 50 feet wide. Taxi-way, tie-down area, parking lot, driveways and buildings were added later.

PUBLIC BUILDINGS AND SERVICES

SCHOOLS

When settlers first came to the county, children were taught in the home, either by the parents or by a teacher hired by them. When there was a sufficient number of children in a community to justify a special building, a school district would be organized and a one room school house built. Early schools were financed by money from the sale of Section No. 16 in each township which was designated as the "school section." Each township had several school buildings so that every family would be within walking distance of a school. In 1883 there were 109 schools with 6147 pupils in Carroll County.

As the population increased, high schools were built, and nearly every township in the county had its own high school. Most of these were maintained until the school consolidation in the 1950's.

Carroll County is now serviced by two school corportations in the county and two corporations primarily outside the county.

Twin Lakes School Corporation

This corporation was organized on January 1, 1963, and serves Adams and Jefferson Townships in Carroll County and several townships in White County. Schools are located at Monticello, Yeoman and East Lawn.

The Yeoman School for grades 1 through 6 is located on an eight acre site. The original school was built in 1916, and an addition was built in 1958. The school has twelve classrooms with a capacity of 360 students.

The Monticello School has grade 7 through 12 in two buildings on a sixty-five acre site. Both buildings were rebuilt after the old ones were damaged in the tornado April 3, 1974.

The East Lawn School is located 1 mile north of Carroll County on White County Road 1300 East which connects with Carroll County Road 500 West.

Delphi Community School Corporation

Organized on July 1, 1964, this school corporation serves Tippecanoe, Deer Creek, Madison, Rock Creek, Liberty and Jackson Townships. School buildings are located in Pittsburg, Camden and Delphi.

The Pittsburg school with grades 1 through 5 is located on a two acre site at the top of the hill in Pittsburg. It has six class rooms with a capacity of 180 students.

The Camden Elementary School, first used for the 1969-70 school year is located on the same one and one-half acre site as the old high school which burned down. The old gymnasium did not burn, and is connected to the new building. With 17 classrooms, the building has a capacity of 510 students.

Three schools are located in Delphi. Hillcrest Elementary School, built in 1950, is located on a twenty acre site in South Delphi. A first addition was built in 1960 and a second in 1969. Hillcrest has a total of twenty-five classrooms, with a capacity of 750 students.

The Middle School for grades 6, 7 and 8 is located in the old high school building on one city block, on about one and one-half acres, on Monroe Street. The old building was built in 1915, a newer section in 1937, and a gymnasium and school lunch room, and band room were added in 1958.

There are twenty-one class rooms with a capacity of 630 students.

The High School was built in 1970 on a twenty-acre site south of Delphi. The school has a capacity of 1200 students. During 1976, a new administrative office building, tennis courts, and baseball diamond were added.

Carroll Consolidated School Corporation

Organized on January 1, 1959, the corporation serves Washington, Carrollton, Burlington, Democrat and Monroe Townships. Schools are located in Burlington and Flora. The Burlington School, used for grades 1 through 6, was built in 1912 on three acres of land in Burlington. It has a capacity of 330 students.

The Flora School, grades K through 8, is located in town on a one and one-half acre site. It was built in 1934 and has a capacity of 900 students.

Carroll High School, built in 1961 two miles east of Flora on State Road 18 on a forty-acre site, has twenty-one classrooms with a capacity of 630 students.

Rossville Consolidated School Corporation

This corporation was organized August 1, 1957, and serves Clay Township in Carroll County, and two townships in Clinton County. The school was built in 1967 on a thirty-five acre site south of Rossville, and has grades Kindergarten through 12. It has a capacity of 1200 students.

CHURCHES

The first church organized in Carroll County was the Methodist Church at Delphi in November, 1826. Other churches representing many denominations were organized wherever enough people were available in other parts of the county. The story of the early churches is well presented in "History of Carroll County Indiana, 1882" by T. B. Helm and "History of Carroll County" by J. C. Odell in 1916.

From the beginning, the church has been the center of activities for a community, and continues to have an influence on everyone in the community.

There are now about 35 churches in the county affiliated with the Carroll County Council of Churches, and about ten other churches.

COURTHOUSES

First Courthouse

The first court in Carroll County was held in the cabin of David Baum near Deer Creek, west of where the Wabash Railroad is now located. In the fall of 1829 the courts were held in a new log schoolhouse in Delphi. In 1830 the court was moved to a new one story frame building eighteen feet square, built on the southwest corner of the public square for the clerk's and recorder's office.

The first Courthouse, a two story brick building fifty feet square, was completed in September 1832, at a cost of $1,351. Painting, inside work, a cupola, plastering and other work required to complete the building made the total cost about $3500. It served the county for twenty-five years.

Second Courthouse

On April 2, 1856 the County Commissioners awarded a contract to build the second Courthouse. It was built of stone and brick with three stories and a basement and measured 65 x 95 feet. The building was completed in 1857 at a cost of $33,387. The clock cost

A view looking south from the Courthouse in Delphi showing the east half of the block south of the Courthouse, and the Courthouse fence which was built in 1857 and removed about 1890.

Second Courthouse in Carroll County 1857 to 1916. The Soldiers and Sailors Monument built in 1893 is still standing but the bandstand has been torn down.

$800, grading the yard $2000, and an iron fence around the yard cost $5697.15. About 1890 the fence was sold to Wm. Bradshaw who moved it to his farm three miles north of Delphi on the Carrollton Road. The farm was sold to the Carney family who sold it to James R. Kremer in 1955. At that time the fence was in such bad shape that it would not hold livestock. It was built with steel and cast iron, and could not easily be repaired. Mr. Kremer sold it for scrap in 1956. The fence weighed about 45 tons.

Third Courthouse

The present Carroll County Courthouse is located on a full block in the center of the business district in Delphi, on the same location where the first two Courthouses were located.

A contract for the new building was let in April 1916, and the cornerstone laid September 4, 1916. The building was completed in 1917 at a cost of $171,000.

During the time of building the Courthouse the business of the county was carried on in the Blythe & Son warehouse which was formerly the Presbyterian Church, located across Union Street from the Methodist Church.

Courthouse Bell

Samuel Davis Gresham was sheriff of Carroll County from 1836 to 1840. During that time he ordered a bell for the Courthouse. The bell was cast in Cincinnati and shipped on boat down the Ohio River and up the Wabash to Lafayette. The boat on which the bell was shipped met difficulty and was sunk in the Ohio River, but was successfully raised later, and the bell finally reached Delphi. It was placed on top of the first Courthouse building, and was clanged to

Wolever Photo

Ceremony for laying the corner stone for the Courthouse in Delphi on September 4, 1916.

CHAPTER I — GENERAL INFORMATION • 19

Third Courthouse in Carroll County built in 1917.

notify citizens of proceedings in the Courthouse. Later it was rung every hour to indicate the time, and was rung on special occasions when the report of a jury or some other important event was scheduled.

It was also used in the second Courthouse built in 1856.

When the second Courthouse was torn down in 1916 to make way for the new one built in 1917, the bell was purchased by Harry Milroy, and for many years was in the yard at his home east of Delphi. Mrs. Mollie Milroy gave it to the county.

In 1967 the Sesqui-Centennial Committee and the Carroll County Historical Society built a frame to hold the bell, and returned it to the rotunda of the Courthouse. The bell and frame weigh 730 pounds. It was rolled outside the Courthouse on July 4, 1976 and rung to celebrate the 200th year for the U.S.

Cannon

The cannon on the northwest corner of the Courthouse lawn has a plaque stating. "In appreciation of the Spanish American War veterans who gave their cannon from this site for World War II. Harry Bohannon Post No. 75 American Legion installs and dedicates this field piece in their honor May 30, 1949:"

Soldiers and Sailors Monument

The Soldiers and Sailors Monument located on the southeast corner of the public square in Delphi was unveiled on July 27, 1893.

At a county reunion of soldiers held at Flora in the summer of 1886, attention was called to the fact that the State Legislature had passed a law empowering County Commissioners to make a special levy for building a Soldiers and Sailors Monument on petition of a majority of the voters in the county. Committees were appointed and petitions circulated in every township. Soldiers meetings were held over the county, and by June, 1889 more than the required number had signed the petition, and the commissioners authorized a two cent levy.

A building committee composed of John G. Troxel, George W. Baum, George McCormick, James W. Wharton and C. J. McGreevey was appointed to select a design and arrange for building the monument.

In June 1892 a design was selected, and a contract given to A. A. McKain of Indianapolis for $11,990. Hannum and Conners of Delphi carried out the contract and erected the monument. John G. Troxel superintended the building of the foundation and George W. Baum the superstructure. J. F. Needler represented Mr. McKain, and Albert Helfer was boss of the workmen.

The monument was constructed of Vermont granite, and a strike at the quarry at Barre, Vermont delayed the work. The monument is 51 feet high and the statue of the color bearer on top is made of bronze.

On four sides are large bronze plates representing war scenes, and bronze plates with the coat of arms of the State and badges of the GAR, WRC and Sons of Veterans.

Murphy Fountain

The drinking fountain located on the southwest corner of the public square in Delphi was built by the city of Delphi with a gift of $3300 by Mr. and Mrs. M. M. Murphy. Mr. Murphy operated a drug store at 112 West Main Street in Delphi from 1878 to 1910. A contract was let in February 1918 for $3290 and the fountain was built of Vermont marble as used in the Soldiers Monument.

Bell used in first and second Courthouse and now in the rotunda of the third Courthouse.

A bronze tablet on the fountain states: "Presented to the City of Delphi, Indiana by Mr. & Mrs. M. M. Murphy who for 40 years were good citizens of our city doing their duties in a quiet unassuming way and helping every cause that stood for better living and better doing."

CARROLL COUNTY JAIL

The first Carroll County Jail was ordered built in Delphi in 1829, and was completed in 1830 on lot No. 101, owned by the county on the north side of the block north of the public square. The address of the house now on that lot is 112 West Monroe Street, and is owned and occupied by George Collins.

The building proved to be inadequate in size and construction, and was replaced in 1839 by another building in the same location at a cost of $550. In 1840 an addition was built at a cost of $1800 for the jailor's house and debtor's room. At that time people could be put in jail for not paying their debts. This did not prove to be an effective method of collecting debts, and the law went out when the new Indiana Constitution was adopted.

In 1871 two lots, number 37 and 38, on the corner of Main and Wabash Streets were purchased at a cost of $3000 for a new jail and sheriff's residence. A stone building for a jail and a brick building for the sheriff's residence were completed in December 1873 at a total cost of $42,000.

The sheriff's residence was replaced, and the jail remodeled in 1955 at a cost of about $60,000. Open House was held on December 9 and 10, 1955. The new stone residence had a combined living and dining room, kitchen, jail office, bath and three bedrooms on one floor with a complete basement. The jail cell block was a two story structure. The entire building was heated with a hot water system and a coal stoker.

COUNTY HOME

A farm of 160 acres located east of U.S. 421 on County Road 100 North was purchased by the county in 1848 at a cost of $2000. The building on the farm burned the next year, and the house was replaced by two hewed-log houses. One was 18 feet wide and 32 feet long with two rooms, and another was 16 feet square. Both were built at a total cost of $120. A brick building was built in 1853 at a cost of $2544.

Part of the present building was built in 1910 at a cost of $40,000. Additions and improvements have been made since then.

For many years, residents of the home furnished labor to operate the farm which provided income to pay the cost of operating the home.

It is now known as Carroll Manor and has a capacity of 38 residents.

Sanitary Landfill

A county Sanitary Land Fill established in 1968 is located on the north end of the County Farm. It is large enough to provide solid waste disposal for the entire county for several years.

COUNTY HIGHWAY GARAGE

The County Highway Garage is located on a four-acre site in the southeast part of Flora. A building constructed in 1948 provides office space and a garage for maintenance of equipment.

PUBLIC PARKS

Two public parks are located in Delphi, and one each in Flora, Camden, and Burlington. The county has two parks. A twelve acre park is located on the banks of Deer Creek in Washington Township along State Road 218. Facilities include camping grounds, picnic table, and a shelter house which can be used year-round. Richard Campbell was caretaker in 1979.

French Post Park is located on a five-acre tract in Rock Creek Township on the south bank of the Wabash River near Lockport. Facilities include a well, summer shelter house and camping grounds. Oliver Widner was caretaker in 1979.

County parks are supervised by a Carroll County Park Board. Members in 1979 were: Steve Nichols, John Reppert, Vern Myer, Robert Moore, and Paul Dean Hile.

FIRE DEPARTMENTS

Fire Departments in the county are located at Delphi, Flora, Burlington, Camden, Cutler, Rockfield and Burrows. Parts of the county are serviced by de-

Picture taken in 1953 of the Carroll County Jail, built in 1873. The jail was remodeled and a new residence for the sheriff built in 1955.

partments located outside the county at Monticello, Idaville, Georgetown, Logansport, Young America and Rossville.

MEDICAL SERVICE

There is no hospital in Carroll County, but one or more is located in each of the five adjoining counties. Ambulance service is available for everyone in the county.

In 1979 there were about 10 doctors in the county.

An article in the Delphi Journal, January 23, 1915 reported 39 doctors in the county: Flora 9, Delphi 10, Camden 4, Burlington 3, Bringhurst 2, Yeoman 1, Ockley 1, Cutler 1, Deer Creek 2, Wheeling 1, Burrows 2, Rockfield 2, and Pyrmont 1.

CARROLL COUNTY PUBLIC HEALTH DEPARTMENT

Prior to World War I, the nursing profession was primarily concerned with giving care to the bedridden. The American Red Cross recommended that nurses be used to teach health and promote vaccination for small pox and immunization against diptheria, whooping cough and tetanus. When the war ended, many Red Cross chapters, including the one in Carroll County, had surplus money in their treasury and were urged to employ Public Health Nurses. The Board of Directors of the Carroll County Red Cross was interested but had trouble finding a nurse qualified for the job. When they learned that Esther (Mrs. Roy) Gregg had training in Public Health, they offered her the job "until they could get someone else," meaning a single person, since very few married women worked outside the home at that time. She began in 1924, and kept the job for 34 years, less five years when their daughter was born. Miss Elsie Delaney was employed as nurse during that time.

At first the project was financed entirely by the Red Cross. Later the township trustees provided some money, and finally the entire project was financed with county funds.

The first work was carried on in the schools with special programs of vaccination and immunization at reduced prices. Polio was practically eliminated in the county by this program. Talks on health at club meetings promoted better nutrition, accident prevention, first aid for injured, etc.

Esther Gregg retired in February 1958. Thelma Trent was appointed in May 1958 and served until December 31, 1979. Shirley Prafka was appointed January 1, 1980.

A County Health Survey was conducted in 1957 and 1958 to find out what health programs were needed in Carroll County. Recommendations for the School Health Programs included: Vision, Hearing, Immunizations, Communicable Diseases, Tuberculin Skin Testing, Pre-school Round-up, Youth Educational Film, and Self-Application Fluoride. Recommendations for County Health Programs included: Tuberculosis, Crippled Children, Polio-March of Dimes, Heart, Mental Health, Red Cross, 4-H Club Health Project, Migrants, Health Educational Programs, and Home Health Care.

A full time Health Department was created when the Carroll County Commissioners established by ordinance the Carroll County Board of Health in 1959. At the first meeting on May 4, 1959, Dr. T. Neal Petry who had served as Health Officer since 1956 was appointed Health Officer for the new department. Prior to that time the job had been filled by local doctors each serving for one year. Nearly four years later Charles L. Burton was appointed as the first Sanitarian, and began work on February 1, 1963.

The Commissioners have passed four County Ordinances involving sanitation, which are implemented by the Board of Health. They are:

1963-1 Food Service Establishments, providing for inspection, requiring permits and fixing penalties.

1963-2 Food Market Ordinance providing for inspections requiring permits and fixing penalties.

1963-3 Private Sewage Disposal: Regulating the installation, construction, maintenance and operation of private sewage disposal systems in closely built up areas and providing penalties.

1968-1 Solid Waste Ordinance: An ordinance regulating the public disposal of garbage and rubbish, requiring permits and providing penalties.

The Health Department has been involved in several activities concerning environment and Public Health. In 1965, 1966 and again in 1976, the department made a pollution survey while the water level in the lakes in the Tippecanoe River was lowered. The department helped establish a sanitary landfill and an animal retention center in 1968. They have helped enforce the Animal Waste Law, and have helped with the many problems of the Area Plan Commission since it was created in 1967. Information was provided for Delphi and Camden when they built their sewage treatment plants, and for Burlington in their plans for a sewage plant. Advice has been given to many individuals regarding the disposal of sewage and other waste, without causing pollution. Special training programs have been provided for those who handle food.

The office of the first County Health Nurse was located in the first room west of the north entrance to the Courthouse. When a full time Health Department was established in 1959 it was moved to the first room west of the south entrance where the County

Mrs. Esther Gregg on the right at a celebration on January 26, 1958 in her honor when she retired as County Health Nurse. Others in the picture are Dr. and Mrs. C. C. Crampton. For several years Dr. Crampton was the oldest practicing physician in Indiana.

Surveyor's office is now located. In 1965 it was moved to the present location in the northeast corner of the Courthouse.

The Health Department is directed by a seven member Health Board appointed by the County Commissioners. Present members and the year they were appointed are: C. L. Wise, M.D., 1963; Arthur O. Weddell, 1969; Marilyn Wagoner, M.D., 1971; Manson Campbell, 1972; John A. Bush, D.V.M., 1974; Harry Jones, D.D.S., 1974 and Mary Lou Blue, 1976. Others who have served are: George W. Wagoner, M.D., Hazel Kirkpatrick, Herb Smith, Max R. Adams, M.D., Charles N. Wilson, D.D.S., Russell D. Callane, Stanley H. Shipsides, D.V.M., Edward S. Emerson, D.V.M., and Jesse Zook. Present employees are: Dr. T. Neal Petry, M.D., Health Officer since 1956; Thelma Trent, R.N., Community Health Nurse since 1958; Charles L. Burton, R.P.S., County Sanitarian since 1963; and Shirley Horn, Vital Statistics Clerk, since January 1, 1979. Others who have served as Vital Statistics Clerks are Ruby Trent, Jane Vorhees, and Mabel Snoeberger.

Jacqueline Davis R.N., has served as school nurse at Carroll Consolidated Schools since March, 1966.

Jacquoline Barnett R.N., was hired by Delphi Consolidated School Corporation in March, 1978. Ruth Johnson served as school nurse in Delphi Schools for a few months in 1962.

Records of births and deaths occurring in Carroll County since 1882, and school enumeration records from 1896 to 1924 are on file in the Health Office. The records of births and deaths were stored in doctor's offices and the school records were in the clerk's office in the Courthouse, until 1959 when they were all placed on file in the Health Department at the Courthouse. School records from 1924 to the present are on file in each school corporation office.

The Health Department issues burial permits, certified birth and death certificates, school enumeration records and genealogy information.

CAMP TECUMSEH

On July 20, 1924, the State YMCA of Indiana purchased 30 acres of Horseshoe Bend on the Tippecanoe River between Delphi and Brookston to establish a camp. A Lafayette newspaper held a contest to name the camp and the winner, Jack Fisher of Battle Ground, won two free weeks at camp. With the naming of the camp, the portion of Horseshoe Bend on which the camp was located became known as Tecumseh Bend, and is still called by that name.

Gradually the camp grew from 30 to 284 acres. In 1952, the camp built a swimming pool and planted 20,000 pine trees to be sold as Christmas trees to provide extra revenue. The trees were not harvested, so the camp now has 30 acres of pine trees.

In 1969, Camp Tecumseh became one of only five camps in the U.S. that is an independent YMCA camp. It is governed by a lay board of directors from Delphi, Lafayette, and the surrounding community. Roy Tulp was hired as the first full time director.

An Adventure Camp was begun in 1972 for 13-17 year olds. Among the trips that are run are backpacking expeditions to the Rockies, Tetons, Wind River Mountains, and the Smokies, canoeing in the Canadian Boundary waters, and bicycle trips to Mackinaw Island, Michigan. 1975 brought the beginning of summer and holiday Day Camp for 5-10 year olds. In recent years programs have expanded to include many more activities, including such things as playground programs, learn-to-swim, trips to Disney World and specialty camps.

The camp is now the largest non-funded outdoor

Entrance to Camp Tecumseh.

Log cabin being built at Camp Tecumseh in 1979.

education center in Indiana, providing educational and recreational programming in the spring and fall for over 30 area public schools. Over 160 social, educational, business and recreational groups use the facilities at the non-profit camp which supports itself completely through usage fees.

Richard G. Marsh has been executive director of the camp since November 1, 1976. In 1978, a major building program began at Tecumseh. The 50 year old cabins are being replaced by log cabins. Each cabin is 25' x 40' and has two living units, each with a capacity of ten people. A new riding stable, outdoor education/day camp pavilion, multi-purpose courts and road repairs are also being completed.

Throughout the many years of operation, the goal of Camp Tecumseh YMCA has been to build Christian character of youth through the preservation and enjoyment of the great outdoors. "Take only memories, leave only footprints" embodies Camp Tecumseh's philosophy of the outdoors.

PUBLIC LIBRARIES

Delphi Public Library

About 1888 a literary club known as the Monday Club was organized in Delphi. During the six or seven years that the club was active, the members often talked about establishing a public library in Delphi.

In the fall of 1896 several former members of the Monday Club organized the Oracle Club primarily for the purpose of establishing a public library in Delphi.

The club sponsored three lectures and at the third which was held in the Presbyterian Church in May 1897, the admission price was one book, and more than 100 books were obtained.

In 1897 a tax rate of two cents per $100 was levied for a library fund, and a public library was established in the Delphi High School. Miss Emma Myers was the first librarian. After taking special courses in Library Science, she classified and catalogued the collection of over 150 books.

About that time it was learned that Andrew Carnegie offered to build a library in any town in Indiana that would meet his conditions. After discussing the matter at several meetings of the Oracle Club, and with the City Council, a public meeting was held in March, 1904 and those who attended were in favor of meeting the conditions to get a donation from Carnegie.

The City Council appropriated $2000 to buy a lot for the library, and approved a tax levee to raise at least $1000 per year for maintenance of the library and building.

A regular Library Board was appointed with the following members: Dr. Frank H. Robinson, James O. Obear, Mrs. John H. Burr, Miss Mary Alice Dodge, Mrs. Mary C. Howe, Charles Harley and James P. Wason. In April, 1904 the school board transferred 2500 books and management of the library to the new Library Board.

In October, 1904 the board rented a room for the library in the rear of the A. T. Bowen and Company bank building which is now occupied by the Carroll Telephone Company. The library was open from 12:30 to 9:30 P.M. This was a great improvement, since the library in the school had been open only during school hours. At that time Miss Iona McCain was librarian and in November Miss Isabelle Rinehart was appointed assistant librarian to serve one hour at suppertime with no pay. Beginning in 1905 she was paid 10 cents for each hour. A janitor was hired for $1 per week.

There were 12 towns in Indiana with Carnegie libraries and a survey of them indicated that they were satisfied with their libraries. An appropriation for $10,000 was approved by Carnegie in January, 1905. Bids were opened July 21, 1905 and a contract signed with W. C. Halstead and Company of Indianapolis for $8050 for the building alone.

Construction began in July and the corner stone was laid Wednesday afternoon, September 20, 1905. The building located at 222 East Main Street, was dedicated June 19, 1906. The total cost of the building including heating, plumbing and wiring was $10,002.40. There were about 3000 books in the library, and by that time there were 50 other Carnegie libraries in Indiana.

Major improvements have included new flourescent light fixtures in 1953, a new roof in 1958 and a gas furnace in 1959 to replace the coal furnace.

For many years a large room in the basement of the library was used for public meetings, but it is now used as a children's library and for special programs for children and adults.

Many individuals and organizations have donated books and other materials for the library. One of the largest was the Howe Fund, which included donations of books and money by Mary C. Howe and her brother William Haskell. Mary C. (Mrs. Newberry J.) Howe helped establish the library, and served as a director until her death, December 9, 1936.

Another outstanding gift of books and money was made by Mrs. Meredith Carney Dial and her husband Thomas. A room was renovated and decorated to be used for Memorial Books and was named the Dial Room.

In 1915 Deer Creek Township levied a tax to help support the library, and service is now available without charge to residents of Delphi and Deer Creek Township. By a special agreement, library card holders in the Flora and Camden Public Libraries may also use the services of the Delphi Library.

There were few administrative changes in the early history of the library. After Miss Emma Myers and Miss Iona McCain, Miss Isabelle Rinehart became librarian in June 1907, and held that position until she married Harry Baum in 1920. Miss Mary Cochrane became librarian in 1920 after being assistant since 1915. She held the position until she retired in June 1960 after a total of 45 years in Library service. Mrs. Irma Crosby acted as librarian until school started, then Mrs. Mary Lamb served as librarian until her marriage in July, 1961. Mrs. Hazel Fry became librarian August 1, 1961 and remained until she retired January 1, 1968.

Mrs. Barbara Hanna was librarian from 1968 to 1975 and Mrs. Betsy McAlhaney from 1975 to 1978. Dennis Noble has been librarian since August 1, 1978.

Members of the Library Board in 1979 were: Audria Clements, president; Abe Alvarez, vice president; Cathy Smith, secretary; Mary Ives, treasurer; Irma Crosby, Linda Perdue, and Robert Walton.

Flora-Monroe Public Library

The Flora Library Board was organized on August 20, 1915. They purchased a lot on North Center Street at a cost of $1183 and built a building costing $9964.25. The Carnegie Foundation furnished $10,000 and the balance was raised by donations.

The Library was opened for business at 9:30 A.M. on Saturday, August 17, 1918. Miss Dawson was the first librarian. Others have been Mrs. Jack (Eleanor) Carter, Mrs. Galen (Kathern) Shope, and Mrs. DeVere (Martha) Hoffman.

The first Library Board was: J. W. Brower, president; E. G. Kitsmiller, vice president; M. V. Eaton, treasurer; and W. T. Lytle, secretary, Mrs. Ethel Goslee, W. V. Pearson, W. B. Kearns, Mrs. Hiram Tinkle and Mrs. Dan Cromer. The present Library Board is: Kenneth McGill, president; Edgar Krauss, Jr., vice president; Mrs. Robert (Karen) Rieffel, secretary; Mrs. Dick N. (Jane) Bishop, treasurer; Mrs. Meredith (Naomi) Butcher, Mrs. Larry (Kathi) Johnson, and Glen Dillman.

The Flora Public Library has merged with Monroe Township to form the Flora-Monroe Township Public Library. In addition to Flora and Monroe Township, the library contracts for service with Democrat, Carrollton and Washington Township.

The Flora-Monroe Township and Delphi Public Libraries have reciprocal borrowing privileges. The library also has a transactual agreement with the Logansport Public Library. Any patron in good standing can use these facilities.

The Flora Public Library has a collection of 2300 volumes, subscribes to 53 magazines and has 600 records available for use. The magazines are kept for a period of five years using the Oblique Storage System. Equipment in the library includes a 3M copy machine, a Kodak movie projector, a Bohn duplicator and a Stereo AM-FM radio and record player.

The basement of the library has been made into a beautiful children's room. On November 19, 1978, an open house was held to dedicate the Maude Ayres Memorial Children's Room. This was a big improvement and allowed more room upstairs for the adults and young people.

Summer finds the library busy with activities. Approximately 200 children are enrolled each year in the summer reading program. Some years there have been as many as three busses required to take the children on the trip that is a treat for those completing the program. Trips are alternated between the Indianapolis Zoo and the Indianapolis Children's Museum.

Other activities are the weekly story hour which draws a large number of the pre-schoolers, and movies which are shown regularly during the winter months at the library and at the nursing home. A book collection is also taken to the Brethren's Home.

Camden Public Library

On January 10, 1928 at the home of Mrs. Florence Baker, the Camden Women's Literary Club voted to start a public library. The Club set 1938, the Golden Anniversary of the Club, for achieving this aim.

Money was raised by various ways, by the Club as a whole and by individual donations of money and books.

A very large gift of books was received from the Nettie Rice Estate and also from Clara Lennon.

The first Board of Trustees appointed consisted of the following members: Dr. Eva Kennedy, Mrs. J. C. Yunker and Mrs. Effie Wyatt.

The first Book Committee was: Mrs. Harold Baker, Mrs. Vurpillat and Mrs. Nell Quinn. All members and friends of the Club contributed much time and effort to the project.

On March 10, 1929 at the Vurpillat Pharmacy the Camden Library was presented to Camden by Mrs. Flora Cripe, president of the Literary Club. Mr. Stangle, president of the Community Club, accepted it for the town.

Mrs. Vurpillat was the first Librarian. From the Pharmacy the Library was moved to the Town Hall room back of Johnson's Store. (now Jackson's store). For the next 10 years the Library was maintained by the Club. As a climax to the Golden Anniversary Celebration in 1938-1939, the Library became a tax supported enterprise.

In 1950, it was moved to a different location in the town building formerly known as the Center Garage. In 1969 the Library Board purchased a lovely old brick home on the corner of Main and Monroe Streets. The Library was moved to its present location in 1970.

Librarians through the years have been: 1940 Nell Quinn with Ruth Edging as assistant; 1942-1973 Ruth Edging. Mrs. Edging retired in December 1973, with a record of 33 years service to the Library. Since 1974 Shirley Schock has been librarian with June Thomas as assistant.

The Library Board in 1979 was: Harold McCormick, president; Rev. Richard Recher, vice president; Nancy Kleckner, secretary, and Mrs. Madeline Kesner, treasurer. Other members were: Mrs. Evelyn Sharp, Mrs. Opal Ringer and Mrs. Myra Gardner.

NEWSPAPERS

WEEKLY PAPERS

A newspaper that is published once each week cannot keep up to date with the latest news. If there are two or more papers in the area published on different days of the week, that adds to the problem. An article in a paper published on Thursday stated: "Grandma Smith is very low. If she dies tomorrow she will be buried on Sunday."

Carroll County has had about fifteen weekly papers, with as many as six being published at the same time. It is difficult to find complete and accurate records on some of them. The following information from several sources is not complete, but does give some facts regarding the many papers in the county.

It is generally agreed that the first newspaper published in Carroll County was the Western Banner. It was published in Delphi by Dr. Robert Weber and Mr. Clymer, beginning on June 24, 1836. They sold it to R. C. Green who had started publication of The Delphi Oracle, about the same time. He sold it to Henry B. Milroy in 1837 and the last issue was printed in 1839.

The Carroll Express was established by A. D. Tweed about 1839 and in 1848 the name was changed to Delphi Herald. Other owners were R. C. Green, Henderson Dunkle, Charles A. Naylor and Thomas B. Helm. It suspended publication in 1850.

Delphi Journal

The equipment was purchased by James B. Scott who established the Delphi Weekly Journal. The first issue was published November 14, 1850. During 1854 and 1855 it was called the Delphi Dollar Journal and in 1856 the name was changed to Delphi Journal. During 1858 and 1859 and again in 1865 and 1866 it was called the Delphi Weekly Journal. After 1867 it was called the Delphi Journal.

This paper was sold to Chas. B. Landis and Victor L. Ricketts in 1887. They published it until July 21, 1910 when they sold it to Noah E. and Bert B. Mayhill. Noah sold his interest in 1919 to Prof. Isaac W. Cripe, Superintendent of Delphi Schools, who kept it for about a year, and sold it back to Noah, who sold his interest to B. F. Ulm on October 18, 1923.

The Mayhill and Ulm partnership continued for 18 years. During this time Mayhill served as Managing Editor and Ulm as Business Manager. For several years during this time B. B. Mayhill was a member of the Indiana State Legislature and members of his family helped with the paper. His wife Dora Thomas Mayhill, served as News Reporter and Society Editor, and wrote many special items. She later wrote and published several books on the History of Carroll County.

Their two sons, Roger and Thomas, also served as editors. Roger was editor for several years until September 1935 when he went to the University of Illinois to do Post Graduate work. Since then he became a Professor in the History Department at Purdue University until the time of his retirement.

Thomas served as editor for a few years, and then moved to Knightstown, where he publishes the Knightstown Banner, the Tri State Trader, Farm Week, and reprints historical books.

In August 1941 the Mayhill family sold their interest to B. F. Ulm, and he formed a new partnership with Leo C. Craig who had been a teacher for 22 years, 15 of which were in the Delphi schools. Leo became Managing Editor, and Mrs. L. H. Smith was employed as Society Editor.

In 1947 Richard Rainbolt purchased the interest

of Buel Ulm in the paper and was a partner until September 1956 when he sold his interest to Leo Craig.

In December 1964 Mr. and Mrs. Leo Craig sold the paper to Mr. and Mrs. Alfred L. Moss of Flora. Mr. Moss was editor and publisher of the Hoosier Democrat, and beginning January 1, 1965 he became editor and publisher of the Delphi Journal. He continued to publish the two papers and printed them both on the recently installed press in the Delphi Journal shop.

Delphi Citizen

The Delphi Times, a Democratic weekly paper which later became the Delphi Citizen was first published in 1848. During the first 30 years a number of people were owners and editors of the paper. Among them were: Jonathan C. Applegate, Milton R. Graham, Frank Burns, J. McCarthy, Joseph R. Horsley, Jasper Keyes, James C. Odell, Patrick H. O'Brian, A. R. Bell, J. A. Cartwright, E. H. Gresham and C. R. Pollard.

In 1879 the paper was purchased by Adelbert B. Crampton. In a few years Mr. Crampton was appointed postmaster and sold the paper to C. R. Pollard and his son-in-law R. M. Isherwood. When Crampton's term as postmaster ended, he wanted to buy the paper but the owners would not sell it to him.

In 1891 A. B. Crampton established his own paper, the Carroll County Citizen and for about five years there were two Democratic papers published in Delphi. The competition between the two papers is indicated by the following quotation from an article written by Mindwell Crampton Wilson in February, 1948 for the 100th anniversary issue of the Delphi Citizen: "Harry Milroy, prominent local resident, whom we think of as a sculptor of those days, was also one of the first cartoonists. His pen and ink drawings were works of art, and he sold them both to the Times and the Citizen. He would draw Dell Crampton and his beard one week and sell it to Mr. Pollard, and the next week he would draw a picture of Pollard and Isherwood hiding behind a barricade from the barrage of words which Dell Crampton had hurled their way and The Citizen would buy it."

In 1896 after a five-year unsuccessful feud, Pollard and Isherwood sold the Times to A. B. Crampton, and the paper became the Carroll County Citizen-Times.

In 1909, A. B. Crampton's daughter, Mindwell and her husband Henry B. Wilson began helping with the paper, and took over the operation in 1915 when A. B. Crampton became governor of the National Military Home at Marion.

In 1924 the name of the paper was changed to Delphi Citizen.

In 1927 the Wilsons sold the Citizen to Mr. and Mrs. Parke Beadle of Parke County who in turn sold to Mr. and Mrs. Wayne Coy of Johnson County in 1931. Gilbert Bailey and Myron Johnson leased the paper from the Coys in August 1933. Gilbert's brother, Allen, and Johnson purchased the paper from the Coys in 1938 when Mr. Coy went to Washington, D.C. to become a high official in the Roosevelt Administration. Upon Allen's death in 1942, his wife, now Jeanne Bailey Moyer, edited the paper until 1946 when the Johnsons purchased her interest in the business. Arthur McDowell, now State Director of Publicity, American Legion, edited the paper for the Johnsons from 1946 to January of 1964. He had been associated with the paper since the middle 30's.

In December 1966 the Johnsons sold the names and subscription list to Alfred L. and Joan E. Moss who had purchased the Delphi Journal two years before from Mr. and Mrs. Leo C. Craig. Beginning in January 1967 the paper was called the Delphi Journal Citizen.

Camden Record

The first issue of the Camden Expositor was published January 8, 1880 by Dr. Carter. Four months later he sold it to Zopher Hunt. Wade W. Farr purchased the paper in November 1901. In June 1913 the name was changed to Camden Record.

The Delphi Journal for August 10, 1933 reported that Mrs. Nettie Warren sold the Camden Record to M. W. Triplet of Hicksville, Ohio.

Thomas Mayhill purchased the Camden Record in 1946, and published it for about two months. The Camden Record was discontinued in August 1946, and the subscription list was sold to the Delphi Journal, the Delphi Citizen, and the Hoosier Democrat.

The Hoosier Democrat

The first issue of the Hoosier Democrat was published September 18, 1897. F. A. Moss who had retired as Postmaster during the administration of Grover Cleveland, was the owner, editor and publisher. He stated in the first issue that it would be a Democratic paper "in the camp of the enemy."

In March 1899 management of the paper passed to Chester A. Keyes and Noah E. Mayhill. They stated that as an independent paper "it shall be no slave to any party."

Mr. Keyes moved to Oklahoma, and sold his interest to Bert B. Mayhill in April 1901. A short time later Burr R. Keyes became the third partner with the Mayhill Brothers.

In August 1908 the Hoosier Democrat became the first newspaper in Carroll County to own a Linotype machine.

The Delphi Journal for April 28, 1904 reported that Allen Huntsinger recently purchased an interest in the Flora Enterprise Sentinel, and moved his family from Camden to Flora.

In March 1909 F. A. Moss purchased the Fountain City Enterprise of Charles E. Nobes. In the meantime the Flora Sentinel owned by Burr R. Keyes and Harry Hanna had merged with the Fountain City Enterprise, and Mr. Keyes had purchased a third interest with Mayhill Brothers in the Hoosier Democrat.

Mayhill Brothers and Keyes sold the Hoosier Democrat to F. A. Moss and his son Ashwell Lynn Moss in April 1909. When F. A. Moss died in August 1916, Ashwell became editor, and became sole owner in February 1931 when he purchased the interest from his mother. In June 1941 the Hoosier Democrat purchased the Carroll County Press from Burr R. Keyes and J. W. Sink and the two papers were merged.

The Carroll County Press had been established in 1911 by Burr R. Keyes and Wade Farr, who had been employed on every newspaper in the county at one time or another. Mr. Farr sold his interest in the Carroll County Press to Keyes and Son and retired from the newspaper business when he was elected County Auditor.

Burr R. Keyes, retiring editor of the Carroll County Press, was the oldest publisher in Carroll County and the Press was the youngest newspaper. Mr. Keyes had been connected with all the newspapers in Flora, including the Fountain City Enterprise, the Flora Sentinel, the Carroll County Press and the Hoosier Democrat. Alfred L. Moss, grandson of the founder of the Hoosier Democrat joined his father at the office in June 1949, and became editor and sole owner when his father retired in 1963.

The Comet

In 1974 Al Moss decided to combine his newspapers and have just one paper for Carroll County. He had been editor of the Hoosier Democrat since 1963, the Delphi Journal since December 1964, and the Journal-Citizen since December, 1966 when the Delphi Citizen was combined with the Delphi Journal.

None of the names would be satisfactory for a county wide non partisan paper so he started looking for a name. Dean Overholser was one of several who helped him think about a name. At that time the Comet Kohoutek was prominent in the news, since it had been discovered on March 7, 1973 and had been visible during the latter months of 1973. One day Dean said: "Why not call your new paper the Comet?" Al agreed "Why not!" and so it was named the "Carroll County Comet" and the first issue was published February 6, 1974.

One fortunate thing about the choice, enough letters were available from the old "Hoosier Democrat" sign to make the new sign "Comet" at the office at Flora. Offices have been maintained at Flora and Delphi to handle news, ads and subscriptions, and one paper is published for the county.

Employees in 1979 in addition to A. L. and Joan Moss were Pauline Robeson and Donna Overholser at Delphi, and the following at Flora: Wayne Duddy, Susan Scholl, LaDonna Allen, Cleve Evans, Chris Clear, Karen Hollis and Chris Denny.

DELPHI DAILY HERALD

Carroll County had at least one daily paper. It was called the Delphi Herald, and the office was located south of the Masonic Temple in the building on the corner of Washington and Front Streets in Delphi.

It was published for about fifteen years beginning about 1897. A copy was placed in the cornerstone of the Presbyterian Church in 1909. At that time the paper was published by F. A. Baker and Son.

An article in the paper in November, 1901 states: "Wade W. Farr, who was formerly a half owner of the Delphi Herald, has purchased the Camden Expositor plant and took possession of the same Thursday."

MONTHLY PAPERS

The Farm News

There is no record of a monthly paper being published in Carroll County, but from October 1941 to December 1978 a special Carroll County edition of the Farm News was printed at Marion, Indiana.

Studies have shown that the success of an organization is often determined by the kind of a job it does in keeping its members and the general public informed about what it is doing. A good program of education and publicity includes information at meetings, reports to members, and news articles in newspapers and magazines. Most larger organizations have a newsletter or magazine for the members, but for a small organization this is too expensive.

This problem was solved by the Farm Bureau and its affiliated cooperatives in Indiana with a publication known as "The Farm News." It was an eight page newspaper published once each month with a special edition available for each county. Pages 2, 3, 6 and 7 were the same for every edition each month, and pages 1, 4, 5 and 8 were different for each county edition. Material for the county pages was collected by a local editor who had reporters from each interested organization in the county report their news for the month. It was assembled and sent to Marion, Indiana where it was edited, printed, and mailed to members in the county. Indiana is the only state that has a paper of this kind.

First Farm News

The first Farm News was published in Grant County in April, 1935. It was a six page paper with 14 paid subscribers for the first issue. A subscription campaign soon resulted in enough subscribers to make the paper eligible for a second class permit which was granted by the postal department in June that year.

During the next two years five more county editions were added. The cooperatives in the six counties organized a non-profit corporation to handle all the details of news gathering, the sale of advertisements, editing and all activities connected with publishing the paper, except the actual printing.

In 1939 six more counties were added. In 1940 arrangements were made for the Indiana Farm Bureau to deduct the subscription price of the paper from the annual Farm Bureau dues. Farm Publications, a closely held corporation was organized to take over the duties of the non-profit corporation, and the Indiana Farm Bureau Cooperative Association took an active part in the paper, and recommended it to county associations. Twenty seven new county editions including the Carroll County edition were started in 1941.

In a few years there were editions for nearly every county in the state with a total circulation of more than 200,000. This made it the third largest newspaper in Indiana. The post office at Marion, Indiana had more second class mail permits than any other post office in the U.S.

For several years the paper went to nearly every farm in Indiana, and to a few readers in every state and in Canada, Puerto Rico, England, Alaska, Africa and Australia.

The Editor

The idea of Farm News was originated by Von O. Pinkerton, the first and only Editor of the paper. Many friends advised him that the idea would not work. One with newspaper experience told him, "No, you'll never be able to get them to collect the news, write it up, and send it in to you regularly; you just can't teach farm people the meaning of a deadline." He tried it anyway, and after a lot of hard work, succeeded beyond the expectations of anyone.

Mr. Pinkerton wrote an article in the April 1975 Farm News reporting some of the problems involved in securing mailing permits from the post office. He wrote: "That first application was granted since a Washington friend of an Indiana politician who was a friend of mine took an interest in what I was trying to do. . . . later difficulties arose because people in the postmaster general's office refused to believe that the Farm Bureau and the Farm Bureau Co-op were two separate organizations. . . . those problems were finally overcome after some three or four personal visits to Washington. . . . even meeting that tall gal who was the receptionist in the postmaster general's office was a revelation. . . . I don't know what she expected, perhaps a part Indian from the wilds of the Midwest, but she offered me a handshake the like of which I'd never seen before. Her hand hung down instead of being extended and having grown up on a farm where we had milk cows, I didn't know whether to pull it or shake it. . . . years later, I was told one was supposed to kiss a hand held like that, but that information came 20 years too late to do me any good."

Purposes

A primary purpose of the paper was to give farmers a news media where they could write what they knew and read what others had to say, about what they had done, were doing, and hoped to do, by belonging to a farm organization. This would encourage members and prospective members to do a better job in building and using farm organizations.

Another purpose was to develop people in every county who would learn to recognize and write news stories telling about the successes and failures in the march of Hoosier farm people toward a better life.

Local Editors

The use of an editor and reporters in each county is one feature that made Farm News different from any other farm paper. Training schools were held each year for local editors and reporters to instruct them how to collect and write news, and encourage them to do a better job. Awards were given each year for counties which did an outstanding job on Farm News, and Carroll County won its share of awards.

Special Editions

Extra pages were added any month when an unusual amount of news was available. The Carroll County edition usually had four extra pages in August to have room for pictures of activities at the County 4-H Fair. The largest edition ever printed was a 48 page edition in Howard County.

Carroll County Farm News

The first edition of Carroll County Farm News was published in October, 1941, and was sent to farmers in Carroll County each month. The last edition was in December, 1978. Organizations cooperating in the new project were the FB, Farm Bureau Cooperative Association, REMC, Production Credit Association, County Agent and the AAA. For many years employees in the FB Co-op office served as local Editor. Mrs. Clayton Million served as editor since 1970.

For the first seven years the Carroll County REMC used the back page for its news, and the paper was often called the REMC paper. It was difficult to keep the mailing list up to date so that all members received the paper, so in 1948 the REMC began their own paper called "Kilowatt Ours."

News about other organizations in the county has varied, depending on who was willing to take the time to write articles. Regular features throughout the nearly 40 years were articles by the County FB president, County Women's leader, Pet and Hobby leader, Rural Youth, Co-op Manager, Production Credit Association, Soil and Water Conservation District, County Agent and many others. Annual meetings of the many organizations have been featured, as well as many special events in the county. Several people who had taken trips wrote articles about their trips.

Beginning in June 1949 a series of articles each month entitled "Meet your Neighbor" featured a story about a farm leader in the county. Articles were written about Clayton Million, Fred Rodkey, S. A. Wickard, Dean Mills, Artus Rodenbarger, Loyd Zook, Joseph E. Peterson, Enos Berkshire, John B. McCormick, Charles Sanderson, Ralph Maggart, Carl Johnson, Leroy Robeson, Harold Frey and Russell Craig.

Out of the Wastebasket

Beginning in January, 1946 and for the next 138 months, an anonymous joker who has never admitted it, wrote an article called "Out of the Wastebasket" and signed it "your little pal, Oscar the Office Boy."

Little Oscar was a bashful and shiftless character who stayed in the office of the County FB Co-op Association and did odd jobs like sharpening pencils, taking the boss's fountain pen to the post office to fill it with ink, licking postage stamps, etc., but mostly he did as little as possible. Sometimes he would save a little money by dropping a letter in the box without a stamp when no one was watching. He scratched around in the wastebasket and came up with all kinds of information and dirt about people and things. He went to meetings, listened to the big people talking, and reported anything he saw or heard that was fit to print.

Fan mail the first month included three post cards. Two were from folks who wondered since when the Farm News got so hard up for something to print that it used junk like that. The other was from "Big Oscar" (Oscar Cooley) who was director of publicity for the IFBCA. Little Oscar even helped Big Oscar on one of his radio programs on WIBC at Indianapolis in November 1946.

A survey of readers in the county revealed that this column was the most widely read feature in Farm News. One reason was that it reported on the really important things of life. One time Little Oscar discussed the problem of how to do a neat job of licking postage stamps and eating popcorn at the same time. Another time he suggested that someone ought to build a clear plastic cover for man holes. That way you could look in and see if anything was wrong without lifting the lid. Also when it was necessary for some one to work in the man hole, he

"Out of the Wastebasket"

could close the lid and still have light without having pedestrians drop in on him.

He reported all kinds of conversations, like the time he heard two farmers talking, and one of them said that he wished the price of hogs would go down. He had sold all but two of his hogs, and was waiting for the price to go down so he could afford to butcher them.

Sometimes when he was tempted to tell everything he heard or saw, he took another look at a picture post card with the picture of a fish with a sad expression on his face. The fish had just been caught and was saying: "If only I had kept my mouth shut."

After looking things over at Old Settlers, he made this observation: "An optimist is a person who thinks he can win a Teddy Bear for a nickel while a pessimist is the same guy ten minutes, three dollars, and no Teddy Bear later."

Pumpkin Seed

It wasn't all foolishness and nonsense (at least not quite all). He never missed an opportunity to give a boost to the FB Co-op or other worthy organizations in the county.

In October 1952 he reported on hearing an argument between Loyd Zook and Lawrence Metzger. The question was: "If I plant a pumpkin seed in my garden and the vine grows through the fence and a pumpkin grows on your side, who does the pumpkin belong to?" He didn't report on who won the argument, but did make the statement: "People work hard to build a bigger and better FB. That's a lot harder work than plantin' pumpkin seeds and the benefits run through the fence and help every farmer whether he gives them $10 or a cussin.'"

Doomsday Jackson

When things were too quiet around the office Little Oscar would take off on his bicycle and see what was going on around town. In June 1956, he reported that he saw Doomsday Jackson mowing his sidewalk. He stopped to see what was going on and reported: "He had one of those new fangled whirly whiz lawn mowers, and was using it to blow the dirt and stuff off the sidewalk. It was doing a real nice job, and a lot easier than using a broom. They say that lazy folks are efficient, so leave it to a guy like my pal Doomsday to figure out the easy way to do things."

Fertilizer Sacks

It was customary in those days for a farmer to keep records by writing things on the barn door. When the barn door got full of figures and information, that created a problem. Little Oscar offered a solution: "Write it on a paper fertilizer sack. When the sack is covered with figures, tear off the outer layer of paper and put it in the sack and start on the second layer of paper." Before that idea caught on, along came bulk fertilizer and spoiled it.

Mousetrap

Little Oscar got in real bad trouble in December 1952. Here is part of the article that month: "I caught my fing r in a mous trap. It's th on I us to slap th l tt r " " on th typ writ r. That's th l tt r b - tw n "w" and "r" on th typ writ r or b tw n "d" and "f" in th alphab t." The article went on in much more detail, but without using the letter "e." The article was followed by an 'editor's note.' "A mouse trap is bad but we are warning you, a noose around the neck is worse. Don't tempt us the second time."

Cousin Susie

In July 1957 Oscar went fishing and talked cousin Susie into writing an article for him. She ended the article with the statement: "Oscar will see you next month if the fish don't get him." He wrote no more articles so the fish must have gotten him.

Merrillee

For several months another character wrote an article "The Gossip Truth" and signed it Merrillee. It was another high class article keeping people up to date on the low down about everyone and everything around the office.

A universal problem for any organization or business is to get people to do things. The Farm News editor had to keep working to get people to write news and had varying degrees of success. The following article in August, 1964 was a new low as far as quality of articles is concerned:

It Don't Make No Difference If You Don't Read This

"The other day I was mindin' my own biznes and along comes my nabor and says: 'How about you doin' something fer me?' Rite away I thot of thre or fore things I wanted him to do fer me sometime, so I gave him the ole buddy and butterup treatment and told him I would do it fer him.

"Then after it was too late I ask him what was it I could do fer him? He explained that the editor of the Farm Noos was trying to pep up his paper by gettin' different folks to rite stuf fer him. My nabor said this was his month to drum up somebody, and I was it. So here I am.

"If there is anything I can't do worse than something, it is to rite anything. The last thing I rote was a pome fer my teecher. Must have been about my third year in the forth grade. It was named: 'My teecher, poetree and mee' and here is kinda how it went:

'My teecher has traveled in many lands
And left her footprints in many sands
Twice has she crossed the see
But she can't make a poet out of mee.'

"There were several more verses but they weren't any better. My teecher never did say if she liked it very good or not, but at least it got me out of the forth grade. My teecher was still in the forth grade when she finally retired.

"I don't no how long a thing I have to rite, but it won't make no difference, cause you won't reed it no how. You will be too bizy reedin' the stuff folks are promisin' so you will vote fer them this fall.

"Speekin' of the lection, I herd one guy who had it sized up about rite. He said he was gonna read everything he could find, listen to all the speeches, and watch everything on television so he would know the why and becauses about everything. Then he says: 'When I go to vote, I'll vote a strait (censored by the editer) ticket, cause that's the way papy and granpapy always voted.'

"At least he was onest, and that's more than you can say fer some of them that is runnin' fer ofis.

"One nice thing about a good lively campaign, if everyone agreed, who would you argu with? Here's another thot about the lection. If you don't have gumption enough to go vote, then you hadn't otta belyaik about who gets elected. It's kinda same way if you don't like to reed this kind of stuf in Farm Noos—why don't you rite something?

"A. N. Onymous."

In spite of bad days like this the editor continued to keep people informed through Farm News. It not only educated and entertained readers for nearly 40 years, but has become one of the best sources of information for this book.

CHANGES IN AGRICULTURE

CHANGES IN U.S.

The story of the revolutionary changes in Agriculture during the last 150 years was well presented by Mauri Williamson, Executive Secretary of the Purdue Agricultural Alumni Association at his exhibit at the Indiana State Fair in 1976.

"1830-1865. The Dawn of Progress. The Age of hoof & harness. The steel moldboard plow, the reaper, and the grain thresher were invented and gave a hint of better things to come. Farm families were leaving the Eastern Seaboard and moving to the fertile lands of the midwest.

"1865-1890. The age of invention. Lots of clever contraptions. Following the Civil War a great industrial revolution took place in American Agriculture. Many high sophisticated farm tools such as the grain binder, the two row corn planter, and the steam engine were developed, and the farmer surged ever westward.

"1890-1925. The Golden Age of American Agriculture. A happy time of threshing rings, county fairs, and apple butter. Sociologically the American Farmer was the prominent force in the land. The farm bloc exerted powerful influence in Washington. The period saw the expansion of small towns, farm organizations, cooperatives, Agricultural Extension, the Agricultural colleges, rural churches, and working together.

"1925-1945. The age of change. The end of horses and steam. Gasoline and electricity takes over. If there was a sad time in American Agriculture this was it. The dust storms, the depression, the drought, surplusses, and the chinch bug emphasized the fact that agriculture was over expended and underdeveloped. Many changes were soon to come.

"1945-1976. The technological age in American Agriculture. The modern farmer feeds the world. Following World War II the scientific mechanization of American Agriculture began. The modern farmer is truly an economist, a scientist and a humanitarian. He has been called on to feed the country and the world in an efficient and economic manner and he has answered that call."

The following table also on display at the exhibit lists some figures showing the changes in Agriculture in the U.S. during the same period:

	1830-1865	1865-1890	1890-1925	1925-1945	1945-1976
No. of farms	1,449,073	4,008,907	6,361,502	6,096,799	2,818,580
Farm Population	13,000,000	24,000,000	32,000,000	39,500,000	8,900,000
% of total Pop.	55.8	47.7	34.6	23.2	4.2
People fed per farmer	4.2	5.6	7.1	10.7	61.4
Investment per farm	$2258	$3833	$5470	$5518	$131,295
Corn Yield Bu. per A.	24.3	27.3	27.9	28.4	86.2

CHANGES IN AGRICULTURE IN CARROLL COUNTY

Changes in Agriculture in Carroll County have followed very closely the pattern shown by Mauri Williamson for Agriculture in the U.S. Farming in Carroll County has become big business. Records at Purdue University indicate that an investment of about $1 million per worker is required for a crop farm in this area in 1979.

An article in the Delphi Journal for February 5, 1912 reported that Dr. Patrick who owned several farms told his tenants that he would give $100 to the one with the highest corn yield. George Booze of Adams Township won with an average yield of 69.85 bushels per acre on 86.17 acres. Yields reported by other tenants were: George Popejoy, 66.82, Jack Popejoy 59.27 and Albert Peterson 57.35.

The Delphi Journal for April 11, 1912 reported that a book entitled "How to Grow 100 Bushels of Corn Per Acre on Worn Soil" had become a best seller. It was written by W. C. Smith, an attorney in Delphi who lived on a farm north of Delphi.

The Delphi Journal for March 14, 1912 reported that Ed Oliver of Newland, Indiana had said: "Half your labor will pay for a farm in four years. Give me half your crop of onions for four years and I will give you a deed for the land." This gives some indication of the price of land at that time.

The most revolutionary changes in agriculture in Carroll County have taken place in recent years, and are shown by the table of figures taken from the Census of Agriculture for the years 1944, 1954, 1964 and 1974.

U.S. CENSUS OF AGRICULTURE FOR CARROLL COUNTY, INDIANA

Year	1944	1954	1964	1974
Number of farms	1682	1645	1217	1042
Ave. Size Acres	134	138	189	217
Value per Acre $	123	273	363	962
Number of Farms with:				
Over 1000 acres	2	1	2	19
Hogs	1277	1165	690	402
Milk Cows	1375	816	150	51
Chickens	1429	1170	359	119
Number of Hogs	65,147	120,098	124,535	131,508
Number Milk Cows	7418	5227	1652	861
No. Chickens 4 Mo. & older	164,831	187,500	124,056	770,426
Value Farm Products Sold:				
Ave. Per Farm $	4202	9657	15,690	57,938
All Crops $	1,261,583	4,553,676	6,956,174	29,164,000
Livestock & L.S. Products $	5,797,924	11,316,505	12,129,457	31,302,000

The table of figures from the U.S. Census of Agriculture shows that during the period of 30 years the size of farms nearly doubled, the value per acre increased nearly eight times, the average value of farm products sold per farm increased nearly 14 times, and there was a change from livestock farming to crop farming. While the total farm sales of livestock and livestock products increased more than five times, the income from sales of crops increased 23 times. In 1944, income from the sale of livestock and livestock products was more than four times the income from the sale of crops. In 1974, income from the two sources was nearly equal.

Hogs

More than 75% of the farms in Carroll County had hogs in 1944, while thirty years later less than 40% had hogs. During the same period the number of hogs on farms in Carroll County more than doubled. Carroll County has more hogs than any other county in Indiana. In the U.S. Carroll County ranks 19th in number of hogs, and second in number per square mile.

Milk Cows

In the early days every farm family, and many living in town, had one or more milk cows. At that time cows in town had the freedom of streets and alleys during the day but not at night. The Delphi Journal for March 24, 1892 reported that the Town Council was considering an ordinance to prohibit cows from running at large on the streets of Delphi. People who had cows opposed the ordinance, while those without cows favored it.

In 1944 more than 80% of the farms had milk cows, but in 1974 less than 5% had milk cows. The total number of milk cows in the county in 1974 was about 12% of the number in 1944.

In 1979 there were only five dairy herds in Carroll County producing Grade A milk.

Poultry

In 1944, 85% of the farms in Carroll County had chickens while in 1974 less than 12% had chickens. During that time the total number of chickens in the county increased 460%. In 1979 there were more than 45 poultry houses with 33,000 or more hens each.

FARM POWER

The following article taken from the July 3, 1976 issue of Prairie Farmer was written by Mauri Williamson, Executive Secretary of the Purdue Agricultural Alumni Association:

> "Technology has advanced but the pioneer ideas are still with us.
>
> "In American agriculture there has always been a direct correlation between advances in technology and general productivity. This advancement has allowed our farmers to produce far more efficiently than those any place else.
>
> "It began with the development of the plow. When a farmer moved west in search of productive land he hung a plow on the side of each wagon. It may have been a wood moldboard plow or, if the farmer was more fortunate, a cast iron moldboard.

"As he eagerly sank the plow into the new land he found that the heavy prairie soils were not at all like the dirt back East. The plows of that time could not scour in all that growth and rotted vegetation.

"In 1837 technology stepped in. A blacksmith in Grand Detour, Illinois, named John Deere, used an old saw blade to fashion a moldboard of steel. It could scour in prairie soils and the new land was opened for farming.

"Farm power also advanced farming. Until that time man's productivity had been limited by the strength of his back.

"In the early 19th century men like Richard Trevethick, William Murdock, and others were experimenting with steam. By 1860 horse-drawn portable steam engines were becoming common sources of power for grain separators, sawmills, and gristmills.

"By 1880 the self-propelled steam traction engine was a reality. We entered a romantic time of threshing rings, plowing matches, and the love affair between man and his favorite steam rig. Many a blacksmith shop echoed with the loud boast of threshermen as they defended and sometimes lied about the virtues of their engine.

"J. I. Case, Frick, Keck-Gonnerman, Reeves, Nichols and Shepard, Advance, Rumely, Gaar Scott, Baker, Avery, and all the rest were names that would capture the imagination of the American farmer.

"If you've ever been a part of a threshing ring (even a water boy), you can't forget the pungent smell of the coal smoke, the scream of the whistle, the big dinners, the itch of the wheat beards, and the settlin' up parties.

"Sadly the princely reign of the steam traction engine was not destined to be a long one. By 1925 production of steam engines had nearly ended. As early as the 1890's attention began turning to the coughing, popping, smelly gasoline engine as the most practical source of farm power.

"The internal combustion engine had been around for some time, but it was not until 1892 that John Froelich mounted a 20-hp. gas engine on a Robinson steam engine running gear. The result is now considered to be the first operative gasoline traction engine. Froelich later organized the Waterloo Traction Engine Company, and for many years produced the popular Waterloo Big Boy. In 1918 Deere and Company purchased this firm and entered the tractor field.

"The period from 1900 to 1920 was a time of rapid increase in the number of companies trying to build tractors. Hundreds of foundries, threshing machine firms, steam engine manufacturers and average people with ideas entered the field. A few of those machines were well engineered and worked satisfactorily. Many were poorly designed and were a poor replacement for a good team of horses.

"The variety of types was a sight to behold. Many had the size and looks of their relative the steam engine. Some were motor plows with the implements mounted underneath or to the side. Man probably invented many new cuss words when trying to attach those plows.

"Some manufacturers produced motor cultivators that replaced the horse. They were built so that the horse-drawn tools that the farmer already owned would be attached. In most cases the operator rode on the implement and controlled the tractor from there. The Moline Universal, the Indiana, and the Avery were well-known tractors of this type.

"In 1902 Charles Hart and Charles Parr of Charles City, Iowa, built what is commonly cited as the first successful mass-produced gas traction engine. This two-cylinder four-to-five-plow 'Hart-Parr No. 1' was the first to be called a tractor. This company later was purchased by the Oliver Chilled Plow Works, forerunner of White Farm Equipment Company.

"The early gas tractors were most practical on large grain farms where they were used primarily for plowing. The steam engine was still considered best for belt work because of its smooth power and high torque.

"The need still persisted for a small, lightweight, inexpensive machine that would be suitable for the small farms of the Midwest. In 1917 that need became a reality. Henry Ford and Son introduced the 'Fordson.'

"It embodied a cast iron unit frame construction. The tractor produced 20 hp and cost about $700. It was noisy, became so hot that you could hardly sit on it, and was practically impossible to start on a cold morning. But it answered the small farmer's dream.

"Over 750,000 Fordsons were sold from 1917 to 1927. In some years they made up almost 50% of the total tractor sales for the U.S. Many other companies soon followed the lead of the Fordson.

"The decade of the 1920's saw the tractor come of age. In 1921, 186 firms produced 68,029 tractors. In 1930 only 38 companies manufactured 196,297 units. From 1920 to 1930 the number of tractors on Indiana farms had grown from 9230 to 41,979.

"In 1924 the horse got some very bad news. It

lost two of its last remaining field chores, planting corn and cultivating. International Harvester introduced the Farmall Regular row crop tractor. With tricycle configuration, high clearance, and ability to turn sharply at the end of the row its versatility was quickly recognized. Soon most manufacturers were producing row crop tractors.

"Can you remember the boys down at the elevator laughing about the rumors that tractors would soon have rubber tires. This was about 1933. All those dire predictions about the bouncing and the getting stuck must have been untrue. By 1935, 14% of the tractors sold were on rubber. By 1950 almost all tractors were rubber-tired. Allis-Chalmers was a leader in the application of rubber tires to farm tractors.

"There are a great many other recent technological improvements, live power takeoff, hydraulics, fast-hitch mounted implements, the high compression engine, diesel power, and now the giant four-wheel-drive tractors are amazing advances. But the daring and colorful work of the early pioneers still seems to be the most significant. Come to think of it, a lot of their ideas and imagination are still with us. Take a look at your tractor sometime. You'll see the result of nearly 100 years of hard work and ingenuity."

OTHER CHANGES

There have been many changes in other things besides Agriculture. Some of these changes are in the following article from the Delphi Journal for November 5, 1931:

"What a Difference 50 Years makes in Life's History. 1881—Fifty years ago women wore hoopskirts, bustles, petticoats, corsets, cotton stockings, high buttoned shoes, ruffled cotton drawers, flannel nightgowns, puffs in their hair—did their own cooking, baking, cleaning, washing, ironing, raised big families, went to church Sunday—were too busy to be sick.

"Men wore whiskers, square hats, ascot ties, red flannel underwear, big watches and chains, —chopped wood for stoves, bathed once a week, drank 10¢ whiskey and 5¢ beer—rode bicycles, buggies or sleighs—went in for politics—worked 12 hours a day—and lived to a ripe old age.

"Stores burned coal oil lamps—carried everything from a needle to a plow—never took an inventory—placed orders for goods a year in advance—always made money.

"1931—today women wear silk stockings, short skirts, low shoes, no corsets, an ounce of underwear—have bobbed hair, smoke, paint and powder, drink cocktails, play bridge, drive cars, have pet dogs and go in for politics.

"Men have high blood pressure, wear no hats, and some no hair, shave their whiskers, shoot golf, bathe twice a day, drink poison, play the stock markets, ride in airplanes,—never go to bed the same day they get up—are misunderstood at home—work five hours a day—play 10—sleep ten —sleep in a twin bed, die young.

"Stores have electric lights, cash registers, elevators, never have what the customer wants—trust nobody—take inventory daily—never buy in advance—have overhead — markup — markdown—quota—budget—advertising—stock control—annual and semi annual—end-of-the-month—dollar day, founder's day, rummage, economy day sales—and never make any money."

CHAPTER II

THE EARLY YEARS

"Go West, young man, go West!" was good advice and while it solved some problems, it created others. As the East became more thickly populated, the vast wilderness and virgin soil in the West offered an opportunity for pioneers to move to new territory and new opportunities. Some moved because of the advantages offered, while others moved West to avoid the problems where they were living. If a person had trouble with his neighbors, relatives, or government, he could load his family and a few belongings in a wagon and go West.

Regardless of the reason for moving, pioneers soon learned that they must depend on others for some kind of help. At first they got together for such jobs as barn raising and log rolling where more help was needed than that provided by the family. Later, as the population increased, it was necessary to form more complex organizations in order to solve the problems created by civilization.

CARROLL COUNTY

Carroll County was named after Charles Carroll of Carrollton, who was at that time the only surviving signer of the Declaration of Independence. He died on November 14, 1832.

Carroll County was created by an act of the Indiana Legislature January 7, 1828 which provided that the county would become a unit of Government on April 1, 1828. In the first election of county officers held in the county April 28, 1828, there were 76 voters.

The first white settlers in Carroll County, the Henry Robinson family, arrived on December 31, 1824. They built a cabin on the hill south of Deer Creek near where Riley Road is now located. About 40 families came in 1825 and settled along the rivers and streams. Most of them came from Pennsylvania, Virginia, Ohio and Kentucky, and many were from families who had migrated from England, Scotland, Ireland and Germany. History records that in May, 1826 when Henry Robinson built a mill along Deer Creek to saw lumber and grind meal, 28 men came to help build the mill. This included every man then living between Wild Cat and Rock Creek. This is the only time that all the men living in Carroll County were at the same place at one time.

The following article is from the Delphi Journal for March 1934:

First Merchant

"Probably the first merchant in the county was Daniel F. Vandeventer from New York, who brought by keel-boat, a stock of goods and placed them in a log storehouse erected by Daniel Baum, Sr., in the yard adjacent to his own cabin on Deer Creek where the Wabash railroad now crosses.

"When the county was organized Mr. Vandeventer was elected clerk and his store served both for store-room and Clerk's office.

"A little later Isaac Griffith bought another small stock of goods, and established a store just south of the mills, which was afterwards owned by himself and Mr. Hasley, on the creek east of Delphi.

First Doctor

"The first practicing physician in the county was Dr. John M. Ewing. Since he had the whole field to traverse alone, his practice became quite extensive but not, as he alleged, very lucrative, for he was a man charitably disposed and performed a large amount of service for which he received no other compensation than the consciousness that he had discharged his duty faithfully. Dr. Ewing married Lydia Ann, third daughter of Henry Robinson.

"On the third of January 1828, a post office was established here and Abner Robinson was named postmaster.

"Among the annoyances to which the early settlers were subjected was the presence, especially in the warm weather, of numerous rattlesnakes. This required uncommon caution in working among the weeds and undergrowth that pervaded the settlements. Their den seemed to be located on the Wilson farm east of Delphi, not far from Deer Creek.

Early Schools

"The first school was taught by Sarah B. Robinson in the summer and fall of 1827 in an old cabin on her father's farm. Aaron Dewey took charge in the winter following. During 1828 the first public school building was erected in Delphi. It was of hewed logs and really a very respectable edifice in the day of its usefulness.

"Prior to the adoption of the public school system of 1852, six buildings appeared to have been built for that purpose in Deer Creek township, all of an inferior quality and pronounced 'bad' by the incoming school officials. New ones were ordered built without delay and in 1854 five new buildings were erected in the township.

"In 1856 a schoolhouse was erected at a cost of $670. Another house was built in 1857 at a cost of $440 and in 1858 another house at a cost of $435 making eight in all. In 1869 ten teachers were hired in the schools of Deer Creek township."

WATER POWER MILLS

When settlers arrived at a new territory and built a log cabin to protect them from the weather, and cleared a small patch of ground to raise crops, the next order of business was to build mills to grind grain and saw lumber. These were located along the small streams where water power was available. An interesting report on early mills in Carroll County was published in the Delphi Journal of July 14, 1938.

"The first mill in the county was located where Mortonville now is, on Deer Creek—that was Robinson's Mill, built in 1826 by Henry Robinson.

"A letter written by Magdalena McCain, wife of Daniel McCain, mentions the first mill. It read:

"There were no mills in reach of us, except Mr. Robinson's Mill, which answered a very good purpose for grinding corn, but even that, because of the severe weather, froze up and we were obliged to make hominy and pound corn to make meal for bread. We had brought two barrels of flour with us, but that we had to use up immediately.

"The Indians were, for a year or two, more frequent visitors at our cabin than were the whites, but they were always peaceable. My husband cleared five acres for our corn, and he soon made our cabin more comfortable. He laid a floor, having hauled logs through the deep snow (for it was over two feet deep) to Mr. Robinson's saw-mill. Mr. Robinson was kind enough to erect a small grist and saw-mill for the accommodation of himself and those who might chance to follow him.

"Later, in 1830, Mr. Robinson constructed a

Wolever Photo

The first mill in Carroll County was built in 1826 by Henry Robinson on the north side of Deer Creek east of Delphi where Mill Street in Mortonville now ends. The mill had several owners and was known by many different names.

merchant mill on Deer Creek. To this structure was added a large addition by the owners, and this new mill became known as the Red Mill. The old Red Mill was operated by Mr. William Gardner, and on March 21, 1911, this mill burned to the ground. (* see note on page 62).

"Robinson's Mill became known as Roach's Mill after a Mr. Roach had purchased it. A Mr. Duke also ran the mill for a while.

"Besides Roach's Mill and the Red Mill, which were driven by water power, Delphi had the Montman Mill which was steam driven. It was located where the Whiteman Elevator now stands.

"Robinson's old saw mill was on a small branch of Deer Creek, just east of the city. It was operated by an overshot wheel. The next saw mill was built in the bottoms, and was supplied by water leading from Deer Creek at a point above, by its own fall.

"An early mill was built on the south bank of the Wabash, a short distance below the steamboat locks, the water being obtained from above the dam. This was run by a turbine wheel. Mr. Platt, the father of United States Senator Moses E. Platt, was the second owner of the mill in the early forties. The senator was born in a two-room frame house near the mill, and it is still standing. The senator, when here on a visit about 1910, readily recognized it as the place of his birth.

"Other mills were built in various townships when the population justified it. The people would haul logs to the mills during the winter on sleds and usually the lumber was shared in the nature of 'toll.' The best walnut and poplar lumber was used in the building of houses, some of which in later years has been utilized in the building of the older homes in the county.

"In 1830 a carding-mill was built on Knight's Branch, a short distance above its entrance into Deer Creek, by James Carney, and was operated by him for several years. In 1832 a saw-mill was built at Lockport on Burnett's Creek by John A. Barnes, and in 1835 he erected a grist-mill. John Newman also built a saw-mill on Rattlesnake Creek in 1834, and a few years later added a flouring-mill.

"In Clay township, John Wagoner constructed the first saw-mill and also a mill to grind wheat and corn. Saw-mills were built in Carrollton township in 1835 and the first grist-mill in 1848.

"The old Adams Mill, on Wild Cat Creek east of Cutler, was built in 1831. Mr. Adams erected a flouring-mill in 1835. Samuel Weaver operated a carding-mill, also manufactured linseed oil, and later owned a woolen-mill at Prince William.

"In Jefferson township, the first saw-mill was built on the Tippecanoe River in 1834, by Anthony Sheets, and he afterwards added buhrs to grind wheat and corn. This mill was located where the Oakdale Dam is now built.

"The first saw-mill in Rock Creek township was erected in 1831 by Emanuel Flood, on Rock Creek. Later, on the same site, a flouring-mill was built by John Mullendore in 1848, known later as the Dougherty Mill."

Adams Mill

The only early mill still in operating condition at its original location in Carroll County is the Adams Mill near Cutler.

Adams Mill near Cutler 1978.

In 1831 John Adams, who came from Pennsylvania, built the first saw mill in the Democrat Township area one mile northeast of Cutler on the Wild Cat Creek. Seeing the need for flour, he added a flouring mill in 1835 on the same millrace with one run of buhrs, which ground both corn and wheat.

The two story structure continued to run until 1842 when the sawmill machinery was removed. Late in 1845 the present building was erected with four buhrs and two turbine wheels. It is fifty feet long, forty five feet wide and sixty feet from the peak of the roof to the water of the tail race below.

In 1860 Warren Adams, son of John, bought the mill and in 1865 started the sawmill again and ran it until 1882.

The mill housed the Wild Cat Masonic Lodge #311 on the third floor of the mill from 1864 to 1867. This was one of two known Masonic Lodges in Indiana to have started life in a flour mill.

The Wild Cat Post Office was on the second floor from 1850 to 1894.

A stove on a concrete floor in a small office on the first floor supplied heat through holes in the ceiling for the Post Office and lodge hall located above.

A merchants store was built near the mill and a small village grew around the mill and was named Boliver in 1837. The covered bridge was built in 1872 and the railroad was laid west of the mill in the same year. The store moved to the new town of Cutler located along the tracks, and the Wild Cat Mill began to disappear as a farm community center.

As early as 1911, the mill generated electricity to light the towns of Cutler, Sedalia and Rossville, and farm homes along the line. No other small towns around had electricity then. The generator was ruined in 1913 by flood waters that reached a depth of 28 inches on the ground floor.

On August 11, 1913, the Wild Cat Utilities Company was incorporated to generate, transmit and sell electric current. Directors were John T. Johnson, Robert F. Johnson, and Jesse Johnson who at that time was owner and operator of the mill. They continued for a few years to supply electric power to the surrounding community. When the need for electricity was more than their generator could supply, a large gasoline engine was added to supply more power. It was run from evening until midnight. Each evening shortly after sundown the peaceful valley of the mill was punctuated with the monotonous "chug chug" of the engine. With each chug the light flickered all along the line, making a very unsatisfactory aid to the water wheel. Later a line was built from the interurban power line at Middle Fork to Rossville to furnish power to the former mill customers.

The mill continued to be used until 1940 to grind wheat into flour and it was sold in bags with a picture of a large horseshoe framing the head of a Wild Cat. It was named "Good Luck Flour" made by the WILD CAT ROLLER MILL at Cutler, Indiana.

In 1941 the mill was purchased by Claude Sheets, a sound engineer for a New York motion picture studio. The dam across Wild Cat was leaking, and Mr. Sheets repaired it with two carloads of cinders shipped on the railroad from Logansport to Cutler. He used the generator at the mill to supply light and heat for his home near the mill. He restored the mill and ground flour and corn meal from June 1943 until 1950, when the state law required that all areas where food was processed must be rodent proof, and other regulations became so strict that he was forced to suspend operation of the mill.

He then filled the mill with antiques and made it into a museum which was visited by many people.

In 1974 Mr. Sheets sold the mill to Jim Broadhurst from Valparaiso, Indiana. He rewired the mill and installed a sprinkler system for fire protection, and has done some work on developing a park and recreation area on part of the 17 acres where the mill is located.

Star Roller Mill

Several water power mills were built along Wild Cat near Burlington beginning in about 1830. The only remaining mill is the Star Roller Mill which was built in 1834 by John Garrison who later sold it to Tom Robinson. After the Civil War the mill was sold to Martin G. Haun, a Civil War veteran, who was trustee of Burlington Township, and served as Councilman, Commissioner, and Auditor in Carroll County. Ownership of the mill remained in the Haun family until 1940 when Earl Haun sold it to a corporation composed of his son-in-law Roy A. Brubaker along with Dale and Russell Rodkey and John T. Johnson.

In addition to operating the mill, the water was used to generate electricity for the mill, and the town of Burlington in the early 1900's.

In 1953 the dam was taken out, the mill race filled and the building was used as a place for grinding and mixing feed. The milling of flour was discontinued because of new food and drug laws. In 1964 the mill was purchased by Charles L. Yeager and Kenneth Shriver who later sold his interest to Mr. Yeager. He expanded the feed mixing facilities and added grain storage bins with a capacity of more than one million bushels, and Star Roller Mill became one of the larger industries in Carroll County.

Adam Porter Mill

In 1857 Adam Porter built a water power grist mill along Deer Creek about a mile west of Camden on land now owned by B. Jesse Zook. A road just west of the house where Roy Greggs lived for many years went south, forded Deer Creek and went to what is now County Road 350 N. The mill was built at the foot of the hill along the north side of the creek. Most of the old mill race can still be seen.

In the 1890's the county built a new road and bridge south of Camden just east of the present location of St. Rd. 75 and travelers no longer needed to ford the creek at the mill.

About 1897, Antoni Karasynski completely dismantled the Porter Mill and moved it to Camden and located it on Lot No. 5, where it now stands on the north side of Main Street west of the Pennsylvania Railroad. He used power from a gasoline engine to again operate the mill as a flour and grist mill for a few years.

In 1922, Frank Snoeberger purchased the idle mill and used it for a coal yard for many years. In February, 1943 the Carroll County Farm Bureau Cooperative Association purchased the coal yard and remodeled the old Porter Mill into an elevator. A cupola was added to the top, a driveway on the west, and an office on the south. The main structure remained with its beautiful timbers and posts, mostly made from large poplar trees, pinned together just like it was built in 1857.

In 1969 the CCFBCA built a new modern elevator north of Flora and closed the elevator in Camden in November 1970. In December 1970 the property was sold to Allison, Steinhart and Zook, Inc., who operated the elevator on the east side of the railroad. The old part of the mill is now used for storage, and the office is used by B. Jesse Zook.

CAMDEN ELEVATOR

In the early 1900's several elevators were built by farmers in Carroll County. In the summer of 1910 a group of farmers around Camden formed a stock company known as the Farmers Grain and Supply Company with James J. Reeder, president, and M. W. Dillon, secretary.

Land was purchased from Sarah A. (Sanderson) Thompson and Charles Flora of the Reliance Construction Company of Indianapolis was hired as architect. The Reliance Construction Company, hired to build the elevator, presented blueprints and plans on September 28, 1910. The building, located east of the railroad on the north side of Main Street, was completed in 1911. The same company later built the elevator at Rockfield using the same plans.

In the fall of 1919 the elevator was sold to LeRoy Urmston on contract for $14,000. Officers of the company at the time of the sale were John U. Shanks, president; and Charles B. Hanaway, secretary.

The Urmston Company paid for the elevator in about five years, and then had financial problems and in the late 1920's went bankrupt. The elevator closed until 1932, was acquired by the Camden State Bank and rented on a year to year basis. On April 1, 1935 it was rented to Steinhart Grain Company of Indianapolis and B. Jesse Zook was appointed as the local manager. He had worked at the Indianapolis office since 1929, and continued as manager of the local elevator for 41 years.

The Steinhart Grain Company was organized in Indianapolis in 1919 and for many years was owned mostly by Farmers Elevators in Illinois and Indiana. The company is now known as Allison, Steinhart and Zook and has its main office located in Camden with B. Jesse Zook, president; John G. Steinhart, vice president; and Dennis L. Zook, secretary.

BLACKSMITH SHOPS

There were many blacksmith shops and they provided a necessary service by repairing machinery and shoeing horses. Some idea of the importance of the horse shoeing business is indicated by the following article from the May 16, 1914 issue of the Hoosier Democrat. "Last Saturday, Wm. Eckerle, one of our three village blacksmiths, sold the past year's accumulation of old worn out horse shoes which he had pulled off and replaced with new ones. There was slightly over seven tons of old shoes."

SOCIAL LIFE OF THE PIONEERS

The early pioneers had a very rich social life which generally centered around their churches. Members of many churches were forbidden to dance, but "singin's" were very popular. These were held in homes and attended mostly by young people.

Quilting bees were also very popular. Women in the community would get together in the evening to make beautiful quilts and comforters, many of which were used as wedding presents. Young men in the community often had a party in the summer house or kitchen, and when the bee was over they would escort the young ladies to their homes.

Wolever Photo

Harry Baum standing beside a pile of old horseshoes in front of his blacksmith shop on the northeast corner of Main and Union Streets in Delphi.

Taffy pulls, apple butter "stirrin's," and apple "parin's" were among the other social events in the community.

Weddings were the big social events, and sometimes were two day affairs with feasting and celebrations.

Other social events such as "spellin' bee's" and "cipherin' matches" were associated with the schools.

Barn Raisings

Early settlers used logs to build the first houses and barns. When saw-mills were available, farmers would cut and haul logs to the mill for lumber for parts of a building. The framework for a barn was usually made from logs hewn by hand and held together with wooden pins.

A farmer would usually hire a carpenter to cut and fit the ends of the beams to form the side of a barn on the ground. When all the sides were completed he would invite his neighbors for a "Barn Raising."

With ropes, poles, and a lot of help, each side of the barn was raised into position and fastened to the other sides with wooden pins. It was quite an art for the carpenter to have everything measured so that the sides would fit together properly.

Usually a barn could be raised in a day's time, and near enough completed that the farmer and carpenter could finish it later.

All the families in the neighborhood came for a barn raising, and with the big dinner at noon and the opportunity for everyone to catch up on the latest news in the community, barn raisings became a vital part in the social life of a community as well as one of the earliest examples of people working together to help each other.

Barns were set on large stones for a foundation in order to keep the sills off the ground. Barns were well built, and many were used for more than 100 years.

Husking Bees

The task of husking or shucking the corn was frequently lightened and enlivened by the "Husking Bee." When dry enough the ears were snapped from the stalks, hauled from the field and thrown in a large pile near the corn crib. The neighbors, old and young, both men and women, were then invited to the "Husking Bee." The center line was marked by a pole or rail supported just above the pile of ears. Sides were chosen by two leaders and the husking began with each side striving to reach the center first.

Sometimes the contest was to see who could husk the greatest number of ears of corn. The finding of a red ear of corn was often used as a reason for special celebration.

The occasion was one of much merriment, usually

followed by a bountiful supper, after which the young folks danced while their parents visited.

Butcherings

Large growing families needed a lot of food to help them keep up with the hard work necessary for farming. With very little money to buy the limited amount and kinds of food available at the grocery stores, it was necessary for a farm family to produce most of their food.

Nearly every family raised a few hogs, and during the winter they would invite their neighbors to help butcher the hogs. Help was needed to lift the hogs into and out of the kettles of hot water so that the hair could be removed. Later everyone helped in cutting up the meat, rendering the lard in large open kettles, and in grinding and stuffing the sausage. Usually someone would throw some tenderloin into the kettle of lard in order to provide some extra good cracklings after the lard was squeezed in the lard press. Once in a while someone would throw a chunk of liver in the lard kettle, and learn the hard way that it would spoil the flavor of the whole kettle of lard.

Hams and bacon were cured with salt and the curing process was finished in a special "smoke house." Meat was hung in the building and a fire was built in a small stove. The stove pipe was then removed so that the smoke filled the building. The curing process required ten to twenty days, depending on how well the fire was maintained. Hickory wood was used to give the meat a better flavor. Hickory smoked meat is still advertised as the best.

Some meat was partly cooked and preserved by covering with lard in large earthenware jars.

Butcherings were among the high lights in the social events of the winter, and dates were scheduled in advance in order to avoid conflicts in dates with other events in the community.

Dried Food

Many kinds of food were dried in order to preserve them for use in the winter. Drying racks, usually made by nailing plastering lath about a half-inch apart onto boards used for sides of the rack, were about twenty inches wide, forty-eight inches long, and an inch and a half in depth. Peaches were cut in half, and apples cut into fourths or eighths, depending on the size of the apple. Some racks were covered with paper on which was spread sweet corn cut from the cob.

These racks of food were placed in a heated building, and sometimes carried out into the sun on a dry day until the food was dry enough to keep. The fruit was easily prepared for meals in the winter. The dried corn was not something a gourmet would rave about, but it was accepted as part of the menu if not served too often.

Flies

The coming of spring brought mixed blessings to the farm family. The stove in the parlor was taken down, giving more living space. Cooking and eating was moved from the small inside kitchen to the larger summer kitchen, which was not heated in the winter.

About that time, along came the flies. With no screen for the doors or windows, they soon picked the house as one of their favorite places. At meal time they would swarm on and over the food. Sometimes a "fly brush" was made by fastening a newspaper onto a handle, then cutting the paper into strips about one-half inch wide. When flies were bad, or if company were present, a younger member of the family was given the job of waving the fluttering strips of paper back and forth over the table, in order to keep the flies moving. They hoped that some flies would get discouraged and go to one of their other favorite stopping places—the manure pile at the barn, or down the path to the little building that has been replaced with modern plumbing.

Dinner Bell

Nearly every farm family had a dinner bell. A ring at noon would bring the entire family to the house for dinner. Some horses seemed to know what it meant, and would turn around in the middle of a cornfield and head for the barn when they heard the bell.

A long and loud ring on the bell at any other time of day would bring all the neighbors because they knew that it was a call for help.

Farm Sales

Farm sales have continued to be an important business and social event in each community. When a farmer retires from farming, or moves to another farm, it is customary for him to have a farm sale to dispose of a part or all farm machinery, livestock and household goods.

A date is set, the sale is advertised in local papers and sale bills posted in public places. On the day of the sale everyone in the community goes, some to buy, and others to visit. A local church or other group usually serves lunch.

When the sale is over, the farmer has disposed of his property. Many of his neighbors have purchased something they need, and everyone has had a good visit with neighbors.

Sale bills listed in old copies of the paper provide an interesting list of tools used at that time.

Threshing Rings

The development of the reaper, binder and threshing separator made it possible for a farmer to raise more grain.

A grain threshing separator built in 1918 and used until about 1935. This was a 22-36 Avery Yellow Kid.

The coming of the steam engine and larger threshing separator led to the organization of Threshing Rings. About ten farmers in a neighborhood would get together, exchange help, and hire someone to thresh their grain. Each farmer would provide some of the help which included bundle wagons to haul the bundles from the field to the threshing machine, pitchers to throw the bundles on the wagon, and wagons with grain beds to haul the grain from the machine. Each farmer would also have a "water boy" with a horse and buggy to haul jugs of fresh water for the men in the fields.

After the grain was cut and shocked the threshing machine would move from one farm to another until the threshing job was completed. On larger rings, they might take a month or more, especially if there were several days of rain.

After the threshing was finished the farmers would get together for a "settlin' up" party. Each farmer would either pay in or receive a sum of money based on the amount of work he had contributed, and the number of bushels of grain he had threshed. Here again the "settlin' up" party was an excuse to get together, exchange gossip, and eat cake and ice cream.

The thing most old timers remember about threshing was the big dinners each day. The whole crew ate wherever they were threshing when it came time for dinner. With no modern methods of refrigeration, the preparation of dinner for a crew like that required a lot of work. The women would begin early in the morning picking chickens, peeling potatoes, baking bread and pies and all the other work necessary to prepare a big dinner. In many communities each family tried to prepare a bigger and better meal than the others, so the men were well fed.

On larger threshing jobs, and during good weather it was no problem to plan where each dinner would be held. However, if farmers each had only a few hours threshing, it was quite a problem to determine who would feed the crew each day. A light rain in the morning might make an excuse to wait until afternoon to start threshing, and be certain of finishing before noon the next day. On some small jobs, they could start early in the morning before the grain was really ready, and be done before noon. The problem was solved in many threshing rings by having the men carry their dinner.

Nothing was more frustrating to a farm woman than to see wagons and a threshing machine coming down the road about eleven o'clock in the morning and no dinner prepared. Some claim that this problem was a primary cause of the threshing rings going out of business. Others say that a more important reason was the development of the combine.

The threshing rings served a useful purpose for nearly a hundred years in the history of this area, and old timers still like to talk about it.

Men who owned threshing outfits formed the Carroll County Thresher's Association, and had an active organization for many years. The Delphi Journal for June 7, 1902 reported that the Association met at Flora and elected Ed Voorhees as delegate and Harve Bowerman as alternate to a state meeting to be held at Indianapolis.

The Delphi Journal for August, 1903 reported that "David Musselman, the hustling farmer east of Camden, claims the threshing championship of northern Indiana for this year. One day last week his machine threshed 825 bushels of wheat in three different townships and in two counties. The machine had to be moved and set four times."

Later the same month the Delphi Journal reported that "the Stranathan Threshing Ring of Madison Township, threshed 27,000 bushels of oats and wheat during the past 16 days. The ring used the Case tractor outfit and moved to nine different jobs, among whom were: Ray McCouch, Sam Sites, Frank Zook, E. W. Bowen, Earl Hefner, Harry Maxwell, Lester Dickinson, Fred Hannell and J. Ren Bates."

The Hoosier Democrat for July 27, 1946 reported that "Edward (Paddy) Voorhees is just now finishing his 60th year as a thresherman. During that three-quarter century span he has, perhaps, threshed with his outfits on more farms and helped to harvest the largest number of bushels of grain than any other person in Carroll County. Now past 81 years of age he stated Wednesday morning that this is his last year to take out his machines."

Much more could be written about threshing rings, and how they were used by farmers to solve their problems by working together.

AGRICULTURAL SOCIETY

On January 22, 1829, the State Legislature passed an act authorizing "Twenty or more citizens of any county, who should see proper to meet at their County Seat, to organize themselves and become an Agricultural Society, with corporate and politic powers." Very little was done as a result of this act, but, on

February 14, 1851 the State Legislature passed another act "for the encouragement of Agriculture." The State Board of Agriculture, created by this act, sent information to all counties. The Delphi Journal of August 28, 1851 had an editorial suggesting that a county organization be formed as provided in the act. A meeting was held in the Courthouse in Delphi on September 20, 1851 to discuss the suggestion and committees were appointed to proceed with details for the organization. After several meetings the Carroll County Agricultural Society was formed.

COUNTY FAIRS

The first County Agricultural Fair in Carroll County was held in Bowen's Grove north of Delphi on Saturday, October 15, 1852. This was an area between Middle School on Monroe Street, and the City Park. The main gate was located near where the brick house at 603 East Monroe now stands. The race track for the fair was located in the valley near the park. An old barn, part of which is still standing on the property owned by Elizabeth Best was used for race horses. A larger barn nearby was used for storage of race carts and hay. Forty two premiums, ranging from 50 cents to $5.00 totaled $63.35. Some items for which premiums were given were: the best cultivated farm, the best five acres of wheat, the best swine and sheep, and the best farm wagon. Awards in the women's department included premiums for the best bedquilt and the best five yards of rag carpet.

The fair was such a success, that the next year, 1853, it was held for two days, October 20 and 21 at Camden. About two acres of ground was neatly enclosed by a high board fence for the fair. Admission fees totaled $83.48 and the amount for premiums and expenses for the fair was $155.55. The county paid $80.00 and $106.00 was received from members initiation fees. There were more than 100 members.

It was reported that thousands of people attended the fair to see the exhibits of livestock and machinery. Premiums were awarded on seventy five articles and products, including domestics, manufacturers, dairy products, farming utensils, livestock, poultry and farm products.

The third Annual Fair was also held at Camden, October 12 and 13, 1854, and was bigger and better.

The fourth Annual Fair was held at Delphi. It was first scheduled for October 11 and 12, 1855, but was postponed until October 25 and 26 because of the unusual amount of sickness prevailing at the time.

The fifth Annual Fair was held at Delphi October 8 and 9, 1856.

Fair at Pittsburg

The sixth Annual Fair of the Carroll County Agricultural Society was held at Pittsburg on September 29, to October 1, 1857. Citizens of Pittsburg built a fence around an area and arranged everything for the comfort of visitors. James Odell was the speaker on the first day.

Exhibits at the fair included horses, cattle, sheep, hogs, wagons, plows, corn planter, clover sower, furniture, clothing, rag carpet, cloth, blankets, leather, saddles, apples, vegetables, butter, cheese, honey, maple sugar, molasses, yeast bread, cakes, jelly, etc., chickens, quilts, shirts, and wheat.

An article in the Delphi Journal October 6, 1857 stated: "we are convinced that the society would be established upon a much firmer basis, be more reliable and much more patronized, if the Fair Grounds were permanently located. We think it would be much better and in the end cheaper than the present mode of rival subscriptions between different points of the county for the Fair."

Fairs at Delphi

The seventh Annual Fair was held at Delphi for three days September 29, 30 and October 1, 1858. The report of the secretary of the society for that year states: "We have located the place for holding our fairs for five years at Delphi, and have enclosed about seven acres of ground with a permanent fence. The attendance at the Fair was larger than on any former occasion, and, as the fair is permanently located, the prospect is that a more general interest will be taken than formerly. The amount received for membership at the gate was $441.80, the amount awarded as premiums was $391.50, leaving a balance of $50.30."

At the ninth Annual County Fair at Delphi in 1860 the admission fee was 20 cents per day per person or $1.00 for a family. Admission charge for earlier fairs was five or ten cents per person.

Fairs were not held every year, and in 1872 the Agricultural Society of Carroll County was reorganized. During the next ten years, about seven fairs were held.

New Fair Ground

The Carroll County Agricultural Society raised $4150.00 by subscription in 1873 and purchased 30 acres of land at $125 per acre from Theodore Snyder. It was located south of Delphi on the north side of the Burlington Road and east of the Plank or Frankfort Road. The roads are now known as County Road 200 N. and State Roads 18, 39 and U.S. 421. This land is where the water tank was erected by Delphi in 1963.

The Delphi Journal for September 2, 1874 reported that: "Work improving the County Fair Grounds is progressing rapidly. Already the Amphitheatre is ready. Floral and Agricultural Halls, two stories high will be finished in another week. Ninety eight horse and cattle stalls and hog and sheep pens will be ready next week. The track is one half mile long. There are four good wells on the grounds and a branch of pure water within a few hundred yards of the grounds on a public road. People are to bring furniture, paintings and antiques."

A few days before the Fair in Delphi in 1876, somebody set fire to the stalls and about one hundred were burned. They were rebuilt in time for the Fair. Part of the amusements scheduled for that year failed to show up, so a committee went to Chicago and secured two other acts.

In 1881 a Fair at Delphi was held during the week beginning September 20. There were more than 1000 exhibits, with 300 premiums ranging from $1.00 to $100.00.

Other Fairs

A County Fair was held in Camden, beginning in 1881, and continued each year with the last being held in 1896. These fairs had exhibits of horses, cattle, hogs, sheep and other farm products. One year the premiums paid were $1,000.

In 1889 the Carroll County Voluntary Agricultural Association was organized for the purpose of holding an Annual Fair at Delphi. It had a capital of $10,000 and 15 directors. Three were from Deer Creek Township and one from each of the other townships. A race track was built on the Fair Grounds south of Delphi, and for several years horse races and annual County Fairs were held.

In 1895 a half mile race track was built at Flora, and Annual Fairs were held there for several years.

Tri-County Fairs were held at Poplar Grove in Irwin Township, Howard County.

STREET FAIRS AT DELPHI

In September 1898, Delphi held their first Street Fair. The second Fair, September 18 to 22, 1899 was bigger and better with pens for all kinds of farm livestock. There were 15 other classes of exhibits in the show. A Fine Arts Exhibit was held in the Courthouse. There were two balloon ascensions each day, and the Hagenback's Trained Animal Show. There were several bands and lots of music. The local paper stated that one reason for the success of the Fair was that there were no gamblers or "Hoochee Couchee" shows. These kinds of activities had killed other fairs in Indiana.

In 1901 the Fair ended with a sale of livestock shown at the Fair.

In 1906 the date for the Fair was changed to October.

These fairs were sponsored by the Retail Merchants Association in Delphi, and conducted by a Fair Committee with Robert C. Pollard, president; and E. E. Barnard, secretary. In 1907 they appointed one representative from each township to help conduct the fair.

The Free Carroll County Horticultural and Agricultural Association was organized on August 22, 1908 with five directors. They were William S. Margowski, Joseph E. Ruffing, George R. Ives, Charles S. Buckley and John W. Childers. The purpose was to establish a free county fair to be held annually in Delphi or vicinity.

County Fairs continued to be held every fall on the streets of Delphi during the first week in October. The Delphi Journal reported that in 1908 the livestock parade was four and one half blocks long.

CARROLL COUNTY FAIR ASSOCIATION

On the evening of March 31, 1921 a large group of farmers and Delphi citizens met in the Assembly Room in the Courthouse and decided to organize the Carroll County Fair Association. They elected seventeen directors, one for each of the 13 townships and four from Delphi. John W. Kerlin served as temporary chairman of the meeting.

Wolever Photo

Methodist Church ladies food stand at the Street Fair in Delphi in 1908. Coffee was listed at 5 cents and doughnuts at 2 for 5 cents.

The board had eight more meetings before the Fair. Most of them were held in the County Agent's office in the Courthouse. At these meetings they adopted a constitution and by-laws and elected officers. They also voted to elect five women from the county at large as members of the Board of Directors. Directors were elected for a three year term, with about one third of the directors being elected each year.

The first officers and directors were: Dr. Guy A. Thomas, president; John W. Kerlin, first vice president; George Sites, second vice president; C. Clay Pearson, secretary and Frank S. Girard, treasurer; directors were: Murrey Gardner, Adams Township; O. C. Hendrix, Burlington; Taylor Fouts, Carrollton; Lloyd Beard, Clay; Bert Lane, Deer Creek; Loren Chittick, Democrat; Wm. Foreman, Jackson; George E. Sites, Jefferson; Elmer Sheets, Madison; J. Frank Shoff, Monroe; John W. Kerlin, Rock Creek; A. L. Burkholder, Tippecanoe; A. A. Newer, Washington; City of Delphi, W. S. Margowski, John H. Mount, C. B. Shaffer, C. Clay Pearson; women representing county at large: Mrs. Yantis Wells, Mrs. Charles Hannell, Mrs. Ward Beard, Mrs. Frank Sanderson and Mrs. Nora Hinkle.

Will E. Brown was elected as general Superintendent of the Fair. Superintendents for the various departments were: Cattle, Charles W. Moore; Hogs, Bert Lane; Poultry and Pet Stock, Lloyd Beard; Agriculture and Horticulture, Fred C. Smith; Machinery, Charles Hargraves; Home Economics Needlework, Mrs. Charles Hannell; Culinary, Mrs. Ward Beard; Art, Mrs. Frank Sanderson; Streets and Alleys, George Roach; Floral, Mrs. Noah Mayhill; Baseball, W. W. Snoeberger; Horseshoe, E. O. Grimm and 4-H Exhibits, A. L. Hodgson.

1921 Fair

The 1921 Fair had 100 pens for hogs, 30 for cattle, 20 for horses, 8 for sheep and 75 to 100 coops for poultry. There were more than 2000 exhibits at the Fair. There was a parade of livestock and on Friday there was a school parade with O. L. Scales in charge in which 700 students from grades one through twelve participated.

One float in the parade, prepared by Madison Township Farm Bureau, called attention to the fact that hides were three cents per pound while shoes were $10 per pair and that hogs were eight cents per pound while bacon was 40 cents per pound. Thursday was Farm Bureau day and another day was dedicated to Industry. Automobiles on display included Ford, Buick, Overland, Willys-Knight and Hupmobile. The American Auto Top Factory in Delphi had a display. Other features included ball games, a horse shoe tournament, bands and free attractions. Merchants were asked to decorate their stores for the Fair. A special exhibit was that of the Fine Arts Department under the direction of Mrs. Frank Sanderson. Featured in the exhibit were pictures by local artists Harry Milroy and Roy Trobaugh, who had a state wide reputation for their art. They continued to have exhibits at fairs for several years.

The total amount of money available for the Fair was about $4000. Carroll County appropriated $500 for the Fair. About $900 was received from concessions and the rest of the money was from donations of $1 to $50 each by 150 individuals and businesses.

Expenses totaled $3700, of which $1400 was for premiums. Other expenses included printing and advertising, judges, lumber and material for tents and cost of free attractions.

1922 Fair

An interesting and unusual feature at the Fair in 1922 was a contest to guess the number of "O's" on the front page of a newspaper. James Riley won $10 for the nearest guess of 1850. The correct number was 1866. Other features included a double parachute leap, a 150 foot dive, acrobatic stunts, high bar performing, comedy act and a parade of school children. The Historical Society had a display of relics in the Assessor's Office.

Mrs. Roy Gregg, the County Health Nurse, was in charge of a baby show.

1923 Fair

The County Fair, held the first week in October, 1923 had several free attractions that cost the Fair Association a total of $850. One act used four well trained bears and other acts featured roller skating and wire walking. An unusual feature was the Bucking Ford. It was a Model T Ford with the rear axle moved forward so that the car was almost balanced on the axle. A fast start would cause the front end of the car to leave the ground, and the car would run on one axle with the back end of the car dragging on the ground. A quick stop would put it back on all four wheels.

Mrs. Charles Buckley was in charge of a display of relics in the DAR room. Items on display included a compass that came over on the Mayflower, and a six dollar bill used at the time of the Boston Tea Party. Another item was a combination spoon, knife and fork saved by a Carroll County soldier who had tunneled his way out of the Libby Prison. He was Daniel Ferrier, a soldier in the Civil War and father of Miss Myrtle Ferrier.

Will Gros displayed a puzzle which he had carved out of wood 49 years before. It consisted of tiny wheels and swinging bells and measured about 6x4 inches. It was enclosed in an ordinary glass bottle with a common sized stopper.

There were a total of 215 entries exhibited at the fair in 1923.

1st. Vice Pres.
Elmer E. Sheets

2nd. Vice Pres.
B. W. Lane

President   John W. Kerlin

Secretary
C. E. Schnepp

Treasurer
Harry E. Reed

Carroll County Fair Association
Delphi, Ind., Oct. 7, 8, 9 and 10, 1924

Township Directors
C. V. Hoover, Adams
Harry Maxwell, Burlington
John Sink, Carrollton
Clarence Frye, Clay
Wm. Ashba, Deer Creek
E. E. Stephens, Democrat
W. W. Snoeberger, Jackson
George E. Sites, Jefferson

General Superintendent, William Ashba

Township Directors
Burton Honan, Madison
J. Frank Shoff, Monroe
John W. Kerlin, Rock Creek
A. L. Burkholder, Tippecanoe
Roy Caldwell, Washington

Directors at Large
Mrs. Catharine Brackenridge
Mrs. Wm. Klepinger
Mrs. John Kennard
Mrs. Blanche Balser
Mrs. Chas. Doctor

Directors City of Delphi
C. B. Shaffer
C. O. Julius
Paul Quick
C. Clay Pearson

Delphi, Indiana   192

SUPERINTENDENTS

Horses
Ira Moore

Cattle
Wm. Haslet

Swine
Hiram Kerlin

Sheep
Ira Moore

Poultry
Rolla Gwinn

Grain Fruit and Vegetables
Fred C. Smith

Culinary
Mrs. Ed. Blythe

Needle Work
Mrs. Carrie Cox

Floral
Mrs. Melvin Deeter

Fine Arts
Harry Milroy

Club
H. T. Ebbinghaus
H. E. Ackerson

Relics
Mrs. Chas. Murphy

Horse Shoe Tournament
John Kennard

COMMITTEES

Attractions
Harry Reed
C. B. Shaffer
C. Clay Pearson
Ralston Wilber

Premium
B. W. Lane
H. E. Ackerson
Fred C. Smith
Mrs. Melvin Deeter
Mrs. Carrie Cox

Publicity
Harry Brewer
G. A. Shaffer
Forrest Orr

Concessions
John Hamling
Haughey Mount
E. E. Pruitt

Letterhead used by the Carroll County Fair Association in 1924 listing officers, directors, superintendents and committees.

The Association was organized in 1921, and conducted a Street Fair in Delphi each year for 10 years.

1924 Fair

There were 501 exhibits at the County Fair in Delphi on the first week of October, 1924. These included 61 quilts and coverlids. The usual displays of flowers, Home Economics exhibits and girls' 4-H Club exhibits were on display in various rooms in the Courthouse.

Pictures by Roy Trobaugh and sculptures by Harry Milroy were on display.

Boys and girls in 4-H took part in a parade Friday afternoon. Free acts included trapeze and acrobatic acts, a trained goat and donkey act and a double parachute leap each day, and a balloon ascension on Wednesday.

1925 Fair

Special attractions at the Fair held from October 6 to 9, 1925 included Japanese acrobats and jugglers, and Frisko's Trained Seals.

Many churches and lodges had food stands, and the Courthouse was full of interesting exhibits. More livestock was on exhibit, and there were 50 more coops of poultry than in the previous year.

1926 Fair

Again the Fair was held in Delphi on the first week of October, 1926 with the usual rides, red lemonade and hot dog stands, fortune tellers and shows and games of all kinds.

Free attractions included acrobats, aerialists and high pole artists. As usual, health posters made by school children were on display in the Courthouse. The Department of Agriculture had a large soil map on display.

Merchants had exhibits in front of their stores. An exhibit by L. M. Pletcher Hardware Store was lighted by a Delco Lighting Plant furnished by M. F. Justice of Flora.

1927 Fair

The Fair held September 27 to 30, 1927 was bigger and better than ever. It filled so many streets that motorists going through town on the state roads complained because they had to use side streets.

Free acts included Miss Bench Bentum, a world famous high diver and three acrobatic clowns.

The Grange had a display showing the differences between old and new methods of farming.

J. J. Hufty exhibited a combination shot gun and rifle, and his fireplace with old fashioned kettles and ovens. F. M. Denman of Flora had a number of old time musical instruments on exhibit. Another interesting exhibit was an old fashioned cane which could be used as either a cane or a chair.

In addition to the usual 4-H exhibits, 10 calves which had placed in the Indiana State Fair were exhibited by members of the Flora Jersey Calf Club.

1928 Fair

A special attraction at the County Fair in Delphi from October 2 to 6, 1928 was a show put on by George Popejoy and his trained dog, a white Collie named Teddie. George had trained his dog for eleven months, and this was his first public performance. His show was popular at many fairs and other events later that year.

Another interesting act used trained seals with juggling and balancing acts.

John Harness, the Apple King from Burlington Township, had an exhibit displaying 18 varieties of apples.

There were a total of 409 exhibits entered in the Fair.

Cattle were in pens on East Franklin Street, sheep were on Market Street, hogs were on Union Street and horses were in a building formerly occupied by Carroll County Lumber and Coal Company. Chickens were in a building at the Bradshaw Wagon Works on South Washington Street and other exhibits were in the Courthouse. The tallest stalk of corn brought in by Leland Carrigan of Rock Creek Township measured 17'4" and was on display in the Assembly Room of the Courthouse. Mrs. Pearl Allen of Delphi presented a mounted bald eagle to the Museum. A freak chicken brought in by Ralph Reagon stood upright like a person, and had to lie down to eat.

1929 Fair

The County Fair was held at Delphi the week of October 1, in 1929. There were 25 horses exhibited at the Fair. Seventy 4-H girls had exhibits, and there were 48 in boys 4-H projects showing pigs, lambs and calves.

Last Street Fair

The last Street Fair held in Carroll County was held at Delphi on September 16 to 20, 1930. There were 430 exhibits. Livestock pens were on West Franklin Street and on North Wabash Street. Chickens were in the Wason Building north of the Courthouse on the corner of Franklin and Market Streets. 4-H Girls' exhibits, flowers, fancy work, horticulture and art exhibits were located on the three floors of the Courthouse.

For several years the County Fair Association had spent more money than they had received, and the Association was in debt. The county had been subsidizing the Fair, as much as $2000 in some years. The county withdrew their support of the Fair in 1930.

It was necessary to borrow money to pay bills, and the directors signed a note to secure the loan.

The Fair Board met in July 1931 and decided not to sponsor a Fair that fall, but to try to raise enough money to pay the indebtedness, and be ready for a Fair the next year.

Final Meeting of Fair Board

The following article in the Delphi Citizen, December 3, 1931 records what appears to be the final meeting of the Carroll County Fair Association:

"Officers and directors of the Carroll County Fair Association met last Saturday in the County Agent's office and voted to continue the organization although they did not sponsor a Fair the past year. It is hoped that the Fair may be revived next fall.

"Money to pay the indebtedness contracted at the holding of the 1930 Fair was appropriated by the county council this fall. The debts of the Association have been paid in full, which leaves them in good position for sponsoring another Fair.

"Practically all of the former officers were re-elected; they are: president, Frank Riley, re-elected; first vice-president, C. V. Hoover, replacing George Sites, who is now out of the county; second vice-president, Mrs. B. B. Mayhill, re-elected; secretary, Charles E. Schnepp; treasurer, E. R. Smock; directors; C. V. Hoover, Adams Township; Marion Thomas, Burlington; Van C. Blue, Carrollton; William Ashba, Deer Creek; Frank Moss, Democrat; Frank Redenbacher, Clay; Burton Honan, Madison; J. Frank Shoff, Monroe; Dr. W. H. Lane, Jackson; C. L. Million, Rock Creek; Walter Casad, Jefferson, taking the place of George Sites; Leroy Robeson, Washington, taking the place of Roy Caldwell who has moved into another township; Frank Riley, Tippecanoe; directors at large: Mrs. William Klepinger, Mrs. Lawrence Whistler, Mrs. Sam Sites, Mrs. Robert Van Natta and Mrs. B. B. Mayhill."

A 4-H Fair and Festival was held in Delphi in 1931, and has been held at Flora since then. That story is in Chapter VI.

HORSE THIEF DETECTIVE ASSOCIATION

People who steal things are lazy (like everyone else) so they specialize on stealing things that are plentiful, are easily transported, and can be sold quickly at a good price. For a period of about 50 years, people specialized in stealing horses, because they met all the requirements. Chicago was the market for stolen horses.

In 1866 the Indiana General Assembly enacted a bill which authorized citizens to organize "Horse Thief Detective Associations," for the "purpose of detecting and arresting horse thieves, counterfeiters, incendiaries and all other felons and bringing them to justice: to aid each other in recovery of stolen property and for mutual protection and indemnity against such thieves." They worked with sheriffs and other police officers. Some of the members were appointed by the Board of County Commissioners as constables, and had all the authority of regular constables. In some cases they had authority to make an arrest where the county sheriff could not.

Records in the Courthouse at Delphi show that at least eleven such organizations were incorporated in Carroll County. The first one, recorded December 7, 1874 was the Wild Cat Horse Protection Company which had headquarters at School #8 in Burlington Township. They had 20 charter members.

The Horse Thief Detective Company of Pittsburg was recorded June 12, 1882 with 16 charter members.

The Deer Creek Horse Thief Detective Association with 17 charter members was organized October 12, 1889; the Cutler Detective Company July 30, 1900 with 20 members, the Rockfield Detective Association October 13, 1905 with 15 charter members; the Auterbin Detective Company of Cutler, October 21, 1905 with 20 members, the Flora Detective Association May 19, 1906 with 21 charter members with W. H. Linton, president; James J. Moss, vice president; George V. Brown, secretary; Jesse V. Bright, treasurer and U. M. Blue, Captain. In 1908 the Flora Association elected Dr. O. F. Campbell as Captain and re-elected the other officers.

The Burlington Detective Association was organized May 19, 1906 with H. L. Huddleson, president; S. S. Cleaver, vice president, Palestine Hanna, secretary; Amos Brubaker, treasurer; John H. Oyler, Captain, and 24 other charter members.

The Indiana State Legislature amended the state law March 9, 1907, and under this new act the Pittsburg Horse Thief Detective Association was organized May 9, 1908 with O. F. Hornbeck, Clark Davidson and W. H. Phillips as trustees. Other charter members were Frank E. Delzel, Joseph H. Davidson, John A. Pollard, N. C. Henderson, Evan Julien, Elias Harner and B. F. Rush.

On December 11, 1909 the Delphi Horse Thief Detective Association was organized with Albert E. Peterson, Joseph F. Lowe and Manson H. Sibert as trustees. Other charter members were Walter Radabaugh, John Davis, James Lowther, James A. Neff, James L. Neff, Everet Lowther and Nelson Mullendore.

The Camden Horse Thief Detective Association was organized August 16, 1911. Trustees were Plato Robison, C. E. Baker and Ellis Armstrong. Other charter members were Charles Northcutt, Charles McGruff, Perry Rule, William Bell, Foss Sieber, Isaac Wolf and Charles Appleton.

There were probably several other associations in the county that were not incorporated. There is no record of any of these officially disbanding but they gradually went out of business as horse stealing became less prevalent.

John Kennard of Yeoman reported that he joined the Pittsburg Association in 1914. They held regular meetings in the upstairs of a store at Pittsburg operated by a man called "Jugaway" Bill Smith, where the Landmark Restaurant is now located. Dues in the Association were $1.00 per year, and Mr. Kennard reported that about a year after he joined "everybody just stopped going to the meetings" and it went out of business.

An activity of an Association in the county was reported in the Delphi Journal, July 1926: "The Horse Thief Detective Association of Cutler has just announced its stand relative to petty thievery that has been going on in that vicinity and has announced that it will offer a reward of $25 for an affidavit against theft and an additional $25 for conviction of the thief or thieves as the case may be."

The Delphi Journal for January 10, 1901 had the following article: "The recent report of J. W. Volpert of Peru, secretary treasurer of the Horse Thief Detective Association of Indiana is of unusual interest. The need for such a state organization is apparent in the boldness now being shown by the horse thieves. In the three states, Indiana, Ohio and Illinois there are 167 Associations, over half of which are located in Indiana. The Association of Miami County is a fair example of those existing throughout the state, with nearly 150 members and over 100 of them sworn in as special deputy officers. The reports for 10 years show 110 stolen horses, 92 of which were recovered and a total of 200 thieves arrested and convicted."

A booklet listing the proceedings of the sixty-seventh Annual Session of the National Horse Thief Detective Association at Marion, Indiana October 4-5, 1927 indicates that the organization was very much alive and active at that time. The report lists 291 companies in 62 counties in Indiana with 8763 members. The largest company was "Cass" in Cass County with 375 members, and the smallest was "Six Mile" in Jennings County with five members. Marion County had the largest number with 28 companies and 1007 members. Montgomery was second with 25 companies and 672 members.

Ten new companies were organized in 1927, and one of these was Green Lawn in Carroll County. There were seven companies listed from Carroll County. The officers, company No. and number of members were: Burlington, No. 164, S. E. Carey, president; D. F. Beck, secretary; Ross Kesler, Captain; 10 members; Cutler No. 69, J. M. McCarty, president; Russell K. Sink, secretary; Frank Enoch, Captain; 30 members; Pittsburg No. 92; James D. Riley, president; W. F. Maxwell, secretary; John L. Kennard, Captain; 24 members; North Fork No. 111, Owen Kirkpatrick, president; E. J. Mechling, secretary; C. J. Hufty, Captain; 15 members; Rockfield No. 102, Dean Adams, president; I. A. Rosenbarger, secretary; Harve Dilling, Captain; 15 members; Bringhurst No. 376, Tiffon Wilson, president; Richard M. Nimmiur, secretary; 56 members; and Green Lawn No. 85, Bennie Rice, president; Jessie Zinn, secretary; Clint Wagner, Captain; 38 members.

Four delegates from Carroll County elected to attend the National Convention were: Irvin Flora, Cutler; Wilford Hufty, Pittsburg; I. A. Rosenbarger, Rockfield; and Bennie Rice, Green Lawn.

KU KLUX KLAN

The Ku Klux Klan was organized in Pulaski, Tennessee in 1865. This was just after the Civil War, and during the period of reconstruction in the South. In many areas the local government was unable to deal with the many problems, so citizens organized Klans to render swift justice as they saw it. They called themselves the Invisible Empire Knights of the Ku Klux Klan. The Klan was based on the principle of freedom of thought, speech, press and assembly; complete separation of the Church and State; and free public schools in which no sectarian theories would be taught.

Membership was limited to white protestant native born Americans and all others were excluded. They justified this on the fact that other races and religions had organizations in which membership was limited to their own people. While the Klan claimed that they had nothing against other races and religions, their activities quite often made life miserable for negroes, Jews and Catholics.

The Klan grew more violent in its methods but not guilty of all crimes committed in its name. Other groups disguised themselves as Klansmen to perform violent acts. In 1871 Congress passed the Force Bills which gave the President power to suppress the Klan as a conspiracy against the government. The Klan disappeared soon after.

A new KKK was organized in 1915 in Atlanta, Georgia and grew rapidly, reaching a membership of about 5 million members in the United States.

Indiana

The Ku Klux Klan was very strong in Indiana in the early 1920's. In May 1924, D. C. Stephenson, Grand Dragon of the KKK in Indiana made the following statement: "There's been a lot of talk going around and there's going to be a lot more, and the fiery cross is going to burn at every crossroads in Indiana, as long as there is a white man left in the state." He also asked the Klan to back the 18th Amendment and rid the country of bootleggers. Under the leadership of D. C. "I-am-the-law" Stephenson, the organization took credit for electing at least one governor, U.S. Senators, mayors and thousands of lesser officials. Stephenson was convicted in 1925 of the murder of an Indianapolis young woman and sentenced to a life term in the Indiana State Prison. Early in 1928 the Attorney General of Indiana filed two suits asking that the Klan be dissolved. The suits were never tried, but public opinion was getting very strong against the Klan. The Indianapolis Times waged a savage campaign against the Klan, and for this the paper was awarded the Pulitzer Prize in 1928. This ended the growth and political power of the Klan in Indiana. In 1944 the KKK in the U.S. dissolved because it could not pay $500,000 due in back taxes.

Carroll County

While membership records were secret, there were a large number of members in Carroll County. Many natives admit that they were members, but do not want their names used. One former member said: "It seemed that every time we met they took up a collection and expected everyone to throw in $10. A representative from the State organization was usually there to take the money, and that's the last we saw it." It was reported that one minister operated a profitable business by using white bed sheets to make robes and sold them to members.

A State meeting of the Klan was held in Delphi on June 28, 1923. The program was complete with music, speaker, refreshments and ended with a torchlight parade and the burning of a fiery cross.

Deer Creek No. 20 held their regular meetings on the third floor over Elles & Orr's Drug Store, now Orr's Drug Store.

On September 24, 1923 the Klan held a rally in the Community Park at Flora.

In 1924 a speaker at a Klan meeting claimed that the Farm Bureau with its Cooperatives and other activities was a scheme for the Jews to get control of Agriculture.

RURAL FREE DELIVERY

The story of the first Rural Routes in the U.S. in 1896 is told in Chapter III. The first Rural Route in Carroll County was established at Delphi in August, 1898. Mr. F. M. Dice from the Post Office Department spent two or three days in Carroll County checking various routes, and recommended a route about 21 miles long in Deer Creek, Adams, Jefferson and Tippecanoe Townships. The August 18, 1898 issue of the Delphi Journal described it as follows: "Starting at Delphi the Route takes the road to the Carrollton bridge and up the hill to the schoolhouse, thence NE about 3/4 mile to road leading to Hopedale, follows this road to N. Line of John Pearson's farm. W. & N. to the road which runs through Hopedale, striking this road half a mile W. of Hopedale Post Office. Thence 1/2 mi. W. Thence 1 mi. N. 1½ mi. W. past the home of John B. Ellis (The Loco Post Office) and strikes the gravel road. From there the Route follows the gravel road coming in over the Range Line Road to Pittsburg and through W. Delphi."

James H. B. Whistler resigned his position as Deputy Postmaster and was appointed carrier, at a total pay of $300 per year. He visited everyone along the Route and explained to them that their only obligation was to put up a proper box along the Route for their mail. Failure to put up a box would be regarded as an indication that they did not desire mail delivery service. Delivery was started on August 15, 1898 and by December 1 there were 227 names on the Route. The amount of business on the Route was twice the amount required by the government to maintain a Rural Route. A great many people had the impression that Rural Free Delivery "would last until after the election."

Mail was delivered every day except Sunday and regular holidays. The carrier was allowed to charge patrons for delivering packages and telegrams, receive subscriptions for newspapers, and perform other services providing it did not interfere with delivery of mails. Some carriers hauled laundry for their patrons. Passengers could be hauled, but they were not permitted to handle the mail. Carriers also had a small supply of stamps and post cards.

The second Rural Route was at Flora and began delivery May 2, 1900. John Sparks was the first carrier. The Route was 26 miles long and served over 200 families. It was described as follows: "East from Flora past Dr. Cook's farm, South to Joel Overholser farm, East to Dan Landis', South to Bringhurst and Darwin Pike, East to Walnut Stump, North to Flora Pike, East to Widow Cook's, North to Jasper Landis', West to Gravel Hill Schoolhouse, North to Van Blue's, West to John Cartwright farm on the Delphi and Flora Pike, South to Gillam Schoolhouse, East to Flora."

Two more Routes were established in the county in October, 1900. A Route 26 miles long at Camden was described as: "Running West on the gravel road to the John Wise farm, thence South ½ mile, thence East one mile, thence South one mile to Schoolhouse No. 2, thence East a mile and a half, North 3/4 mile and East along the line of the gravel road to Carrollton Township and following the same line continues East to the Michigan gravel road, thence North 1 mile, West on the gravel road to the Carnell farm, thence N. 2 mi., thence West a mile and 3/4 to Schoolhouse No. 8, thence S. a mile and 3/4 to the Campbell farm, thence West 2½ mi. to Camden."

A second Route at Delphi, 25 miles long: "runs from Delphi, South to Pyrmont on the Dayton gravel road, thence East on the road North of Wildcat to Schoolhouse No. 1 in Clay Township on the Prince Wm. Road, about 2½ mi. this side of Prince William.

Farmers with their mail boxes in front of the Post Office at 113 W. Franklin St. in Delphi in October 1900 when the second Rural Route at Delphi was established south of Delphi in the area now served by Route 4.

Some of the names on the mailboxes are: George Trawin, John Nipple, L. A. Calvert, Daniel Anderson, Henry Gushwa, J. B. Dickinson, C. E. Wile, Z. A. Redding, H. S. Rohrabaugh, P. E. Schnepp, Samuel H. Haslet, W. Swain, John A. Din, L. D. Marion, A. A. Rohrabaugh, Robert Turpie, W. H. Robinson, John H. Shultheis, Elias Barner, W. K. Morrison, Samuel Milroy, A. P. Smock, Margaret Shaw and W. S. Haslet. Boxes were made by a steel post company in Adrian, Michigan.

From there the line follows the Pr. Wm. Road to the Weidner farm beyond the blacksmith shop, thence E. past Frazier Thomas', thence North to Joe Hanna's farm, thence E. 1 mi., thence N. 2 miles thence West past John D. Wilson's coming into Delphi over the Camden Road."

Will S. Smith was the first carrier on the Route and by this time the pay was increased to $500 per year. In the winter, Mr. Smith carried a lantern in his buggy to help keep warm. Some carriers had a small charcoal stove in their buggy.

In October, 1900 the postage rate for first class letters was raised from one cent to two cents per ounce for delivery on Rural Routes. It was estimated that it cost about $1 per person per year to operate a Rural Route and it was generally agreed that the benefits justified the costs. In 1902 the pay for rural carriers was increased to $600 per year if the Route was 25 miles long.

The Delphi Journal for August 1901 stated: "Farmers who live along the lines of rural free delivery mail Routes are soon to have the advantage of the United States weather bureau's forecasts of the weather. Arrangements are being made by the post office department and the weather bureau to have the mail carts equipped with signals which will be displayed on the sides. Mail carriers will receive their weather predictions for the day before they start on their Routes in the morning, and will put up the proper signals on both sides of their carts."

Two more Routes out of Delphi began on February 1, 1902. William Culler was carrier on a Route going East, and Edward Montgomery on a Route West and North. A Route was also established at Bringhurst and this made seven Routes in the county serving a total of 1000 families.

An article in the Delphi Journal on May 8, 1902 reported that Mr. Sam Rathbone, special agent in charge of the middle division of RFD recently moved from West Virginia to Indianapolis. He went home to supper one evening and his wife said: "Sam, I don't believe this RFD business is any good. I think it is going to ruin the country." He asked why and she told him that the price of chickens had gone up from 35 to 50¢ and eggs from 12 to 18¢ a dozen. The man delivering these to her had been reading the market reports in the daily papers and had been able to keep up with current prices. Mr. Rathbone had no answer handy.

The September 14, 1977 issue of the Carroll County Comet reported that the Delphi Journal 75 years ago stated: "On Monday two new Rural Routes were put in operation. One is Route 2 out of Bringhurst of which Charles McCracken is carrier, the other is Route No. 2 out of Flora with W. G. Canter as carrier."

On November 1, 1902 the Route out of Burrows was 22 miles long with 135 houses, occupied by 675 people.

In the fall of 1903 another Route was established at Camden. It was 24 miles long and served 134 homes.

By September 1904 there were 15 Routes in the county, and it was estimated that another 30 or 35 would be required to cover the county.

By April, 1905 there were seven Routes out of Delphi serving 3462 people in 767 houses. The Routes had a total of 182 miles, with 153 miles of gravel and 29 miles of dirt roads. Carriers on the Routes were: 1-Gus Johnson, 2-Joe Montgomery, 3-Mead Titlow, 4-Alonzo Mitchell, 5-Charley Stewart, 6-Wm. Culler and 7-Frank Lyons.

A new Route was started at Flora with L. D. Davis carrier, a Route at Cutler with Clyde Bonebrake carrier, and another at Camden with Charles Rice carrier.

The Delphi Journal for September 23, 1906 had the following report:

"Gus Johnson is the oldest rural carrier in Carroll County. We do not mean that Gus has reached an age where he should be chloroformed but that he has been driving a Rural Route wagon longer than any other carrier in Carroll County. Not only has Gus Johnson been driving a wagon longer than any other carrier in Carroll County but he has a record that cannot be surpassed by any carrier in the state. He has been a carrier for the past six years and during the six years he has been in government service he has not missed a trip over his Route. Another remarkable thing about his service as a rural carrier comes from the fact that during all the time he has been in the service he has used the same wagon and changed horses but once. He has used a wagon manufactured by the Delphi Wagon Works which is surely a great test and recommendation for their wagon. We might also say that since Gus has been in the service he has wooed and won a bride. This may not be anything out of the ordinary but nevertheless it occurred.

"'No. 1' can be seen on his wagon and his Route is one of the best Uncle Sam has to offer in the county to his carriers. He goes West on Monroe Street to the canal bridge and then over the new stone road to Pittsburg. On leaving Pittsburg he goes over the Range Line gravel road to the Pleasant Run Schoolhouse and then turns East and goes to the Carrollton Hill where he turns North to Hopedale. At Hopedale he turns West and then South and back over the Range Line road.

"Gus Johnson has been an efficient carrier, always looking out for the interests of his patrons and there are few carriers who have a higher regard for their needs. He says he likes the job and is as well pleased with the work as he was the first week. While he has made nearly two thousand trips and traveled nearly fifty thousand miles in the little wagon, just big enough for one, he has offered no complaint of either the heat or the cold weather."

The description of R. 1 in the article is slightly different than the original Route. It was later changed to include all the original Route, plus other territory as the Route was made longer.

On January 1, 1913 the new parcel post system went into effect. The post office handled packages up to 11 pounds in weight and six feet in length and girth combined. The rate was five cents for the first pound and three cents for each additional pound. Insurance was 10¢ per pound.

On June 9, 1914 a parcel post wagon was shipped by W. H. Bradshaw of the Delphi Wagon Works to Loveland, Ohio. This wagon was the first to be built and placed in service under specifications by the Postmaster General A. S. Burleson.

In 1914 the pay for rural carriers was raised to a maximum of $1200 a year.

As Rural Routes were established, mail was delivered to small local Post Offices saving the cost of a contract Route for this purpose. Later the small Post Offices were closed, and more money was saved. In May, 1915 the Post Office at Pittsburg was closed at a savings of about $300 per year. This Post Office had been in operation for 79 years. Routes 1, 2 and 3 from Delphi went through Pittsburg and served the former patrons of the Post Office.

On September 1, 1915 Tippecanoe County began using automobiles to deliver mail on Rural Routes, and the change was soon made on all Routes. This made it possible to have longer and fewer Routes.

TELEPHONES

The first record of a telephone conversation was on March 8, 1876 when Alexander Graham Bell told Thomas A. Watson, "Mr. Watson, come here, I want to see you." That was the beginning of a new way of life for people in the U.S.

A few private telephones were installed in 1877. The first exchange using a switchboard was installed in New Haven, Connecticut on January 28, 1878. Names were used for the first year, but as the number of subscribers increased, it became difficult for the operators to learn everyone's name. In 1879 each subscriber was given a number.

The American Bell Telephone Company was organized in March, 1880, and installed telephones in the larger cities. By 1881 nearly every large city in the U.S. had a telephone exchange. The first long distance line for public use was opened on January 12, 1881 between Boston, Massachusetts and Providence, Rhode Island, a distance of 45 miles.

In 1894, the first telephone patents expired, and independent companies began installing telephones in small towns and rural areas.

In June, 1914 a transcontinental telephone line was completed across the U.S. Service began at a ceremony on January 25, 1915. Alexander Graham Bell, in New York City talked to Thomas Watson in San Francisco.

During the conversation Mr. Bell repeated their first conversation held 39 years earlier by asking Mr. Watson to come here. This time Watson answered, "It would take me a week to get there now!"

At first it took 23 minutes to make a call from New York to San Francisco, and the cost was $20.70.

Dial telephone service began in Norfolk, Virginia on November 8, 1919. By 1931 nearly 1/3 of the homes in the U.S. had telephones, and by 1977 95% had telephones. There were about 70 telephones per 100 people in the U.S. in 1979.

Other kinds of communication developed along with the telephone.

The first radio station was KDKA, Pittsburgh which began in March, 1920. Radio station WBAA at Purdue is the oldest radio station now operating in Indiana.

The first television was on April 7, 1927 when Herbert Hoover, Secretary of Commerce talked in Washington, D.C. and the picture was carried on telephone lines to New York. The first T.V. station in Indiana was W9XG at Purdue University, which went on the air on December 31, 1931.

The invention of the transistor in March, 1947, led to rapid improvements in all systems of communication. Before the development of the radio and television, the party line telephone was the main source of news and entertainment.

The Party Line

There were about ten telephones on each line, and for many years this was a primary source of news, gossip and entertainment. When someone on the line was called, all the phones on the line would ring. Each person had a different ring. One long ring was for central, and a certain number of long rings, or short rings or a combination of long and short rings were assigned each subscriber. Number 1 was a short ring and number 2 was a long ring. A person with number 111 would have three short rings, while a person with number 211 would have a long and two short rings. Everyone knew the ring for others on the line, and many people "listened in" to see what was going on. In some cases this was handy. In case of an emergency a person could ring anyone on the line, and almost everyone on the line would get the message. By calling someone on another line, twice as many people would get the message.

Old timers say that some who "eavesdropped" were careless and had their telephone close to a loud ticking clock or some other noise that made it possible for others to tell when they were listening.

In 1901 the State Legislature passed a law imposing a fine as high as $500 for giving out information obtained by eavesdropping on a telephone line.

Telephones in Carroll County

When the first patents on telephones expired in 1894 many independent companies were organized. Most of them were small, and no official records of their activities are available.

One of the first telephone lines in Carroll County was built by Dr. A. H. Coble of Rockfield. In 1895 he installed a line to Lockport and Hopedale for his personal use. In 1896 he built a line to Camden and Flora, and in 1897 extended it to Bringhurst, Cutler and Burlington.

Beginning in 1895 local newspapers had many news articles about telephones. While these articles do not provide all the information, they do indicate that many telephones were installed at that time.

The following excerpts are from the Delphi Journal:

> July 30, 1896. "Mutual Telephone Company of Logansport is arranging to run toll lines into every small town in Carroll County and the rates will be greatly reduced."

June 17, 1897. "Carroll Telephone Company has completed its line between Delphi and Monticello and the line is now open for business. It is probable branch lines will be built into Sleeth and Yeoman connecting also with those towns. It is probable that a connection will be made at Monticello with the line between Rensselaer and Lafayette. If this is done Delphi will be connected with 25 or 30 other towns in northwest Indiana."

July 15, 1897. "Telephone service can be obtained over the long distance lines at Gregg's Music Store to Georgetown, Hopedale, Camden, Rockfield and Flora. The rate to all these points is 25¢ except to Camden which is 15¢."

August 12, 1897. "Telephone connections will be made with Burlington within 30 days. To Dr. A. H. Coble we are indebted for this new line because of his construction of new lines. Burlington line will run through Bringhurst and Cutler. Dr. Coble uses the standard Bell telephone instruments."

October 14, 1897. "Burlington telephone line completed but difficult to talk between Delphi and Burlington. Breaks, cracks and sputterings and stutterings. Hope this can be stopped soon. New telephone card issued Monday for Carroll Telephone Company. Gives all additions since last card was published and straightens out many changes. Those who do not have a new one should waste no time getting one."

April 7, 1898. "Local telephone exchange now connected by way of Monticello with Idaville, Burnett's Creek, Lake Cicott and Logansport, and it will be only a few days before we can talk with Reynolds, Chalmers, Rensselaer and all important points in White, Jasper and Newton County, and other counties in northern Indiana."

June 2, 1898. "Telephone communication has been established between Delphi and Frankfort by local exchange by way of Bringhurst."

April 20, 1899. "Delphi will soon be in communication with telephone exchange in Indianapolis."

April 4, 1901. "The Farmer's Mutual Telephone Company has been organized, connecting a large number of farmers between Camden and Deer Creek on an independent telephone line which is soon to be installed. The organization was effected last Saturday at the Fouts Schoolhouse where a meeting was held and the following organization formed: Bennie Carnell of Camden, president; U. E. Tesh of Camden, vice president; Frank Shanks of Deer Creek, treasurer; E. C. Rice of Camden, secretary; Dr. McNeal and Frank Shanks trustees."

June 26, 1901. "The Independent Telephone Company is running a telephone line from Kokomo to Burlington."

July 28, 1901. "Last Thursday the Central Union Telephone Company sent a man to Flora to take out all the local phones. This company has been working in opposition to the local telephone company for several years, charging nothing for service, but the people refused to accept their generosity and they were forced at last to abandon the fight."

November 23, 1905. "Independent telephone business in state safe and sound. Three hundred sixty eight independent telephone exchanges in state, doing a good business with 175,000 telephones in state. No company has been in hands of receiver."

Delphi

Early in 1895, Wm. Bradshaw of Delphi made plans for the Indiana Telephone and Construction Company to put an exchange in Delphi. However, in January 1896, the Delphi City Council voted to give a telephone franchise to Indiana Harrison Construction Company. A survey showed that 65 places were wanting telephone service at rates of $2 per month for a business and $1 per month for a residence.

In January 1896, H. Kerlin and Son and E. W. Bowen organized the Carroll Telephone Company with 60 shares of stock at $100 each, and signed a contract with Indiana Harrison Construction Company for a telephone exchange in the city, with lines to Flora and Pittsburg. About the time the lines were completed, Dr. Edward Walker purchased a con-

Telephone operators at the switchboard at Delphi when exchange was converted to dial equipment on January 10, 1960. Left to right: Fannie Simons, Beatrice White, Fay Wood, Jean Walters, Kate Loveland, Opal Wood, Inez Johnson, Julia Schilling and Margaret Gerard.

trolling interest in the company and took control on August 1, 1896.

In 1897, lines were extended to Burlington and Monticello. In 1902, lines were built in the rural areas near Delphi and telephones were installed in about 150 farm homes. The rate was $1 per month.

The first switchboard and office for the Carroll Telephone Company was located upstairs in the building at 116 East Main Street above where the Delphi Journal and the Oracle Press were located in later years. The office was moved upstairs above the Bradshaw Insurance Agency at 111 East Main Street, and in 1939 was moved to the present location at 123 East Main Street.

In October 1939, the Carroll Telephone Company purchased the telephone exchange at Idaville and converted it to dial in 1959.

The exchange at Delphi was converted to dial on January 10, 1960.

The Carroll Telephone Company became a subsidiary of Mid-Continent Telephone Corporation on February 1, 1971. Three Delphi men who had a total of 120 years of service with the company retired on this date: John Walker, president of Carroll Telephone Company had been lineman for 32 years; Charles A. Wood, plant superintendent had been with the company since 1922; and Robert W. Wood, general manager and treasurer, had been affiliated with the company since 1934.

Five other employees remained with the company. They included: Owen W. Delaney, lineman since 1953; David A. Wood, maintenance man in the central office, and with the firm since 1946; and Fred A. Collins, six years as lineman and other duties. Clerks in the front business office who remained were: Mrs. Asa (Laurene) Cohee, employed over 20 years, and Mrs. Owen (Thelma) Delaney who had been in the office for 12 years.

Present employees include: Charles E. Peek, manager since February 1, 1971; Sheryl Dyer, Virginia Timmons and Louise Sales, office; David A. Wood and Rick Randol, central office; Fred Collins, Harold Stayer, Doyle Moore and Jack Kelly, installer repair and Marlene Collins, housekeeper.

Flora and Bringhurst

At least seven telephone companies were organized in the Flora and Bringhurst area between 1896 and 1905.

The first record of telephones in the Flora area was the incorporation of the Flora and Logansport Telephone Company on November 18, 1896. Its purpose was to construct and operate telephone lines between Flora and Logansport and other towns. Officers were Albert H. Coble, president; Addison Michael, vice president; Charles E. Noble, secretary; Jacob H. Flora, treasurer, and James R. Cromer, director.

Mrs. Martha Patty, Cashier, Mrs. Marjorie Peterson, Mrs. Faye Edging and Mrs. Pearl Mocherman, operators until the change over to the new dial system at the Flora Telephone Exchange.

The Delphi Journal for May 7, 1897 reported that the Flora Telephone Company was trying to secure a connection with the Central Union Telephone Exchange at Logansport. The line had been built from Flora to Logansport and as far into the city as Sycamore Street near the Eel River where the city authorities enjoined the company from going any further.

About a year later the Carroll County Commissioners granted the Central Union Telephone Company of Logansport the right to place its poles on the right of way of highways in the county, and they took over the line built by the Flora and Logansport Telephone Company.

Early in the spring of 1898 Dave E. Miller installed a telephone switchboard in his drug store in Bringhurst. It was connected with toll lines to Burlington, Frankfort and Delphi.

The Delphi Journal for March 27, 1902 reported that the Flora Mutual Telephone Company was organized with A. J. Cook, president; J. H. Coplen, treasurer and Dr. W. E. Callane, secretary. Directors were A. J. Cook, Rev. A. G. Crosswhite, Harve Bowerman; solicitors were J. J. Moss, Frank Woods, Rev. A. G. Crosswhite, J. M. Hendrix, and Del Burkebile. The company was capitalized at $5000 consisting of 200 shares of stock at $25 per share. As soon as the stock was sold they planned to purchase the Flora and Bringhurst telephone systems.

The issue of the Delphi Journal for May 12, 1904 reported that stockholders in the proposed Flora and

Bringhurst Cooperative Telephone Company elected the following officers: Dr. W. E. Callane, president; Rev. A. G. Crosswhite, vice president; E. E. Eikenberry, general manager and J. H. Coplen, treasurer. Trustees were W. F. Wagoner, R. S. Tidrick and Harvey A. Thomas.

In November 1904 the Flora Telephone Company was organized by the following ten people: Dr. F. P. Lyons, Dr. E. L. Peter, Dr. W. E. Callane, J. H. Coplen, R. R. Bright, Harve Thomas, Henry Rinehart, W. F. Wagoner, Van C. Blue, and W. S. Viney. They purchased the telephone company in Flora, and the Miller Company in Bringhurst. This made a total of 700 telephones for the new company, and ended the competition between telephone companies for a short time.

In March 1905 the Bringhurst Cooperative Telephone Company was organized with 25 subscribers. Officers were: W. J. Nimmins, president; C. Retherford, secretary, and A. B. Cohee, treasurer. Directors were: D. H. Carter, A. B. Coble, and R. S. Tidrick.

The Flora Company refused to make a connection with the new company at Bringhurst, so the telephone war was on again.

The Bringhurst Company continued in business until May, 1911 when they sold the system with 53 phones to the Cutler Cooperative Telephone Company at a price of $3360.

In July 1905 the Home Telephone Company was organized in Flora with Harry E. Soesbe, manager of the Bell system at Frankfort as president; Harvey E. Studebaker, vice president; and Joseph E. Studebaker, secretary-treasurer. The new system was installed and began operation early in 1906.

In 1915 Warren Knapp was employed as manager of the Flora Telephone Company.

In 1929 the Flora Telephone Company, owned by Mr. and Mrs. Warren Knapp and Mr. and Mrs. Charles Cockrane, was sold to the United Telephone Company of Indianapolis, which had been incorporated March 10, 1926.

Dial Telephones

After operating the Flora Telephone Company for several years the United Telephone Company built a new building at 16 East Main Street and installed equipment for dial telephones. The change-over from the switchboard to the automatic dial system was made at 1:01 A.M. Sunday, January 15, 1961. A 125 foot microwave tower was installed to connect the Flora exchange with the company's Monticello exchange for long distance calls, and later that year it was possible for the 1230 telephone subscribers at Flora to make direct dial calls throughout North America without the assistance of an operator.

The Delphi Journal for January 19, 1961 gave information about the telephone operators:

Mrs. Marjorie Peterson and Mark McCracken tried out the new dial system shortly after cutover in the new office of the Flora Telephone exchange.

"The thirteen telephone operators 'lost their jobs' with the dial system.

"Mrs. Jack (Roberta) Gillam has been night supervisor for six years. Operators included: Mrs. Leon (Margaret) Viney, Mrs. Norman (Marjorie) Peterson Jr., Miss Roselyn Penn, Miss Dorothy Myer, Mrs. Russell (Pearl) Mocherman, Mrs. Mills (Vella) McKinley, Mrs. Junior (Betty) Maxwell, Mrs. Billy (Wilma) Garrison, Mrs. Jay (Faye) Edging, Mrs. Ernest (Mabel) Dunham, Mrs. Dean (Betty) Briggs, and Mrs. Kathryn Minnix.

"Mrs. Minnix has been an operator for 16 years. Mrs. Mocherman has 14 years time accrued and Miss Dorothy Myer has 13 years. Mrs. McKinley and Mrs. Edging, night operators since June 1951, have worked 9½ years each."

Mrs. Robert Patty and Mrs. Ray Cook continued as cashier and assistant in the new office. Mark McCracken continued as maintenance man.

Cooperative Telephone Companies

Beginning in 1902 several small towns and rural communities organized cooperative telephone companies. Information about them was obtained from Official Records in the Courthouse, articles in newspapers, records of the telephone company and from people who were involved. The information is not complete, but does indicate the great interest in telephones, and demonstrates how people helped each other get this new service.

Deer Creek Telephone Company

Articles of Incorporation for The Deer Creek Cooperative Telephone Company were signed on May

18, 1902. Directors for the first year were: A. A. Cook, Perry Johnson, James D. Zartman, Samuel Mitchell, Charles V. McCloskey, Daniel M. McCloskey, and A. A. Newer, who purchased the first share of stock on July 1, 1903. A total of 75 stockholders each purchased a share of stock at $30. Anyone who wanted a telephone installed was required to buy a share of stock. Many of the stockholders helped set poles and put up wire in order to get service.

John West was probably the first lineman. Others were: Willie Seagraves, Clay Shanks, Fred Lantz, Victor Henry, and Frank and Bill Mullin.

The first switchboard was in the Roy Landis home in the north edge of Deer Creek, which was later remodeled for the Lutheran parsonage. The switchboard was moved to the residence later owned and occupied by the John Martin family. The company later purchased the property belonging to Mrs. Emma Hornbeck, and the switchboard was located there until it was replaced by dial equipment.

Roy Landis was the first operator. He was assisted by Mrs. Vena Bryant, who continued, either part or full time, as long as the switchboard was used. Other operators were: Mr. Branblett, Roy Burt, Pauline Wilson, Nina Robeson, Lottie Williams, Maxine Spencer, Olive Gill and Mrs. Effie Cornell, a sister to Mrs. Bryant.

The Deer Creek Telephone Company was sold to the Camden Telephone Company in July 1962 and was converted to dial at 2:00 P.M. Saturday, February 2, 1963. At that time there were approximately 307 phones with 40 extensions in the exchange. The property where the switchboard was located was sold to Ralph Dyke.

The trustees at the time of the sale were: Harve Lenon, chairman; Leroy Robeson, vice chairman; Orton Peters, secretary; Roy Yeakley, treasurer and general manager; Ira Nelson, Oris Shanks and Harry Plank.

Yeoman Telephone Company

In 1902 a number of people living in and near Yeoman organized a Cooperative Telephone Company. It took them about a year to secure a franchise on the territory, and on September 8, 1903 they filed Articles of Association which were approved by the Secretary of State on January 12, 1904.

The company started with a capital stock of $1000 and built lines to provide telephone service for stockholders. In 1905 they borrowed $500 to purchase telephones to rent to others along the lines.

In 1905 the directors by unanimous vote decided that "anyone who calls central between 9:00 P.M. and 5:00 A.M., only when it is an emergency, and that is to be determined by central, be made to pay 10¢ and the same be given to the central girl for being bothered."

For years the telephone rent was paid quarterly. In 1915 the directors voted that "no subscriber can be delinquent more than two quarters."

In 1919 an addition was made to the office building, and in 1947 the company purchased a new Stromberg-Carlson switchboard which was used until 1955.

On May 22, 1953 a storm severely damaged the telephone system. Temporary repairs were made to restore service and the directors applied for and secured a 35 year loan of $170,000 from the Rural Electrification Administration. The system was completely rebuilt with about 80 miles of line and a new building was constructed where new modern dial telephone equipment was installed. The system was built large enough to provide service to the ever increasing demand from customers along the Tippecanoe River and Lake Freeman.

On October 9, 1955 the cut-over was made and the Yeoman Telephone Company became the first automatic dial system in the county. Floyd W. Oberkrom was lineman and plant superintendent beginning in 1955. Mrs. Wayne Norris who became chief operator in 1952 continued as bookkeeper and office manager. She was replaced by Florence Nicewander who retired in 1972 and was replaced by her daughter Shirley Larson. The officers and directors in 1955 were: Robert R. Million, president and general manager; Fred Gaumer, vice president and Glenn Davis, secretary. Other directors were Clarence Davis and Arthur Ward.

In 1967 E. O. Teach was president; William M. Goslee, secretary and George Breeze, treasurer. Other directors were: John Million, Charles Ginn and Martin Baum.

In 1979 John Crowell was president; Jerry Lilly, vice president; Dwaine Wigner, secretary-treasurer;

Office of Yeoman Telephone Company built in 1955. This is the only one of the many cooperative telephone companies organized in Carroll County that is a locally owned independent company operating one exchange.

Dean Goslee, manager and Floyd Oberkrom, plant superintendent. Shirley Larson was bookkeeper and Mrs. Melvin (Donnabelle) Brown had been records clerk since 1972. Pat Million and Glenn Davis were directors. There were about 1000 customers in 1979.

Rockfield Telephone Company

The Rockfield Cooperative Telephone Company was organized in February 1903 with 58 stockholders. Officers were: John W. Kerlin, president; P. M. Byrum, secretary and W. H. Galbreth, treasurer.

In 1907 there were 70 stockholders and 117 telephones. John W. Kerlin was president; A. L. Surface, vice president; P. W. Van Gundy, secretary and Thomas Robinson, general manager. Trustees were: Samuel Clauser, C. L. Million and A. M. Rankin.

In 1913 there were 72 stockholders, and officers were: A. L. Surface, president; Charles Raber, vice president; P. M. Byrum, secretary and T. W. Moore, treasurer.

In 1960 the Rockfield Company was purchased by the Camden Telephone Company.

Camden Telephone Company

On February 26, 1903 a few citizens met at the Odd Fellows Hall in Camden to make plans for organizing a telephone company. Temporary officers elected were: C. E. Baker, president and G. B. Wingard, secretary. A committee was appointed to draft a Constitution and By-laws.

Four meetings were held in March, and people in Camden and the surrounding area were contacted to see if they were interested in telephones. Soliciting committees were in charge of F. G. Armick, in Camden; Enoch Sieber, west of town; Jesse Martin, east; Jesse Plank, north; and James Lesh, south of Camden. Twenty in Camden, and four in the country signed up during March.

On April 2, 1903 the Camden Cooperative Telephone Company was organized. Officers elected were: U. E. Tesh, president; Leo Whorley, vice president; G. B. Wingard, secretary; C. E. Baker, treasurer and E. A. McFarland, general manager. Trustees elected were: Jesse Plank, for a term of one year; F. G. Armick, two years and O. W. Wyatt, three years.

The Constitution and By-laws adopted at the meeting provided that each member would own and maintain his own telephone. If the telephone was damaged by lightning, it was to be taken to the central office where it would be repaired by the company. Twenty seven members signed the Constitution and By-laws. Each member agreed to pay an equal share of the amount needed to install a switchboard and build lines. Each member was asked to make an initial deposit of $20. Members were asked to contribute more money as it was needed.

During April, the trustees purchased 104 poles, 100 eight pin crossarms, and one barrel of insulators from the Rockfield Telephone Company, at a total cost of $154. They purchased a switchboard and telephones from the Swedish American Telephone Company for $347. John Fessler was hired at $2 per day to begin setting poles on May 19, 1903.

The residence of Miss Grace Armstrong on East Main St. was leased at $5 per month and the switchboard installed. Telephones were connected as the lines were built. The rate for a telephone on a party line was $1 per month.

Arrangements were made with other telephone companies in the county for each company to build and maintain one half of the line to connect the companies. Toll charges of 10 cents per call were divided equally between the companies.

Articles of Incorporation were approved and filed on March 17, 1904. The company was incorporated for a period of 50 years. By the end of 1906 there were 61 shareholders with 65 shares of stock, and a total of 170 telephones on the line.

Perry Rule was elected general manager in January 1905, and served until John Graham was elected in January 1908.

In 1908 a house on lot No. 22 owned by Mrs. Bunker was purchased for the office, and the switchboard was moved there on June 6, 1908.

At the stockholders meeting in January 1915 it was reported that there were 260 telephones on the Camden line, and that toll free service was available to most other exchanges in the county except to Delphi.

At the Annual Meeting of the Camden Cooperative Telephone Company held in February 1958, the telephone company was dissolved, and a new Camden Telephone Company was formed with the Articles of Incorporation being filed with the Secretary of State of Indiana on December 4, 1958. At that time there were 47 stockholders, and the officers were: W. O. Pettiner, president; Claude Wickard, vice president; Lloyd Yerkes, secretary; Harold Wyatt, treasurer and John McCain, manager and board member. Forrest Appleton was plant superintendent assisted by John McCain. Mrs. Hanna Appleton was office secretary. The new company applied for and received a loan from REA to rebuild the system and convert it to dial telephones.

The Camden Company purchased the Rockfield Telephone Company in 1960, and the Burrows and Deer Creek Telephone Companies in 1962. Additional money, making a total of about $750,000 was borrowed from REA.

The overhead lines were replaced with underground cable. A new dial telephone system for Camden and Rockfield was installed in Camden and put in operation at 12:01 A.M. Sunday, August 20, 1961.

The first switchboard operator at Camden was Mrs. Laura Lennon Sterling who was assisted by her sister, Mrs. Emma Porter. Mrs. Aaron Wingard was the next operator, and Mrs. Dora Keyes was operator for several years prior to Miss Sulie Ward, who was the last switchboard operator at Camden. Miss Ward had worked seven days a week for 37 years with no vacation. Others assisting were her two sisters, Misses Myrtle and Martha Ward, and Miss Fay Dilling. The switchboard was open from 5:00 A.M. to 9:00 P.M. seven days a week. Emergency calls were answered at night.

New dial equipment was installed in a building in Deer Creek, and the telephones were converted to dial at 2:00 P.M. Saturday, February 2, 1963. A building was constructed at Burrows, and dial equipment installed. The telephones at Burrows were converted to dial on May 19, 1963. This was the last exchange in Carroll County to convert to dial telephones. This made it possible for people with telephones in Carroll County to make a direct call anywhere in the United States. Toll free service was provided between Delphi and the Camden companies. In addition Camden subscribers could call Flora and Idaville, and Deer Creek subscribers could call Flora and Burlington. There were a total of 1370 telephones on the Camden exchange in 1979.

In 1966 the Camden Telephone Company installed a new tower for the use of mobile telephones. The tower, erected January 14, 1966 is 150 feet high with a 19 foot antenna, and can be used by mobile dial telephones within 25 miles of the tower. This was the first and is still the only service of this kind in Carroll County. About 35 or 40 were using this service in 1979.

Officers of the Camden Telephone Company in 1979 were: W. O. Pettiner, president; Joe Sullivan, vice president; Mrs. Hanna Appleton, secretary-treasurer; Lloyd Yerkes and E. E. Johnson, directors and Jack Ford, manager.

Burrows Telephone Company

The first meeting to discuss "putting in" a telephone system at Burrows was held on February 2, 1903 and the Burrows Cooperative Telephone Company was organized in March 1903 with 47 subscribers served by 25 miles of line.

The first officers were: M. J. McGreevy, president; W. F. West, vice president; N. G. Martin, secretary and O. N. Glasscock, treasurer. Trustees were: J. E. Dixon, S. A. Wason and Jerome Justice. B. F. Eyman was general manager.

J. H. (Hank) Hinkle operated the first switchboard which was located in his Burrows home until 1907, when property was purchased and a new building constructed for the switchboard and office. Some who served as operators were the Frank Kennedy daughters, Mrs. Aaron Wingard, Isaac Cain, John Graham, K. L. Riggle, Charles Hoover, Josephine Daniels and her sister Myrtle Williams, Mrs. White, Mrs. Lillian Grant, Mrs. A. E. Wentzell, and Mrs. Vera Stewart, who began November 15, 1955. She had the honor of being the last "Hello Girl" in Carroll County when the system was converted to dial on May 19, 1963.

In 1962 the Burrows Telephone Company was purchased by the Camden Telephone Company. Officers of the Burrows Company in 1962 were: Carl Yeakley, president; Fred Benner, vice president; John Benner, secretary; R. O. Justice, treasurer and Frank Mullin, director. William and Frank Mullin were linemen.

Cutler Telephone Company

The Cutler Cooperative Telephone Company was incorporated in February, 1906 with William N. Draper, president; Noah Plank, secretary; William Smith, treasurer and George Phillips, general manager. William S. Hazlet, George W. Shanklin and James D. Long were directors.

In May, 1911 the Cutler Cooperative Telephone Company purchased the Bringhurst Cooperative Telephone Company which then had 53 telephones.

The system was converted to dial telephones, and in 1971 the company was purchased by Mid-Continent Telephone Company.

Burlington Telephone Company

The Burlington Telephone Company was organized December 28, 1914 with 20 stockholders and a capital of $2100. The first officers were: William T. Hindman, president; J. P. Haun, secretary; H. B. Summers, treasurer and S. D. Lowe, general manager. Other directors were: Joseph S. Tam, Ellis Logan, and Pratt W. Stonebraker.

The first switchboard was installed and maintained by Stephen Lowe in a room on the second floor of the livery stable. It was operated by Mrs. Lucille Mercer. After a fire destroyed that building, a switchboard was installed at the corner of Michigan and 6th Street near the site of the present Indiana Bell station.

Carroll County Cooperative Telephone Association

In August, 1903, 25 delegates representing the Cooperative Telephone Companies in the county met at Camden and organized the Carroll County Cooperative Telephone Association. They planned to establish a Co-op Telephone switchboard to handle all the calls between the exchanges in the county. In July, 1904 they reached an agreement to exchange calls with all telephone systems in the county at a cost of 10¢ per call, with the money to be divided equally between the companies involved in the call.

The Association was still active in 1930. The Delphi

Journal March 13, 1930 reported that directors from six exchanges met at the Perry M. Byrum home in Rockfield and elected the following officers: W. G. Million, president; Earl Stewart, vice president; and P. M. Byrum secretary treasurer. Exchanges in the Association were: Yeoman, Rockfield, Deer Creek, Burrows, Camden, Cutler in Carroll County and Idaville in White County. They had a total of 2500 phones, and the rate was about $1 per month.

Carroll County Cooperative Telephone Company

In March 1920 a company was organized to sell stock and raise enough money to buy all the telephone exchanges in the county and have toll free service for the entire county. Edward Smock was treasurer, and others selling stock were Emory Flora, E. W. Bowen, C. M. Kerlin, William Brown, W. G. Klepinger, R. C. Julien, Robert Ray, Noah Landis, and B. F. Ulm. They applied to the Public Service Commission for permission to buy the companies, but in November, 1920 the PSC decided that there should be no change in ownership of the exchanges in the county.

MARKETING FARM PRODUCTS

One of the major problems of the early settlers was to find a market for their farm products. Some grain and meat was hauled by wagon to Chicago or Indianapolis, but this was slow and expensive. About 90% of the surplus produce was loaded on barges and floated down the river to New Orleans where the produce and barge were sold. The crew returned by commercial steamboat.

Each farm had a few cows and chickens for their own use, and surplus eggs, cream and butter was traded at the grocery store for necessary supplies. For several years each town had one or more stations that collected eggs, milk and cream and some was shipped on the interurban to processing plants.

The Delphi Journal for July 6, 1911 reported that an egg had hatched in the Richard and Company Poultry Yard. Hot weather had caused the egg to hatch, and the chicken was alive and well.

Several cooperative creameries were organized in the county, but most of them did not stay in business very long. In many cases they were promoted by companies selling machinery and equipment.

Several stores operated huckster routes selling groceries and collecting farm produce. Many old timers can remember that when they were kids, one of the highlights of the week was when the huckster came. That usually meant candy, and other good things to eat. The wagon or truck was built with shelves for groceries, and usually had a crate on the back or top for poultry, and a barrel with kerosene for lamps. One of the last huckster routes in the county was operated by Lanes store in Bringhurst, and was discontinued in 1946.

Packing Plant

The following is part of an article written by Wm. C. Smith, first president of the Carroll County Historical Society and printed in the Delphi Citizen August 21, 1930 as one of a series of articles entitled "Up the River of Time."

"From 1840 to 1871, Delphi was one of the largest pork packing centers of Indiana, and after the canal began operations and became the great highway of commerce of the Wabash country, the pork packing industry in Delphi finally centered in the firm of Spears, Dugan & Co., consisting of James Spears, James P. Dugan and Reed Case.

"Case came to Delphi in 1836, and was a canal contractor and built the canal through Delphi and the steamboat locks at the Pittsburg Dam. In 1838 he formed a partnership with James Spears of Lafayette and they did business under the name of Spears & Case. This firm built the cut off from the canal to their warehouse that stood where the Kerlin elevator now stands so that canal boats could run up to it.

"In 1845 James P. Dugan became a member of the firm of Spears & Case and the firm became known as first stated. In 1863 this firm constructed the large packing house in the east end of Delphi just south of the Camden road where it crosses the interurban track and Robinson's Run, on the bank of that stream. This stream, after the packing house was built, became known as "Gut Creek" because all the entrails from hogs slaughtered were thrown into it, where they were washed into Deer Creek and from it into the Wabash River. Imagine if you can the condition of these streams when this packing plant was packing a thousand head of hogs per day which they did in the palmy days of its business. There are yet men and women living who remember the condition of those streams at that time.

"This packing house was constructed of stone quarried near its site and stood until 1885, when it was torn down and the stone and timbers were used in the construction of the Dodge Paper Mill.

"There is a crayon picture of this packing house in the relic room in the Courthouse which shows that it was a large enterprise. And there was a railroad switch leading from the Wabash railroad to it.

"This packing house did a large business until the year of 1871 when Spears and Case died and the business soon thereafter ceased, and that was the death of the pork packing industry in

Delphi. We have before us an old letterhead of the firm of Spears, Dugan & Co., printed in the early seventies on which is printed a cut of their buildings, and that they were packers of 'Pork, Beef and dealers of Sugar Cured Hams, Pork, Lard, etc.'

"If one who has never heard of this industry should now visit the site of it, he would find but a slight depression in the surface of the ground of many feet in length and breadth, now covered with a heavy sod, and he would never suspect that it was once the location of one of the largest packing houses in Indiana which slaughtered a thousand head of hogs a day. It was so large that it attracted the attention of the Armour plant in Chicago and its representative came to Delphi to consider the proposition of buying and enlarging it. Then Delphi had but one railroad, and it was slowly killing the canal, and the representative said that shipping facilities were not sufficient.

"When this plant was running farmers within a radius of 100 miles of Delphi drove their hogs to it on foot. One who has never driven hogs knows nothing about the task of driving hogs to market. In those days it never occurred to the farmer that he could easily haul his hogs to market in wagons, they thought they had to be driven. A big, fat hog is slow in motion unless he becomes stampeded or frightened, and then he makes some pretty swift movements until he becomes winded and becomes so contrary that he simply will not go forward unless seized and moved forward by force. Hog drivers got along pretty well in spite of rough, muddy roads which was then the condition of all roads, unless they came to bridges and culverts across rivers, creeks and branches and upon these they had their troubles galore. A hog, like an elephant, will not cross a bridge if he becomes in the least suspicious of it. If he sees a ray of light between the cracks of the flooring or if the sides are open he refuses to cross the bridge and no persuasion will coax him across either. He has to be seized and forced across. Sometimes the drivers would fight droves of hogs for hours in trying to get them across bridges which not only wore the hogs out but the drivers as well. All kinds of decoys and devices were used to fool the hogs and sometimes they worked but more often they didn't. Straw was scattered over the floors of bridges and shelled corn was thrown before the hogs and run ways were made at the approaches so the hogs could not break off at the sides which did not remedy the matter much.

"It took two days to drive hogs from Wild Cat to Delphi and the writer's father said that it took him four or five days to drive his hogs from Howard county 35 miles to Delphi. At night the drivers would drive their hogs in a farmer's barn lot, feed them and put up with the farmer over night and all farmers welcomed these drivers as there was a feeling of neighbourliness prevailing then.

"It has been said that when this packing house was in full operation that the streets of Delphi resembled a big hog pen. All the roads leading into Delphi and all its streets was simply crowded with droves of hogs accompanied with their drivers shouting loudly the language used by hog drivers and cracking their long black snake whips. It is easy for one familiar with hog driving to close his eyes and see in dreams, and hear again, these vast droves of hogs with their drivers slowly winding their way through our now peaceful, quiet streets to the big packing house at the east end of our city.

"In our packing houses of today not a thing is wasted. They say that even the squeal of the hog is utilized. It was not so when our packing house was in operation. Only the hams, sides, shoulders, hair and a part of the back bones, spare ribs and livers were used, the rest was given away or dumped into the creek. The hair was spread upon the fields surrounding the plant to dry. There were but few houses if any, in Mortonville then and the land now occupied by it was used to spread the hog's hair upon until it became in proper shape to ship."

Farmers Cooperative Packing Company of Indiana

Probably the most ambitious program for marketing farm products was the organization of a $1,000,000 Farmers Cooperative Packing Company of Indiana in April, 1920. It was organized to "buy, sell and deal in hogs, cattle, sheep, poultry and to slaughter same and dispose of its products and to provide cold storage for butter, eggs, meat of all farm products and equip and hold all real estate necessary to carry on the industries and business above mentioned." Officers were: David L. Musselman, president; Wade P. Thompson, vice president; Auda Gee Studebaker, secretary attorney; Fred H. Engle, treasurer. Others on the Board of Directors were: John H. Mourer and James D. Ball.

In June, 1920 a group from White and Carroll counties visited packing plants in North Dakota. They came back with a report that the plant would require about five times as much money as they had planned.

They proceeded with plans and the Delphi Journal for September 18, 1920 showed a drawing of the proposed plant and reported the selection of a site near Delphi. The proposed location was northwest of Delphi where the Belt Railroad crosses the old state road. The Delphi Commercial Club agreed to donate 34 acres of land valued at $10,000 where a part of the stone quarry is now located. They also offered 50 lots in the Commercial Club addition for homes for employees of the plant. These lots were valued at $100 each. Plans were made to build the plant in 1921, and it was estimated that 90% of the livestock would be hauled to the plant in trucks.

Several issues of the Delphi Journal during the winter carried large advertisements offering to sell stock to raise money for the plant. After a few months there was no further information in the papers, so it is likely that not enough stock was sold to complete the project.

The records show that the packing plants which they visited in North Dakota went out of business after a few years because they could not raise enough capital to continue the business.

Hog Point

Sometimes an area is given a name because of some special activities in that area. An example is Hog Point, an area west of Carroll County where the Tippecanoe River empties into the Wabash River.

Mrs. Milton Buck reported that farmers would ear mark their pigs in the spring and turn them loose in the woods to eat acorns or anything that they could find during the summer. In the fall the farmers would have a hog roundup and drive them to the point bounded by the Wabash River on the south and the Tippecanoe on the west. There they would load the hogs on barges and ship them to a packing plant at Lafayette.

Chicago Grain Market

According to an article in the Centennial Issue of Prairie Farmer, January 11, 1941 the records show that in 1838 a total of 78 bushels of wheat was received in Chicago. More arrived in 1839 but there were no facilities for handling or storage, and 1678 bushels were loaded from farm wagons directly to a small lake ship and taken to a lake port in New York. In 1841 the price of wheat in Chicago was $1 per bushel, and was 40 to 50 cents per bushel at interior points. Farmers hauling wheat to Chicago had trouble finding a market, and often received much less than the market price. In 1848 the first wheat was shipped to Chicago by railroad. The Chicago Board of Trade was organized in 1848, and some order was established in the grain market.

Cooperatives

Farmers, business men, cooperatives, organizations and people all have one thing in common. Some succeed and others fail.

T. L. Canada and T. K. Cowden of Purdue University made a study of Agricultural Cooperatives in Indiana from 1885 to 1939. Their study indicated that during the 55 year period, 640 cooperative marketing and purchasing associations were formed in Indiana.

Most of this development took place after 1910, only 43 associations having been formed prior to that date. Over one half of the 640 associations were organized during the six year period, 1917 to 1922. In 1919 alone, 101 organizations were started.

The peak in the number of active associations was reached in 1924 when 420 organizations were operating. In 1939, only 218 cooperatives were doing business, but the total volume of business was more than three times the volume in 1924.

During World War I and the following years, many farm organizations and cooperatives were organized and some succeeded far beyond the expectations of those who organized them. Professional promoters took advantage of the opportunity and promoted business ventures which were doomed to failure.

In the late 1800's many small cooperative creameries were organized in Indiana, and a few in Carroll County. In most cases a high powered salesman would organize a creamery association and sell stock to farmers in the area. He would then sell high priced equipment to the association, and move on to a new territory and the cooperative would soon fail.

Many worthy projects were promoted by people who had a genuine interest in the improvement of their community, but failed because they could not raise enough money to get the project started.

Grain Marketing Associations

A larger number of grain marketing cooperatives have been organized in Indiana than any other type of association. Nearly one half of the 191 grain marketing associations were started in 1919 and 1920. About 30% of all the grain marketing cooperatives were still active in 1939.

Livestock Marketing Associations

The rapid expansion in livestock marketing associations occurred between 1917 and 1922 when 78 percent of the organizations were formed. In 1923 there were 131 active associations, and by 1939 only 21 were operating.

Most of the associations formed were shipping associations that pooled farmers' livestock for rail shipment to terminal markets. With improved highways and truck transportation the need for the shipping association no longer existed in many areas of the state.

In 1939 the cooperative marketing of livestock was still the most important type of cooperative activity in the state from the standpoint of dollar volume of business. Well established cooperative commission firms were operating on practically all the terminal markets patronized by Indiana farmers.

Purchasing Associations

Cooperative purchasing developed later in Indiana than most of the other types of cooperative activity. There were two peak periods in the formation of purchasing organizations, one in 1919-1920 when 33 associations were started, and the other from 1928 to 1930 when 42 were formed.

About 140 purchasing associations were formed in Indiana during the 55 year period. In 1931, 104 were active, and in 1939, about 90 were still in business.

In 1909 only five percent of the total number of cooperatives were purchasing organizations, by 1939, 43 percent of the total were classified as purchasing associations.

The rate of survival of cooperative organizations is about the same as for other business organizations. The same rules apply to both, they must supply a need, and must be operated on sound business principles.

---

* An article on page 36 copied from the Delphi Journal of July 14, 1938 stated that the old Red Mill at Delphi burned in August, 1910. Robert Brookbank thought that this was not the correct date, so he checked with Robert Wood who saw the mill burn when he was a boy, and recorded it in his diary on March 21, 1911.

A report signed by Thos. V. Martin in the Delphi Fire Department Record dated March 22, 1911 stated: "At 9:55 P.M. Company answered alarm, Burning of the 'old Red Mill.' The mill and surrounding buildings being out of the city and beyond the reach from any of the city plugs the company could do nothing but keep in readiness to fight any fire that might start from the millions of brands of fire sent up from the big fire. The 4th hose reel was taken to the plug at the corner of North St. and Prince William gravel road, in readiness in case fire should get a start in that vicinity. The reel from the city house was taken to the corner of Wilson and Main but neither was used. Loss was only to value of timber in the mill and buildings."

The fire department probably spent the night watching the fire, and the report may have been dated the next day when they finished the job.

A picture taken by Andrew Wolever, dated March 22, 1911 entitled "Ruins of the Red Mill" showing the foundation of the mill and smoke from the recent fire was probably taken the morning after the fire.

Based on this information we have changed the date of the burning of the old Red Mill from August 1910 to March 21, 1911.

The Delphi Journal did not report the burning of the mill. The fire probably was not considered as important news, since no other building was damaged, and the mill had been abandoned and used only by tramps for several years.

CHAPTER III

GRANGE

The National Grange of the Patrons of Husbandry, the first and the most important farm organization that developed in the post Civil War period was organized December 4, 1867 by Oliver Hudson Kelley, a clerk in the Office of the Commissioner of Agriculture in Washington, D.C., and six associates. It was patterned after the Masonic Order and was to bind farmers together for "Social intercourse and intellectual advancement."

EMBLEM

The Grange emblem is seven sided, representing the Seven Founders and the seven degrees of membership. The "P of H" stands for "Patrons of Husbandry," the official name of the organization. The sheaf of wheat signifies their belief in the importance of agriculture.

Subordinate Granges

Local units are called Subordinate Granges. When a Subordinate Grange disbands the charter is returned to the National organization and all property is sold at auction. The money is held in trust for 10 years and during that time is available for the starting of another Grange in that location.

Degrees

Subordinate Granges meet at least monthly and confer the first four degrees. The fifth degree known as the degree of Pomona is conferred by the Pomona Grange, which is the county or district organization. The State Grange confers the degree of Flora which is the sixth degree. The National Grange confers the seventh degree which is the degree of Ceres.

First Local Grange

Potomac Grange No. 1, the first local Grange, was organized January 8, 1868 in Washington, D.C. Mr. Kelley resigned his job and spent full time organizing state and local Granges. His first success was Fredonia Grange No. 1 in Chautauqua County, New York, April 16, 1868. Minnesota was the first State Grange, organized February 23, 1869. By 1873 there were Granges in 44 states. The Panic of 1873 gave farmers a greater need for organization. By the end of 1874 there were twenty thousand Granges and in 1875 there were 858,050 members, the largest membership ever recorded.

Purpose

At the Seventh Annual Convention of the National Grange in St. Louis in February 1874, they adopted the "Declaration of Purposes of the National Grange." The general purpose was "to labor for the good of our Order, our Country, and Mankind." This was interpreted to include home improvement, legislation, education, better farming practices, cooperative buying and selling and anything else that might improve life on the farm.

Other statements on policy included "to avoid imposition and dispense with middle men as far as practicable" and "to inculcate morality and temperance, foster education and cultivate brotherly love."

Business Ventures

Many of the local Granges organized cooperatives for marketing farm products, and cooperative stores for purchasing farm supplies, but most of these were not incorporated. The local stores pooled their orders and purchased many items on a statewide basis for better prices. In several states the Grange made agreements with manufacturers to sell items to members at a discount of 20 to 25%. Items in the agreements included plows, cultivators, sewing machines, parlor organs and mowing machines. In some states, trading cards were issued to members and local merchants agreed to give a 10% discount to Grange members on anything purchased in their store. This was one of the reasons for rapid increase in Grange membership, but the practice was soon discontinued because the stores had too many complaints from non-members. In Iowa the state Grange manufactured 250 harvesting machines and sold them at about one-half the price of other harvesters.

In 1874 the National Grange purchased patents on many kinds of farm machinery and made plans to build factories in seven states.

The crash came and the Iowa Harvester Factory failed in 1875 and bankrupted the state Grange. Other failures followed, and many people dropped out of the Grange for fear that they might have to pay some of the losses. By 1889 the national membership was only 106,782, the lowest on record. They then returned to the basic principles with which they had started, and membership gradually increased.

Some of the stores and cooperatives organized by the Grange were incorporated and operated on a set of rules based on those of the 28 weavers of Rochdale, England, who organized the first successful consumers' cooperative. Many of them are still in business. An outstanding example is the Cooperative Grange League Federation Exchange, Inc. (commonly called GLF) organized in Ithaca, N.Y. in 1920. It was sponsored jointly by the Grange, Dairymen's League and the Farm Bureau and operated in New York, New Jersey and Pennsylvania. July 1, 1964 it merged with other cooperatives to form Agway, Inc. which now supplies manufacturing, purchasing, and distribution services and farm product processing and marketing service for farmers in 12 states. It is now the second largest regional cooperative in the United States.

Several State Granges are operating successful cooperatives to provide service to their members. Two insurance companies that serve Grange members are the National Grange Mutual Insurance Company of Keene, New Hampshire, and the Farmers and Traders Life Insurance Company of Syracuse, New York, which is a Grange sponsored company licensed to do business in 27 states and the District of Columbia.

Montgomery Ward

One of the early principles of the Grange was to "dispense with middlemen as far as practicable." A young man by the name of Montgomery Ward lived in Chicago and had worked as a traveling salesman in the rural areas of the Midwest. He learned about Grange activities and decided to do something about it. In 1872 he issued a catalogue, a single sheet on eight by twelve paper, headed: "Grangers Supplied by the Cheapest Cash House in America." It went on to state: "At the earnest solicitation of many Grangers, we have consented to open a house devoted to furnishing farmers and mechanics throughout the Northwest with all kinds of merchandise at wholesale prices." By 1874 this catalogue was eight pages, and for 1875 contained seventy-two pages. The business grossed several million dollars per year. For several years the company served Grange members only, but as the business grew its service was extended to the general public. Montgomery Ward & Company was not the first mail order house in the United States, but it was the first to cater directly to rural patrons.

Grange Stores

In many areas where the Grange stores were doing a good business, there was much talk of the day of the "Middleman" being over, and that other stores would soon be out of business. In many towns the local merchants got together and decided that each would sell one commodity below cost, and draw trade from the cooperative store. It speaks ill for the loyalty of the members to their own business organization to record the fact that the plan generally worked.

Sovereigns of Industry

The Grange was not the only organization that tried and failed in establishing stores. Labor groups organized the "Sovereigns of Industry," a secret order which was active from 1874 to 1879. They had a membership of about 40,000 members in the East and Middle West. In 1875 there were 310 Councils, and 101 had some kind of retail business. When the hard times of the late seventies left members short on cash, the stores extended credit to meet competition and soon failed.

LEGISLATION

While the Grange is often considered as a social organization, it has maintained a legislative department which has had much influence on agriculture and the nation. In the early years much emphasis was placed on the regulation and control of railroads when it seemed that freight rates were too high. Following the Civil War, came a period of rapid expansion in railroads. It was generally supposed that competition between rail lines would control prices, and little thought was given to any kind of Government regulations. After a brief period of ruinous rate wars, the railroad companies got together and agreed on rates. When the price of corn was 15¢ per bushel in Iowa and $1 per bushel in the East, it was obvious that freight rates were too high.

In the early 1870's the four northwestern states of Illinois, Iowa, Minnesota and Wisconsin passed laws sponsored by the Grange restricting the railroads. In November 1876 the U.S. Supreme Court upheld these and similar laws and established the fundamental principle that the state which permitted a monopoly retained unto itself the right to regulate and control that monopoly.

It was obvious that states could not solve all the problems of the railroads, so the principle was applied on the national level by the passage in 1887 of the Interstate Commerce Act. Later legislation applied this principle of monopoly control to all public utilities. The Sherman Antitrust Act of 1890 provided that the self regulating features of the competitive market should be preserved by the prevention of monopolies and other practices which operated to restrain trade or destroy competition.

The following quotation is from a book written by W. L. Robinson, published by the National Grange, called "The Grange—1867-1967, First Century of Service and Evolution."

> "The adoption of these two laws which were the heart of the Granger legislation became one of the landmarks of economic history. The modified capitalistic system which developed in the United States under the guidelines of these progressive laws avoided the errors which had developed in Eastern European capitalism, which made their system vulnerable to socialism.
>
> "Thus, the regulation of monopolies and the preservation of the competitive system in the U.S. has resulted in the greatest economic development, the widest ownership of production, the most liberal distribution of profits, and the highest standard of living of any major country of the world. Without the Granger Laws this would not have been possible, and indeed, the U.S. might well be a socialistic nation today.
>
> "Since these historic beginnings, the same principles have been applied to communications, air transportation, and the regulation of commodity and stock exchanges.
>
> "The fundamental concept in government-business relations in our nation flows from Granger Laws. Under them, monopolistic tendencies of capitalistic business have been controlled by regulatory laws so as to preserve the benefits of competitive enterprise, the ingenuity of man and human dignity, and still have the benefits of large-scale production from the incentive of free men."

Government Agencies

The Grange also played a prominent part in the creation of the U.S. Department of Agriculture and the many agencies serving agriculture. Before this time the National Grange made plans to collect information on the condition of crops throughout the country and pass it on to members of the order.

The Morrill Act of 1862 providing for Land Grant Colleges in each state was passed before the Grange was organized, but very little was done until ten years later when the Grange helped establish many of the colleges.

The Grange was active in sponsoring the Hatch Act of 1887 creating the Agricultural Experiment Station, the Smith-Lever Act of 1914 creating the Agricultural Extension Service, the Smith-Hughes Act of 1917 providing for Vocational Education, and the Rural Electrification Act of 1936 providing for Rural Electrification.

RURAL FREE DELIVERY

One of the greatest improvements in rural life for which the Grange was largely responsible was Rural Free Delivery of mail. Residents in larger cities had their mail brought to their door every day, but rural people had to go to the post office for theirs.

In a discussion in a local Grange in the Central West, a woman raised the question why farmers should not have their mail delivered as it was in the cities. A resolution which resulted from this discussion was approved by the Pomona and State Grange and then by the National.

For several years the Grange tried to get Congress to consider RFD, but Congressmen could think of all kinds of reasons why it was not practical. One Senator from Pennsylvania said, "Delivery of the mail by this Government to the doors of the farmers will destroy the rural life of which America is so proud. The center of rural life is the country post office, where farmers gather to meet each other when they get the mail. All that will be swept away by this Socialistic scheme!" The debate filled 40 pages in the Congressional Record. When the bill was finally passed, the vote in the Senate was 27 to 25. Congress appropriated a small amount of money to try it on a small scale, and hoped that the project would fail and that they would hear no more about it.

Appropriations for 1893 and 1894 totaled only $30,000, and the Postmaster General decided that this was not enough to start an experimental service. In 1896 Congress appropriated $10,000 more, and the total of $40,000 was used to start routes in several states. The first route was at Charles Town, West Virginia, the home of Hon. William L. Wilson, then Postmaster General. At the end of 1896 routes were in operation in thirty states.

The annual report of the Post Office Department for 1897 stated: "There has been nothing in the history of the postal service of the United States so remarkable as the growth of the Rural Free Delivery System." Some of the benefits mentioned in the report were: increased postal receipts, increase in value of farm land along the routes with some estimates as much as $5.00 per acre, improvement in roads used by the rural carriers and better prices for farm products because producers received market information.

In 1898, National Grange officers discovered that the proposed appropriation for the Post Office Department did not include anything for continued RFD service. When this was called to the attention of Congress, they not only restored the amount but increased it so the RFD could be expanded even more.

The first Rural Route in Carroll County was established on August 18, 1898. This story is told in Chapter II.

Parcel Post

For about 25 years the National Grange recommended the establishment of a parcel post system for the transportation of small packages by mail. Regular mail was limited to four pounds per package, and the rate was one cent per ounce or 16¢ per pound. The Parcel Post Law was finally enacted on August 24, 1912 and became effective on January 1, 1913. At first the packages were limited to no more than 11 pounds in weight and six feet in length and girth combined. The rate was five cents for the first pound and three cents for each additional pound. Insurance rate was 10¢ per pound.

WOMEN

The National Grange was the first American Association of any general sort to give women full equality and a vote in the organization. A resolution adopted in 1885 recommended that women be allowed to vote in elections. This was thirty five years ahead of the 19th amendment ratified in 1920 giving women the right to vote.

Women have always taken an active part in the Grange. Several times during the organization of the Grange, the men became discouraged and might have given up except for the encouragement and financial support given by the women.

In 1976 at the 110th Annual Session of the National Grange in Atlantic City, New Jersey, Jenny Gorbusky, Director of Women's Activities, presented to John Scott, the National Master, a check for $300,000 to be used in paying off the balance of the debt on the National Headquarters Building of the Grange in Washington, D.C. The women raised most of the money by selling 150,000 copies of the National Grange Bicentennial Year Cookbook. A mortgage burning ceremony was held in March at the Headquarters Building, and each Subordinate Grange was sent a sample copy of the mortgage to burn at one of the March meetings, to help celebrate the occasion.

JUNIOR GRANGES

In addition to programs for women, the Grange has activities for all members of the family.

One of the original purposes of the Grange was to "advance the cause of education among ourselves and for our children by all just means within our power." To help accomplish this purpose the National Grange in 1888 approved the organization of Junior Granges for children from 5 to 14 years of age. There is a provision that those who became members of a Junior Grange at an early age may continue until they are 16. At either 14 or 16, the junior members join the regular Grange and take part in the activities along with older members in the family. This helps make the Grange a family organization, and is given as one of the reasons that the organization has lasted more than 100 years.

INDIANA GRANGE

The first Grange in Indiana was organized in Vigo County in 1869. By the end of 1874 there were 1900 Granges in Indiana, or an average of about two for each township in the state.

The Indiana State Grange was organized at a meeting in Terre Haute on February 28, 1872 by O. H. Kelley, Secretary of the National Grange. The second meeting of the Indiana State Grange was held at Monticello on November 18, 1872, and the third at Valparaiso on November 26, 1873. Valparaiso papers in speaking of the meeting said: "The town was full of strangers, more than could find accommodations at hotels, boarding or private houses and more than one hundred had to sleep in the Courthouse or such other public places as they could find."

Annual meetings of the Indiana State Grange are held at various places in Indiana. Some have been at Lafayette and Logansport and two were held in Delphi in 1924 and 1931.

State Meetings at Delphi, 1924

The 54th Annual State Grange Convention was held at Delphi on October 19 to 24, 1924, with about 300 present. General Headquarters were at the Dame Hotel; Committee Headquarters were in the Assembly Room in the Courthouse, and General Sessions were held in the K of P Hall and in the Armory, now the City Building. The opening session was held in the Presbyterian Church.

Meals were served at the Baptist and Methodist churches, as well as at local restaurants.

Noah Landis served as chairman of the Reception Committee representing three local Granges, Star in the West, Welcome Inn and Colburn.

All State Grange officers were present, as well as S. J. Tabor, Master of the National Grange, and E. A. Eckert, Master of the Illinois State Grange.

While in Delphi, the delegates visited the Historical Room in the Courthouse, and were taken by auto to visit the Oakdale Dam under construction on the Tippecanoe River. They also visited Camp Tecumseh and Purdue University.

1931 Grange Meeting

The 61st session of the Indiana State Grange was held at Delphi in October, 1931. General sessions were held at the IOOF Hall, and a banquet one evening was at the Presbyterian Church.

Speakers on the programs included Yantis Wells, Mayor of Delphi; Fred Wheeler, president of Delphi Chamber of Commerce; Prof. C. A. Smith of the Delphi Lions Club; and E. A. Eckert, Master of the Illinois State Grange. C. T. Amick, President of Delphi Lions Club presided at one of the sessions.

Entertainment included a quartet with Loyal Hoshaw, Grover Kite, E. O. Grimm and Harry Reed accompanied by Mrs. Charles Stewart. Mrs. Mabel Fraser sang several numbers accompanied by Mrs. Mary Harper Smith.

Ladies from the Welcome Inn Grange at Radnor presented a program one evening called: "The Old Maids' Convention."

Among the many Grange members in Carroll County who have attended the state meetings as delegates from the county were: J. S. Pearson, J. P. Haan, L. Snyder, George Gilleford, Charles Billings, J. B. Bard and wife, R. T. Barbour and wife, G. M. Sibray and wife, W. J. Nimmins and wife Laura, J. L. Sheets, E. P. Wingard and wife, N. J. and Martha J. Smith, William Young, Mary Young, Bertia McMahan, Josiah and Lydia E. Looker, Manford and Etta Kelsey, Taylor Bard, Mrs. Mary Bard, Hester Smith, Taylor B. Fraser, Laura Fraser, Charles H. Smith, Ray Aiken, Orpha Jackson, Charles Jackson, Laura Jackson, James A. Smith, Lucy M. Smith, Obe Campbell, Lulu Campbell, Newman Viney, Lydia Viney, Wilber Doolittle, Cecil Doolittle, Martha E. Huntley, Eli Craig, Della Craig, Loyd Zook, Eunice Zook, Charles Phillips, Mrs. Saide Phillips, Raymond L. Dillman, Ester Dillman, John F. Allen, Mrs. Pearl E. Allen, Glenn and Edna Davis, Ira E. Fetterhoff, J. C. and Mrs. Ruth Lowery, Harry and Elva Griffith, Jesse E. and Opal Wise, Charles Frantz, Mrs. Elizabeth Frantz, Wm. Spry, Mrs. Gladys Spry, Omer and Della Wilson, Agnes C. McCouch, Courtney and Maude Clawson, Bruce and Mary Draper, Chris Brummett, Pearl Brummett, Rev. Homer Farthing, Carrie Farthing, Charles W. Thompson, Mildred Thompson, Lester Dickinson, Irene Dickinson, Raymond Todd, Geneva Todd, Mark and Zola Hefner, Roscoe Quick, Zelpha Quick, Paul Wilson, Margaret Wilson, Larry Gruber, Nellie Gruber, Harold A. Allen, Dorothy Allen, Aaron Randle, Elva Randle, Robert Pearson, Ethel Pearson, John Dempsey, Dennis McCouch and Opal Dunn.

Loyd E. Zook served as Chaplain of the State Grange from 1931 to 1952. Mrs. Zook accompanied him to the meetings and played the piano. Mabel J. Crowell was State Lecturer from 1933 to 1936.

CARROLL COUNTY GRANGES

There have been 33 Subordinate or local Granges in Carroll County. Information on 27 of these was furnished by Charles E. Dillon of Cass County who has been State Secretary for several years. Information on six more is from local newspapers. Twenty-three of these were organized in 1873. They were: Carroll #94 at Pittsburg; Rock Creek #121, Rock Creek Township, April 29; Jefferson #122, Jefferson Township, May 1; Delphi #130, Delphi, May 2; Jay #163, Rock Creek Township, May 9; Oak #173, Rockfield, May 29; White Grove #191, Jefferson Township, June 13; Clay #212, Clay Township, June 23; Camden #219, Camden, June 24; Union #222, Jackson Township, June 26; Madison #257, Madison Township, July 25; Adams #276, Lockport; Woodville #291, Woodville, August 11; Lockport #364, Lockport, September 6; Monroe #429, Bringhurst, October 2; Carrollton #501; Burlington #657, Burlington, November 21; Mt. Pleasant #746, Jefferson Township, December 11; Paint Creek #775, Washington Township, December 12, Carrollton #776, Carrollton, December 13; Commercial #855, Pyrmont, December 23; Sugar #910, Burlington, December 27; and Oakland #911, Wild Oak, December 27.

Three were organized in 1874 and they were: Cline #1051, Carrollton, January 15; Oakdale #1177, Pittsburg; and Pacific #1752, Washington Township, March 4.

Star in the West #2057 was organized on January 3, 1890. Success #2125 in Burlington Township was organized on March 1, 1901; Welcome Inn #2227 in Madison Township, March 1, 1922; Tipwa #2300, Tippecanoe Township, October 2, 1924; and Jefferson #2314, Jefferson Township, April 27, 1926. The last were: Rock Creek #2345, January 24, 1934 and Monroe #2346, March 13 organized by Jesse E. Wise.

Carroll County Central, the Pomona Grange was located in Delphi.

Star in the West #2057

One of the more active Granges on which records are available was the Star in the West #2057, organized on January 3, 1890 in the southern part of Monroe Township near Cutler. The first officers were: James Bard, Master; N. J. Smith, Overseer; W. W. Pitman, Lecturer and George D. Trobaugh, Secretary. Minutes of their meetings show that they did an active business in such items as Eureka Oil, Cady Clipper Tobacco, sugar, baking soda, cloves, cinnamon, pepper, allspice, Carolina Head Rice, oyster crackers, rolled oats and binder twine.

Charles W. and Mildred Thompson were active members until they died in 1954. Officers listed for 1946 were: Raymond Dillman, Master; Wm. Clem, Overseer; Josie Smith, Lecturer and Charles Smith, Secretary.

Welcome Inn Grange #2227

The Welcome Inn Grange was organized March 10, 1922 at Radnor with 46 charter members. Officers elected were: G. L. Clawson, Master; George Lucas, Overseer; Loyd Zook, Lecturer; Josephine E. Rohrabaugh, Secretary. Regular meetings were set for the first and third Friday nights of each month. The Welcome Inn Grange was active until about 1965.

At a meeting in March 1929, a debate was held: "Resolved that a man has more determination than a woman." Mabel Jakes Crowell and Mrs. John McCouch were on the affirmative and Perry Rule and Arthur Kite were on the negative.

In April 1932, the Welcome Inn Grange and the Plains Grange from Tippecanoe County debated on the subject: "Resolved that the woman should carry the pocket book."

Tipwa Grange #2300

The last active Grange in the county was Tipwa Grange in Pittsburg. It was organized at a meeting in Pittsburg on September 25, 1924 and voted to disband in 1979. Loyd E. Zook of Welcome Inn Grange in Radnor was in charge of the first three meetings. They signed up 47 Charter Members and held the first official meeting on October 30, 1924. The first officers were: Clifford Bitler, Master; Frank Imler, Overseer; Mrs. Fren Smith, Lecturer; Mrs. Pearl Bitler, Secretary; and W. F. Riley, Treasurer. Meetings were held every Thursday night with an attendance of about 50. During the summer, meetings were changed to Tuesday night so they would not interfere with band concerts at Delphi. In May 1942, meetings were changed to the first and third Thursday nights.

The official spelling of the name when it was organized was "Tippwa." The Grange selected this name because the meeting place was located between the Tippecanoe and Wabash rivers. This spelling later was changed to "Tip-wa" and then to the present "Tipwa."

For several years meetings were held in various buildings in Pittsburg. In 1942 the Hudson building was purchased and used for Tipwa Grange meetings. Mr. Wm. Spry donated some wood, and the members cut it to use for fuel to heat the building in winter months.

In November 1948 the Grange appointed a committee to investigate the possibility of constructing a new building. Members of the committee were: John Kennard, Chairman; Russell Craig, Arlie Hughes, Pat Holloway and John Gingrich. In June 1949 land northwest of Pittsburg was purchased from Charles Kerlin to build a 32' x 66' building. Members donated part of the labor, and the building was completed by

Tipwa Grange float in Old Settlers parade at Delphi, August 13, 1955.

February 1950, and was dedicated on May 21, 1950. It was completely paid for by September 1953. Landscaping was done in 1953 by boys from the Delphi High School.

While the building was used primarily for Grange meetings, it was also used for other groups, such as Boy and Girl Scouts, Rural Youth, Farm Bureau and other community activities. In 1951 the Camden High School held their Prom in the Grange Hall.

Tipwa Grange was incorporated in 1957. In 1959 there were 140 members.

Programs at meetings included talks and discussions on many topics of local interest. County Agents discussed problems of livestock and poultry raising, and new methods of crop production. Dr. J. M. Haggard, a veterinarian discussed Brucellosis and other livestock diseases. Cora Zell St. Amand, HDA discussed nutrition. Members were encouraged to attend Farmers' Institute meetings. Sometimes the discussion was on proposed legislation affecting agriculture and resolutions were passed and sent to members of the Legislature.

Entertainment was usually provided by members, and often they would exchange programs with other Granges or other organizations, such as Farm Bureau and local schools.

Contests added variety to the program. In September 1929, Courtney Clawson was appointed to represent the men and Mrs. Larry Gruber to represent the women. Each group was given $1 and requested to see how much they could earn on the money by the first of the year. That was during the time that the size of dollar bills was being changed. The women were given a large dollar bill and the men a small one. The women won the contest by earning $31.39 while the men earned $27.50.

Debates were held on a wide variety of subjects such as: "The relative merits of living in the city or country. Should women work outside the home? What is the smartest animal on the farm? What should we do with worn-out machinery? Should women serve on the jury? What do you think of chain letters? Does it pay to butcher livestock on the farm? More corn grows in a crooked row than in a straight row. Women are better drivers than men."

In March 1930, members of the Tipwa Grange had a debate: "Resolved that a well planned meal is more essential than a well prepared meal." The debate was won by the men on the negative side.

Community activities included such things as collecting old clothes for the needy, sewing for Red Cross, giving flowers for ill and deceased, sponsoring Boy and Girl Scouts, providing meals for workers at Blood Mobile and election boards, providing transportation for voters at elections, and sponsoring fox drives.

For many years the Grange served lunches at farm sales. While this did not make much money it did provide a needed service for the community. For several years the Grange had a food tent at the Old Settlers celebrations at Delphi.

Clarence Eyer Syrian Relief Project

In 1948, John T. Roth, Master of the Tipwa Grange, received a letter from Clarence Eyer, a former member of the Grange. Mr. Eyer was teacher of Vocational Agriculture in the Delphi Schools before he left with his family to be Agricultural Advisor to the Syrian Government. In this letter he described the living conditions of the 110,000 Arab refugees who had been driven out of Palestine into Syria. He reported that the Syrian government was supplying them with food and some shelter, but could not afford to provide them with clothing. They badly needed blankets and clothing of all kinds.

The Grange responded by organizing the "Clarence Eyer Syrian Relief Project." With the help of many individuals and other organizations including the Farm Bureau and Home Economics clubs, they collected 2700 pounds of clothing and sent it to Mr. Eyer.

Other Activities

The Tipwa Grange had a float in the Fourth of July parade in Delphi for several years and won several prizes.

In 1958 the Grange nominated Bill and Wanda Duff for the "Young couple of the Year" contest sponsored by the State Grange.

Officers of the Tipwa Grange for 1978 were: Mabel Burt, Master; Harold Allen, Overseer; Wanda Duff, Lecturer; William Duff, Treasurer; Dorothy Allen, Secretary; Phyllis Porter, Chaplain and Dennis McCouch, Steward.

Among those who have served as Master are: Clifford Bitler, Frank Lybrook, R. G. Gamble, Wm. Glenn Davis, C. R. Clawson, John T. Roth, Larry E. Gruber, Jesse E. Wise, Russell C. Craig, Chris Brummett, Raymond Todd, Donald Duff, William Duff, Robert Duff, Dan Lybrook, Buddy Holloway, Robert Pearson, John E. Dempsey, Richard Sheldon, and Mabel Burt.

Exhibit at Fair

At the County Fair in Delphi in October 1929, the Granges in the county built an exhibit on the stage in the Assembly Room in the Courthouse. It was a miniature Community Center with a Grange Hall, church and school.

Active Granges in the county at that time were: Star in the West, Welcome Inn, Tipwa and Jefferson.

Essay Contests

In October 1935, Dennis McCouch won first place in the State Grange Essay Contest on the subject: "How the Grange Can Promote Highway Safety." The first prize was $5 and a silver medal furnished by the American Automobile Association which joined with the Grange in sponsoring the contest. In 1934 he received a bronze medal for second place in a similar contest.

In 1936 Helen Zook won the State Grange Essay Contest on the subject: "Causes of Highway Accidents in my Grange Community." Both Mr. McCouch and Miss Zook were active members of the Welcome Inn Grange.

In 1952, Glenda Fisher of R 4, Delphi, was named the winner of first place in Indiana in the Nation-wide Essay Contest jointly sponsored by the National Grange and the American Plant Food Council. The subject of the essay was: "Conservation Farming for Abundant Living." She received a cash prize of $100 for her essay which was submitted through the Welcome Inn Grange in Carroll County. A total of 276 essays were entered in the State Contest.

Stuffed Toy Contest

Beginning in 1977 the National Grange has conducted the Stuffed Toy Contest co-sponsored by the Fairfield Processing Company, Danbury, Connecticut and McCall's Pattern Company, New York City.

Brenda Draper of Bringhurst, a senior in Carroll Consolidated High School and a member of Tipwa Grange, won a $50 savings bond when a stuffed toy which she had made was judged best at the National Grange Convention in 1978. The award was presented by Mary Cain of Lafayette, Director of Women's Activities for the Indiana State Grange.

For the contest in 1978, Grange members in Indiana made 1396 stuffed toys. More than 1000 of these were given to the Greater Lafayette Community Centers, and 100 were donated to the Lafayette Fire Department for distribution at Christmas.

GRANGE ACHIEVEMENTS

Aaron Jones, Worthy Master of the National Grange, speaking before the National Grange meeting in Portland, Oregon, in 1904, summed up Grange achievements in these words:

> "A generation has passed, crowded with greater advancement than any similar period in the world's history, since our organization was founded to meet conditions essential to public welfare. It was consecrated to develop the best type of social conditions, to foster and promote good citizenship, to develop agriculture, to secure equity in the business relations of the agricultural classes with the industrial and commercial interests of our country. . . . The Grange removed the isolation of the farm homes, inculcated and promoted education, fostered and secured better schools for our children, raised the standard of intelligence among the farming population, developed the latent talent of its members, making them logical thinkers and writers and fluent speakers, understanding the relation of agriculture to the varied and complex social, industrial and commercial interests of our country and the world. These glorious results were attained by steadfast adherence to the principles of our Order and methods suggested by the founders of our Fraternity."

Officers of Tipwa Grange #2300, in 1979: Seated left to right: William Duff, Treasurer; Dorothy Allen, Secretary; standing: Harold Allen, Overseerer; Mabel Burt, Master.

FUTURE OF THE GRANGE

Albert S. Goss, Master of the National Grange from 1941-1950 asked the following question: "How long will the Grange live?" He answered by saying: "I believe it will live as long as it continues to serve the welfare of Agriculture and the Nation. Whenever it becomes ingrown and selfish, and the members look on it only as a means of bringing them pleasure, entertainment or profit, it will fade away."

The National Grange has survived for more than 100 years and is still active. In 1978 there were 5290 Subordinate Granges in 40 states with more than 500,000 members.

CHAPTER IV

EXTENSION SERVICE

The Cooperative Agricultural Extension Service is the largest adult education program in the world, and has played an important part in the greatest advancement in agricultural technology ever experienced. The name indicates that it is a cooperative program, with federal, state, and county governments working together to finance and implement the broad educational program. It had its beginning during the administration of President Abraham Lincoln.

THE MORRILL OR LAND GRANT ACT

In a message to Congress on December 5, 1861 President Abraham Lincoln made the following statement: "Agriculture, confessedly the largest interest of the Nation, has not a department or bureau, but a clerkship only, assigned to it in the Government. While it is fortunate that this great interest is so independent in its nature as not to have demanded and extorted more from the Government, I respectfully ask Congress to consider whether something more cannot be given voluntarily with great advantage."

On July 2, 1862 President Lincoln signed the Land Grant Act which created the first United States Department of Agriculture and gave each state certain public lands which they could sell and use as an endowment to start a university. Since there were no public lands available in Indiana, the grant gave Indiana 609 sections of land in Nebraska. This was sold at an average price of 54 cents per acre, and provided about $200,000 for the university.

PURDUE UNIVERSITY

Purdue was founded in 1869 when the Indiana General Assembly accepted a generous offer of 100 acres of land and $150,000 in money by John Purdue of Lafayette on condition that the agriculture school be located in Tippecanoe County and named Purdue University, and that he be appointed a life time member of the Board of Trustees. Other citizens of Tippecanoe County added $50,000 to the offer and Purdue University was established and opened for its first full year on September 16, 1874 with six instructors and 39 students. The School of Agriculture was established in 1879, and Professor Charles L. Ingersoll conducted experiments with wheat and fertilizer on plots located just south of the present Stewart Center building.

In 1880 a new series of seven plots covering ten acres were laid out on the west side of Marstellar Street where the Ag. Administration, Forestry and Horticulture buildings are now located. Experiments were carried out with different varieties of small fruit, vegetables, grasses, other farm crops and crop rotations.

Professor Ingersoll went to Colorado University in 1882, and was replaced by William C. Latta, who remained with Purdue University until he retired in 1923. He continued as a consultant for the university until he died in 1935.

Agricultural Experiment Station

The Hatch Act of 1887 provided $15,000 for each state for an Agricultural Experiment Station. The Station was established at Purdue on July 1, 1887, but was not very active until the Smith Act of the Indiana Legislature in 1905 provided funds for the Experiment Station. George I. Christie came to Purdue in 1905 to be in charge of the Experiment Station.

Farmers' Institutes

In 1882 the Indiana State Board of Agriculture sponsored Farmers' Institutes at Columbus and Crawfordsville. In 1888 they worked with county Farmers' Associations and sponsored Farmers' Institutes at Franklin and Anderson. This created more interest, and in 1889, the Indiana State Legislature passed a bill giving Purdue University the job of administering Farmers' Institutes. Professor William C. Latta went to work on the job and 50 Institutes were held in Indiana that winter. The next year, Institutes were held in 90 counties, and by 1894 there was at least one in every county with many counties having several.

State leaders who have been in charge of Farmers' Institutes are: W. C. Latta, 1889-1923; W. Q. Fitch, 1923-1937; H. E. Young, 1937-1941; and O. W. Mansfield, 1941-1960.

First Boys' and Girls' Clubs

In 1904 a Boys' Corn Club was organized in Hamilton County, and in 1907 an act by the Indiana Legislature authorized the Farmers' Institute to sponsor Boys' Clubs. In 1908 there were 5,000 boys in Corn Clubs in 35 counties. Later, clubs in Sewing, Canning, and Poultry were organized for girls. In 1912, Zora Mayo Smith was appointed as the first State Club Leader, and club work became part of the Agricultural Extension Service at Purdue University. In the 1920's the name was changed to 4-H Clubs.

Extension Service

In 1906 some work was started in Agricultural Extension as a part of the Experiment Station. In 1909 the Maish Act in Indiana, provided $10,000 for extension work of the Experiment Station.

In 1911 Purdue University established a Department of Agricultural Extension, and the same year the Indiana State Legislature passed the Clore Bill which provided $10,000 for 1911, and $30,000 per year after that for use in Agricultural Extension.

First County Agents

The Land Grant colleges throughout the U. S. working through the Experiment Stations, Extension Services and Farmers' Institutes, were looking for better ways to get information to farmers. On November 12, 1906 a County "Demonstrator" was hired in Smith County, Texas to work with farmers in the county. The idea spread and by 1911 Southern states had 508 "Demonstrators" working in counties. While they were not called County Agents, they were doing the work later assigned to County Agents.

Leonard B. Clore, who sponsored the Clore Bill in 1911, was appointed Agricultural Advisor in LaPorte County on October 1, 1912. This project was sponsored by the LaPorte County Crop Improvement Association, the Crop Improvement Committee of the Chicago Grain Exchange and Purdue Extension Service.

INDIANA VOCATIONAL EDUCATION ACT OF 1913

In February 1913, the Indiana State Legislature passed the Vocational Education Act which provided for state and local funds to employ a County Agent in each county. Purdue University Extension Service was named to administer the program. The law instructs the County Agent "to co-operate with Farmers' Institutes, Farmers' Clubs and other organizations, conduct practical demonstrations, Boys' and Girls' Club and contest work and other movements for the advancement of agriculture and country life and to give advice to farmers on practical farm problems and aid the county superintendents of schools and the teachers in giving practical education in agriculture and domestic science."

On June 1, 1913, Thomas A. Coleman was appointed State Leader for County Agents. At that time there were four County Agents in Indiana. They were Leonard B. Clore, appointed for LaPorte County, October 1, 1912; Ralph Chitty, Montgomery County, January 1, 1913; Harry James Reed, Park County, February 1, 1913 and John Seremis Bordner, St. Joseph County, April 1, 1913.

The Vocational Education Act of 1913 provided for the County Agent to be appointed annually by the County Board of Education subject to the approval of Purdue University and the State Board of Education. The County Board of Education was made up of the County Superintendent of Schools, and the Trustee in each township. When the County Board of Education changed political complexion, there was often a change in County Agents. The frequent changes, and despair among County Agents of anything like permanent employment in one county, made it difficult to keep all the counties supplied with agents. In 1920 there were agents in 72 counties, and by 1930 there were still only 74.

Amendment in 1937

An amendment approved by the General Assembly March 11, 1937 changed the procedure for hiring County Agents. The amendment included the following statement: "The office of County Agricultural Extension Service is hereby created in each and every county of this state, and all appointments shall be made in the manner herein provided, and subject to the provisions of this Act. The County Council shall appropriate annually, not less than one thousand dollars, which shall be used in paying the office help, expenses of the County Extension Service Agents, rent, office supplies, equipment, and other incidental expenses. The County Agricultural Extension Service in each county may consist of County Agricultural Agents, Home Demonstration Agents, and 4-H Club Agents to be appointed by the Board of Trustees of Purdue University, upon the recommendation of the President of the University. All appointees shall become members of the staff of Purdue University.

"It shall be the duty of the Director of the Agricultural Extension Service to appoint such other personnel as may be necessary to carry on the work of the County Agricultural Extension Service."

This solved the problem of political influence in the appointment of County Agents. All 92 counties in Indiana now have Agricultural Extension Service offices in operation, with relatively little annual turn over in personnel. Nearly every county has an Extension Advisory Committee made up of representatives of all organizations interested in Extension work in the county. This committee usually names an Executive Committee to advise and help direct the work of the Extension Agents.

SMITH-LEVER ACT

Several Federal laws affecting the Agricultural Extension Service have been enacted by the U. S. Congress, but it is generally agreed that the most important legislation was the Smith-Lever Act approved on May 8, 1914. This act provided an annual appropriation and describes the work of Agricultural Extension by stating that it "shall consist of giving instructive and practical demonstrations in agriculture and home economics to persons not attending or resident in said colleges in the several communities, and imparting to such persons information on said subjects through field demonstrations, publications, and otherwise: and this work shall be carried on in such manner as may be mutually agreed upon by the Secretary of Agriculture and the State Agricultural College or Colleges receiving the benefits of this Act."

DIRECTORS OF EXTENSION

Directors of Extension at Purdue have been: George I. Christie, 1905-1928; Thomas A. Coleman, 1928-1941; Leroy E. Hoffman, 1941-1962; and Howard G. Dieslin, since 1962.

EXHIBIT TRAINS

The Exhibit Train was one of the methods used by the Purdue Agricultural Extension Service to get information to people. The first Exhibit Train started a tour in December 1905. The Lake Erie and Western Railroad furnished the cars and the Extension Staff filled them with exhibits and furnished specialists to go along with the train. On this first train, G. I. Christie gave lessons on Corn Judging. During the tour they made 82 stops, and had a total of 20,000 people visit the train.

The Delphi Journal for March 29, 1906 had the following article: "The Seed Gospel Train on the Monon Railroad yesterday morning was an object of much interest and over 1,000 people were at the depot to greet it. Superintendent Hendricks and the entire High School were at the depot to pay their respects to Purdue and learn something about seed corn. Hundreds of farmers were in the crowd and enjoyed the one half hour talk. The special was run under the auspices of the Monon Railroad, Purdue University, the Indiana Grain Dealers Association and the Indianapolis News. Briefly the talk was along this line: 'Select good seed corn, test it carefully, plant it well, tend it well, and don't husk it until it is matured and dry.'"

Nearly all the railroads in Indiana cooperated on this project and furnished trains without cost to the University. The Indiana Traction Lines furnished Interurbans for several exhibits. On March 22-27, 1915, a Dairy Feed Exhibit on an Interurban car made 25 stops and was viewed by 4,537 people.

The Delphi Journal reported that on March 12, 1927 an Interurban equipped with all kinds of farm devices that could be operated by electricity made stops at Burrows, Rockfield and Delphi.

The last Exhibit Train was March 3-28, 1947 and was a demonstration of all the latest in Agricultural Services at that time. Subjects covered were: corn, dairy, horticulture, soils, wheat, onions, alfalfa, livestock, poultry, fruit and vegetables, muck crops, farm and home. There were eight exhibit coaches with 23 exhibits, two sleeping cars and one dining car for the Purdue staff, an electric generating car and one railroad car and crew of several men. There were 21 from Purdue who made the entire trip, and about 45 specialists spent some time on the train. The train traveled a total of 2,400 miles, made 56 stops and was visited by 66,415 people. The train stopped in Delphi on March 25, 1947.

During the period of 42 years that Exhibit Trains were operated, they made a total of 1440 stops and were visited by 408,137 people.

SHORT COURSES

Another method used by the Extension Department was to conduct Short Courses. Members of the staff at Purdue, along with local leaders would go to a county and conduct a school lasting from two days to two weeks. The first was held in Rushville on December 16-21, 1907 with an attendance of 125 people. The subjects discussed were Corn and Livestock. The last was in Nappanee on February 3-4, 1942 with 1210 people. The subjects were Animal Husbandry, Agronomy and Home Economics.

During the 35 years there were a total of 362 Short Courses with an attendance of 432,447 people.

The following reports on three Short Courses in Carroll County are typical of the many held in the county.

A Short Course was held at Flora on February 24, 25, and 26, 1916. Local people in charge of the project were: Dr. A. J. Cook, chairman; H. A. Thomas, assistant chairman; and S. H. Gasaway, secretary treasurer. There were eight instructors, and they gave lessons on Soils & Crops, Horticulture, Dairy, Animal Husbandry, Poultry, and Weed Eradication. For the ladies there were sessions on Domestic Science, Household Economy, and Health.

The following is from the monthly report of the County Agent, H. E. Ackerson regarding a Short Course held at Flora, January 7 and 8, 1926.

"Business men of Flora cooperating with the Farm Bureau and other organizations put on a very successful two day Short Course and 2,508 different people attended some one of the sessions. One man and one woman in each township who were responsible for the publicity in their community was a big factor in getting out the large attendance. Three hundred twenty persons attended the Banquet on Friday evening which was addressed by Prof. G. I. Christie, Director of the Experiment Station at Purdue.

"The Community Club at Flora, a very live organization of business men and farmers, sponsored the Short Course and saw that everything possible was done to insure its success.

"The Indiana Condensed Milk Company furnished two Club cows and their progeny from the Sheridan Calf Club for study purposes at the Short Course. These two herds including ten animals in all made quite an interesting exhibit.

"A pure bred Jersey Calf Club and Cow Testing Association are being organized in the Flora Community as a result of the Short Course."

Two thousand fifty people attended one or more sessions of a Short Course at Flora on January 7 and 8, 1930. Prof. K. E. Beeson conducted sessions on Soils and Crops, and Prof. E. A. Gannon talked on Feeding and Breeding of Dairy Cattle. Sessions for the ladies included talks by Miss Zaring on Home Management and Miss Muehl on Foods.

The highlight of the meeting was a Home Talent Show attended by more than 1000 people the first evening. There were ten numbers composed entirely of local talent from all parts of the county.

A Banquet was held on the last evening at which more than 200 people in attendance heard an inspiring talk by Dr. R. P. Schultz.

COUNTY FAIR EXHIBITS

Beginning in 1911 the University prepared exhibits on a variety of subjects, and rented them for use at County Fairs at a cost of $35 for a set of exhibits. The exhibits were also shown at the State Fair each year.

CARROLL COUNTY FARMERS' INSTITUTES

Institutes were organized on a county basis, with county officers, and a chairman for each township or area where Institutes were held.

Programs included subjects of interest for the entire family with entertainment provided by local talent. Sometimes there would be an exhibit of farm crops with prizes given by local merchants.

Institutes were among the first organizations to sponsor 4-H Clubs and often used club members on the program.

When a two day Institute was held, it was customary for Purdue University to furnish speakers for the first day, and people in the local community provided the program for the second day.

Many Farmers' Institutes have been held in Carroll County, but only a few have been reported in the local papers. The following information from local papers is not a complete report, but gives some indication of the importance of Farmers' Institutes for many years.

The Delphi Journal reported on the Annual Farmers' Institute held at Flora, December 9 and 10, 1892. Another was reported as held in Flora on December 8 and 9, 1893. Since these were reported as Annual Institutes, it is likely that the first was held in 1890, which was the first year for many county Institutes in Indiana.

A news article in the Hoosier Democrat for January 12, 1901 reported that the attendance at an Institute held in Flora on January 4 and 5, 1901 was the best of any Institutes yet held in the county. A number of topics of general interest were discussed. One subject of especial interest was a talk on the Hessian Fly by Mr. Kime.

A contest for prizes on Agricultural products brought out some good exhibits. A prize of 50 pounds of flour offered by Miller and Kern for the best exhibit of yellow corn was won by Jake Logan. W. R. Meyer exhibited white corn and won a similar award given by E. G. Kitzmiller.

The chairman of the Institute offered a prize of $3 for the best half bushel of potatoes, and $2 for the second best. These awards were won by W. T. Hanaway who took first and Noah Fouts second.

In June 1901 more money was appropriated to hold a greater number of Farmers' Institutes each year. On February 1 and 2, 1904 one was held at the Deer Creek Lutheran Church.

On February 12 and 13, 1906 an Institute in Delphi was referred to as the "first one held in Delphi for several years." Officers listed for the meeting were Dr. A. J. Cook of Monroe Township, president, and S. T. Sterling of Jackson Township, secretary. Subjects on the program included "Clover, Hogs, Mothers and Daughters, Corn, Fertilizer and Growing Crops for Canning Products."

Another Institute was held at Owasco on February 22, 1906.

In 1907, one day Institutes were held at Delphi, Camden, Yeoman, Ockley, Deer Creek and Burlington. A two day Institute was held at Flora.

In February 1909, an Institute was held at Pyrmont, and J. W. Eikenberry gave a talk on "Farms and Farmers." The same year at Deer Creek, Taylor Fouts and A. A. Newer were speakers.

J. W. Eikenberry was chairman of the Farmers' Institute at Deer Creek on February 9 and 10, 1910. Subjects discussed included: "Poultry, Clover, Sanitation, Potatoes, Sheep, Soybeans, Seeds, Farm Boys and Girls, Gasoline Engines, and Past, Present and Future of Farming."

In 1913 Perry Rule was county chairman of Farmers' Institutes. Local chairmen were W. V. Polk, Burlington; W. J. Landis, Sharon; J. F. Jervis, Cutler; J. W. Reiff, Delphi; Perry Rule, Camden; Isaac Swatts, Pyrmont; T. W. Schnepp, Yeoman and D. V. McCloskey, Deer Creek.

The Bringhurst Poultry Association helped with the Farmers' Institute held January 4-9, 1915. Officers of the Association were: Roy Lane, president; Ora Platt, vice president; Charles E. Barnard, treasurer; Guy Coplen, superintendent; L. N. Cook, assistant superintendent; Wm. Nimmins, clerk and J. J. Moss, secretary.

An Institute was held at Burlington on January 19 and 20, 1915 and the local speaker was John R. Harness, the Apple King.

Farmers' Institutes continued to be held at various locations in the county. In 1921 there were nine Institutes with a total of 37 sessions. The attendance totaled about 7,000 people, or nearly 200 per session. There were 869 paid-up members, or an average of 96 per Institute. At a meeting of officers to make plans for the next year, everyone was present except George Sites. He answered the roll call by long-distance telephone, and explained that he could not get his automobile started. They counted him present.

In 1925 there were 11 Institutes with Roy Caldwell, county president, and Ray Rush, secretary. Local officers were: Ray Rush, Tippecanoe; Ross Wagoner, Camden; Chas. Sieber, Delphi; Earl Stewart, Rockfield; Albert Caldwell, Wheeling; Perry Rule, Madison; Glenn Kennard, Yeoman; Clarence Stout, Burlington; Walter Bowen, Cutler; F. C. Ayres, Bringhurst and Vernie Stephen, Deer Creek.

Ten Institutes were held in Carroll County in January and February 1929. Chairmen of the Institutes were: Frank Riley, Pittsburg; Russell Sink, Cutler; Fred Myers, Bringhurst; Earl Downham, Deer Creek; Jesse Benner, Rockfield; Sam Maxwell, Yeoman; Truman Snoeberger, New Hope; Carl K. McCarty, Burlington; Joseph W. Neibel, Camden and I. N. Landis, Wheeling.

Farmers' Institutes continued to be held in the county, but were fewer in number, and by 1936 the only meeting in the county was at Cutler on January 20. Another was held in Cutler in December 1938. Officers were: Otto Odell, chairman; Chalmer Trobaugh, vice chairman; Mrs. Bert Pullen, secretary and Larry Strong, treasurer.

This is a copy of an article written by Mrs. Clark Metsger, S & E Leader of Burlington Township Farm Bureau published in the April 1940 issue of Hoosier Farmer about the Farmers' Institute program which was held at Burlington on February 14, 1940.

"The Burlington Township (Carroll County) Farm Bureau sponsored a Farmers' Institute in connection with the regular February meeting at the school gymnasium. An estimated 300 persons attended.

"Corn and small grains were exhibited by the Vocational Department. The 4-H Club girls baked cakes and cookies. The Home Economics Club displayed several projects including quilts, crocheted bedspreads, and laces, health posters were shown by the school children. Other exhibits showed brown and white eggs, hobbies, and antiques.

"M. K. Derrick gave a talk in the afternoon on 'Seeds and Fertilizers.' Mrs. Scholl spoke of the 'Social Conditions and Moral Problems of the Day.' Rosemary Bowman gave a reading, and music was furnished by Ross Garrison and Ralph Rinehart. A "Penny Supper" at 5:30 P.M. was well attended, and the money was used to buy song books for the Farm Bureau.

"The school orchestra opened the evening session by playing several numbers. George Harvey gave a talk on the advantages and accomplishments of Farm Bureau. A piano duet was played by Mrs. Austin and Mrs. Barnard, and a clarinet duet by Gene Towe and Francis Ferguson. A short play, 'The Family Album,' closed the program."

TRI-COUNTY INSTITUTES

Several meetings were held at Burnettsville for a Tri-County Institute for Carroll, Cass and White Counties. At a meeting in January 1939, Charles Mourer was elected president, Mr. and Mrs. Ardis Landis of Carroll County, Mr. and Mrs. Thomas Barnes of White County and Mr. and Mrs. Frank Pownell of Cass County were elected vice presidents, Wilbur Young, secretary and Ed Eldridge, treasurer. Speakers were Rev. H. H. Western and Rev. Howard Jenkins. Talks were also given by two 4-H boys, Loyal Cripe and James Pierce.

At the Institute held on January 24 and 25, 1940, speakers were Okel F. Hall and Mrs. O. A. Scipio.

On February 9, 1951, 95 attended an Institute. Speakers were Mrs. Frank Kirkpatrick of Frankfort and Alfred Hessler, Fountain County.

On February 8, 1952, 73 attended. Speakers were Richard Wilsey and Calvin Purdue of Acton.

The 51st Annual Tri-County Farmers' Institute for Cass, Carroll and White Counties was held in Burnettsville on Tuesday, February 7, 1956, with sessions in the morning, afternoon and evening. This was reported as one of the oldest and largest Institutes in Indiana.

Officers were: Roy Best, president; Mrs. John A. Girard, secretary; and Ivan Meeker, treasurer. Vice presidents were: Mr. and Mrs. Del McVay of Carroll County, Mr. and Mrs. Bud Scott of Cass County and Mr. and Mrs. Wilbur Young of White County.

Speakers on the program were: Mrs. Clarence Cecil of Muncie, and Gordon Richardson of Brookston, a Vocational Agriculture teacher in Morocco High

School and an International Farm Youth Exchange delegate to Turkey in the summer of 1954.

Entertainment was furnished by the Lake Cicott school, and by Bob Hurt, a magician from Lafayette.

Prizes of one dollar, fifty cents and twenty five cents were given to first, second and third place winners in exhibits which included corn, soybeans, wheat, rye, oats, cakes, rolls, cookies, eggs, handicraft, sewing, and samples of wood.

The 53rd and last Tri County Institute was held at Burnettsville on February 4 and 5, 1957.

Officers were Sam McVay, president; Mrs. John A. Girard, secretary; and Bert Fisher, treasurer. Vice presidents were: Mr. and Mrs. Raymond Nicoll, Carroll County; Mr. and Mrs. Delbert Guy, Cass County and Mr. and Mrs. Coy Best, White County.

Money in the treasury was donated to the International Farm Youth Exchange.

CARROLL COUNTY EMERGENCY WAR AGENT

During World War I, the slogan "Food will win the War" led to the appointment of several Emergency War Agents to help farmers produce more food. Harry E. Ackerson was appointed for Carroll and White Counties, and served from September 16, 1917 to January 1, 1918.

J. W. McFARLAND, FIRST COUNTY AGENT

By 1917 all the states in the U.S. had enacted laws authorizing the appointment of County Agents as provided in the Smith-Lever Act of 1914. More than one third of the states had appointed some County Agents. Indiana led the list with 41 agents, with several counties on the waiting list.

The method of getting a County Agent was to have 20 or more land owners sign and present a petition to the County Board of Education, along with $500 to help pay for furniture and soil testing equipment for the office.

In January 1918, the following petition was presented to the County Board of Education: "To the County Board of Education of Carroll County, Indiana:

> "We, the undersigned owners of real estate situated in Carroll County, Indiana, used for farming purposes, and being interested in agriculture, do hereby petition for the appointment of a County Agent in and for the County of Carroll, State of Indiana. (Signed)
>
> "William C. Smith, James A. Shirk, C. M. Kerlin, Sell S. Doty, John W. Kerlin, W. G. Klepinger, G. W. Julien, Oscar Leatherman, John T. Jervis, Harry Baum, Fred Ferling, E. R. Smock, C. W. Montgomery, C. S. Redding, T. E. Page, H. E. Newell, Charles Johns, Floyd M. Johns, R. Clark Davidson, C. V. Hoover, Frank Shoff, T. W. Armstrong."

Purdue University recommended John Wm. McFarland, a middle aged practical farmer, and he was approved by the County Board of Education at their meeting February 16, 1918. He had been Emergency War Agent in the county since January 16, 1918. He served as County Agent until he died on November 8, 1918 following an 11 day illness from influenza, pneumonia and other complications.

One of the first activities of the new County Agent was to hold meetings and demonstrate the treatment of oats for smut. Several farmers volunteered to sow a part of their field with seed treated with formaldehyde, and the rest with untreated seed. When the crop was harvested, farmers in the neighborhood were encouraged to visit the demonstration farms and see how much the yield of oats was improved by treatment for smut.

Several Farmers' Institutes were held in the county, and the County Agent was a speaker at some of them.

Boys in Agriculture classes in school were shown how to make rag doll testers for seed corn. Mr. McFarland encouraged the movement to put a Vocational Agriculture Department in the Delphi High School.

An organization with a representative from each township was formed to encourage farmers to build more silos in order to make better use of feed for cattle.

Poultry raisers were encouraged to pen up or sell their roosters in order to produce higher quality eggs.

COUNTY DEMONSTRATOR

In April 1918, a campaign was started to secure a County Demonstrator to help women with their problems on foods, canning, and use of substitutes. It was necessary to raise $150 for equipment for the office, and contributions were made by several townships, and various organizations and individuals. The County Agent worked with the County Council of Defense in raising the money and selecting someone for the job. Mrs. Nancy Ellis was hired, and began her work June 1, 1918 by giving demonstrations on the use of potato flour as a substitute for wheat flour. Women were encouraged to use only one third as much wheat flour as they had been using. People were encouraged to raise family gardens, and use new foods that could be produced on the farm. One new food promoted was "Schmear Kase" made from sour milk. Some people objected because that was a German name, so the name was changed to "cottage cheese."

One woman from each township was appointed on a committee to help Mrs. Ellis with her work. Mrs. John Todd was elected chairman of the committee.

PAUL S. LOWE, COUNTY AGENT 1919

The Carroll County Board of Education met January 9, 1919 and approved Paul S. Lowe of Boone County as County Agent. He had been recommended by the Purdue Extension Department in December. The board also reappointed Mrs. Nancy Ellis to take charge of the Home Economics work. The State and Federal Government paid the salary of both agents, and the county had appropriated $1500 to pay part of the office and traveling expenses.

One of the first activities of the new County Agent was to call a meeting of farmers in the county to organize a County Farmers' Association. County Associations were being organized in many counties in Indiana to help the County Agent with his work in the county.

The meeting was held at the Courthouse in Delphi at 1:30 Saturday afternoon February 22, 1919 with about 200 farmers present. Officers elected were: Taylor Fouts, president; Perry Rule, vice president; Dr. Ren C. Julien, secretary and J. A. Shirk, treasurer.

One of the first orders of business was to arrange for a Farmers' Institute in every township. Five townships were not organized so the following people were appointed temporary chairmen in their townships: Frank S. Girard, Adams; John K. Todd, Deer Creek; Roy P. Martin, Madison; Earl Stewart, Rock Creek and Charles Ginn, Tippecanoe.

In December 1920 the name of the Farmers' Association was changed to Carroll County Farm Bureau. The history of that organization is continued in Chapter VII.

Money appropriated for the Agricultural Department in Washington D.C. was reduced, and, effective July 1, 1919, less money was available for office expenses in the county. The July 31 issue of the Delphi Journal had the following notice signed by County Agent Lowe: "Will have to discharge stenographer July 31, 1919. After the above date I will be in my office Monday afternoon and all day Saturday as regular office days. On any other day of the week the office will be open at no special time except by special appointment." P. S. Lowe resigned as County Agent January 1, 1920.

A. L. HODGSON, COUNTY AGENT 1920-1922

The County Board of Education appointed A. L. Hodgson as County Agent on March 16, 1920 and he served until March 15, 1922. In 1979 he was living in California.

At first the County Agent had no office secretary, so he had to do his own office work, until Mary Mason was hired as secretary.

During 1920 the County Agent drove 5400 miles and conducted 24 culling demonstrations for poultry. In one case a farmer culled and sold about one-third of his hens. In a week the remaining hens were laying more eggs than the entire flock laid before they were culled. During July and August 1921 there were 10 culling demonstrations with an average attendance of 50 people. Forty-one and eight-tenths percent of the hens were culled, and only 13.5% were considered as good layers.

Those two years were a period of great activity for the Agricultural organizations in Carroll County. The Farmers' Institutes continued with meetings in nearly every township. 4-H Clubs were expanded to include more projects. More than 500 4-H members were reported in 1921. Mrs. Hodgson helped train members of Girls' 4-H Clubs and also directed the Choir at the Methodist Church in Delphi. The County Farmers' Association organized several Shipping Associations for livestock. Several Breeders' Associations were organized by purebred livestock producers. Several test plots for corn were used to demonstrate improved practices in raising corn. Farmers were encouraged to raise soybeans, a new crop in the county. In the fall of 1920 a Soybean Conference sponsored by Purdue University was held on the Taylor Fouts farm with an attendance of more than 1000 farmers from four states.

Many people did not realize that the County Agent was involved in all of these activities, and didn't appreciate the good job he was doing in the county. In February 1922, the Board of Education voted not to hire a County Agent for Carroll County. Some members thought that it was costing too much money. The County Agent was one of the highest paid officials in the county. Many realized that he worked more hours than other officials, while some people thought that he wasn't working if he wasn't in the office when they wanted to see him.

In March 1922 the County Farm Bureau hired Mary Mason as secretary and she kept the County Agent's office in the Courthouse open two days each week as Farm Bureau headquarters.

H. E. ACKERSON, COUNTY AGENT 1923-1928

On May 1, 1923 the County Board of Eduction appointed Harry E. Ackerson as County Agent, to begin work on June 1. He came from Westfield, in

Hamilton County, and had served two years as Agent in Miami County. He had also served as Emergency War Agent in Carroll County in 1917.

The County Agent continued to use the Farm Bureau in promoting the Extension program in the county. A committee appointed by the Farm Bureau helped determine which activities were important in the county. The County Agent attended Farm Bureau meetings in every township. In 1925 the County Farm Bureau secured a motion picture machine through the cooperation of a number of business men in the county. It was a 32 volt machine and could be used at several schools where an electric light plant was available. There was an attachment for the projector so that it could also be used in the few places with 110 volt electricity. In the other places where there was no electricity, the County Agent would load five 6 volt auto batteries into his car and use them to run the machine. A set of fully charged batteries would provide power for a show for one evening. The machine was used at many township Farm Bureau meetings and Farmers' Institutes, and the County Agent was usually the operator.

4-H work continued to increase in Carroll County with active clubs in all parts of the county and a 4-H exhibit at the County Fair each year.

In 1924 the first 4-H Camp was held August 18-22 at Camp Tecumseh, with 35 boys and girls from Carroll County attending the camp.

Crop Activities

Since corn was the main crop in Carroll County it was logical that some of the major projects for the Extension program were concerned with corn. In the 5-Acre Corn Club five silver and seven bronze medals were given in 1924, and four gold, six silver and seven bronze medals were awarded in 1926. Another project sponsored was the 1-Acre Corn Club for boys in 4-H.

Farmers were encouraged to test seed corn for germination. Three community seed corn testing stations were provided in the county where a farmer could have his seed corn tested at a cost of one and one half cents per ear. In 1926, the germination on all corn tested was less than 60%.

Soybeans were becoming an important crop in the county, recommendations were made on new varieties, and demonstrations were held to encourage farmers to inoculate their soybean seed.

There were several orchards in the county, and demonstrations were held to show owners how to prune their trees. A spray ring was organized by several orchard owners in order to have better equipment for spraying trees.

In one demonstration it was shown that certified seed potatoes could produce twice the yield of ordinary seed potatoes.

With a need for more legumes for dairy cattle, a series of Farm Bureau meetings had a program on the use of limestone and sweet clover. In 1926 ten carloads of limestone were shipped to Flora for farmers in the area. It was shoveled from the car to wagons and spread on the fields by shoveling off the wagon. Earl Newell figured out a way to use a regular manure spreader to spread limestone and the idea was used by other farmers.

In 1927 farmers in Carroll County sowed 306 acres of alfalfa.

Livestock Projects

In 1924 the first Ton-litter Club was organized in the county with 33 members (a litter of pigs weighing 2000 pounds at the age of six months). The project was continued for several years. Other Gold Medal projects included colt, beef and sheep.

In 1923, 23 dairy herds with 276 cattle were tested for Tuberculosis. In 1927, 51% of the cattle owners signed a request and all cattle in the county were tested for T.B.

Several Dairy Cow Testing Associations were formed in order to help dairymen select their better cows.

Recommendations were made for better feed for livestock. It was reported that one farmer began feeding a better ration to his cattle on Thursday and by Sunday had doubled the milk production.

Demonstrations were held on better methods of caring for sheep and lambs and some farmers claimed that the new practices would double their income from sheep.

On July 21, 1925 about 100 people on a State Poultry Tour visited the Shoff farm in Carroll County.

Not to be outdone, the beekeepers in the county organized and held meetings to learn more about taking care of bees.

Home Economics Activities

In 1924 five new Home Economics clubs were organized in the county making a total of 14 local clubs. All 13 townships were entered in the Millinery Project, with 47 women attending the project lesson. On January 7, 1925 a county Millinery Round-up was held at the Flora Community Building with 226 present.

In 1926 the first Women's Camp was held at Camp Tecumseh with 12 women attending the entire program, and many others attending part of the sessions. In 1927 there were 53 in attendance.

Other Activities

A survey of the county showed that 75% of the farms had Canada thistles. Some had discovered them recently, while one farm reported that they had had thistles since 1888. In 1924 four meetings were held in the county with an attendance of 56 people who were given information on the latest methods of controlling Canada thistles.

In 1926 the Extension Service, with the help of the Flora Community Club and the County Farm Bureau, sponsored a two day Short Course at Flora. A total of 2508 people attended one or more sessions, and there were 320 at the Banquet for the final session with Prof. G. I. Christie, Director of the Experiment Station at Purdue as the speaker.

In the fall of 1926 the State Corn Husking Contest was held on the Pullen farm near Flora. Seventy five business and professional men representing the Flora Community Club and 25 farmers representing the Carroll County Farm Bureau helped with the contest which 2500 people attended.

A new weed in the county was quack grass, and in 1927 meetings were held to inform farmers about methods of controlling it.

In 1927 Farmers' Institutes were held in 10 townships with a total attendance of 2822 people.

In 1927 the Banker-Farmer Tour for the Lafayette District with 150 people visited the Claude Wickard farm to look at hogs, and the Taylor Fouts farm to see soybeans.

On August 15, 1928 a National Soybean meeting attended by 150 people was held at the Taylor Fouts farm, where the first soybeans in this part of Indiana were raised. They also visited the farms of Roy Caldwell and Chester Joyce.

The County Agent worked with Purdue University and Northern Indiana Power Company and helped make a study of the practical uses of electricity on the few farms where it was available. Power uses studied included electric ranges, refrigerators, milking machines, and motor driven feed grinders.

On March 31, 1928 Harry E. Ackerson resigned as County Agent because of ill health.

RALPH MAGGART, COUNTY AGENT 1928-44

Ralph Maggart was appointed County Agent on May 7, 1928 and served until March 31, 1944. This

Ralph Maggart, County Agent from May 7, 1928 to March 31, 1944.

was the longest term served by any County Agent in Carroll County, and he was one of the few County Agents in Indiana who was a native of the county where he served. One of a series of articles in the Indiana Farmers Guide in 1931 concerning County Agents said:

"Directing agricultural extension work in his home county is a bit unusual but that is the combination in Carroll where R. J. Maggart reigns as County Agent, and it has all the earmarks of a good arrangement if one may judge from the extensive projects underway. Here are just a few of them:

"Twenty two percent of the county's crop land in legumes, a Home Economics club in every township with a membership of more than 500 farm women, 150 farmers enrolled in a swine sanitation project, 75 active members in the 4-H Jersey Calf Club, 125 purebred club heifers that paid for themselves in the first lactation period, 42 farmers keeping farm records, 65 using big team hitches, 300 signed up for 4-H Club work this year, between 5,000 and 6,000 acres in soybeans, 12 farmers keeping beef production records and 6 in the colt club.

"Incidentally while driving around the county keeping the host of projects going smoothly, he also succeeds in managing his own farm where he lives about 2 miles east of Delphi."

RECENT COUNTY AGENTS

During the 35 years since Ralph Maggart completed his 16 year term in 1944 there have been 7 County Agents in Carroll County. They are: Robert A. Van

80 • CARROLL COUNTY RURAL ORGANIZATIONS

Ralph J. Maggart, County Agent 1928 to 1944 also operated his farm east of Delphi where this picture was taken in 1950.

Harold R. Berry, County Agent 1952-1960.

Dale R. Kasten, County Agent from April 1, 1960 to October 14, 1973.

Howard McCarty, County Agent 1947 to 1952.

Charles McCoy, County Agent from January 15, 1974 to May 8, 1977.

Slyke, April 1, 1944 to March 31, 1946; Alfred P. Nelson, April 1, 1946 to November 30, 1947; Howard McCarty, December 1, 1947 to January 5, 1952; Harold R. Berry, January 6, 1952 to March 15, 1960; Dale R. Kasten, April 1, 1960 to October 14, 1973; Charles McCoy, January 15, 1974 to May 8, 1977 and Steve Nichols since September 6, 1977.

CHAPTER IV — EXTENSION SERVICE • 81

Steve Nichols, County Agent since September 6, 1977.

Cora Zell St. Amand, Home Demonstration Agent 1947 to 1950 and Jeanne Muller, Home Demonstration Agent 1950 to 1951.

Members of Carroll County Home Economics clubs who sang special numbers at a program honoring Miss Jeanne Muller at the REMC Auditorium October 29, 1951. Left to right: Miss Dora Fossnock, Mrs. Orpha Goslee, Mrs. Lucille Neuenschwander and Mrs. Mabel Fossnock.

Members of Carroll County Home Economics clubs who sang special numbers at a program honoring Miss Jeanne Muller at the REMC Auditorium October 29, 1951. Left to right: Mrs. Marcellini, Mrs. Fred Clem and Mrs. Harold McKinney.

ASSISTANT COUNTY AGENTS

Earl F. Downen served as the first Assistant County Agent in Carroll County from November 1935 to March 1937. He worked in Carroll and Clinton Counties spending half time in each county. Much of his time was spent working with 4-H and other young peoples organizations, but he also helped on other programs in the Extension Office.

Other Assistant County Agents have been: Ted L. Brown September 1, 1954 to August 31, 1958 and Monte Alderfer, September 16, 1959 to February 28, 1963.

These men helped with all phases of the Extension Program, but were responsible for the Better Farming Better Living Program in which they worked with a small number of young farm families and not only helped them do a better job of farming, but also helped them with the many problems involved in better living.

EMERGENCY WAR FOOD AGENT

Reba J. S. Briggs served as Emergency War Food Agent from June 6, 1944 to November 30, 1945. During this time most of her work was with poultry, gardens, canning, school lunches, nutrition classes and Home Economics Clubs.

HOME DEMONSTRATION AGENTS

The First Home Demonstration Agent in Carroll County was Mary M. Thompson Powers who served from August 1, 1946 to June 30, 1947. Others were:

Cora Zell St. Amand July 1, 1947 to September 30, 1950; Jeanne Muller October 1, 1950 to October 31, 1951; June H. Lowther January 1, 1952 to March 1, 1955; Elaine E. Kull Liley May 1, 1957 to October

June H. Lowther, Home Demonstration Agent, 1952-1955.

Elaine Kull Liley, Home Demonstration Agent, 1957 to 1964.

Norma Sullivan, Home Demonstration Agent since March 19, 1973.

31, 1964; Kay Ellen Ayler December 7, 1965 to July 31, 1966; Diana Rohrer October 1, 1966 to August 31, 1967; Elizabeth Combs September 1, 1967 to November 15, 1972, and Norma Sullivan since March 19, 1973.

4-H ASSISTANTS

Those who helped in recent years with 4-H activities during the summer were: Margaret Hedderick, Frieda Burgitt, Mary Ann Newell, Marjorie Schnepf, June Fine, Mollie Sheldon, Mary Ellen Scott, Madonna Jervis, Joanna Scott, Debbie Shoemaker, Barbara Martin, Cindy Maxwell, Betty Leinberger and Leanna Johns.

YOUTH AGENTS

On June 27, 1977 Reneé Krieg was hired as the first full time Youth Agent in the county. She remained on the job until June 15, 1979 and on June 23, 1979 she added McKee to her name and moved to Fountain County.

Bruce Ragan was hired as Youth Agent and began work June 18, 1979.

EXTENSION OFFICE

The first County Agents' office was located in a room in the northwest corner of the first floor of the Courthouse and was moved to the Post Office after it was built in 1937. In 1976 the office was moved to its present location south of Delphi.

OFFICE SECRETARIES

As is true with most successful organizations, much of the work at the County Agents' office has been done by the secretary.

Mary Mason was office secretary from 1920 to 1935. Others have been Lillian Haines Thompson, 1935 to about 1938; Jane Witter Titus to June 1940; Lenore McCarty Allen, June 1940 to August 1943. Secretaries during the next 7 years were: Alyne Bowman, Kathleen Pollard, Jean Pruitt Ferrier, Phyllis Steinman, Phyllis Franklin and Mrs. Annabel Hanna. Secretaries since 1950 have been Elsie Overley Myers, 1950 and 1951; Magdalene O'Farrell Mears, May 1951 to 1959; Pat Toole Porter, October 1959 to May 1960; Darilee Peter Robbins, May 1960 to October 1964; Carmen Blocher Killingsworth, October 1964 to 1971; Marsha Blocher 1971 to fall of 1972; and Cathy Peterson Smith since 1972. Patsy Pullen Jennings has served as office secretary several times for a short period of time.

CHAPTER IV — EXTENSION SERVICE • 83

Renee' Krieg, Youth Agent from June 27, 1977 to June 15, 1979.

Bruce Ragan, Youth Agent since June 18, 1979.

The Carroll County Extension Staff 1979. Left to right: Jill Meek, Cathy Smith, Joan Rogers (Program Assistant), Renee' Krieg, John Foley, (Area Administrator) Norma Sullivan, Steve Nichols, and Mary Sheldon.

Sandy Maxwell and Jill Meek have served as extra help in the office recently.

EXTENSION COMMITTEE

Since 1937 the activities of the County Agricultural Extension Agent have been directed by an Extension Committee made up of representatives from each township and from each organization that is concerned with the Extension program.

Each year this committee meets in November, reviews the work of the Extension staff, makes plans for future activities and elects an executive committee to direct the program for the year.

Members of the Extension Executive Committee elected in November 1978 were: Dr. Lawrence Stauffer, president; Richard Denhart, vice president and Mrs. John (Virginia) Bush, secretary. Other members on the Extension Board for 1979 were: Mrs. Herbert (Mildred) Been, Ron Guckien, Dan Lybrook, Mrs. Joe (Louann) Starkey, Larry Trapp, Don Ramsey, Carol Bordner, Mrs. Pat (June) Million, Jerry Blue, Jerry Hendress, Kenneth Orem and Mrs. Leo (Clara) Rider.

ACTIVITIES

Each of the many people involved in Extension work in Carroll County has made valuable and important contributions toward a better life for people in the county. Much of the information on these activities is available in newspapers, annual reports and other records in the Extension Office.

Members of the County Extension Executive Committee at a meeting at the County Agent's office on January 26, 1950. Left to right: John C. Peterson, chairman; Lloyd Burgitt, Robert Hedde, Fred Hannell, Charles T. Black, Mrs. Charles Harter and Miss Frieda Burgitt.

Members of the staff in the Extension Office have continued to direct 4-H Club activities, arrange winter schools for adults and help people find solutions to their many problems. The Extension Service was involved in many events, including the Prairie Farmer WLS Farm Progress Show on the Miles T. Martin farm in 1954.

Many new organizations have been formed to help solve new problems, while other organizations, after completing the job for which they were organized, have ceased to function. The County Agent helped organize the Soil & Water Conservation District, the Area Plan Commission, the County Community Development Committee and other organizations as they were needed. Information about many of these organizations and activities are in other parts of this book.

On the following pages are reports on a few of the many activities in which the Extension Service has been involved.

Livestock

Methods of feeding hogs in the 1930's were influenced greatly by the many meetings with John Schwab and others from Purdue University who emphasized the importance of proper feeding and Sanitation in hog production. The records show that in 1930, about 90 farmers attended a Swine School when the temperature was below zero.

Nearly every farmer had a few milk cows, and they were encouraged to use better feeding and production methods. A Dairy Herd Improvement Association was organized for farmers who wanted to know more about the milk production of their cows.

A Cooperative Creamery at Crawfordsville provided a better market for cream for many farmers in the county. For several years there were four trucks hauling cream from Carroll County to Crawfordsville.

In 1930 the Indiana Poultry Cooperative Marketing Association opened a plant in Monticello to process and market eggs and poultry. This provided a market for more than 300 poultry producers in the county. Eggs were collected on regular routes once each week in the winter and twice each week in the summer. Marketing on the basis of grade and quality provided an incentive for farmers to produce better eggs and poultry.

A report of the County Agent shows that in 1931 there was only one farm in the county with more than 1000 hens, about 20 with more than 500, 150 with 300 to 500, 500 with 100 to 200, 700 with 50 to 100 and 300 with less than 50.

As the types of farms and numbers of livestock changed, the Extension Service supplied information and advice to those who needed it to decide on changes in their farming operation. The Extension Service and the Agricultural Experiment Station at Purdue provided valuable information to farmers to help them control diseases and solve the many other problems in livestock production.

Carroll County Livestock and Meat Caravan

On February 7, 1952, 222 people visited the Carroll County Livestock and Meat Caravan held at the REMC auditorium in Delphi. Twelve exhibits were set up around the auditorium wall and eight specialists from Purdue were present to explain exhibits and answer questions. A program was held from 11:00 to 12:00 noon and from 1:00 to 2:00 P.M. Masters of ceremony were John C. Peterson and Leo Craig.

The Carroll County Rural Youth had a food stand.

Those on the committee who helped set up and take down exhibits were: Fred Hannell, Truman Plank, Eldon Robeson, Lawrence Douglas, Clyde Cook, Robert Hedde, Sr., Fritz Schnepf, Harry Wilson and Charles Meade.

Robert Clawson of the REMC was in charge of the public address system.

Miss Frieda Burgitt and Mrs. Alfred Anderson were in charge of registration.

The Carroll County Home Economics Chorus sang several numbers.

Hoosier Gold Medal Club

For many years the Indiana Livestock Breeders Association sponsored Gold Medal Clubs for hogs, colts, sheep and calves.

In the Hoosier Ton-Litter Club, a gold medal was presented if a litter of pigs weighed 2000 pounds or more at 6 months of age. Silver and bronze medals were awarded for lighter weights. Twenty three

Truman Plank and Melvin Fisher talking things over with G. P. Walker at the Meat Caravan.

litters were entered in the contest in Carroll County in 1939.

In the Hoosier Thousand Pound Calf Club, a gold medal was given for a calf weighing 1000 pounds at one year of age. Silver and bronze medals were awarded for lighter weights. In 1939 there were 59 calves in the club in Carroll County.

Similar awards were made in the Hoosier Gold Medal Colt Club and the Hoosier Gold Medal Sheep Club.

Medals were presented at the Annual Banquet of the Indiana Livestock Breeders' Association during the Agricultural Conference at Purdue. Special recognition was given by the Purdue Agricultural Alumni Association to those who won a number of medals.

Hundreds of farmers have won medals in the project and farmers in Carroll County have won their share.

Horses

The first gold medal Colt Club to be organized in Carroll County was formed in Burlington Township in November, 1926. The first five farmers to join the club were Carlisle Humes, Garland McCarty, Clifford Cleaver, Harry McCarty, and Roy Bowman.

In 1929 a demonstration on big team hitches was conducted in the county by P. T. Brown of Purdue. About 65 farmers attended the demonstration, and many of them used the big team hitch on their farms.

In September 1929 the Burlington Gold Medal Horse and Colt Club show was held with 45 horses shown in five classes. Businessmen in Burlington donated merchandise for prizes. A horse pulling contest was held at the show.

Interest in horses declined rapidly as more and better tractors became available.

Rural Electrification

Perhaps the greatest change in farm life during this time came as a result of building rural electric lines in the county. For many years the County Agent and the Extension Service had encouraged more and better uses for electricity on the farm, and Ralph Maggart was active in helping organize the REMC which made electricity available to farmers in the county. Other County Agents have supplied information to help farmers make better use of electricity.

Agricultural Adjustment Program

As a result of the Great Depression which began in 1929, the Agricultural Adjustment Administration, known as the AAA was created in 1933 to help farmers control surplus farm products by reducing production. During 1934 the production of hogs was reduced 25% and corn production reduced 24%.

The County Agent helped conduct educational programs and helped the first committees get the program organized. The Extension Office has continued to help with the education and information necessary to administer the program.

Crops

A drastic change in corn production resulted from the development of Hybrid Corn. In former years much emphasis had been placed on the proper selection and testing of seed corn. By 1939 more Hybrid Seed Corn had become available, and many farmers in the county began producing seed for their neighbors.

The Five-acre Corn Contest was started in 1914 as a cooperative enterprise between the Indiana Corn Growers' Association, the Agronomy Division of the Department of Agricultural Extension, and County Agents. It was a yield contest in which 284 farmers participated the first year, 21 of whom produced 100 bushels or more per acre with 112 bushels per acre being the highest.

In 1932 the contest in Carroll County was won by Roy Snoeberger with a yield of 132 bushels per acre. This was the highest yield ever recorded in Carroll County up to that time. Other winners in the contest that year were John Snoeberger, 129 bu.; Carl Yeakley, 100.4 bu.; Clarence Dilling, 97 bu. and Miles T. Martin, 89 bu.

By 1954 corn yields were being determined for over 4000 contestants in the U.S. and this was the first year of yields over 200 bushels per acre, which was duplicated in each of the six years that followed, with 241 bushels per acre being the highest.

The name of the Indiana Corn Growers' Association has been changed to the Indiana Crop Improvement Association.

In 1931 Taylor Fouts raised the first lespedeza in Carroll County. The next year about 12 or 15 farmers raised lespedeza, a new forage crop for hay and pasture.

The first sudan grass raised in Carroll County was in 1932 when Ralph Rinehart and Orliff Coghill each raised 10 acres.

Farm Records

On Tuesday afternoon August 28, 1928 agricultural and grade school teachers met at a Teachers' Institute at Delphi High School, and J. C. Bottom of Purdue gave a talk on Farm Budgeting and Farm Record Keeping. Several teachers had their students keep farm records as a school project that winter. Mr. Bottom had just started work at Purdue, and this was his first county meeting in Indiana. Since he did not have an automobile he borrowed a Model T Ford from another Extension worker to make the trip.

On December 30, 1933 about 20 farmers met at the Courthouse at Delphi and organized a Farm Record Association for Carroll County. Officers elected were: Webb Robeson, president and John C. Peterson, secretary treasurer.

J. C. Bottom from the Farm Management Department of Purdue met with the Association on January 26, 1934 to help members get started on the record books. They agreed on the following prices to use for valuation of opening inventories: dairy cows $30 to $40 each, ewes $3 to $7, hogs $3 per hundred pounds, hens $ .50 each, corn $ .36, wheat $ .74, oats $ .30, rye $ .48, soybeans $ .70 per bushel, clover hay $12 per ton and fodder $ .16 per shock. Fourteen farmers completed their records for the year and had them summarized by Purdue University. Each farmer received a report showing detailed figures for his farm, along with the average figures for all farms.

The 14 farms in Carroll County averaged 238 acres and had an assessed valuation of $57 per acre. The average labor income for the year was $1516. Labor income was the amount a farmer had left for his work after paying all expenses including interest on investment. In addition to this he had a house to live in, and products raised and used on the farm.

Those who had their records summarized in 1934 were: Mrs. Lloyd Beard, W. H. Bowman & Son, Melvin F. Fisher, Frank Hedderick & Son, Fred Hershberger, J. C. Humes, Ralph Maggart, Arthur R. Mullin, H. E. Newell & Son, W. F. Peterson and Sons, Elmer Reiff & Son, Webb Robeson, Walter H. Barnhart, and Merritt E. Johnson.

During the first three years the Association charged each member $2 to help pay the cost of summarizing the records. The University later assumed this expense, and the County Association donated a balance of $24.20 in the treasury to the Carroll County 4-H Club Exhibit Association in 1940. Officers in 1940 were: Earl B. Newell, president and Walter Barnhart, secretary treasurer.

In 1941, 22 farmers had their records summarized at Purdue. This included 14 record keepers who had not been in the program in 1934. They were: Ben Metzger, F. G. Schnepf, Oren Eikenberry, J. W.

Farmers in Carroll County who met at the County Agent's office on January 11, 1952 with A. M. Nichter of Purdue University to have their farm record books checked and completed for summary by the University. Seated, left to right: Joseph E. Peterson, Earl B. Newell, Mr. Nichter, Leroy and Eldon Robeson. Standing, left to right: John C. Peterson, Robert C. Wingard, Walter Barnhart, Cleo Metzger, Oren Eikenberry, William Dickinson, Delbert Eikenberry, Truman Plank, John B. McCormick and J. W. Eikenberry.

Eikenberry, Marvin V. Jervis, Robert C. Wingard, Frank Barnhart, Leroy Robeson, Floyd Smeltzer, Lee F. Flora, John B. McCormick, Wm. Dickinson, Earl B. Newell and Truman Plank.

This program has been continued by Purdue, but in recent years there have been fewer records with a more complete and detailed analysis of each record. Over the years this program has provided the University with accurate records of actual farming operations in Indiana, and has given farmers an opportunity to compare the figures on their farm with the average figures for similar farms in their area.

Carroll County Farm Management Association

The Carroll County Farm Management Association was organized in 1949 with 33 members. Officers who served for the first two years were: Ralph Maggart, president; George Sites, vice president and Charles T. Black, secretary treasurer.

The Association was active for about fifteen years, and during that time arranged for many meetings in the county where members and guests were invited to eat a meal and hear a program and discussion on some current problem affecting agriculture. They also sponsored Farm Outlook meetings.

For nine years members joined with the County Purdue Ag Alumni Association and sponsored a chicken barbecue. Following is a brief report on five of them.

Chicken Barbecues

The Carroll County Farm Management Association and Purdue Ag Alumni Association sponsored the first chicken barbecue in the county at the Delphi Park, Thursday evening, September 17, 1953. Seventy five broilers were served to 106 people. Chicken was barbecued under the supervision of Wayne Detwiler, Extension Poultry Specialist at Purdue.

Local members who helped were: Kenneth Newell, Ralph Sullivan, W. S. Weaver, Charles Black, Eldon Robeson, John Burke, Homer Wilson, Raymond Todd, Don Bowman and Harold Berry, County Agent.

Dr. Earl Butz of Purdue spoke on "Farm Horizons Beyond the Line Fence."

Members of the Association used metal barrels to make charcoal pits for barbecuing chicken, and these were used for several years for an annual chicken barbecue.

The Second Annual Barbecue was held at Delphi City Park August 17, 1954. Over 150 people attended and heard R. L. Kohls of the Purdue Agricultural Economics Department discuss "A Loaf of Bread."

Two hundred fifty pounds of chicken were barbecued by Homer Wilson, Kenneth Newell, John Burke, Ralph Sullivan, Charles Black and Harold Berry.

Lowell Ward and Wm. Dickinson prepared the slaw, Raymond Todd was coffee maker, and Gardner Martin was in charge of other food supplies.

The Fifth Annual Chicken Barbecue by the County Farm Management Association and the Purdue Ag Alumni Association was held at the Delphi City Park on Thursday evening August 22, 1957. Gardner Martin was county president.

The Eighth Annual Chicken Barbecue was held on August 25, 1960 with 125 present. The speaker was Lawrence Senesh, from the Department of Economics, Purdue.

The Ninth Annual Chicken Barbecue was held at Delphi City Park, on Thursday evening, August 17, 1961 with 165 present. Rev. Joe Wick, minister of the Christian Church in Lafayette spoke on "Therapy of Laughter."

On August 16, 1962 a Pork Barbecue was held at the Fairgrounds in Flora with 115 present. The speaker was Bill Anderson, from the Producers Marketing Association. Officers elected were: Kenneth Newell, president, Eldon Robeson, vice president and Joseph E. Peterson, secretary treasurer.

This was the last public barbecue sponsored by the Farm Management Association.

Purdue Agricultural Alumni Association

In 1928 W. O. "Brick" Mills was hired as field agent for the School of Agriculture at Purdue. His job was

Officers of the Carroll County Farm Management Association for 1951 were left to right in front row: Truman Plank, secretary treasurer; Eldon Robeson, vice president and Lee Flora, president. The officers for 1950 in the back row were: Charles T. Black, secretary treasurer; George Sites, vice president and Ralph Maggart, president. The new officers were elected at the farm outlook meeting, sponsored by the Farm Management Association and the extension office, held at Delphi High School on October 10, 1950.

to work with graduates of the School of Agriculture, and help them do a better job of farming.

One of the first projects was to distribute the newly developed hybrid seed corn to individual farmers, and let them produce seed for themselves and their neighbors. Several farmers specialized in this and the production of hybrid seed became a major part of their business.

In 1931 the Carroll County Agricultural Club was organized to help farmers keep records and get them summarized. Officers were: Will Ginn, president; Byron Jervis, vice president; Orville Wilson, secretary treasurer and Earl B. Newell, chairman of the program committee.

In 1934 the Carroll County Purdue Ag Alumni Association, with Webb Robeson as chairman, sponsored an essay contest. There were five essays written, and the contest was won by Keith Sink. He was given free tuition to a Short Course in Agriculture at Purdue.

Officers of the Carroll County Purdue Ag Alumni Association for 1950 were: Miles T. Martin, president; Taylor Fouts, vice president and Joseph E. Peterson, secretary treasurer.

Officers for 1951 were: Harold Thompson, president; Earl Newell, vice president and Raymond Todd, secretary treasurer.

Officers for 1953 were: Raymond Todd, president; Don Bowman, vice president and Dorothy Newell Mills, secretary treasurer.

Operation Brainpower

The Carroll County Purdue Ag Alumni Association sponsored a project known as Operation Brainpower. On January 3, 1959 seventy high school students interested in Agriculture and Home Economics were taken to Purdue for Ag Opportunity Day. Students heard talks by President F. L. Hovde, Dean Earl L. Butz, Dean V. C. Freeman, and Dean D. C. Pfendler. A campus tour included the new Recreational Gym, housing facilities and classrooms. Students were guests of Purdue at the Purdue-Michigan basketball game.

On December 29, 1959, 131 students and 29 drivers made a similar trip, and on February 17, 1962 another group of 131 students were taken to Ag Opportunity Day.

On a similar tour February 16, 1963 students were guests at a Purdue Variety Show in the Loeb Theater.

About 35 counties in Indiana sponsor this project, and from 700 to 1500 high school students are taken

Officers for 1950 and 1951 who attended the Carroll County Purdue Ag Alumni Association banquet March 24, 1951 were left to right: Joseph E. Peterson; Chester Biddle of Remington, State Ag Alumni president; Gordon Graham, Purdue Ag Alumni Field Secretary; Taylor Fouts; Raymond Todd; Earl Newell; Miles T. Martin; Glenn Sample, Speaker and Editor of the Hoosier Farmer; and Harold Thompson.

to the University each year. About 35,000 students have been exposed to a college campus since the program began.

Purdue Ag. Alumni Association Fish Fry

One of the highlights in the activities of the Purdue Ag Alumni Association is the Annual Meeting and Fish Fry held each year as a part of the Agricultural Conference at Purdue.

This started in 1928 when Claude Harper, Professor of Animal Husbandry; and Fay C. Gaylord, Professor of Horticulture, prepared chicken and noodles (at 60¢ a plate) for 300 alumni crowded into the "large" laboratory of the Agricultural Engineering Building. Professor Aitkenhead was head of the department and this building was known as "Aitkenhead's Castle."

Purdue President, Edward C. Elliott, in his speech, declared the meeting to be characterized by the most noise, noodles and enthusiasm he had ever witnessed. Greetings were extended by Dean J. H. Skinner and Indiana Governor Harry Leslie. This set the pattern of addresses and entertainment by prominent persons for the next 50 years.

It was at one of these meetings that President Elliott, in discussing the importance of organization, made the statement: "Consider the banana, whenever it leaves the bunch it gets skinned."

In 1944 the chicken and noodles was replaced by a Fish Fry prepared by the famous Akron Jonah Club. The minutes of the 1945 meeting recorded "more than 600 hungry, howling Ags were served all the fish they could eat."

For several years the meetings have been held in the Purdue Armory with a capacity crowd. In 1976 there were nearly 2500 in attendance, and they ate 1,716 pounds of fish.

Maurice L. Williamson, Executive Secretary of the Purdue Ag Alumni Association since 1953 has been in charge of the event, which is the largest Alumni gathering in the nation. His report on the meeting for 1979 stated:

> "Twenty-five hundred wildly enthusiastic Purdue Ags practically trampled each other to get a good seat for the Purdue Ag Annual Meeting and Fish Fry in January. 'Circus' was the theme, with the Peru Festival Circus doing the daring deeds. Governor Otis Bowen was the wild animal trainer (logically), and Purdue President Arthur G. Hansen was the human cannonball—a role in which he has earned considerable experience. Next year, the Fish Fry will be held on Friday, January 18. 'Riverboat' is the theme. Be there."

These meetings are always attended by many Purdue Ag Alumni from Carroll County.

Outdoor Cookery

An unusual project lesson was held on June 18, 1956 when 200 women in Carroll County attended a special interest lesson on Outdoor Cookery. There was no Home Demonstration Agent at the time, so the lesson was given by Harold Berry, County Agent. He reported it as "The most work I put in on any teaching activity."

The lesson demonstrated equipment, safety, and many meat and vegetable items that could be prepared on the charcoal grill. The meeting was concluded by feeding the group a pork chop dinner. Starke and Wetzel furnished the pork, and it was prepared with the help of a committee from the Farm Management Association which included: Miles Martin, Ray Todd, W. S. Weaver, Charles Beale and Ted Brown.

For several years many meetings included a meal with chicken or pork chops cooked on the open grill. One year the county served a pork chop luncheon for people on a State Swine Tour.

Mosquitoes

In the spring of 1952, Wilbur Bitler of Delphi asked Harold Berry, County Agent, if something could be done about the mosquito problem in Delphi. A community program was organized, and more than $500 was donated for a spraying program from June 2 to August 8. This was the first community mosquito control program in Delphi.

Land Judging

The first 4-H Land Judging Contest in Carroll County was held August 8, 1952 on the Carl Jester farm south of Delphi with the help of Kenneth Pyle of the Soil Conservation Service.

Community Development Committee

The Agricultural Extension Service at Purdue was set up to help farmers with their individual farm problems such as kinds and varieties of crops, cultivating methods and fertilizer use. Rapid technological development had great social impact on communities, and farmers became concerned about more than just the problems of producing and marketing agricultural products.

In the 1930's a Land Use Planning Program was developed in which local people were asked to make plans for better land use, and to make long range plans for their areas. This resulted in more requests for the Extension Service to assist with social and community problems.

In about 1958 an experimental Community Development Committee was established in Perry County. During the next few years several other counties organized Community Development Committees. The Extension Service helped select local leaders to set up the committees, and then supplied technical information when requested by the committees which had no official power except to give advice and make recommendations.

An outstanding example of the results of the work of a committee was the establishment of the Parke County Covered Bridge Festival which was organized with the help and encouragement of the Community Development Committee in Parke County.

Carroll County Community Development Committee

In 1963 the County Extension Committee made a list of leaders in Carroll County, and during the next year 68 of them were interviewed by Dale Kasten, County Agent, and Henry A. Wadsworth from Purdue University. People were asked to name the things that they thought were needed in Carroll County in order to make it a better place in which to live. The most frequent suggestions were: more recreational areas, more industry, and some kind of county planning and zoning to provide more homes for people without interfering with the use of better farm land for agricultural purposes. Several were concerned about education, especially for adults, and vocational training. Some were concerned about having better medical facilities and law enforcement. A few suggested that the best way to solve the problems of Carroll County was to divide it among the adjoining counties.

Each of the people interviewed was asked to name five people in the county whom they thought would be qualified and willing to serve on a County Committee to study the problems in Carroll County and make suggestions for improvement.

A total of 182 people were suggested, but 18 were suggested more often than others. Seventeen of these agreed to serve on the committee.

The first meeting was held on July 15, 1965 with 13 of the 17 members present. Members have continued to meet nearly every month. Three of the original members have died and three have resigned, but the other eleven were still active members and attended about 75% of the meetings in 1978. New members have been selected by the committee to maintain a membership of 15 to 20 on the committee. Beginning in 1977 some women were added to the committee and spouses of members were invited to attend the meetings.

The committee operates without any publicity, and their names have never been published. This is because they feel that it is easier to get things done if no one cares who gets the credit.

The committee has no authority and takes no official action. Members study a wide variety of problems, and invite others to meet with them in order to get reliable information on problems and recommendations on how conditions in the county might be improved.

When members agree on something that needs to be done to improve conditions in Carroll County the members work as individuals and as members of other organizations to get the changes made.

Some of the problems studied and on which some progress was made include county planning, road numbering system, sanitary landfill for solid waste disposal, ambulance service and more opportunity for vocational education.

Other problems were studied and no solution was found. An attempt was made to establish an emergency telephone number for the county. In some communities it is possible for a person to dial a special number and get help for any emergency, such as a fire, accident or illness. With residents of Carroll County served by six telephone companies inside the county and about eight companies outside the county, it is a physical impossibility to have the same emergency number for everyone to use unless major changes are made in equipment in the telephone exchanges.

Recently the committee has been working with the U. S. postal service, ambulance service and the fire departments to establish a uniform numbering system for homes in the county in order to make it easier in case of an emergency to find where a person lives.

The County Agent has served as secretary of the committee and has helped get specialists to meet with the committee and discuss problems.

PLANNING AND ZONING

State legislation provides for several kinds of planning commissions in Indiana, and in most cases the County Agent is designated as a member.

In February 1966 a petition signed by 20 taxpayers was presented to the County Commissioners requesting that they establish County Planning and Zoning in Carroll County. A public hearing was held with 40 interested citizens of the county taking part in the discussion. County Commissioners were: Lee Flora, Ren Groninger and Carl Dittman.

In April 1966 the County Commissioners established a County Plan Commission and appointed a nine member board. As provided in the law, four members were: Dale Kasten, County Agent; Charles Ritzler, County Surveyor; Leonard Ireland, School Superintendent and Carl Dittman, County Commissioner. Others appointed to the board were: John C. Peterson, John Harvey Todd, Fred Martin, Kenneth Frey and Lewis Mullin.

The County Plan Commission was authorized to work in all unincorporated areas in the county. After several meetings members recommended that an Area Plan Commission be established to include any town or city that wanted to be in the program.

An Area Plan Commission was created in July 1967. On September 27, 1967 the commission selected the firm of Beckman, Swenson and Associates of Fort Wayne to prepare a comprehensive plan and zoning ordinances for the county. The firm and the Plan Commission spent the next four years preparing the Plan and Ordinances which were approved early in 1971 by the County Commissioners, the city of Delphi and the towns of Burlington, Camden and Yeoman. Flora chose to continue with their own Plan Commission which had been operating for several years.

The new Zoning Ordinances became effective on May 24, 1971. A referendum was held at the same time as the general election in November 1971 in Democrat Township and voters decided not to participate in the program.

The first members of the Area Plan Commission were: Dale Kasten, County Agent; Charles Ritzler, County Surveyor; Leonard Ireland, representing the schools; Henry Rozhon and Glen Harner representing Delphi; Ralph Rohrabaugh representing Camden, Burlington and Yeoman; John T. Johnson appointed by the County Council and John C. Peterson appointed by the County Commissioners.

The County Agent has been secretary of the Commission, John C. Peterson has been chairman and Charles Ritzler, vice chairman for the entire period, except during the first year when Ralph Rohrabaugh was vice chairman. Other members of the Plan Commission in 1979 were: Rex Hinkle, appointed by the Council; Glen Harner and Herbert Isaacs representing Delphi, Robert Ayres representing the school corporations and Bob Wyatt representing the towns of Camden, Yeoman and Burlington.

About 265 building permits per year were issued during the first seven years. A. Ray Myers has been Zoning Administrator and Roy Slavens has been Assistant Zoning Administrator. Roberta Sparhawk has been office secretary since April, 1979.

Members of the Board of Zoning Appeals in 1979 were: Cecil Glick, chairman; Glen Harner, secretary; Rex Hinkle, Kenneth Yeakley and Albert Burkle. Lewis N. Mullin has been attorney for both the APC and Board of Zoning Appeals since they were organized.

New members of the Area Plan Commission for 1980 were: Burton Billiard, appointed by the County Council to replace Rex Hinkle; John P. Sumpter, appointed by the Mayor of Delphi to replace Herb Isaacs; and Frank Simmerman, appointed by the towns of Camden, Burlington and Yeoman to replace Bob Wyatt.

EXTENSION-RESEARCH SUPPORT COMMITTEE

The Indiana Extension-Research Support Committee, Inc. was recently formed to provide a structure by which the local people can have input in program development, participate in guiding program decisions, and in providing budgetary and legislative support at the local, state, and national levels.

The State Committee will study the needs for Extension and Research, and make recommendations to the State Legislature for appropriations of money for the more urgent projects.

The committee will meet with similar committees in other states and make recommendations to the U.S. Congress for appropriations. Members of the committee appointed from Carroll County are: John B. McCormick, Dan Lybrook and W. S. Weaver.

CARROLL COUNTY EFNEP PROGRAM
By Norma Sullivan

The Expanded Food and Nutrition Program (EFNEP) was initiated in 1968 by the Extension Service as an educational nutrition program to improve the nutritional level of diets of low-income families. This program is an integral part of the Extension Home Economics and 4-H Youth Programs.

The adult phase is charged with providing a food and nutrition educational program to enhance the quality of the family's nutrition. The progression of families from EFNEP to other home economics programs enables the families to participate in educational programs in family living areas in addition to nutrition.

The 4-H phase of EFNEP is charged specifically with providing educational programs for youth from low-income families. While meeting this need, the goal of Extension is to encourage participating youth to pursue other opportunities through involvement in additional 4-H programs for meeting the 4-H mission of developing responsible youth citizenship.

The three distinguishing features of EFNEP are that it is: A. Intensive education on an individual and/or small group basis, B. Conducted by Extension paraprofessionals and/or volunteers trained and supervised by Extension professionals, C. for low-income families and youth.

The program started in Carroll County in 1968, as one of the original counties in Indiana in the program.

Carroll County has two program assistants who each work half-time or 20 hours a week. Program Assistants who have served in Carroll County include: Betty Ann Duke, Betty June Dawson, Rosanna Fife, Frances Shull, Pam Logsdon, Dorothy Murray, Carol Johns, Joan Rogers and Mary Catherine Sheldon.

FACTS

Fast Agricultural Communication Terminal System, known as FACTS is a system with computer terminals in each of the 92 County Extension Offices in Indiana connected with 18 terminals on the Purdue Campus and 10 more at Purdue's Regional Offices throughout the state. All terminals are connected with the central computer system at Purdue.

A development grant for $1.16 million from the W. K. Kellogg Foundation of Battle Creek, Michigan to the Indiana Cooperative Extension Service in 1976 got the program started in Indiana, which was one of the first states to have a program of this kind. Each county paid for a part of the cost of the local terminal, and pays the cost of operation, estimated at $1800 to $2000 per year. The terminal in the Carroll County office was installed in February and was ready for use in April, 1979.

A wide variety of information including weather and market reports, and the latest developments in research is available to farmers, homemakers and others in Indiana at no cost to them. This information is available much sooner than it would be in bulletins or by mail.

The terminal in each Extension Office is programmed to help people make decisions on a number of problems, including Farm Building Plans, Crop Rotation, Garden Planning, Livestock Feeding Programs, Insect Control, Weed Control, Estate Planning, Income Tax Management, Home Insulation, Budget Planning and many others. 4-H Enrollment Records and other records in the County office will be kept on the computer.

CHANGES IN AGRICULTURE

During the 60 years since the first County Agent was appointed in Carroll County there have been more changes in agriculture than during any other period in history, and the County Agent, as the local representative of the Extension Service has been involved in many of these changes.

During a period of 28 years, from 1932 to 1960 the number of horses and mules on farms in the U.S. declined from 17.3 million to 3.1 million.

The number of tractors on farms increased from 1 million in 1932 to 4.5 million in 1972.

From 1934 to 1972 the average yield per acre for corn in the U.S. increased from 28.8 to 95.5 bushels per acre. During the same period the total production of soybeans increased from 23 million to 1.3 billion bushels. Fertilizer sales increased from $120 million in 1933 to $2.1 billion in 1970. The number of people fed by one farmer increased from 9.8 in 1930 to 51 in 1972.

ROLE OF EXTENSION SERVICE

The Cooperative Extension Service continues to be the largest, most successful informal educational organization in the world. It is a nationwide system funded and guided by a partnership of federal, state, and local governments that delivers information to help people help themselves through the land-grant university system.

The system was based on the belief that human progress could be enhanced if the products of research could be translated to lay language and made available to individuals for a higher quality of decision making. Research from universities, government, and other sources is utilized to help people make their own decisions. The success of this system in developing the world's most productive agriculture has been recognized throughout the world.

There is a Cooperative Extension Service in each of the 50 states, the District of Columbia, Puerto Rico, Virgin Islands and Guam. More than a million volunteers help multiply the impact of the Extension professional staff.

Extension programs are nonpolitical, objective, and based on factual information. The Extension Service dispenses no funds to the public, and is not a regulatory agency, but it does inform people of regulations and of their options in meeting them.

Extension has the built-in flexibility to adjust its programs and subject matter to meet new needs. Activities shift from year to year as citizen groups and Extension workers who are close to the problems recommend changes. The citizens themselves cast the final vote by electing to take part in the Extension programs that serve them best.

CARROLL COUNTY EXTENSION AGENTS

H. E. Ackerson 9-16-17 to 1-1-18 Emergency War Agent White & Carroll Counties
J. W. McFarland 1-16-18 to 2-16-18 EWA
  2-16-18 to 11-12-18 County Agent
P. S. Lowe 1-1-19 to 1-15-19 EWA
  1-16-19 to 1-1-20 County Agent
A. L. Hodgson 3-16-20 to 3-15-22 County Agent
Harry E. Ackerson 6-1-23 to 3-31-28
Ralph J. Maggart 5-7-28 to 3-31-44
Robert A. Van Slyke 4-1-44 to 3-31-46
Alfred P. Nelson 4-1-46 to 11-30-47
Howard McCarty 12-1-47 to 1-5-52
Harold R. Berry 1-6-52 to 3-15-60
Dale R. Kasten 4-1-60 to 10-14-73
Charles McCoy 1-15-74 to 5-8-77
Steve Nichols 9-6-77

Assistant County Agents

Earl F. Downen 11-1-35 to 3-9-37
Ted L. Brown 9-1-54 to 8-31-58
Monte Alderfer 9-16-59 to 2-28-63

Youth Agents

Reneé Krieg 6-27-77 to 6-15-79
Bruce Ragan 6-18-79

Home Demonstration Agents

Nancy Ellis 6-1-18 to 6-30-18 EWA
Reba J. S. Briggs 6-6-44 to 11-30-45 EWA Assistant
Mary M. Thompson Powers 8-1-46 to 6-30-47
Cora Zell St. Amand 7-1-47 to 9-30-50
Jeanne Muller 10-1-50 to 10-31-51
June H. Lowther 1-1-52 to 3-1-55
Elaine E. Kull Liley 5-1-57 to 10-31-64
Kay Ellen Ayler 12-7-65 to 7-31-66
Diana Rohrer 10-1-66 to 8-31-67
Elizabeth Combs 9-1-67 to 11-15-72
Norma Sullivan 3-19-73

CHAPTER V

EXTENSION HOMEMAKERS

INDIANA EXTENSION HOMEMAKERS ASSOCIATION

The Indiana Home Economics Association was organized at Purdue University during "Farmers Week", January 17, 1913 with 58 charter members, and with 10 clubs paying dues.

The objects of the Association, as stated in its constitution were: "To promote the general knowledge of home economics; to bring into affiliation all organizations dealing with the subject; to secure the teaching of home economics in the schools of the state."

Mrs. Virginia C. Meredith was elected the first president and made the following statement: "Every community needs organized groups of women to guide in a common sense way spirited discussions about whatever will make Indiana homes, better homes. This is the aim of this association."

At its first meeting a resolution was adopted requesting a legislative appropriation of $100,000 for a Home Economics building at Purdue. This request was repeated from time to time until 1923, when the building was secured.

At the first Annual Meeting on January 15, 1914 the State Treasurer reported $7.50 on hand. By 1927 there were 309 clubs with 10,142 members. In 1977 there were 3,000 clubs with 53,000 members in Indiana.

In 1951 the name was changed from Indiana Home Economics Association to Indiana Home Demonstration Association. In 1966 the name was changed to the Indiana Extension Homemakers Association, and county clubs changed their names at the same time.

Club Creed

In 1930 the State Association sponsored a contest for a creed. From the 60 entries the following creed, written by Mrs. C. W. Horne of Hendricks County was adopted: "We believe in the present and its opportunities, in the future and its promises, in everything that makes life large and lovely, in the divine joy of living and helping others and so we endeavor to pass on to others that which has benefited us, striving to go onward and upward, reaching the pinnacle of economic perfection, in improving, enlarging and endearing the greatest institution in the world, the home."

Association Prayer

In 1936 the State Association Prayer submitted by T. M. Sample of Shelby County was adopted:

"Dear Lord, with thankful hearts we come,
For family and friends and home,
And for the sunshine and the rain,
That ripens fields of golden grain.
'Lord of the harvest,' bless us still;
We are submissive to Thy will;
What e'er our harvests are to be
Our hope and trust are yet with Thee."

This may be sung to the tune: "He Leadeth Me."

Meredith Loan Fund

The 25th Anniversary was celebrated in 1937 by establishing the Mrs. Virginia C. Meredith Loan Fund. In 1941 this fund was combined with a loan fund established in 1932, to provide money for juniors and seniors at Purdue. The fund is supported by contributions from clubs.

The seal of the Extension Homemakers Association has had only a few minor changes since it was designed by Venus Klein of Kosciusko County and officially adopted by the Association in 1933.

Associated Country Women of World

In 1939 the Indiana Home Economics Association became affiliated with the National Home Demonstration Council, and sent a delegate to London for the meeting of the Associated Country Women of the World which was organized in 1930 and meets every three years at various places in the world. Indiana usually has one or more delegates. Mrs. Fred L. McCain of Carroll County, who was President of the Indiana Extension Homemakers Association in 1972-73 was the official delegate to the world meeting at Oslo, Norway in 1971. She also attended other meetings at East Lansing, Michigan in 1968, Perth, Australia in 1974 and Nairobi, Kenya in 1977.

Homemakers Exchangees

In 1962 Mrs. Rosanne Scott, Muncie, was sent to Australia as the first Homemaker Exchangee.

In 1965 Delma P. Maio from Brazil was the first Homemaker Exchangee brought to Indiana.

Both programs have been continued, and several women in Indiana have had an interesting visit to other countries, while many others have had the pleasure of entertaining foreign guests in their homes.

Twin Pines

A campaign which was started in 1947 by the State Home Economics Association raised $30,000 by contributions from Home Economics members throughout the state and in 1953 the money was loaned to establish Twin Pines, a cooperative home for women at Purdue. The loan was repaid in 1971.

Twin Pines, one of about seventeen cooperative housing units on the Purdue campus, is a white frame two-story house located at 322 Waldron St. near the center of the Purdue campus, and has adequate facilities for 27 students.

Membership in a cooperative house is a type of scholarship since it provides inexpensive housing for deserving students who have a definite financial need.

The house is organized on a democratic basis, with officers and members responsible for the total operation of the house. Students share responsibility of household operation, and each student spends an average of 7 to 8 hours per week on duties including meal preparation, house cleaning and maintenance.

Applicants for the house must be residents of Indiana, and must have their application approved by their County Extension Homemakers Association.

CARROLL COUNTY

According to annual reports in the office of the County Agent, Mrs. Taylor Fouts was the first woman in Carroll County to contact Purdue about Home Economics Extension work. The first club in Carroll County was organized in Washington Township in 1917. Some of the early clubs were organized as women's auxiliary to the township Farm Bureau. By the end of 1924 there was one club organized in each township, and a county club was organized. It was organized as a non-profit organization, affiliated with the Cooperative Extension Service of Purdue University, and all women of Carroll County were eligible for membership in a local Home Economics Club.

An article in the constitution states: "The purpose of this association shall be to help make better homes, by promoting social, educational, religious and general welfare of the various communities of the county by the study of Home Economics, and to promote the high ideals which are the foundation for a happy and useful life."

Carroll is one of the few counties in Indiana that has continued to have a club organized in each township. In 1939 Carroll County was one of only six such counties and was honored by having members serve as hostesses at the tea table on January 12 at the Purdue Agricultural Conference. Those who served were: Mrs. Vernie Stephen, Mrs. Imogene Austin, Mrs. Cleon Smith, Mrs. Charles Starkey, Mrs. Miles T. Martin, Mrs. Lloyd Beard, Miss Margaret Mabbitt and Mildred Allen.

COUNTY PRESIDENTS

Those who have served as Carroll County Presidents are: Mrs. Ed Blythe, Mrs. Charles Doctor, Mrs. C. V. Quinn, Mrs. Lawrence Whistler, Mrs. Glen Stair, Mrs. Grace Benner, Mrs. Wilbur Grantham, Mrs. Charles Cunningham, Mrs. Vernie Stephen, Miss Margaret Mabbitt, Mrs. Jesse Yeager, Mrs. Junior Shanks, Mrs. Burton Honan, Mrs. Harry Wilson, Miss Frieda Burgitt, Mrs. Harold Thompson, Mrs. Mary Ratcliff Cox, Mrs. Marie Hanrahan, Mrs. Joseph E. Peterson, Miss Pauline Robeson, Mrs. Fred McCain, Mrs. Wayne Langston, Mrs. Orton Zook, Mrs. Keith Sink, Mrs. Elwood Burkle, Mrs. Wayne Forgey, Mrs. Charles Jones, Mrs. Kenneth Kelly, Mrs. Doyle Miller, Mrs. Junior Snider, Mrs. Dean Appleton, Mrs. Gene Jennings, Mrs. Lewis Mullin, Mrs. Robert Quinn and Mrs. Richard Smith.

In 1979 there were about 650 members in 27 active clubs in Carroll County. The clubs were: Adams, Aim-Hi, Burlington, Carrollton, Carrolltonettes, Classie Lassies, Clay Harmony, Cutler, Deer Creek, Dolly Madison, Double Dozen, Flora, Forty-Niners, Friendly Circle, Goal Getters, Home Endeavor, Jackson, Jefferson, Jr. Home Endeavor, Lib-

Carroll County Home Economics Club officers elected at the Home Economics Achievement Day, October 26, 1950 at the Cutler School. Left to right: Miss Frieda Burgitt, president; Mrs. Ira Fisher, treasurer; Mrs. Harold Thompson, first vice president; Mrs. Harry Wilson, past president; Mrs. Robert Ratcliff, second vice president; Mrs. George Peterson, publicity chairman; Mrs. Roy Bowman, secretary and Miss Jeanne Muller, Home Demonstration Agent.

erty Belles, Modern Homemakers, Modern Mrs., Monroe, Rock Creek, Silver Belles, Sycamores and Washington.

County officers for 1978-79 were: Mrs. Robert Quinn, president; Mrs. Richard Smith, first vice president; Mrs. Charles Childers, second vice president; Mrs. Ted Sidenbender, secretary; Mrs. Robert Hicks, treasurer; Mrs. Tom Goltz, publicity; Mrs. Bill Dittman, Health and Safety and Mrs. Lewis Mullin, past president and advisor.

Officers elected for 1979-80 at the Achievement Day program held on April 4, 1979 were: Mrs. Richard Smith, president; Mrs. Charles Childers, first vice president; Mrs. Robert Hicks, second vice president; Mrs. Tom Goltz, secretary; Mrs. Bill Dittman, treasurer; Mrs. Keith Hollowell, publicity; Mrs. Ed Nelson, Health and Safety and Mrs. Robert Quinn, past president and advisor.

EXTENSION HOMEMAKERS PAST PRESIDENTS CLUB

In 1951 Miss Frieda Burgitt, president of the Carroll County Home Economics Club called a meeting of the past presidents of the club. The first meeting was held at the home of Mrs. Burton Honan in Madison Township and as a result the Carroll County Home Economics Past Presidents Club was formed. For several years the group got together three or four times a year for a cooperative luncheon and then had a special program or just visited in the afternoon. A special money making project by the members was selling Clearjel, a special starch used for thickening fruit pies, which makes the filling clear instead of milky as it is when regular corn starch or flour is used. Proceeds from this project were used to purchase memorial books for deceased members. These books were placed in libraries in the county. Money was also used to send the president of the County Extension Homemakers Club to the State Extension Homemakers meeting at Purdue each year in June.

In recent years meetings have been held only in the spring and fall because of the many activities of the past presidents. Meetings continue to be well attended.

Carroll County is one of the few counties in the state of Indiana that has a Past Presidents Club. Officers elected for the 1979-80 year were: Mrs. Maxine Snider, president and Mrs. Patsy Jennings, secretary treasurer.

PROJECT LESSONS

The Extension Homemaker Clubs sponsor one or more project lessons each year. A specialist from Purdue presents a project lesson to leaders from each club, and these members pass the information to others at their club meetings. Subjects to be used as project lessons each year are selected by a vote of the membership. If a subject receives several votes but not enough to be one of the project lessons, it may be used for a "special interest" lesson at a county meeting, and anyone interested may attend.

Some of the many project lessons have been: Millinery, Wise Use of Leisure Time, Rugs, Pillows, Embroidering, Crocheting, Sewing, Discipline-Develop-

Extension Homemakers officers for Carroll County for the year 1979-80 elected at the Achievement Day program April 4, 1979 to assume office July 1 are, from left, Mrs. Richard Smith, Friendly Circle, president; Mrs. Charles Childers, Modern Mrs., first vice president; Mrs. Robert Hicks, Carrolltonettes, second vice president; Mrs. Tom Goltz, Junior Home Endeavor, secretary; Mrs. Bill Dittman, Junior Home Endeavor, treasurer; Mrs. Keith Hollowell, Home Endeavor, publicity; Mrs. Edward Nelson, Carrolltonettes, health and safety and Mrs. Robert Quinn, Modern Homemakers, past president and advisor.

ing Responsibility, New Trends in Hair Styles, Cleaning and Care of Sewing Machine and Adjusting Tension, Interior Decorating, Picture Arrangements, Legal Rights and Responsibility of Individuals and Family Members, Use of Pork in Family Meals, Weight Control, Facing Family Crisis, Using Leftovers, Sewing with Knits, Information at Time of Death, Personal Touches in the Home and Landscaping Around the Home Including Garden and Flowers, Holiday Decorating, Party Foods, How to Live More Relaxed, Cooperative Buying, Code Practices, Recipes without Sugar-Low Calorie, Recognizing a Swindler, Ladies' Self Defense, and One Dish Meals. For several years the clubs sponsored a demonstration on Flower Making at the County Fair.

Special Interest lessons have included China Painting Series, Kitchen Planning Workshop, Craft Workshop, Refinishing Furniture, Sewing for the Home Series, Crafts from Scraps and Throwaways, Microwave Cooking, Weight Control Series, Vacation Spots in Indiana, Fitting Patterns and Alterations, Beginning Sewing, Advanced Sewing, Tailoring and Men's Wear Workshop.

During World War II the Home Economics Clubs helped sponsor a Canning Center at Delphi. During the year 1944, 5,000 cans of food were processed at the center.

During 1941 the clubs helped collect aluminum, and in 1942 they encouraged more than 1000 families to raise a Victory Garden.

Millinery Project

One of the first projects selected by the clubs was the Millinery project, in which all thirteen township clubs participated in 1924. Eighty seven members of Home Economics Clubs attended a lesson in the spring to learn more about making hats. The project was completed at a Millinery Round-up at the Flora Community Building on January 7, 1925. There were 178 ladies at the covered dish dinner at noon, with a total attendance of 226 for the afternoon program. A playlet "Le Remede" was given with participants being women from every club in the county. Three demonstrations were given by local leaders on Sectional Hat Crowns, Ribbon Trimmings and Brim Making.

Clothing Project

The women took up the Clothing project for 1925 under the supervision of Helen McKinley of Purdue University. At a school held in April, 14 local clubs in the county each had two representatives. During the month 17 meetings were held by the clubs and 250 women received the benefit of this demonstration. One lady remarked: "I have been cutting and fitting clothes nearly all my life, but I learned several new things about altering patterns at the demonstration."

This project was carried on for another year, and was completed at the Annual Achievement Day meeting at the Flora Community Building on January 18, 1927. One hundred and two women braved the wintery blasts and snow drifts to attend the meeting which was in charge of Miss Meta Martin of Purdue. Two playlets were presented, demonstrating the work carried on throughout the year, and a style show was staged.

Nutrition Project

The clubs voted to take the Nutrition project for 1927. Lessons were given by Flora Miller of Purdue. Members had exhibits at the County Fair in Delphi in September, displaying the various well planned meals explained in these project lessons.

The Nutrition project was continued, and it was estimated in 1929 that 559 homes were reached with the project, including 59 women who were not members of a Home Economics Club.

4-H Activities

Each year an exhibit is held during the 4-H Fair showing various items that Extension Homemakers have made. Each club may show an article in each of the two categories chosen. First, second, and third awards are given in each category.

Each year the County Extension Homemakers Club pays expenses for two girls to attend State Fair Girls' School held during the State Fair.

The clubs in the county also pay for girls' 4-H pins which are presented at the achievement programs in the fall.

A private Fashion Revue is held before the 4-H Fair and girls model the garments they have made in their clothing project. At the public Fashion Revue held on Wednesday evening during the County 4-H Fair the County Extension Homemakers Club plans the program, furnishes flowers, decorates the stage, the county president presents ribbons and the Fashion Revue chairman presents flowers to the champion and reserve champion in each division of clothing.

The Fashion Revue is an educational activity which places emphasis on selecting, constructing, selecting accessories and modeling a garment. The objectives are: to encourage 4-H youth to build self confidence and poise; to develop understanding of "self" in order that the individual may select and make clothing which is becoming to the individual and expressive of her personality; to develop skills necessary to plan, select and construct clothing using available resources; to develop the ability to select suitable and becoming accessories; to develop good posture and good grooming habits; to develop the ability to choose from current fashion that which is suitable to the lifestyle and figure characteristics of the individual.

The categories that may be entered in the State Fair 4-H Fashion Revue are: School Wear, Suit or Coat, Dress Up Wear, Formal Wear, Separates and Free Choice.

A County Grand Champion and Reserve Grand Champion is presented with awards from Mr. and Mrs. Myron Beesley and Mr. and Mrs. Fred McCain.

Homemakers Fashion Show

The Homemakers Fashion Show is held each year. Women in clubs make their own garments and model them in a Public Fashion Show held in the spring. They model in State Fair Divisions which are: Classy Lads and Lassies, Mod Mamas and Papas, Gracious Grandmas and Grandpas and Professionals. Categories are: Family Outfits, Dresses, Coat or Suit, Separates, My Choice and Evening Wear. Winners in the county are eligible to go to the state contest and model during the State Fair.

Fall Frolic

All the Carroll County Extension Homemakers Clubs participated in the Fall Frolic which was held at the Camden Community Building in October 1971. The name was later changed to Fall Event.

Each club donated several items of food to be sold at the Country Store. Proceeds were used to meet expenses for the County Extension Homemakers organization. Each club was permitted to show a table of crafts and project lesson ideas.

The Fall Event was an opportunity for all to share ideas for Christmas and other holidays. A Country Store booth at the County Pork Festival in June 1979 replaced the Fall Event.

Valentines

In the 1950's the State Home Demonstration Club decided on a state project in which Home Demonstration Club members donated Valentines and stamps or money to be given to the residents of Riley Hospital and the State School for the Deaf at Indianapolis to send to their friends and relatives.

In 1979 Extension Homemakers Clubs in Carroll County were the only clubs in Indiana still continuing with this project. Each year a committee of officers of the county organization either takes or mails the Valentines and stamps to the children. In 1979 there were 2742 Valentines and $90 in stamps donated by clubs in Carroll County.

JANE AWARD

A resolution passed at the 1971 Annual Meeting of Indiana Extension Homemakers established the Jane Award to identify women in Indiana who have contributed to building leadership in others and who have done things that need to be done without expecting any material reward in return. The first Jane Award was given by the state organization to Janalyce Rouls to express the appreciation of a grateful organization.

"Any women, any age, who is a leader in any community is eligible. Nomination forms are filled out by a leader in the community who is acquainted with the nominee.

Those in Carroll County who have received the Jane Award are: Mrs. Eldon (Wilma) Robeson, 1972; Mrs. Wayne (Helen) Forgey, 1973; Mrs. Junior (Maxine) Snider, 1974; Mrs. Geneva Jones, 1975; Mrs. B. Jesse (Anna Myrle) Zook, 1976; Mrs. Robert (Grace) Deel, 1977; Mrs. Lawrence (Mary Ellen) Johnson, 1978; Mrs. Elwood (Betty) Burkle, 1979 and Mrs. Milton (Pat) Rodgers 1980.

EXTENSION HOMEMAKERS CLUB CHORUS

A Carroll County Home Economics Club Chorus was organized on June 26, 1936 with 13 charter members. Members in November that year were: Mrs. Maude Smith, Mrs. Charles Cunningham, Helen L. Shepard, Lorene Grantham, Gladys Hoffman, Grace Grantham, Mary Mullin, Hazel Coble, Dene Million, Mary E. Hufford, Katherine Sommers, Dora Fossnock, Mabel Fossnock, Mrs. Guy Clauser, Bernadine Maxwell, Lena Hannell, Katherine Weil, Flossie Cox, Lou Greenup, Geneva Reef, Mrs. Hazel Zook, Emma Sheets, Alma Pierce, Ruth Beard, Olive Plank, Agnes Metzger, Ruby Martin, Ruth Edging, Leah Brechbeil and Miriam Fabiarske.

Directors and Accompanists

The first director of the Chorus was Edith Dickinson and the second was Edith Peters. Mrs. Mildred Shanks became director in 1949. Mrs. Daniel (Lucille) Brown directed the Chorus from 1951 until June 30, 1976 and was awarded a plaque for 25 years of service. Mrs. William (Peggy) Martin and Mr. Joseph Spence each served as director for a short time. Mr. Claude Sumner has directed the Chorus since 1978.

Accompanists have been Goldie Mitchell, Mrs. Mark (Mary Catherine) Carter and Joan Smith. Mrs. Carter served from 1950 to 1976, and was awarded a 25 year plaque presented by William E. Luhman, Director of Purdue Musical Organizations, during the Annual Chorus Festival held in the Purdue Music Hall on June 11, 1975. Mrs. Brown accepted the award for Mrs. Carter who was on vacation.

Annual Chorus Festival

The Chorus sings each year at the Annual Chorus Festival at the June meeting of the State Extension Homemakers Association held in the Music Hall at Purdue. In recent years the Chorus has had more than 1000 women from about 40 counties in Indiana.

The Carroll County Chorus sang "Shades of 1964" for their afternoon presentation at the Festival in 1975. Mrs. Glenn Eikenberry was president of the Chorus and Mrs. Daniel (Lucille) Brown was the director. Other members of the Chorus at the Festival were: Vera Spangler, Frances Gross, Blanche Loy, Anna Freitag, Carrie Yerrick, Beth Rodkey, Alta Nagele, Mabel Deel, Barbara Cory, Reba Shanks, Ruth Bordner and Peggy Martin.

Trip to Washington, D.C.

One of the highlights of the Chorus came in 1950 when 40 from Carroll County went with about 500 Chorus members from Indiana to sing on the evening of Indiana Day, July 12, at the Sesquicentennial Celebration in Washington D.C. The Indiana Chorus was led by Albert P. Stewart of Purdue, and they were accompanied on the piano by Governor Henry F. Schricker for part of the program. The 40 who went from Carroll County are named under the picture.

To help raise money for the trip the Home Economics Clubs in the county put on a show "Carroll County Varieties" at the Delphi High School Auditorium on April 13, and at the Flora Community Building on April 14, 1950.

Officers and Members 1979

Officers of the Carroll County Extension Homemakers Chorus for 1978-79 were: Mrs. Naomi Eikenberry, president; Mrs. Mary Loser, vice president; Mrs. Wanda Shonk, secretary treasurer; Claude Sumner, director and Joan Smith, accompanist. Members practice the first and fourth Tuesday afternoons, al-

Carroll County Chorus members and some other people from Carroll County took a trip to Washington, D.C. on July 10, 1950. Left to right, seated: Mrs. Joe St. Amand, Mrs. J. F. Shanks, Mrs. Paul Oyler, Mrs. Russell Oyler, Mrs. Kenneth Cripe, Mrs. Chalmer Loman, Miss Elsie Parker, Mrs. Wilma Parker, May Rhine, Mrs. Joe Snyder, Mrs. Truman Plank, Mrs. Miles Martin, Mrs. Ross Downham, and Mrs. Blanche Hinkle. Standing: Mrs. Rex Day, Mrs. Ruth Yocum, Mrs. Ross Eikenberry, Mrs. Flo Sheets, Mrs. Robert Jordan, Mrs. Mae Frantz, Mrs. Daniel Brown, Mrs. Herbert Jervis, Miss Eleanor Simmons, Mrs. Roy Bowman, Miss Mildred Reynolds, Mrs. William Bordner, Mrs. Robert Reef, Mrs. Raymond Nicoll, Raymond Nicoll, Mrs. Levi Furst, Mrs. Martha Ginn, Mrs. Edgar Fountain, Sr., Mrs. Clark Metsger, Mrs. Fred Rodkey, Mrs. Orvel Campbell, Miss Reba Shanks, Mrs. Charles Hendrix, Mrs. Mabel Stout, Mrs. Murtie Rinehart, and Mrs. Flora Taylor.

Farm Bureau Quartet singing at the Home Economics Variety Show April 13, 1950. Left to right: Howard Smith, Reuben Smith, Orvel Schock and Charles Pearson.

"Trio and the Nose" with Mrs. Paul Oyler, Mrs. Kenneth Cripe and Mrs. Russell Oyler at the County Home Economics Variety Show at Delphi and Flora April 13 and 14, 1950.

Fredona Lesh and Charlene Johnson tap danced at the County Home Economics Variety Show at Delphi and Flora April 13 and 14, 1950.

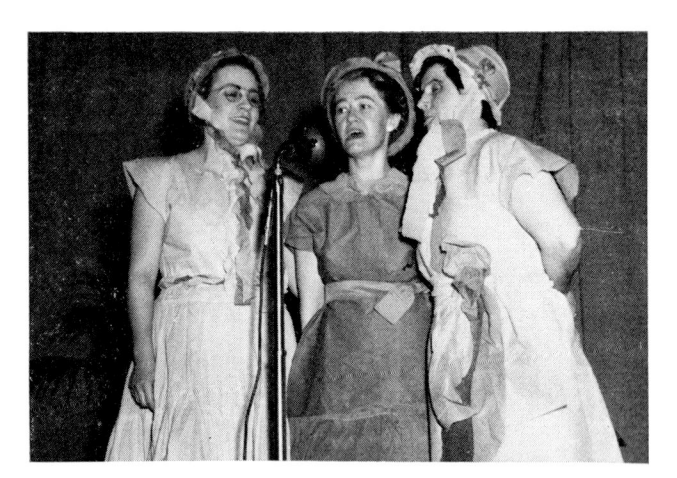

Carroll County people who were present at the Home Economics Variety Show held at Delphi and Flora, April 13 and 14, 1950, enjoyed an evening of outstanding entertainment. Proceeds from this show were used to help defray expenses of chorus members on their trip to Washington, D.C. in July. Some of the participants were "The Apple Sisters," left to right: Mrs. John Roth, Mrs. Carl Draper, and Mrs. Joe St. Amand.

ternating between Delphi and Flora, with Mr. Sumner as director.

Members in the Chorus in 1979 living in Carroll County were: Ruth Barnhart, Carol Brewster, Ruth Bordner, Carolyn Burkle, Phyllis Cook, Mabel Deel, Naomi Eikenberry, Pat Frey, Frances Gross, Jane Kearns, Mary Loser, Blanche Loy, Donna McCarty, Frances Newhouser, Alta Nagele, Glenda Oyler, Beth Rodkey, Reba Shanks, Wanda Shonk, Vera Spangler, Frieda Urban, Terry Wine, Ruth White and Carrie Yerrick. Members living in White County were: Margaret Anliker, Eleanor Biddle, Mary Lane and Jean Rancatore.

Originally the Chorus included only members of a Home Economics Club. Since 1961 membership has been open to any woman who likes to sing and the name was changed to Choral Club.

LOCAL EXTENSION HOMEMAKERS CLUBS

Many of the early clubs were organized as an auxiliary of the Township Farm Bureau, and only a wife of a FB member was eligible to belong. Membership dues were $1 per year, and meetings were held at the same time and place as the Township FB meeting. When the Farm Bureau membership was changed to include the entire family, the auxiliaries reorganized as Home Economics Clubs and any interested woman could belong.

Most of the clubs that have been organized in the county are still active. A few have become associate clubs, meet only a few times during the year and don't have project lessons. One club continued only as a social club.

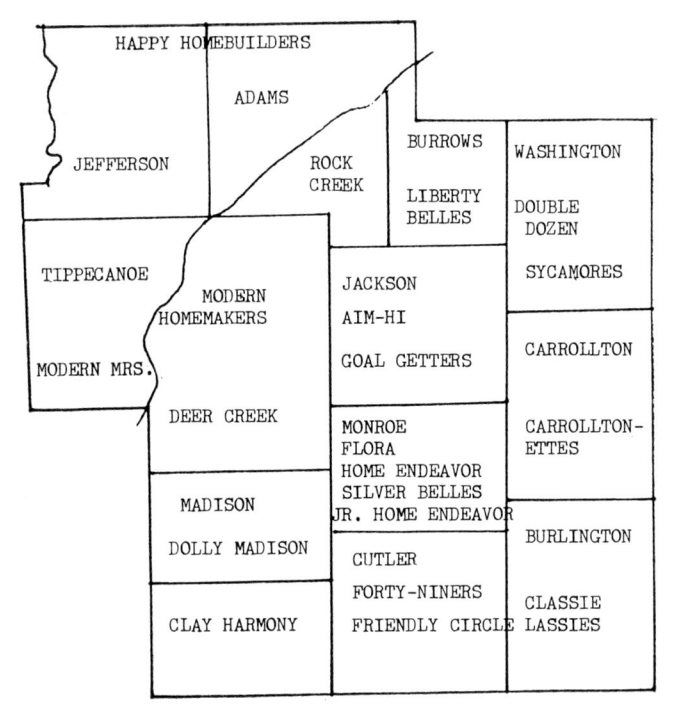

Carroll County map showing location of 31 Extension Homemaker Clubs.

Active clubs have regular meetings and participate in the many project lessons sponsored by the county club. Local clubs help pay for pins for 4-H members who complete their projects in Girl's 4-H Clubs. All clubs participate in the Extension Homemakers exhibit at the County 4-H Fair. Most clubs help in the Valentine project, and other local community activities.

Members of clubs gave food for participants in the first Carroll County Diabetes Bike-a-Thon sponsored by the American Diabetes Association on October 7, 1979.

Complete records are not available on the early history of all the clubs in the county, but the following reports on 31 clubs are listed in alphabetical order.

Adams

In January 1925, a number of ladies met at the Adams Township school building and organized the Township Home Economics Club with the help of Miss Lella Gaddis of Purdue and Mrs. Ed Blythe of Delphi. Officers the first year were: Mrs. Charles (Mary) Hoover, president; Mrs. R. H. (Dene) Million, vice president; and Mrs. Levi Blickenstaff, secretary-treasurer.

Meetings were held for about three years and then, because of lack of interest, were dropped until the club was reorganized in February 1931, under the direction of Mrs. Lawrence Whistler. Officers elected were: Blanche Reiff, president; Dene Million, vice president and Leone McManus, secretary-treasurer.

The club has carried on many projects and activities. In 1957 it was the first club in the county to entertain a group of patients from Logansport State Hospital. Other activities have included support of many 4-H projects, gifts to servicemen, support of United Fund, Red Cross, IFYE and many other community projects. In 1979 the club donated $100 for the new 4-H Building Fund.

When the White County Memorial Hospital was built, the club members sponsored a drive for funds for the Hospital which amounted to more than $2000, from people in Adams Township and the club was awarded a bronze plaque which hangs in the foyer of the hospital. A few years later the club had raised enough money from special projects to make an additional $5000 contribution to White County Memorial Hospital.

In 1979 the club sponsored its 34th annual bus trip. They went to Indianapolis where they attended a musical at Beef and Boards. Some areas visited in former years included Chicago, Detroit, Frankfort, Kokomo, Holland, Michigan; Amishville at Berne, Mammoth Cave, Parke County and Brown County.

Many members have held offices for a number of years. Two charter members, Blanche Hershberger and Leone McManus, are still active in the club.

Officers for 1979-80 were: Mrs. Evelyn Crowell, president; Mrs. Pete Rodgers, 1st vice president; Mrs. Doyle Miller, 2nd vice president; Mrs. Beth Miller, secretary; Rhonda Long, treasurer and Mrs. Norma Peterson, reporter.

Aim-Hi

The Aim-Hi Club was organized at a meeting on December 21, 1948 at the home of Mrs. Edwin Wise of Camden. Officers elected were: Mrs. James E. Minich, president; Mrs. Dallas Wise, vice president; Mrs. Edwin Wise, secretary and Mrs. Robert Yerkes, treasurer. There were 29 charter members, and total membership was limited to 36.

The club supported many local projects and canvassed the town of Camden for the United Fund Drive in 1978.

Officers in 1979-80 were: Mrs. Glen Sell, president; Mrs. Dean George, 1st vice president; Mrs. Richard Kendall, 2nd vice president; Mrs. John Rodgers, secretary; Mrs. Ray French, treasurer and Mrs. Steven Ashby, reporter.

Burlington

On February 20, 1923, the Burlington Home Economics Club was organized at a Township Farm Bureau meeting at the school. The ladies organized into "Women's Auxiliary of Farm Bureau" with 13 members. Dues were $1 per year with money being used to help the Farm Bureau.

In May the name was changed to Ladies Home Economics Club. At the same time the dues were lowered to 25 cents per year. Mrs. Clarence Johnson was the first president.

In 1926 the club meeting place was changed from the school to homes of members. The highest membership in the club was 64 in 1926. The club has used all project lessons offered by the Extension Service.

The club also helped on the Burlington Centennial celebration in 1978. Pearl Garrison, 89, was presented a potted plant on Mothers' Day as the oldest member in 1978.

In 1979 there were 21 members, including Pearl Garrison and Beth Rodkey who were charter members.

The 1979-80 officers were: Mrs. Carl (Ina) Milburn, president; Edith Bell, 1st vice president; Mrs. Loris (Esther) Stout, 2nd vice president; Mrs. Harold (Eileen) Pullen, secretary and reporter and Mrs. Lloyd (Mary) Williams, treasurer.

Burrows

A club was organized on May 17, 1919 at the home of Mrs. Ed Heddrick in Burrows. Officers were: Mrs. Della Wagoner, president; Mrs. Helen Scott, vice president and Isey Lowe, secretary treasurer. It was first called "Community Club" and had 50 members in 1920.

The Delphi paper for January 14, 1922 reported that the Burrows Home Economics Club furnished hot lunches to Burrows school children who did not go home for lunch.

The club disbanded in 1962 and three years later the Liberty Belles Club was formed to take its place.

Carrollton

The first meeting in Carrollton Township was in the summer of 1921, at the home of Mrs. D. J. McCain. Officers were: Mrs. Charles McCloskey, president; Mrs. Warren Todd, vice president and Mrs. Jasper Quinn, secretary treasurer. It was reorganized on March 25, 1925 with 33 members. Mrs. Russell Zartman was elected president.

In 1978 the club donated money for Valentines for Riley Hospital and cheer cards were sent to shut-ins throughout the year. Iris McCain gave a report of Homemakers Conference and showed how to display the American flag. Jane Kearns demonstrated how to make silk flowers. Special meetings were held at the Dinnerbell Restaurant at Burlington.

In 1979-80 the club was an associate club. Officers were: Mrs. Ethel Landes, president; Mrs. George Flora, 1st vice president; Miss Margaret Mabbitt, 2nd vice president; Mrs. Robert Wingard, secretary; Mrs. Susie Landes, treasurer and Mrs. Edith Barber, reporter.

Carrolltonettes

The Carrolltonettes Home Economics Club was organized in May 1952, by a committee consisting of Mrs. Fred McCain, Mrs. Charles Meade and Miss Margaret Mabbitt. Mrs. Jr. Snider sponsored the club. The first meeting was held in June 1952 at the home of Mrs. Meade who chose the name for the club. Mrs. McCain was the first president and there were 18 members.

In 1978 the Carrolltonettes donated money to the Carrollton 4-H Club to help sponsor a 4-H Queen candidate at the Fair and sold pecans as a money-making project. The club members helped a family in Pittsburg at Christmas by donating canned goods, clothing and toys.

Officers for 1979-80 were: Mrs. Craig Martin, president; Mrs. Ed Nelson, 1st vice president; Mrs. Ernest Minich, secretary; Mrs. William Seward, treasurer and Mrs. Roy L. Ousley, reporter.

Classie Lassies

This club was organized in 1970. The first officers were: Carol Schwarzkopf, president; Esther Braden, vice president; Loretta Lambert, secretary; Phyllis Miller, treasurer and Barbara Erwin, reporter. There were seven of the charter members in the club in 1979.

The club flower is the carnation, club colors are blue, green and gold, and the club motto is "Look Inward, Look Outward, Look Upward." Members sold subscriptions for Farm Wife News at a Farm Progress Show.

Officers for 1979-80 were: Delores Wertz, president; Mrs. Ron Cottrell, 1st vice president; Mrs. Mark Smith, 2nd vice president; Mrs. Bill Northcutt, secretary; Mrs. Joe Scott, treasurer and Mrs. Jim Avery, reporter.

Clay Harmony

The Clay Township Club was organized at a Township Farm Bureau meeting at the Owasco School on February 14, 1921 as an auxiliary to the

Township Farm Bureau. With 19 charter members, the club met every two weeks on the same night as the Farm Bureau.

On March 31, 1921 they had a demonstration on "Dress Forms" and five forms were made then. Eventually 21 forms were made.

On January 18, 1933 a meeting was held at the home of Mrs. Earl Bolinger and the club was reorganized as the Clay Harmony Club. Officers elected were: Mrs. Orpha Miller Goslee, president; Mrs. Mary Hufford, vice president; Mrs. Ruth Stong, secretary and Mrs. Ruth Metzger, treasurer. Meetings were held in the afternoon in the home of members.

The club has sponsored many interesting trips including Chicago, Michigan City Prison, Friendship Gardens, Dunes Park, Murat Temple at Indianapolis, Women's Prison, Jim Gerard Show, Schools for the Deaf and Blind, Goodwill Industries at Indianapolis, the Journal and Courier Plant and Vogue Cleaners at Lafayette, Twin Pines at Purdue, a two-day trip to Detroit, Michigan and Canada, the Covered Bridge Festival in Parke County and Nashville in Brown County.

In 1979 Mrs. Orpha Goslee, an active member of the club, was the only surviving charter member of the original club.

Officers for 1979-80 were: Mrs. Robert Shultheis, president; Mrs. Ruth White, 1st vice president; Mrs. John Burkle, 2nd vice president; Mrs. Maurice Eller, secretary; Mrs. Orville Shultheis, treasurer and Mrs. Meredith Greenwood, reporter.

Cutler

A club was organized at Cutler in 1920 with 20 charter members and dues of $1 per year. Mrs. Ed Stephens was the first president.

Meetings were held each month either in the home of a member or at the Cutler Presbyterian Church. Project lessons were given by project leaders but in more recent years programs for the meetings were given on current topics of interest to the members. In June, 1979 a program was given on the Flag. The 19 members in 1979 were all over 60 years of age.

A special activity one year was to pack and send 66 Christmas boxes to boys and girls in service. Another time members helped a family who had lost their home by fire. Special music was planned for each meeting.

Officers for 1979-80 were: Mrs. William (Ruth) Bordner, president; Naomi Sparks, 1st vice president; Alice Pope, 2nd vice president; Hazel Draper, secretary; Daisy Webb, treasurer and Florence Porter, reporter.

Deer Creek Township

Deer Creek Township was organized in January 1924, at a meeting at the Courthouse with County Agent H. E. Ackerson. Miss Nellie Flanangham was the demonstrator from Purdue and had been giving lessons to other organized clubs.

Edith Holmes was elected president; Nora Shortridge, vice president; Ruby Martin, secretary treasurer; Elsie Pearson and Lydia Watson, project leaders. Others present were: Edna Menaugh, Nellie Cree and Zena Shelley. They decided to meet the second Thursday in February and 44 attended the February meeting.

Deer Creek Township Club women have continued to meet each second Thursday afternoon, have received project lessons, helped with 4-H, given Valentines for Riley Hospital, had auctions, invited other club members as guests, had special programs and members have had exhibits at the 4-H Fair.

For several years the members of the Deer Creek Township Club furnished food for a cooperative dinner for those who reside in the Carroll County Home the second Thursday in August. The Delphinium Girl's 4-H Club provided devotions and a program for the July Home Economics meetings.

Officers for 1979-80 were: Helen Anderson, president; Mary Benjamin, 1st vice president; Clara Sims, 2nd vice president; Elizabeth Peterson, secretary; Irene DeWinton, treasurer and Gertrude Sheets, reporter.

Dolly Madison

The Dolly Madison Club in Madison Township was organized at a meeting on March 11, 1959 in the home of Pearl Mays, and was named after the famous wife of President James Madison. The club limited their membership to 18 so that they could meet in homes. The constitution has since been amended to allow unlimited membership. Officers elected for the new club were: Mrs. Carl (Joan) Mays, president; Mrs. Don (Marlene) Ramsey, vice president; Mrs. Don (Maxine) Hathaway, secretary and Mrs. Orville (Frances) Hathaway, treasurer.

Mrs. Carl Mays is the only charter member still in the club.

Five of the members in 1979 were daughters or daughters-in-law of women who had been active members. Husbands are guests at the March Anniversary Dinner Party held at a restaurant each year. Guest Night was traditionally held in May when other clubs were entertained. A "forgotten patient" at the Logansport State Hospital was remembered each month and was given Christmas and Birthday gifts. Food articles were brought to the December meeting to be given to a needy family. For several years a Tupperware Party has been held in October and this has been a consistent money-making project. A family picnic was held each summer and a tour for members and guests was planned each year. Some of the places visited were: Logansport State Hospital, Indianapolis School for the Blind, Colonial Bakery, Tippecanoe Upholstery, Seiferts Potato Chips in Fort Wayne, and Stewarts Furniture in Frankfort.

Although the twelve charter members were all young homemakers from Madison Township, the members in 1979 were from several townships and ranged in age from grandmothers to new brides.

Officers for 1979-80 were: Mrs. Carol (Fern) Walters, president; Mrs. Emmett (Pat) Frey, vice president; Mrs. Allan (Linda) Eller, secretary; Mrs. William (Linda) Graves, treasurer and Mrs. Dan (Cindy) Gottschalk, reporter.

Double Dozen

The Double Dozen Club of Washington Township was organized on February 12, 1959 and got its name from the fact that it was the 24th club organized in the county. The motto is: "Never Content Yourself by Doing Second Best." Colors are yellow and white and the flower is the yellow snapdragon.

The first officers were: Virginia Marcellino, president; Margaret Yeakley, vice president; Merila Downham, secretary; Elizabeth Downham, treasurer and Helen Forgey, reporter.

There were 24 charter members and those still active in the club in 1979 were: Perrietta Appleton, Betty Bell, Elizabeth Downham, Helen Forgey, Marilyn Guckien, Marilyn Hile, Flora Bell McKinney, Virginia Marcellino, Mary O'Donnell, Louann Starkey and Margie Yeakley.

The club had many projects including the following: it contributed to the Retarded Children School at Delphi, supported local 4-H clubs, contributed to Carrollton Kindergarten, helped with various drives, sent Valentines to Riley Hospital, donated Christmas gifts for patients and participated in the "Adopt-a-patient" program at Logansport State Hospital, donated a picnic table to the County Park at Deer Creek, helped with county Fashion Shows and took many trips to points of interest. The club has had two county Home Economics presidents, Helen Forgey, 1970 and Perrietta Appleton, 1975-76; two townships 4-H leaders, Helen Forgey and Lona Yeakley and two Jane Award winners, Wilma Robeson and Helen Forgey.

Officers for 1979-80 were: Mrs. John Guckien, president; Mrs. George Marcellino, 1st vice president; Mrs. Bill Dyke, secretary; Mrs. George Downham, treasurer and Mrs. Eldon Robeson, reporter.

Flora

Nine women met on July 30, 1937 at the home of Mrs. Otis Myer to organize Flora's first Home Economics Club under the Purdue Extension Program. They were: Mrs. Walter Mitchell, Mrs. Edward Colvin, Mrs. Fred McPherson, Mrs. Wilbert Kenrick, Mrs. Ross Briggs, Mrs. Paul Burns, Mrs. Clarence Payne, Mrs. Lloyd Mocherman and Mrs. Otis Meyer. The club had 39 members at the end of the year.

The first officers were: Mrs. Wilbert Kenrick, president; Mrs. Lee Fetterhoff, 1st vice president; Mrs. A. A. Flora, 2nd vice president; Mrs. Lloyd Mocherman, secretary and Mrs. Otis Myer, treasurer. In 1979 these officers were all living, and Mrs. Mocherman was an active member of the club.

During World War II the club members collected books for servicemen, made soldier kits, bought stamps and bonds, sponsored U.S.O. drives and was aided with some of its food problems by the assistance of the Emergency War Food Assistant, Reba J. S. Briggs.

At the August 1978 meeting a Show and Tell program was given by members who brought an antique article and told special things about the article. In the fall 84 gifts were collected for the Mental Health Association to use as Christmas gifts for patients in the Logansport State Hospital and local nursing homes.

Officers for 1979-80 were: Helen Dobler, president; Mrs. Blanche Loy, vice president; Neva Hundley, secretary; Ruth Wilson, treasurer and Florence Mitchell, reporter.

Forty Niners

The Forty Niners Club in Democrat Township was organized by ten members who met in the home of Mrs. Doyle (Juanita) Jervis in December 1949. They elected Mrs. Kenneth (Ann Louise) Kelly, president; Mrs. Harold (Alberta) Bowen, 1st vice president; Mrs. Herbert (Grace) Jervis, 2nd vice president; Mrs. Harold (Dorothy) Allen, secretary; Mrs. Max (Katherine) Watkins, treasurer and Mrs. Harold (Phyllis) Cook, publicity.

In their first year as a club, they were host to the County Achievement Day held on October 26, 1950 at the Cutler High School.

In 1978 Mr. Koehler of Koehler Bros. Nursery spoke at guest night and Mrs. Lee Eckert of the Basket Shop showed a variety of baskets. Diane Stout was winner in her category at the County Homemakers Fashion Show and went on to win second at the State Fashion Show. In July the girls from the local 4-H Club held a dress revue at the club meeting. Dan Brickey, a physician's assistant, gave an informative lesson on household first aid.

Officers for 1979-80 were: Mrs. Dale Huffer, president; Mrs. Howard Egelhoff, 1st vice president; Mrs. Gayle Stout, 2nd vice president; Mrs. Henry (Vera) Shepherd, secretary; Mrs. Vernon (Mildred) Hausenfluck, treasurer and Mrs. Ric (Vickie) Ayres, reporter.

Friendly Circle

The Friendly Circle Club was organized in June, 1950. Their motto is "Work and Win", colors are yellow and green and the flower is the yellow rose.

Charter members still in the club in 1979 were: Winifred Landes, Frances Pullen, Rose Pullen and Margaret Sibbitt.

Special projects have included contributions to Mental Health and a Christmas party each year. Trips outside the county each year have included visits to Purdue Kitchens, National Homes, Kroger Egg Plant at Wabash, Honeywell Foundation, American Container Company, and the Benjamin Harrison Home. The club celebrated its 25th anniversary dinner in 1975 at Bachelor Run Church and Becky Eikenberry was guest speaker. The club also participated in the Bicentennial Program at the Little Theater at Delphi High School and won second place.

In 1978 club members gave a program at the Brethren Home and served cookies and punch to the residents. The local EMT's gave a program and showed the members the inside of an ambulance.

Officers for 1979-80 were: Mrs. Jim Allbaugh, president; Debbie Hood, vice president; Rosanna Fife, secretary; Donnabell Myer, treasurer and Pat Witter, reporter.

Goal Getters

The third Home Extension Club in Jackson Township was formed in October 1969. Justine Crume, president of the Aim-Hi Club, opened the first meeting. Officers elected for 1970 were: Jody Patty, president; Charlotte Wallace, 1st vice president; Janis Hanaway, 2nd vice president; Bonnie Richter, secretary and Suanne Jones, treasurer. A total of 22 members were in the club in 1970.

A committee composed of Sandy Keen, Mary Walters and Suanne Jones selected the name of "Goal Getters" for the club. The motto chosen was: "Keep Your Eye on the Goal." Mint green and yellow were chosen for the club colors and the yellow rose as the flower.

Guest night was held once a year. At Christmas the members went caroling and took boxes or baskets to the Senior Citizens or shut-ins. In 1978 "Our Senior Citizens" was a special project. Members took favors to them at their lunchrooms, took them to Dr. appointments, beauty shop appointments, grocery shopping and other errands. One Saturday members washed windows for the Senior Citizens who asked for help. In May 1978 Senior Citizens were invited as special guests and all enjoyed a delicious supper and played Bingo.

In 1979 there were nineteen members, including the following charter members: Nancy Biederwolf, Dorothy Frye, Cecilia Griffey, Janis Hanaway, Melodie Hodges, Birdie Lake and Kay Spence.

Officers for 1979-80 were: Mrs. William Lake, president; Mrs. Ernest Spence, 1st vice president; Mrs. Gary Penn, 2nd vice president; Mrs. George Hanaway Jr., secretary; Mrs. Paul Wedlhuizen, treasurer and Mrs. Dale Griffey, reporter.

Happy Homebuilders

A group of women from Jefferson and Adams Townships met at the home of Mrs. Russell (Margaret) Pearson to organize a Home Economics Club in 1950. Mrs. Paul (Louise) Smith was elected president.

Some of the charter members were: Mrs. Russell (Margaret) Pearson, Mrs. Paul (Joan) Mikesell, Annabelle Hanna, Mrs. Cloid (Ruth) Crawn, Martha Hankins, Mrs. Paul (Louise) Smith and Mrs. David (Betty Lou) Smith.

The club met in the evening and since most members had small children husbands were used as baby sitters and this gave the women a night out.

Some women from White County also became members of the club later.

Some of the other women who served as presidents were: Mrs. Joe (Louann) Starkey, Mrs. Don Hankins, Mrs. Alden Schroeder, Mrs. John D. Coble, Mrs. Joe Hildebrandt and Mrs. Vicki Criswell.

The club was very active for many years with the membership as high as 25. At the time it was disbanded in 1975 there were 6 members who were: Vickie Criswell, president; Betty Ward, secretary; Ruthie Crawn, treasurer and Ruth Crawn, Doris Crawn and Marjorie Miller.

The club sponsored trips to Cincinnati, Indianapolis, Lafayette and Kokomo, helped take older folks to the election polls to vote, helped police the girl's rest room at the 4-H Fair, helped in the Country Store in the fall and other county Home Economics projects.

The last business meeting was held at the home of Mrs. John (Betty) Ward on November 12, 1975 when members voted to stop meeting as a club and encouraged each member to join another club. The money left in the treasury was used to purchase Christmas gifts for the Mental Health program.

The members and their husbands had a farewell supper as a club on December 27, 1975 at the Sportsman at Monticello.

Home Endeavor

The Home Endeavor Club at Flora was organized at the home of Mrs. Charles Gibson on October 5, 1945 by Mrs. Marion Gibson, president of the Monroe Township Club; Mrs. Mark Carter, president of the Flora Club; Mrs. Mildred Fouts, County Home Economics Club president; Mrs. Monroe Meade, a friend of Mrs. Fouts; Mrs. Reba J. S. Briggs, Emergency War Food Agent and Mrs. Joe (Cora Zell) St. Amand who was a former Home Economics teacher and later was County Home Demonstration Agent.

The first officers were: Laura Dillman, president; Mrs. Jack Voorhees, vice president; Mrs. Charles Gibson, secretary; Annabelle Smith, treasurer and Mrs. Jack Smith, publicity chairman.

Home Endeavor was suggested for the name of the club by Mrs. Robert Sibray. The club flower chosen was the pink rose and the colors gray and pink. Lessons were given on Pressure Cookers, Wall and Floor Coverings, Sugar Stretchers and Lampshades by Mrs. Cora Zell St. Amand. Social Diseases and Childbirth were discussed by Mrs. Esther Gregg, County Health Nurse.

Flea Markets and White Elephants Sales have been used as money making projects. Donations have been made to the EMT Ambulance Service, Santa Fund, 4-H Foundation, Meals on Wheels, County Rest Room at the Flora Park, Senior Citizens and Valentines and stamps to Riley Hospital.

Programs have included guests speakers, and reports on trips by members. One program was a traditional Coming Out party for a Mexican girl. Husbands of members were guests at some meetings.

Officers in 1979-80 were: Mrs. Keith Hollowell, president; Mrs. Russell Hicks, vice president; Mrs. Virginia Gibson, secretary; Mrs. Edna King, treasurer and Mrs. Leroy Matson, reporter.

Jackson

The Jackson Township Club was organized early in 1922 with Mrs. Guy Coplen, president; Mrs. Grover Sink, secretary and Mrs. Ross Wagoner, treasurer.

In 1978 the club contributed to the Camden Youth Program, the County Chorus, and donated stamps and Valentines to Riley Hospital.

A book was placed in the Camden Library in memory of Inah Caldwell, one of the members.

Money for projects was raised by an auction of food, plants and miscellaneous items.

The County Nurse, Thelma Trent, presented a program on breast cancer. Several members of the club presented reports on places of interest they had seen during the year.

Officers in 1979-80 were: Mrs. Claude Wise, president; Mrs. Raymond Rueger, vice president; Mrs. Mary Dittman, secretary; Mrs. Fedora Harrison, treasurer and Mrs. Edith Patty, reporter.

Jefferson

The Jefferson Township Club was organized by County Agent A. L. Hodgson in the fall of 1920 at a meeting at the Oak Grove Church, as an auxiliary to the Township Farm Bureau, and met at the same time as the Farm Bureau.

First officers were: Mrs. Bill Coppock, president; Mrs. W. G. Million, vice president and Mrs. Tom Armstrong, secretary-treasurer.

In 1979 the members held all day meetings at homes and had a carry in dinner or ate at a restaurant. They did not receive project lessons but had special programs.

Officers in 1979-80 were: Mrs. Charles Mummert, president; Florence Redding, 1st vice president; Mary Kilmer, 2nd vice president; Elnora Scott, secretary; Eleene Shaffer, treasurer and Gladys Roth, reporter.

Junior Home Endeavor

The Junior Home Endeavor Home Demonstration Club was organized on October 12, 1970 on the twenty-fifth anniversary of the Home Endeavor Club by Mrs. Charles Gibson, Mrs. Lowell Johnson and Mrs. Tom Cowell.

Officers installed by Mrs. Gibson and Mrs. Cowell were: Mrs. Lowell Johnson, president; Mrs. Tom Click, vice president; Mrs. Ed Stephens, recording secretary; Mrs. Stanley Langston, treasurer and Mrs. John Angle, publicity chairman.

The new club started with eleven members and gained four new members in a year.

The new club was presented by Mrs. Gibson to the older club as a surprise at their twenty-fifth anniversary party.

Four charter members of the new club had mothers or mothers-in-law who were charter members of the older club.

Members and their mothers were: Mrs. Lowell Johnson, Mrs. Richard Johnson; Mrs. James Reed, Mrs. Charles Gibson; Mrs. Ed Stephens, Mrs. Robert Sibray; and Mrs. Bill Dittman, Mrs. Junior King. Mrs. Weldon Hicks, a charter member of the new club was also a sister to Mrs. Gibson and Mrs. Johnson.

In May of 1978 members rode their bikes from Flora to Delphi, toured the museum, had a picnic and rode back to Flora. In August they had a progressive supper and sold helium balloons at the Fair and Old Settlers. During the year the club supported many community activities, had project lessons, parties and special programs including one on Women and Patriotism by Mrs. Anne Briggs.

Officers for 1979-80 were: Mrs. James Cripe, president; Mrs. Lowell Johnson, vice president; Mrs. Terry Kinzer, secretary and Mrs. Bill Dittman, treasurer.

Liberty Belles

Ten women met with Kay Ayler, HDA and Mrs. Hazel Zook at the home of Mrs. Maxine Snider on December 1, 1965 to organize a club at Burrows. They elected Mrs. Maxine Snider, president; Mrs. Catherine Martin, vice president; Mrs. Amy Snipes, secretary and Mrs. Mildred Been, treasurer.

The colors chosen were red, white and blue and the flower the red rose.

A $25 Savings Bond was cashed along with $3.21 from the Burrows Home Demonstration Club, which was disbanded in 1962, and put in the treasury for use in starting the Liberty Belles Club. Seventeen members were in the club in 1966.

The club has had several projects since its organization. An auction was held in 1967 with the proceeds going to the Carroll County Retarded Children's Organization. In 1968 contributions to Dollars for Scholars, Cancer Fund and Heart Fund were made, and in 1969-70 Christmas boxes were mailed to men in the service and cheer plates were given to shut-ins. In 1971 all club members participated in the County Chorus Talent Night and won second place. Members cleaned roadsides with the help of 4-H Clubs in Liberty and Rock Creek Townships and hosted a Mother-Daughter guest night. Also in 1971, Peggy Martin won first place in her group at the County Homemakers Style Show. In 1972 secret pals were drawn for the first time. Club members entertained husbands twice in 1973 and had a family picnic in August. In 1974 Mary Bickett won first in Mod-Mama's Family Outfits at the County Homemakers Style Show. Mrs. Maxine Snider was elected County President and received the Jane Award. Valentines were given for distribution to the Deaf School and Riley Hospital at Indianapolis.

Officers in 1979-80 were: Mrs. Raymond Gardner, president; Mrs. Robert Heckard, vice president; Mrs. Richard Rinehart, secretary; Mrs. Paul Snipes, treasurer and Mrs. Herbert Been, reporter.

Madison

The Madison Club was organized in March 1925, as an auxiliary of the Township Farm Bureau. There were 23 members with Lena Hannell, president and Zelda Maxwell, secretary treasurer.

The club was reorganized as an Extension Homemakers Club and in about 1974 became an Associate Club. Since then the club has been meeting seven or eight times each year for social gatherings with varied and special programs.

The club members have entertained their husbands each year with a meal at a nice eating place followed with entertainment. In 1977 the club celebrated their 25th year of these parties.

For almost as many years the club has had an annual breakfast each June in a members home, with many varied and interesting programs.

The membership in 1979 was 16. The largest number of members at any time was approximately 48.

Officers in 1979-80 were: Mrs. Tom (Chestine) Witter, president; Mrs. Truman (Evelyn) Zook, vice president and Mrs. John (Anna) Maxwell, secretary treasurer.

Modern Homemakers

The Modern Homemakers Club was organized on February 5, 1948 at a meeting at the Extension Office in the Post Office at Delphi.

Cora Zell St. Amand, HDA; Mrs. Paul Sims, president, and Mrs. Earl Newell and Mrs. Joseph E. Peterson, members of the Deer Creek Township Club helped organize the new club.

The motto adopted by the club was: "Be a Good

Members of the Modern Homemakers Home Economics Club at a meeting in 1948, left to right front row: Geneva Todd, Opal Campbell, Bernadine Eastwood, Elva Randle, Lura Cain; middle row; Margaret Burkle, Thelma Sines, Jane Smith, Nadine McCarty, Mabel Thomson, Gladys Landis; back row: Pauline Humbarger, Maxine Humbarger, Lucile Quinn, Rachel Haggard, Mabel Weaver, Marjorie Newell and Dorothy Myers.

Homemaker, not Just a Housekeeper." Colors chosen were salmon and wedgewood blue and the flower was the gladiolus.

The first officers were: Margaret Burkle, president; Annabelle Coffey, vice president; Geneva Todd, secretary and Nadine McCarty, treasurer. Project leaders were Mabel Thomson and Bernadine Eastwood.

The first regular meeting was held February 25, 1948 in the home of Mrs. Earl Newell with 18 members present. The first project lesson on "What's New in Household Equipment" was given by Doris Peterson of the Deer Creek Township Club.

There were 26 charter members, and total membership was limited to 36. The new club won the attendance prize in the county for their first year, 1948 and again in 1949.

Members in 1979 who had been in the club since 1948 included Louella Limp, Gladys Landis, Dorothy Myers, Lucile Quinn, Helen Roth and Mabel Weaver.

This was one of the first evening clubs and husbands were used as baby sitters.

The club anniversary was observed each year with a dinner meeting usually with guests. August and December are also "party" meetings.

Officers in 1979-80 were: Mrs. Joe (Mary Catherine) Ward, president; Mrs. Albert (Margaret) Burkle, vice president; Mrs. Devon (Maxine) Yoder, secretary; Mrs. Jack (Augusta) Burkhalter, treasurer and Mrs. Eugene (Mabel) Weaver, reporter.

Modern Mrs.

The Modern Mrs. Club was organized on January 4, 1949 by Miss Frieda Burgitt, Mrs. Rose Morrison, Mrs. Bessie Swaim, and Mrs. Madie Thompson assisted by Mrs. Cora Zell St. Amand, HDA.

Sixteen members joined the new club and elected Jean Fountain, president; Mary Ratcliff, vice president; Phyllis Steinman, secretary and Marion Myers treasurer.

Officers for 1979-80 were: Mrs. Charles Myers, president; Mrs. Edna Cedarquist, 1st vice president; Mrs. Don Huffman, 2nd vice president; Mrs. Harold Wilson, secretary; Mrs. Ed Littman, treasurer and Mrs. Dale Craig, reporter.

Monroe

A club was organized in Monroe Township in 1920 as an auxiliary to the Township Farm Bureau. Meetings were held four or five times each year. The first officers were: Mrs. George Thomas, president; Lena Burns, secretary and Mrs. Frank Shoff, treasurer.

The club was reorganized at a meeting held December 1, 1925 at the Flora Community Building. There were 20 present, and all became charter members. Officers elected were: Mrs. George Thomas, president; Mrs. David Jenkins, vice president and Mrs. Fred Voorhees, secretary treasurer.

Charter members were: Mrs. George Thomas, Mrs. Fred Voorhees, Mrs. Lawrence Whistler, Mrs. Harry Quinn, Mrs. J. W. Eikenberry, Mrs. Dora Wingard, Mrs. Harvey Thomas, Mrs. John Unger, Mrs. Rufus Flora, Mrs. Raymond Dillman, Mrs. Will Angle, Mrs. Dave Jenkins, Mrs. Roy Eller, Mrs. Dave Oaks, Mrs. Charley Jackson, Mrs. Luther Rude, Mrs. Tiffin Wilson, Mrs. Luther Ross, Mrs. Robert Wertz and Miss Eva Sheets.

Officers for 1979-80 were: Mrs. Lee (Elva) Voorhees, president; Mrs. Don (Esther) Wagoner, 1st vice president; Mrs. Glen (Helen) Wagoner, 2nd vice president and Mrs. Wayne (Freida) Langston, secretary treasurer.

Rock Creek

On January 3, 1924 a Farmers' Institute was held at Rockfield with 75 in attendance. Following the Institute, Mrs. R. A. Ogg, the Institute speaker, helped the ladies organize a Home Economics Club with 18 members the first year. Nellie Foust Martin was president; Bernice Mullendore, vice president; Goldie Smith Landes, secretary and Marie Flora, treasurer.

The club was first organized as the Rockfield Club, but in 1939 the name was changed to Rock Creek Extension Homemakers Club.

It has been a very active club with project lessons, trips and picnics. Trips included visits to Chicago, Indianapolis and Cincinnati, and places of historical interest in Carroll County. The club has provided help for 4-H members and boys in the military service, and has donated magazines for patients at Long Cliff, and Valentines for children at Riley Hospital.

In 1933 each member donated three eggs for the Student Loan Fund of Carroll County.

In 1934 they planted flowers and shrubs in a small park at the east end of Rockfield, and placed a large rock in honor of Harry Bohannon, a local boy who was the first casualty from Carroll County in World War I.

One year they made $106 by selling vanilla.

Officers for 1979-80 were: Mrs. Grace Deel, president; Mrs. Doris Smith, 1st vice president; Mrs. Hazel Mullin, 2nd vice president; Mrs. Wiladean Snoeberger, secretary and Miss Margaret Bowman, treasurer.

Silver Belles

The Silver Belles Home Extension Club held its first meeting in 1963 with 12 members. Connie Collins was the first president, and in 1979 was the only charter member still active in the club which then had 17 members. The name was chosen because it was the twenty fifth club to organize in Carroll County and at that time had the youngest members. Their object was to become better informed in the work of the home. The club colors are blue and silver and the motto is: "The Better the Deed, the Better the Day." Meetings are held in homes of members.

The club has taken one or two trips each year including a day in Nashville in Brown County, dinner and outdoor theater in Indianapolis, and shopping and dining in Lafayette. Each Christmas season they have a candy-cookie exchange at their December meeting. In September 1978, Mrs. Anne Briggs, a local attorney gave a presentation on Patriotism.

The most involved activity in recent years has been the sponsoring of a food stand at various events in the Flora Park. Members started by serving at the Bicentennial Fall Festival with outdoor cooking of ham and beans and chicken and noodles in black open iron kettles. This was a great success, so they continued at the Carroll County 4-H Fair the next year with a chicken-noodle dinner. Members had a hot dog stand at the Lena Burns sale and sponsored a Pepsi wagon at the Pork Festival in 1978 and 1979, featuring Polish sausage and hot dog sandwiches.

The Silver Belles Club has supported many community projects. They donated money for a pager when the Flora EMT Service was established, and gave money for the Helping Hand Fund sponsored by the Flora Psi Iota Sorority. The club built a showcase for use at the County 4-H Fair, purchased corsages for the 4-H Fashion Revue at the Fair, and sponsored a trip to Indiana Beach for members of the Happy-Go-Lucky 4-H Club.

The newest project, planned as an annual event, was the awarding of a scholarship to a graduating senior from Carroll High School who has been active in Girls' 4-H. The first award was a gift of $300 given in 1979 to Annette Wyant.

The officers for 1979-80 were: Glenda Oilar, president; Beverly Angle, 1st vice president; Shirley Hatfield, 2nd vice president; Rita Sorrells, secretary treasurer and Mrs. Carolyn Schiele, reporter.

Sycamores

The Sycamores Club was organized in May 1977. The first officers were: Sheila Yeakley, president; Barb McKinney, vice president; Terri Marcellino, secretary and reporter; Caren Johnson, treasurer and Dottye Robeson, cheer. Meetings are held in the homes of members.

Projects which the members have sponsored were: selling noodles at Burlington Sesquicentennial, baked food auction to raise money for 4-H, Tupperware parties, picnic with husbands, swimming party, and special things for meetings to create interest. There were 15 in the club in 1979. The ages of the members range from 21 to 32 and all had young children.

Officers for 1979-80 were: Sue Lane, president; Dottye Robeson, vice president; Kathi Johnson, secretary and Caren Johnson, treasurer.

Tippecanoe

Twenty eight women of Tippecanoe Township met on April 16, 1924 in Athletic Hall at Pittsburg and organized a Home Economics Club. Mrs. Ed (Minnie) Blythe talked on "Club Organization." Those present were: Belle McCormick, Mrs. Guy Thomas, Mary Spring, Etta Gibson Coble, Eva Overholser Lynch, Florence Goslee Maxwell, Adelia Maxwell, Julie Hildebrand, Lena Ireland Barnes, Bessie Henderson, Elizabeth Shepard, Belva Guthrie Vaughan, Louise S. Blanchard, Amy Brown Whitley, Elsie Tyler, Fern Young Smith, Miss Loe Giles, Ethel Hornbeck Lybrook, Merle Henderson Robertson, Pearl Robinson Bitler, Madie Brown Thompson, Blanche Carmichael Martin, Helen Robinson Anderson, Flossie Hornbeck Clawson, Agnes Arnott Brookbank, Grace Latshaw Patton, Florence Dunkard Henderson and Margaret Lybrook Brookbank.

The first officers were: Adelia Maxwell, president; Pearl Bitler, vice president and Martha Klepinger, secretary treasurer.

The first project lesson was on Making Flowers. The next year the lessons were on Sewing and Dress Forms and a charge of 25¢ a club was made each time the county demonstrator came.

In the 1930's members started the first hot lunch program in Pittsburg school. Other activities for the club have been serving dinners at public sales, providing leaders for girls 4-H Club, filling Christmas baskets, filling kits for boys in service, exchanging flower seeds, paying $10 for and planting shrubery at Pittsburg school, entertaining other clubs, buying a kitchen stove for the Pittsburg school, making night gowns for Red Cross, assembling bedside kits, helping on Cancer Drive, giving books in memory of local people and furnishing boosters for 4-H.

An unusual project was the sharing of a Floor Wax and Furniture Polish recipe: ½ lb. Beeswax, 1 lb. paraffin, ¼ pt. raw linseed oil and 1¼ pts. turpentine, heat over slow fire.

The last officers of the club were: Mabel Burt, president and Mary Benjamin, secretary treasurer.

Former charter members still living in 1979 who were members in 1978 when the club disbanded were: Helen Anderson, Flossie Clawson and Ethel Lybrook.

Washington

The first club in Carroll County was organized in Washington Township. In the spring of 1917 a meeting was held at the home of Mrs. Edith Cooper in Deer Creek. Mrs. Cooper was elected president and Mrs. Iva Downham and Mrs. Flora Cornell were selected as demonstrators to go to meetings at Delphi to get information to present at club meetings. For several years the club held all day meetings and then changed to afternoon meetings.

The club was reorganized in 1924, and is one of three Home Economics clubs in Washington Township.

For several years the club entertained the 4-H girls at a picnic dinner and program in the afternoon. The club has sponsored several trips and for several years has held a Christmas dinner and party in December with husbands as guests.

In 1978 the club members did the Crop Drive and contributed a monetary gift to the Indiana 4-H Foundation. The year brought three new members and one member, Eva Sidenbender, was elected County Publicity Chairman.

Officers for 1979-80 were: Mrs. Ted (Eva) Sidenbender, president; Mrs. Virgil (Gladys) Joyce, 1st vice president; Mrs. Thomas (Ruthina) Forgey, 2nd vice president; Mrs. Leroy (Charlene) Robeson, Jr., secretary; Mrs. Lawrence (Mary Ellen) Johnson, treasurer and Miss Pauline Robeson, reporter.

CHAPTER VI

4-H AND FFA

4-H EMBLEM, PLEDGE, MOTTO, CREED

4-H EMBLEM

A four-leaf clover with the letter "H" on each leaflet, meaning the development of Head, Heart, Hands and Health, is the official 4-H Club emblem.

4-H PLEDGE

I pledge my HEAD to clearer thinking; my HEART to greater loyalty; my HANDS to larger service, and my HEALTH to better living for my club, my community, my country and my world.

4-H CLUB MOTTO

To Make the Best Better

NATIONAL BOYS' AND GIRLS' CLUB CREED

I believe in Boys' and Girls' Club Work for the opportunity it will give me to become a useful citizen.

I believe in the training of my HEAD for the power it will give me to think, to plan and to reason.

I believe in the training of my HEART for the nobleness it will give me to become kind, sympathetic and true.

I believe in the training of my HANDS for the dignity it will give me to be helpful, useful and skillful.

I believe in the training of my HEALTH for the strength it will give me to enjoy life, resist disease and make for efficiency.

I believe in the great trinity of Club Work—the home, the school and achievement.

I believe in my country, in the State of Indiana, and in my responsibility for their development.

In all these things that I believe, I am willing to dedicate my service for their fulfillment.

STATE 4-H HISTORY

According to an article in the October 1975 issue of the Carroll County Farm News, A. B. Graham is recognized by many as the father of the organized youth club movement. As Superintendent of Schools in Clark County, Ohio in 1902 he sponsored corn and garden clubs with 85 boys and girls participating.

The first record of club work in Indiana was in February 1904 when John Haines, Superintendent of Schools in Hamilton County, called a meeting of all boys interested in "growing a patch of corn." Ninety three responded, and each was furnished seed corn. Township trustees and merchants provided prizes for the best ears of corn exhibited by the boys that fall.

The article in Farm News continued:

"Dr. G. I. Christie, who joined Purdue University's staff in 1905 and later directed the Indiana Extension program, is credited, along with the Indiana Corn Growers Ass'n, with promoting the organization of Junior clubs in Indiana.

"Commenting on the work in the early years, Christie observed: 'These contests have not only interested the boys and girls and the teachers of industrial subjects, but they have secured the support of the patrons for the school work in general. The result of all this work is better schools, better pay for the teachers, more interested boys and girls, better farming, better homes and a better country life.'

"By 1912, boys and girls club work had grown to the point that employment of a state-wide supervisor was advisable. (This came only a year after the Indiana General Assembly passed the Clore Act, creating County Agent positions.) Z. M. Smith, principal of Jefferson Township High School at Goldsmith (Tipton County) was hired for the job.

"Purpose of the work, as outlined at that time, was to encourage rural and village boys and girls to become interested and efficient in farm and home activities, to provide careful organization and field follow-up in such projects as growing field crops and gardens, canning and finding markets. The agent was to seek the cooperation of schools, business interests and other organizations in the pursuit of these objectives.

"Smith and Christie soon visualized an organization that would bring into close cooperation the county superintendent of schools, the county agent, the township trustees and men and women in each district. They saw this type of cooperation necessary to success. The state would need to provide the boys and girls with bulletins outlining the best practices in each project area and with report forms to complete. Local leaders would be necessary to encourage and advise the youth.

"In the early years Smith traveled the state by buggy, train, interurban, car and even on foot, selling the idea and developing clubs. By 1915, there were 28 local club leaders and that same year the first Junior Club exhibit was held at the State Fair with the showing of a class of market hogs.

"The cloverleaf and the H's have been associated with club work since early in the century. Speakers of that day often likened the three H's— Head, Heart, Hands—in education to the three R's. Pins with three-leaf and four-leaf clovers were given as awards in 1909 and 1910. Although "hustle" was once suggested for the fourth H, the word "Health" was officially added at a 1911 meeting in Washington, D.C.

"Throughout the following decade, clover pins with four H's became popular and synonymous with boys and girls club work in Indiana. Four-H also appeared on canning labels as early as 1913. It was not until the early 20's however, that people began to refer to the corn, canning, and other boys and girls clubs as 4-H Clubs.

"The first Indiana Boys' and Girls' Club Roundup was held at Purdue in 1918. Three years later the Chicago-based Club Congress, a nation-wide program recognizing top 4-H'ers, was born. Then in June 1927, the state sent delegates to the first National 4-H Club Conference in Washington.

"Working cooperatively with the Extension Service, Kiwanis Clubs of Indiana sponsored the first Junior Leader Training Conference at Shakamak State Park in June, 1932. In 1940, Rotary Clubs of Indiana, joining with Extension, began sponsoring District Adult Leader Training Conferences. Although the sites and training formats have been changed over the years, these programs are still underwritten by the two civic groups. Many businesses and industries have also sponsored 4-H programs, projects, trips and endeavors through the years.

"In the early 30's, older rural youth who had not opted for college but who missed their previous association with 4-H and school sought an interest group. Organizations were formed in Carroll, Tipton, Blackford and Parke counties. In late 1935, the state 4-H Club office at Purdue began a service to these out-of-school young adults. This developed into the Rural Youth Program. Although enrollment dropped during World War II, it has since shown great gains. Today, Rural Youth embraces all single young adults . . . not just those living in the rural area.

"After nearly 30 years as State Leader, Smith retired June 30, 1941. Harry F. Ainsworth, a former vocational agriculture teacher, replaced him and served until his sudden death November 21, 1946. J. C. Ralston, a longtime state 4-H staff member, became acting state leader November 22, 1946, and continued until May 31, 1947. At that time, Harold B. Taylor was named state leader. He served until August 16, 1966.

"Under Taylor's guidance, Indiana 4-H enrollment increased from less than 54,000 to more than 90,000, ranking sixth nationally. Adult leaders increased from 3,000 to 13,000 and the number of 4-H project areas from 26 to 49.

"In 1962, the Indiana 4-H Club Foundation was created and a youth training center developed at the old Ross Civil Engineering Camp, 12 miles southwest of Purdue. The People-to-People and International Farm Youth Exchangee programs, the State Fair sponsored achievement trips, and the soil judging programs were also established during Taylor's tenure.

"Dr. E. L. Frickey replaced Taylor in 1966 and served until September 15, 1975. Dr. R. J. Frist, assistant director of the Indiana Cooperative Extension Service and state 4-H and youth leader, is currently 4-H department head at Purdue.

"During Frickey's nine years of leadership, 4-H enrollment in Indiana more than doubled. Today, more than 162,000 youths are enrolled in organized clubs and groups with an additional 40,000 plus participating as TV members.

"4-H has expanded into the urban and inner-city areas in recent years with more than 45% of its membership now living in cities over 10,000, in suburbs of cities over 50,000 and in the central city areas.

"Major advancements have also been noted in professional staff development and in the volunteer leadership training programs. Several new human development projects have been added to relate to today's youth, but much of the enrollment continues in the project areas developed years ago—such as clothing, foods and the animal sciences.

"Success of Indiana's 4-H program can be attributed not only to its dedicated professional leadership but also to the many loyal volunteer adult leaders. Its success also stems from the support of civic groups, businesses and industry... and most of all from the youth who have worked to make the best better."

CARROLL COUNTY 4-H CLUBS

One of the first records of 4-H activity in Carroll County is an article in the Delphi Journal for September 28, 1916 which states:

"Pig Club in Delphi will have an exhibit Saturday, September 30. The club is composed of boys and girls of the county who during the past summer have been raising pigs scientifically under the direction of Prof. Hummel of the Delphi High School. Children receive credit for the work done during the summer."

Purebred livestock breeders in the county helped sponsor the project, which was called the Corn-Pig Club. The Delphi Journal for April 20, 1918 reported that 25 purebred gilts would be given by local Poland China Breeders to pig club members in the county if they completed their project.

The Delphi Journal for February 5, 1920 reported:

"Gearold Clawson, Delphi High School graduate of 1918 joined the pig club that year and became champion Junior Livestock Judge of Indiana. He receive a two month course at Purdue in Animal Husbandry and is now going to Manchester College to teach stock judging and to carry on his work in the college. Clawson says that his success has been due entirely to the Dr. Ren C. Julien Pig Club of Delphi High School and asks that every boy in the school who has the opportunity to join it do so, for it may determine for him the future of his life."

Poland China Pig Club

The Delphi Journal for December 25, 1920 reported that Poland China breeders organized a pig club at Flora, and furnished a purebred gilt for each boy.

Raymond Calvert was teaching agriculture in the Flora schools, and helped encourage several of the boys to join the club. He later moved to Lafayette where he was a well known Doctor for many years.

E. E. and Charles Eikenberry were advisors for the boys and told them the best method of feeding and caring for the hogs. Boys who were given Spotted Poland China pigs were: Walter Moss, Charles T. Black, Noah Yeater, Wilber Yeater, Frank Sink, Harold Oaks, Junior Metsker, Elmer Gillam, Charles Eikenberry, Otis Beamer and Charles Spitler. Those who received Big Type Poland China pigs were: Willard Veach, Wm. Brown, Gero Flora, Wayne Eikenberry, Loren Ayres, Castyle Fouts, Russell Oyler, Carey Oyler, Kenneth Ginn, Ralph Ginn, Robert Wingard and Leon Ray.

Other 4-H Clubs

In 1918 J. W. McFarland was appointed as the first County Extension Agent in Carroll County and became active in organizing 4-H Clubs. Farmers' Institutes also sponsored clubs, and used club members on their programs. One report stated that the success of Institutes was due largely to the part boys and girls played in the programs. Teachers in schools, and many local leaders helped, and club work grew rapidly.

During 1920, a total of 178 girls' clubs were organized in 32 counties in Indiana, with an enrollment of 2280 members. Projects were: Sewing, Canning, Baking, Home Keeping, Garden, Poultry and several kinds of livestock.

One of the first projects of the County Farm Bureau after it was organized in 1919 was to help sponsor 4-H Club work. At a County Farm Bureau meeting at Camden in March 1921 a group of 48 girls in the Canning Clubs in and near Camden sang for part of the program. Prof. T. A. Coleman, the speaker, said that he knew of no other county in the state that was doing things in a bigger way than in Carroll County.

Canning and Sewing Clubs for girls were organized in many townships. Some of these were sponsored by the Township H. E. Clubs.

Clubs in 1921

1921 was the first big year for 4-H in Carroll County, and there were more than 500 boys and girls in 4-H Clubs. Forty of them attended the 4-H Club Roundup at Purdue May 3 to 6. Canning Club girls from Deer Creek, Wheeling and Burlington put on a stunt at the Roundup. These were the first Canning Clubs in the county. A Bread Judging team from Carroll County was awarded a loving cup for winning first place in a contest at the Roundup. Members of the team were: Hazel Razler, Fern Brown and Bernice Johnson.

A Guernsey Calf Club was organized in 1921 with 17 members, and calves were imported directly from the Isle of Guernsey. A. L. Hodgson, County Agent at that time, reported that these were the first purebred Guernsey cattle in the county.

One of the early girls' 4-H Clubs was the "County Seat Sewing Club" in Delphi. Mrs. Lewis Wise was leader, and in 1921 the officers were: Mildred Wise, president; Frances Wingard, vice president; Mary Angel Cartwright, secretary and Helen Louise Shaffer, treasurer.

Several 4-H Clubs were organized in the Radnor and Ockley schools. The "Hen and Chicks" Club was organized with Jean Chissom, president; Catherine Norton, vice president and Wm. Haslet, secretary treasurer.

Officers of the "I will Work" Pig Club were: John Shaffer, president; Wm. Hannell, vice president; Dale Goslee, secretary treasurer with Leo Craig as leader.

The "Golden Rule" Canning Club, had Golden Rule, one of the Perry Rule triplets as president; Margaret Long, vice president; Catherine Norton, secretary; Katheryne Reppert, treasurer and Mrs. Charles Hannell as leader.

Officers of the "Willing Workers" Canning Club in Tippecanoe Township were: Geneva Ginn, president; Kathryn Ulery, secretary and Blanche Boone, treasurer. The Corn Club in Tippecanoe Township had Jack Swatts, president; Emery Crowell, vice president; John James, secretary and Howard Ginn, treasurer.

Officers of a Canning Club at Flora were: Eva Morrical, president; Kathleen Bingaman, vice president and Mildred Craig, secretary treasurer.

Officers of a Sewing Club at Flora were: Beulah Moss, president; Mary Hankins, vice president; Helen Myer, secretary and Marjorie Sines, treasurer.

Officers of the Washington Township Poland China Pig Club were: Robert Dillon, president; Lowell Shanks, secretary and Lyman Smith, treasurer.

Officers elected by the Carroll County Calf Club were: Francis Sites, president; Glenn Jester, vice president; Sylvia Galloway, secretary and Mildred Jones, treasurer.

There were 47 plots checked in the One Acre Corn Club, with an average yield of 83.77 bushels per acre. John E. Snoeberger had the highest yield with 122.57 bushels per acre. He also won third in the Junior Class at the International Livestock Show.

Washington Township One Acre Corn Club was organized with seven boys. Officers were: James Dillon, president; Leon Smith, vice president; Charles Guckien, secretary and Homer Myers, treasurer.

The records show that in 1923 Mrs. Roy Gregg organized a club in Madison Township with 10 girls.

In 1924 Hilda Bowen of Delphi became the first volunteer County Leader for 4-H Girls' Clubs. She helped organize clubs in five townships with 75 members.

In 1925 Edna Kirkpatrick, a teacher in the Delphi schools served as County 4-H Leader and enrolled 178 members in Girls' Clubs.

In 1926 there were 200 girls enrolled in 4-H Club work in Carroll County. The largest club was the "Sunshine Club" in Burlington Township with 57 members led by Miss Marie Miller.

Beef Club

The Baby Beef Calf Club was organized in 1924, and the first show was held at the County Fair at Delphi in October. It was one of the best attractions at the fair. The calves were sold at auction on Friday, the last day of the fair, at prices ranging from $9.00 to $12.25 per cwt.

Seven 4-H beef calves were shown at the County Fair at Delphi September 10 to 16, 1925. They were sold at auction, and the prices ranged from $12.75 to $15.00 per cwt.

John Benner had the first place calf and was awarded a gold watch by the American Angus Breeders Association. He also won a silver cup for his calf at the Cleveland Calf Show.

In 1927 the Carroll County Shorthorn Breeders Association gave $50.00 to be awarded to 4-H Club members showing Shorthorn calves.

Jersey Calf Club

In April 1926 the Flora Community Club helped secure 40 purebred Jersey calves for 4-H Club members in the county. A member of the Community Club was assigned to help each 4-H Club member for the year.

Drivers for the trucks collecting milk and cream for the Indiana Condensed Milk Company and Schlossers Creamery helped encourage boys and girls to enroll in the club. In June 36 boys and girls attended a calf club fitting demonstration conducted by E. A. Gannon of Purdue. The club members were shown how to dress up their calves for the show. This club with its 40 members had over 95% attendance at all meetings.

All 40 calves were exhibited at the County Farm Bureau Picnic in Flora on August 25, and $200 prizes were awarded. The Cow Testing Association displayed the cow with the highest production record of any cow in the Association, along with butter cartons representing the amount of butter produced by the cow in one month.

In 1927 the Community Club helped secure 20 more calves, and cooperated with the two creameries in placing nine purebred Jersey bulls on farms in the vicinity. Seven members of the Calf Club showed calves at the Indiana State Fair and five entered the National Dairy Show. They won their share of prizes at both shows. Velma Berkey showed the Grand Champion Jersey heifer, and won sweepstakes over all breeds at the State Fair. She was awarded a trip to Washington, D.C. and a trip to the National Dairy Show at Memphis, Tennessee. Three other members of the club won second, third and fourth at the State Fair.

Members of the club showed their calves at the Central Indiana contest sponsored by the Indiana Condensed Milk Company. Dan Todd won $25 for first place, and Paul Flora won $15 for second place.

In order to encourage the production of better legume hay and pasture, the Indiana Condensed Milk Company supplied each of the 27 members with 10 pounds of alfalfa seed and enough limestone for one acre. Schlosser Brothers Creamery gave 1½ bushels of soybean seed and inoculation to each of the 30 club members. Members who raised alfalfa exhibited alfalfa hay at the show the next year.

In 1928 there were 14 more purebred Jersey heifers distributed to 4-H members at a cost of $110 to $175 each. This made a total of 74 members in the Flora Calf Club.

In 1929, 65 continued as members and 11 new members were added.

The Calf Club Show continued to be held with the County F.B. Picnic at Flora. In 1930, more than 3000 people attended the event on August 13 when Edgar D. Bush, Governor of Indiana, was the speaker. One of the features of the 4-H Dairy Calf Show was a special class for calves produced by former 4-H calves.

4-H PICNIC

The first picnic for boys and girls 4-H Club members was held at Delphi in June, 1921. More than 400 attended. The afternoon was spent playing games followed by a wiener roast. Delphi Businessmen's Association furnished lemonade, the County Farm Bureau 25 gallons of ice cream, and E. H. Dame, five gallons of ice cream. Members of the Guernsey Calf Club drew lots to see who got which calf. The cost of the calves ranged from $148.55 to $181.58.

The Carroll County Farm Bureau has invited 4-H members to attend the Annual County FB picnic nearly every year.

STATE FAIR

At the State Fair, September 1921, exhibits from Carroll County Canning Clubs occupied one third of the space devoted to canning, and won one third of the prize money. An essay contest was held to determine which girls got to go to State Fair Girls' School, which was being held for the third year. Carroll County has continued to be well represented every year at the Indiana State Fair.

INTERNATIONAL LIVESTOCK, HAY AND GRAIN SHOW

Club members from Carroll County who won trips to the International Livestock Show in Chicago in 1921 were: Sylvia Galloway, Kenneth Quinn, Charles Jester, Robert Townsley, George Loveland, Hilary Nichter, Areline Lytle, John E. Snoeberger, John Greenwalt, Robert Munson and Thomas Sanderson.

They went to Chicago on the Monon Railroad, and were accompanied by Mr. A. L. Hodgson, the County Agent. They saw an ear of corn that was 30 feet high and 20 feet in circumference. It was made from 60 bu. of corn with the ears cut in half and nailed on a framework the shape of an ear of corn.

They had a club rally, and demonstrations by club members. Each state was asked to sing a favorite song and give one yell. Indiana won the prize for giving the best yell.

In 1927 Virgil Joyce, in his third year of 4-H Club work, was awarded the Sweepstakes Prize on his Ten

Ear sample of yellow corn at the International Grain and Hay Show in Chicago. Others from Carroll County who won awards at the show were: Will Joyce, Roy Snoeberger, Taylor Fouts and Chester Joyce.

Many more from Carroll County had exhibits at the show in later years.

CAMP TECUMSEH

August 18-22 1924, 95 boys and 150 girls attended a 4-H Camp at Camp Tecumseh for one week. There were 34 from Carroll, 152 from White, 40 from Benton and 19 from Grant counties. With leaders, chaperones, and employees at the camp, there were nearly 300 people.

That was the first year for Camp Tecumseh, and buildings were not completed. Some of the campers slept in tents. Each camper furnished food and was asked to bring the following: 1 lb. bacon or ham, 12 potatoes, 6 ripe tomatoes, or 1 can tomatoes or beets, 1 can pork and beans, ½ lb. butter, 1 glass jelly, 18 eggs, 1 can fruit, 12 apples if available, 6 lemons, 1 dozen cookies; ½ lb. rice. small head cabbage, 1 live chicken (fry or hen), 1 qt. green beans, 1 lb. sugar, 1 can condensed milk, 1 loaf bread and 1/8 lb. cocoa.

There were five cooks and 15 helpers at the camp, and each day about 15 or 20 boys and girls "volunteered" to help. Usually their services were "volunteered" by camp leaders who kept watching for excuses to assign KP duty. One evening they fried 50 chickens, prepared a kettle of mashed potatoes and 3 dishpans of fried potatoes, a kettle of green beans, and other food.

The Carroll County Farm Bureau furnished a picnic dinner and entertainment one day. Entertainment included the Sites Trio, Balser Quartet and the Moore Singers of Wheeling.

4-H members from Carroll County who attended the camp were: Eva Chapman, Thelma Yeager, Everett Chapman, Robert Clawson, Virgil Joyce, Lloyd Joyce, Robert Wason, Robert Sanderson, John Snoeberger, Leland Carrigan, Max Holmes, Olive Black, Vera Holmes, Lucile Sanderson, Annette Landis, Vera Black, Perry Million, John Million, Thelma Rice, Dorothy Lyon, Jean Kramer, Mildred Sneathen, John C. Peterson, Joseph E. Peterson, John Disinger, Geneva Rice, LaVonne Airhart, Josephine Wagner, Lorene Schock, Katherine Shaffer, Lucile Schock, Laura Temple, Hazel Rice, Bertha Hasselbring and Katherine Landis.

Lucile Sanderson was selected as one of the two star campers.

4-H Camp was again held at Camp Tecumseh in 1925 from August 17 to 24. Carroll County was represented with 47 girls the first four days, and 21 boys the last four days.

In 1926 the attendance was 56, and in 1927 there were 39 from Carroll County. Beginning in 1926, Chief Eagle Feather and Princess Silver Heels, full blooded American Indians were at Camp Tecumseh, and for several years campers had the opportunity to visit with them and learn more about Indians.

Carroll County continued to send delegates to 4-H Camp Tecumseh every year until 1935, and during a few years since then. A few counties in Indiana have continued to send representatives, and a regular 4-H Camp is held at Camp Tecumseh in June each year.

CARROLL COUNTY FAIRS

The Carroll County Fair Association was organized in 1921 and held a Street Fair at Delphi each year through 1930. A major feature at the Fair was the exhibits by 4-H boys and girls.

Temporary pens were built on the streets for livestock, and Girls' 4-H exhibits were displayed in the Courthouse.

4-H members were in the parades held during the fairs.

In 1924 there were 60 4-H exhibits at the County Fair at Delphi. Winners of first prize were given their awards on the speakers stand on the last day of the fair.

In 1927 the 4-H Club exhibit at the fair included 11 pigs, 6 pens of lambs, 2 beef calves, 4 exhibits of corn and 13 Jersey calves. Ten of these calves had placed in the Indiana State Fair where they were exhibited by members of the Flora Jersey Calf Club. Exhibits by girls 4-H members included sewing, baking and canning displays.

In 1929, 70 girls and 48 boys had 4-H exhibits.

More details about these fairs are in Capter II.

Delphi: 1931 4-H Fall Fair and Festival

For a few years the County Fair Association had trouble getting enough money to pay expenses. In July, 1931 the board met and decided not to have a fair that year. A short time later the Delphi Chamber of Commerce voted to sponsor a 4-H Fall Fair and Festival at Delphi on October 1, 2 and 3.

Fred Wheeler, chairman and Wm. B. Smith, secretary of the Chamber of Commerce worked with Ralph Maggart, County Agent, and made plans for a big celebration. Merchants and others including the

Carroll County Farm Bureau who had supported the County Fair responded with enthusiasm and supported the new project. The theme of the Festival was "Get acquainted with your neighbor—you might like him."

The committee arranged to have a Ferris Wheel, Merry-go-Round, and a Seaplane ride. All other activities were by local people.

Jason Been had just become the first person in Delphi to own an airplane, and the day before the fair he flew over 30 nearby towns in his new airplane and dropped 15,000 hand bills promoting the Festival.

On the first day, Thursday, October 1, Delphi merchants allowed 50¢ per bu. for wheat in exchange for merchandise. Farmers traded 103 bu. of wheat that day.

Pork Barbecue

The big event of the day was a pork barbecue at noon. Eleven pigs weighing 140 pounds each were roasted, beginning at 7 o'clock Wednesday evening. Roscoe Fraser of Monticello was in charge of the barbecue. There were 1500 pounds of pork, 3000 slices of bread, 12 dozen buns, lots of wieners and other food, but it was not enough to feed the crowd of about 2500 people who came, and many went away hungry and disappointed.

Tug of War

After on Old Fiddlers Contest Thursday afternoon, there was a Tug of War across Deer Creek, with farmers on one side, and merchants on the other. After a while the merchants gave up, and farmers were declared winners.

Mr. W. S. Margowski who was in charge of the contest said that the last Tug of War had been held twelve years before, and he was on the losing merchants team that got pulled through the waters of Deer Creek.

Each contestant was given a new pair of overalls. There was one contestant representing each township, and an equal number from town. Those in the contest from Delphi were: Paul Quick, George Vaughn, Glenn Chad, Larry Boone, William Givler, Grover Kite, Hugh Davies, John Todd, Pete Olson, Lon Perigo, William Hawley, Charles Roskuski and L. M. Conley. Those from the county were John Kennard, Leonard Seward, Walter Ringer, Fred Hershberger, Carl Johnson, Walter Barnard, Paul Hunt, Henry Fair (who weighed 290 pounds), Willard Allbaugh, J. F. Haines, Matt Hanrahan, Chalmer Loman and John C. Peterson.

A report of the events in the Delphi Citizen stated that after the contest Mr. Margowski was unable to find the rope which he had borrowed for the event. An old timer who was in the contest and for obvious reasons wanted to remain anonymous reported that the rope was cut into short pieces and distributed among the winners as souvenirs.

4-H Day

Friday was 4-H Day and much of the day was directed to judging the many 4-H exhibits. Cash prizes totaling $200 were awarded. 4-H livestock was penned on West Franklin St. Girls 4-H exhibits and a flower show were in the Courthouse. There were demonstrations, contests, and a dress revue. The Home Economics Clubs also had exhibits. A feature on the program in the afternoon was a water fight between

The crowd watching the Tug of War across Deer Creek on October 1, 1931.

The bridge was built in 1893 to replace a covered bridge built in 1849 at the same location. The steel bridge was replaced by the present concrete bridge in 1936. Riley Dam shown in the picture was completed in July 1930.

two teams representing the Delphi Volunteer Fire Department.

Youth Day

Saturday was designed at Youth Day and featured a Pushmobile Race around the Courthouse. There were nine teams of three members each in the contest. The winning team was John Mount, Raymond Leatherman and Paul Griffith. Other features on the program included a Hog Calling Contest won by Frank Redenbacher, and a Husband Calling Contest won by Mrs. Lon Miller.

Entertainment Contest

An Entertainment Contest with W. B. Smith as M.C. was held each evening. A crowd of 4000 attended the first night, and about 8,000 each of the next two nights. Every township in the county was represented and more than 500 people were on the program. The winner Thursday evening was the Kitchen Kabinet Orchestra from Madison Township Farm Bureau. The Camden H. S. Minstrel Band won the second night and the Carrollton Township Clown Band won on Saturday night. A popular feature on the show each evening was the Dixie Boys Quartet from the Ford Motor Plant in Detroit.

It was estimated that 20,000 people attended the Festival, and too many of them were there on the day of the free barbecue. Complaints by those who did not get enough to eat was a major reason that the Festival was not held the next year.

Fall Festival at Flora 1932

After the problems encountered in the 4-H Fall Festival in Delphi in 1931, no one was enthusiastic about trying it again in 1932. Since the 4-H Dairy Calf show had been held at the County Farm Bureau picnic at Flora in August for several years, it was decided to include all 4-H exhibits in the event. The County Farm Bureau contributed $100 and the Flora Community Club $400 for prizes and expenses. The three day show began on Thursday, August 18 with the 4-H Dairy Calf Show. The next day 4-H pigs, lambs and beef calves were on display. Girls' 4-H exhibits and a flower show were in the Flora Community Building both days.

On Saturday there was a Horse Pulling contest with 15 teams of horses competing. The County Farm Bureau had a basket dinner at noon and a program with C. A. Wilson, President of the Chicago Union Stockyards as the speaker.

In the afternoon there was a Band Concert, a Balloon Ascension and several contests. Mrs. Charles Wray of Carrollton Township won a Nail Driving contest; Mrs. Mattie Greider of Deer Creek Township won a Dinner Calling contest and Mrs. Omer Gangloff of Washington Township won an Egg Carrying contest.

Saturday evening, about 3,000 people attended a local talent show with acts from all parts of the county.

Fall Festival at Flora 1933

The 4-H Club Festival was again held at Flora in connection with the County Farm Bureau Picnic, on August 17, 18 and 19. There were 25 beef calves, 23 pigs, 18 lambs and 28 dairy calves.

The County Farm Bureau Picnic was held on Friday with I. H. Hull, Manager of the Indiana Farm Bureau Co-op Association as speaker.

Thursday night a show was put on by the Purdue Threshing Crew.

Friday night the business men of Flora furnished part of the program with a Minstrel Show and Rube Band. The program included numbers by 4-H members from every township.

On Saturday a Horse Pulling contest was in charge of Evan Sanderson and Russell Harter.

Fall Festival at Flora 1934

The 4-H Club Festival was held at Flora on August 16, 17 and 18 with 75 more exhibits than in 1933. The Community Art and Garden Club also had exhibits in the Community Building. Livestock was exhibited on Thursday and a Horse Pulling Contest was held on Saturday.

Each day there was a Balloon Ascension with a Triple Parachute Jump. The Hillbilly Musicians and the Rube Band furnished music.

About 1,000 people attended the County Farm Bureau Picnic on Friday to hear Larry Brandon, vice president of the Indiana Farm Bureau.

4-H AGRICULTURAL EXHIBIT ASSOCIATION

Articles of Incorporation were filed and approved on August 5, 1935 for the Carroll County 4-H Agricultural Exhibit Association, Inc. The seventeen members on the first Board of Directors were: Charles Tansey, Adams Township; Charles Thompson, Burlington; Robert Wingard, Carrollton; Clarence Frey, Clay; Charles T. Black, Deer Creek; Hal Shaffer, Democrat; W. H. Lane, Jackson; Leon Kasten, Jefferson; Obe Campbell, Madison; Oren Eikenberry, Monroe; Turpie Martin, Rock Creek; Frank

Riley, Tippecanoe; Lewis McFatridge, Washington; Haughey D. Mount, Delphi; Lynn Ledman, Flora; W. O. Pettiner, Camden and Herman Weaver, Yeoman.

Incorporators were: Haughey D. Mount, W. H. Lane and Charles Tansey.

Officers for 1935 were: Frank Riley, president; W. H. Lane, vice president and John C. Peterson, secretary treasurer.

A 4-H Fair was held at the Community Park in Flora August 16 and 17, 1935 and has continued to be held there every year. Livestock was in temporary pens in the park, and girls' exhibits were in the Community Building.

In 1960 the directors voted to include the chairman of the girls' 4-H leaders in the county as a member of the board of directors. Those who have served were: Helen Forgey, Frances Zink, Marilyn Nance and Doris Peterson.

In 1970 it was provided that directors representing each township would be elected in November by parents of 4-H members in the township. Three are nominated in October by 4-H leaders and extension council members in each township. One third of the directors are elected each year for a period of three years, and a director can serve for only two consecutive terms, but may serve again after being off the board for one term.

Among those who have served as president of the Exhibit Association were: Frank Hedderick, John Harvey Todd, Leroy Robeson, Sr., Harry Wilson, Charles Meade Sr., Lowell Spesard, Ralph Hughes and Don McCain.

Some in addition to the County Agents, who have served as secretary or treasurer have been: John McGill, Harry Foster, Loyd Zook, Fritz Schnepf Sr., Lee Flora, Meredith Ayres, Dwaine Ward, Jack Moss and John T. Downham.

Officers for 1979 were: Don McCain, president; Dick Rinehart, vice president; Doris Peterson, secretary and Dix Weaver, treasurer. Other members were: Dan Snell, Bob Crume, Jerry Lilly, Richard Oilar, Robert Smith, Dr. John Bush, Jim Powlen, Bob Dillman and Ron Swayze. Robert White, Dan Hinkle, Charles Meade, Jr., and John Burkle were newly elected to begin their term in January 1980.

4-H FAIR BUILDINGS

The first permanent building for the 4-H Fair at Flora was the 54'x108' hog barn built in 1938 with a capacity of about 200 hogs. The dairy barn was built in 1939. Both were paid for by the Flora Community Club and the cost was about $2,000.

In 1950 the Flora Community Club purchased and moved a barn to the grounds to be used as a beef cattle barn. This was known as the Hinkle barn and was used until about 1970. The Flora Community Club built the Commercial Exhibit Building in 1959 and rest rooms in 1961.

In 1968 the stage was removed and the floor under the stage cemented in the building in the park owned

Carroll County 4-H Exhibit Association members 1978-79 who attended a directors meeting November 21, 1978. Seated left to right: Mrs. John (Doris) Peterson, Steve Nichols, Renee' Krieg, Ralph Hughes, Jack Moss, Dr. John Bush. Standing: Richard Oilar, Ron Swayzee, Robert Smith, John T. Downham, Robert Crume, Dix Weaver, Bob Dillman, Paul Miller, Ed Nelson and Dan Snell.

by the Community Club and used for 4-H and Home Economics Club exhibits.

Livestock Scales

In 1955 a set of portable scales for weighing livestock was donated by Bassett and Talbert, Carroll County Farm Bureau Cooperative Association, Kerlin Elevator and Feed Mill, Delphi Lumber Company, Union Bank & Trust Company, Stuntz Yeoman Company, George Todd & Son, Hargraves Motor Sales, Mount's Hardware, Wertheimer Cattle Company and Ranger Products.

The Carroll County Pork Producers have purchased two sets of portable scales for weighing hogs.

4-H Cattle Barn

The Carroll County Farm Bureau Cooperative Association sold the material and supervised the volunteer labor to build a 60'x105' pole building for cattle at the 4-H Fair Grounds at Flora. The building was constructed in about a week, beginning February 25, 1957. More than 130 volunteers helped build the building. They were supervised by Jack Goslee, Manager of the Co-op Lumber Department at Yeoman, and Reed Goslee and Don Roth, who were building pole barns for the Co-op Association. Charles Meade Sr. was building chairman, and was assisted by Harold Tully, Frank Mullin, Lee Flora, Ted Brown and Harold Berry.

About 8 volunteers from each township were secured by the directors of the County 4-H Exhibit Association. Directors in 1957 were: Richard Cree, Adams Township; Rex Hinkle, Burlington, Charles Meade Sr., Carrollton; Kenneth Frey, Clay; Charles T. Black, Deer Creek; Rev. E. E. Morris, Democrat; Harry Wilson, Jackson; Roy Slavens, Jefferson; Frank Mullin, Liberty; Lee Flora, Madison; Fritz Schnepf Sr., Monroe; Ren Groninger, Rock Creek; James Riley, Tippecanoe; Leroy Robeson, Washington; Robert Steinhart, Camden; Dave Crutchfield, Yeoman; Richard Ayres and Richard Leiter, Flora; and Leo Craig, Delphi. Officers were: Harry Wilson, president; Charles Meade Sr., vice president; Harold Berry, secretary and Fritz Schnepf Sr., treasurer.

The building was wired for electricity with wiring material furnished by the County Commissioners. Labor was donated by Rural Youth members supervised by Herb Isaacs of the Carroll County REMC. Among those who helped were: Bob McCain, Kenneth Yeakley, Eldon Robeson and Jim Flora.

The total cost of the cattle barn was $7696.11 most of which was paid with money appropriated by the County Council, and it was built on land given to the county by the Flora Community Club.

Wash racks measuring 10'x40' were built July 22, 1957 at a cost of $167.73.

On June 13, 1958 Charles Meade Sr. supervised the installation of cattle ties in the cattle barn, and forms for a loading chute. Those who helped were: Harry Wilson, Raymond Cline, Junior and Max Snider, Danny Hinkle, Burton and Jim Billiard, Robert Crume and Fred Jones.

In 1963 another beef wash rack was constructed at a cost of $263.14 with money donated over a period of years.

In July 1974 an addition to the cattle barn was constructed at a cost of $3785.

Ralph Sullivan Ford Grant

In 1962 Ralph Sullivan was one of 14 farmers in the U.S. to be selected for one of Ford's Third Annual Efficiency Awards. The award program was sponsored by Ford Almanac, a publication of the Ford Motor Company, and Sullivan was chosen for his success in growing corn.

The award of $2,000 could be given to any worthy cause selected by the recipient, and Ralph named the Carroll County 4-H Club Exhibit Association. The award was presented at a banquet at the Carroll Consolidated School, and the money was used to help pay for a new building to house a show ring.

Show Ring

A 70'x105' building housing a show ring, stage, Junior Leaders stand and office was built in July 1962 at a cost of about $7,000, all of which was donated by individuals, organizations and businesses.

In July 1966 a dressing room was added to the building at a cost of $1,743.15 which was donated by Extension Homemakers Clubs, Farm Bureau, the Exhibit Association and individuals. Stone for both building projects was donated by Delphi Limestone Company.

The Carroll County Rural Youth furnished an amplifier for use during the Fair. In 1963 it was replaced with a larger system which was rented each year.

Hog Barn

The old hog barn on the fairgrounds was wired on February 27, 1958 with 27 lights and 12 electric outlets. Herb Isaacs supervised the job and his helpers were: Rex Hinkle, Keith Sink, Junior Snider, Fritz Schnepf Sr., Charles Beale, Charles T. Black and Martin Justice Jr. The Flora Community Club furnished $90 for material for the job.

The hog barn was razed in 1976 and replaced by a 52'x152' pole barn with concrete floor with a 24'x32' addition on the north side for wash pens and special pens for the champion hogs. The building has 120 pens with a capacity of about 300 hogs.

Carroll County Farm Bureau Cooperative Association built the building and Charles Jacobs of Flora did the concrete work. Electrical work was done by Perdue's Electrical Service of Delphi. Pens were purchased from Circle F. Builders of Reynolds and were installed by 4-H members and adult leaders.

The total cost was about $33,000 with only $12,000 available at the time it was built. Of this amount the Carroll County Pork Producers gave $5,000, the county appropriated $4,000 and $3,000 was from donations. More money was donated during the Fair, and the rest was borrowed, with the directors of the Exhibit Association signing the note. The final payment on the building was made in February 1979.

Officers of the Exhibit Association in 1976 were: Charles Meade Sr., president; Lowell Spesard, vice president; Dwaine Ward, secretary and John T. Downham, treasurer.

4-H Community Building

In 1979 plans were made to construct a building on the Carroll County 4-H Fairgrounds in the Flora Community Park. The proposed building would include a large banquet room with kitchen and rest room facilities and would be used for exhibits during the 4-H Fair. The building would be available throughout the year for 4-H activities, banquets, annual meetings, wedding receptions, auctions, family reunions etc. It would be similar to the buildings used as a community center at the Cass and Clinton County fairgrounds.

A building fund was started to secure the funds necessary to start construction, and about $10,000 was raised during the 4-H Fair in 1979. Contributions were made by many individuals and organizations. The largest single amount was from the sale of a black lamb donated to the Fair Association by the Paul Fife family. The lamb, sold at auction, was purchased by Bright National Bank and Jackson-Lee-Pearson, Inc. Each paid $1,600 for a half interest in the lamb, making a total of $3,200 for the building fund.

4-H FAIR BOOK

Each year a 4-H Fair Premium List and Program Book was printed which listed the rules and regulations governing the various projects, and a list of activities during the Fair. It also listed the special awards that were given for different projects. Beginning in 1942 and until 1977 the book was financed by the Carroll County REMC. Before 1942 it was financed by various other business concerns in the county. Beginning in 1978 the book has carried advertisements by many individuals and businesses, and money from advertising has provided part of the revenue to help operate the Fair. Junior Leaders sold the ads for the Fair Book.

4-H BEEF AUCTION

The first 4-H Beef Calf Auction at the 4-H Fair at Flora was held on Friday evening, August 17, 1945 at an Auction Ring set up in the ball diamonds in the park at Flora. The project was in charge of County Agent Robert VanSlyke and a committee of Robert VanNatta, Robert Hedde and Walter Barnhart. Ralph Rinehart was auctioneer and about 40 calves were sold.

The grand champion owned and exhibited by James Dickinson of Madison township was an Angus calf weighing 1,040 lbs., and purchased by John De-LaCroix, manager of the Carroll County Farm Bureau Cooperative Association for $31.50 per hundred, totaling $327.

The first prize Shorthorn steer owned and exhibited by Jane Thompson of Monroe township was the second high animal. It weighed 1,020 lbs. and was purchased by the Todd Seed Corn Co., for $25 per hundred, totaling $255.

The first prize heavyweight owned and exhibited

Comet photo
Buyers of the black lamb sold at auction at the 1979 4-H Fair. Left to right: Rex Overholser, Adolf Haines and Lowell Craft representing the Bright National Bank; Tim Hoopingarner representing the Paul Fife family who donated the lamb; Bill Pearson and Pete Jackson, representing Jackson-Lee-Pearson, Inc. Each paid $1,600 for a half interest in the lamb, making a total of $3,200 for the building fund.

James Dickinson and his Grand Champion Steer at the County 4-H Fair in 1945. The steer was purchased at the auction by the Carroll County Farm Bureau Cooperative Association for $31.50 per hundred pounds and weighed 1,040 pounds.

by Joyce Pullen was purchased by Keener Packing Co., for $19.75 per hundred, totaling $176.71. It weighed 895 lbs.

The cattle averaged $18.14 and sold for a grand total of $6,282.28.

The buyers of the animals were Jack Hawkins, Delbert Smith, Mel Boller, Hi Grade Food Co., Kuhner Packing Co., Keener Packing Co., Carroll County Co-op, Bollei Farrer Co., Todd Seed Co., Kingan & Co., Fred Roskuski and Guy Sibbitt.

A donation of $250 was given by a group of business men in Carroll county, showing their appreciation to the 4-H boys and girls for their splendid efforts in making this show and sale possible. The donators were: Fred Wheeler Implement Co., Hoosier Democrat, Flora Produce, E. E. Landis, Day Hardware, J. C. Lowery, Kerlin Elevator, Aschanhort Insurance, Voorhees Lumber Co., Bishop & Lane, Budrow Hardware, Eaton and Cripe Motor Sales, Elmer Cripe & Co., Carter Funeral Home, Bright National Bank, Ora Shirar, Mann Chevrolet Co., Fred Clawson Grocery, Julius Clothing Co., Producers Commission Co., Charles Stouse Service Station, Dr. Wilson, Thompson's Drug Store, Leiter Funeral Home, Wm. Eckerle Co. and Pioneer Seed Corn.

The auction was changed from Friday to Thursday night in 1947 and is now in charge of Ralph Rinehart's sons, Martin and J. R.

The auction, one of the highlights at the Fair, has been expanded to include hogs, sheep and rabbits as well as cattle, and has been supported by many individuals and businesses. Those who purchased 4-H livestock at the auction either in 1978 or 1979 were: The Andersons, Angle Bros. Trucking, Ayres Hardware, Berry Feeds, Bright National Bank, Business Assoc. of Greater S.W. Monticello (Ken Murray), Camden Hog Market, Camden State Bank, Carroll County Farm Bureau Co-op, Carroll Lumber Co., Cutler Grain & Feed Co., Dean Todd Seeds, Delphi Limestone Inc., Dye Lumber Co., Erny's Fertilizer Service, Esserman Tire Service, Fairacre Farm (Bill Pickart), Fleet Supply Inc., Green Tree Feeds, Hanenkratt Grain Co., Heinold Commodities, Heinold Hog Market, Jackson-Kitchell Inc., Jackson-Lee-Pearson, Dr. Harry Jones, Kerlin Elevator, Kerlin Feed Mill, Logansport Livestock Yards, Mann Chevrolet-Buick, Inc., Martin Farms Inc., McManus Family, Meadowview York & Hamp Farm (Dan Snell), Greg Michael, Mid States Feeder Pigs, J. B. Miller, Monticello Implement Co., Moorman Feeds (Dan Altman), Morning Star Fertilizer, Nichols Durocs, Oakridge Farms, Patchett Sales & Service, Pearson Farm Service, R. E. Pearson Sales & Service, Pioneer Seed Corn Co., Premier Feeds, Premier Hybrids Inc., Pure Seed Processing, Rehm Grain & Nutrena Feeds, Rinehart Auction & Real Estate, Ritchey Dog House, Robeson Equipment, Inc., Seedomics Hybrid Corn Co. Inc., Smith Construction Co., Smith Tire Service, Star Roller Mills, Stoney Pike Sale Barn, Tenbrook Sales, Thompson Funeral Home, Triangle Feeds, Union Bank & Trust Co., United Feeds, Inc., Waddells IGA, Whiteman Bros. Elevator, WILO Radio, Wilson Farm Service, Wilson Foods Corp., and Zinn Kitchens Inc. Donors or Boosters were: Yeager & Sullivan, Triangle Feeds Inc., and Star Roller Mills.

Many others have helped on committees for the auction on show ring management, weighing, health paper checking and tabulation.

4-H FAIR QUEEN CONTEST

A 4-H Queen Contest was first sponsored by the Delta Theta Chi Sorority in Flora, and supported by the Flora Community Club. Winners are eligible to compete in the State Contest at the State Fair.

The 4-H Fair Queen committee chairman in 1978 and 1979 was chosen by the 4-H Exhibit Association and she picked the committee of girls to serve with her. Marcia Abbott Eppers served as chairman for 1979 along with Carolyn Wood, Donna Sales, Barbara Hughes, Teresa Maxwell, Shelia Myers, Debbie Jones, Carol Baker, Teresa Zinn and Nancy Michael.

Carroll County 4-H Fair Queens have been: Jane Williams Kearns 1958, who was also third at the State Fair; Jerilyn Jones Kennedy 1959; Kay Shriver Riegel 1960; Pat Todd Petrie 1961; Louann Milner Collins 1962; Darlene Allen Coble 1963; Ann Miller Emery 1964; Debbie Mann Jones 1965; Kathy Graf Davis

1966; Lindy Ayres Fowler 1967; Carolyn Howe 1968; Pat Long Hendershot 1969; Renita Draper Carman 1970; Rita Dittman Zawisza 1971; Debbie Miller Groninger 1972; Kris Shriver McGill 1973; Cheryl Gooding Layman 1974; Joni Ayres 1975; Loretta Leazenby Scagnoli 1976; Connie Griffith 1977; Cindy Langston 1978 and Louann Frey 1979.

Several meetings with the contestants were held prior to the fair and girls received instruction on hairstyling, make up, fashion and physical exercise. Contestants were sponsored by 4-H Clubs, individuals, organizations and businesses.

The Queen and members of her court assisted in giving out ribbons, trophies and other errands at the auction and during judging of livestock at the fair.

CARCASS EVALUATION

For several years the Carroll County Farm Bureau has sponsored a Carcass Evaluation Program at the County 4-H Fair. Cattle and hogs were butchered after being shown at the Fair, and awards given on the basis of dressing percentage and quality of meat. In some years samples of the meat were displayed at the FB booth during the last two days of the Fair.

Beginning in 1969 the County FB and the Carroll County Pork Producers have sponsored a pork chop barbecue for 4-H hog and beef club members and their families. On Tuesday evening August 5, 1969 at the Merchants Building at the Flora Park there were more than 150 present representing the 36 families with 4-H members who entered 57 hogs and 19 calves in the contest.

The pork chops were barbecued by Dale Kasten, Raymond Zink and Bob Pickett. The meal was in charge of Mrs. Raymond Zink, Mrs. John Burkle, Mrs. Raymond Romein, Mrs. Roy Slavens, Mrs. Roscoe Hoffman, Mrs. Clayton Million and Mrs. Emmett Frey.

Marion Stackhouse of the IFB Commodity Department, Raymond Zink and Charles Hanna were in charge of the evaluation meeting after the supper.

Richard Curts won the Champion Beef Carcass trophy given by the Cyanamid Company, and Dennis Funkhouser won the Champion Swine Carcass trophy sponsored by the Camden-Flora Elevators.

On August 16, 1979, 65 4-H Club members who competed in the Swine Evaluation contest were given awards and were paid by Wilson Packing Company for their hogs on the basis of grade at the Evaluation Meeting sponsored by the Carroll County Farm Bureau. Barbecued pork chops and other food was provided by the Carroll County FB for the 4-H Club members and their parents.

Those who received the top 10 places in the contest were: Monica Lamb, Jay Bush, Julie Crowel, Deb Maxwell, Annette Wyant, Lori Trapp, Bill Reiff, Tom Miles, Nick Cronk and Liesl Stauffer.

4-H ENROLLMENT

Records at the County Extension Office indicate

Carroll County 4-H members who attended the Stark & Wetzel Banquet for the first 4-H Commercial Beef Feeders of Carroll and Clinton Counties on September 27, 1954. The calves were sold to Stark & Wetzel Stockyards on September 23, and the carcassas shown September 25. Left to right, front row: Bill Kearns, Monroe Township who received the trophy for first choice carcass; Bob Bordner, Gary Deboy, Martin Wagoner and Larry Fellows, Democrat, receiving commercial carcass trophy from J. A. Crabb, Frankfort plant manager. Second row: David Hoshaw and Carol Flora, Madison Township, and Patricia Ann Meade, Carrollton Township.

Cooks at the Pork Chop Barbecue at the Community Park at Flora August 16, 1979. Left to right: Emmett Frey, Jim York, Don Willy, Francis Humbarger and Gene Jennings.

The meal was furnished by the Carroll County Farm Bureau for 4-H members who were in the carcass evaluation contest and their immediate families.

that nearly 10,000 different boys and girls have been in 4-H Club work in Carroll County. The total enrollment has been about 32,000 but about 70% of these were members the previous year. The largest number on record was an enrollment of 907 in 1956. The enrollment for 1979 was 584 and 541 completed one or more projects. Over the entire period the enrollment has been 40% boys and 60% girls. About 85% of those who enroll each year complete one or more projects.

Members must be at least 10 years of age during the year and not more than 18 years of age at th beginning of the year enrolled, so a member may be in a club for 10 years. Until 1964 a member could continue in 4-H work until age 20 or a total of 12 years. Abut 50 projects are available in Carroll County and members may enroll in as many projects as they can complete during the year. Some very active members have completed as many as 100 projects during the time they were in 4-H. Mini 4-H for boys and girls 8 and 9 years old was started in Burlington Township in 1978. In 1979 Burlington and Clay Townships each had a Mini 4-H Club with 26 enrolled in the two clubs.

4-H is big business. In 1978 there were about 5.5 million 4-H members from 9 to 19 years of age in programs directed by nearly 600,000 adult and teenage volunteer leaders in the U.S. Members participated in programs in more than 3,000 counties of the United States, as well as the District of Columbia, Puerto Rico, the Virgin Islands and Guam.

4-H AWARDS

About fifty companies and foundations offer awards on a national basis, and most of these are available to members in states and counties that care to participate in the program. It is up to the Extension Agent and 4-H leaders in each county to decide which awards will be offered in the county. For many years 4-H members in Carroll County have won their share of state and national awards.

Prize money and ribbons financed by an annual appropriation of $4,500 by the Carroll County Council are given for each of the several hundred classes of 4-H exhibits at the Fair. In addition to these awards, about 65 business firms, organizations and individuals in Carroll County offer special awards for members in the county. Among those who gave special awards in Carroll County in 1978 were Carroll County REMC, Indiana Electric Assn. & Indiana REMC's, Flora Community Club, County Farm Bureau Co-op, County Farm Bureau, Crawford Petroleum, Delphi Limestone, Inc., Camden State Bank, Union Bank & Trust Co., Delphi Merchants, Camden Lions Club, Mr. and Mrs. Miles T. Martin, Randolph Bakery,

REMC photo
Pictured above, left to right are the 1951 4-H Farm and Home electric project winners of Public Service Company of Indiana awards: Lois Peterson, Democrat Township; Sue Rush, Carrollton Township and Dan McCain, Deer Creek Township. Ralph Melin, manager of the Public Service Company in Delphi, is holding the award of Peter Morris, who was from Democrat Township.

REMC photo
4-H Electric Project REMC Award Winners in 1954 left to right: Harold Zook, Jerry Williams, Stephen Peterson, John Beale, JoEtta Henderson and Anne Wilson.

Waddell's IGA, Brosman's IGA, Stephan's IGA, Wallmann's Certified Foods of Delphi, Payne's Stores, Mr. & Mrs. Myron Beesley, Mr. & Mrs. Fred L. McCain, Extension Homemaker Clubs, Judy Thelen, Township Farm Bureau Organizations, The Andersons, Blazers Saddle Club, Carroll County Pork Producers, Todd Tybrid Corn Co., Radio Station WSAL, Kerlin Feed Mill, Monroe Meade Memorial Trophy, C & C Energy Inc., Dr. A. A. Anderson Veterinarian, Camden and Flora Elevators, Logansport Livestock Yards, Inc., Mr. and Mrs. John Lind, J Bar D Quarter

CHAPTER VI — 4-H AND FFA • 125

Girls' electric REMC award winners in 1956 left to right: Inga Cox, Donnabelle Plank, Mertha Zook and Joy Carol Greenlee.

REMC 4-H Electric Award winners in 1959 left to right: Dix Weaver, Dana Ruegamer, Sam Rhine, David McCain and David Peterson.

4-H Electric Exhibit REMC Award winners in 1957 standing: Karen Johns, Joetta Joyce, JoEllen Wagoner, Charlotte Hanna; kneeling David Peterson and Stephen Peterson.

4-H Electric REMC Award Winners in 1965 left to right: Phil Martin, Richard Scott, Mike Starkey and Jerry Moss.

Horse Farm, Carroll County 4-H Horse & Pony Club, Bradshaw Insurance Agency, Inc., Mr. & Mrs. Bob Simmons, Rainbow Restaurant, Mr. & Mrs. Merritt Hardt, Roy Robertson, Sharon Montgomery, Jackson Township Farm Bureau, Yeager and Sullivan, Inc., Whiteman Brothers Elevator, Rural Youth, Dimitt Registered Hampshires, Burlington State Bank, Erny's Fertilizer Service, Marsha Floyd, Smith Tire Service, Sisson Jewelry Store, Ric-Mar Bassetts, Oliver's Boarding Kennels, Shirar Feed Co., Inc., Sedalia Elevator, AMPI, Carroll County Soil & Water Conservation District, Ralph R. Rodkey, Inc., Jackson-Lee-Pearson, Inc., County Hybrid Seed Producers, Carroll Lumber Co., Inc., Delphi Greenhouses, the Bright National Bank, Action Realty, Don & Kym Wyant, Steve Dimitt and Robert Lovelace & Family.

It would be impossible to list all awards won by 4-H members, but on the following pages is a brief description of some of the major awards, and a list of some in Carroll County who have won the awards.

STATE FAIR GIRLS' SCHOOL

Each county is entitled to send two girls between 16 and 19 years of age, to the school held each year since 1919 during the Indiana State Fair. Girls participating can not participate in any other activities during the duration of the school as a full schedule takes all of their time.

CARROLL COUNTY RURAL ORGANIZATIONS

At the August 1957 4-H Fair Morris Clem, Farmers Mutual Insurance agent, presented wrist watches to Bethan Guge and Janella Guge of Burlington and David Peterson of Deer Creek; front row, division champions in the 4-H Fire Prevention activity, and fountain pens to reserve champions, Mertha Zook of Deer Creek, Joyce Snoeberger of Rock Creek, Colleen Bailey of Madison, and Eric Johnson of Burlington, second row. Fifty girls and boys participated in making farm and home surveys and studying fire prevention activities. Judith Hodges of Jackson, Sonia Landis of Monroe, Sandra Sidenbender of Washington, and Bethan Guge of Burlington, health and safety leaders, received a trip in the fall of 1957 for getting six or more members to participate in their clubs.

Objectives are: to develop a greater appreciation for the whole state of Indiana through an enjoyable experience at the Fair, promote personal growth, clarify career opportunities, make personal decisions and develop leadership skills and provide new insight into government, culture and human relations.

Twelve Honor Girls are selected from among the delegates each year, based on the vote of the delegates and final selection by the staff. These girls return the following year as group leaders and program assistants. From the Honor Girls one is selected as Assistant Director, who returns and is in charge of the program the next year.

Sherri Flora was an Honor Girl in 1977 and returned as Assistant Director in 1978.

Carroll County has sent more than 100 delegates to the School.

Those who attended in 1978 were Debbie Maxwell and Michelle Sullivan. Janet Connaway and Dee Sanderson attended in 1979. Dee was chosen an Honor Girl to return in 1980.

STATE FAIR BOYS' SCHOOL

Since 1974 or 1975 there has been a State Fair Boys' School similar to the school for girls. Those from Carroll County who attended in 1978 were Daniel Brower and Chris Burkle and Curtis Yeakley and Lonnie Spesard attended in 1979.

STATE FAIR CAMP

For many years 4-H leaders who helped at the State Fair and 4-H boys and girls who exhibit livestock have stayed at the State Fair Camp, located in a section of the buildings used for State Fair Schools.

NATIONAL 4-H CLUB CONGRESS

The National 4-H Club Congress which began in 1921 is an event where all 50 states send 4-H girls and boys to Chicago the week after Thanksgiving for a week of fun and education, with expenses paid by state and national donors. To win the honor, a 4-H member must submit an Achievement Record Book which is judged on the basis of 4-H activities. About 45 from Indiana go each year. The Indiana State Fair sponsors 16 and National Donors and companies sponsor others.

Among those from Carroll County who have won the trip and the basis for the award were:

1938 Ray Robertson, District Judging

1938 Carolyn Hedderick, Foods and Nutrition, second in nation

1941 Charles Mourer, State Fair, first on hogs

1942 Margaret Hedderick, Achievement, National Presidential Award

1949 Fritz Schnepf Jr., Achievement

1950 Robert Crume, Poultry, National winner

1951 Marjorie Schnepf, Canning

1954 Ray Gish, Achievement, Lafayette District

1955 JoEtta Henderson, Achievement

1957 Mary Jo Thompson, Frozen Foods

1958 Virginia Peterson, Public Speaking

1962 James Thompson, Achievement

1969 Jeff Moss, Electric, National and David Martin, Achievement

1970 Jerry Moss, Electric National

1971 Randa Zink, Citizenship and Madonna Jervis, Public Speaking

1973 Teresa Zink, H. E. Record, Consumer Education

1975 Barbara Martin, Poultry

1976 Barbara Moss, Safety, National winner

1977 John Moss, Electric, National winner

NATIONAL 4-H CONFERENCE

This program began in 1927 as a camp in Washington, D.C. It was later changed to a conference held annually in April at the National 4-H Center in Washington, D.C. Indiana's four delegates are chosen on the basis of 4-H Achievement records and personal interview. The purposes of the conference are leadership and citizenship training, with involvement in national 4-H program concerns and developments.

Ray Robertson attended in 1938 and Jerry Moss in 1972.

WAKANDA

Wakanda (formerly Ouibachi) is a week-long program at the Hoosier 4-H Leadership Center during July. The program emphasizes the importance of physical, social, mental and spiritual development, for 13-15 year old 4-H members. Objectives are to help them develop a good feeling about themselves and the things they can do, to help increase their confidence in themselves and others, to help them feel more at home with themselves and others and to help them learn leadership skills.

WASHINGTON D.C. TRIPS

The trip which started in 1952 was sponsored by Stark and Wetzel of Indianapolis. Delegates were picked on their over all Achievement Records in 4-H. About 16 delegates from the state were selected each year. The last year for this trip was 1965. Those who have gone on the trip from Carroll County were:

1954   JoEtta Henderson
1956   Mary Jo Thompson and Bill Kearns
1957   Edwin Cox and Patricia Meade
1958   Martha Schnepf and Gary Crume
1959   Meredith Ayres
1960   Ron Dickinson
1961   Jim Thompson
1962   Carolyn Peterson
1963   Marsha Jones and Terry Snider

The Stark & Wetzel trip was replaced in 1966 by the REMC Achievement Trip to Washington, D.C. Each year 18 boys and 18 girls in Indiana were selected on the basis of their overall 4-H record. Those who have taken the trip were:

1967   Dianne Forgey
1968   Myron Sink
1969   Madonna Jervis
1970   Randa Zink
1972   Harold Zink
1973   Teresa Zink
1974   Barbara Moss
1976   John Moss

Each year the Indiana State Fair awards a trip for four from Indiana to New York City and Washington, D.C. Winners from Carroll County have been Twillie Tully in 1955 and David Peterson in 1963. Both won the trip on their Electric Project.

STATE FAIR ACHIEVEMENT TRIP

A week's trip, sponsored by the State Fair is awarded each year to 35 winning contestants in 4-H activities at the State Fair. These include winners in demonstrations, judging, public speaking, fashion revue and the tractor operators contest. The trip includes visits to Williamsburg, Washington, D.C., Philadelphia, Gettysburg and the National 4-H Center. Some winners from Carroll County have been:

1958   Virginia Peterson, Public Speaking

1960   Pat Wagner, Dianne Ward, Team Demonstration

1964   Dianne Minneman, Home Furnishings Judging

1967   Mary Ellen Scott, Clothing Judging and Jeff Moss, Electric Demonstration

1970   Rick Ayres, Tractor Driving Contest

1974   Denise Hummel, Home Furnishings Demonstration

1975   Joetta Johns, Meat Products Demonstration

4-H KEY CLUB AWARD

A new program, the 4-H Key Club award for 4-H Club boys and girls in Carroll County and in Indiana was launched on June 7, 1956 at the annual 4-H Club Roundup at Purdue University. It was offered through the National 4-H Club Committee, and sponsored jointly by the Purdue University Agriculture Extension Service and the Cities Service Oil Company.

The program is based on 4-H Records of Achievement, and gives recognition to 4-H Club members who have shown consistent growth in their club work, have developed their leadership ability, and have been helpful members in their club and community. It is also to encourage boys and girls to continue their work in 4-H. Winners must have completed at least three years in the Junior Leader project and five years in 4-H.

Awards in the program are gold keys with the recipients name engraved, mounted on bracelets for the girls and tie clasps for the boys. Each recipient also receives a certificate. Winners of the award become life members of the Indiana 4-H Key Club.

The new program had already been organized in six states and was soon extended to a national basis.

The first state meeting was held in 1958 at Purdue University, and later meetings were held at Purdue University or the Hoosier 4-H Center. In 1971 the meeting place was changed to the Indiana State Fairgrounds, a more centralized location. The 1972 meeting was held at the Farmers Building at the State Fairgrounds on August 20.

Awards for 1956, the first year, were presented to the following 4-H members in Carroll County: Martin Rinehart, Mary Jo Thompson, Bill Kearns, Patricia Meade and Murray Langston, Monroe Township; Janet Joyce, and Joetta Joyce, Washington; Judith Miller, Clay; Twillie Tully, Jefferson; Byron Gilbert, and Kenneth Orem, Burlington; Myra Carter, Martha Carter and Lewis Ruman, Democrat; Martha Schnepf, Marcia Langston, and Jeris Eikenberry, Monroe; Robert Peterson, Adams; Dwaine Ward, John Elston, Glenda Fisher and Virginia Fisher, Madison Township.

Award winners for each year since then have been, 1957: Lois Downham, Nan Beck, Nancy Chapman, Jane Williams, Brenda Flynn, Gary Crume, Edwin Cox, Carole Welch, Donnabelle Plank, Virginia Peterson and Robert White.

1958: Lou Ann Pearson, Darilee Peter, Jane Ann Jones, Connie Briggs, Harold Craft, Cullan Eikenberry, James Thompson, Mary Ann DuVall, Catherine DuVall, Meredith Ayres, Jerry Wagner, Marta Porter, Myrna Billiard, Barbara Barnes, Christina Forgey, Emmett Herr and Max Snider.

1959: Charles Meade Jr., Caroline Sue Dant, Carolyn Verrill, Carolyn Peterson, Nancy Vinard, Donna Hodges, Barbara Johnson and Ron Dickinson.

1960: Tom Billings, Marsha Jones, Ronald Myer, Jerry Arthur Thomas, James Thompson and Patricia Todd.

1961: Barbara Adams, Linda Adams, Joann Cripe, Madonna Eller, Roger Frey, Ward Frey, Delores Hanna, Joseph Huse, Myra Sue Johnson, Marilyn McCain, Henry Milburn, Dwight Pullen, Mary Lou Schnepf, Kay Shriver and James F. Tarkington.

1962: Donald Billings, Richard DuVall, Janet Scott, Terry Snider, Hilda Vass and Tom Wagner.

1963: Vicki Sue Johnson, Duane Pullen, Joe Thomas, Pat Wagner and Jean Ann Ward.

1964: David Peterson, Gene Humbarger, Leveda Smith and Betty DuVall.

1965: Martha Kay Weaver.

1966: Sue Markley.

1967: Pam Fossnock, Thomas E. Flora and Dix Weaver.

1968: Dianne Forgey, Lynn Allan Brown, Barbara Jo George and Mary Ellen Scott.

1969: Nancy DuVall, Madonna Jervis, Linda Merson, Evy Sheldon, Marilyn Shultheis, Rebecca Smith, Randa Zink and Jeffrey Moss.

1970: Janet Mays and Judy Mays.

1971: Caryn Craig, Teresa Childers, Joe McCain, Jerry Moss, Clyde DuVall and Mollie Sheldon.

1973: Mary K. Geheb, Barbara Martin and Teresa Zink.

1974: Kathy Cory, Dean Cripe and Harold Zink.

1975: Barbara Moss and Mary Jo Mays.

1977: John Moss, David Maxwell and Joetta Johns.

1978: Michelle Sullivan, Dee Sanderson, Sherri Flora and Susan Ramsey.

1979: Debra Maxwell, Linda Mays, Lori Kremer, Annette Wyant and Kirk Schwarzkopf.

FARM BUREAU 4-H CHICAGO ACHIEVEMENT TRIP

At a meeting of the directors of the Carroll County Farm Bureau on March 25, 1949 County Agent Howard McCarty suggested that the County FB sponsor an Achievement Trip to Chicago for four outstanding 4-H members each year. The FB approved the plan and agreed to pay $150 per year for the expenses

Carroll County 4-H Achievement delegates to Chicago, November 29 to December 1, 1949. Left to right: Robert Crume, Robert Lee Hendrix, Howard and Nadene McCarty, chaperones, Barbara Sue Van Meter and Marjorie Ann Shnepf.

CHAPTER VI — 4-H AND FFA • 129

Left to right: Howard McCarty, Max Douglas, Gordon Jones, Wanda Hughes and Sue Landis, at the railroad station at Delphi, November 28, 1950 as they are ready to leave for their 3-day tour of Chicago. The trip was sponsored by the Carroll County Farm Bureau as an award for outstanding achievement in 4-H Club work. Miss Jeanne Muller, home agent, attended the national home agents' conference in Chicago, and remained to accompany the local group on the tour.

Winners of the Farm Bureau 4-H Achievement trip November 26, 1951, ready to board the train for their trip to Chicago.

Left to right: Mr. and Mrs. Howard McCarty, chaperones; L. E. Hoffman, Director of Extension at Purdue; Shirley Hughes, Marilyn Newby, Robert Simmons, and Jim Sharp. Mr. Hoffman did not go with the group, but was at the right place at the right time to get in the picture.

of two girls, two boys and two chaperones. This amount of money was increased in later years.

Award winners were selected by the County Agent, Home Demonstration Agent, County FB officers and 4-H Adult Leaders, on the basis of the member's achievement record, including number of years in club work, number of projects completed and other activities, including junior leadership.

This trip was awarded each year, except 1968, beginning in 1949 and continued through 1971. Winners in 1971 did not take the trip until June 16, 17 and 18, 1972. This trip was replaced in 1977 by the National Citizenship Shortcourse.

Places visited in Chicago during the Achievement trips included the International Livestock Exposition, Field Museum, packing plants, special radio and TV shows, Aquarium, Planetarium, Museum of Science and Industry, Board of Trade Building, Chinatown, Maxwell St. Market, Federal Reserve Bank and other Chicago sights.

Following is a list of those who went on the trip each year:

Farm Bureau 4-H Trips To Chicago

Year	Girls	Boys	Chaperones
1949	Barbara Sue Vanmeter Marjorie Ann Schnepf	Robert Lee Hendrix Robert Crume	Mr. & Mrs. Howard McCarty
1950	Sue Landis Wanda Hughes	Max Douglas Gordon Jones	Howard McCarty Jeanne Muller
1951	Shirley Hughes Marilyn Newby	Robert Simmons Jim Sharp	Mr. & Mrs. Howard McCarty
1952	Anita Douglas Olive Carr	Gene Appleton Richard Porter	Mr. & Mrs. Harold Berry
1953	Joan Benner Mary Helen Mears	Ray Gish Meredith Carter	Mr. & Mrs. Harold Berry
1954	Rachel Morris Patricia Maggart	Carol Flora Martin Rinehart	Mr. & Mrs. Harold Berry
1955	Carolyn Jones Judith Henderson	Jeris Eikenberry Bill Kearns	Mr. & Mrs. Harold Berry

1956	Mary Jo Thompson Twillie Tully	Murray Langston Kim Black	Mr. & Mrs. Harold Berry
1957	Glenda Fisher Martha Schnepf	Gary Crume Harold Craft	Mr. & Mrs. Ted Brown
1958	Barbara Johnson Virginia Fisher	Cullan Eikenberry Dwaine Ward	Mr. & Mrs. Harold Berry
1959	Janet Bailey Virginia Peterson	Ronald Dickinson Meredith Ayres	Mr. & Mrs. Harold Berry
1960	Mary Ann DuVall Carolyn Peterson	Charles Meade Jr. Jim Thompson	Mr. & Mrs. Monte Alderfer
1961	Carolyn Verrill Marilyn McCain	Stephen Peterson Charles Snider	Mr. & Mrs. Monte Alderfer
1962	Marsha Jones Jo Ann Cripe	James R. Scott David L. Peterson	Mr. & Mrs. Kenneth Yeakley
1963	Marilyn Crain Marlene Todd	Richard Crane Don Billings	Mr. & Mrs. Peter Liley
1964	Diane Mullin Karen Kahler	Eric Johnson	Mr. & Mrs. Junior Snider
1965	Betty DuVall Leveda Smith	Terry Overholser Stanley Clem	Mr. & Mrs. Dwaine Ward
1966	Jane Ann Long Kathryn Felthoff	Joe Forgey Tom Flora	Mr. & Mrs. Bill Duff
1967	Diane Herndon Jane McIlrath	Dix Weaver	Mr. & Mrs. Ron Lauster
1969	Ellen Childers Kay Funkhouser	David Martin Jeff Moss	Mr. & Mrs. Junior Snider
1970	Nancy DuVall Madonna Jervis	Phil Martin	Mr. & Mrs. Raymond Romein
1971	Mollie Sheldon Randa Zink	Joe McCain Jerry Moss	Mr. & Mrs. Kenneth Orem

NATIONAL 4-H CITIZENSHIP SHORTCOURSE

This is held in Washington, D.C. at the National 4-H Center. Each Shortcourse is a week of learning, hard work and fun. The program includes assemblies, discussions and tours of our Nation's Capitol. This trip replaces the 4-H Achievement Trip to Chicago, sponsored by the Carroll County Farm Bureau from 1949 to 1971. The County Farm Bureau pays $100 each for three delegates, and the County Junior Leaders organization sponsors one. Each delegate pays about one half the cost of the trip. Those who attended in 1978 were: Michelle Sullivan, Curtis Yeakley, Mark O'Farrell, and Annette Wyant.

Delegates from Carroll County in 1979 were: Lori Kremer, Leanna Johns, Linda Mays, Bill Leinberger and Chris Burke.

TENURE AWARDS

The Women's Department of the IFB sponsors the Tenure Award program. Certificates of recognition are given to one girl and one boy in each county who have completed at least 10 years of 4-H Club work. Awards are furnished by the FB Insurance Company. At first the awards were presented at the Indiana State Fair on Farmers' Day. Beginning in 1976 the awards have been presented at District FB meetings in July.

In addition to giving recognition to outstanding 4-H members, the program helps to encourage Indiana 4-H members to remain in 4-H Club work. Winners in Carroll County have been:

1956 Janet Lou Joyce, Martin Rinehart
1957 Mary Jo Thompson, William Kearns

CHAPTER VI — 4-H AND FFA

1958 Joetta Joyce, Dwaine Ward
1959 Lou Ann Pearson, Harold Craft
1960 Virginia Peterson, Meredith Ayres
1961 Carolyn Peterson, Jim Thompson
1962 Mary Ann DuVall, James Thompson
1963 Barbara Adams, Tom Wagner
1964 Diane Mullin, Dick Welch
1965 Kathryn Felthoff, Max Langston
1966 Betty DuVall, Joe Forgey
1967 Cindy Segraves, Dan Snell
1968 Jane Ann McIlrath, Dix Weaver
1969 Sue Markley, Myron Sink
1970 Evy Sheldon, Jeff Moss
1971 Madonna Jervis, Clyde DuVall
1972 Randa Zink, Richard Scott
1973 Pam Burge, Rick Ayres
1974 Linda DuVall, Harold Zink
1975 Barbara Martin, Tim Burke
1976 Barbara Moss, Mark Schwarzkopf
1977 Joetta Johns, Brad Burton
1978 Sherri Flora, John Moss
1979 Michelle Sullivan, Curtis Yeakley

STATE JUNIOR LEADERS CONFERENCE

Four State Junior Leader Conferences of one week each sponsored by the Indiana District of Kiwanis are held annually during June at the Hoosier 4-H Leadership Center. County quotas are six percent of the Junior Leader enrollment for the previous year. The program is designed to develop leadership, understanding of group dynamics and an awareness of self and others and is carried out with the guidance of Junior Leader Council members elected at each conference to conduct the next year's program.

Those who attended in 1978 were: Melody Huff, Susan Smith, Lori Trapp, Jackie Weller, Phil Archer, Jay Bush, Kirk Schwarzkopf and Lonnie Spesard. Scott Jennings, Carmen Bruner, Danny Smith, Rita O'Farrell and Sherri Duff attended in 1979.

Carroll County delegates were sponsored by Delphi Limestone and the Burlington Kiwanis Club.

STATE JUNIOR LEADER COUNCIL

At each of the four weeks at State Junior Leader

Carroll County delegates to the district 4-H Junior Leaders Training Conference at Purdue, April 4, 1951. Front row, left to right: Carol Flora, Madison Township; Dan Lybrook, Tippecanoe; Gerald Fry, Liberty; County Agent Howard McCarty; Fred D. Blue, Carrollton; Phillip Campbell, Washington; and Richard Mears representing the county Rural Youth. Second row: Mrs. Charles Harter, county Farm Bureau S & E leader; Mary Helen Mears, Deer Creek; Jean Bowman, Deer Creek; Linda Wilson, Democrat; Joyce Caldwell, Jackson; Joyce Meek, Washington; Diana Jennings, Rock Creek; Carol Wilson, Monroe; and Rebecca Jane Quinn, Liberty. Back row: Miss Jeanne Muller, home agent; Mary Lou Shaffer, Adams; JoEtta Henderson, Madison; Mary Furst, Tippecanoe; Lois Powell, Carrollton; Wilma McIlrath, Burlington; Gladys Ruegamer, Democrat; Wilma Haslet, representing Rural Youth; Roger Zook, Burlington; Bill Roach, Deer Creek; Douglas Wagoner, Adams; Dean Shoff, Monroe; Bob Duff, Deer Creek; Wayne Replogle, Jackson; and Miles Martin of the county Farm Bureau.

Conference, the delegates elect five boys and five girls to the Council. These 40 Council members plan and conduct all activities at the following year's conference. They also serve as 4-H representatives at many area, state and national activities.

Those who have been elected from Carroll County were: Marlene Todd, 1963; Mara Bowman, 1968; Dean Cripe, 1974; Brad Burton, 1975 and John Moss, 1977.

CAMP MINIWANCA

This is a two-week conference held at a camp near Muskegan, Michigan for 17-21 year-olds interested in self-development of leadership skills. This is an Achievement and Participation trip, formerly sponsored by the Danforth Foundation of Purina Mills and now sponsored by the American Youth Foundation. Those who have attended were: Fritz Schnepf Jr., 1949 and Twillie Tully, Mary Jo Thompson and Bill Kearns in 1957.

ANIMAL SCIENCE WORKSHOP

This three-day educational conference has been held on the Purdue Campus since 1973. It is sponsored by the departments of Animal Sciences and State 4-H and Youth at Purdue. The purposes include: acquiring a greater appreciation and knowledge of animal agriculture, career opportunities, leadership development; and helping other 4-H members. Participants must be entering their sophomore, junior or senior year in high school during the fall semester. Each county may be represented by one delegate per species category (Swine, Beef, Sheep, Poultry, Dairy and Horse).

Those from Carroll County who attended in 1978 were Lonnie Spesard, JoAnne Connaway, Annette Watson and Phil Burkle.

Those who attended in 1979 were: Kari Ayres, Susan Flora, Susan Sturdivant and Janet Connaway.

PLANT SCIENCE JAMBOREE

This is a three-day workshop, held on the Purdue Campus, in June with four delegates per county—two in Field Crops and two in Horticulture. Technical subject matter, information and career exploration opportunities are emphasized.

The program is sponsored by the Indiana Crop Improvement Association, the Crops Division of the Indiana Farm Bureau Cooperative Association, Inc., and the United Farm Bureau Insurance Companies, in cooperation with the Department of Agronomy, Horticulture and 4-H and Youth at Purdue.

Those from Carroll County who attended in 1978 were: Jeff Rider, Michelle Sullivan, Alan Wyant and Bill Leinberger.

Those who attended in 1979 were: Janet Draper and Kathi Ennis.

NATURAL RESOURCES LEADERSHIP CAMP

Natural Resources Leadership Camp is held during July at the Hoosier 4-H Leadership Center. Counties may send two delegates between 13 and 16 years of age. The program includes learning experiences in four areas of conservation: Soil, Forestry, Wildlife and Entomology. Local sponsors pay the camp costs of each delegate.

Those from Carroll County who attended in 1978 were: Becky Floyd, Lisa Sanderson, Scott Ackerman and Bobby Floyd.

In 1979 Rita Leinberger and Erin Garrison attended.

Delegates were sponsored by Todd Hybrid Corn Company and Carroll County Soil and Water Conservation District.

Becky Floyd who attended the Natural Resources Leadership Camp as a delegate from Carroll County in 1978 was selected as one of the Junior Counselors who helped with the camp in 1979. She was selected as one of six Indiana 4-H members to attend the National 4-H Wildlife Workshop in Washington, D.C. on August 6 to 11, 1979. This was sponsored by the Atlantic Richfield Foundation.

STATE 4-H CHORUS

4-H Club members 15 or older during the year may apply for membership in the State 4-H Chorus. Auditions are conducted by the Purdue Musical Organization Staff at locations around the state. The Chorus sings annually at the 4-H Club Roundup and at the State Fair.

Those from Carroll County who have been chosen were: Bonnie Howard, Jerry Moss, Nancy Carmichael, Lori Kremer, Ray Wilson and Gary McCarty.

STATE 4-H BAND

4-H Club members at least 15 or older during the year may apply and final selection is made by State 4-H Band directors. The band plays annually at the 4-H Club Roundup.

Those from Carroll County who have been chosen were: Kathy Markley, Dee Sanderson, Kay Walton, Kimbra Zolper and Kevin Robeson.

Left to right: Fritz Schnepf Sr., Mrs. Harry Wilson, Ellwyn Weiss, Harry Wilson, and J. T. Downham, visiting at the 4-H achievement program held at the REMC auditorium at Delphi on January 17, 1952. Weiss, a native of LaGrange County and a student at Purdue University, showed colored slides he had taken while an Exchange Student in Finland in 1951. He was sent as one of the two from Indiana as a part of the fourth annual International Farm Youth Exchange project, sponsored by the Purdue Collegiate 4-H Club. The trip was financed by many organizations, including the Farm Bureau, Farm Bureau Co-op, and 4-H organizations in Carroll County.

INTERNATIONAL 4-H YOUTH EXCHANGE IFYE

This international project, known by the initials IFYE, was started in 1948 as a post-war venture in human relations among young people in all countries. It was first called International Farm Youth Exchange and the name was recently changed to International Four-H Youth Exchange. Carefully selected 4-H members are sent to live with farm families in other countries where they live with one or more farm families. Young people from those countries are invited to live with farm families in the U.S. There were 14 exchangees the first year. Some of the families in Carroll County who have had foreign students in their homes were: Fritz Schnepf Sr., and Truman Plank in 1957; Robert Ayres, in 1960, Fred Martin, in 1963 and Carl Mays, in 1973.

Programs are available for a 4-H member to go as an individual or as a member of a group. More than 60 countries have participated and about 2,000 delegates from the U.S. have gone abroad while over 2,000 farm youths from these countries have come to the U.S.

Monte Alderfer who was assistant County Agent in Carroll County from 1959 to 1963 had been an IFYE exchange student to India.

IFYE CARAVAN

A nine-week international summer program, grouped for individuals during the year they become 17 or finish their junior year through the year they reach 19. The Caravan program is supported by funds raised by the Collegiate 4-H Clubs with counties having an individual selected is obligated to raise $300 toward the total expenses. Individuals are also expected to pay $300 toward total expenses.

IFYE REPRESENTATIVES

A ten-week to five-month program for single individuals 20-25 years old on date of departure. Individuals selected are expected to contribute $300 and the county in which they reside is expected to raise $300 toward the total cost. Collegiate 4-H Clubs raise the remaining funds necessary.

COMMODITY MARKETING

One representative from Indiana is selected each year to participate in an expense-paid tour of the Chicago Board of Trade and the city of Chicago, sponsored by the Chicago Board of Trade. Selection is made on the basis of the 4-H member's Achievement Record Book. Danny Hinkle was the winner in 1957.

AMERICAN INSTITUTE OF COOPERATION

A national meeting has been held annually since 1925 to increase understanding and appreciation of cooperative principles in the American business system. It is sponsored by cooperatives in Indiana and other states. 4-H is represented by six state-wide representatives, two each from the State Junior Leader Council, the Natural Resources Leadership Camp and the Indiana Junior Horticultural Association. Rural Youth is also represented by two delegates. A young couple is sent each year by the Carroll County Farm Bureau Cooperative Association and the Carroll County REMC. More details about AIC and the delegates from Carroll County are in Chapter VIII.

SHARE THE FUN

This is a local talent program put on by 4-H members in each county each year.

Categories available are: Curtain Acts (not more than five entertainers) and Group Acts (five or more). County winners advance to the area contests, with area winners performing at 4-H Roundup. Curtain Acts should not be more than three minutes long and Group Acts not more than eight minutes long.

In 1955 the 3 J's, the Joyce sisters of Washington Township, represented Indiana at the Share the Fun Breakfast at the National 4-H Club Congress in Chicago.

ROUNDUP

This program, started in 1918, is a three-day conference held annually at Purdue University during late June or early July. The program is developed to interest about 3,000 4-H Club members, ages 14 to 18, and to inspire them to continue in 4-H work. Quotas are based on 10 percent of the previous year's enrollment of boys and girls 14 years old and over, with a minimum of 10 delegates per county. Housing is provided in various dormitories at the University.

Those who attended in 1978 were: Denise Clevenger, Susan Flora, Lisa Brower, Susan Burkle, Kim Sutton, Julie Funkhouser, Laura Spesard, Michelle Oilar, Lisa Kearns, Rita Leinberger, Kimbra Zolper, Alan Wyant, David Brower, Scott Jennings, Max Victor, Jeff Scott, Danny Smith, Brian Burton, Norman Anderson, Mike Floyd and Paul Rider.

Those who attended in 1979 were: Cathy Archer, Lisa Spesard, Linda Byers, Cecilia Burke, Lisa Burnworth, Annalea Robeson, Teresa Hertenstein, Millie Howard, Robert Lambert, Amy Brown, Anita Wyant, Chris Meade, Tim Redding, Bob Floyd, Mark Abbott, Mark Peterson, Joe Downham, Phil Johns, Roger Mays and Dirk Abbott.

SCHOLARSHIPS

National Award Programs

Approximately 200 educational and college scholarships (usually $1,000 each) are given annually at the National 4-H Congress in Chicago to winners in the various achievement programs. State Achievement Record winners in the various contests are automatically entered to represent Indiana in these contests.

National Scholarship Funds

Approximately ten scholarships are available to Indiana 4-H'ers and are awarded annually on the national level. Present offerings include: Agribusiness Careers, college freshman in Agriculture; Alpha Gamma Rho—college freshman in Agriculture; Animal Science—college junior, majoring in Animal Science; Edwin T. Meredith—college freshman, any four-year course; Veterinary Medicine—any student enrolled in College of Veterinary Medicine.

State Fair School Scholarships

Thirteen scholarships for further instruction in Indiana colleges and universities are available for delegates making the best records in their high school and in the State Fair Schools.

Preference for scholarships will be given to those who have graduated from high school, who rank in the upper third of their graduating class and who hold no other scholarships.

All scholarships are for the purpose of fee remission and are not given in cash. Some schools give complete fee remission and others are partial. The amounts vary according to the college. Scholarships are awarded on the basis of the following: High School grades, State Fair School participation, Personal interview, Record of community activities, 4-H Club, Church, School and community interests and a test given at State Fair Schools.

State 4-H Scholarships

Forty-six 4-H scholarships to Purdue University are available annually. The amount varies, based on need as established through the Financial Aids Department.

No complete list of scholarship winners is available but among those from Carroll County who have won scholarships were: Lucille Million, 1947, State Fair School; Fritz Schnepf Jr. 1948; Robert Crume, 1950; Marjorie Schnepf, 1951; Edwin Cox, 1957; Tim Burke, 1976; and John Moss, 1977, $1,000 at National 4-H Club Congress.

HOOSIER 4-H LEADERSHIP CENTER

The Indiana 4-H Foundation was organized in 1961 for the specific purpose of providing financial support for the establishment and maintenance of a 4-H Leadership Training Camp in Indiana. The site selected in 1962 was the Ross Civil Engineering Camp located on 210 acres of scenic woodland along the Wabash River about 12 miles southwest of Lafayette. Buildings and equipment at this location were installed in the 1920's and were used as a summer training camp for Purdue University Civil Engineering students. In 1960 this method of training was discontinued and the camp was closed.

The Indiana 4-H Foundation leased the camp and added several buildings. A lodge has overnight facilities for 68 persons, and a campground has 24 camp sites for camping trailers. The dining hall has a capacity of 250 persons, and two dormitories for summer use accommodate 90 persons each. An old church was recently moved to the grounds and used as a Memorial Chapel. The Camp which is open year round is used for many 4-H activities and is available for meetings of other groups.

In January, 1979 an Indiana 4-H Leaders Forum was conducted at the Hoosier 4-H Leadership Center. This was followed by 30 regional adult 4-H leader workshops, sponsored by the Indiana Rotary districts. Nearly 1,200 4-H leaders participated in these workshops held in February and March. Junior Leader training programs were held on two different weekends in March and involved 150 teenage leaders.

A great number of state activities were held in June, after schools closed and before county fairs started. The first activity in June was the State 4-H/FFA Judging Contest involving nearly 1,000 youth. At the same time, four weeks of State Junior Leader Conferences were conducted at the Hoosier 4-H Leadership Center with 550 Junior Leaders participating.

The month of June was capped with one of the most successful 4-H Roundup programs ever held. More than 2,400 young people participated. All 4-H Roundup delegates were taken to the Hoosier 4-H Leadership Center for project training.

The Indiana 4-H Foundation is a non-profit organization governed by a board of 21 directors. As a result of a membership drive in 1979, 1400 individuals, groups and businesses contributed a total of $30,000. This money was used to make necessary repairs and improvements to the buildings and facilities at the camp.

DuVALL'S COMPLETE 147 YEARS OF 4-H

Jeffery and Gregory, twin sons, and the youngest of thirteen children in the Clyde DuVall family, each completed 10 years of 4-H Club work in 1978, and made a total of 147 years of club work for the family. Members of the family completed about 425 4-H Club projects. In addition to all the achievements of her 13 children, Mrs. Mary DuVall has completed 20 years of leadership with the Merry Maidens 4-H Club of Jefferson Township. She was awarded a 20 year trophy at the annual 4-H Club Roundup at Purdue June 27, 1979.

4-H activities for the family began in 1952 and projects ranged from foods, clothing and crafts to dairy, swine and wildlife. Many awards were presented to members of the family with the Key Club Award going to Catherine and Mary Ann in 1958, Richard 1962, Betty 1964, Nancy 1969 and Clyde in 1971. The Farm Bureau Achievement trip to Chicago was won by Mary Ann in 1960, Betty in 1965 and Nancy in 1970.

Catherine (Chaney) the oldest of the 13, completed 10 years of 4-H work and was an assistant leader with her mother after her freshman year at Ball State University. She is currently living in Tucson, Arizona, and is teaching nursery school there. She also does volunteer work with the Boy Scouts of America.

Mary Ann completed 12 years of membership in 10 different project areas. She attended Ball State University and is teaching in the Tipton School in Logansport.

Richard participated in 12 different project areas during his nine years with the program. He went on to attend Findlay College in Ohio and after graduation from Seminary he located in Granby, Connecticut, where he is a minister.

John completed eight years of 4-H work in the sheep, dairy and wildlife projects. He presently lives at R. 4, Monticello, and is engaged in farming.

Betty (Lewis), after completing 10 years with major emphasis in clothing and foods, went on to attend the International Business College in Ft. Wayne and

The Clyde DuVall family of Jefferson Township, R. 4, Monticello, has completed 147 years of dedication to 4-H in Carroll County. They are pictured, front row, from left: Jim, Gregory, Jeffery, Clyde, Larry and Harry DuVall; back row: Richard, Clyde "Ike" (father), Mary (mother), Catherine (Chaney), Mary Ann, Linda, Nancy (Martin), Betty (Lewis) and John Duvall.

is a secretary for the United Methodist Church in Monticello.

Harry and Larry, twins, each completed nine years with dairy being their main project. They each received several county dairy awards along with showmanship awards going to Larry, five years and Harry, three. Larry went on to Purdue University and is presently employed by Allis Chalmers in West Allis, Wisconsin. Harry lives near Yeoman and is employed by Globe Valve.

Nancy (Martin) completed 10 years of 4-H in seven different project areas. She attended Ball State University and lives in LaVesta, Nebraska, where she is a grade school teacher.

Clyde presently lives at R. 4, Monticello, and is employed by Premier Feeds of Monticello. He completed 10 years of project work with most of his awards coming from the dairy project. He currently is running the family dairy with his younger brother, Gregory.

Linda completed 10 years of project work with 36 first placings in 12 different areas. After graduation from Twin Lakes High School, she attended Wright's Beauty School in Logansport and is now a beautician in Logansport.

Jim completed 10 years with most of his emphasis in lamb, dairy and swine projects. He is currently farming in the Yeoman area and is interested primarily in swine.

Jeffery and Gregory, the last of the 13, bring to a close the membership life of a very closely knit and active family. They each completed 10 years with dairy and swine being their biggest projects. Jeffrey is currently at home farming and Gregory is a student at Purdue, commuting from home.

Even though the last of the Clyde DuVall family has completed 10 years, they will not be forgotten. The experiences they have gained can never be taken away from any of them, and they will stay in the records forever—as the largest, most active 4-H Family of Jefferson Township of Carroll County.

4-H JUNIOR LEADERS

The Carroll County Junior Leaders organization is a group of 4-H boys and girls 14 years old and older who have had at least two years of 4-H. Their main purpose is to act as assistants to the regular leaders, and turn in a completed record book to the Adult Leader. They have meetings of their own nearly every month of the year, sponsor Share the Fun programs, operate the Junior Leader Food Stand during

4-H Junior Leader officers in 1954 seated, left to right: Jeris Eikenberry, president; Doyal McIlrath, Patricia Meade, JoEtta Henderson, LaDene Wagoner, Jane Williams and Meredith Carter. Standing: Kenneth Orem, Carol Flora, Brenda McKinley, Jack Black, Linda Snoeberger and Sue Rusk.

the Fair, help with the County Judging and Demonstration Contests and help in the shelter house and with the livestock at the Fair. A special program was given at the December 1978 meeting entitled "This is Your Life So Far, Reneé Krieg." At this meeting it was revealed that Reneé would become Mrs. Jim McKee in June.

Officers for 1979 were: Lori Kremer, president; Dee Sanderson, vice president; Susan Smith, secretary; Lori Trapp, treasurer; Anita Wyant and Lisa Kearns, recreation leaders; Annette Wyant, Janet Connaway, Bill Leinberger, Dan Smith, Rita O'Farrell and Phil Archer, Board of Directors.

Officers for 1980 were: Dan Smith, president; Lisa Kearns, vice president; Julie Funkhouser, secretary; Carmen Bruner, treasurer and Rita O'Farrell and Scott Jennings, recreation.

ROTARY ADULT TRAINING CONFERENCE

Since 1941 the Rotary Clubs have been financing a meal for adult leaders who attend a school. Meetings are held each spring, and have been in Kokomo, Monticello, Flora and Delphi. The most recent one was held at Delphi on March 6, 1979. 4-H adult leaders from about nine counties in the area attended the meeting and were given suggestions and ideas to use in conducting 4-H meetings.

CHAPTER VI — 4-H AND FFA • 137

Raleigh Fosbrink from Purdue speaking at the Rotary 4-H Leaders Training meeting held at the Delphi United Methodist Church March 6, 1979. Seated at the head table are: Renee' Krieg, Youth Agent; Mrs. Tom Freeman, Tom Freeman, Rotary president and Dennis Mellon, Rotary secretary treasurer.

4-H ADULT LEADERS BANQUET

The first recognition banquet honoring 4-H Adult Leaders in Carroll County was held on Wednesday evening, November 3, 1948 at Conrad's Sportsman near Monticello. This was one of several banquets sponsored in counties by members of the Indiana Chain Store Council. Delphi merchants who sponsored the banquet were: Forrest Sprague of the Ben Franklin Stores, Max Daugherty of the Delphi A & P, Jack Bloyd of the Delphi Kroger Store, and Ray Sterzik of the Federated Stores.

Charles Van Nuys representing the Indiana Chain Store Council was a guest.

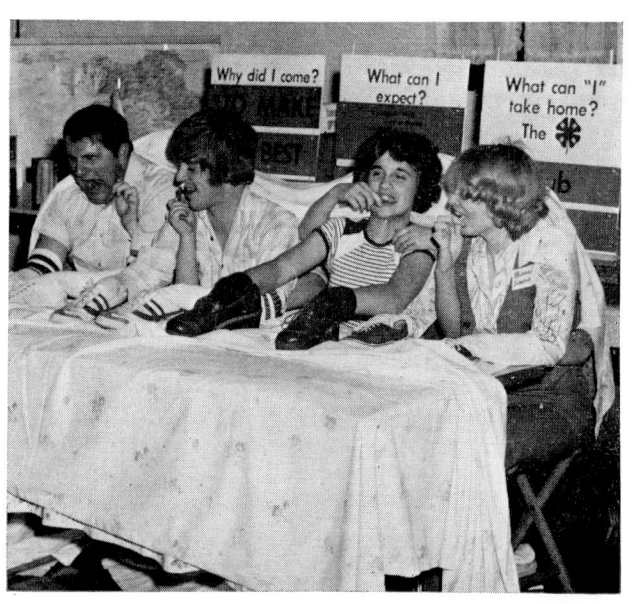

The winning Share-the-Fun act The Smear Family which was presented at the Rotary Leaders Training School for 4-H Leaders March 6, 1979 at the Delphi United Methodist Church. Left to right Ron Slavens, Bill Reiff, Cindy Peterson, and Carmen Slavens. The extra hands helping brush teeth are unidentified.

4-H Leaders who attended the Rotary Training School at the Delphi United Methodist Church March 6, 1979. Seated left to right Mrs. Donnabelle Brown, W. S. Weaver, Brad Burton, Jeannie Martin, Caren Johnson, and Renee' Kreig. Standing Richard Reel (Youth Agent LaPorte County), Meredith Ayres, Doris Peterson, Raleigh Fosbrink (Purdue Staff), Mona Downhour, Meg Burnworth, Barbara Hughes, Allen Hughes, Kay Ross, and Bill Peek (State 4-H Staff).

An interesting talk was given by L. M. Busche of Purdue on his recent trip to Germany.

County Agent Howard McCarty and Home Agent Cora Zell St. Amand presented the leaders present with leadership certificates for the number of years each had served as an adult leader. 4-H leaders present and the townships in which they served were: Mrs. Harold Wyatt, Carrollton; Mrs. Harold Wilson, Democrat; Mrs. Gene Maxwell, Tippecanoe; Mrs. Joe Henderson, Madison; Mrs. Dwight Beard, Clay; Mrs. Richard Milner, Monroe; Mrs. Samuel Sinn, Washington; Mr. and Mrs. Raymond Nicoll, Adams; Lawrence Douglas, Carrollton; W. S. Weaver, Deer Creek; Paul Harrington, Democrat; Horace Pryor, Jackson; Robert L. Brown, Jefferson; Harold Thompson, Monroe and John T. Downham, Washington.

All leaders were given favors of 4-H automatic pencils as compliments of the Indiana Chain Store Council.

This Annual Banquet has continued to be one of the highlights for adult leaders. Many Delphi merchants have helped sponsor the project. The banquet for 1978 was held at the Delphi Methodist Church on November 16.

The 4-H Adult Leaders Banquet for 1979 was held at Honan Hall in Delphi on November 15. An Eastman Kodak Outstanding Leader Award was presented to Milton Rodgers. The Camden Lions Club gave a monetary award to Jon Zink, Curtis Yeakley and Dee Sanderson for Achievement Record books.

The banquet was sponsored by Delphi Merchants: Bassett & Talbert, Beesley's Department Store, Brosman's IGA, Culligan Water Conditioning, Kerlin Feed Mill, Loy Roofing Company, Production Credit Association, R. E. Pearson Sales, Dr. & Mrs. Larry Stauffer, Thompson Funeral Home, Todd-McLemore Motors, Inc., Union Bank & Trust Company, Wallmann's Certified Foods, Whiteman Bros. Elevator, Wilson Farm Service and Wynkoop Pharmacy.

Leaders for 1979 and the number of years they had served were: Mrs. Melvin (Donnabelle) Brown, 10; Ron Slavens, 5; Mrs. Milton (Pat) Rodgers, 7; Milton Rodgers, 6; Jim Flora, 6; Charles Meade Jr., 5; Mrs. Jim (Mary) Martin, 2; Jim Martin, 3; Gene McCarty, 7; Connie Clark, 1; Mrs. John (Doris) Peterson, 25; Bob Duff, 13; Mrs. Kevin (Kay) Ross, 1; Mrs. Dan (Bonnie) Snell, 4; Dan Snell, 4; Mrs. Dean (Joyce) Sanderson, 5; Larry Trapp, 1; Dean Cripe, 1; Mrs. Clyde (Mary) DuVall, 20; Tim Burke, 1; Mrs. Robert (Betty) Randolph, 27; Terry Snider, 1; Mrs. Carl (Joan) Mays, 10; Mrs. Don (Judy) Thelen, 1; William Maxwell, 8; Don Calvert, 4; Mrs. Dale (Meg) Burnworth, 5; Mrs. Richard (Mona) Downhour, 5; Meredith Ayres, 21; Mrs. Allen (Barbara) Hughes, 2; Allen Hughes, 2; Mrs. Craig (Jeannie) Martin, 3; Mrs. Ed (Caren) Johnson, 3; Robert Scott, 8; Jeff Shanks, 9; Rick Ayres, 3; Mark Redding, 3; Mrs. Chuck (Janet) Spooner, 1; Mrs. Kent (Sharon) Montgomery, 5; Brad Burton, 2; Mrs. John (Marsha) Stoner, 4; Harold Sprague, 6; Charles Geheb, 11; W. S. Weaver, 42; and Dix Weaver, 3.

Some former leaders who have served 15 or more years and the year they retired were: Roy Slavens, 31 years and Junior Snider, 30 years in 1978; Charles Meade Sr., 20 years and Wayne Landes, 18 years in 1977; Miss Reba Shanks 37 years in 1970; Mrs. Cora Zell St. Amand, 16 years in 1963; Richard Harlow, 32 years in 1959; Hubert T. Ebbinghaus, 35 in 1957 and Harold Thompson, 22 years in 1955.

More than 1,000 adults have served as leaders for 4-H Clubs in Carroll County.

NORTHERN INDIANA ENTOMOLOGY FIELD DAY

The first Northern Indiana Entomology Field Day was held on June 30, 1979 at the Leatherwood Farm located northeast of Delphi. This was attended by 65 4-H Club members from Northern Indiana. Plans were made to have this field day again in 1980 at the same location. Brian Metzger of White County, Greg Hellman of Allen County and Bruce Ragan of Carroll County assisted members of the Purdue staff in giving help to 4-H members on suggestions for catching insects and methods of displaying them at the 4-H Fair. Awards given were: Identification books, nets, Entomology boxes, killing jars and pens. Those attending brought their own sack lunches and drinks were furnished.

Part of the Carroll County 4-H Leaders who attended the Leaders Banquet on November 17, 1978 and the number of years they had served. Left to right: W. S. Weaver, 41; Junior Snider, 30; Robert Duff, 12; Meredith Ayres, 20; Mrs. Robert (Betty) Randolph, 26; Charles Geheb, 10; and Mrs. John (Doris) Peterson, 24.

FALL CROP SHOW

The 4-H County Fair has been held early in the year before most farm crops were ready to show. Crop shows have been held in November or December for 4-H and FFA members to exhibit their crops. For several years these shows were held at Bassett and Talbert's showroom when it was located in the building on the corner of Main and Market Streets in Delphi. Later the show was held in the REMC auditorium in Delphi. These were sponsored by the Delphi Chamber of Commerce with the help of local merchants, county organizations and seed companies.

The shows in 1978 and 1979 were held at the Carroll High School Agriculture room.

4-H FAIR PICTURES

Each year at the Carroll County 4-H Fair pictures are taken of winners in various projects exhibited. These pictures taken by the Carroll County Comet are a few of the winners in 1979.

Comet photo
4-H Fair Foods 1979 left to right: Donelle Craft, Tara O'Farrell, Michelle Oilar, Michelle Sullivan, all champions and Deb Maxwell, Reserve Grand Champion.

Comet photo
4-H Fair 1979 Plant Science and Forestry left to right: Brett Loman, Reserve Grand Champion Forestry; Jane Shanks, Grand Champion Plant Science.

Comet photo
4-H Fair 1979 Woodworking, left to right; John Brown, Grand Champion; Neal Lybrook, champion; Monty Edging, champion; Scott Jennings, Reserve Grand Champion.

Comet photo
4-H Fair 1979 Junior Clothing, left to right: Deanna Wilimitis, Lana Lowery, Liesl Stauffer, all champions.

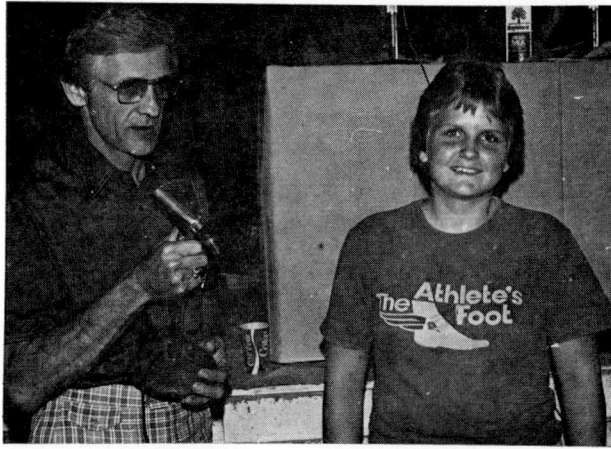

Comet photo
4-H Fair 1979. Carla Gangwer, right, of Democrat Township received the first "Outstanding 4-H Achievement Award" at the Carroll County 4-H Fair auction on Thursday evening. The award was presented by Richard Oilar of Flora, member of the 4-H Exhibit Association. The donor of the award is unknown. Selection is based on achievement and the amount of work demonstrated by the individual named. Next year the Exhibit Association and 4-H Leaders will choose the winner.

140 • CARROLL COUNTY RURAL ORGANIZATIONS

Grand Champion Barrow of the 1979 4-H Fair shown by Liesl Stauffer. Those in the picture left to right were: Susan Abbott, second Runner-up of the Queens Court; Liesel Stauffer, Dean Berry, Jerry Jenkins, Lori Kremer, Miss Congeniality of the Queen's Court and Ben Stauffer, brother of Liesl.

4-H Fair, 1979 Crafts, left to right: Wendy Bailey, David Lybrook, Deb Maxwell, Rene Franek, and Matt Leahy, all champions.

4-H Fair 1979 winners in Gardening, left to right: Maggie McCormick, champion; Shawn Martin, Reserve Grand Champion; Bernie Leinberger, champion.

4-H Fair, 1979. The Grand Champion wether lamb of the 4-H Fair was sold by David Downhour to Ritchey's Dog House at Burlington for $1.15 per pound. Left to right kneeling, Downhour and his nephew, Nathan Beckner. Behind, Mrs. Joyce Ritchey and 4-H Fair Queen Luanne Fry.

The 1979 Overall Showmanship Award in memory of Mark O'Farrell was presented to Rita O'Farrell. In the picture left to right: Dave Kilmer; Carol and Paul O'Farrell donors of the award and Rita O'Farrell.

CHAPTER VI — 4-H AND FFA • 141

Carroll County 4-H Fair Dress Revue winners in senior division for 1979, left to right: Dee Sanderson, Sherri Duff, Ann Wagoner, Lori Kremer, Grand Champion; Myron Beesley presenting engraved tray to Grand Champion; Lisa Burnworth, Reserve Grand Champion; Annette Wyant and Jerri Moore.

4-H Fair 1979, Child Development winners, left to right: Ann Wagoner, champion; Beth Wallace, Reserve Grand Champion; Janet Rodgers, Grand Champion.

4-H Fair 1979 Home Furnishings winners left to right: Connie Abbott, champion; Sherri Duff, Grand Champion; Liesl Stauffer, champion; Tara O'Farrell, Reserve Grand Champion.

FUTURE FARMERS OF AMERICA

Courses in Vocational Agriculture under the National Vocational Act were first established in 1917. A number of local departments developed so-called "Agricultural Clubs."

Thirty-three delegates representing 18 states met in Kansas City, Missouri in November 1928, and organized the Future Farmers of America.

In 1938 the organization purchased 28½ acres of land which was part of George Washington's estate near Alexandria, Virginia and established the National FFA Camp, where the National Headquarters are now located.

Membership is open to students 14 to 21 years of age who are enrolled in Vocational Agriculture in a public school. Girls were first admitted to membership in 1969. In 1978 there were 509,735 active members in 8,148 FFA Chapters in every state in the U.S. and Puerto Rico. The Virgin Islands had an affiliated chapter.

Through active participation in the FFA, members learn by taking part in and conducting meetings, speaking in public, participating in contests based on occupational skills, earning awards and recognition and becoming involved in cooperative efforts and community improvement. The FFA offers the opportunity for achieving a personal goal of becoming productive citizens in our democracy.

THE MOTTO

> LEARNING TO DO
> DOING TO LEARN
> EARNING TO LIVE
> LIVING TO SERVE

FFA CREED

"I believe in the future of farming, with a faith born not of words but of deeds—achievements won by the present and past generations of agriculturists' in the promise of better days through better ways, even as the better things we now enjoy have come to us from the struggles of former years.

"I believe that to live and work on a good farm, or to be engaged in other agricultural pursuit, is pleasant as well as challenging; for I know the joys and discomforts of agricultural life and hold an inborn fondness for those associations which, even in hours of discouragement, I cannot deny.

"I believe in leadership from ourselves and respect from others. I believe in my own ability to work efficiently and think clearly, with such knowledge and skill as I can secure, and in the ability of progressive agriculturists to serve our own and the public interest in producing and marketing the product of our toil.

"I believe in less dependence on begging and more power in bargaining; in the life abundant and enough honest wealth to help make it so—for others as well as myself; in less need for charity and more of it when needed; in being happy myself and playing square with those whose happiness depends upon me.

"I believe that rural America can and will hold true to the best traditions of our national life and that I can exert an influence in my home and community which will stand solid for my part in that inspiring task."

THE FFA EMBLEM

The National Emblem is made up of five symbols, each of which has unique significance.

The cross section of an ear of corn, which forms the outline of the emblem represents common agricultural interests since corn is native to America and is grown in every state.

The rising sun, signifies progress and the new day that will dawn when all farmers are educated and have learned to cooperate.

The plow, is the symbol of labor and tillage of the soil.

The eagle, signifies the national scope of the organization.

The owl, is the symbol of knowledge and wisdom.

Within the FFA emblem are the letters "FFA" and the words "vocational agriculture" signifying the integral relationship of this educational program.

The FFA colors are National Blue and Corn Gold. These colors should appear in connection with all meetings and in the equipment and paraphernalia used.

INDIANA FFA CHAPTER

As a result of a meeting of Vocational Agriculture teachers at Purdue, the Indiana FFA Chapter became the 19th State Chapter on September 6, 1929. All of the Indiana State FFA conventions have been held on the campus at Purdue.

At the 50th Annual Convention held June 19-21, 1979 a six foot granite marker weighing 4,500 pounds was placed in the northwest corner of the lawn at the Agricultural Administration Building. The marker, made of stone from Mt. Rushmore, South Dakota, was inscribed with a message paying tribute to the past members, advisors and friends of FFA. More than 1,000 FFA members attended the convention and helped dedicate the marker. At the same convention the FFA also sealed a time capsule to be opened in 25 years, or the year 2004. It contained information on the principal activities as well as the list of chapters and officers in Indiana.

The Indiana FFA has a leadership camp at Trafalgar which began in 1968. Another project is the FFA Barn with exhibits at the Indiana State Fair.

In 1979 there were 216 FFA chapters with more than 11,000 members in Indiana.

DEGREES

The four degrees of active membership are: "Greenhand," "Chapter Farmer," "Hoosier Farmer," and "American Farmer."

To be a "Greenhand" one must be regularly enrolled in a class in Vocational Agriculture and must possess facilities for and have a satisfactory program of supervised farm practice. The student must express a desire to be a member of this organization and agree to abide by its regulations, must be recommended by the local executive committee on a basis of these regulations, and must receive a majority vote of the members present in a regular meeting of the local chapter.

To be a "Chapter Farmer" one must have completed at least one year in Vocational Agriculture and be enrolled in Vocational Agriculture. The member must have earned and deposited in the bank or otherwise productively invested at least $25.

To be a "Hoosier Farmer" one must have completed two years of Vocational Agriculture, or earned and invested at least $200 and be able to pass certain tests.

To be an "American Farmer" one must have made and invested $500 and be able to pass certain tests.

Degrees are conferred when a member accomplishes the required work in the Vocational Agricultural Program in the school. Local chapters determine when a member is eligible for the first two degrees. The state organization determines eligibility for the third degree and the national organization confers the fourth degree.

The FFA Alumni Association was organized in 1971 for former FFA members and present and former Vocational Agriculture teachers.

DELPHI FFA CHAPTER

The Vocational Agriculture Class of the Delphi Chapter received its charter to the FFA in April 1938. The official name is "Future Farmers of Delphi High School."

Officers of the chapter for the first year 1938 were: Bernard Schmitter, president; John Bowman, vice president; Loyal Cripe, secretary; Kenneth Vaughn, treasurer and James Pierce, reporter.

Other members for 1938 were: Ivan Ashby, Robert Austin, Clayton Beard, Donald Bowman, Donald Buck, Robert Martin, Robert Cripe, Edgar Fountain Jr., Frank Hanaway, Wayne Rule, Herschel Smith, Ralph Baum, Harold Bussell, Robert Farmer, Hobart Hanaway, Vernon Isley, Robert Jones, Gene Maxwell, John Mullin, Fred Newman, Wm. Schnepp, Dick Swickard, Ernie Scott, Dick Coble, Ralph Gerbens, Charles Huffer, Bruce Kite, Clay Maxwell, Clayton Mullin, Ed. Hufford, Robert Schnepp, Charles Shultheis and Jack Bowman.

Stuart F. Guthrie was Vocational Agriculture teacher in Delphi for three years, from the fall of 1936 to the spring of 1939. During that time he organized the largest pig club in the state of Indiana, and for two years held a corn show in Delphi. Boys in the classes won a total of $110 in the National Farm Record Book contest during the three years.

In the spring of 1938 four members of the Delphi Vocational Agriculture class won prizes in the National Farm Record Book contest sponsored by the International Harvester Company and the Extension Service. Winners were: Ernest Scott, $25; Gene Maxwell, $10; Clayton Mullin, $10; and Jack Bowman, $5. This was the largest number of winners in any one high school in the U.S. Also in 1938, John Bowman and Dick Swickard won an essay contest and went to the State 4-H Conservation Club Camp at McCormick's Creek State Park.

In 1939, four members of the class won the trip awarded for participation in conservation activities. They were: Ivan Ashby, Vernon Isley, John Bowman and Dick Swickard. There were 125 from Indiana at the camp in 1939.

A typical example of the activities of the Delphi Vocational Agriculture class was a sheep shearing demonstration on April 4, 1939. Stuart F. Guthrie, the teacher, took his class to the Chris Schoff farm where Henry Mayo of Purdue showed them how to shear sheep. They used electric clippers. At least one sheep was sheared by each of the following: Bruce Kite, Herschel Smith, James Pierce, Michael Guckien, Robert Fountain, Max Martin, Robert Maxwell, Gene Maxwell, Kenneth Newell, Donald Stewart, Edgar Fountain Jr., Robert Martin, Wm. Schnepp, Ernest Scott, Kenneth Vaughan and Robert Brown.

Clarence Eyer was employed as Vocational Agriculture teacher at Delphi in the fall of 1939. He continued the projects for Vocational Agriculture boys and in December started a series of evening classes for adults. Another project was the printing of 500 "NO HUNTING WITHOUT PERMISSION" signs to sell to landowners in the area.

Dick Balser of the Delphi Chapter was secretary of the Indiana FFA in 1943, was elected president in 1944 and again in 1945. This was the first time that anyone had served as state president for two years.

FFA CORN HUSKING CONTESTS

The FFA of Delphi sponsored a Corn Husking Contest at the Ed. L. Kite farm four miles north of Delphi on the Carrollton Road on September 27, 1939. The members of the committee in charge of the contest were: Ed Kite Jr., Kenneth Vaughan, Herschel Smith and Gene Maxwell. Ernest Rohrabaugh, a neighbor, furnished a team and wagon for the contest. There were 20 contestants, and the winners were: Ed Kite Jr., first; Fred Newman, second; Robert Martin, third; Hobart Hanaway, fourth; Donald Stewart, fifth and Michael Guckien, sixth.

The County Contest was held October 2, 1939 at the Clarence Stout farm in Burlington Township with about 100 people present. There were 12 contestants from the six Vocational Agriculture classes in Carrollton, Camden, Flora, Burlington, Cutler and Delphi. Lloyd Cripe of Camden won the contest.

The FFA held a Corn Husking Contest on the Earl Newell farm in 1941. Contestants were: Kenneth Newell, Paul Ashba, Wayne Zinn, Donald Duff, George Hildebran, Robert Schmitter and Robert Fountain.

Robert Martin of Carrollton Township won first among 12 contestants in the District Vo-Ag Corn Husking Contest at the Fred Wagner Farm near Brookston in October 1941. He husked 905 pounds of corn in 40 minutes. He placed tenth in the State Contest held in Perry Township, south of Indianapolis where there were 24 contestants.

DELPHI FFA 1947-48

The years 1947 and 1948 were busy ones for the Delphi FFA Chapter directed by W. S. Weaver, Vocational Agriculture teacher in the Delphi High School from 1945 until 1976. The members of the Chapter rented 60 acres of land near Burrows, and conducted experiments with several kinds of crops and fertilizers. The boys set out $40 worth of fruit trees and sprayed about 100 trees for themselves and another 100 trees for neighbors. One fall the students made 50 gallons of cider from apples given to the boys from one of the orchards they had sprayed.

The chapter was one of the largest and best in Indiana. All 60 boys in the chapter took an active part and completed more than 600 different activities. Many of the members received special awards during the year. The Delphi FFA during the 1947-48 school year won eight first place awards in District and State Contests, plus the National Silver Emblem award which is one of the highest FFA honors given in the U.S.

Several members raised a new breed of white turkeys which are smaller than regular turkeys. The advantage of the smaller turkey was that "you do not have to eat turkey for a month after Christmas."

Members of the chapter sprayed lawns with 2-4-D to control weeds, used a new chemical for treating seed potatoes, and learned to test milk. FFA members conducted a regular monthly broadcast over Radio Station WASK at Lafayette. For a Public Service Project the students checked bicycles and issued stickers for those judged to be safe.

Bill Duff was president of the chapter for two years, and was awarded the Hoosier Farmer Degree. Some of the other members were: Jesse Wilson, Bill Roach, Quentin Clem, Max Hughes, Orton Zook Jr., Dale Brewer, Leonard Brummett, Alan Fross, Ed Brown, Richard Brown, Bob Gerard, Harold Griffey, Jim Tribbett, Richard Mears, Jim Scott, Don Burton, Glenn Calvert, Francis Wright, Don Huff, Jack Peters, Dale Craig, Merrill Hughes, James McClean, Wayne Swatts, Leroy Amstutz, Wayne Zook, Dick Brewer, Don Hankins, Clark Carr and Bradley Capper.

DELPHI FFA 1950

At the State FFA Convention at Purdue University in April 1950 members of the Delphi Future Farmers of America Chapter again won many honors. With an audience of more than 700 FFA members and guests, Bill Roach won the most coveted of FFA

CHAPTER VI — 4-H AND FFA • 145

Left to right: Roscoe Quick, Deer Creek Township Farm Bureau president; W. S. Weaver, vocational agriculture teacher; Charles T. Black, secretary-treasurer of Deer Creek Township Farm Bureau and members of the FFA chapter of Delphi High School with a ton of fertilizer presented to them by the Deer Creek Township Farm Bureau in May, 1949.

awards, first place and a cash award of $115 in the State Public Speaking Contest. The subject of his speech was: "Let's Make Farming Safer." Bill represented the state at the Regional Contest in Iowa that summer.

Roger Cain obtained the Hoosier Farmer Degree for projects carried over a three year period.

The Delphi chapter won the Gold Emblem and the award of $35 that went with it. The chapter also won $50 for placing first in Farm Fire Prevention activities and $25 for Farm Safety activities. The News Letter published by the chapter was awarded first place for the third consecutive year. The Reporter's Book compiled by Bill Roach won second place in the contest and Jack Peters and Bob Hankins won third place on their Treasurer's and Secretary's books, respectively.

The members planted over a thousand trees on their home places and also set out 300 locust trees for George Brewer. The members learned to prune grape vines and fruit trees. The chapter furnished Duroc gilts for several members and obtained war surplus materials from which members made heat hovers for tractors, canvas covers for machinery and goggles for use in the farm shop. Several members entered judging contests in the County Vocational Agriculture and 4-H projects.

The Indiana Farm Bureau sponsored many FFA activities, and helped pay the expenses of the state officers and American Farmer Degree winners to Kansas City, Missouri where the National FFA Convention was held each fall.

DELPHI FFA 1953-1954

In 1953 and again in 1954 members of the Delphi FFA Chapter attended the American Institute of Cooperation meeting as a result of winning an award sponsored by the Indiana Farm Bureau and the Indiana Farm Bureau Cooperative Association for having the most outstanding cooperative projects of any FFA Chapter in Indiana. This was the first time that any chapter had won the award for two consecutive years.

Those who went to the AIC meeting at the University of Missouri at Columbia, Missouri in 1953 were: Dan Lybrook, Ralph Hughes, Eddie Carr and John Furst.

In 1954 the AIC meeting was held at Cornell University in Ithaca, N.Y. Those who went were: Don Robbins, Ralph Hankins, Carol Flora and Roger Wilson. W. S. Weaver, their teacher, and Pat O'Hara, Farm Youth Director for the IFB accompanied the boys on both trips.

In 1954 the chapter also won a trip to the IFBCA Warehouse at Indianapolis. Those who went on the trip were: Don Robbins, Bob Brown, Jim Raderstorf, Cloyd Spear, Louis Dunn, Roger Wilson, John Furst, Roy Ward, Jerry Jeffries, Kim Black, Bill Peterson, W. S. Weaver, Ronnie White, Harold Zook, Frank Herron, George Hanaway, Gerald Frey, Joe Robinson, Tom Armstrong, Stanley Boyles, Ralph Hankins, Carl Peters, Dean Burton, Ralph Hughes, Dan Lybrook and Jerry Sneathen.

DELPHI FFA 1976

This was the first full year of the "Food for America" program in which the story of Agriculture was presented to 500,000 elementary school students.

A World Conference on Agricultural Education was held at the National FFA Convention in Kansas City, Missouri in November, 1976. Two hundred representatives from 24 countries discussed methods of improving agriculture and increasing the world food supply.

DELPHI FFA 1978-79-80

Officers of the Delphi Chapter for 1978-79 were: Jim Garrison, president; Kevin Cripe, vice president; Brad Hatke, secretary; Norman Anderson, treasurer; Scott Jennings, reporter and Chuck Veach, sentinel.

Officers for 1979-1980 were: Greg Stonebraker, president; Kevin Cripe, vice president; Mark Abbott, secretary; Scott Jennings, treasurer; Paul Jeffries, reporter and Curt Duff, sentinel. All of these boys attended the National FFA Convention at Kansas City, Missouri, November 6-10, 1979.

Those who have served as Vocational Agriculture teachers in Delphi were: Stuart Guthrie, fall of 1936 to spring 1939; Clarence Eyer, fall of 1939 to spring of 1942; Ray Hurt, fall of 1942 to spring of 1944; Arden Russell, fall of 1944 to spring of 1945; W. S. Weaver, fall of 1945 to spring of 1976; Dan Gottschalk, fall of 1976 to spring of 1977; Chester Peacock, fall of 1977 to spring of 1978; Wm. Morrison, fall of 1978 to spring of 1979 and Bruce Cunningham since July of 1979.

FLORA FFA JUDGING TEAMS

Harold Thompson was Vocational Agriculture teacher at Flora High School from 1937 to 1956. During that time he coached many livestock judging teams and several of them won high honors.

In 1940 a Dairy Team composed of Kenneth Cooke, Charles Dillman, Paul Johnson and Bill Wertz, won the Indiana State Fair Judging Contest. They won the right to represent Indiana at the National Dairy Show which was held at Harrisburg, Pennsylvania that fall.

In 1941 a Dairy Judging Team composed of Richard Flora, Merle Kuns, James Mummert and Robert Smith won the Indiana State Fair Judging Contest. They competed in the National Judging Contest at Memphis, Tennessee, that fall with Robert Smith being high individual in the judging of Brown Swiss cattle.

A team of four boys coached by Mr. Thompson won the Livestock Judging Contest at the Indiana State Fair in September 1947. This gave them the right to represent Indiana at the National Junior Judging Contest which took place at the International Livestock Exposition held in Chicago in December. Members of the team were: Bertis Berkshire, Fritz Schnepf Jr., Kenneth Sharp and Tom Allen, who was second high man in the entire State Contest and won a $75 scholarship to the Purdue University School of Agriculture.

At the show in Chicago the team again won first place. Fritz Schnepf Jr. was the high individual, and received a camera and a $300 scholarship. Tom Allen was second and received a $150 scholarship. Bertis Berkshire was fifth and Kenneth Sharp tenth. There were 98 individuals in the National Contest.

In 1949, the Dairy Judging Team from Flora, directed by Harold Thompson, won the Biltmore Trophy at the International Jersey Cattle Show in Memphis, Tennessee. Competing against 23 judging teams from 14 states, the team placed highest in the 4-H Section in which it was entered, and also had a higher score than the team from Kendallville which won in the FFA Section. Members of the team were: Tom Allen, Robert Kingery, and Marjorie Schnepf, with Max Douglas as alternate.

The Monroe Township and Carroll County Farm Bureau and Carroll County Farm Bureau Cooperative Association helped pay the expenses of the team for their trip.

Another Livestock Judging Team from Flora, coached by Harold Thompson, won first place at the Eastern National Livestock Judging Contest held at Timonium, Maryland, on November 12, 1955. Members of the team were: Harold Craft, Martha Schnepf, Patricia Ann Meade and Mary Jo Thompson. Mary Jo Thompson was high individual in the entire contest, Patricia was second and Martha third, thus giving the top three placings to girls on the Flora team.

The team was presented a trophy, $50 in cash and ribbons at a banquet. Expenses for the teams' trip to Maryland were paid by eleven local organizations and businesses.

FLORA FFA

Teachers of Vocational Agriculture at Carroll High School in recent years have been: Harold Thompson, 1937-1956; Leon McGaughey, 1956-1960; Billy Joe Latham, 1960-1961; Steve Mills, 1961-1970; George Fox, 1970-1973; Joe Gottschalk, 1973-1974 and Ted Howard since 1974. Jack Moss has been Agriculture teacher in Jr. High at Flora since 1971 and has been sponsor of the Junior High FFA Chapter composed of seventh and eighth grade students.

Officers of the Carroll High School FFA for 1979 and 1980 were: Joe Downham, president; Dave Bowman, vice president; Chris Wilimitis, secretary; Doug Sibbitt, treasurer; Dan Gangwer reporter; Mike Barnard, sentinel; Tim Redding, historian and Ted Howard, advisor.

Activities have included contests in Public Speaking, Agricultural Demonstrations and Parliamentary Procedure. Judging contests have included livestock, crops, entomology and soils. The FFA also sponsors a livestock judging contest for all high school students. Special events attended by members have included the State FFA Convention at Purdue, the National Convention at Kansas City, Missouri and summer leadership camps.

In 1979 the club farmed 21 acres, including 13 acres belonging to the school corporation and 8 acres donated by Dr. Bush.

Each year the club has a banquet for members and their parents. At the banquet April 25, 1979 awards were given to: Lonnie Spesard, highest grade average in agriculture class; Tony Rudd, outstanding chapter leader; Brad Crum, Star Chapter Farmer Degree, highest senior award, based on performance in the areas of scholarship, leadership and the member's farming program; and Chris Wilimitis, Star Greenhand Award for being the outstanding first year member.

The Hoosier Farmer Degree, available only to the top 4% of all members in the state has been awarded since 1973 to Rick Ayres, Terry Voorhees, Dale Orem, Larry Skiles and Randy McIlrath. The American Farmer Degree for the top one half percent of members in the U.S. has been awarded to Rick Ayres and Larry Skiles, who also served as President of the District in 1977-78.

Members of an Agriculture Advisory Board for 1978-79 were: Steve Mills and Meredith Ayres, Monroe Township; Bob Gangwer and Ed Wagoner, Democrat; Joe Scott and Ruel Crum, Burlington; Hubert Bowman and Benny Redding, Carrollton; George Downham and Craig Martin, Washington; Dick Pulley, Ag. Business and Jerry Hendress, Young Farmer.

ROSSVILLE FFA

Students from Clay township in Carroll County attend school at Rossville, in Clinton County, and several have been active in the FFA Chapter.

The Delphi Journal for September 14, 1961 reported that the Rossville High School Judging team participated in the State Livestock Judging contest. Members of the team were: Roger Frey, Gordon Biery, Jim Need and Gordon Cripe. They were coached by Charles Wolf, Vocational Agriculture teacher.

The Indianapolis Stockyards Marketing Institute presented clocks and desk pens to the winners. The team won $250 from the Indiana State Fair for expenses to go to the American Royal Livestock Show in Kansas City, Missouri to judge in October. The team also won a large rotating trophy presented by Hygrade Foods, Inc. and a smaller trophy for being the high team in judging cattle. Awards were presented at a banquet held on September 4, at the Atherton Center at Butler University.

At the American Royal Livestock Show, James Need won a gold award and Roger Frey and Gordon Biery won bronze emblems. As a team they won one of 13 silver awards. Alternate member Gordon Cripe was a gold medal winner in the livestock showmanship contest.

Bobby Mohler of the Rossville Chapter was a member of the National FFA band that played in several concerts at the event.

The Delphi Journal for September 5, 1963 reported that the Rossville High School Livestock Judging team of David Need, Gary Kuhns, Ron Beery and Ron Larson won third in the state competition held August 23 at the Indiana State Fair.

CUTLER FFA

The Wildcat FFA Chapter in the Cutler High School was organized in 1943 and was active until the school was closed in 1958. Vocational Agriculture teachers at the Cutler School during the last few years were: Harold McKinney, Mr. Patchett and Hubert Rule.

During that time members of the Chapter won several awards in the District and State Judging Contests with teams entered in Dairy, Livestock, Poultry, Crop and Land Judging Contests.

Among those who were active members of the FFA during the last few years were: Gary Deboy, Richard Mundell, Don Reef, Martin Wagoner, Larry Fellows, David Clem, Dana Hudson, Jerry Reef, Jack McCarty, Carl Mocherman and Meredith Ayres, who was the only member awarded the Hoosier Farmer Degree in 1958.

BURLINGTON FFA

Burlington FFA received their charter in 1952. At that time Charles Wolf was Vocational Agriculture teacher and Doyal McIlrath was elected the first president.

In 1954 Doyal McIlrath, Dewey McIlrath, Dick Eller and Kenneth Orem received the Hoosier Farmer degree.

Ronnie Hodson was a member of the National FFA Chorus in 1955.

In 1957-1958 Kenneth Orem was elected state treasurer and received the American Farmer Degree in 1958.

CAMDEN FFA

There was an active FFA Chapter in the Camden High School for several years until the school closed in 1965. Merrill Jacks, Clayton Mullin and Mr. Davies were teachers. The last Vocational Agriculture teacher at Camden was John R. Dunn. The last officers of the FFA at Camden were: Jim Hodges, Maurice Wolf, Joe Wallace, Jerry Walters, Ron Flora and Mike Groninger. Among those who were active in the chapter and later operated farms in the community were: Harold Herr, Carl Forgey, Galen Snoeberger and Gary and Larry Penn.

The chapter raised money by selling garden seeds. Many of the members attended the State Conventions at Purdue University and several Farm Progress Shows. Field trips were taken to Chicago to visit the Board of Trade, the International Livestock Show and other points of interest. Members participated in several soil and livestock judging contests.

BURNETTSVILLE AND TWIN LAKES FFA

Students from Adams Township in Carroll County attended High School at Burnettsville and were active in an FFA Chapter organized about 1954 by J. McDaniels, the Vocational Agriculture teacher. Richard Harlow taught Vocational Agriculture for about two years and was succeeded by Donald E. Huff who began teaching at Burnettsville in July 1958.

Schools were consolidated in 1963 and the Burnettsville High School students moved to Twin Lakes High School at Monticello. Mr. Huff continued as Vocational Agriculture teacher at Monticello until July 1967. Don Purkhizer has been Vocational Agriculture teacher since 1967.

During these years students from Adams and Jefferson Townships took an active part in the FFA program at the Twin Lakes School.

AGGRESSIVE YOUNG FARMERS

A recent project of the FFA was the Aggressive Young Farmers organization. The Delphi Chapter for former students of the Delphi Community School Corporation was organized in November 1976. Charter members were: Arni and Jan Bol, Gary and Sue Cleaver, Larry and Connie Davies, Dan and Cindy Gottschalk and Phil and Teresa Maxwell.

Members who joined later were Larry and Donna Thompson, Murray and Christina Gingrich and Larry and Marla Storm.

Officers for 1977 were: Gary Cleaver, chairman; Cindy Gottschalk, secretary and Dan Gottschalk, advisor.

Officers for 1978 were: Arni Bol, president Donna Thompson, secretary; Teresa Maxwell, treasurer and reporter and Dan Gottschalk, advisor.

Officers for 1979 were: Larry Thompson, president; Phil Maxwell, vice president; Sue Cleaver, secretary; Teresa Maxwell, treasurer and reporter and Dan Gottschalk, advisor.

The chapter has 10 monthly meetings each year at the homes of members. A recent program included discussion of Roberts Rules of Order of Parliamentary Procedure. At another meeting Rev. William Heinrich presented a program and movie on Almond Farming in California.

The chapter sponsors several trips during the year, including the State Fair, Farm Progress Show, State Young Farmers Tour and the State Young Farmers Convention, held February 22-24, 1979 at the Indianapolis Convention Center.

Members take an active part in community activities by contributing to such things as the Ambulance Service and furnishing money for prizes and awards at the White and Carroll County 4-H Fair.

SOIL SAVERS

Another Young Farmers Chapter associated with the FFA in the Delphi School was organized February 13, 1979. They named their organization "Soil-Savers". Charter members were: Alan and Barbara Hughes, Steve and Terri Brummett, Ed and Marsha Oilar, Doug and Chris Duff, and Dan and Cindy Gottschalk. Officers were: Alan Hughes, president and Marsha Oilar, secretary.

NEW GENERATION YOUNG FARMERS

The Young Farmer Chapter associated with the Vocational Agriculture department of the Carroll High School, and named New Generation Young Farmers is primarily designed for persons between the ages of 21-35 and is intended to fill in the spaces between the Agriculture High School classes and the local Adult Farmer classes. Monthly meetings are held at the member's homes except during planting and harvest months. Topics have ranged from local speakers to a field trip to the Ralston Purina Research Farm at St. Louis, Missouri.

Members of the New Generation Young Farmers in 1979 were: Bill and Jodi Pickart, Craig and Jeanne Martin, Dave and Marilyn Minich, Larry and Kathy Johnson, Ed and Wanita Wagoner, Ed and Caren Johnson, Jerry and Mara Hendress and Darryl and Sue Lane. Adult advisor was Ted Howard of Carroll Consolidated High School.

CHAPTER VII

FARM BUREAU

In 1910 the Binghampton Chamber of Commerce in Broome County, New York, invited local farmers to join, and named them on an agricultural committee. The Chamber already had several other committees, and referred to them as the "Traffic Bureau," and the "Manufacturers Bureau" etc. so it was only natural to refer to the committee of farmers as the "Farm Bureau."

On March 20, 1911 Binghampton County hired a County Agent, and he used the "Farm Bureau" of the Chamber of Commerce as the organization to help him with extension work in the county. On January 1, 1913 the County Agent helped organize the Broome County Farm Improvement Association in order to work with a larger number of farmers in all parts of the county. In 1914 this new organization was merged with the Chamber of Commerce Committee and the name was changed to Broome County Farm Bureau.

As County Agents were appointed in other counties, farmers were encouraged to organize and help them carry on the work of extension. Some county groups called these organizations "Farm Bureau" while others used such names as "Better Farming Association" and "Soil and Crop Improvement Association."

AMERICAN FARM BUREAU FEDERATION

By 1919 there were 12 state organizations, and representatives of these organizations met at Ithaca, New York to consider the formation of a national organization. Plans were made for a meeting at Chicago on November 12-14, 1919 at which 500 delegates and visitors from 31 states met and organized the American Farm Bureau Federation. Indiana was the first state to join the new national organization, which was ratified by 28 states with a total of 400,000 members. Dues for AFBF were set at 50¢ per member. J. R. Howard of Iowa was elected president. The main office for the American Farm Bureau Federation was established in Chicago, and a legislative office was opened in Washington, D.C.

Agreement between AFBF and USDA

As farmers became better organized with state and national organizations, they became interested and active in more than just the Extension Service. Farmers used their new organization for the purchasing of farm supplies, marketing of farm products, and for the promotion of legislation for agriculture. These commercial activities created a problem for the Extension Service. Business men objected to the promotion of business activities by a County Agent. Other farm organizations objected to the help the Farm Bureau organizations were receiving from the Extension Service. Recognizing these problems, the AFBF and the USDA on April 22, 1921, signed an agreement which included the following statement:

"Since these County Extension Agents are part of a public service as defined in the Smith-Lever Act and receive some part of their salary from public funds, they are to perform service for the benefit of all the farming people of the county whether members of the Farm Bureaus or not, and are to confine their activities to such as are appropriate for public officials to perform under the terms of the Smith-Lever Act. The County Agents will aid the farming people in a broad way with reference to problems of production, marketing, and formation of Farm Bureaus and other cooperative organizations, but will not themselves organize Farm Bureaus or solicit memberships, receive dues, handle Farm Bureau funds, edit and manage the Farm Bureau publications, manage the business of the Farm Bureau, engage in commercial activities, or take part in other F.B. activities which are outside their duties as Extension Agents."

INDIANA FARM BUREAU

In January 1919, a meeting was held at Purdue to discuss the formation of a state organization of farmers. Purdue leaders prominent in the meeting were

Dean J. H. Skinner, T. A. Coleman, and Prof. W. C. Latta. A committee named at this meeting arranged for a state meeting in Indianapolis in February. Forty representatives from 15 counties met and appointed a committee to make a survey of farmers in several counties to determine interest in a state organization. Another committee was appointed to draw up a Constitution and By-Laws to present at a state meeting in March.

On March 25, 1919, 400 delegates representing "Farmers' Associations" and "Better Farming Associations," as many of them in Indiana were called, met at the Claypool Hotel in Indianapolis and organized the Indiana Federation of Farmers' Associations. By the time of the first state convention on November 18, 1919 there were organizations in 54 counties, and by the end of 1919 there were 81 counties with Farmers' Associations. A brief statement of purpose approved at the organization meeting was: "an organization of the farmers, by the farmers, to protect the interests of farmers; and by education, legislation and other honorable means, to promote the largest good for all the people."

In the beginning, Farm Bureau leaders saw the danger of entangling alliances. Although feeling very friendly toward the County Agricultural Agent and Purdue University, pioneers in the movement specified that a County Agent, or a representative of the college could not be a delegate or hold office in the new Farmers' Organization.

John G. Brown of Monon was elected president of the new state organization. A newsletter called the "Organized Farmer" was published. An editorial in the issue for June 1919, stated: "We are not for class legislation, but a square deal between the three general classes—producers, distributors and consumers—The farmers represent the land owners, the homemakers, the law-abiding element. Hence this great movement of organizing and federating the farmers will make for the stability and perpetuity of our civil and religious institutions."

The second Annual Convention of the Indiana Farmers' Association was held on November 16, 1920 and the second convention of the AFBF was held on December 6, 7, and 8 at Indianapolis.

In December 1923 the name of the state organization was changed to Indiana Farm Bureau Federation, and the name of the newsletter was changed to Hoosier Farmer.

There is no complete record of membership in the Indiana Farm Bureau for 1919, but in 1921 membership reached 64,420, a figure not to be attained again until 1946. The membership for 1979 was 284,048, which was the largest membership ever reached by any state. The AFBF had more than three million members in 1979.

Farm Bureau Districts

During the first year meetings of the new State Farmers' Organization were held nearly every month. At a meeting in April it was decided that Indiana would be divided into ten districts, with one director from each district. The ten district directors, together with the state officers, made up the Board of Directors for the state organization. These same districts have been used by most of the cooperatives organized by the Indiana Farm Bureau.

Carroll County was located in District 3 with seven other counties: Benton, Cass, Clinton, Jasper, Newton, Tippecanoe and White. The first director for the district was C. W. Hickman of Tippecanoe County who served during 1919. E. E. Reynolds of Tippecanoe County was director in 1920 and C. S. Moore of Clinton County served in 1921. Burton D. Honan of Carroll County was elected in 1922 and served four years as district director. Guy McMullin of White County served from 1926 to 1930, and Arthur E. Arnott of Jasper County served from 1931 to 1958. Lawrence Holloway of Clinton County has served as director since November, 1958.

Those who have served as director of the Women's Department representing District 3 have been Mrs. Ida Chenoweth, Tippecanoe County; Mrs. Austin (Effie) Cochran, Clinton; Mrs. O. W. Stevens, Tippecanoe; Miss Vivian Henderson, Carroll; Mrs. Nelson

Arthur E. Arnott of Jasper County served as Director of District 3 Farm Bureau from 1931 to 1957.

Rupe, Cass; Mrs. W. B. Combs, Clinton; Mrs. James (Blanche) Viney, Carroll and Mrs. Kenneth Walters, Jasper County.

Mrs. Harvey Bupp of Newton County has been secretary treasurer of District 3 Farm Bureau since 1956.

Women in Farm Bureau

When the Indiana Federation of Farmers' Associations was organized it was a men's organization. Only three women attended the first Annual State Convention November 18, 1919. One of the first concerns of the new organization was the low quality of rural schools and they felt that women might solve that and other problems.

The Hoosier Farmer of February 1922 reported: "FARM WOMEN TO HAVE PART IN FEDERATION AFFAIRS:—The Executive Committee of the Indiana Federation of Farmers' Associations has decided to call a conference of farm women, near the middle of February, at which meeting consideration will be given to the introduction of farm women's problems in the program of State Federation work. Each county will be asked to send one delegate to this conference and any other farm woman will be welcome to attend the meeting.

". . . It is the feeling that through the combined efforts of farmers and their wives the Federation can render a greater service than is possible under the present system of organization."

A later issue of Hoosier Farmer reported on the first conference held on March 7, 1922: "The scores of delegates that filled the Palm Room of the Claypool Hotel cheered the six women speakers—the first in the history of Indiana Farm Bureau, as they made point after point . . . speaking out clearly in favor of better homes, better schools, better roads, better churches, and a richer and varied rural social life. . . ."

Mrs. Charles W. Sewell of Benton County was one of the speakers at that first meeting on March 7, 1922. Seven years later she was named head of the Women's Department and then served as chairman of Home and Community Activities of the AFBF for 16 years. She expressed her philosophy in these words: "You can't be loyal indefinitely to a fertilizer bag, an oil drum or an insurance policy." The injection of moral and spiritual values by the women made a significant contribution to the growth and stability of Farm Bureau.

Since a primary interest of the new women's branch of the state organization was the improvement of rural schools, it was only natural to select a teacher as head of the new department. They selected a man, L. A. Pittenger, a farmer and teacher from Delaware County, who was a director of the state organization. He later became president of what is now Ball State University.

For a few years the Women's Department operated as a separate organization, and held separate meetings. Women's groups were organized in several counties. One woman in each of the ten Farm Bureau Districts was appointed, and on February 3, 1923 the committee of ten District Women's Leaders met at Indianapolis and outlined a more extensive and definite program.

Wm. H. Settle, new president of the state organization appointed Mrs. Verna Hatch as chairman of the Women's Department, but it was not until three years later that she was considered the department head.

Women began to take a more active part in township, county and state meetings, and helped establish the Indiana State Fair Girls' Camp, with each county paying the expense of one 4-H girl to this ten-day camp.

President Settle called a meeting of one woman in each Farm Bureau District on October 27, 1926. On that date the Social and Educational Department was officially organized as a part of the Indiana Farm Bureau, and Mrs. Verna Hatch was named as head of the department. Indiana was one of the first states in the nation to have a Women's Department. Women who have served as head of the department were: Mrs. Ed (Verna) Hatch, 1926-28; Mrs. Harry (Gertrude) Modlin, 1928-29; Mrs. Charles W. (Edna) Sewell, 1929-35; Mrs. Benjamin (Lillie) Scott, 1935-47; Mrs. Russell (Ethel) Cushman, 1947-55; Mrs. Paul (Nellie) Flinn, 1955-57 and Mrs. Guy E. (Lois) Gross, since 1957.

The name of the S & E Department was changed to the Farm Bureau Women's Department by official action of the Farm Bureau Board of Directors on March 7, 1957.

Indiana Farm Bureau Presidents

Indiana Farm Bureau Presidents have been: John G. Brown, 1919-1922; Wm. H. Settle, 1923-1934; Lewis Taylor, 1935-1936; Hassil E. Schenck, 1937-1957; George Doup, 1958-1976 and Marion Stackhouse since 1977.

Tax and Legislative Department

In the early days in Indiana, the great majority of people were farmers. Many farmers were elected to the State Legislature so there was no great need for a farm organization to look after farmers' interests in the legislature. Nearly everyone owned property, and the tax on property represented a reasonable measure of ability to pay and a measure of benefits received. As the state grew and the population increased in the cities, it became evident that farmers needed an organization to represent them at the legislature. As business and professions developed, the property tax became out of date and was no longer a tax based on ability to pay, nor was it a fair measure of benefits received.

It was only natural that when the IFB, first called Indiana Federation of Farmers' Associations, was formed one of the first activities concerned taxes and legislation. This has continued to be one of the most important activities of the IFB. In the fall of 1920 the president of the state organization appointed a committee of five to draft a program, and attend the session of the State Legislature in the interest of organized agriculture. The program of the committee was based on strict economy in government and a broadening of the tax base. Many counties also appointed committees to help the state committee at the legislature.

For sixty years the Indiana Farm Bureau has represented farmers at the legislature, and has had a significant influence on legislation. During this time many people have served as representatives for FB. Anson Thomas had served more than 30 years when he retired in 1961. Among the many others who served were: George Harvey, Samuel L. Thompson, Vance L. Denney, Hollys Moon, and many other employees and elected officials.

During 1979 the IFB was represented in the legislature by William F. Marvel, William A. Hadley, Meredith M. Kincaid, Wilber M. Schakel and James Barnett.

Glenn W. Sample, as first vice president of IFB, helped create Ivy Tech in 1963, and in recent years has spent full time directing the activities of Ivy Tech until he passed away on January 5, 1980.

The following pages outline a few of the many acts of the Indiana Legislature affecting farmers.

State Legislature from 1921 to 1979

1921

In 1921 the legislature passed a Pure Seed Law which was badly needed because Indiana had become the dumping ground for low grade seeds from other states. The legislature also passed a Blue Sky Law which protected investors in stocks, bonds and securities. Another law of interest to farmers was one which permitted interurbans to haul livestock.

1923

In August 1922 the state FB organization appointed a legislative committee for the 1923 session. The committee worked out a program to be offered by organized agriculture, and on January 15, 1923 met with representatives and discussed the program with them. This was the first time in Indiana that representatives of agriculture had met with members of the legislature to discuss a program with them.

One of the laws passed by the 1923 legislature was the Indiana Agricultural Cooperative Act, which was vetoed by Governor McCray. A tax of two cents per gallon on gasoline, and a higher fee for a license for heavy trucks helped relieve property taxes. Another law permitted counties to pay as much as $1,000 for a County Agent. Attorney fees for large ditches was reduced from four percent to one percent. The State Board of Accounts was given permission to investigate all contracts made by local officials. Another law reduced the bond limit for gravel roads.

One unique feature of the 1923 session was that it was referred to as the "Farmers' Legislature."

1925

The 1925 session re-enacted the Indiana Agricultural Cooperative Act and Governor Ed Jackson signed it on February 23. This bill was passed by 91 to 0 in the House and 37 to 2 in the Senate, which proved that the Indiana Farm Bureau was gaining influence in the State Legislature. This bill was sponsored by I. Harvey Hull, a member of the legislature who was a director of the IFB, and later was manager of the IFBCA. Many of the agricultural cooperatives in Indiana have been incorporated under the act.

A bill was enacted which increased the gasoline tax from two to three cents per gallon, this money to go to the State Highway Fund for road construction and maintenance.

A bill was passed which set up rules and regulations whereby TB testing for cattle was made compulsory in Indiana. The department of livestock and the statistical department were established at Purdue University. A bill was passed which placed regulations upon the sale of unpasteurized or raw milk in Indiana. A great deal of effort was put forth to secure an amendment to the State Constitution, which would make possible the enactment of a Net Income Tax Law.

1927

An important bill passed by the 1927 legislature provided that public officials could not spend more money than had been appropriated. This was one of the best checks upon public expenditures that has ever been enacted into law in Indiana.

Another law provided for the reassessment of real estate. A survey showed the farm land was assessed at approximately 21 percent more than its cash value.

There were many other bills ranging from control of the corn borer to changes in tax laws introduced in this session. The FB took a stand on all that affected agriculture. An unusual record was established in this session of the legislature—every major bill favored by the FB was enacted into law, while not a single major bill which the FB opposed was passed.

In 1927 the IFB established a permanent Department of Taxation and Legislation with Lewis Taylor, first vice president of IFB as director of the new department. According to the minutes of the board meeting, the policy of the department was "To study tax problems and legislation pertaining to them."

1929

Not many important bills were passed by the 1929 legislature, but the discussion on some bills brought to the attention of the people of Indiana the necessity of working out a program of tax equalization between real property and other types of income. A resolution was passed asking the governor to appoint a committee to make a study of new sources of revenue to finance the state government.

1931

The 1931 legislature was primarily concerned with tax laws. A bill providing for a tax on corporations failed to pass by two votes. A bill was defeated which would have diverted six and one-half million dollars from the State Highway Commission fund to the general fund. A bill was passed providing for the voters in the 1932 election to vote on an amendment to the State Constitution to provide for an income tax in Indiana.

A bill was passed which provided that budgets for 1932 and 1933 could not exceed the 1931 budget. The Governor's Committee on Taxes was continued for two years.

It was during the 1931 session that the first FB demonstration was staged. One thousand farmers were called in to council with the senators and representatives. The attitude was much improved after the visit.

1932 SPECIAL SESSION

In 1932 the IFB presented a petition with 40,000 names to the Governor requesting him to call a special session of the Indiana Legislature to consider taxes. Several thousand farmers went to Indianapolis to present the petition and the Governor called the special session to meet on July 7.

Among the first bills passed was one providing that about $12,000,000 of the state highway funds be sent to counties, cities, and towns to replace money being raised by property taxes. A bill was passed which limited total budgets to $1.50 per hundred dollars of assessed valuation. A bill was passed which merged 23,279 miles of township roads with the county highway system, and another bill declared a five-year moratorium on three-mile gravel road bonds.

Several other bills were passed reducing government expenses, and the total result was a reduction of about $30,000,000 in property taxes.

1933

A bill known as the "Milk Dumping Bill" was passed which made it unlawful to interfere with the transportation of any agricultural or dairy product upon the public highway. This stopped strong-arm methods used in milk strikes, and provided for differences to be settled around the conference table.

A bill provided that livestock buyers be required to furnish a bond guaranteeing payment of all purchases of livestock. A law was repealed which had required all trucks hauling livestock to the Indianapolis market to be cleaned after livestock was unloaded. This saved farmers about $40,000 per year.

Another bill provided for the payment of $600 by the state to each teaching unit. This amounted to about $12,000,000 which had formerly been paid by property owners.

The most important act was the passing of the Gross Income Tax Bill, which was estimated would raise $14,000,000 in the first year. The Intangible Tax Bill was passed, which provided for a tax rate of 25 cents per hundred dollars of value, and was estimated to raise $1,500,000 per year.

1935

The most important act of the 1935 legislature was the passing of the Indiana Statewide Rural Electric Membership Act, which made possible the development of the great REMC system in Indiana.

1936 SPECIAL SESSION

A Special Session was called in 1936 to enact the Public Welfare Act. This was necessary to meet the requirements of the National Welfare Act. It provided that the county provide 20%, the state 30% and the federal government 50% of the total cost.

1937

A bill was passed which made the Bond Moratorium Law continuous, and outlawed three-mile gravel road bonds for all time.

The maximum property tax rate was changed to $1.25 in rural areas and $2 in cities and towns.

1939

In 1939 an attempt was made to lower the rate on the Gross Income Tax. The senate held a public hearing in the state house attended by about 10,000 farmers. No change was made on the Gross Income Tax rates.

The State Highway Department took over 383 miles of streets where state highways went through cities and towns. This provided property tax relief for the cities and towns.

A law was passed which set up grades, weights and standards for eggs. This gave the producer some incentive to produce better eggs, and gave the consumer some indication of the quality of eggs he purchased. Before this law was enacted an egg was an egg until it hatched.

Bills affecting the REMC's provided that directors could be paid for their time, and provided for the election of only a part of the board each year.

1941

Six bills were introduced which would have been detrimental to the development of REMC's in Indiana. All were defeated. One would have required a license fee of $5 on each weighing, measuring and metering device in Indiana. This would have cost about $23,000,000. Another bill would have permitted public utilities to build less than one mile of line without first securing a permit from the Public Service Commission. This would have permitted utilities to split up territory so that the required number of patrons could not be secured by the REMC to develop their project.

A bill introduced by the moving picture industry was defeated. This bill prohibited any free moving pictures, regardless of whether it was a school, educational, advertising or almost any other type of exhibition, unless it was held in a regularly licensed theater.

Another bill which did not pass was known as the Lawyer Bill. This bill would have required that all adjustments, settlements, contracts and agreements be written by a lawyer. It would also have provided that no one could appear before any board, commission or hearing unless he was a lawyer.

A new law provided that property could be assessed for taxes at less than market price.

1943

A law regarding the operation of farm machinery on the highway provided that no license was required to move tractors and machinery from one part of a farm to another. A license fee of $3 was required for tractors on the highway for any other purpose, and a special farm machinery license was available at $3 for machinery such as seed cleaning or paint spraying equipment.

1945

A Bangs Eradication Bill was passed which provided for the control and eradication of Brucellosis in cattle in Indiana.

A Diagnostic Laboratory was created at Purdue University to be operated by the Department of Veterinary Science.

A Farm Research Department was established at Purdue University to find new uses for agricultural products. Among the projects to be worked on were plastics, synthetic rubber, and alcohol from farm products.

The REMC Act was amended to provide for the transfer of small sections of electric lines from one electric company to another.

The Soil Conservation Act of Indiana was amended to make it easier to establish and operate Soil Conservation Districts.

A Flood Control Commission was created to help prevent damage from floods, and to help preserve water resources in the state.

Township trustees were authorized to help financially with procurance and operation of township fire fighting equipment.

1947

A bill was enacted for marketing research to improve the marketing, handling, storage, processing, transportation and distribution of agricultural products.

A law was passed prohibiting the sale of alcoholic beverages on the Indiana State Fairgrounds during the period of the State Fair.

A law was enacted which made the teaching of the effects of alcoholic drinks, tobacco, sedatives and narcotics upon the human body mandatory in grades four through eight of the public schools of Indiana.

A Holding Company Law was enacted granting school corporations the power to lease school buildings.

An act was passed creating a study commission to be known as "The Commission on Domestic Animals and Poultry Diseases." Their job was to prepare a re-codification of all Indiana laws and regulations relating to the control and eradication of communicable diseases in domestic animals and poultry.

Several bills were enacted to provide for consolidation of schools.

1949 AND 1951

Probably the most important act of these two legislatures was the re-codification of all the animal health laws into one law summarizing about 60 laws which had been passed from 1867 to 1949. No material changes were made in the laws, but only about one third as many words were used. This job was started in 1949 and finished in 1951. New laws were then enacted which provided for a longer tenure in the State Veterinarian's office, and provided for better control of TB, Rabies and Bang's Disease (Brucellosis). The Indiana State Livestock Sanitary Board was given the responsibility of working with the State Veterinarian in enforcing the animal health laws.

1953

Frequent outbreaks of vesicular exanthema in hogs in Indiana had been traced to the feeding of raw garbage. A law was passed prohibiting anyone from feeding uncooked commercial garbage.

1955

The program for the eradication of Brucellosis in Indiana was set up about one year when the state legislature approved a suggestion made by a member of the IFB Livestock Committee and created a state revolving fund of $100,000 to be loaned to counties to pay their share of the cost of the program. The money was repaid to the state by county funds available the next year in the county budget.

1957

The legislature passed a bill to create a new Veterinary Science School at Purdue University.

The gasoline tax was raised two cents per gallon to provide money for roads, and a surtax was added to the Gross Income Tax to provide funds for other needs.

1959

Provisions were made for a more uniform value to be used in assessment of personal property throughout the state, and the value of personal property for tax purposes was set at one third of its true cash value.

1961

A new law permitted the creation of an Indiana seaport on Lake Michigan.

1963

Indiana Vocational Technical College was established for vocational training and education. This program was expanded by action of the legislature in later years.

A law provided that farm land rezoned for other purposes be assessed at its value as farm land as long as it was used for farming.

Major changes were made in Indiana Tax laws. An increase in the amount paid by the state for schools helped many counties reduce the tax on property. The tax package enacted shifted farmers from a three eighths percent gross tax to 2% of adjusted gross income, and resulted in a lower tax for most farmers.

A two percent retail sales tax was enacted, but farmers were exempt on payments for production items. Changes were made in the tax on corporations to provide more revenue.

1965

Property tax relief provided by the retail sales tax and other elements of the 1963 "tax package" was retained.

All laws regarding water management were codified into one law. The new law placed control of county ditches in the hands of a local ditch board composed of the county commissioners and the county surveyor, and established simplified procedures for construction and maintenance of drains.

A new department of Natural Resources was created and took over activities that had been in several other departments.

1967

A Diagnostic Laboratory was established in Southern Indiana for poultry and livestock farmers.

A law provided for inspection of meat and dairy products by the State Board of Health.

A Motor Vehicle Inspection law was enacted.

1969

A provision was made for uniform traffic control devices for streets and highways in Indiana.

The State Fish and Game Laws were re-codified.

The Gas Tax was increased two cents per gallon and truck license fees were increased. The State Excise Tax replaced the property tax on motor vehicles effective in 1971.

Two million dollars was provided for a Food Science Laboratory at Purdue.

1971

A bill provided for regulation of pesticides and another set standards for confinement feeding of livestock and poultry.

Single member legislation districts were established for both the Senate and House.

Farm service buildings were exempt from inspection by the Indiana Administrative Building Council.

Approval was voted to allow a farm truck license to be purchased at one half price after August 1 each year.

1972

New legislation dealing with habitual traffic offenders was enacted.

A law provided for township trustees to be elected for an unlimited number of terms and another provided that 18 year olds could qualify as candidates for delegates to State Party Conventions.

A law was changed to provide for reassessment in all counties at the same time.

1973

Major changes in the tax laws provided for lower property taxes. The state sales tax was increased to 4%, and the extra money was used to reduce the property tax bill by 20%. Property tax levies were frozen at the 1973 level, and counties were permitted to collect income tax to provide money for the county.

The use of high phosphate detergents was left on the outlawed list for home laundry use, but was legalized for use by farmers in cleaning dairy and egg cleaning equipment.

1974

Fifteen million dollars was transfered from the local road and street fund to the State Highway Commission, making it possible to complete the Interstate Highway Construction Program in four years instead of ten years. Provision was made for this money to be repaid over a period of years from Federal Highway Trust Fund allocations.

A new law provided for only part of the county council to be elected at one time.

A new law was enacted which granted authority for any civil city, town, township or county to lease a building in a program similar to the School Building Holding Company Act of 1947.

Amendments were made to the annexation laws providing more protection for people living in the area.

1975

Money recovered in malpractice suits was limited to $500,000 with $100,000 coming from the insurance company and the remainder from a compensation fund established by the state of Indiana financed by contributions by all insurance companies. Attorney fees were limited to 15% of any amount paid by the compensation fund.

A Direct Primary Law was enacted which provided that party candidates for governor, lieutenant gov- and U.S. senator would be nominated by a Direct Primary instead of a State Political Convention.

Several changes were made in the Indiana Probate Code, including a provision for unsupervised administration of an estate.

The J.P. Court system was replaced by a County Court system to handle small claims.

1976

A change in the refund of taxes paid on motor fuel not used on the highway permitted a farmer to either apply for a refund each six months or claim a credit when he paid his State Income Tax.

Inheritance tax laws were codified and a few changes made.

A new formula was approved for distributing money from the state to schools.

Several changes were made in activities permitted by county and township government.

A new Criminal Code was adopted for the State of Indiana.

1977

Changes in the inheritance tax laws and Probate

Code provided that many small estates would not be required to file a State Inheritance Tax Return.

Controls were provided to limit the amount of increase in taxes resulting from higher valuation in the reassessment of real estate.

A new law was added which permitted livestock producers to register a brand for their livestock.

A committee was created to develop a program for the evaluation of state government agencies and made recommendations for termination of some of them.

Changes were made in eminent domain procedures which helped protect the interest of the land owner.

A law created a new pension program for police and firemen.

An "Open Door" law was passed which provided that government agencies make more of their meetings open to the public.

A new law provided rules and procedures for a county to establish parimutual betting activities.

1978

Seventy eight million dollars was appropriated out of the general fund for use on state and local streets and roads.

Tax relief was provided for the elderly, and for those who did certain work on their homes to conserve energy.

A "Sunset" bill was passed requiring government departments, agencies and programs to justify their existence.

The tax on motor fuel was simplified and included in the pump price.

1979

Provisions were made to build a new Agricultural Research Building at Purdue. Money was allocated to Purdue for various research projects, including research on gasohol and other alcohol products made from farm products.

A special reduction in property taxes was provided for homeowners and the rate on the State Gross Income Tax reduced.

A complicated set of controls was placed on local government units limiting the amount of property tax they could collect.

Additional exemptions were provided in the Inheritance Tax laws.

Legislation was passed requiring that the advertised price at a gasoline station be the same as that displayed on the pump. Gasohol sales were exempt from the State Sales Tax.

Fertilizer spreaders were exempt from the motor fuel tax.

Major changes were made in the financing of local schools. More money was provided by the state, and the cost of transportation was no longer included in the overall property tax limit for schools.

Legislation added cattle, dairy products and soybeans to the list of farm commodities which may be subject to a check off program if approved in a referendum by growers of each product.

Legislation was passed requiring a city annexing territories to develop a written fiscal plan and establish a definite policy relating to the annexed area.

New legislation required the elimination of the monthly fuel adjustment charge on a utility bill, and made this a part of the total bill.

Livestock Marketing

One of the first commercial projects of the Farm Bureau was to find a better way to market livestock. Most livestock was sold to local buyers who would buy livestock from local farmers and ship the livestock in carload lots to a terminal market. Some larger farmers, or sometimes a few neighbors, would have enough livestock to ship a carload to the market. Someone had to go along with the load to see that the animals were properly handled and sold when they arrived at the terminal market. Commission firms at the terminal markets had been closely associated with local livestock buyers, and were accused of taking more interest in selling livestock for them than for farmers.

In 1920 the state organization established a livestock marketing department and hired Mr. P. C. Ohler to manage a section of the stockyards at Indianapolis to handle livestock shipped by FB members. The new department charged one cent per head on hogs, sheep and calves, and four cents per head on cattle. This was much cheaper than sending someone with a load of livestock.

Producers Commission Association

In order to do a better job of selling livestock at Indianapolis, the Producers Commission Association was organized and started business on May 15, 1922. D. L. Swanson was the first manager. Scott Meiks was manager from 1926 until 1946 and Richard Cummins was manager from 1946 until 1970.

By December 1922 the PCA was handling 25% of the total market receipts, which was more than the total handled by the next three firms operating in that market. During the first seven months the PCA handled $1 million worth of livestock. PCA charged the same commission as other firms, and after paying operating costs, refunded the difference to Farm Bureau members who shipped livestock.

During 15 years (1923-1937) Producers handled an average of about 35% of the sheep, 25% of the hogs and 22% of the cattle each year at the Indianapolis market. During this time they refunded to FB members 25% of the commission paid for selling livestock. This was an average of $35,033.01 per year. During the first 25 years PCA refunded more than $800,000 to member patrons in cash refunds on commission charged.

In the early 1940's the volume of livestock at the Indianapolis market declined, and in 1946 Producers Commission Association had no net earnings.

Producers Marketing Association

Much of the livestock was being sold through local markets so in order to continue to be of service to livestock producers, the Commission Association was reorganized in 1946 as the Producers Marketing Association and established about 30 branch markets in Indiana. Some were established to assemble and ship hogs to packers, and others included an auction market for all livestock.

Most of the hogs assembled at the branch markets were sold through Eastern Order Buyers, Inc., a subsidiary owned jointly by PMA of Indiana and Producers Livestock Association of Ohio.

Branch Markets

A hog market established by the Producers Marketing Association at Logansport opened on March 3, 1947. A market study revealed that after the Producers Market was established at Logansport, the price paid for hogs in that area was 30 to 50 cents per hundred pounds nearer the market price at Indianapolis than it was before the market was established. The Wilson Packing Company plant was built at Logansport in 1968 and provided a market for hogs in the area. The Producers Market at Logansport was closed in 1971.

A market for hogs was opened at Klondike near Lafayette in 1948, and an auction market for all livestock was added in June 1950 with an open house on July 8, 1950. The auction market continued until December 1977. At that time Kenneth Murray, market supervisor for the PMA markets in Indiana stated:

"When we started our operation at Klondike back in 1950 there were over 100 such auctions in Indiana. Now there are only about 35 and half of them are up for sale.

"We are going for more direct or feedlot selling of cattle. The PMA takes the packer-buyer directly to the feedlot where the sale or transaction is made. Then the animals are shipped directly to the facility where they are weighed and shipped on to the packer."

Bernard Dauby, manager of the Klondike branch reported that during 1979, $12,000,000 worth of livestock was handled through the branch at Klondike.

Other Services

PMA was a member of the National Livestock Producers Association, Chicago, with similar Producers Livestock Associations from coast to coast. Services to farmers included the sales of all kinds of livestock, the procurement of all species of feeder livestock and breeding stock, market reports and many feedlot services as needed by farmers.

One service the Association provided was to handle futures contracts on livestock so that farmers could hedge their feeding operations. Several farmers and some employees took advantage of the service to speculate on futures contracts. The Association became over-extended financially and suffered a loss of more than $1,400,000 in June 1970. This loss more than wiped out the total value of all the preferred and common stock and it was necessary for PMA to file for bankruptcy. The Indiana Farm Bureau came to the rescue and loaned enough money to preserve the corporate structure. The PMA operating with Gene Shaver as manager continued to provide a livestock agency for farmers in Indiana.

During 1979 PMA, with 26 branch markets, marketed more than one million head of livestock in Indiana with a value of 225 million dollars.

Federated Marketing Service

When World War I ended, prices of farm products fell drastically.

A report by the U.S. Department of Agriculture shows that during the year 1920 the price of butterfat fell 22.4%, from 67¢ to 52¢; corn fell 53%; from $1.45 to 68¢; Wheat fell 16.8%, from $2.50 to $2.08; hogs fell 29.4% from $14.50 to $10.25; cattle prices declined 29.4% from $17.00 to $12.00. Prices continued to decline during 1921, and the price of wheat dropped to 60¢ a bushel and hogs to $6 per hundred. The price decline for these two years was the most severe ever recorded by the USDA.

In 1923 Congressman Finley Gray reported to the U.S. House of Representatives that during the previous two years, one third of the farmers of America had lost their farms and another one third were bankrupt, but were permitted to remain on their farms because their creditors did not want to take possession.

Prices of supplies farmers purchased remained high and this created a demand from farmers for the new Federation of Farmers' Association to do something about it for them. During 1919 and 1920 several county organizations pooled orders of members for fertilizer, twine and other farm supplies in order to get a better price.

During these two years the state organization published prices of twine and other supplies, and helped local associations get a better price.

In Henry County a local dealer for a major implement company agreed to sell machinery to Farm Bureau members at a special 10% discount. When the machinery manufacturer learned about this they refused to supply him with machinery, and he was forced out of business.

On December 13, 1920, the Federation, the Indiana State Grange, and the Indiana Farmers' Grain Dealers' Association organized the Federated Marketing Service to purchase farm supplies for farmers in the state. Its purpose was to gather and pool orders to get a better price. Local farmer elevators and shipping associations when available were used as local points for collecting orders and distributing supplies. In other areas the work was handled by county and community committees.

During 1921 the marketing service handled about $200,000 worth of fertilizer, coal and twine, refunded $1,656.42 to members, and ended the year with a net worth of $2,912.87. During January and February 1922 the marketing service lost money, and ended the two months with a net worth of only $195.09. The Grain Dealers' Association withdrew from the service and it was reorganized in March 1922 by the Federation of Farmers' Associations and the Indiana Grange. Louis F. Shuttleworth was hired as full time manager and business increased. During 1922 the service handled two million pounds of twine at a savings of about two cents per pound. A contract was signed with a fertilizer company to buy fertilizer in carload lots at a discount of $1.50 per ton in addition to the regular trade discount of seven percent. The Marketing Service contracted for the entire output of a coal mine, and added dairy feed to the list of supplies handled. By October 1922, the net worth was $5,151.56.

At the beginning of 1923, the Federation of Farmers' Association took over the interest of the State Grange in the Federated Marketing Service, and reorganized it as the Indiana Farm Bureau Purchasing Department. Mr. Shuttleworth was retained as manager, and business continued to increase.

At the end of the year October 31, 1923 the net worth had increased to $13,454.65. Sales for the year included about 12,000 tons of fertilizer, 1,275,000 pounds of twine, 16,000 tons of coal and 900 tons of feed.

Branch Warehouses

The Purchasing Department worked through county representatives who were directly responsible to the state office. During 1924 and 1925, ten warehouses were established in the state. In each case the county Farm Bureau members would approve the project and agree that they would not carry on purchasing activities that would compete with the branch warehouse. Farm Bureau members loaned enough money to the state organization to finance the warehouse in their county, which was controlled completely by the State Purchasing Department.

During 1924 the feed department was greatly expanded. In 1925 the department started handling clover and grass seeds. During 1925 feed was sold at a guaranteed price for future delivery, but the department did not protect itself by hedging. Money was lost by speculating on the grain market. Nine of the ten warehouses lost money, and the Purchasing Department ended the year with a deficit of $12,082.

The manager resigned, and I. Harvey Hull, who had been a director since 1922, was hired as the new manager on February 14, 1926. The story of the development of the IFBCA is in Chapter VIII.

International Fund

The IFB International fund is supported by contributions from FB members through their township and county organizations. The money is used to help support the Country Women's Council, the Associated Country Women of the World, Farmers and World Affairs and the International 4-H Youth Exchange.

The Associated Country Women of the World (ACWW) was organized in 1930 and has more than eight million members, representing Farm Bureau, Homemaker clubs and other women's organizations throughout the world. One of their projects is "Pennies for Friendship" with a goal of eight million pennies representing one penny per member each year. This money is used for a special project each year as determined by the ACWW Council.

Farmers and World Affairs (FWA) is a non-profit educational organization founded in 1956. It works primarily in cooperation with farm organizations to help the American Farmer become better informed, more concerned and more effective in building a world of peace and freedom. FWA is supported by voluntary contributions and by grants in aid of foreign currencies from the Bureau of Educational and Cultural Affairs of the U.S. State Department. FWA takes no position on political questions, either domestic or foreign, but believes that the well-being of our country depends on the democratic participation of well-informed citizens.

The IFYE program is explained in Chapter VI.

Modlin Memorial Fund

Gertrude C. Modlin, who had been state chairman of the Social and Educational Department of the IFB for about two years, died suddenly of a heart attack on November 24, 1929 while on her way to attend the Annual Convention of the IFB at Indianapolis.

In January 1930, the directors of the IFB elected Mrs. Charles W. Sewell of Otterbein as chairman of the S & E Department. One of her first acts was to call a meeting of S & E directors and set up a loan fund as a tribute to Mrs. Modlin. The loan fund was established to provide loans at a low rate of interest for members of FB families who needed money for education.

Ex-Governor Frank Lowden of Illinois, who was a speaker at the state convention, heard about the fund and contributed the first hundred dollars. Many township Farm Bureau organizations made a regular contribution to the fund each year.

In 1941 the Modlin Memorial Committee decided to give a $50 scholarship in each of the 10 FB districts for a boy or girl to attend the Agricultural Short Course at Purdue. In 1946 the program was expanded to provide two scholarships in each district, and one could be used for the Homemakers Short Course at Purdue. The Homemakers Short Course was discontinued in 1955, and since then the scholarships could be given to anyone at least 17 years of age, a member of a FB family for at least two years, and enrolled in a school of higher education as a full time student and on campus at the time the award was given.

The amount of each scholarship was raised to $75 in 1952, to $100 in 1958, to $150 in 1973 and to $200 in 1977.

In 1960 the Farm Bureau Foundation Inc. was organized to carry on the project started by the Modlin Fund.

Students in Carroll County who won a scholarship were: Eldon D. Robeson, 1947 and 1948; Elizabeth Ann Mears, 1949; Donald A. Shanks, 1950; Helen Rodgers, 1952; Patsy Pullen, 1954; Dan Lybrook, 1955; Catherine L. DuVall, 1960; Marilyn McCain and Terry Snider, 1962; Aleta Marie Scott, 1963 and 1964; Nancy DuVall, 1970; Mary Ellen Scott, 1971; Madonna Jervis, 1972; Tim Burke, 1975 and Mike O'Farrell, 1976.

Rural Church Improvement Contest

Awards are presented each year at the Farm Bureau Women's Conference in February to three rural churches in each district, based on improvements made during the previous year.

Some of those from Carroll County who received the award were: Radnor Methodist, 1965; Yeoman Methodist, 1967; Burrows Presbyterian, 1972; Pyrmont United Brethren and Lockport, 1973; Radnor Methodist, 1974; Hickory Grove, 1977 and Oak Grove, 1978.

Indiana Agricultural Marketing Association

The Indiana Agricultural Marketing Association was organized in November 1961 as an affiliate of the Indiana Farm Bureau. The purpose of the new organization was to improve marketing conditions and prices for farm products.

Tomato growers were the first to use the services of the new association, and were later joined by snap bean and sweet corn growers and swine producers.

The Indiana FARM FRESH MARKET was organized as a division of the IFMA. This division is made up of a group of fruit and vegetable growers in Indiana who market their products directly to the consumer. Each year a map is published showing the names and location of members in Indiana, and lists the produce they have for sale.

Golden Gate Special

An article in the July 1946 issue of the Hoosier Farmer announced that the Hoosier Farmer and the IFB had made arrangements with Mr. and Mrs. Vernon Hinkle to conduct a 14-day tour to California, from December 3 to 16, for Farm Bureau members to attend the AFBF Convention at San Francisco, December 8 to 12.

Members of any FB family in Indiana were eligible for the trip, and the cost was less than $200 per person for all expenses except for the four days in San Francisco. The article stated that a special train called the "Hoosier Farmer-Indiana Farm Bureau-Golden Gate Special" had been chartered for the first 500 to make reservations.

By July 30 there were 700 reservations, and about 40 to 50 more were being received each day. Arrangements were made to take more people, and when the day arrived, there were nearly 1,100 people on four trains.

A few days before the trip, John L. Lewis had his coal miners go on strike, and there was no coal for the locomotives. The group went from Indianapolis to St. Louis on chartered busses, and continued the trip on trains with oil burning diesel engines. The coal strikes were over by the end of the trip, and the trains returned to Indianapolis as scheduled.

Each of the four trains had a baggage car, a lounge car, an observation car, two dining cars and eight pullman cars. The total length of the four trains was more than a mile and they stayed within a few minutes of each other for most of the trip.

In addition to the convention, those who went on the trip saw the Grand Canyon, Hollywood, Reno, Great Salt Lake, Eagle River Canyon, the Royal Gorge and many other points of interest along the way.

The entire trip was made without a single accident, and with no major illness. The trip broke several records. It was the largest delegation from any state ever to attend a National Convention. It was the largest civilian group ever moved over that much distance by railroad. At each sight seeing place it was the largest civilian group ever to stop at one time.

The people traveled 6,500 miles on five railroads, and stayed at eight hotels and all of the restaurants and hotels reported that they had never had a better group of people. No "Souvenirs" were reported taken and there was no stealing, drinking or gambling. Farm Bureau members from 84 counties in Indiana were on that trip. The 39 from Carroll County were: Theodore W. Baum, Mr. and Mrs. Roy K. Blue, Clarence Cleaver, Mr. and Mrs. L. D. Dickinson, Mr. and Mrs. J. Earl Fouts, Mr. and Mrs. Taylor Fouts, Mr. and Mrs. Clark A. Haines, Mr. and Mrs. Robert Hedde, Miss Vivian Henderson, Mr. and Mrs. Warren M. Knapp, Mrs. Pearl Mabbitt, Mr. and Mrs. Miles T. Martin, Mrs. Orpha Meade, Mr. and Mrs. Ralph Reagon, Mr. and Mrs. Artus Rodenbarger, Mr. and Mrs. Evan Sanderson, Mr. and Mrs. Orvel C. Schock, Claude R. Wickard, Mr. and Mrs. Ralph Goslee, Mr. and Mrs. Earl Newell, Mr. and Mrs. Ross Shoff, Mr. and Mrs. Charles Sanderson and Mrs. Amel Spring.

Pacific All West Expedition

The Golden Gate tour was so popular that the Hoosier Farmer and IFB conducted another tour September 11-23, 1947. More than 1,200 people from 85 counties in Indiana went on the 8,000 mile trip which included many points of interest in the Western United States as well as parts of Mexico and Canada. There were three trains with 33 pullman cars and nine diners.

Hoosier Travel Service

There were so many requests for more trips, that the Hoosier Travel Service was organized in May 1948 to arrange and conduct educational and recreational trips throughout the world for Indiana farmers. Hassil E. Schenck, President of the IFB was named president of the organization and Glenn W. Sample, vice president of the IFB was named manager.

The "Hoosier Harvest Special" tour was conducted August 19-30, 1948 to the Grand Canyon and Yellowstone National Park.

On December 9-19, 1948 there was a "Hoosier Christmas Special" to Washington, D.C. and Canada.

The "Hoosier Farmer Northwest Expedition" began August 14, 1951.

The Travel Service continued for many years to arrange and conduct tours for Indiana farmers.

Citizenship Seminar

The first young people's Citizenship Seminar sponsored by IFB was held at Franklin College, Franklin, Indiana in June 1975. The Seminar is designed for juniors or seniors in High School with leadership potential and with the ability to speak to groups of

Those from Carroll County who got on the special train at Delphi on August 14, 1951 for the Hoosier Farmer Northwest Expedition were left to right: Maude Heddrick, Bringhurst; Theodore Baum, Delphi; Earl and Mrs. Maude Newell, Delphi; Mrs. William Guckien, Madonna Guckien, and William Guckien, Camden. They visited Glacier National Park, Sun Valley, Yellowstone, Grand Teton, and Rocky Mountain National Parks, Father Flannigan's Boys' Town and many other points of interest.

people after the Seminar, and who would also be proud to represent their county.

Subjects covered in the four-day Seminar were: the American Way of Life; People and Governments Around the World; American Private Enterprise; and the American Political Systems.

The Seminar is planned as an investment in the future, and will assist students to become better informed citizens and to have a better understanding of their duties and responsibilities as good citizens.

Students selected to represent Carroll County were Barbara Moss and Debbie Frey in 1975; Brad Jennings and John Moss in 1976; Linda Mays, Lori Trapp and Julie Frey in 1977 and Scott Jennings in 1979.

Safety Seminar

Since 1973 the IFB has sponsored a four-day Safety Seminar each summer for freshmen and sophomores in High School, at the Columbus Youth Camp located in Bartholomew County between Columbus and Nashville.

Each County FB pays $35 for the expenses of each delegate from the county.

Students from Carroll County who have attended were: Barbara Moss and Larry Frey in 1973; Brad Jennings in 1975; Linda Mays, Lori Trapp and Julie Frey in 1977; Jennifer Dittman and Scott Jennings in 1978.

AFBF Leadership Conference

The AFBF sponsors a four-day conference each year during April at the Lake of the Ozarks in Missouri. The conference provides education, information and motivation for young men and women to avail themselves of opportunities to make maximum contributions to the society in which they live. Our economic system, representative government, the the farm-to-table food industry, agriculturally-related career opportunities, citizenship and responsibilities and safety were stressed in developing understanding.

About 125 delegates from all parts of the United States attend the conference. Delegates from Indiana are selected from students who attended the Safety Seminar a previous year and their expenses are paid by IFB.

Representatives from Carroll County have been: Brad Jennings in 1977 and Jennifer Dittman in 1979.

CARROLL COUNTY FARMERS' ASSOCIATION

County Agent Paul S. Lowe called a meeting of farmers on Saturday afternoon February 22, 1919 in the Assembly Room of the Courthouse at Delphi. About 200 farmers attended the meeting to consider a proposed Constitution and By-laws which had been prepared by a previously appointed committee. With a few minor changes, the farmers approved the Constitution and organized the Carroll County Farmers' Association, and set the date of March 4 for a special meeting to elect officers for the year. Officers elected were: Taylor Fouts, president; Perry Rule, vice president; Dr. Ren C. Julien, secretary and J. A. Shirk, treasurer. Prof. G. I. Christie of Purdue spoke on the subject of "Farmers' Organizations and Their Relation to the Business Men in the Cities and Towns." A resolution was passed asking the State Legislature to retain the law regarding County Agents. Dues were set at $1 per year and any land owner, renter or worker on farms was eligible to be a member. Fifty one paid their dues and by the end of the year there were 386 members.

The Constitution provided that the leader of the Farmers' Institute in each township would be a director of the new organization. Each director was to appoint six men in his township to study the needs of farmers in their locality and report these needs or requests to him. The chairman would report to the County Agent, who was ready to respond to all requests for service.

Five townships did not have an organization to sponsor Institutes, so the county president was authorized to appoint a director to represent each of these townships. Those appointed were: Frank S. Girard, Adams Township; John K. Todd, Deer Creek; Roy P. Martin, Madison; Earl Stewart, Rock Creek and Charles Ginn, Tippecanoe.

The Democrat Township Breeders' Association of Cutler, organized and operating successfully for several years, requested that they be accepted as the township unit of the new organization. The request was granted.

A list of directors for the first few years is not available. News articles during that time indicate that in addition to ones already named as officers or directors, others who were leaders during the first few years were: C. V. Willey, Walter Ayres, George Cohee, Claude R. Wickard, Sam D. Smith, Burton D. Honan, Paul Girard, Will Klepinger, Charles Doctor, Elmer Sheets, J. Frank Shoff, George Sites, Bill Foreman, Elliott Crowel, Harry Griffith, W. G. Million, Sylvester Robinson, George Thomas, Bill Bordner and Edgar Logan.

On September 27, 1919 representatives from seven County Farmers' Associations in the area met in the County Agent's office in the Courthouse in Lafayette to consider rates to be paid for corn husking. They recommended a rate of six cents per bushel.

Name Changed to Farm Bureau

On Thanksgiving night 1920, representatives from 35 towns in northeast Indiana met at Wabash and made plans to merge the Indiana Federation of Farmers' Associations, the Indiana State Grange, and the Farmers' Grain Dealers Association of Indiana, into a new organization to be known as the Indiana Farm Bureau. These plans for merger did not materialize, but on December 4, 1920 the directors of the Carroll County organizations changed the name to Carroll County Farm Bureau. In December 1923, the name of the state organization was changed to Indiana Farm Bureau.

Farm Bureau Dues

Membership dues were $1 during 1919, and were then raised to $5. Of this amount the county and township organizations each received $2 and the state and national organization each received fifty cents. In December 1920 the directors voted to allow women to belong to Farm Bureau for $1 if one member of the family already belonged. Later the rules were changed so that the $5 membership fee included the entire family.

Farm Bureau dues remained at $5 for a family membership until 1948 when dues were changed to $10. Dues were raised to $15 in 1967 and to $20 in 1978.

County Farm Bureau Membership

Membership in the Farm Bureau grew rapidly during the first three years. There were 386 members in 1919, 1,117 in 1920 and 1,257 in 1921. Membership declined for a few years, and this number was not reached again until 1948 when the membership was 1,351. The membership for 1979 was 2,165. A complete list of the number of members and the county officers for each year is at the end of this chapter.

Farm Bureau Field Men

In the early 1930's the Organization Department of the IFB employed two field men to help counties with their membership campaigns and other activities in the county. George R. Harvey was selected to work in the north half of Indiana.

By 1940 the number of field men was increased to

This picture was taken at the Courthouse at Delphi about 1920. Pictured left to right: Bill Foreman, Elliott Crowel, Claude R. Wickard, Charles Doctor, C. V. Willey, Burton D. Honan, Harry Griffith, W. G. Million, Elmer Sheets, Dr. Ren C. Julien, Sam D. Smith, Sylvester Robinson, Frank Gerard, George Thomas, John W. Ashby, Al Hodgson, Bill Bordner and Edgar Logan. Mr. Hodgson, County Agent, was the only one still living in 1979.

five, and Lewis Deardorff was employed for Districts 1 and 3. When the number of field men was increased to 10, E. H. (Gene) Wilson was employed on June 1, 1950 for District 3 and Mr. Deardorff continued in District 1.

Donald E. Henderson served as field man in District 3 from June 1959 until December 31, 1965. Hollys Moon served until June 1970 and Earl Roberts until July 1972. Wilson Justice served for a few months in 1972. Jim York has served since 1974 as one of 15 field men in Indiana. He represents the IFB in six counties, including Carroll.

Livestock Shipping Association

Local livestock shipping associations were formed in many communities. Jefferson Township Shipping Association shipped a carload of livestock on December 26, 1921. There were 70 hogs and one calf. The hogs sold for $8.75 per 100 pounds. The total cost including freight and commission was 51½ cents per 100 pounds. A committee appointed to solicit more members for shipping associations included: Loyal Hoshaw, Burton D. Lane, Fred C. Smith, Oscar Leatherman, Ira Moore, Sam Sites, Frank Imler, Will Klepinger, Harry Holmes, Earl Newell and James Smock.

In January 1922 a County Shipping Association was organized at Delphi with Burton D. Lane, president; Roy Martin, vice president and Fred C. Smith, secretary treasurer. Other directors were Walter Dobbins and Will Klepinger. During one week in December 1922, one carload of cattle and five carloads of hogs were shipped from Carroll County to the Producers Commission Association at Indianapolis.

Burton D. Lane acted as manager of the County Shipping Association, until Harry Holmes was selected as manager in February 1924. Among those who served as local managers were: Wilbur Crowell, Adams Township; Lloyd Beard, Clay and Madison; Guy Sibbett, Democrat; Albert Atkinson, Yeoman; E. E. Stephens, Cutler; Fred Voorhees, Flora; H. G. Kerlin, Delphi and A. A. Newer, Camden.

In the year ending in May 1924 Farm Bureau members in Carroll County received about $600 refund from the Producers Commission Association which amounted to about 30% of the commission paid. In 1925 farmers in Carroll County received a refund of $495.11 or about 25% of the commission paid.

Scott Meiks who became manager of the Producers Commission Association in 1926 was the speaker at the County Farm Bureau picnic August 16, 1922 and was also the speaker at a county meeting for livestock farmers in the Community Building at Flora on August 12, 1924. In January 1925, 108 farmers from Carroll County made a trip in four busses to visit the Producers Commission Association at the Indianapolis Stockyards.

When trucks replaced the railroads for hauling livestock, farmers hauled their livestock directly to the terminal market, and the shipping associations went out of business.

Farmers in Carroll County continued to market their livestock through the Producers Commission Association. In 1933 more than 300 farmers in Carroll County received a total of $879.96 refund from Producers in amounts ranging from 11 cents to $24.40 per farmer.

After branch markets were established by the PMA, annual meetings were held in each market area. At meetings for the Logansport and Klondike branches, Carroll County was well represented in attendance, and by local talent on the programs.

A Market Advisory Committee was established in each market area and many Carroll County livestock producers served on these committees.

Robert Hedde served for several years as director of the PMA representing the eight counties in the Third District.

CARROLL COUNTY FARM BUREAU PURCHASING DEPARTMENT

One of the early acts of the CCFB was to establish a Purchasing Department so that members could pool their orders and buy farm supplies at a better price. One person in each township was named to collect the orders, usually at a township Farm Bureau meeting, and members would then get their supplies directly from the railroad car when it arrived. The first supplies handled were fertilizer, twine, feed, fence and coal. Farmers were encouraged to use high analysis fertilizer and save handling so much fertilizer. They learned that the lower analysis fertilizer which they had been using was manufactured as a high analysis fertilizer, and then had sand added to it so farmers would think they were getting more fertilizer.

Harry Holmes of Deer Creek Township was the first County Purchasing Agent. He reported that the department handled $38,000 in business for 1924.

Wm. Lee Henderson was named County Purchasing Agent in December, 1926. In addition to pooling orders and ordering supplies in carload lots, he kept a barrel of motor oil in his corn crib and sold oil by the quart or gallon. One of the best customers was Russell Craig who operated two truck routes collecting cream for the Co-op Creamery at Crawfordsville.

On June 4, 1927 the County Farm Bureau directors

met and organized the CCFBCA. Activities of the Cooperative Association are reported in Chapter VIII.

An interesting article about the early activities of the Cooperative Association written by Leo C. Craig is included with his biographical sketch in Volume II.

MEMBERSHIP CAMPAIGNS

For many years a major activity of the County Farm Bureau was a membership campaign to get new members. This was known as the annual "Roll Call," and a County Roll Call Captain with the help of someone in each township would organize a campaign in which solicitors would call on every farmer in the county and ask them to become a FB member.

Many farmers looked forward to the opportunity to visit with their neighbors and tell them about their organization. The following stories are just a few of the many that could be told.

During the FB membership campaign in 1944, Wayne Hiatt, and Tom Hendricks bet Miles T. Martin and Ralph Rinehart a steak dinner that they couldn't go out and get enough members in one day to make 100 FB members in Deer Creek Township. Miles and Ralph won the bet, and Tom Hendricks being manager of the FB Co-op Hatchery insisted that they eat chicken instead of steak, and that they put it off until Wayne Hiatt's broilers were large enough to eat. Everyone agreed and Wayne furnished the chicken and Tom and his wife invited the other three and their wives to their home for the dinner. Tom reported on the dinner: "Ralph and Miles ate so much that they were not seen for a week. Just between you and me, I'll never bet with them again."

The following story appeared in several magazines and papers during a membership campaign.

"Could this happen to you?

"This little story came to my attention a few days ago. Perhaps it is not too exaggerated to have some degree of truth to it. A neighbor of mine who had never belonged to the Farm Bureau sent his little boy to borrow a copy of the Hoosier Farmer from his neighbor. In haste, the boy knocked over a bee hive and in 10 minutes looked like a wart summer squash. His father ran to his assistance and, failing to notice

Township Roll Call Captains met at the Country Club at Delphi on Saturday evening, September 29, 1951 to make plans for the Roll Call for Farm Bureau members for 1952. Miles Martin was County Roll Call Captain, and Glenn Workinger was Field Man for the Organization Department of Indiana Farm Bureau.

Standing left to right: Russell Clawson, Perry Million, Beryl Beckner, Charles Sanderson, Carl Johnson, Oren Eikenberry, Wayne Lohrman, Charles Meade, Ellis Kuszmaul, and Glenn Workinger. **Seated:** Ralph Reagon, Homer Wilson, Clarence Cleaver, Russell Pearson, Clarence Frey, Raymond Dillman, Sam Sinn and Miles Martin.

F. L. Walkey and George Kenzlor of West Lafayette entertained at the County Farm Bureau Victory Supper October 27, 1950, for volunteer solicitors who helped complete a successful Farm Bureau membership campaign.

the barbed wire fence, tore and ruined a $9 pair of trousers.

"The old cow took advantage of the gap in the fence, got into the field and killed herself eating green corn. Hearing the commotion, my neighbor's wife ran out the door, upset a four gallon churn of cream into a box of little chickens, drowning the entire batch.

"The baby, being left alone, crawled through the cream into the parlor, ruining a new $50 rug. During the excitement, the oldest daughter eloped with the hired man, the dog broke up 11 setting hens and the goat got out and chewed the tails off four dress shirts on the clothesline.

"Moral: Don't ride on your neighbor's membership. Renew your membership today in the Farm Bureau."

During the FB membership campaign in Carroll County in 1947, a special effort was made to see everyone who might be eligible to belong. A card was provided for each solicitor to list the reason given by those who refused to join. One hundred and eighty two cards were turned in, and the following is a list of reasons given for not joining Farm Bureau:

45—no reason
27—may join later
21—not farming enough to consider themselves eligible
18—didn't think it would benefit them
9—religious objections
3—don't believe in it
7—short on money (sickness, etc.)
1—dues too high—should be $3
4—could not attend meetings
4—afraid of landlord or some member of family
2—partner belongs and that's enough
29—sore about something
    6—sore at some individual
    10—sore at Co-op
    1—sore at REMC
    7—sore about problem in township
    5—just plain sore
2—belonged to Farmers' Union
1—buys enough that Co-op should pay his dues
1—don't know enough about it
3—Farm Bureau in too many commercial activities
1—too many social activities and not enough business
1—too much graft
1—Farm Bureau has too much of his money now
1—hasn't received full value for his $5 last year
1—just time to quit
———
182 total

SOCIAL AND EDUCATIONAL DEPARTMENT
By Mrs. Miles T. Martin in 1950

"The first S & E leader of Carroll County was Mrs. C. V. Quinn. Mrs. Quinn tells us that the County Farm Bureau Chairman received word from the state office to select a woman as leader of a women's organization in connection with the Farm Bureau. As the county was already organized for the Home Economics Clubs and Mrs. Quinn was president, they asked for her help. She accepted the office. She wrote to the Home Economics leader in each township to secure the name of a lady to serve with the Farm Bureau. This is how the first leaders of the county were selected. The first year's work was mainly getting organized. In our records for 1928 we find that the State S & E leader, Mrs. Verna Hatch was present at one of the County Farm Bureau board meetings and discussed 'The part of the S & E Department in the Farm Bureau.' Claude R. Wickard was County Farm Bureau chairman at this time.

"Mrs. Sam Sites succeeded Mrs. Quinn as S & E leader and served three years. Mrs. Sites planned with the townships for a schedule of exchange programs. One project was to organize male quartets, the winning quartet to be sent to the State Fair and the State winners to receive prizes. Monroe Township Quartet won the County Contest and was sent to the State Fair in 1929. In 1930 announcement was received of a poster contest for boys and girls.

"Mrs. Lloyd Beard was elected S & E leader in 1932 and served three years. In one of the county director's meetings Mrs. Ida Chenoweth, District S & E leader, was present and talked on 'Standard Township Outlines.' The first mention of a Public Speaking

Contest was given at a District Farm Bureau meeting. The project of each township to have a quartet was creating much interest. Mrs. Beard promoted the sale of Co-op flour by having the townships serve 'Butterfly' suppers of pancakes and sausage at their meetings. Carroll County won second placing in the state in this project. Anyone who attended one of these suppers will remember the good pancakes and the fun of seeing who could eat the most.

"May 15, 1934 the S & E directors met at the home of Mrs. John Witter for a cooperative dinner and made the County Farm Bureau Flag. They planned a meeting for June 12th to dedicate the flag.

"In the wool pool project Mrs. Beard won first placing in the district and state and received a wool comforter as a prize.

"Mrs. John Witter succeeded Mrs. Beard and served two years. During this time the beginning of the membership campaign of the REMC project was started—the S & E's promoted the publicity in the township meetings. As this was of great interest to all the meetings were well attended. In the wool pool project the county won first in the state and Mrs. Witter received a wool blanket. The S & E Alumnae held a dinner meeting at Mrs. Witter's home on June 16, 1936. At the County Picnic at Delphi City Park, the county was honored by having for their speaker Ed O'Neal, President of the AFBF. Other counties nearby were invited to attend.

"Mrs. Castyle Fouts was elected S & E leader. The exchange of programs between townships was stressed and carried out. The REMC project was the main topic. The County directors of the REMC passed a resolution to have a drawing in each township Farm Bureau meeting during April and that one free house wiring job and one free barn wiring job be given the winners. Mention is made of finding a Chorus director and an Orchestra leader. In the second year of Mrs. Fouts term she resigned on account of illness and Mrs. Lloyd Beard finished her year.

"Mrs. Nona Logan was the S & E leader for 1939 and 1940. The outstanding achievement at this time was the organization of a County Farm Bureau Band of boys and girls of Farm Bureau families. Band uniforms were also made. There was a night program in connection with the County Farm Bureau Picnic, each township gave a number, with a prize given to the township with the most outstanding number. A county meeting in conjunction with the Burlington Township Farm Bureau was held at the home of Mrs. Logan. Henry Schricker, Lieutenant Governor, was the speaker. Ice cream and cake was served to 300 persons. The Farm Bureau Queen contest was first mentioned at this time. June 28, 1940 the County S & E Alumnae met for an afternoon tea at the home of Mrs. Logan. Mrs. Cochran, District S & E outlined activities of the S & E Department. There were 42 present.

"Mrs. Charles Tansey served as S & E leader for four years 1941 through 1944. The County Farm Bureau Office was established during this time. The Banquet for Rural Youth given by the County Farm Bureau was given for the first time and the Township S & E leaders were called on to assist. One of the projects was the Cake Baking Contest. Mrs. Tansey entertained wherever she went with her wit and witticisms.

"Vivian Henderson succeeded Mrs. Tansey and served as County S & E leader for two years. Vivian was a former Rural Youth member. She grew up in the Farm Bureau and Co-op work as her father, Lee Henderson, was Carroll County's first Co-op Manager, and she worked in the office at times. This experience has been invaluable to her in her many activities in Farm Bureau work. In February 1945 there was an Alumni dinner meeting of the past County presidents and County S & E leaders. June 4, 1946 an Alumnae meeting of S & E leaders was held at a tea at the Flora Christian Church. Mrs. Russell Cushman, State S & E leader was the speaker and Mrs. O. W. Stevens, District S & E leader was a guest. In 1946 Eldon Robeson received a Modlin Scholarship for the Short Course at Purdue. During this time Carroll County had their first Home Demonstration Agent, Miss Mary Thompson. After serving two years Vivian was elected District S & E leader.

"Mrs. Miles Martin succeeded Vivian Henderson and served three years. One new project was the organization of a County Farm Bureau Chorus for mixed voices. During the three years the Chorus sang at County meetings, twice in the District program at the State Fair and at the Annual Logansport Amboy Producers Commission Association meeting at Peru. In 1948 our first County Pet and Hobby Club leader, Mrs. Charles Harter, was named. Another new project was a Farm Bureau tent at the 4-H Fair at Flora with a guessing contest to create interest. In 1947 the County won a District Modlin Scholarship to the Purdue Short Course, won by Eldon Robeson and another scholarship in 1949 won by Donald Shanks. In 1949 for the first time Purdue University offered a 6-weeks Homemakers Short Course for young women, comparable to the Short Course for boys. The S & E department offered scholarships for this course also and Elizabeth Mears of our county won a scholarship. Joan Hannell also attended the Short Course. Mrs. Charles Tansey was a contestant in the

CHAPTER VII — FARM BUREAU • 169

Public Speaking Contest. In 1949 for the first time the townships were 100% in contributing to the Modlin Memorial Fund, also every township met the requirements of a Standard Township."

PET AND HOBBY CLUBS

Indiana Farm Bureau, the only State Farm Bureau organization with a program for younger children, has Pet and Hobby Clubs for children up to 10 years of age who are members of a FB family. The first township Pet and Hobby Clubs were organized in 1940, and meetings are held at the same time and place as township Farm Bureau meetings.

Pets may include any living thing and hobbies include making or collecting anything in which members are interested. Collections include buttons, stamps, coins, pottery, animals, dolls, match folders, marbles, bottles, seashells, candles, paper napkins, postmarks, pictures of wild flowers or birds, etc.

The Club Motto is: "Love, Learn and Laugh." The Promise is: "I promise to Love my pets; to Learn which are my friends or enemies; I promise to Laugh and be happy."

The job of a county leader is to help the township leader, and to have charge of the county contests and projects.

Those who have served as county leaders in Carroll County were: Mrs. Charles Harter, March 1948-49; Mrs. Pete Fischer, 1950-55; Mrs. Charles T. Black, 1956-57; Mrs. Cliff Bosworth, 1958-63; Mrs. Roy Slavens, 1964-69; Mrs. Barbara Richardson, 1970-71; Mrs. Eldon Robeson, 1972-75 and 1978-79; and Mrs. Mabel Mullin, 1976-77.

A Poster and Banner Contest is held at the County FB meeting in March each year. The Poster Contest is for preschool children through age seven and the Banner Contest is for eight through ten years of age. County winners are eligible for the District Contest at the fall series of District Women's meetings. Winners in the district are displayed at the FB Women's Conference in February.

A Hobby Show is held in June at the County FB Talent Night program, and a Flower Show and Pet Parade is held the day of the Farm Bureau Picnic at the County 4-H Fair.

A statewide Pet Parade is held each year on Farmers' Day at the Indiana State Fair.

An Amateur Contest for Pet and Hobby Club members is held each year in the Farmers' Building at the State Fair.

Clay Township Farm Bureau Pet and Hobby Club members in December 1950. Front row, left to right: Linda Metzger, Roger Frey, Stanley Miller, Wayne Remaly, Eddie Remaly and Ward Frey. Back row: John Gochenour, Edith Metzger, Judith Miller, Marilyn Butler, Donna Neuenschwander, Carol Frey, and Mrs. Kenneth Miller, leader.

Jackson Township Pet and Hobby Club, February 21, 1951. Seated, left to right: Susan McCain, Charlotte Hughes, Marilyn McCain, Judy Hughes, Billy Schock, Jr., Donnie McCain and Richard Leslie McCain. Standing is Mrs. Charles Hughes, Pet and Hobby leader.

Pet and Hobby Club members who attended a meeting April 3, 1951 in Monroe Township. Front row, left to right: Kay Lynn Shriver, Edwin Chapman and Johnny Smith. Back row: Mrs. Floyd Chapman leader, Bobby Johnson, Darrell Chapman and Becky Smith.

Madison Township Pet and Hobby Club April 4, 1951. Front row, left to right: Marilyn Porter, Patty Wagner, Dickie Simmons, Diane Ward, Marjorie Humbarger, Dale Humbarger, Susan McCormick and Martin Mears. Back row: Mrs. Mark Porter leader, Tommy Wagner, Sanford Pearson, Joe Porter, Bill Redmon, Donald Peterson, Eric McCormick and David Porter.

Deer Creek Township Pet and Hobby rhythm band entertaining at the county Farm Bureau meeting at the REMC auditorium at Delphi on June 29, 1951. Left to right: Susie Beale, Judy Draper, Sheryl Beale, Charmion Black, Johnny Gingrich, Mertha Zook, David Peterson, Freddie Draper, Johnny Beale, David Beale and Stephen Peterson. Virginia Fischer accompanied them at the piano. Mrs. Russell Cushman, state S. and E. director, was the speaker for the evening.

Burlington Township Pet and Hobby Club members August 8, 1951. Left to right around the table: Gale Stout, Ronnie Crain, Alan Stout, Mark Beckner, Roger Beckner, Richard Stout, Dean Beckner, Wayne Beckner, Mary Jo Thomas, Elaine Robertson, Mrs. Rosella Robertson leader, Barbara Crain standing, Eddie Robertson and Marilyn Crain.

Deer Creek Township Pet and Hobby Clubbers who won a cup for achievement in February, 1952. Front row, left to right: Sheryl Beale, Mary Ruth Burkhalter, Mary Ann Newell, Susan Beale (holding cup), Dale Wagoner, Charmion Black, and Richard Newell. Second row: Freddie Draper, Jimmy Arborsal, Charles Beale, Betty Wagoner, David Peterson, Judy Draper, Marcia Alberts, Linda Wagoner, Johnny Gingrich, and Treva Zook. Back row: Mrs. Charles Black (township leader) Maxine Pullen, Carolyn Peterson, Virginia Peterson, Stephen Peterson, David Beale, Carol Schmitter and Mrs. Pete Fischer (county Pet and Hobby leader).

MEETINGS

Much of the work of Farm Bureau is carried on in meetings of various kinds. Regular or special meetings for many purposes have been held on a Township, County, District, State or National basis.

Following is a brief report on a few of the meetings.

National Farm Bureau Meetings

Annual meetings of the American Farm Bureau Federation have been held in December or January. About half of them have been held in Chicago, and the others at various locations throughout the United States. The purposes of the meetings are to elect officers, determine policy for the organization and to keep members informed about activities of the AFBF.

Indiana and Carroll County have been well represented at National meetings. The record was set in 1946 when about 1,100 people from Indiana including 39 from Carroll County attended the Annual Meeting in California. Thirteen from Carroll County attended the AFBF Convention at Dallas, Texas in December 1950. Twenty one members of Rural Youth and several others from Carroll County attended the AFBF Convention at Seattle in December 1952.

Gene Jennings, chairman of the Carroll County Farm Bureau was elected as one of the delegates to represent Indiana at the AFBF Convention at Phoenix, Arizona, January 6-8 in 1980.

State Farm Bureau Meetings

Carroll County has always been represented by several official delegates and others who attend the Annual Meeting of the Indiana Farm Bureau held at Indianapolis in November or December. This has usually been a three day meeting with the first two days used for reports on activities of interest to members. The third day has been for delegates to elect officers and adopt resolutions which determine the policy of the state organization for the coming year.

A state meeting for the Women's Department has been held in February each year and several from Carroll County have attended these meetings.

Annual meetings of affiliated cooperatives have been held at Indianapolis at various times during the year. In December 1979, for the first time in several years, the Annual Meeting of the Indiana Farm Bureau and the Indiana Farm Bureau Cooperative Association were held at the same time in the Convention Center at Indianapolis.

Special state meetings have been held whenever there was a need to get special information to members, or to have members help determine a policy for the IFB. One such meeting was in 1932 when several thousand farmers, including a large delegation from Carroll County, went to Indianapolis to present a petition with 40,000 names to the Governor requesting him to call a special session of the State Legislature to consider taxes.

District

Farm Bureau members in eight counties in District 3 Farm Bureau have been holding four regular meet-

Part of the group from Carroll County who went by bus to the S & E Conference at Indianapolis in February 1952. Left to right: Mrs. Charles Hughes, bus driver, Mrs. Charles Davis Vaughan, Mrs. Pete Fischer, Mrs. Walter Parrett, Mrs. Everett Snell, Mrs. Fritz Schnepf Sr., Mrs. Kenneth Shriver, Mrs. Raymond Shriver, Mrs. Charles T. Black, Mrs. Clarence Cleaver, Mrs. Truman Zook, Mrs. Robert Ward, Mrs. Charles Snow and Mrs. Charles Harter.

Anson Thomas, director of the tax and legislative department, and George Harvey, director of research, Indiana Farm Bureau, who conducted the Farm Bureau district tax school at Delphi, November 27, 1950.

ings each year, and special meetings to help farmers with record keeping, tax reporting, estate planning and other problems.

At one of the meetings which has been a banquet each year since 1955, awards have been given to counties based on the activities and accomplishments in the county during the past year. Carroll County Farm Bureau has won its share of these awards.

County

An Annual Meeting is held in the county each fall to elect officers, adopt resolutions and report activities of the organizations to members.

A County Picnic has been held each summer, usually at the same time as the County 4-H Fair.

For several years a County Meeting has been held in June with a Home Talent Show and a Pet and Hobby Show.

A County Meeting usually has been held to make plans for the annual "Roll Call", and a victory supper was often held after the campaign was completed.

Several county meetings have been held to train new officers for their duties. The County Farm Bureau entertained members of the Carroll County Rural Youth at several meetings.

The first Annual County Farm Bureau Meeting was held December 9, 1919. Officers elected for 1920

172 • CARROLL COUNTY RURAL ORGANIZATIONS

Those from Carroll County who attended the Farm Bureau district tax school at Delphi, November 27, 1950. Seated, left to right: Lee Flora, Richard Snoeberger, Roy Snoeberger, Mrs. Charles Calton, Mrs. Harry Wilson and Mrs. Charles D. Vaughan. Standing: Roy Gardner, John C. Peterson, Charles Calton, Harry Wilson, Clarence Frey, Joseph Peterson, Robert Reiff, S. A. Wickard, Loris Stout, Levi Furst and Jacob Huffer.

Those from Carroll County who attended the district Farm Bureau meeting at Antioch on July 9, 1952. Left to right: Mrs. John C. Peterson, Mrs. Charles Harter, Mrs. Charles Snow, Mrs. Truman Zook, Mrs. Robert Simmons, Mrs. Cliff Bosworth, Mrs. Cleon Carter, Mrs. Elwood Burkle, Truman Zook, Mrs. Clarence Cleaver, Ivan Burkle in front of Mrs. Cleaver, Miles Martin, Mrs. Robert Ward, Clarence Cleaver, Mrs. Paul Vollenweider, and Robert Ward. John C. Peterson, not in the picture, was behind the camera.

CHAPTER VII — FARM BUREAU • 173

Township S & E directors who were presented corsages at the annual Carroll County Farm Bureau meeting October 25, 1949 left to right: Mrs. Homer Wilson, Deer Creek Township; Mrs. Cliff Bosworth, Burlington; Mrs. John Wise, Jackson; Mrs. Wayne Lohrman, Democrat; Mrs. Lowell Ward, Madison; Mrs. Wilbur J. Wilson, Monroe; Mrs. Robert Simmons, Jefferson; Mrs. Orpha Goslee, Clay; Mrs. Richard Wysong, Rock Creek; and Mrs. Miles T. Martin, county S & E director.

Members of the nominating committee meeting in the home of Charles Sanderson to select nominees for each county Farm Bureau office for 1952. Seated, left to right: Mrs. Clifford Bosworth, Burlington and George Sites, Deer Creek, chairman of the committee. Standing: Taylor Fouts, Carrollton; John McCormick, Madison and Charles Sanderson, Jackson. Mrs. Blanche Viney of Jefferson Township also served on the committee but was not present when the picture was taken.

Directors of the Carroll County Farm Bureau who attended a directors meeting on April 9, 1979. Seated, left to right: Mrs. Raymond (Cecile) Nicoll, Mrs. Clayton (Esther) Million, Mrs. Emmett (Pat) Frey, Mrs. Gene (Patsy) Jennings, Mrs. John (Carolyn) Burkle, Mrs. Richard (Mary) Sheldon and Mrs. James (Maxine) White. Standing: Charles Hanna, Francis Humbarger, Gene Jennings, Raymond Nicoll, Richard Denhart and James White.

Officers of the Carroll County Farm Bureau for 1952. Left to right: Clarence Cleaver, Deer Creek Township, newly elected president; Mrs. Charles Harter, Carrollton, re-elected S & E leader; Fritz Schnepf, Monroe, newly elected vice president; Mrs. Pete Fischer, Deer Creek, re-elected Pet and Hobby leader; and Mary Ellen Kempf, re-elected secretary treasurer. Mr. Cleaver had served for three years as county vice president and was elected president to succeed John C. Peterson, who had served for seven years as county president and declined to accept the nomination.

Past County Farm Bureau officers honored at a County Farm Bureau meeting February 9, 1952. County S and E leaders seated left to right: Mrs. John Witter, Mrs. Charles Tansey, Mrs. Miles Martin and Mrs. Charles Harter. Standing County presidents Taylor Fouts, Burton D. Honan, Sam D. Smith, George Sites, Loyd Zook, Miles T. Martin, John C. Peterson, and Clarence Cleaver.

were: Burton D. Honan, president; Claude R. Wickard, vice president and Dr. Ren C. Julien, secretary treasurer. Lewis Taylor, secretary of the Indiana Farm Bureau was the speaker.

At the Annual Meeting in December 1920, a ten pound box of chocolates was offered to the township having the largest percentage of members present at the meeting. The prize was won by Adams Township with nine out of 57 members present. A County Legislative Committee was appointed with the following members: Mrs. W. E. Kirkpatrick, Mrs. Paul Girard, Perry Rule and E. W. Bowen.

Other members of the County Tax and Legislative Committee during the first 15 years were: F. S. Girard, A. A. Newer, George Thomas, Fred C. Smith, Arthur Mullin, John Reeder, Burton D. Honan, George Guard and Webb Robeson.

Corn to Europe

At a County Meeting at Camden in March 1921, 227 people heard T. A. Coleman from Purdue explain the relief plan proposed by Herbert Hoover, Wartime Food Administrator. A committee appointed in charge of the program was Taylor Fouts, Fred C. Smith and Stanley Gasaway. In March, 21 farmers in the county donated and delivered 3,000 bushels of corn to Flora and Delphi. Elevators shelled and loaded the corn without charge, and the railroads gave free transportation to the mills where it was processed for shipment to Europe. Whiteman Bros. Elevator provided shelling and loading for corn delivered to Delphi. A total of 431 carloads of corn were donated by farmers in the corn belt for the program.

PICNICS

The first County Farm Bureau picnic was held on August 21, 1919 in Lyon Grove east of Flora. The committee on location was John Todd, Frank Balser and George Hunt. The program committee was Taylor Fouts, Frank Girard and Dr. Ren C. Julien. One of the events of the day was a Horseshoe Pitching Contest.

The second county picnic was held September 1, 1920 at the Community Park in Flora. People came to the picnic in 587 automobiles. The program included songs by Mary and Mabel Sites of Jefferson Township. Boys and girls in 4-H Club work had their picnic at the same time and place.

The Carroll County Farm Bureau continued to have a picnic each summer, usually in August, and most of them have been held at Flora. For several years they have been held during the 4-H Fair.

Scott Meiks, manager of the Producers Commission Association at Indianapolis was the speaker at the picnic in 1922 and 1924. Wm. H. Settle, President of the IFB was speaker in 1923.

Special music at the 1922 picnic was a duet by Pauline Todd and Beth Billiard. In 1924 a joint picnic was held at Camp Tecumseh with the White County Farm Bureau and music was furnished by the Balser Quartet with Dean and Burr Balser, Raymond Coble and Harry Haslet.

1929 Picnic

The picnic for 1929 was a special event with about 1,500 people in attendance. Speakers were: Hon. Fred Purnell, Representative of the 9th District of Indiana, and G. E. Metzger from the Illinois Agricultural Association.

A Quartet Contest was held, and the winner was a quartet from Monroe Township with Ora Shirar, Walter Price, Ernest Sink and Leslie Hausenfluck. The quartet was on a program on Radio Station WLS on January 6, 1930.

Charles Gard of Clay Township won the Old Fiddlers' Contest. Another quartet on the program was the FB Alabama Quartet from Clay Township with Rev. Allen, Clarence Frey, Ed Carpenter and Henry Shepard.

Hilda Bowen of Delphi led games and contests for girls at the picnic for several years.

1934 Picnic

Larry Brandon, vice president of the IFB was the speaker at the picnic in 1934 with about 1,000 people present.

In the afternoon a Softball Game between directors of the Carroll County Farm Bureau and the directors of the Carroll County Farm Bureau Cooperative Association resulted in a 34 to 14 win for the Co-op directors.

Elizabeth Stephens was in charge of games for girls. A Sack Race was won by Joan Rodenbarger, Esther Flora and Helen Smith.

Music was furnished by the Clay Township Orchestra and the Scott-Robeson-Yeager Orchestra from Rock Creek and Washington Townships.

A Hog Calling Contest was just getting a good start when Mrs. Lloyd Beard, County S & E leader, read a telegram from Scott Meiks from the Producers Commission Association at Indianapolis asking them to stop the contest because hogs were leaving the Indianapolis Stockyards.

1935 Picnic

Edward O'Neal, President of the AFBF was a speaker at the FB picnic held in the City Park in Delphi in 1935.

The meeting started at 10:00 a.m. with a baseball

game in charge of Artus Rodenbarger and Leroy Wade.

Other counties in the FB District were invited and furnished part of the program which included a quartet from White County and an orchestra from Benton County.

County and Township S & E Directors were on the committee for the noon meal.

Miles T. Martin was in charge of parking automobiles, and Lloyd Beard, Fred Martin and Ralph Maggart served as water boys.

1940 Picnic

Dr. J. Raymond Schultz was speaker at the picnic in 1940. Another feature on the program was the first public appearance of the County Farm Bureau Band with 25 members directed by Omer Collins. An Entertainment Festival that evening attracted a crowd of 1,200 people. An Amateur Contest was won by the Camden Trio with Marjorie Shonk, Margaret Hedderich and Marjorie Wise accompanied by Mrs. Clarence Hyman.

1943 Picnic

Entertainment at the County Farm Bureau picnic in August, 1943 included a cornet trio by Joe Carey, Dick Grantham and Charles Heiland.

There were two quartets from Madison Township. One was made up of Leonard Clawson, Claude Zook, Loyd Zook and Russell Clawson. Members of the other quartet were Roy Martin, Bert Goslee, Harry Maxwell and John B. McCormick.

1949 Picnic

L. H. Hess from the Soil Conservation Service was speaker at the picnic in 1949. There were several special numbers on the program including the Three J's and the County Chorus, and both represented the county at the Indiana State Fair program in September. Other numbers on the program were a reading by Sue Starkey, a solo by Mrs. Mildred Shanks, and a Whistling Solo by David Smith accompanied by Mrs. Pearl Crowell.

Special guests at the picnic were those who had been members of the Farm Bureau for each of the 30 years since it was organized in 1919.

Taylor Fouts, one of the 30 year members who served as the first president of the CCFB paid tribute to the 50 who had been members for 30 years by pointing out that 12 of them had served as directors and three as president of the CCFBCA. Six were among the 21 incorporators of the Carroll County REMC in 1935. Four of the women had served as County S & E Directors.

The 50 who qualified as 30 year members in 1949

Twenty two of the 50 who had been members of the FB for 30 years, and were at the Farm Bureau picnic, August 26, 1949. Front row, left to right: C. R. Clawson, J. W. Eikenberry, Charles G. Black, W. G. Million, Roy Richter, John L. Witter, Roy Cornelison, Obe Campbell, and Lloyd Metzger. Back row: William Douglas, Artus Rodenbarger, Clarence Frey, Taylor Fouts, S. A. Wickard, George E. Sites, Mrs. Monroe Meade, L. D. Dickinson, Mrs. Mildred Shanks, Mrs. Ben Metzger, Warren H. Todd, William M. Wingard and Miles T. Martin.

were: Wilbur Crowell, Adams Township; Clifford E. Cleaver, Wm. Douglas, Mrs. Clarence Stout, Burlington; John T. Billings, Taylor Fouts, Mrs. Pearl Mabbitt, Mrs. Orpha Meade, Otto Platt, Mrs. Mildred Shanks, C. E. Sibbitt, Warren H. Todd, Claude R. Wickard, S. A. Wickard, Carrollton; Frank Barnhart, Lloyd Beard, Clarence Frey, Mrs. Ben Metzger, Lloyd Metzger, Edward P. Troxel, Clay; Charles G. Black, Mrs. George Julien, Earl B. Newell, Mrs. John A. Shaeffer, George E. Sites, Deer Creek; O. L. Hausenfluck, Artus Rodenbarger, Democrat; Roy Cornelison, Miles T. Martin, Roy Richter, John Witter, Jackson; Charles W. Jones, Cecil S. Million, W. C. Million, Everett E. Scott, Paul Vollenweider, Jefferson; Obe Campbell, L. D. Dickinson, Burton D. Honan, Marvin Shultheis, Madison; J. W. Eikenberry, W. B. Kearns, Mrs. Virginia E. Stephens, Wm. M. Wingard, Monroe; C. R. Clawson, Nelson Giles, Mrs. Hattie Henderson, Frank Imler, Tippecanoe; A. A. Newer and S. D. Smith, Washington.

Every 10 years the County FB has honored those who have been members since 1919. In 1979 there were only two charter members who had been members every year. They were Miles T. Martin and John L. Witter.

The Carroll County FB has continued to have a picnic each year during the 4-H Fair at Flora. 4-H members have been invited to the dinner and a Flower Show and Pet and Hobby Parade has been held in the afternoon.

Other speakers at picnics have been: 1931, Paul V. McNutt, later Governor of Indiana; 1936, Larry Williams, Manager of Country Life Insurance Company of Illinois; 1946, John Haramy of Indianapolis; 1948, Hassil E. Schenck, President IFB; and 1956, Paul Johnson, Editor of Prairie Farmer.

"Danny and His Dainty Dollies" as they entertained with novelty numbers at the County Farm Bureau picnic August 17, 1951. Left to right: Fred Hedderick, Wayne Caldwell, Walter Sprinkle, Jim Sullivan, Gardner Martin, Frank Kessner, Danny Caldwell and John Berkshire. They were accompanied at the piano by Shirley Sprinkle.

Farm Bureau at County Fair

For many years the County Farm Bureau has had an exhibit at the County 4-H Fair at Flora. In 1949 there was a contest to guess the number of beans in a jar.

In 1964, 72 gallons of milk donated by milk producers in the county were given away. For the last few years visitors at the Farm Bureau exhibit have been given popcorn, sausage and other farm products.

"One Horse" Meeting

For several years a county meeting was held in December for newly elected officers of the Township Farm Bureau organizations in order to help them plan their work for the year.

There were 50 present at the meeting in December 1949 and a survey of those present revealed that only one owned a horse.

A special feature on the program that day was a demonstration on how to wrap a Christmas package. Fritz Schnepf, Sr. and Claude Remaly wrapped the package with each of them using one hand. They did a good job and demonstrated the fact that people can do a good job when they help each other.

Early Township Meetings

Meetings were held in every township during 1920, and several townships had their own picnic. Washington Township held a picnic on June 12 in John P. Hinkle's Grove with more than 500 present. There were 133 automobiles. Tippecanoe Township held a picnic at Frank Imler's Grove and Jefferson Township at Delmar Clark's Grove.

Townships continued to have active organizations with large crowds at the meetings. In January 1921 about 200 attended an oyster supper at Burrows served by the ladies of the Presbyterian Church. Entertainment was provided by a quartet composed of Paul Martin, Everett Flora, Roy Snoeberger and Kenneth Bohannon with Mrs. Mabel Jayne Mullin as accompanist.

Deer Creek Township met in 1921 at the Presbyterian Church at Delphi with ladies of the church serving ice cream and cake. Music was furnished by the Make Merry Quartet, Mrs. A. L. Hodgson, Mrs. Gwinn Smith, Dean Balser and Loyal Hoshaw.

Ladies in Jefferson Township organized a Ladies Auxiliary Farm Bureau with Mrs. Wm. Coppack as president. They put on a program in April at Carrollton Township with 350 present. Guests were from Jackson, Washington, Deer Creek and Jefferson Townships. Mrs. Charles W. Sewell of Otterbein spoke on "Keeping up with Father and the Boys."

Carrollton Township School

An example of the many projects sponsored by Township Farm Bureau organizations was the campaign by Carrollton Township FB to get a ball diamond and lights for their township school. A finance committee with R. E. Grubb, Rev. Jack Yarian, Fred Hood, Mrs. Mildred Fouts and Margaret Mabbitt solicited donations from people in Carrollton Township and collected about $1,000. A ball diamond with lights was presented to Willard Allbaugh, township trustee, by Elmer Spitler, president and Mrs. Charles Harter, S & E at a Township FB meeting at the school on June 27, 1946.

Three hundred people attended the meeting for the ceremony and a program was presented which included singing by the Carrollton Township FB Men's Chorus, and songs by Gaylord Archibald accompanied by Pauline Fouts at the piano.

After the meeting members ate ice cream and cake, and watched two ball games.

MORE FUN

In the early days of Farm Bureau, men would get together about once a month for a township meeting, discuss such things as the Export Debenture Plan and the McNary-Hagen Bill, pool their orders for twine, coal and fertilizer and go home.

When the S & E Department was organized the Township Farm Bureau meeting was attended by the entire family and for many farm families this was the main event of the month. With no television, few radios, theaters and other kinds of entertainment, people learned to entertain themselves, and the Township Farm Bureau provided the excuse to get together. In many townships there were more than 100 people at each meeting.

One of the early projects of the S & E Department was to have one township arrange a good program and present it at several other township meetings. Local talent was used in the programs, and a large number of people learned to entertain others.

Various talent contests were held, and for several years an Entertainment Festival was held in connection with the 4-H Fair. This created more interest and got more people involved in entertaining.

The Delphi Gang

Orvel Schock and Rev. O. P. Manker got a crew together from Delphi and vicinity and put on a show in nearly every township in the county and in several neighboring counties. Some programs had a band made up of anyone who could play a musical instrument and had time to go to the meeting. They practiced as they played and everyone had fun.

A quartet which went to most of the meetings usually consisted of O. P. Manker, Orvel Schock, Grover Kite and Burr Balser. Sometimes Dean Balser substituted for Orvel Schock.

Albert Smith entertained with his interesting stories and helped with a dialogue known as "Bear's Oil."

For several years a cast from Deer Creek Township Farm Bureau put on plays to entertain at other township meetings. Some of the titles were: "Jim Taylor Joins the Farm Bureau," "Harvest Days," "Too Much Chicken," and "The Calamity Howler."

Magic

George Peterson was one of several who entertained with a program of magic. On one program George had his neighbor Amm Corn helping him.

Taylor Fouts, chairman of the program committee; Mrs. Almer Armstrong of the Indiana Farm Bureau Co-op Association, speaker of the evening; Mrs. Everett Snell, Carrollton Township S. and E. leader; Mrs. Charles Harter, county S. and E. leader and Raymond Huse, Carrollton Township Farm Bureau Chairman at the Carrollton Township Farm Bureau meeting May 10, 1951.

Part of the group who had just finished eating at the oyster supper in Carrollton Township on January 11, 1951. Seated around the table, left to right: Bob McCain, Taylor Fouts, Roy Blue, Larry Landis, Laurel Beck and Raymond Dillman in front. Standing: Evan Sanderson and Rev. Stephenson.

178 • CARROLL COUNTY RURAL ORGANIZATIONS

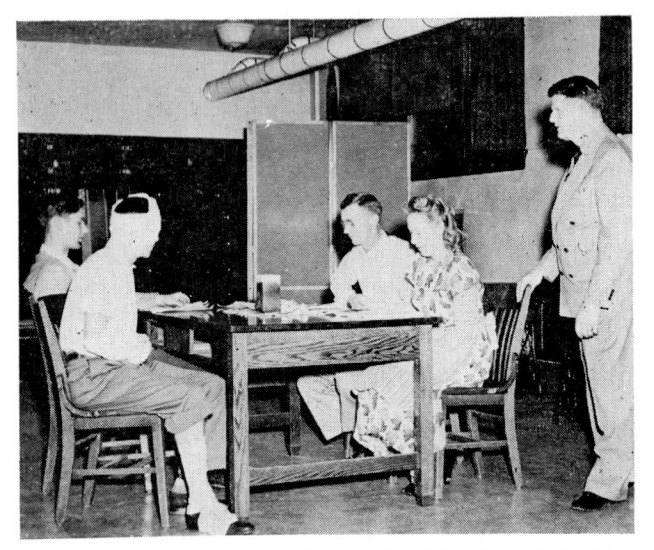

A play, "A Typical Farm Bureau Family" directed by Mrs. Truman Zook and written by Mrs. Homer Wilson, was given at the Deer Creek Township Farm Bureau meeting, April 17, 1950. Members of the cast were, left to right: Jesse Wilson, Don Huff in bandages, Gerald Hanawalt, Doris Hanawalt, and Ralph Reagon.

When it came time to pull a pigeon out of a hat, Amm noticed just as he was ready to hand George the hat, that the pigeon was not in the hat. In full view of the audience he took the pigeon out of his pocket and put it into the hat. That show was remembered longer than the ones that went as planned.

Fan Dance

The Fan Dance, made popular at the World's Fair in Chicago, was a widely discussed subject, so it was only natural that a few eyebrows were raised when it was announced that the next feature on the program at a township Farm Bureau meeting was a Fan Dance. The curtain went up and no one was on the stage. As the audience waited with varying degrees of anticipation or shock, a guy on each side of the stage pulled on a piece of string and a common ordinary fan tied to the string in the middle of the stage jumped up and did it's dance.

Other Entertainment

For many years local talent was used for programs at township and county meetings, and contests of various kinds were held. A large number of people were involved, and it would not be possible to mention everyone. The following are just a few, and give some indication of the kinds and variety of entertainment.

Washington Township had a quartet of 4-H girls, Lorene Hayes, Lavon Johnson, Evelyn Bowman and Charlene Yeager.

A quartet in Carrollton Township included John McCain, Lloyd Sink, Franklin Kintner and Joe Wagoner.

In September 1933 a quartet from Monroe Township won the State Contest and placed second in the National Contest in Chicago, where they sang at the AFBF Convention and on Radio Station WLS. Members of the quartet were Mr. and Mrs. Ora Shirar, Mrs. Melvin Fisher and John McCloskey, Jr.

Lee Seward played the guitar and harmonica while his sister Eva whistled. Lee also played the guitar and sang. For several years he had a regular show on Radio Station WOWO at Fort Wayne. One of his favorite songs was "I've Got No Use for the Women," but Nancy came along and changed that.

Joseph E. and John C. Peterson entertained as Slim and Spud by telling stories about Gourd Corn, Bears, Snakes, Ducks and other important subjects.

Carroll County was well represented at the Indiana State Fair in 1946 with a Whistling solo by David Smith, accompanied by Pearl Crowell, a reading by Mrs. Charles Tansey and a solo by Gaylord Archibald.

In 1949 entertainment for a county meeting was

Indianapolis News Photo

Monroe Township Farm Bureau Quartet, left to right: Ora F. Shirar, Mrs. Shirar, Mrs. Melvin Fisher and John J. McCloskey. The Quartet won first place in a contest at the Indiana State Fair in September 1933, and won second place in a national contest in Chicago where they sang at the AFBF Convention and on Radio Station WLS.

CHAPTER VII — FARM BUREAU   179

provided by the "Sacs Sisters" (Paper, Burlap and Gunny). They were Bill Fouts, Jim Jones and Lowell Morgan of Cass County.

In 1951 Peggy Fischer won first place with her readat the State Amateur Talent Program at the State Fair.

Kenneth Yeakley and Joe Spitznagle of Washington Township played the part of Homer and Jethro.

Jackie Walters entertained as a ventriloquist with her friend Elmer.

Raymond Romein entertained with his musical saw for about 33 years.

In 1968 Bonnie Howard won the Share the Fun Contest with her solo.

In 1968 Kevin and Lori Kremer represented the county at the State Fair Entertainment program.

The Three J's, Jalene, Janet and Joetta Joyce of Washington Township were popular entertainers at many meetings for about 15 years prior to 1960. In 1954 they won the county, district and state contests and attended the National 4-H Club Congress where they were on the program at the Share the Fun breakfast on December 1, 1955 at the Conrad Hilton Hotel in Chicago.

The Clay Township Farm Bureau Orchestra with

Kenneth Yeakley and Joe Spitznagle impersonating Homer and Jethro at a Rural Youth supper, sponsored by the Carroll County Farm Bureau on January 31, 1956.

The Clay Township orchestra playing at the Deer Creek Township Farm Bureau meeting at Delphi in January 1950. Left to right: Bob Jones, drums; Mrs. Ben Metzger, piano; Charles Gard, violin; Mrs. Mabel Fossnock, guitar; Dennis Huffard, trombone and Earl Disinger, banjo.

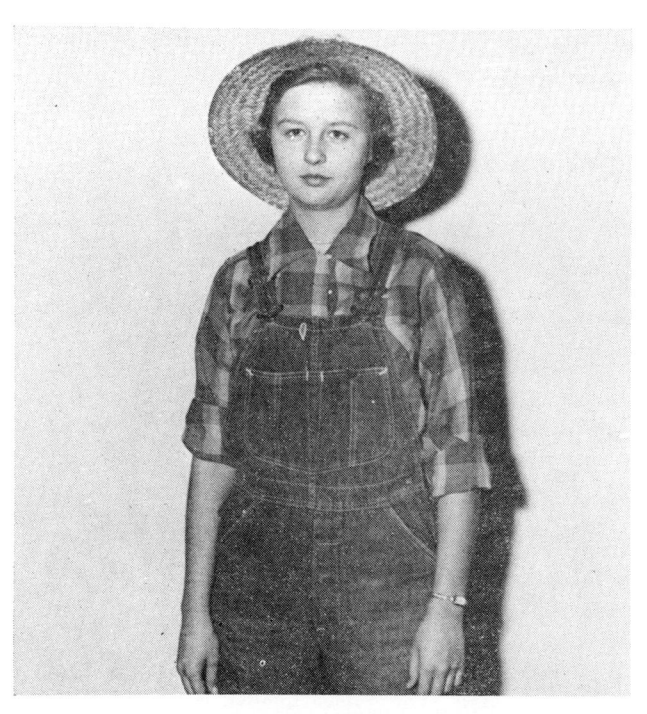

Miss Peggy Fischer, daughter of Mr. and Mrs. Pete Fischer of Delphi, was first-place winner in the state-wide Farm Bureau amateur talent program, staged at the State Fair on Friday, September 7, 1951. Peggy presented a humorous reading and competed in the 15-year-and-up age group.

Jerry Daniels and Sandra Cassell, Carroll County entertainers in 1950s.

Robert Wise and his accordian at the County Farm Bureau meeting October 25, 1950.

Charles Gard and his violin played at many meetings in the county for several years.

Jeris Eikenberry played many piano selections.

The singing Hathaway family entertained at many meetings.

Jane Ann Jones entertained with monologues.

The Harmonettes of Burlington Township entertained with musical numbers by Carol Jane Hood, Jane Williams, Betty Moyer and Sandra Bell.

Mrs. Garland McCarty and daughter Lenore furnished music at a District Farm Bureau meeting at Delphi in January, 1940.

The Clay Township Trio made up of Mrs. Emmett Frey, Mrs. John Burkle and Mrs. Roger Frey accompanied by Mrs. Roy Newhouser, sang at many meetings.

Amateur Contests

When the 4-H Fair was moved to Flora in 1932, Ora Shirar and the Flora Community Club conducted an Amateur Contest at the Fair. This was a popular feature at the Fair and continued for several years.

An Amateur Contest sponsored by the County Farm Bureau was held at the County 4-H Fair on Tuesday and Wednesday evenings, July 29 and 30, 1952. Mrs. Charles Harter, County Farm Bureau S & E leader was chairman, and was assisted by Township S & E leaders. The Flora Community Club awarded $40 in cash prizes for each evening's contest. A Group Act with five or more people with an act of not more than ten minutes, or a Curtain Act with five or less people requiring not more than five minutes could enter the contest. Only one contestant was allowed for each township and one each for Flora and Delphi. Elimination contests were held in several townships.

Jane Ann Jones of Flora won the contest the first evening, and a group from Democrat Township won the second evening. They presented a skit "Finishin School." In the act were Mr. and Mrs. Cleon Carter, Mr. and Mrs. Truman Plank and Mrs. Alice Sledge.

Second place was won by the Carroll County Rural Youth Chorus.

All three acts represented Carroll County at the District Rural Entertainment Festival at Lafayette on October 6.

Tom Fouts, better known as Captain Stubby, got his start at an Amateur Contest at the County Fair.

Carroll County Farm Bureau Chorus

Mrs. Miles T. Martin, County S & E, and Lewis Deardorff, District field man organized a Carroll County Farm Bureau Chorus, and had their first meeting on June 27, 1947. Mrs. Mildred Shanks was the director and Miss Lesta Hausenfluck was the pianist. Some members were: Mrs. Miles T. Martin, Miss Myna Robertson, Mrs. Everett Keyes, Mrs. John Wise, Peggy Lou Barnard, Mrs. Orton Zook, Mrs. George Peterson, Mr. and Mrs. Taylor Fouts, John Furnham, O. L. Hausenfluck, Mr. and Mrs. David Smith and Howard Smith.

Their first public appearance was at the County Farm Bureau Picnic at Flora on August 14, 1947. For the next few years they appeared on many programs in the county.

Mary Jo Thompson, left, daughter of Mr. and Mrs. Harold Thompson of Flora; and Dawn Flora, right, daughter of Mr. and Mrs. Russell Flora of Monroe Township, entertaining at the county Farm Bureau training school at the Flora Library on December 7, 1951.

County Farm Bureau Band

A County Farm Bureau Band made up of 30 boys and girls from Farm Bureau families in every township was organized in 1940. The band was directed by Omer Collins of Logansport. Mrs. Clark Metsger and Mrs. Nona Logan were appointed to get material to make costumes for band members. A band concert and an ice cream social helped raise money for the uniforms.

Twenty five members of the band played at the State Convention of the Indiana Farm Bureau at Tomlinson Hall on November 13, 1940. The band continued for only a few years, and in 1949 the costumes were sold to Taylor Fouts for $1 each.

Members of the band listed in the Hoosier Democrat for July 19, 1941 were: Donald Zartman, Frances Sanderson and Margaret Landis all of Carrollton Township; Pauline and Eldon Robeson and Donnabelle Seagraves, Washington; Robert and Ladene Rodkey, Treva Metsger, Lois Congram, Mary Crume, Beverly Snyder, and Joaquin Bowman of Burlington; James Clawson, Pattie Brewer and Phyllis Jean Craig of Tippecanoe; Douglas Million, Ralph Hanna and Helen Smith, Adams.

OTHER ACTIVITIES

The County Farm Bureau has been involved in many activities. Several projects supporting 4-H are listed in Chapter VI.

County officers and others have written many news items for local papers, the Hoosier Farmer, the Farm News and Newsletters to members.

Each year the County Farm Bureau and the County FBCA have sold State Fair tickets at a reduced price before the Fair. Three thousand tickets were sold each year during 1946 and 1947.

Farm Bureau members have always helped their neighbors in time of need. Many helped their neighbors after the storm that hit Carroll County in May 1953.

On April 14, 1963 a group from Clay Township donated 50 hours of work to help clean up storm damage at Moran in Clinton County.

Several in the northwest part of Carroll County helped clean up the damage caused by the tornado at Monticello on April 3, 1974.

4-H Achievement Programs

Clay Township Farm Bureau is the only Township Farm Bureau in Carroll County which now has regular monthly meetings. Other Township Farm Bureau organizations meet from one to four times per year. Every township has a meeting in the fall to give 4-H awards and pins to boys and girls in the township who have completed 4-H projects. In most townships this is a supper meeting, and the program usually includes slides showing 4-H activities during the past year. Each Township Farm Bureau pays for 4-H pins for boys, and the Extension Homemaker clubs pay for 4-H pins for girls.

Public Speaking Contests

For several years beginning in the early 1930's the Farm Bureau sponsored Public Speaking Contests for women. Of the many winners in the district contest, pictures are available of Mrs. Charles Tansey who won in 1951, and Mrs. Alice Sledge, the winner in 1952.

Some members of the Carroll County Farm Bureau Band which was organized in 1940 and directed by Omer Collins, second from right. Monroe Meade, County FB chairman, is holding banner at left in picture.

Mrs. Charles Tansey who served as County Farm Bureau S & E Director from 1941 to 1944 won the Women's Public Speaking Contest in the Third Farm Bureau District in 1951.

Carroll County Farm Bureau Queen Contest

For several years, beginning in 1940, the Carroll County Farm Bureau and affiliated organizations in the county conducted a County Queen Contest. Different rules were used for each year, and no complete record of winners is available. During some years the County Queen was selected by the Carroll County Rural Youth. One year the votes for the queen were based on the sale of paint by the Carroll County Farm Bureau Cooperative Association.

The County Queen was crowned each year at the County Farm Bureau Picnic in August, and was eligible to enter the state contest usually held during the Indiana State Fair. During some years the State Queens were crowned during a ceremony at the State Fair and in other years they were crowned at the Indiana Farm Bureau Convention in November. During most years the County Queen was a guest of the Farm Bureau Insurance Company at a banquet during the Indiana Farm Bureau Convention.

Among those who won the Carroll County Queen Contest were: Pauline Robeson and Marjorie Shonk, 1940; Marion Mourer, 1943; Evelyn Crowell, 1944; Laverna Zook, 1945; Norma Dietz, 1946; Eva Lu Pearson, 1947 and Peggy Lou Barnard, 1948.

Essay Contests

For several years the County Farm Bureau sponsored an essay contest, and the winner was given a two day trip to the IFB Convention at Indianapolis.

In 1928 there were 34 contestants and the contest was won by Geneva Shaffer of Washington Township on the subject: "Why Dad and Mother Should Belong to Farm Bureau."

Charlene Yeager of Washington Township won the contest in 1929 on "Why Farmers Should Organize."

In 1977 the essay contest was replaced by the Farm Wife of the Year contest.

Sheep Dipping

In 1937 the Carroll County Farm Bureau purchased a sheep dipping outfit. It was a large metal tank on a wagon with gates and chutes arranged so the sheep could be driven through the tank filled with sheep dip containing lime and sulphur to help control ticks and lice.

The records show that 2,972 sheep were dipped in 1938, 2,810 in 1939 and 2,143 in 1941. The outfit was operated by Harold Kaston in 1938, and by Oliver Wooley of Flora in later years.

In 1947 the outfit was sold to Taylor Fouts for $16.

Operation Traffic Count

On October 16, 1956 a traffic count was made at several road intersections in each township to help determine which roads were used most.

One hundred forty Farm Bureau members donated their time for the day to help make the survey. The information was used by the County Commissioners in making a long range plan for road improvement in the county.

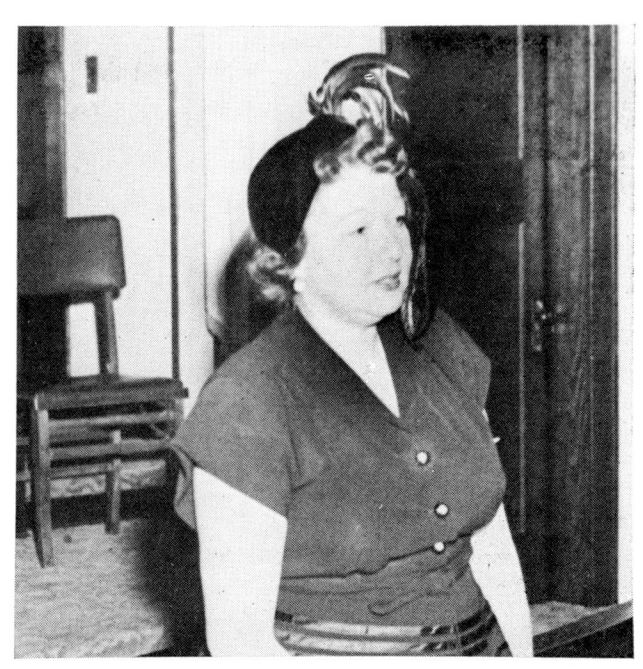

Mrs. Alice Sledge of Democrat Township won the Women's Public Speaking contest at the District Farm Bureau meeting at Fowler on January 9, 1952. The subject of her talk was "Making American Democracy a Reality."

Pork Demonstration

Carroll County Extension Homemakers County Officers and Club Presidents were dinner guests of the Carroll County Farm Bureau at 6:30 p.m. April 8, 1978 at Mom's Place in Burrows operated by Maxine and Junior Snider. A salad smorgasbord was served to 38 guests.

The program was a Pork Demonstration by James York, District Farm Bureau field man and John Baugh from the Indiana Farm Bureau Commodity Department, who cut up half of a pork carcass and gave many tips on how the different individual cuts could be prepared for meals.

Packages of fresh pork as door prizes were given to Iris McCain, Esther Million, Mabel Burt, Wilma Snipes, Hazel Mullin and Helen Anderson.

On March 1, 1979 James York gave a Pork Carcass Demonstration as a lesson for County Extension Homemaker project leaders at the REMC auditorium at Delphi.

Operation Citrus

In November 1970 the Board of Directors of the Carroll County Farm Bureau approved a new program known as "Operation Citrus," a Farmer-to-Farmer marketing program sponsored by Farm Bureau. The Indiana Agricultural Marketing Association, an affiliate of the Indiana Farm Bureau, made arrangements with the Florida Agricultural Marketing Association sponsored by the Florida Farm Bureau, to ship oranges and grapefruit from Florida directly to Farm Bureau members in Indiana. The fruit was ordered in November and delivered in December.

This program has been continued each year, and has been expanded to include orange, grapefruit and lemon concentrate from Florida and cheese from Wisconsin.

The produce is delivered by truck to a central location in the county where it is picked up by those who had placed orders.

Farm Bureau Safety Lane

For several years the Carroll County Farm Bureau and the Farm Bureau Insurance Company operated a Safety Lane for automobiles. One was on August 5, 6, and 7, 1946 in Delphi where 254 cars were checked for safety.

The lane was operated by two men from the IFB Insurance Department. Local people who helped were Mr. and Mrs. David Smith, Miss Lucile Million and Donald Mullin, general agent for the Farm Bureau Insurance Company in Carroll County.

Cars were checked for brakes, wheel alignment, lights, horns and windshield wipers. Each driver was given a card showing what was right or wrong with his car. The principal defect was lights, with brakes in second place.

No charge was made for the test, and cars which passed the test had an "approved" sticker put on the windshield. Many people whose cars failed the test had their cars repaired and came back for the safety sticker.

This free testing service was begun by Farm Bureau in 1940, but was discontinued during the war. In 1941, 41.4% of the cars tested at the safety lanes in Indiana were found to be unsafe and in 1946 the percentage of unsafe cars was about 44.

Crime Prevention

To help reduce crime in Indiana the Indiana Farm Bureau offers an award of $500 for information leading to the arrest and conviction for Arson, Malicious Injury to Property or Theft committed on the premises of a member.

The Farm Bureau Insurance Company in 1976 organized a program known as CRIME TRAP, (Total Registration of All Property). This program encourages members to mark their property with an identification number, using a pen that writes with "invisible" ink, which can be seen only under an ultra violet light.

A form is provided for members to list their property along with the identification number, serial numbers and other means of identification. This information is then filed with law enforcement agencies, making it easier for them to identify stolen property when it is found.

Picture Projectors

In 1925 the Carroll County Farm Bureau secured a 35 mm silent moving picture projector with the help of several business men in the county. A glass slide was prepared for each business that made a contribution, and these slides were shown when the machine was used.

The machine weighed about 50 pounds and was listed as "semi portable." It operated on 32 volts and was convenient to use in schools in the county with 32 volt electric plants. In schools with 110 volt electric service a rheostat was used to reduce the voltage to 32. The machine used a 600 watt lamp, which required 20 amperes on either 32 or 110 volt service.

This created a problem because many buildings were not equipped with wiring circuits and fuses designed for a 20 ampere load.

In meeting places where no electricity was available, the machine was operated by five 6 volt batteries. These were usually hauled in an automobile and connected to the machine with a long extension cord. A set of fully charged batteries would operate the machine for an evening show. The County Agent usually operated the machine, and it was used for several years at Township Farm Bureau meetings.

County Agents in other counties with a similar movie projector sometimes used a generator powered by an automobile. One rear wheel of the auto would be blocked up so it would turn and run the generator which was fastened under the running board of the auto.

In 1941 a 16 mm sound projector was purchased by the Carroll County Farm Bureau, the Carroll County REMC and the AAA.

In 1947 the projector was replaced with a later model machine purchased by the Carroll County Farm Bureau and Carroll County Farm Bureau Co-op Association. In 1949 a 35 mm machine was purchased to show film strips and slides.

All of these machines were used to provide programs in many Township Farm Bureau meetings.

In 1947 the CCFB directors sold the original 32 volt machine to Joseph E. Peterson for $5. In the meantime someone had stolen the lenses and the heavy duty extension cord used with the machine. A box of glass slides with the machine listed several of the business men who had helped pay for the machine.

A slide shown at the beginning of each show stated: "This Farm Bureau motion picture machine has been made possible through the cooperation of the following business firms. It will be to your interest to patronize these firms and tell them that you saw their ad here."

A few of the Delphi merchants named on slides were: Carroll County Loan and Trust Company, Blythe & Sons, and Lewis Morrison. Some from Flora were: Oaks and Minix, E. E. Landis, Carroll County Loan, Trust and Savings Company, Flora Produce, Indiana Condensed Milk Company and Northcutt Bros. Others in the county included: W. C. Smock Company, Burrows; Cutler Bank, Cutler, and Soyland Seeds, Camden (Fouts Bros.), The Producers Commission Association had a slide, and one for State Farm Mutual Auto Insurance Company listed the IFB as State Agent. Local agents listed were: A. A. Newer, Camden; Wilbur Doolittle, Delphi; E. E. Stephens, Cutler and Lloyd Beard, Rossville.

Another slide stated: "Have you paid your Farm Bureau Dues for 1927? Do it now! and be a member of the 999 FB Club."

Other slides with the words for songs were used for community singing.

County Farm Bureau Scholarships

Beginning in 1967 Carroll County Farm Bureau has given scholarships each year to High School graduates who plan to take further training. Two scholarships were awarded the first year and four each year after that.

The first scholarships were $50 each, and in November 1975 the amount was increased to $100 per scholarship. Applications were placed with the Guidance Counselors in each High School attended by Carroll County students.

Those eligible to receive a scholarship must be: a resident of Carroll County for at last one year, a member of a Farm Bureau family, a senior at one of the four High Schools serving Carroll County, be enrolled for further education and show signs of social adjustment and cooperation in High School.

Scholarship winners have been:

1967 Sharon Wilken and Gary Duff
1968 Rebecca Smith, Karen and Linda Kremer, Wm. Anderson
1969 Mary Ellen Scott, Nancy DuVall, Jeff Moss, Stanley Hathaway
1970 Joan Wilken, Mary Fassnacht, Janene Sieber, Dennis Funkhouser
1971 Teresa Burke, Pamela Sue Sheetz, George Mears, John Duggleby
1972 Deborah Ann Mills, Elaine Campbell, Eddie A. Hanna, Jerry W. Frey
1973 Cindy Hathaway, Madonna Kremer, Tom Petry, Harold Ray Zink
1974 Kathy D. Miller, Terri Cook, Kim D. Groninger, Gentry L. Johnson
1975 Susan E. Duff, Bethany E. Zook, Leonard E. Fultz, Neal Harper
1976 Kimberly Hathaway, Jane Hicks, Larry Lucas, Edward Irmeger
1977 Kay Ellen Walton, Tamara Jo Cook, Jeff Been, John Moss
1978 Linda Jeanne Mays, Teri Diane Reiff, David Dean Appleton, David Jay Scott
1979 JoAnne Connaway, Loretta Ann Kremer, Phillip D. Burkle, Kevin L. Robeson
1980 Douglas Barnard, Gayle Abbott, Carrie Ayres, Denise Clevenger

YOUNG FARMERS

In 1970 the IFB started on a new program for organizing Young Farmer groups in each county. The program was for any farmer up to 30 years of age.

The first meeting in Carroll County was held March 11, 1970 at the Suburban Restaurant in Flora. Meredith Ayres and Calvin Fieleke were selected to be in charge of the organization. Those who attended the meeting were: Gerald Hanna, Ann Hawkins, Meredith Ayres, Joe Fountain, Harry DuVall, Larry DuVall, Vicki Richardson, Mr. and Mrs. Calvin Fieleke, Raymond and Mrs. Zink, County FB Women's leader; Mr. and Mrs. Bernard Green of Benton County; Earl Roberts, District Farm Bureau field man, and Charles Hanna, President of the Carroll County Farm Bureau.

The first state meeting was a two day session held at the Marott Hotel in Indianapolis with about 140 from all parts of Indiana. Estel Callahan was director of the program for Indiana Farm Bureau.

Sharon and Meredith Ayres were one of three Young Farm couples in the United States to win a National Young Farmer award at the second Annual National Convention of Young Farmers in 1970.

Mr. and Mrs. Gerald Hanna attended the Young Farmers Conference at Indianapolis February 25, 1974 and Mr. and Mrs. Craig Martin attended in November 1976.

Vickie and Rick Ayres were among the 175 Hoosiers who participated in the Annual Young Farmers Conference for young farmers and their wives held February 5 and 6, 1979 at the Marriott Inn in Indianapolis.

In 1979 Mr. and Mrs. Jerry Frey were elected as directors for the state organization representing District 3. Jerry also was one of the three finalists in the Indiana Young Farmers Discussion Contest sponsored by the IFB at the State Convention at Indianapolis in December 1979.

Those from Carroll County who attended the Annual Young Farmers Conference at Indianapolis on February 4 and 5, 1980 were: Gail and Brad Burton, Ruth and Gary Forgey and Janice and Jerry Frey.

CIMCO 44

Farm Bureau Public Relations Committee

At a meeting of the Public Relations Committee of the Carroll County Farm Bureau on March 3, 1961 problems of Carroll County were discussed. Those attending the meeting were: Ralph Maggart, Carl Johnson, Marion Langston, Fannie Blue, Esther Million, Don Willy, Dale Kasten, Charles Hoover, Robert Clawson and Gene Wilson. It was decided that each one present would invite someone else to meet with the committee the next month in order to get other organizations and business groups involved in the program.

There were 20 people at the next meeting on April 3 at the County Agent's office in Delphi. Those present who were not at the previous meeting were: Monte Alderfer, Ted Brown, Pauline Robeson, Al Moss, Dick Bishop, Kenneth Cooke, Ancil Bowley, Art McDowell, Norwood Gentry, Fred Chandler and Donald Henderson.

After discussing the problems in Carroll County, and what might be done about them, the chairman, Ralph Maggart, appointed Ted Brown, chairman; Marion Langston, Al Moss, Pauline Robeson, Dale Kasten, Art McDowell and Norwood Gentry as a sub-committee to make plans and recommendations.

This sub-committee met on April 20 and recommended that a committee be appointed to represent all parts of the county, and all occupations and interest groups. They suggested that the FB Public Relations Committee appoint three members from each township, and that the County Agent and HDA be members of the committee making a total of 44 members.

The sub-committee recommended that projects considered be ones that would benefit all county residents. Some areas suggested were: county planning, United Fund, vocational training for youth and adults, consumer credit, education, bookmobile, restoration and marking of historic points in the county, county road numbering, and youth counciling and guidance.

CIMCO 44 Organized

These recommendations were presented at a committee meeting on May 2, 1961 in the County Agent's office. The 18 members present approved the recommendation of the sub-committee, and the suggestion made by Al Moss that the new organization be called CIMCO 44. This stands for Carroll Improvement Membership Committee of 44. Those present at that meeting who had not attended a previous meeting of the committee were: Elaine Kull, Mr. and Mrs. Fred McCain, John C. Peterson, J. Marcus Haggard and Leo C. Craig.

On June 5, 37 members of CIMCO 44 met at the County Agents office. Ralph Maggart served as temporary chairman and Pauline Robeson as temporary secretary. The members decided that the new organization should not depend on any other group or organization for financial support, so they passed the hat and collected $11 to be used for postage and

Members of the Public Relations committee of the Carroll County Farm Bureau at a meeting on March 3, 1961. Left to right: Marion Langston, County Farm Bureau vice president; Dale Kasten, County Agent; Carl Johnson, County Farm Bureau president; Charles Hoover, manager of the County Farm Bureau Cooperative Association; Ralph Maggart, former County Agent; Robert Clawson, manager of the County REMC, Don Willy, County Farm Bureau insurance manager; Mrs. Clayton Million, County Farm Bureau secretary and Mrs. Fannie Blue, County Farm Bureau Women's Leader.

other expenses. The date of regular meetings was set for the first Monday night in each month, and a committee was appointed to nominate officers to be elected at the next meeting. Members of the nominating committee were: J. Marcus Haggard, Mrs. Truman Plank and Mrs. John Kirkpatrick.

At the next regular meeting July 3, officers elected were: Robert Clawson, president; Marion Langston, vice president; Marie Hanrahan, secretary and Robert Hedde, treasurer. A committee appointed to prepare a Constitution and By-laws for consideration at the next meeting was Art McDowell, Fred Martin and Gardner Martin.

The Constitution adopted at the next meeting held at Rockfield on August 7, 1961 provided that when one member resigned or quit attending meetings, the two remaining members in a township would appoint a replacement.

One of the purposes named in the Constitution was to study the needs of the county, and to work with all individuals and organizations who seek to better the county in any matter. Another purpose was to "create an atmosphere, free of politics, where matters vitally affecting our county can be discussed with a view of affecting a solution." Also on the list was the preservation and marking of historical places in the county.

Regular meetings the first Monday night of each month, with an average attendance of 20 to 30 members, were held at different places in the county with members from the host township providing a meeting place and refreshments.

The organization continued for five years, with new officers each year. Others who served as president were: John C. Peterson, Charles Hanna, Lewis Mullin and Ren C. Groninger. Other vice presidents were: John Temple, Fred Martin and Elwood Burkle. Other secretaries were: Elaine Kull Liley and Dale Kasten.

United Fund

One of the first community projects undertaken by CIMCO 44 was the United Fund for Carroll County. The subject was discussed in 1961 at the November meeting at Burlington and the December meeting at Camden. The idea was approved, and Art McDowell,

Ren. C. Groninger and Marion Langston were appointed to represent CIMCO 44 on a committee with one member from each Township: John Temple, Adams; Ancil Bowley, Burlington; Raymond Huse, Carrollton; Paul Miller, Clay; Joseph T. Ives Jr., Deer Creek; Stanley Anderson, Democrat; Carl Baker, Jackson; Robert Mills, Jefferson; Merlin Mullin, Liberty; Lee Flora, Madison; Devere Hoffman, Monroe; Delmar Galbreth, Rock Creek; Lloyd Anderson, Tippecanoe and Michael Hinkle, Washington.

This committee continued with plans and finished organizing the United Fund for Carroll County in 1962 and 1963.

Historical Sites

At the regular meeting at Camden December 5, 1961, Faye Wise gave a talk and displayed a map of Carroll County on which she had located many points of historical interest. Robert Bradshaw, vice president of the Carroll County Sesquicentennial Committee met with CIMCO 44 on April 4, 1965 and discussed historic spots in Carroll County.

The Carroll County Sesquicentennial Committee, celebrating the 150th year for the state of Indiana in 1966 printed and distributed a map of Carroll County showing points of historic interest in every township.

At a meeting held at the County Agent's office in Delphi on February 5, 1962 a historical committee: John Temple, Ren C. Groninger and Lewis Mullin presented a drawing by Mrs. Berdena Peter of a proposed placemat to be used in eating places interested in boosting Carroll County. The plan was approved, placemats printed and used in restaurants and at banquets throughout the county.

A stone arch built over Burnetts Creek in 1841 so that the Wabash and Erie Canal could cross over the creek is located east of Lockport along the Towpath. An unusual engineering project, the arch is still in good condition and members agreed that it should be marked. Jesse Brothers of Rockfield furnished and set a stone marker shown in a picture on page 6. Later the county commissioners obtained an easement from Ira Leslie who owned the property at the north end of the arch and built a stairway so that people could get a better view of the arch.

Parke County

At a meeting at the Hickory Grove Church on December 7, 1964, Reuben Dooley, Manager of the Parke County REMC told of the progress made in 12 years by a similar committee in Parke County. Their main project was the Parke County Covered Bridge Festival which attracts large crowds each year.

The Parke County Committee had also promoted the building of recreational facilities, and had encouraged several small industries in the county.

County Parks

Realizing a need for parks and recreation areas in Carroll County, CIMCO 44 made a survey of the county and proposed several locations for parks. The committee recommended that a camping site be established at French Post Park near Lockport, and encouraged the Flora Rotary Club with their camp site at Adams Mill near Cutler.

Telephones

CIMCO 44 had several meetings with representatives of the telephone companies in the county to study the possibility of providing toll free telephone service to all parts of the county. Like other organizations that have worked on this project they gave it up as not practical at that time.

Trash Disposal

One of the problems considered by CIMCO 44 was that of trash disposal. A lot of trash was being thrown out along the roads in the county and presented several problems. It was unsightly, unsanitary, and in some cases interfered with traffic. Specialists from Purdue and the State Board of Health, and Charles Burton, County Sanitarian, were on the program at several meetings.

After studying the problem the committee encouraged the County Commissioners to establish a sanitary land fill at the County Farm. This did not completely solve the problem, but it did provide a place where people could legally dispose of their solid waste.

Road Numbers

For several years the FB and other organizations in the county had recommended that roads in the county be named or numbered, and signs installed to identify them. This would help people find where others lived, and would help the county highway department in identifying roads. The project was discussed at several meetings, and the committee recommended a system that had been adopted by several other counties in the state. The county council appropriated money, the county surveyor's office prepared a map showing road numbers, and the county highway department installed and is maintaining signs at each crossroad.

Economic Report

At the regular meeting held April 1, 1963, County Agent Dale Kasten gave a report on a Masters Thesis by Monte Alderfer, who had recently been a Better Farming Better Living Agent in Carroll County. The title of his thesis was: "An Analysis of the Factors Affecting the Economic Development of Carroll County, Indiana." The report showed that the income of people in Carroll County averaged less than for people in surrounding counties, and that 29% of the workers living in Carroll County were employed outside the county. An average of 88 people were moving out of the county each year to get a better job.

The committee decided to take the responsibility of preparing an Economic Report on Carroll County in order to study the problem and suggest changes to improve the economic and social status of people in the county.

Several meetings were held with speakers including L. Tim Wallace, Hank Wadsworth and James Guthrie of Purdue University to discuss the problem.

At the regular meeting on July 3, 1963 at the Burrows Presbyterian Church, four committees were appointed to work on the Economic Report. Members of the committees were: Agriculture: Raymond Dillman, John Allbaugh, Fred Martin, John Crowel, Milton Bowman, Elwood Burkle, Kenneth Frey, Ernest Minich and Bill Martin; Recreation and Tourism: Lewis Mullin, Ren C. Groninger and Orville Shultheis; Supporting Services: Charles Hanna, Pauline Robeson, Esther Million and John C. Peterson; Industry and Commerce, Art McDowell.

When the report was completed, members were convinced more than ever of the importance of the many projects on which they had been working and realized that there were many more opportunities for improving conditions in Carroll County.

County Planning

Several meetings were held on the subject of County Planning, and how it might be used to improve conditions in Carroll County. At a meeting in the Courthouse at Delphi on April 6, 1964, 55 members and guests of CIMCO 44 heard Charles Sargent, Purdue Agricultural Economist, discuss community, county and area planning and zoning. He defined planning as a group of people deciding on how land should be used in the future, and zoning as the legal method of putting the plan into effect. He stated that purposes of planning and zoning include the preservation of good farm land for agricultural use; protect residential, retail and commercial areas; reserve areas for industry, schools, parks and public buildings; develop highways and roads and control traffic; control unsightly areas and provide for sanitation.

At a meeting at the Methodist Church in Burlington on October 5, 1965 Don Henderson, fieldman for the IFB presented a colored slide show designed to help people become aware of the advantages of planning and what it can do in solving problems in a community. He reported that more than half the counties in Indiana had some kind of planning and zoning.

The last meeting of CIMCO 44 was held at the home of Robert Clawson on November 7, 1966. In some townships, new members had not been appointed to replace those who dropped out, and fewer people attended the meetings. The Extension Service had organized a Community Development Committee, sometimes refered to as "Super CIMCO" which had the same general purpose as CIMCO 44. Those present at the meeting decided to disband the organization, and continue to work as individuals and through other organizations to improve conditions in the county. A report on the Community Development Committee is in Chapter IV, on page 90.

FARM BUREAU INSURANCE

In April 1925 the Indiana Farm Bureau signed a 10-year contract with the State Farm Mutual Insurance Company in Bloomington, Illinois to provide Automobile Insurance to members of the IFB. For several years this was a satisfactory arrangement. State Farm was a small company that needed a market and this gave them access to the farm market in Indiana. Farm Bureau members were able to buy good insurance at a fair price, and the IFB received a commission which provided money to operate the state organization.

In 1934 a committee was appointed to investigate and make recommendations about renewing the contract which was to expire in 1935. A majority of the committee members recommended that the contract be renewed. A minority, including Arthur Arnott of Rensselaer, recommended that the Indiana Farm Bureau organize its own Auto Insurance Company. When the committee on Insurance reported to the board of the IFB, the directors being evenly divided and unable to agree, decided to present the matter to the delegates at the Annual State Convention.

1934 State Convention

Members who attended the 1934 Annual Meeting of the IFB in Tomlinson Hall in Indianapolis on November 21-23, 1934 agreed that it was one of the most exciting conventions ever held.

President Wm. H. Settle was strongly in favor of renewing the Insurance Contract. Low prices for farm products had caused many farmers to drop their membership in Farm Bureau. In 1933, memberships in Indiana hit an all time low of 23,000. Mr. Settle appreciated the certainty of $30,000 each year from the Insurance Company, and doubted that a FB owned Insurance Company could do any better. About half of the directors and delegates agreed with Mr. Settle. Farm Bureau leaders who had been active in the rapidly growing Farm Bureau Cooperative Association realized the advantage of farmers owning their own Insurance Company.

Election of the president would decide the issue. Mr. Settle was so sure of being elected that the Insurance Company had a band ready to march into the hall to help celebrate the victory when he was elected.

Running against President Settle for election was Lewis Taylor, vice president of the IFB, who was in favor of organizing an Insurance Company. A simple majority of votes of the 152 voting delegates was necessary for election. On the first ballot, Settle had 64, Taylor 69, Maurice Douglas 6, and Hassil E. Schenck, 13 votes.

A second ballot gave Settle 61, Taylor 82, Douglas 4 and Schenck 5. Lewis Taylor was elected president, and the band went home without playing.

This left the office of vice president vacant, and the delegates unanimously elected Hassel E. Schenck as vice president. Mr. Schenck was a delegate and as a member of the rules committee had presented a minority report which the delegates liked. Mr. Schenck became president when Lewis Taylor died in December 1936 while attending the Annual Convention of the AFBF in California.

Farm Bureau Mutual Insurance Company

The first order of business facing the newly elected officers was the formation of a Mutual Insurance Company. The Farm Bureau Mutual Insurance Company of Indiana, Inc. was organized and licensed to transact business on February 26, 1935. During the first year the company sold 3,341 policies, collected $120,628.85 in premiums, and ended the first year with a surplus of only $148, and assets of a little more than $400. Many people were skeptical of the new company, but it grew rapidly and in 1979 was the largest Auto Insurance Company with headquarters in Indiana, and ranked second among all companies selling Auto Insurance in Indiana.

For several years the Insurance Company did not provide much income for the state organization, and this created a problem. In 1937 the state officers and all except one of the employees at the state office voluntarily agreed to collect only $3,000 per year of their pay.

The Farm Bureau Fire and Tornado Insurance Company was incorporated October, 1945, and licensed to do business on February 21, 1946. On May 1, 1948 it was merged with and became a division of the Farm Bureau Mutual Insurance Company.

On January 1, 1966 the Farm Bureau Mutual Insurance Company changed it's name to the United Farm Bureau Mutual Insurance Company.

Hoosier Farm Bureau Life Insurance Company

In 1936 the IFB made a survey of members to determine interest in starting a Life Insurance Company. Plans made and presented at the State Farm Bureau Convention in 1936 were approved by the delegates. The Hoosier Farm Bureau Life Insurance Company was chartered on March 25, 1937 and received authority and license to do business on June 11, 1937.

Guaranteed Surplus Contribution Certificates totaling $32,410 were sold to individuals, Township and County Farm Bureaus, and to local and State Farm Bureau Cooperatives. This money was all repaid during 1945. More than 2,000 charter applications were received, and amounted to more than $2,000,000. This was ten times the minimum legal requirement to start a Life Insurance Company in Indiana.

The Farm Bureau Life Insurance Company had $100,000,000 insurance in force by early in 1953 and reached $1 billion in April 1972, after operating for 35 years. In October 1977, the company reached the $2 billion mark, and by the end of 1979 nearly $3 billion worth of Life Insurance was in force.

On June 30, 1964 the Hoosier Farm Bureau Life Insurance Company changed its name to the United Farm Bureau Family Life Insurance Company, and in 1979 was the largest Life Insurance Company licensed to sell insurance only in Indiana.

The Auto and Life Insurance Companies have the same directors, management and agency force with at least one office in each of Indiana's 92 counties. The companies have about 600 agents and employ about 2,000 people.

Farm Mortgage Company

The Farm Bureau Insurance Companies established a Farm Mortgage Company to loan money on Farm mortgages and Miles T. Martin was appointed Carroll County representative in August, 1944. The program was discontinued after about five years.

Rural Acceptance Corporation

In 1953 the Indiana Farm Bureau and the Farm Bureau Mutual Insurance Company organized the Rural Acceptance Corporation to finance the sale of automobiles. In 1959 the service was expanded to include other loans.

Superior Parts

On January 1, 1954, Superior Parts, Incorporated was organized as a subsidiary of the Insurance Company, as a salvage yard to handle wrecked vehicles for the Insurance Company. The yard was first located in Boone County, until a new highway went through the yard and made it necessary to relocate. There are now two salvage yards, one near Logansport and one near Bedford. Some parts are used in repairing insured autos, and others are sold.

Rural Insurance Agency

In 1959 the Rural Insurance Company was organized as a wholly owned subsidiary of the Farm Bureau Mutual Insurance Company. It has contracts with other insurance companies for the writing of policies not written by the Farm Bureau companies. This makes it possible for agents to offer a full line of insurance to all customers.

Indiana Farm Bureau Offices

The first office for the Indiana Federation of Farmers' Associations was in Room 369 in the English Hotel in Indianapolis, but soon moved to the Lemcke Building on East Market Street. Lewis Taylor, secretary of the organization moved everything in two suitcases.

When the Farm Bureau Mutual Insurance Company was organized, the Farm Bureau needed more room, and in 1936 moved to the Old Trails Building at 309 West Washington Street. In 1941 the Indiana Farm Bureau, the insurance companies and the Indiana Farm Bureau Cooperative Association moved to the Majestic Building at 47 South Pennsylvania Street. This building was later owned and occupied by the IFBCA. In 1945 the insurance companies moved across the street to the Century Building.

In 1947 the U.S. Government took over this building and the insurance companies moved to the Union Title Building at 155 East Market Street. The insurance companies purchased the Meyer-Kiser Security Trust Building at 130 East Washington Street and moved there in 1949. A new twelve story building was built east of this building in 1969, and both buildings are now occupied by the IFB and the insurance companies and some affiliated organizations.

FARM BUREAU INSURANCE IN CARROLL COUNTY

During the ten years that the IFB had a contract with the State Farm Mutual Insurance Company to sell insurance to farmers in Indiana, there were many farmers in Indiana selling insurance as agents for the company. When the contract was cancelled by action of the delegates at the State Convention in 1934, most of the agents kept their contract with the State Farm Insurance Company and many of them continued to be members of the FB and took part in other FB activities.

It was necessary to find new agents to represent the new Farm Bureau Mutual Insurance Company which was licensed to do business on February 26, 1935. On March 16, 1935 the CCFB directors appointed Lloyd Beard, manager of the Implement Department of the CCFBCA, to represent the FB Insurance Company in Carroll County. In April, 1935 the County FB was incorporated, and became the official representative of the insurance company in the county. Lloyd Beard continued to sell insurance, and John C. Peterson, secretary of the CCFB and Ross Wagoner, manager of the CCFBCA bulk oil plant, were also appointed as solicitors to sell insurance in the county. In January 1936, Keith Sink, Charles Nance and Richard Hawn were appointed as special agents, making a total of six agents in the county.

When the new Hoosier Farm Bureau Life Insurance Company began operating on June 11, 1937, it was necessary to have someone spend full time on insurance. Ernest Stephens was hired as the first General Agent for the county.

Ralph Rinehart was appointed General Agent in

Ernest Stephens, first General Agent of the Farm Bureau Insurance Company in Carroll County. He served from 1937 to 1940.

March 1940. Insurance agents in April 1942 were: Ralph Rinehart, John Kennard, Marjorie Shonk, Monroe Meade and Ross Wagoner. Members of the Insurance Committee in April 1942 were: Artus Rodenbarger, Roy Richter, and Joe Snyder.

For the month of December 1943, Mr. Rinehart ranked first in the state in the production of Automobile Insurance and third in Farm Liability Insurance.

In recognition of this achievement the Indiana Farm Bureau Insurance Company purchased $13,100 in War Bonds in Carroll County. The bonds were purchased through Lloyd Beard, county representative for the Lafayette Production Credit Association.

In 1944 the commission paid to the County Farm Bureau on the sale of insurance in Carroll County was $162.91 from Auto and $119.26 from Life Insurance, making a total of $282.17 for the County Farm Bureau. In July 1945 the County Farm Bureau appointed Leroy Robeson, Clarence Frey, Wayne Zinn; Artus Rodenbarger and Mrs. Gale Crowell as members of the County Insurance Committee.

In February 1946 Charles Thompson and Lloyd

Ralph Reagon began as Agent for Farm Bureau Insurance Company in Carroll County February 14, 1949, and was Agency Manager from August 1955, until he died in November 1958.

Metzger were hired as special agents. Ralph Rinehart resigned as General Agent, but continued as a special agent. In March 1946 Donald Mullin was hired as General Agent.

Ralph Reagon began as special agent on February 14, 1949 and became General Agent on June 27, 1949. Charles Thompson continued as special agent in Burlington, Democrat, Clay and Madison Townships until he died in 1954.

On November 23, 1949 the Carroll County Farm Bureau signed a contract with the Farm Bureau Insurance Companies in which the county organization agreed to provide office facilities and other services for which they would be paid by the insurance companies.

On October 25, 1949 there were 1,195 Farm Bureau Auto Insurance policies in Carroll County. In 1950 Ralph Reagon was one of seven Farm Bureau Insurance agents in Indiana to be awarded a trip to Washington, D.C. to attend the National Association of Life Underwriters Convention. Ralph qualified by writing $288,000 worth of Life Insurance in one year.

Morris Skiles served as special agent in 1951 and Donald Duff was special agent in 1953.

Agency Managers

In August 1955, Ralph Reagon was promoted to Agency Manager for Farm Bureau Insurance in Carroll County. Other agents in the County Farm Bureau office at that time were Ray Robertson and

Charles Thompson, Farm Bureau Insurance Agent, 1946 to 1954.

Donald Willy. For several years Mr. Reagon had been a member of the Century Club which required an annual sale of $100,000 of Life Insurance. In 1955 he qualified for the Quarter Million Club, requiring $250,000 in production.

Dave Morehouse became a special agent late in 1955. In April 1956 the Carroll County agency moved to the number one position as compared with the 90 agencies in the state, topping the next highest group by some $40,000 in Life Insurance production.

In April 1957 Carroll County was the first county in Indiana to reach the goal of $1 million sales in one year. Agents at that time were Ralph Reagon; Agency Manager; Donald Willy, Ray Robertson and Dave Morehouse.

Ralph Reagon died in November 1958 and Donald Willy was named Agency Manager. Ray Robertson was transferred to Benton County as Agency Manager.

At the annual agents convention at French Lick in October 1960 Donald Willy was recognized as a successful Agency Manager. He had gained membership on the All-American team, a top sales club, four years of the five since he became an agent.

Insurance Agents

Among those who have served as Farm Bureau Insurance Agents in Carroll County since 1958 have been: Harry Watts, Tom Brooks, John Price, Harold McCormick, Gene Mellinger, Roy Slavens, Perry Haskins, John Young, Don Connelly, Steve Jordan,

Arnold Teel, District Farm Bureau Insurance Adjuster and Michael Fife, Carroll County Farm Bureau Insurance Agent at the Farm Bureau Office in Delphi.

Farm Bureau Insurance Employees at the Delphi Office in March 1979. Left to right front row: Mary Hildebran and Betty Ward. Back row: Don Willy, Rudy Gardiner, Randy Sheets and Dick Williams.

Charles Walgumuth, Gordan Logan, William Landis, Marvin Manges, Larry Goodwin, Charles Anderson, Jerry Berkshire, Russ Cable and Ray Kilmer. Agents in 1979 were: Dick Williams since 1970, Michael Fife since 1972, Randy Sheets and Rudy Gardiner since 1978 and Don Gritten 1979. Donald Willy was agent beginning on August 1, 1955 and has served as Agency Manager since November 1958.

District Insurance Adjusters

Richard Blackwell was employed in September 1947 as Insurance Adjuster for Carroll, Cass, Clinton, Tippecanoe and Howard counties and was located in the Farm Bureau office in Delphi. In July 1950 he was replaced by James R. Wehlege. Arnold Teel has been the adjuster since August 1961.

County Farm Bureau Office

For nearly 25 years the office of the Carroll County Farm Bureau was located in the County Agent's office. In 1943 it was moved to the office of the Carroll County Farm Bureau Cooperative Association at 120 East Franklin Street.

On August 1, 1955 the Farm Bureau and Insurance office was moved to 108 North Washington Street and was moved to 103 West Franklin Street on February 15, 1958.

In 1962 the CCFB purchased a lot on the corner of Washington and Monroe Streets and constructed an office building. Open house for the new office was held on August 10 and 11, 1962. Later another lot was

CHAPTER VII — FARM BUREAU 193

purchased north of the building and plans made to enlarge the office building.

On September 14, 1973 the Farm Bureau directors approved the location for a branch office at 40 South Center Street in Flora with open house in February 1974.

Office Secretaries

While the County Farm Bureau office was located in the County Agent's office, Mary Mason did the work for both the Farm Bureau and the County Agent until 1935. From 1935 until 1943 the Farm Bureau work in the County Agent's office was done by Lillian Thompson, Jane Witter and Lenore McCarty.

Employees in the Farm Bureau office at Delphi in January, 1980: Marlene Collins, seated and Vonda Pennington, standing.

Employees at the Farm Bureau Insurance office at Flora in December 1979 are left to right: Don Gritten, Virginia Lyons and Dick Williams.

Lenore McCarty Allen, Secretary of Carroll County Farm Bureau from 1941 to 1946.

Carroll County Farm Bureau building at the corner of Washington and Monroe Streets in Delphi.

194 • CARROLL COUNTY RURAL ORGANIZATIONS

Jesse and Vivian (Henderson) Hoover with their daughter Sue Ellen in 1951. Jesse was District Field Man for Indiana Farm Bureau, and Vivian was Carroll County S and E director in 1945 and 1946, and County secretary from 1947 to 1949. She was also District S and E Director.

Jane Witter served as secretary from 1938 to 1940; Lenore (McCarty) Allen from 1941 to 1946; Vivian Henderson from 1947 to 1949 and Mary Ellen (Kempf) Pauley from 1949 to 1956. Others who helped part time during this period were: Rosella Zinn, Dorothy Newell, Mrs. Homer Wilson and Mrs. Ruth Howell. Among those who have served as office secretary for the Farm Bureau and Insurance Company since 1956 have been: Connie Spitler, Carol McFatridge, Laurie Ritchie, Eleanor Wilken, Marjorie Newell, Dare Strycker, Linda Perdue, Diana Klopfenstein, Peggy Draper, Donna Bieghler and Dale Noonkester.

Those working in the office in 1979 were: Mary Hildebran since 1963, Virginia Lyons since 1964, Betty Ward and Marlene Collins since 1974 and Vonda Pennington who started work when Mary Hildebran retired in 1979.

Hospitalization Insurance

In January 1947 the Farm Bureau directors discussed Hospitalization Insurance for members in Carroll County. The first county to start selling Farm Bureau Hospitalization Insurance was Wayne County in 1943. By 1947 there were 34 counties in Indiana in the program. Carroll County directors voted to have a Hospitalization program and set the dates of February 18 to March 20, 1947 for the campaign. During this charter campaign any Farm Bureau member was eligible for the insurance without a physical examination, providing there were at least 850 applications. A campaign was organized with at least four solicitors in each township, and every Farm Bureau member was offered the opportunity to get in the new program. The campaign ended with 1,013 applications. Farm Bureau Hospitalization Insurance became effective in Carroll County at 12:01 p.m. on March 15, 1947.

Mary Ellen Kempf Pauley, office secretary for the Carroll County Farm Bureau from 1949 through 1956.

Mrs. Homer (Mildred) Wilson, Secretary of the Carroll County Farm Bureau in 1950.

CARROLL COUNTY FARM BUREAU, INC., DELPHI, INDIANA

YEARS	MEMB.	PRESIDENT	V. PRESIDENT	S&E DIRECTOR	SECRETARY
1919	386	Taylor Fouts	Perry Rule	(Women's Department	Dr. R. C. Julien
1920	1117	Burton D. Honan	Claude Wickard	after 1957)	Dr. R. C. Julien
1921	1257	Burton D. Honan	Claude Wickard		George Sites
1922	719	Sam Smith	Chas. Doctor		George Sites
1923	765	Sam Smith	Chas. Doctor		George Sites
1924	623	George Sites	E. E. Stephens		Mary Mason
1925	573	George Sites	E. E. Stephens		Mary Mason
1926	764	E. E. Stephens	George A. Thomas		Mary Mason
1927	615	E. E. Stephens	George A. Thomas		Mary Mason
1928	695	Claude R. Wickard	Obe Campbell	Mrs. C. V. Quinn	Mary Mason
1929	635	Claude R. Wickard	Obe Campbell	Mrs. Sam Sites	Mary Mason
1930	773	Claude R. Wickard	Obe Campbell	Mrs. Sam Sites	Mary Mason
1931	787	J. W. Eikenberry	Arthur R. Mullin	Mrs. Sam Sites	Mary Mason
1932	584	J. W. Eikenberry	Arthur R. Mullin	Mrs. Lloyd Beard	Mary Mason
1933	514	J. W. Eikenberry	Arthur R. Mullin	Mrs. Lloyd Beard	Mary Mason
1934	523	Arthur R. Mullin	Miles T. Martin	Mrs. Lloyd Beard	Mary Mason
1935	470	Arthur R. Mullin	Miles T. Martin	Mrs. John Witter	John C. Peterson
1936	426	Loyd E. Zook	Clarence Cleaver	Mrs. John Witter	John C. Peterson
1937	516	Loyd E. Zook	Clarence Cleaver	Mrs. Castyle Fouts	John C. Peterson
1938	441	Monroe Meade	Artus Rodenbarger	Mrs. Lloyd Beard	Ernest Stephens
1939	466	Monroe Meade	Artus Rodenbarger	Mrs. Nona Logan	Jane Witter
1940	465	Monroe Meade	Ben Metzger	Mrs. Nona Logan	Jane Witter
1941	479	Monroe Meade	Ben Metzger	Mrs. Chas. Tansey	Lenore McCarty
1942	582	Miles T. Martin	Russell Craig	Mrs. Chas. Tansey	Lenore McCarty
1943	700	Miles T. Martin	Russell Craig	Mrs. Chas. Tansey	Lenore Allen
1944	792	Miles T. Martin	Russell Craig	Mrs. Chas. Tansey	Lenore Allen
1945	843	John C. Peterson	Oren Eikenberry	Vivian Henderson	Lenore Allen
1946	937	John C. Peterson	Oren Eikenberry	Vivian Henderson	Lenore Allen
1947	1237	John C. Peterson	Oren Eikenberry	Mrs. Miles Martin	Vivian Henderson
1948	1351	John C. Peterson	Clayton Million	Mrs. Miles Martin	Vivian Henderson
1949	1295	John C. Peterson	Clarence Cleaver	Mrs. Miles Martin	Vivian Henderson
1950	1324	John C. Peterson	Clarence Cleaver	Mrs. Charles Harter	Mrs. Homer Wilson
1951	1356	John C. Peterson	Clarence Cleaver	Mrs. Charles Harter	Mary Ellen Kempf
1952	1373	Clarence Cleaver	Fritz Schnepf	Mrs. Charles Harter	Mary Ellen Kempf
1953	1378	Clarence Cleaver	Fritz Schnepf	Mrs. James Viney	Mary Ellen Kempf
1954	1462	Clarence Cleaver	Ray Robertson	Mrs. James Viney	Mary Ellen Kempf
1955	1486	Clayton Million	Estal Mullin	Mrs. James Viney	Mary Ellen Kempf
1956	1518	Clayton Million	Mark Porter	Mrs. James Viney	Mary Ellen Pauley
1957	1500	Clayton Million	Mark Porter	Mrs. James Viney	Connie Spitler
1958	1466	Clayton Million	James Riley, Sr.	Mrs. Fannie Blue	Carol McFatridge
1959	1473	Carl Johnson	Clayton Million	Mrs. Fannie Blue	Eleanor Wilken
1960	1492	Carl Johnson	Marion Langston	Mrs. Fannie Blue	Esther Million
1961	1523	Carl Johnson	Marion Langston	Mrs. Fannie Blue	Esther Million
1962	1544	Marion Langston	Junior Snider	Mrs. Fannie Blue	Esther Million
1963	1562	Marion Langston	Junior Snider	Mrs. Fannie Blue	Esther Million
1964	1595	Marion Langston	Junior Snider	Mrs. Fannie Blue	Esther Million

CARROLL COUNTY RURAL ORGANIZATIONS

YEARS	MEMB.	PRESIDENT	V. PRESIDENT	S&E DIRECTOR	SECRETARY
1965	1644	Junior Snider	Charles Hanna	Mrs. Fannie Blue	Esther Million
1966	1681	Junior Snider	Charles Hanna	Mrs. Fannie Blue	Esther Million
1967	1706	Junior Snider	Charles Hanna	Mrs. Fannie Blue	Esther Million
1968	1614	Junior Snider	Charles Hanna	Mrs. Fannie Blue	Esther Million
1969	1697	Charles Hanna	Charles Hanna	Mrs. Frances Zink	Esther Million
1970	1743	Charles Hanna	Raymond Zink	Mrs. Frances Zink	Esther Million
1971	1734	Charles Hanna	Meredith Ayres	Mrs. Frances Zink	Maxine Snider
1972	1767	Meredith Ayres	Charles Hanna	Mrs. Maxine Snider	Pat Robbins
1973	1821	Meredith Ayres	Charles Hanna	Mrs. Maxine Snider	Pat Robbins
1974	1817	Meredith Ayres	Charles Hanna	Mrs. Maxine Snider	Pat Robbins
1975	1855	Meredith Ayres	Charles Hanna	Mrs. Maxine Snider	Pat Robbins
1976	1975	Meredith Ayres	Gene Jennings	Mrs. Maxine Snider	Pat Robbins
1977	2144	Meredith Ayres	Gene Jennings	Mrs. Maxine Snider	Carolyn Burkle
1978	2216	Gene Jennings	Francis Humbarger	Mrs. Maxine Snider	Carolyn Burkle
1979	2165	Gene Jennings	Francis Humbarger	Mrs. Maxine Snider	Carolyn Burkle

TOWNSHIP FARM BUREAU OFFICERS

Township Farm Bureau Chairmen and Women's Leaders serve as members of the board of directors of the Carroll County Farm Bureau. During the first few years some townships elected a special representative to serve as director of the county organization.

There is no complete record of those who have served as officers of the Township Farm Bureau organizations. The following list includes nearly everyone who has served as chairman of each Township Farm Bureau.

ADAMS

F. S. Girard
Paul Girard
George Wooden
Wilbur Crowell
Orvel Schock
George W. Peterson
A. D. Moore
Clayton Million
Howard Smith
Earl Wakeland
John Wagoner
Gale Crowell
Raymond Nicoll
Russell Pearson
Robert Ward
Donald L. Dill
Douglas Million
Roscoe Hoffman

BURLINGTON

Edgar Logan
Spud Harness
Clarence Johnson
Clarence Stout
Wm. M. Douglas
Jake F. Harness
Garland McCarty
Verne Avery
Charles Thompson
Joe Snyder
Ross Garrison
Ralph Rinehart
H. J. Eastman
Rex Hinkle
Fred Rodkey
Leonard Shriver
Ray Robertson
Verne Wise

John R. Harness
C. I. Moss
Beryl Beckner
Marion Langston
Keith Sink

CARROLLTON

Taylor Fouts
Warren H. Todd
Jesse McCain
Monroe Meade
S. A. Wickard
Bert McCain
Robert Wingard
Glenn Booth
Manford Wagoner
Clyde Cooke
Glen Zartman
Fred Hood
Homer Thomas
Elmer Spitler
Evan Sanderson
Robert Simmons
Raymond Huse
Robert Rodgers
Charles P. Dillman
Lawrence Vass
Carl Overholser
Raymond Dillman

CLAY

Isaac Swartz
Ed Fenstermacher

Clarence Frey
Frank Redenbacher
Eli Ritchey
Edward Fossnock
Leroy E. Wade
Walter H. Barnhart
Ben Metzger
Roy Cornelison
Lloyd Metzger
Cleo Metzger
Claude Remaly
Lawrence Metzger
Walter Irmeger
Kenneth Frey
Ermal Greenwood
Virgil Irmeger
Marion Ward
Carl Clem
Emmett Frey

DEER CREEK

John K. Todd
Burton W. Lane
Harry Holmes
Andrew Gerbens
Sam G. Sites
Newell Cox
Earl B. Newell
Clarence L. Cleaver
Charles T. Black
Joseph E. Peterson
Wayne Hiatt
John C. Peterson

Milton Bowman
Miles T. Martin
Homer Wilson
Roscoe Quick
George E. Sites
Truman Zook
Robert Pullen
Verl Wagoner
Reuben Smith
Gene Jennings

DEMOCRAT

Noah Flora
Walter Ayres
Walter E. Bowen
Artus Rodenbarger
Charles R. Fellows
Lloyd Unger
Hal R. Shafer
J. C. Humes
Charles Thompson
O. L. Housenfluck
Joe Flora
Ralph Reagon
Clifford Darling
Robert McCarty
Wayne Lohrman
Cleon Carter
Donald J. Wilson
Thomas Cowell
Meredith Ayres

JACKSON

G. A. Hunt
George Cohee
Wm. R. Foreman
Frank Hedderich
Albert Cree
Arthur Ritchey
Earl Chapman
Webb Robeson
Melvin Fisher
Coy C. Shanks
John L. Witter
Roy Richter
Gardner Martin
Silas Yost
Walter Sprinkle
Dean McCain
Charles Sanderson
John Wise
Raymond Ringer
Wilmer Hodge
John Berkshire
Everett Brown
Hershel Trapp

JEFFERSON

George E. Sites
W. G. Million
Sam M. Maxwell
C. B. Million
Lawrence Landis
Charles Crook
Herbert Million
Frank Hawn
Robert E. Burke
John Kennard
John Burke
Lawrence Fry
Charles R. Hanna
Forrest J. Redding
Paul Vollenweider
Francis Dimmitt
Don Hankins
Roy Slavens

MADISON

Roy P. Martin
Elmer Sheets
Harry B. Miley
Howard Cleaver
J. Ren Bates
Obe Campbell
Harry R. Maxwell
Loyd E. Zook
Glen Stair
Hobart Wolfe
Joe Henderson
Claude Zook
Orville Ward
Orton Zook
Lee Flora
Lowell Ward
Mark Porter
Wayne Clawson
John B. McCormick
Donald Hathaway
Carl Mays

MONROE

J. Frank Shoff
John Unger
George Thomas
D. C. Jenkins
Elmer Kuns
J. W. Eikenberry
Oren Eikenberry
Fritz G. Schnepf Sr.
Myron Jenkins
Rush McCarty

Carl C. Johnson
Harold H. Thompson
Raymond Dillman
Ralph Rinehart
J. C. Yunker
Floyd Chapman
Wm. W. Warnick
Kenneth H. Myer
Beryl Beckner
Delbert Eikenberry

ROCK CREEK AND LIBERTY

Earl Stewart
C. V. Willey
Charles Montgomery
Nelson Guthrie
Charles Sanderson
Leon Kasten
S. A. Wasson
Arthur Hildebrand
Robert Hedde
Walter Martin
Keith Sink
Donald Mullin
Enos Berkshire
Ren C. Groninger
Richard Wysong
W. R. Hanawalt
Fred Kuszmaul
Dave Morehouse
Virgil McFatridge
Merlin Mullin
Lee Sterrett
Junior Snider

TIPPECANOE

Charles Ginn

W. G. Klepinger
Sylvester Robinson
Wm. L. Henderson
Larry Gruber
C. R. Clawson
Edgar Fountain
Russell Craig
Fred Gerard
Robert VanNatta
Levi Furst
Warren Wood
George Treida
James Riley
Marvin Henderson
Robert Scott
Fred J. Stewart
Frank Lybrook
James White
Raymond Zink

WASHINGTON

Sam D. Smith
Cecil Stephens
H. C. Urick
Nelson Hinkle
David Chapman
W. C. Fouts
Earl A. Downham
A. A. Newer
O. C. Seward
Oral Caldwell
J. T. Downham
Leroy Robeson
Samuel O. Sinn
Joe Starkey
Paul Seward
Eldon Robeson

Those in charge of the Women's Department of the Farm Bureau when it was organized in 1928 were known as Social and Educational directors. In 1957 the name was changed to directors of the Women's Department. The following list includes nearly every woman who has served as leader in each of the townships.

ADAMS

Miss Janice Blackwell
Mrs. Roy Wilburn
Mrs. Arthur Mullin
Mrs. George W. Peterson

Mrs. Albert Moore
Mrs. Clayton Million
Mrs. Charles Tansey
Mrs. T. O. Peterson
Mrs. John Wagoner
Mrs. Gale Crowell

Mrs. Raymond Nicoll
Mrs. Russell Pearson
Mrs. Robert Ward
Mrs. Donald L. Dill

BURLINGTON

Mrs. Wm. M. Douglas
Mrs. Robert F. Johnson
Mrs. Clyde Langston
Mrs. Charles Thompson
Mrs. Nona Logan
Mrs. Veaux Bowman
Mrs. Clark Metsger
Mrs. Fred Rodkey
Mrs. Nina Rinehart
Mrs. Blanche Hinkle
Mrs. Ray Robertson
Mrs. Cliff Bosworth
Mrs. Ross Garrison
Mrs. Marion Langston

CARROLLTON

Mrs. Taylor Fouts
Mrs. S. A. Wickard
Mrs. Manford Wagoner
Mrs. Willard Allbaugh
Mrs. Larry Landis
Mrs. Monroe Meade
Mrs. Homer Thomas
Miss Rosetta Brown
Mrs. Charles Harter
Mrs. Wayne Archibald
Mrs. Joe Fouts
Mrs. Raymond Huse
Mrs. Castyle Fouts
Mrs. Everett Snell
Mrs. Fannie Blue
Mrs. Elver Pullen
Mrs. Raymond Dillman

CLAY

Mrs. Lloyd Beard
Mrs. Edward Fossnock
Mrs. Orpha Goslee
Mrs. Ruth Wade
Mrs. Walter Barnhart
Mrs. Wm. Frain
Mrs. Dallas Frey
Mrs. Raymond Douglas
Mrs. Clarence Shultheis
Mrs. Garrott Kamstra
Mrs. Elwood Burkle
Mrs. Harriet Metzger
Mrs. Kenneth Frey

Mrs. Virgil Irmeger
Mrs. John Burkle
Mrs. Emmett Frey

DEER CREEK

Mrs. Sam G. Sites
Mrs. Miles T. Martin
Mrs. Newell Cox
Miss Irene DeWinton
Mrs. Earl B. Newell
Mrs. Clarence L. Cleaver
Mrs. Asa Cohee
Mrs. John Rowe
Mrs. Joseph E. Peterson
Mrs. Homer Wilson
Mrs. Truman Zook
Mrs. Robert Pullen
Mrs. Donald Draper
Mrs. Verl Wagoner
Mrs. Paul Jeffries
Mrs. Kenneth Newell
Mrs. Reuben Smith
Mrs. Jack Pritchard
Mrs. Nelson Sines
Mrs. Gene Jennings

DEMOCRAT

Mrs. Artus Rodenbarger
Mrs. Doctor Hill
Mrs. Ben Lowery
Mrs. Pauline Largen
Mrs. Hal R. Shafer
Miss Nellie Wilson
Mrs. Marvin Jervis
Mrs. Odin Fidner
Mrs. Paul Wilson
Mrs. George Shaffer
Mrs. Floyd Lohrman
Mrs. Ren Fetterhoff
Mrs. Clifford Darling
Mrs. Earl Clem
Mrs. Wayne Lohrman
Miss Pauline O'Dell
Miss Fay Humes
Mrs. Charles Thompson
Mrs. Ralph Overholser
Mrs. Cleon Carter
Mrs. Ruth Draper Bowman
Mrs. Tom Brooks

JACKSON

Mrs. George Hunt
Mrs. Harold Jones
Mrs. John L. Witter

Mrs. Fred Case
Mrs. Robert Hammer
Mrs. I. E. Roberson
Mrs. Melvin Fisher
Mrs. Milton Bowman
Mrs. Robert Fisher
Mrs. Voris Chapman
Mrs. Walter Sprinkle
Mrs. Everett Keys
Mrs. John Wise
Miss Doris Wagoner
Mrs. Gardner Martin
Mrs. Frank Hedderich
Mrs. Walter Parrett
Hilda McKay
Mrs. Raymond Ringer
Mrs. Myna Ruth Roberson
Mrs. Everett Brown
Mrs. Joe Barnard Jr.

JEFFERSON

Mrs. George E. Sites
Mrs. Glen Kennard
Mrs. Patrick Graham
Mrs. Hazel Coble
Mrs. Charles Mummert
Mrs. W. H. Casad
Mrs. Owen Downham
Miss Lucille Casad
Mrs. Arylis Bernfield
Mrs. Lawrence Fry
Mrs. Frank Lybrook
Mrs. Robert Simmons
Mrs. Forrest J. Redding
Mrs. Blanche Viney
Mrs. Paul Vollenweider
Mrs. Charles R. Hanna
Mrs. Melvin Roach
Mrs. Barbara Richardson

MADISON

Mrs. John McCouch
Mrs. Chester Maxwell
Mrs. Clarence Shultheis
Mrs. Leonard Clawson
Miss Helen Zook
Mrs. Loyd Zook
Mrs. Joe Henderson
Mrs. Orpha Goslee
Mrs. Lee Flora
Mrs. Dale Cleaver
Mrs. Lowell Ward
Mrs. Bob Simmons
Mrs. Marie Hanrahan

Mrs. Francis Humbarger
Mrs. Ralph Wagoner
Mrs. Mark Porter
Mrs. Tom Porter
Mrs. Carol Flora
Mrs. Dale Fossnock

MONROE

Mrs. D. C. Jenkins
Mrs. G. L. Whistler
Mrs. Glenn Eikenberry
Mrs. Fred Clawson
Mrs. Dora L. Wingard
Mrs. Harold H. Thompson
Mrs. Rush McCarty
Mrs. Blanche Loy
Mrs. Bryan Allen
Mrs. Raymond Dillman
Mrs. Charles Ross
Mrs. John Herndon
Mrs. Wilbur Wilson
Mrs. Fritz G. Schnepf Sr.
Mrs. Wm. W. Warnick
Mrs. Kenneth Myer
Mrs. Beryl Beckner
Mrs. Delbert Eikenberry
Mrs. Carl C. Johnson

ROCK CREEK AND LIBERTY

Mrs. Jesse Benner
Miss Mary Allread
Mrs. Fred Martin
Mrs. Fred Benner
Mrs. Herbert Burke
Mrs. Paul Gregg
Mrs. Ward Been
Mrs. Dewey Zinn
Miss Opal Mullin
Mrs. Everett Stewart
Mrs. Frank Hinkle
Mrs. Arthur Mullin
Mrs. Ellis Kuszmaul
Mrs. Richard Wysong
Mrs. W. R. Hanawalt
Mrs. Charles Snow
Mrs. Estal Mullin
Mrs. John Myers
Mrs. Fred Kuszmaul
Mrs. Junior Snider

TIPPECANOE

Mrs. W. F. Riley
Miss Vivian Henderson

Mrs. Charles Davis Vaughan
Mrs. Fred Gerard
Mrs. Dale Maxwell
Mrs. Robert VanNatta
Mrs. Marvin Henderson
Mrs. Larry Gruber
Mrs. Melvin Jackson
Mrs. Raymond Romein

Mrs. Frank Lybrook
Mrs. Opal Vaughan
Mrs. George Treida
Mrs. Lynn Brookbank
Mrs. Earl Eis
Mrs. James White
Mrs. Raymond Zink
Mrs. Harold Greer

WASHINGTON

Mrs. Leroy Hardy
Mrs. Bert Hayes
Mrs. Vernie Stephens
Mrs. Lyman Smith
Miss Pauline Robeson
Miss Lavon Johnson

Mrs. Cleon Smith
Miss Clarice Downham
Mrs. James McLeland
Mrs. Bertha Seward
Mrs. Ross Downham
Mrs. Freida Campbell
Mrs. J.T. Downham
Mrs. Eldon Robeson
Mrs. Wilmer Downham

CARROLL COUNTY FARM BUREAU

1979 Committees

ADMINISTRATIVE

Don Willy
Francis Humbarger
Gene Jennings
Emmett Frey

MEMBERSHIP

Patsy Jennings
Junior Snider
Eldon Robeson
Maxine White
Charles Hanna
Francis Humbarger
Pearl Sines
Bob Dittman
Pat Frey

EXECUTIVE

Gene Jennings
Maxine Snider
Pat Frey
Carolyn Burkle
Wilma Robeson
Francis Humbarger

POLICY DEVELOPMENT

Francis Humbarger
All Township Presidents
Francis Zink
Maxine Snider
Charles Hanna

YOUNG FARMER

Jerry Frey
Rick Ayres

NOMINATING

Joe Peterson
Charles Hanna
Clarence Cleaver
Maxine White
Carl Mays

PUBLIC RELATIONS

Carolyn Burkle
Emmett Frey
Don Willy

Pat Frey
Patsy Jennings
Gene Jennings

LOCAL AFFAIRS

Charles Hanna
Gene Jennings
Wilma Robeson
Patsy Jennings
Francis Humbarger

COMMODITY

Emmett Frey—Hogs
Meredith Ayres—Dairy
Gene Jennings—
  Field Crops
Francis Humbarger—
  Field Crops
Carl Mays—Beef

SCHOLARSHIP

Pearl Sines
Maxine Humbarger

Doris Peterson
Maxine Snider

COUNTY 4-H PICNIC

Pat Frey

COUNTY TALENT

Maxine Snider

COUNTY ANNUAL MEETING

Gene Jennings

COUNTY SPRING MEETING

Francis Humbarger

LEGISLATIVE CO-ORDINATOR

Meredith Ayres

NATURAL RESOURCES

Francis Humbarger

CHAPTER VIII

FARM BUREAU COOPERATIVE ASSOCIATION

INDIANA FARM BUREAU COOPERATIVE ASSOCIATION

The previous chapter tells about the experience of the IFB Purchasing Department. After five years of operation the department had a deficit of $12,082, and several of the directors wanted to abandon the project before it bankrupted the entire organization. On February 14, 1926, I. Harvey Hull was hired to manage the department.

I. Harvey Hull

Mr. Hull had an unusual background which made him qualified for his new job. He was born in 1884 on a farm in Livingston County, Illinois. His father was a progressive farmer who organized the first rural telephone co-op in Illinois. Mr. Hull graduated from law school at Northwestern University in 1909, and returned to the farm in Illinois.

At the Farmers' Institute in Pontiac in 1912 he made the motion that started the Livingston County Farm Bureau, the fourth County Farm Bureau to be organized in Illinois. He was a member of the committee which hired the first farm advisor (County Agent) in the county.

In 1913 he moved to LaPorte County Indiana and helped organize the Hanna Cooperative Livestock Shipping Association, and was elected president. He helped hire L. B. Clore as the first County Agent in Indiana.

Mr. Hull was elected the first president of the LaPorte County FB in 1919, and two years later was elected to the Board of Directors of the Indiana Farm Bureau. As a farmer and cattle feeder in 1920 he learned the hard way that farmers needed a stronger organization to protect them from bankruptcy due to rapidly falling farm prices. Being convinced that farmers needed a law to authorize them to form cooperatives he ran for and was elected to the Indiana State Legislature. In 1923 he introduced a bill providing for farmer cooperatives. It was passed by the legislature but vetoed by the Governor. In 1925 he again introduced the same bill and it became law.

When Mr. Hull was appointed manager of the Purchasing Department, he was named on a committee with Lewis Taylor and Jim Mason to develop a plan for the reorganization of the Purchasing Department. The plan was presented at a joint meeting of the directors of the IFB and the directors and executives of the Purchasing Department on July 26, 1926. The plan was to sponsor a local co-op in each county to be owned and controlled by the local farmer members. The state association would be owned and controlled by the county co-op associations.

After debating the plan all day it was adopted. It was agreed that the county Farm Bureau would nominate one board member for each co-op association, and that local farmer stockholders must be Farm Bureau members.

Visit to Branch Warehouse

On his first visit to a branch warehouse Mr. Hull found that he had trouble getting the local manager to even notice him, until the manager learned that he was the "boss." That convinced Mr. Hull that if the branches were to be successful, they must be owned and controlled by local people, so that almost anyone who came in would be a "boss" and get some attention.

Incorporation

By ending speculation, and improving other business practices, Mr. Hull was able to end the year 1926 with a net worth of $26,006 for the department. On February 1, 1927 the Indiana Farm Bureau Purchasing Department was incorporated under the Indiana Cooperative Act of 1925, which Mr. Hull had introduced in the State Legislature. On March 6, 1930 the Secretary of State approved changing the name to Indiana Farm Bureau Cooperative Association, Inc.

Marvin J. Briggs

In February 1927, Marvin J. Briggs, a farmer in Miami County, was employed as the first general field man for the IFBCA. Mr. Briggs had been active in Farm Bureau membership activities, and had been a speaker at Farmers' Institutes for Purdue University.

Mr. Hull and Mr. Briggs spent much of their time visiting county Farm Bureaus explaining to them how they could organize a county FBCA and become a part of the state program. Twenty seven counties were organized in 1927, 25 more in 1928, and by 1931 a total of 77 county cooperatives had been formed. In each case the directors of the County Farm Bureau became the directors of the County FBCA.

Finance

Local associations were financed by having members sign bonds agreeing to be liable for a limited amount of money, usually $100. These bonds were then used to borrow money from a local bank. No bank ever lost any money on loans secured by bonds, even though there were a few failures during the first years. Earnings of the associations were used to repay the loans, and patrons were issued stock certificates to indicate their share of ownership. Each stockholder had one vote regardless of the number of shares owned. No one was allowed to own more than 1/11 of the stock.

The county associations each purchased a small amount of stock in the state association to provide working capital. Earnings by the state were used for further expansion, and stock was issued to the county associations to indicate their share of ownership in the state association.

Part of the earnings were distributed in cash. The Delphi Journal for January 24, 1929 reported that the IFB Purchasing Department gave cash refunds of $75,000 to FB members in Indiana in 1928.

The Indiana Plan

Over a period of time, and through trial and error, the IFB and IFBCA developed what has been known as the Indiana Plan for Cooperatives. It is based on the Roachdale plan, which provides for one vote per member, limited interest on capital, and distribution of savings to patrons in proportion to patronage.

The essentials of the Indiana plan are:

1. Build local co-ops in each county owned and controlled by member farmers.
2. Build capital by issuing part of the earnings in the form of stock certificates. This was set at 25% at first.
3. Build a state wholesale cooperative owned and controlled by the county association and financed in the same way.
4. Build a strong educational program emphasizing member and local co-op responsibilities and dedication. Keep members, employees, officers and the general public informed regarding the objectives, history, principles, and record of performance of the cooperative.
5. Build industrial activity and interstate cooperatives where advisable.

This was called the Indiana Plan because it was developed and first used in Indiana. It has been used successfully in several other states.

Ohio Farm Bureau developed their cooperative with the state organization controlling local branches. At the American Institute of Cooperation meeting at Columbus, Ohio in 1929, one of the features was a debate between Murray D. Lincoln of Ohio and Harvey Hull of Indiana. They discussed the relative merits of the Indiana Plan with local control, and the Ohio Plan with central control. The Ohio chain of branches had been well managed and seemed to be sound. A few months later the depression hit, and the Ohio system began to collapse. Officials from the IFBCA helped Ohio organize local co-ops according to the Indiana Plan. Indiana also helped Pennsylvania and Tennessee organize using the Indiana Plan.

Because of the early successes, Ed O'Neal, President of the American Farm Bureau Federation asked Mr. Hull to organize all the FB co-ops in the country. Three meetings were held in Chicago but representatives from different states could not agree on whether a national organization should be set up as a department of the AFBF or as a separate organization.

At the next AIC meeting in Baton Rouge, Louisiana, several state co-op leaders who had heard of the meeting in Chicago told Mr. Hull that they would like to join a national cooperative. Some were representatives of state Farm Bureau co-ops, some were affiliated with the Farmers Union, while others were with independent co-ops.

National Cooperatives, Inc.

After several more meetings in Chicago, National Cooperatives, Inc., was organized on February 23, 1933 with I. Harvey Hull elected as president. Membership in the new co-op was open to any state or regional co-op that cared to join. This was one of several national organizations created by State and Regional Co-ops.

FERTILIZER

When the Indiana Federation of Farmers Associations was organized in 1919, most of the fertilizer in Indiana was manufactured and sold by six major companies. It was sold through local farmers who were paid a commission, usually 10% for taking orders from their neighbors. Most fertilizer was sold on credit, so the price was high enough to include this service. There was little competition in the fertilizer industry, so when farm prices fell in 1920, fertilizer prices remained about the same. Several county associations tried to pool orders and get a better price from the fertilizer companies, but all they could get was the local agent's commission.

At a meeting in northern Indiana in 1921, farmers voted to go on a buyers strike, and not buy any fertilizer until the price was reduced. This brought the problem to the attention of the state organization, which then purchased 5,000 tons of fertilizer and sold it to members at cost. The fertilizer industry lowered the retail price and refused to sell any more fertilizer to the state organization. One manufacturer announced that he would not sell to "any bunch of scab farmers." He failed to realize that farmers were the only ones who bought fertilizer.

For two years the state organization purchased fertilizer from small manufacturers, shipped it in carload lots, and sold it for cash, which made it possible to sell at a lower price. Sometimes ingredients were purchased and farmers mixed their own fertilizer, thus saving part of the manufacturing cost. The state organization was able to purchase some ingredients directly from the mines in Montana and Georgia, resulting in even lower costs.

When competition resulted in lower prices for fertilizer, the fertilizer companies were losing money, and got together and agreed not to sell any fertilizer to the new farmers organization.

Tennessee Copper and Chemical Co.

At this time the Tennessee Copper and Chemical Company, a copper mining and smelting concern in eastern Tennessee, was having problems. The fumes from the smelting process killed all the vegetation for miles around. When the government made it quit releasing the gas into the air, the company condensed it to a liquid and dumped it into the river. That killed the fish, so the company was in trouble again.

The by-product which needed to be disposed of was sulfuric acid, an ingredient necessary for the manufacturing of fertilizer, but they were not in the fertilizer business and were not interested in building a sales organization. There was a surplus of sulfuric acid and it could not be sold at a good price.

When the farmers organization and the copper company learned of each others problems, they got together and solved both of them. The copper company built a plant to manufacture fertilizer, and the farm organizations in Indiana, Ohio, and Michigan agreed to sell the entire output of fertilizer.

Production started in the fall of 1923, and in 1924 Indiana sold 13,250 tons of fertilizer. By 1929 the volume reached 43,944 tons. Fertilizer was sold at the prevailing market price, and a refund to members averaged about $3 per ton. For a few years the refund was in cash, but beginning in 1926, 25% of the refund was in the form of common stock and the money was kept for expanding the business.

Participating Contract

In 1931 the Farm Bureau Co-op Association and the Tennessee Copper and Chemical Company entered into a new kind of agreement known as a participating contract. The Copper Company agreed to manufacture fertilizer, and the FB Co-op Association agreed to sell it. At the end of the year any profits on the entire operation were divided equally between them. This agreement was satisfactory for both parties, and continued until 1939.

During this time, transportation methods were changing. Farmers were hauling their livestock to terminal markets in trucks, and it was convenient for them and saved the cost of freight, if they could haul the fertilizer home in their trucks. The plants operated by the Chemical Company were not located in the right places to take advantage of this change. In 1939 the IFBCA built a fertilizer plant at Indianapolis and joined with the Ohio FBCA to build another plant at Lockland, near Cincinnati, Ohio. In 1940 Indiana, Illinois, Michigan and Wisconsin Co-ops built a fertilizer plant at Schererville, Indiana. A 50,000 ton fertilizer acidulation plant to produce superphosphate was added in 1945. In 1953 a plant was built south of Columbia City and was named the Briggs Fertilizer Plant in honor of Mr. M. J. Briggs. Another plant was purchased in 1950 near Jeffersonville, Indiana. Other plants have been added and equipment was added to produce granular fertilizer at the Indianapolis plant in 1954 and at other plants in 1957. In 1966 a new facility was built at Indianapolis to produce a liquid plant food.

CF Industries, Inc.

The Central Farmers' Fertilizer Company, usually called CF Industries, Inc., is the largest plant food manufacturer in the world, and is owned by 19 regional cooperatives, including IFBCA which has about $15 million invested in the company. CF Industries buys the entire production of several large phosphate and potash mines to supply the needs of its many fertilizer processing plants.

CF Industries began shipping potash from Carlsbad, New Mexico in 1959 from a plant owned by National Potash Company. In 1964 CF Industries signed an agreement with Noranda Mines, Ltd. of Canada for the sinking of two shafts to the potash ore beds in Saskatoon, Saskatchewan. This plant, the Central Canada Potash Co. Ltd., started operation late in 1969.

CF Industries owns and distributes the entire output of the Plant City Phosphate Complex, Plant City, Florida. This plant produces about 400,000 tons of phosphate products per year. During 1966 phosphate fertilizer from this plant was delivered to 3,600 delivery points in 40 states. The first carload of fertilizer from the plant to arrive in Indiana was delivered to the Indianapolis plant on January 8, 1966.

On February 11, 1969, CF Industries took over ownership and operation of a phosphate chemical plant near Bartlow, Florida. This 2,800 acre site, formerly owned by International Minerals and Chemical Corporation, had an annual production capacity of one million tons of concentrated phosphate fertilizer.

In 1978, CF Industries completed construction of a phosphate plant with a capacity of one million tons per year on a 20,000 acre site owned by CF Industries in Hardee County, Florida.

CF Industries owns several plants to produce nitrogen fertilizer, including one at Donaldsonville, Louisiana which is the world's largest single nitrogen manufacturing facility. Part of the ammonia produced at the Donaldsonville plant is shipped in refrigerated river barges to storage terminals located along the Mississippi River and its tributaries. Some is also moved to off river storage terminals in Iowa, Illinois and Indiana through a 2,000 mile pipe line built in 1969 by the Gulf Central Pipe Line Company at a cost of $70 million.

Central Nitrogen, Inc.

The increase in corn acreage in recent years has resulted in a need for more nitrogen fertilizer. About 80% of all nitrogen produced in the U.S. is used on farms, so it was logical for farmers to build a plant to supply their growing needs.

Beginning in 1962, farmers in Indiana, Ohio and Illinois, working through their cooperatives, built a $20 million nitrogen fertilizer plant on a 208 acre site on U.S. 41 about five miles north of Terre Haute, Indiana. The new company was named Central Nitrogen, Inc. Cooperatives involved were the IFBCA; Landmark Co-op Association, Columbus, Ohio; Illinois Farm Supply Company, Bloomington, Illinois and CF Industries which later purchased the interests of other co-ops in the plant.

The plant was dedicated on October 22, 1963. Those from Carroll County who attended the ceremony were: Charles Hoover, Charles Black, Charles Hanna and James Stewart. The first carload of fertilizer shipped from the new plant at Terre Haute to an Indiana Co-op went to the Chalmers branch of the White County FBCA.

FEED

Until early in the 20th century, livestock on farms were fed whatever feed was available on the farm. Little was known about the need for supplement feed for livestock and very little commercial feed was available.

The manufacturing of mixed feeds began as a means by which packing houses, elevators, and mills could profit from their wastes and by-products. Early feed legislation required the feed manufacturers to place a tag on each bag of feed giving the percentage of protein, carbohydrates, fats and fiber of the feed and a list of ingredients.

The protein content could legally be derived from bran, meat scraps, cotton seed meal, weed seeds, or any other source. The amount of each ingredient was never given, although the source of protein makes a tremendous difference in the value of the feed.

Agricultural colleges and experiment stations began research on feeds and had a lot of information about the relative value of different ingredients in feeds. No one cared except the farmer who fed the feed, and he had no way of knowing what he was getting in the feed he bought.

The Indiana Farm Bureau, through its Purchasing Department, started its feed program in 1922. Its first effort was to work out an open formula for each kind of feed and to put a special tag on each bag of feed telling the exact amount of each ingredient.

The IFB then joined with Ohio and Michigan Farm Bureaus and asked the livestock departments of the three state's agricultural colleges to recommend formulas to be used for feed. This group, known as the "College Conference Feed Board," met frequently and gave the Farm Bureaus the best known formulas for each feed.

In 1930 the Farm Bureau Cooperative, along with the cooperatives of Ohio and Michigan, set up the Farm Bureau Milling Company, and each state organization made an identical contract with the same company to have its open formula feed made by a single mill.

In 1930 the co-ops made plans to build their own feed mill and began raising money for that purpose, but the depression in 1931 made it more difficult to raise money. Several local co-ops had installed grinding and mixing equipment, and were mixing their own feed. Others were encouraged to do the same, and plans for a central mill were dropped.

When the value of vitamins and semi-liquid ingredients was revealed through continued research, it became evident that the local co-op could not economically buy or accurately control the mixing of all the synthetic and natural products required. In 1943 plans were again made to build a central mill.

Demand for mixed feed increased during World War II, and feed companies could sell all the feed they could manufacture. The feed company that had been supplying the FB Milling Company gave a notice that the manufacturing of feed for the co-ops would be discontinued in 1943.

Fortunately, the FB Milling Company was able to buy an excellent and well located mill at Hammond, Indiana, and used it to supply local co-ops with open formula feeds from April 1943 until the mill was closed in July 1969. The IFBCA built a feed mill at Loogootee in 1965 and one at Indianapolis in 1968. Another feed mill built at Rochester in 1969 has a capacity of 50,000 tons per year. Much of the feed processed at the three feed mills is delivered by bulk trucks that haul 24 tons each and have the most modern system of unloading by using air. Quality of the feed is maintained by the use of a laboratory located at each mill. Special ingredients which cannot be tested in an ordinary laboratory are checked at the Product Research Laboratory operated by the IFBCA at Indianapolis.

The IFBCA and several other regional co-ops carry out a joint research program at six feed testing farms. These farms are scattered from coast to coast, with the nearest one being the IFBCA Poultry Breeding and Research Farm near Lafayette.

OIL

When the IFB Purchasing Department was organized in 1923, the average life of motors in farm tractors was about five years. A study at Purdue University indicated that the use of good oil could increase this by 25%, and save the farmers of Indiana about $1,500,000 per year on tractor engine depreciation.

For two sessions of the State Legislature the IFB tried to get a law passed requiring that lubricating oil be sold on specification, with a label on the container giving the specifications of the oil. This would enable farmers to know what kind of oil they were buying, and give them the opportunity to buy good oil if they cared enough to read and understand the label. The oil companies opposed these bills, and they did not become law.

The Purchasing Department then tried to buy oil with guaranteed specifications, but even the oil companies producing good oil would not guarantee it to be uniform and meet specifications.

In 1926, Montgomery County Farm Bureau was the first in the state to begin distribution of petroleum products to their members, and built the first county bulk oil plant in March 1928. By 1934 there were 76 bulk oil plants owned by county associations in Indiana.

Contracts with Oil Companies

In 1927 the IFB Purchasing Department contracted with the Standard Oil Company to deliver oil to Farm Bureau members at the regular price, and pay the Purchasing Department a commission which would then be refunded to the members. This agreement was temporary and lasted only about one year. The same plan was tried with other oil companies, and with the same results. The oil companies used the agreement to establish routes in the county, and then cancelled the agreement and kept as many of the customers as they could.

Oil Compounding Plant

In 1930 the IFBCA built an oil compounding plant at Indianapolis, which bought the ingredients, tested them to see that they met the proper specifications, and blended them into oil with guaranteed specifications. The first batch of oil was compounded in May 1930. The oil was sold at the same price charged by major oil companies for their good grade of oil which was not guaranteed. The IFBCA hoped to save money for farmers by providing them with a better oil for their engines. While the primary concern was not to make money in the process, the plant paid for itself in the first nine months. In order to increase volume, Indiana, Ohio and Michigan Farm Bureau Co-ops joined together to form the Farm Bureau Oil Company on October 8, 1930. In 1936 the FB Oil Company became a part of United Cooperatives, Inc. In 1958 a new push button oil plant built by United Cooperatives in Indianapolis provided more accuracy and efficiency in the compounding of oil.

True Love and Good Oil

In the early 1930's a motion picture "True Love and Good Oil" was prepared and shown in every county and 700 townships in Indiana. This silent movie, developed and photographed by the staff of the FB Co-op Association, dramatized the story of good oil. All actors in the movie were also members of the staff. Ed Stephens of Carroll County, a field man for the IFBCA, played a leading role as the stubborn farmer who had nothing to do with new fangled ideas promoted by FB. He tried to keep his daughter from eloping with the son of a neighbor who was a FB leader. In the chase the engine in his auto burned out because he was using poor oil. The young couple, with FB Co-op oil in their engine, went merrily on their way and lived happily ever after.

Oil Wells and Refinery

In the late 1930's several good oil wells were developed in Posey County in southwestern Indiana. The IFBCA built a refinery at Mt. Vernon in 1940. Pipe lines were laid from wells in the area, and barges were used on the Ohio River to haul crude oil from other wells to the refinery.

During 1941 and 1942 the IFBCA leased land for oil wells in Kentucky and in Gibson County, Indiana. The first oil well owned by the Co-op Association began producing about 100 barrels of oil per day in December 1941. Enough good wells were brought into production to supply practically all the crude oil needed by the refinery. This made it possible for the IFBCA to take crude oil from the wells, process it and deliver high quality petroleum products to county associations in all parts of Indiana.

Major improvements were made at the refinery to increase its efficiency and capacity to meet the growing demand by farmers for petroleum products. The capacity of the refinery exceeded the available supply of oil in the area so it was necessary to use foreign crude oil.

The first foreign crude oil was processed at the refinery in August 1976, and one and one half million barrels were processed during the balance of 1976. The Co-op Association entered into an agreement with the British Petroleum Corporation for crude oil produced in the North Sea. In 1977 this new source supplied 35% of the crude oil used in the refinery. In 1978 the IFBCA joined two other co-op refineries in a drilling project in West Africa.

Oil Pipe Line

In the fall of 1952 the IFBCA began construction of an oil pipe line 230 miles long from the refinery at Mt. Vernon to carry petroleum products to terminals within 75 miles of every county in the state. The pipe line and terminals cost over $5 million. About half the money was borrowed, and the other half raised by selling preferred stock and debenture bonds. More than the necessary amount of money was subscribed by December 1952.

A terminal along the Ohio River at Aurora was already being used to supply southeastern Indiana. The first new pipe line terminal was at Switz City in Green County, the second at Jolietville in Hamilton County, and the third at Peru in Miami County. The line which crossed under four rivers was eight inches in diameter to the first two terminals, and four inches in diameter from Jolietville to Peru. The first section of line to Switz City was completed and put in operation on February 18, 1953. The line was completed to Jolietville by September 2, and to Peru a short time later. About 30 people represented Carroll County at an open house at Peru on October 21, 1953.

Storage tanks with a total capacity of 22 million gallons were built at the three terminals. Three times during the next five years additional storage tanks were added, and by June 1958 the total storage capacity was 33 million gallons. Booster pumps were added in 1958 to increase the capacity of the line by 50%. Since then many additional improvements have been made and more storage capacity added to meet the ever increasing needs of Indiana farmers for petroleum products.

1979 Annual Report

The Annual Report of the IFBCA for its 53rd year of operation ending on August 31, 1979 reported record sales of $1,039,693,000. This was $139 million more than the previous record for sales set in 1978. Net earnings for the 1979 fiscal year were $2.1 million. Total consolidated assets of the IFBCA and its subsidiaries on August 31, 1979 amounted to $305 million, an increase of $50.5 million over the value of assets on August 31, 1978.

The following is a part of the report of the Petroleum Division in the Annual Report of the IFBCA for 1979:

"In 1979, 187 holes were drilled in the Illinois Basin and at sites in Texas and Oklahoma, 90 of which had sufficient production to develop as commercial wells. At present, these domestic drilling activities provide approximately 1,800 barrels of crude oil per day, a small but significant percentage of the refining capacity at Mt. Vernon, which exceeds 22,000 barrels per day. The Cooperative's domestic exploration efforts are significant because they exemplify the changes that should be made in our national energy policies. State and federal laws, regulations, controls, and tax policies form an almost insurmountable barrier of disincentives to a strong, domestic energy industry. A strong, domestic energy industry, initiated and capitalized by the American people, is critically essential to national security and stability. However, until the economic disincentives are removed, and until a strong, domestic industry is reestablished, the Cooperative must continue to seek foreign sources of crude oil to meet the needs of member cooperatives and their member-patrons.

"To date, the Cooperative's refinery at Mt. Vernon has refined roughly 235,000 barrels of crude oil received from its participation in off-shore drilling activities in Ghana, West Africa. In 1978, the government of Ghana granted a license to Agri-Petco International, owned by the Cooperative and by two other regional cooperative refiners, to explore for crude oil in an 1844-square-mile area now called the Salt Pond Field. . . . The Cooperative is also interested in other exploration efforts in West Africa.

"At the same time that the Cooperative is intensifying its efforts to find new domestic and foreign sources of crude oil, it is continually searching for ways to streamline and improve the efficiency of its refining, transportation, and distribution system. In 1978, the Cooperative completed the modification of the catalytic cracking unit at the refinery, at a cost of $3.8 million. This modification reduces throughput costs at the refinery and permits increased daily production of gasoline. In 1979, the Cooperative will spend $150,000 to investigate the best means to boost refinery capacity by 20 percent. The core of the highly-efficient distribution system is the 300-plus petroleum servicemen, who averaged liquid fuels deliveries of 750,000 gallons in 1979, up nearly 35,000 gallons from the average deliveries in 1978. Twenty-two petroleum servicemen individually delivered more than one million gallons of diesel fuel, gasoline, heating oil, and Gasohol in 1979.

"The Cooperative is also taking a penetrating look at the future energy needs of member cooperatives and their member-patrons. The most economical forms of energy may change in the future, from petroleum to Gasohol, to alcohol, to solar, and even to energy forms not yet discovered. Gasohol may not be the long-term answer, but it can lead to new and better alternatives, and the Cooperative is committed to the search for those new and better alternatives. In nine months, Gasohol grew in volume from an initial order of four 50-gallon barrels of alcohol to deliveries of 1.25 million gallons per month. The alcohol used to make Gasohol required distillation of 325,000 bushels of corn, demonstrating that Gasohol represents an alternative fuel, and an alternative market for grains. Gasohol was introduced in September 1978, at the annual meeting of the Starke County Farm Bureau Cooperative Association, Inc. It was first offered for retail sale in November 1978 by the Porter County Farm Bureau Cooperative Association, Inc. Today, most county associations are making tank deliveries of Gasohol in place of unleaded gasoline, which permits the Cooperative System to stretch its very tight supplies of gasoline by 10 percent."

TRANSPORTATION

In September 1938 the IFBCA purchased a fleet of 10 trucks to haul oil and petroleum products to the county oil plants. By charging the same rate as the railroads charged for full tank cars, the association paid for the trucks in less than a year.

By 1966 there were 25 tanker trucks traveling nearly two million miles per year and hauling 8,200 gallons per trip to deliver petroleum products from the refinery and the three pipe line terminals to the 92 counties in Indiana.

In 1964 a van delivery service was begun to deliver supplies from the IFBCA Indianapolis warehouse to the county associations. Each van could haul 45,000 pounds of freight, and deliver merchandise at a lower cost than by the smaller trucks used by the county associations. Routes were established and deliveries were made to every county each week. Tank trailers with 10,500 gallons capacity were used to deliver anhydrous ammonia from the plant at Terre Haute to the counties.

The IFBCA also owns and operates several barges to haul oil and fertilizer from New Orleans to Indiana. Large 25,000 ton barges are used to haul fertilizer from Florida to New Orleans, where it is transferred to river barges.

The IFBCA also owns and operates about 3,000 railroad cars to haul grain.

The cooperative was among the first to ship grain east in 100-car unit trains, and can load these trains at six of its sub-terminals and export facilities.

20TH CENTURY PIONEER

I. Harvey Hull, general manager of the IFBCA from 1926 until 1946, and president of the board from 1946 until 1950, wrote an article for the Farm News in 1967 entitled "20th Century Pioneer" in which he stated:

"By patronizing his own cooperative, the Indiana farmer has built his own oil department until he now owns and operates his own oil wells, his own gathering lines, his own refinery—the very best—his own pipe lines from Mt. Vernon to Peru, his own trucking service from pipe line stations to every county co-op bulk plant in the state, and his own county co-op plant and trucks which can deliver to every farmer in the state.

"This did not cost him one cent, but it did require loyalty and team work. Now he gets his petroleum products at cost. If there are any earnings in the business, they belong to him. Without knowing it, he has built and paid for a $24 million state oil plant plus his local set-up.

"Now to fully understand the significance of this story, contrast it with what happened elsewhere.

"When our oil program began to look encouraging, we sent Phil Papet down to Kentucky, his native state, to build some local cooperative bulk plants to join with us. It would have been good for both Indiana and Kentucky farmers.

"He succeeded in setting up three or four county co-ops and was starting them in the oil business. At each place where we set up bulk plant service, the price of fuels was reduced in a very short time, but the poor, shortsighted Kentucky farmers sold their plants, and soon prices were back up and the oil companies were again making a good profit on their oil sales. Those farmers have since paid for the plants that they do not own and will continue to pay for more.

"For years, Kentucky farm petroleum prices were higher than in Indiana. Indiana farmers—don't forget this story!"

GRAIN MARKETING

In 1920 there were about 600 local elevators in Indiana owned by farmers. Some of these were cooperatives, but since there was no special law for cooperatives in Indiana, there was no uniformity in their ownership and operation. Many of the managers of farmers elevators got together and organized the Indiana Farmers Grain Dealers Association. It gave some service in management problems, but never entered the field of securing of supplies or terminal marketing of grain. Nearly all of these elevators have gone out of business, or have been taken over by larger elevators. One exception is the Lafayette Cooperative Elevator Company which is still in business, and is affiliated with the IFBCA to serve farmers in Tippecanoe County.

In December 1923 the U.S. Grain Growers Association was organized by the leading national farm organizations to help market grain. It had no direct affiliation with local cooperatives and never functioned.

Wheat Pools

State organizations organized wheat pools in 1923 and 1924. The Indiana Soft Wheat Growers Association, commonly known as the Wheat Pool was organized in May 1924. Farmers would deliver their wheat to a local elevator and receive a part of their money. The grain would be sold during the year and farmers were paid the balance of their money after all grain was sold.

In 1924 about 9,000 farmers pooled 1,300,000 bushels of wheat. Twice as many farmers signed up for 1925, and volume grew to about three million bushels. During those two years farmers received about $1.40 per bushel for wheat compared to a price of $1.20 to $1.25 during harvest.

In 1926 the Indiana pool handled nearly five million bushels of wheat for about 20,000 members. The price of wheat went down after harvest, and members lost money, so many farmers quit using the pool. Local elevators and farmers had no interest in the pool unless it could pay them a better price for grain.

Federal legislation provided money to loan to farmer cooperatives so that they could pay members for their grain when it was delivered. Many farmers needed their money, and did not want to wait for payment by the pool. Counties in western Ohio and central Illinois joined with Indiana, and the name was changed from Wheat Pool to Central States Soft Wheat Growers Association in 1926. Farmers wanted to sell other grain on the same basis, so the name was changed to Central States Grain Association in 1929, and it handled wheat, corn, oats, soybeans, barley and rye.

Ohio and Illinois organized their own grain marketing co-ops, and on March 1, 1935 the name of Central States Grain Association was changed to Indiana Grain Producers, Inc. It handled grain for about 125 elevators in Indiana, and in 1936 handled eight million bushels of grain. This was the largest amount handled by any grain organization in Indiana that year.

Federal Farm Board

In 1929 the Federal Farm Board was established by the Agricultural Marketing Act of that year. Its purpose was to supply the service that was needed by the scattered and disorganized farm grain co-ops by financing and merchandising their grain. The Farmers National Grain Co-op was organized as a National Sales Agency for state and regional grain cooperatives. It had branch offices in every major grain market in the U.S. The local elevators had no control over the Federal Farm Board, and soon lost interest. It was dissolved in 1933.

Lessons Learned

This long series of trials with varying degrees of success and failure indicated two things: first, a local co-op elevator without central service operated with great difficulty and high mortality; second, a central grain marketing service without affiliated local gathering units was not successful.

Indiana Grain Cooperative

The high rate of failure of small locally owned co-op elevators, and of central marketing services without local elevators, convinced the IFBCA that a genuine democratically controlled, federated cooperative was necessary for the successful marketing of grain.

The IFBCA put up the initial capital and on May 31, 1938 organized the Indiana Grain Cooperative. The facilities of Indiana Grain Producers, Inc. were purchased with M. D. Guild continuing as manager. Most of the local units that owned the common voting stock and used the service of the new grain co-op were local units already affiliated with IFBCA.

During the first year, about eight and one half million bushels of grain, worth over $4 million were handled. In 1948, the tenth year, more than $66 million worth of grain were handled. Net worth at the end of ten years was nearly $5 million, and net earnings for the first ten years was nearly $7 million. On January 1, 1950 Indiana Grain Cooperative was merged with, and became a department of, the Indiana Farm Bureau Cooperative Association and was called Indiana Grain.

Even in the rather poor grain year of 1967, Indiana farmers sold more than $111 million worth of grain through their co-op with about $1.5 million in net savings.

Grain Terminals

In July 1938 the Indiana Grain Cooperative purchased the Indianapolis Public Elevator, a one million bushel terminal, from the Indiana Grain Producers, Inc. More grain storage bins added later increased the total storage capacity to over nine million bushels and the drying capacity was increased to 7,700 bushels per hour. In 1942 the Indiana Grain Cooperative took over the 750,000 bushel capacity Gold Proof Elevator at Louisville, Kentucky. Both of these elevators quickly paid for themselves using the standard service charge used by other elevators.

A terminal was acquired at Princeton, Indiana in 1966. An elevator at Toledo, Ohio, on the St. Lawrence Seaway, was purchased in 1960. It had a capacity of 400,000 bushels and more bins were added to make a total storage capacity of 4,750,000 bushels.

In 1967 the co-op acquired a 6.5 million bushel terminal in Chicago. A terminal was built in 1970 at Redkey, near Dunkirk, Indiana, and in 1975 a $7 million terminal with a capacity of five million bushels was built at Clymers, near Logansport, Indiana. This terminal was badly damaged by an explosion in May 1977, and was out of business until the fall of 1979 while being reconstructed at a cost of $4.6 million. An expansion program at a terminal purchased in 1973 in Baltimore, Maryland, begun in 1978 and expected to be completed in November 1980 at a cost of $14 million, will double the annual throughput capacity to 125 million bushels. Other terminals are at New Albany and Evansville, Indiana and Cincinnati, Ohio.

Grain Exports

The first grain exported by the Indiana Grain Cooperative was on June 2, 1949 when a boat was loaded with soybeans at the Baltimore Terminal and shipped to Italy. This shipment totaling 305,000 bushels required three trains to haul it from Indiana to Baltimore.

The report of the IFBCA showed that for the year ending August 31, 1979 the Grain Marketing Department handled 184 million bushels of grain valued at $699 million. About 60% of the grain was exported.

In 1978 about 40% of the grain produced in the U.S. was raised by members of the nations 7,500 farm cooperatives, yet the cooperatives handled only 9% of the grain exported from the U.S.

Seeing the need and an opportunity for cooperatives to handle more exported grain, the IFBCA in 1979 joined with five other cooperatives in the U.S., one in Canada and three in Europe, and purchased a controlling interest in Alfred C. Toepfer Export, Inc. with headquarters in Hamburg, West Germany.

The Toepfer Company, founded in 1919, is an international grain trading organization, with 43 offices in 17 countries, and handles about ten percent of the world's international grain trade. Other cooperatives in North America in the venture were: Gold Kist, based in Georgia; Land O'Lakes, based in Minnesota; Agway of New York; Citrus World of Florida; Landmark of Ohio; and the United Cooperatives of Ontario, Canada.

European cooperatives in the program were located in Holland, Germany and France.

Cebeco-Handelsraad, located in Rotterdam, Holland, is a Central Dutch Supply Cooperative which does a business of $2.2 billion per year with 75,000 farmer members. Most members are livestock farmers who buy an average of two tons of mixed feed per year per acre of land operated. This cooperative is the largest mixed feed producer in the world, and also one of the largest feed importers in Europe.

The German Raiffeisen Supply Central Cooperative, representing 12 regional cooperatives, sells 50% of the mixed feed sold in Germany, and does a business of $7.5 billion per year. Another member in Germany is GIG, a cereal import company.

UNCAC, a central federated organization in France, does a business of $1.25 billion per year and is one of the largest marketers of French cereals.

SEED

Before the IFB was organized, the Extension Service and Agronomy Department at Purdue had been encouraging farmers to raise more clover. Since very little clover was being produced in Indiana, it was necessary to use seed grown in other areas. Many seed dealers were selling seed grown in the southern U.S., southern Europe and South America. This seed looked good and grew well the first year, but did not live through the winter. Seed grown in the northern U.S. and northern Europe was better adapted to the Indiana climate, and would survive for several years.

Farmers were getting discouraged and many quit raising clover because they could not be sure that they were getting good seed. To help solve the problem, Congress passed the Seed Staining Act which provided that a certain portion of the contents of each bag of seed must be stained a color to indicate the country of origin. This helped but it did not solve the problem because much of the seed raised in the U.S. was not adapted to Indiana.

In 1923 the IFB Purchasing Department began to distribute seeds that were bought and processed by the Michigan Farm Bureau. The IFB rented an elevator and seed warehouse in Indianapolis and bought and processed seed. By 1926 the seed operation was one of the larger activities of the Purchasing Department.

Other companies were always selling seed for less money, but farmers soon learned that they could depend on their own organization to provide them with adapted seed, and were willing to pay the higher price.

In 1944 the IFBCA purchased the Crabbs, Reynolds, Taylor Company at Crawfordsville, the largest seed processing plant in the state, and processed seed for the association, and also cleaned seed for growers in Indiana.

Farmers Forage Research, Inc.,

In 1958 IFBCA joined with nine other co-ops in the U.S. to form Farmers Forage Research, Inc. This organization was formed for the purpose of expanding basic and applied research in the improvement of alfalfas, clovers and grasses. Grants were made to Purdue University, to be used in expanding research activities. FFR worked with other colleges and the USDA in development of improved varieties for the betterment of American agriculture.

In 1962 FFR purchased a 72 acre farm near Battle Ground, Indiana, to be used for research in developing better varieties of legumes, grasses and other crops. In 1979 the cooperative introduced four new seed varieties developed by FFR. These seed varieties included: Hi-ply alfalfa; FFR-717C hybrid corn; FFR-929W, a new white corn variety; and C-43, a new, short season corn hybrid adapted for use in northeastern Indiana. FFR continued to expand research on new soybean varieties.

Hybrid Corn

When farmers in Indiana began using hybrid corn the IFBCA was one of the first to get in the business. A drying plant was built at Indianapolis, with several farmers producing seed for it. When Purdue University developed and released Golden Cross Bantam sweet corn, the first field of commercial seed was raised on a farm in Adams Township near Lockport in Carroll County and was processed at the Indianapolis plant.

When the hybrid seed growers in Indiana organized a marketing cooperative, the IFBCA withdrew from seed producing and processing in order to avoid duplication. Most county associations continued to retail seed corn.

IFBCA joined with three other regional cooperatives and organized Cooperative Seeds, Inc. to aid in research, development and marketing of high quality seeds. The new inter-regional cooperative built a seed corn processing plant in Boone County, Indiana, to handle 200,000 bags of seed corn per year beginning in the fall of 1978. The goal is to supply 25% of the seed corn used by Indiana farmers.

CROP CHEMICALS

The Annual Report of the IFBCA for the eight months in their fiscal year of 1977 stated:

"Crop chemicals have become a more significant part of the cost of farm production. Most of these chemicals are manufactured by either national or multi-national firms. Studies of this large segment of industry disclosed that expenditures of many millions of dollars for research and development are required to isolate a compound that has weed or pest control capabilities. Several million more dollars are then required for EPA clearance. Just to locate a compound and make it ready for market not only requires tremendous expenditures, but it also consumes years of time.

"On the average, it takes nearly $20 million to isolate the compound, another $15 million to $30 million to obtain approval by EPA for agricultural use and, on the average, this consumes six to eight years of time. This type of product development requires tremendous company capital and other resources. As a result these products are usually controlled by corporate giants that operate in a broad field of chemical products and over a large part of the world.

"Until last year, cooperatives had had very little effect on helping the farmer to reduce costs of farm chemicals. Universal Cooperatives did acquire an atrazine label last year and was able to purchase some atrazine tech from an overseas source. This atrazine tech was shipped to a formulating plant in the United States where it was formulated and packaged under the Universal label. It is estimated that all farmers, whether they purchased from their cooperative or some other source, saved $60 million to $70 million on the product they purchased in the spring of 1977."

POULTRY

During the late 1920's several attempts were made in Indiana to market eggs through cooperatives, but they were not successful. A study soon revealed that Indiana eggs were of low quality and not uniform. Egg producers in California were able to buy their feed in the Midwest, ship it to California, and ship the eggs to New York where they got enough premium in price to pay the extra costs. It was evident that in order to produce uniform high quality eggs it was necessary to have uniform high quality chickens. This was a case where the chicken came before the egg.

A survey by County Agricultural Agents in 1930 showed that 25% of all baby chickens hatched in Indiana were dying of pullorum disease before they were two weeks old. A high percent of hens in flocks were dying each year from a disease known as range paralysis.

The IFBCA made a study of the poultry industry, and working with Dr. L. P. Doyle of Purdue University developed a plan for the improvement of poultry in Indiana. The two objectives of the plan were to improve the health of poultry flocks in Indiana, and to improve the quality and number of eggs produced.

The state association established poultry breeding farms where hens were trap nested to improve the strain of poultry. Chickens hatched from these improved flocks were used to establish flocks to supply eggs at the county hatcheries. All hens were tested for pullorum, and all flocks were inspected for paralysis. Any hens showing pullorum were removed from the flock. If paralysis was found, the flock was not used to produce eggs for the hatchery. The state association furnished incubators for the counties, and supervised the operation of the county hatchery in order to secure a uniform performance and to protect the reputation of the Co-op brand of chickens. Every hatchery manager spent one week each year at a school conducted by the State FB Co-op and Purdue University where they were told about the best methods of hatchery operation and disease control. The county association operated the hatchery, and located and supervised local flocks to supply eggs for the hatchery.

Both pullorum and paralysis are infectious, contagious and hereditary. Neither can be cured. In order to start the new program it was necessary to find flocks that were free of the diseases. The State Livestock Sanitary Board was working on a plan to control pullorum disease by testing and eliminating the infected hens in each flock. At that time there were only three flocks in the State of Indiana certified as free of pullorum.

It took four months to find 40 flocks without paralysis. When the 40 flocks were tested for pullorum, ten were so highly infected that they could not be used. Several had to be tested three times before the reactors were eliminated. Only one flock had no reactors in the first test.

A hatchery was established in Indianapolis, and in the spring of 1933 the first chicks were hatched from these flocks. Reports from 326 customers showed that less than two percent of the chickens had died during the first two weeks, as compared to the previous rate of 25%. Three of the original flocks developed paralysis, and were eliminated from the program.

During the next few years hatcheries were established in several counties in Indiana. By 1942 there were 23 Farm Bureau Co-op hatcheries in Indiana. During 1941 the hatcheries produced a total of about four million chicks. By 1946 there were 35 Farm Bureau Co-op hatcheries in Indiana with a total capacity of 2,750,000 or two carloads of eggs at one time, and they hatched about eight million chickens that year.

When enough disease-free flocks were developed, work was started on the development of better strains of poultry to lay more and better eggs. During the first 20 years, the average production of eggs per hen increased from 86 to 168 per year, and considerable improvement has been made since then.

During these years the IFBCA lost money on the hatchery department, because of the high cost of controlling diseases. There is no way to measure the benefits of this program to farmers in Indiana.

As a result of the disease control program started by the IFBCA, other hatcheries in the state took more interest in the control of disease, and pullorum and paralysis are no longer a major problem for Indiana poultry producers. Private hatcheries soon learned to buy their eggs from FB Co-op flocks. This took advantage of the costly research and development by the FB Co-op hatcheries, and helped improve many more farm flocks. By 1946 the loss of baby chicks from pullorum disease was only 10% for all hatcheries in Indiana, and was less than three percent for all FB Co-op hatcheries.

The following article was taken from the April 1968 Carroll County Farm News:

Poultry Research Farm at Lafayette

"When the IFBCA began our egg marketing program, local commercial buyers had never bought eggs on a graded basis, and farmers had no incentive to improve quality or uniformity of their eggs. We decided in the very beginning to pay the farmer according to quality and uniformity.

"It resulted in rapid improvement in egg quality, so that after one year, Dr. J. Holmes Martin of Purdue University made the statement to a meeting of chain stores that for many years Purdue had tried to improve the quality of eggs in Indiana by urging that buyers pay for them on a graded basis. He added that in one year's time, the Indiana Farm Bureau Cooperative Association, by paying a premium for quality eggs, had done more to improve egg quality than the unheeded recommendations of Purdue had been able to accomplish in many years. Indiana was beginning to get a reputation for quality eggs that would sell.

"By 1949, there was still need for constant quality research of various breeds. There was talk of hybrid strains like hybrid corn. Dr. Martin, who was by this time completely sold on the cooperative way, called a meeting on May 26, 1949 of all hatcheries in Indiana. He told of the possibilities of hybrid breeding and the need for research that would be too costly for individual hatcheries. He urged that all the hatcheries of Indiana, both cooperative and proprietary, unite to form a research cooperative which would buy, finance, and operate a research farm.

"Fifty-eight hatcheries joined forces, bought a 150-acre farm near Lafayette, hired Glenn Searcy, a highly capable manager well trained in genetics and poultry husbandry, and started research.

"Indiana Farm Bureau Cooperative Association, although already operating two research farms in Indiana, joined in this united effort, and before long found themselves the sole owner and operator as the proprietary hatcheries withdrew.

"During the 19 years of operating the research farm, two superior breeds have been developed—the Princess 55 and the Duchess 60. A year ago the United States Department of Agriculture, after testing 118 different breeds in the United States and Canada, ranked Princess 55 among the top eight.

"A year ago last September, the editor of Poultry Tribune, a national trade publication, called to say that our Duchess 60 had again won the National Poultry Tribune Trophy that is given each year to the bird with the highest three-year average income in the Pennsylvania Random Sample Test. The 3 year average income over chick and feed cost was $2.45.

"This award was presented at the Northeast Poultry Producers' Association Convention in Harrisburg, Pennsylvania."

FARM MACHINERY

Beginning about 1930, the IFBCA tried to make arrangements with various implement companies to supply tractors and other farm machinery to members. Several contracts were tried, but were not satisfactory. Often it was the same old story. The Co-op Association would sell a new line, and when it was accepted by farmers, the company would cancel the contract and establish other dealers in the area.

Co-op Tractor

The IFBCA, working with other state cooperatives, designed and built an entirely new kind of tractor. It was the first farm tractor with a high compression engine and designed entirely for use on rubber tires. The tractor was assembled by the Duplex Machine Company, Battle Creek, Michigan with a Chrysler Industrial engine and a Clark rear end. It would run 40 MPH, and could be used for both a tractor and truck. The first tractor was produced in 1936.

A demonstration was held in every county in Indiana and the tractor was driven instead of being hauled from one county to another. At a demonstration in Hamilton County the tractor failed to perform. It would start but would not run very long. After several attempts and failures the demonstration was cancelled and the crowd went home in disgust. Mechanics found that someone had put a handful of confetti in the gasoline tank. The story was published, and another demonstration was held. More Co-op tractors were then sold in Hamilton County than in any other county in Indiana.

The demonstration in Carroll County was held on the S.A. Wickard farm in July 1936. A total of 270 of the new Co-op tractors were sold in Indiana in 1936.

Bulletin No. 38 "Cooperative Purchasing by Indiana Farmers" issued by the Farm Credit Administration in June 1939 stated: "Five large-scale cooperatives—the Indiana Farm Bureau Cooperative Association; the Ohio Farm Bureau Cooperative Association; Farm Bureau Services, Inc. of Michigan; Farmers Union Central Exchange, of St. Paul, Minnesota; and the Consumers Cooperative Association, of North Kansas City, Missouri—were the principal parties to the contract under which the Co-op tractor was manufactured according to specifications developed by the cooperatives. Other state and local cooperative associations have purchased the Co-op tractor for distribution to farmers. From 1935 to April 1938 a total of 1775 Co-op tractors were reported sold in 30 states and Canada. In April 1938 the state and regional farmers' cooperatives interested in the manufacturing of Co-op tractors and other farm machinery organized American Cooperatives, Inc., to serve as a management and distributive agency for the Co-op tractors.

"In 1939, American Cooperatives, Inc. built a machinery factory in Arthurdale, West Virginia, where they built Co-op tractors and other machinery. The Cooperative did a business of $18 million per year."

National Farm Machinery Co-operative

In 1940 the National Farm Machinery Cooperative, organized by IFBCA and 11 other state and regional cooperatives built a manufacturing plant at Shelbyville, Indiana. A new tractor called the Co-op B-2 was designed and six were built in the last week of 1940. More than 500 tractors were built during 1941 until the factory was converted to defense work. Material to build farm machinery was allocated on the basis of the amount used in 1940, and the Co-op had no basis for allocation for farm machinery.

After the war the plant at Shelbyville built corn pickers and other farm machinery. In 1943 the National Farm Machinery Cooperative bought the Ohio Cultivator Company at Bellevue, Ohio, where corn planters, drills and other machinery were built. In 1944, nine carloads (52 per car) of corn planters were shipped to Indiana.

In December 1945 the National Farm Machinery Cooperative contracted with the Cockshutt Plow Company of Brantford, Canada, to build 1,000 tractors and other machinery with the Co-op name for distribution in the U.S. Twenty six tractors were sold in Indiana in 1946. The company developed the first farm tractor with a live power take-off. This was a great improvement, and made the tractor much more useful in the operation of PTO machinery. The first of the new tractors available was a two-plow tractor, the Co-op E-3. Later a three plow tractor, the Co-op E-4, and a large Co-op E-5 were available. A small Co-op E-2 was designed but very few were built. Several new and larger models were built in the 1950's.

In 1961 the Oliver Corporation, a subsidiary of White Motor Company, purchased the Cockshutt Company in Brantford, Canada. Early in 1962 the company discontinued the manufacture of Cockshutt and Co-op implements, and the IFBCA discontinued distribution of heavy farm machinery.

FARM AND BUILDING SUPPLIES

The Farm and Building Supplies Department of the IFBCA was organized to supply county associations with quality building materials. In 1943 the department acquired a lumber mill at Pine Bluff, Arkansas and another at Leola, Arkansas. In 1944 a shingle mill in Canada, and a coal mine in Kentucky were purchased. Several more plants and factories were acquired later, and the department was now able to supply all kinds of buildings and building material. With five lumber yards in Indiana, each doing more than $1 million worth of business per year, and a full line of buildings for machinery, livestock and grain storage, the IFBCA is one of the largest builders of farm buildings in Indiana.

WOOL MARKETING

Marketing of wool was a problem for farmers in Indiana. Most farmers had only a few sheep and sold the wool at a local feed store or quite often to the man who sheared the sheep. Wool was not uniform, and much of it was of low quality, so buyers did not pay much for it. There was no incentive to produce better wool, because buyers did not pay a premium for quality.

In 1921, farmers in Indiana began selling their wool through the Ohio Wool and Sheep Growers Association where it was graded and sold on the basis of quality. About one-third of the wool produced in Indiana that year was sold through the Ohio Association.

Indiana Wool Growers Assn.

On August 20, 1926 the Indiana Wool Growers Association was organized, and ten years later there were 2,300 members. Arrangements were made for the county cooperative associations to take wool to the warehouse at Indianapolis, where it was graded and sold through the National Wool Marketing Association.

The Indiana Wool Growers Association gave awards to counties doing the best job of marketing wool, based on the amount of wool sold, and the kind of an educational program carried on in the county. Carroll County FB won the award in 1939.

Mr. T. I. Ferris was in charge of wool marketing in Indiana from the time the association was organized until October 1947, when the Indiana Wool Growers Association was merged with the Indiana Farm Bureau Cooperative Association.

National Wool Marketing Assn.

In 1929 the National Wool Marketing Association was formed with headquarters in Boston, Massachusetts, where the principal wool market in the U.S. is located.

Membership in the National Association included units in 28 states with 40,000 members. The association handled the largest volume of wool of any agency in the U.S. Farmers marketing their wool through the cooperative received an average of about five cents per pound above the local price.

FARM BUREAU SERUM CORP.

In 1915 the Indiana Swine Breeders organized the Swine Breeders Pure Serum Company, and built a plant near Thorntown, Indiana, to produce serum and virus for vaccinating hogs for hog cholera.

By 1935 there were 43 serum plants in the U.S. but this was the only one in Indiana, and it was the only one in the world that was a cooperative owned by farmers.

Control of the company was acquired by the IFB in 1931 and by the IFBCA in 1937. In 1938 it was merged with and became a department of the IFBCA.

MIDWEST PRODUCERS CREAMERIES, INC.

The Indiana Farm Bureau organized five co-op creameries in Indiana. In June 1932 these creameries organized the Mid-West Producers Creameries, Inc., to help the local creameries do a better job and provide a market for their products. Butter was sold under the brand name "Valley Lea". The organization became regional, with the addition of more creameries in Indiana and surrounding states. Creameries in this area included those located in Crawfordsville, Remington, Kentland, Kokomo and Wabash.

By adopting uniform manufacturing procedures the quality of butter produced by the member creameries was higher and more uniform. This resulted in a better price for the butter. By centralizing the sales of butter the price received was increased by one half to three quarter cents per pound.

The pool buying of supplies and equipment resulted in enough savings to more than pay the cost of the central association.

P & C FAMILY FOODS

The wide margin between the prices paid for products grown on the farm, and the price paid in the grocery store has always been a concern of both the producers and consumers of food.

In 1946 the IFB, IFBCA and the Producers Marketing Association organized the Cooperative Producer and Consumer Family Foods of Indiana, Inc. Marvin J. Briggs, manager of the IFBCA was president and Hassil Schenck, president of the IFB was vice president. Hal Royce, former director of the Livestock Marketing Department of the IFB was hired as manager.

The purpose was to establish grocery stores in all parts of Indiana in order to provide an outlet for cooperative food processing plants, and to provide consumers with high quality foods at a fair price. Any earnings of the stores were to be divided equally between the processing plants and the consumers.

The first store was opened at Veedersburg on August 7, 1946. Other stores were opened in Lebanon and Greensburg. A survey indicated that the area around Lafayette was one of the best in Indiana for operating a grocery store, and several locations were considered. Three locations at Delphi were given serious consideration. They were the old Dame Hotel west of the Courthouse, west of town where the Dairy Queen is now located, and south of town on Co-op Acres where the Lutheran Church is located.

About this time modern supermarkets operated by chain grocery companies were expanding rapidly. These stores operated on a large volume of business with a narrow margin, and it was very difficult for a small store to compete with them.

A survey of the situation showed that a large amount of money would be needed to build stores and a distribution system large enough to compete with the other stores. The directors of P & C Family Foods decided that this money would serve a better purpose if invested in other projects, and the stores were closed.

DISTRICT DIRECTORS

The eight counties in the Third FB District are represented by one member on the Board of Directors of the IFBCA. Charles Armstrong from Clinton

County was the first director and Sam Molter of Newton County was the second. Arthur Mullin of Carroll County was the next director and served from 1930 until 1937. Charles Dunwoody of Tippecanoe County served from 1938 until 1952 and William Justice from Cass County served from 1953 until 1979. Charles Kerber of Tippecanoe County was elected as director from the Third District at the Annual Meeting of the state association in December 1979.

IFBCA FIELD MEN

Marvin J. Briggs was employed in 1927 as the first general field man for the IFBCA. As the size of the business grew, it was necessary to add more field men so that each county would have more help from the state association.

Field men from the IFBCA who worked in Carroll County were: Edward E. Stephens, 1928-1930; Arthur R. Mullin, 1931-1942; Noble Logan, 1942-1947; Claude Connelly, 1947-1948; Marshall Lawrence, 1948-1975 and Doit Morgan 1975-1976. Ed McCafferty has been field man since 1976.

GROWTH OF IFBCA

The first offices of the IFBCA were located in the Old Trail Building at 309 West Washington St. in Indianapolis. In May 1941 the office was moved to the Majestic Building at 47 South Pennsylvania St.

Arthur R. Mullin, director for the Third District from 1930 to 1937, and field man for IFBCA from 1931 to 1942. He served as manager of the Seed and Fertilizer Department from 1942 to 1960. As chairman of the CCFB and secretary of Statewide REMC he helped organize CCREMC in 1935.

and in 1978 it was moved to the Indiana Building located at 120 East Market St.

These moves were necessary to provide more office space for a growing organization. The IFBCA is owned by local co-op associations serving every county in Indiana. In 1979, the state and county associations employed about 4,000 people.

During the ten years ending in 1979, the state and local associations paid more $87 million in local, state and federal taxes, and paid to members in Indiana more than $35 million in cash payments for patronage refunds, common stock redemption and cash dividends.

For the year ending August 31, 1979 the IFBCA broke all previous records by doing a business of more than one billion dollars.

Other Regional Co-operatives

The Farmer Cooperative Service of the U.S. Department of Agriculture in 1977 published Research Report #40 giving information on Supply Operations of 19 major regional cooperatives in the U.S. for the years 1974 and 1975. IFBCA ranked ninth in supply sales in 1975.

The other large cooperatives in order of size were: Farmland Industries, Inc., Kansas City, Missouri; Agway Inc., Syracuse, New York; Farmers Union Central Exchange, Inc., St. Paul, Minnesota; FS Services, Inc., Bloomington, Illinois; Land O'Lakes, Inc., Minneapolis, Minnesota; Southern States Cooperatives, Inc., Richmond, Virginia; Midland Cooperative, Inc., Minneapolis, Minnesota; and Gold Kist, Inc., Atlanta,

William F. and Paulita Justice at a dinner party at Monticello on September 14, 1979. The party was sponsored by managers of Co-op Associations in District Three to give recognition to Mr. Justice who announced that he would retire in December 1979, after serving 26 years as a director of the IFBCA and as president of the Board of Directors from 1971 to 1977.
Mr. Justice lives in Cass County and part of his farm is in Carroll County. In order to show that he claimed both counties, he had license number 9A8 on his auto.

Georgia. In tenth place was Landmark, Inc., Columbus Ohio.

CARROLL COUNTY FBCA

At a meeting of directors of the County Farm Bureau held Saturday evening, June 4, 1927 at Delphi, I. H. Hull, general manager of the newly organized Indiana Farm Bureau Cooperative Association, met with the directors and explained to them how to organize a Co-op Association in the county. The directors agreed to organize the Carroll County FB Co-op Association and signed Articles of Incorporation providing for a capital stock of $10,000 in common stock and $5,000 in preferred stocks. Directors present who signed the Articles of Incorporation were: Andrew Gerbens, Frank Redenbacher, Wm. Lee Henderson, Artus Rodenbarger, C. B. Million, Clarence Stout, George W. Peterson, Arthur Ritchey and Obe Campbell. The Articles of Incorporation were also signed by I. H. Hull and E. E. Stephens, president of the Carroll County Farm Bureau.

Mr. Hull took the Articles of Incorporation to Indianapolis and filed them with the Secretary of State on Monday, June 6, 1927.

DIRECTORS

The Incorporators decided to have 13 directors, with one from each township, and agreed that the chairman of each Township FB would be the first director to represent his township. It was voted to have about one half of the directors elected each year for a two year term. Names were drawn to see which of the first directors would serve for one or two year terms.

Seven directors for a two year term were: George W. Peterson, Adams Township; Clarence Stout, Burlington; Jesse McCain, Carrollton; Andrew Gerbens, Deer Creek; Leon Kasten, Rock Creek; C. B. Million, Jefferson and Artus Rodenbarger, Democrat. Six directors for a one year term were: Frank Redenbacher, Clay; Arthur Ritchey, Jackson; Obe Campbell, Madison; Elmer Kuns, Monroe; Wm. Lee Henderson, Tippecanoe and Earl A. Downham, Washington.

At their first meeting the directors elected Wm. Lee Henderson as president; Mary Mason, secretary and J. A. Shirk, treasurer.

At the next two meetings of directors held on June 18 and 30, 1927 directors discussed and adopted the by-laws and proceeded with plans for completing the organization. Each Township Farm Bureau and the County Farm Bureau bought one share of common stock at $5 each and the president of each organization was authorized to represent his organization at meetings of stockholders. This made a total of 14 stockholders in the new Co-op Association and 13 of them were directors.

On October 15, 1928 the stockholders changed the number of directors from 13 to 14 to include one director at large in addition to one from each township. Claude R. Wickard, president of the Carroll County Farm Bureau was elected as the 14th director. In later years the 14th director was usually the president of the CCFB.

In 1945 the by-laws were amended to provide that the president of the CCFB be the 14th director providing he met the qualifications as set forth in the by-laws. His terms as a director would begin at the Annual Stockholders Meeting following his election as County Farm Bureau president.

When a township directors' term expired a nomination was made at a regular Township FB meeting, and the directors were elected at the Annual Co-op Stockholders Meeting for a term of two years. Directors were paid $1 per meeting and five cents per mile one way.

In 1942 the by-laws were amended to provide for a committee of three stockholders appointed by the Board of Directors to nominate two candidates from each township when the director's term expired. Directors were elected by stockholders at the Annual Meeting.

In 1957 the by-laws were changed to provide for the election of one third of the directors each year for a term of three years instead of one half each year for a term of two years.

The by-laws provide that a director shall be a stockholder of the corporation, and shall be engaged in the production of agricultural products. The by-laws also provide that: No director shall be engaged in any business in competition with the corporation. No director shall become indebted to the association. No director shall be a candidate for political office except with the consent of the majority of the Board of Directors. No person shall be a director of the corporation whose relatives, by blood or marriage, of a degree as close as that of first cousin is in the employ of the corporation.

A complete list of all directors and officers is at the end of the chapter.

FINANCE

When the CCFBCA was organized in 1927, the township Farm Bureau organizations and the CCFB each purchased one share of common stock at $5. This made a total of $70 and is the only common stock that has been sold by the association.

Limited Liability Bonds

Additional money for operating capital was borrowed from local banks. Members signed limited liability bonds in which they each agreed to be liable for an amount of money, usually $100. These bonds were used as collateral to borrow money needed for operation.

These bonds were first used in October 1927 when the association borrowed $9,000 from the Citizens National Bank of Delphi. Mr. C. B. Shaffer, representing the bank, said that the bank officials had examined similar businesses in neighboring counties, and were well satisfied with the directors and the business set up.

Bonds were signed by a total of 339 members to provide money for the first few years. A complete list of names of bond signers is at the end of the chapter.

After signing the bonds, some members were afraid that they might lose their $100 and wanted to be released from the bond. One member made such a fuss about it that the directors agreed to take his name off the bond if he promised not to tell anyone about it. The next day two of his relatives were in asking to have their names taken off the list. No more names were removed from the list.

Only 34 of these bonds were for amounts less than $100. Each of the 305 who signed bonds for $100 or more was issued a share of common stock with a value of $5. A part of the earnings each year were distributed to members in the form of stock, and whenever the earnings of a bond signer who had been issued a share of stock reached $10 or more he was issued a second share of stock. Other patrons were issued a share of stock whenever their share of the earnings was $5 or more.

The money accumulated by issuing stock instead of cash to members was used for further expansion, and to pay off the loans at the bank secured by the limited liability bonds. These loans were all paid off and the bonds burned at a ceremony at the Annual Meeting of the Cooperative Association in 1940.

Since that time some additional money needed for operation has been borrowed from local banks. Recently most of the money needed has been borrowed from the Bank for Cooperatives at Louisville. Some capital has been obtained by the sale of Preferred Stock and Debenture Bonds.

Refunds

During 1927 and most of 1928 the new Co-op Association operated without a warehouse as the Purchasing Department of the FB had been doing for several years. Earnings were refunded to members in cash.

Records of business for the first two years are not available, but the report of the County Agent for 1927 shows that the Co-op Association sold 790 tons of fertilizer, 617 bushels of seed, two tons of feed and 21 carloads of coal during 1927. Members were given a cash refund of $8,300 which was about 11% of sales.

An article in the Delphi Journal for November 29, 1928 reported that $3,568.05 had been paid in refunds to Farm Bureau members in Carroll County on fertilizer, twine, and livestock. The article also reported a total business of $48,600 for 1928 for the FB Co-op Association and the Livestock Shipping Association.

Beginning in 1929 regular annual audits were made of the Co-op Association, and copies of these audits are available.

Sales for 1929 were $90,275 and net savings were $2,301. This was distributed to members. Cash refunds were paid on twine and fertilizer. One half of one percent of all sales, or about $450 was given in common stock.

For the first several years refunds were paid only to FB members. Earnings on business with others was put in a special fund and used for education and advertising. In 1942 the bylaws were changed, and earnings were distributed to all patrons in proportion to their patronge. Common voting stock was issued to producers of agricultural products, while non-voting common stock was issued to others. Both kinds of stock had the same value, but only owners of voting stock could vote at the stockholders meetings. Voting was limited to one vote per member, regardless of the number of shares of stock owned.

During the 1930's the savings on petroleum products ranged from five to 11% and were refunded to patrons, about half in cash and half in common stock. Savings on other commodities ranged from three to eight percent and were refunded in common stock.

During the 1940's savings averaged about six percent on all commodities, and were refunded in common stock.

Since 1974 earnings have been distributed to patrons, 30% in cash and 70% in common stock.

Sales to each customer were recorded and at the end of the year earnings were allocated to each one on the basis of the amount of his purchases. Small amounts were credited to the account as fractional shares, and when these totaled $5 or more, the customer was issued a share of stock. As the amount of business and number of customers increased, this made a lot of record keeping. In 1974 the by-laws were amended to provide that no refund, amounting to less than $2, would be allocated to a customer; and if he did no business with the association for three years, his fractional shares would be transferred to the reserve fund.

Common Stock

For several years interest was paid on common stock at six percent per year. In 1936 the interest rate was changed to five percent. In 1950 the directors voted to discontinue paying interest on common stock, and use the money to purchase the older outstanding stock.

In 1937 the association began purchasing common stock owned by any stockholder who moved out of the county, and also purchased stock owned by estates. In 1943 the association redeemed all common stock that had been issued during the years 1929, 1930 and 1931. The next year stock issued in 1932 and 1933; in 1946 stock issued in 1934 and 1935; in 1948 stock issued in 1936 and 1937; in 1958 stock issued in 1938, 1939 and 1940; and in 1960 stock issued in 1941 and 1942 was purchased by the association. This was the last stock purchased under the program. The association continued to buy stock to settle estates until 1969.

Directors hope in the future to purchase stock from estates, and stock issued in 1943 and later years. This program is designed to keep the association owned by those who are using it.

Fiscal Year

At first, the Co-op Association operated on a calendar year basis. In November 1930 it was decided to close the year on December 1, so that refund checks could be issued in January.

In 1967 the fiscal year was changed to begin on September 1, because that date was much better for records on grain marketing, which by that time had become a major part of the business.

STORES AT DELPHI

On September 15, 1928 the directors of the CCFBCA met and appointed a committee composed of Wm. Lee Henderson, Claude Wickard, Sam Sites, George Peterson, Clarence Stout, J. W. Eikenberry and Arthur Ritchey, to select a location for a warehouse. The committee met October 1, 1928 and recommended that a store be opened in Delphi on October 15, in the Bradshaw Building, formerly the Coomey Tin Shop located at 106 South Market Street. This building was later occupied by the Ben Logan Plumbing Shop. The committee agreed to rent this building at $30 per month, and recommended that Wm. Lee Henderson be hired as manager and be paid $100 per month. The

Wm. Lee Henderson, first manager of the Carroll County Farm Bureau Cooperative Association who served from 1928 until January 1943.

directors met immediately after the committee meeting, approved the recommendation of the committee, and also authorized the purchase of a truck.

At a meeting of stockholders and directors on October 15, 1928, Wm. Lee Henderson resigned as president, and Claude Wickard was elected president and Obe Campbell, vice president. At the same meeting a decision was made to change the location of the warehouse to 210 West Franklin Street because more room was available and the door was large enough to get the truck inside the building. The main products handled at the new store were feed, seed, salt, fertilizer, coal and binder twine.

For several years a purchasing agent in each township took orders from farmers for fertilizer, feed and seed to be delivered to the central warehouse. In 1932 the first feed mixer was installed. For the year 1932, the CCFBCA was the top county in the district on purchases of feed, seed, fertilizer and petroleum products from the IFBCA.

On January 1, 1935 the store was moved to 120 East Franklin Street, and the bookkeeping department was moved from the County Agent's office in the Courthouse to the new store. A grand opening was held on February 16, 1935 with more than 500 people attending. Refund checks for 1934 were given to patrons. Mabel Snoeberger was hired in November 1935 as the first full time bookkeeper for the Co-op Association. The location was also used as the office for the Carroll

218 • CARROLL COUNTY RURAL ORGANIZATIONS

The Carroll County Farm Bureau Co-op Association at 120 E. Franklin St. Delphi. This was the main office and warehouse for the Association from January 1, 1935 until 1963 when the Delphi branch was moved to 1020 South Washington St.

County REMC until 1943 and for the office for the CCFB from 1943 until 1955.

An Implement Department was established at the location in 1935, and incubators for a Hatchery were installed in the fall of 1936.

Electrical supplies for wiring buildings were handled during the period of construction of REMC lines in Carroll County.

In 1963 the Delphi branch was moved to 1020 South Washington Street with an open house on August 10, 1963.

In 1969 the Delphi branch was closed, and the main office moved to the new Central Carroll location north of Flora.

Weather

On January 22, 1936 a heavy snow storm hit Delphi and the temperature dropped to 20 degrees below zero. That night the warehouse at 120 East Franklin

The Carroll County Farm Bureau Co-op Association and REMC office at 120 E. Franklin St. April 9, 1938. On the left is the Co-op office with Wm. Lee Henderson, manager; and Opal Smith bookkeeper. On the right is the REMC office with John C. Peterson, project superintendent, and Margaret Bowman, bookkeeper.

The sign on the poster in the middle reads: "Easter Market will be held here by Ladies Aid of Pyrmont U. B. Church, Saturday, April 16, 10:00 A.M."

St. was completely filled with automobiles belonging to people who did not want to leave their cars outside in the severe weather, and several people stayed in the office for the night.

Later that year two employees went to a fertilizer plant in southern Indiana to get a truck load of fertilizer. Due to bad weather they did not get back to the store until late at night. They stayed in the office for the rest of the night, and were awakened the next morning by a noise that sounded like raindrops on a tin roof, only much louder. Lloyd Beard had come in early to open the store, and was counting the change as he dropped it into the cash register, one coin at a time.

Farm Machinery

An Implement Department was added in January 1935. A contract was signed with the IFBCA to handle a full line of Co-op implements, and another contract was signed with the Massey Harris Company to handle their implements in the county. Lloyd Beard was hired as manager, and the first truck load of Co-op machinery arrived on January 16, 1935.

In 1936 the IFBCA helped develop and build a new kind of tractor, as described on page 211. Four of the No. 2 Co-op tractors were sold in Carroll County to Wm. Lee Henderson and Sons, Robert Hedde and Son, Miles T. Martin and Sons and Wm. F. Peterson and Sons. One of these tractors is still being used and was on display at the Carroll County 4-H Fair in 1977, and belongs to Joseph E. and John C. Peterson.

In 1939 the directors voted to sell only Co-op implements, and continued to sell them until IFBCA discontinued the distribution of farm machinery in 1962. The County Co-op Association continued a parts and repair service until Jack Orr, the mechanic, retired in 1967.

Other Implement Department managers in addition to Lloyd Beard were: Warren Woods, Charles A. Smith, Morris Skiles, Earl Bowman and Orton Zook.

Hatchery

The IFBCA built a hatchery in Indianapolis in 1933, and farmers soon learned about the high quality and disease free chickens produced by the Co-op Association. In 1936 about 8,000 chickens were purchased from the hatchery by farmers in Carroll County, and there was a demand for the County FBCA to operate a hatchery.

In September 1936, Wayne Hiatt was hired as manager of the new hatchery, which was installed in the Delphi store in November 1936. About 50,000 chickens were hatched in 1937 and more than 100,000 in 1938. Wayne continued as manager of the hatchery until he became manager of the Co-op Association in 1943.

Tom Hendricks was hatchery manager from March 1943 until October 1944.

Emma Cullum was hatchery manager from October 1944 until December 1947. She was replaced by Gene Metzger who had been assistant for a year.

Others who managed the hatchery were Bob

Joseph E. and Elizabeth Peterson with one of the four No. 2 Co-op tractors sold in Carroll County in 1936 and still being used in 1980. The picture was taken in 1949.

Wayne Hiatt, manager of the Farm Bureau Co-op Hatchery at Delphi from 1936 to 1943, and manager of the FBCA from February 1943 until September 1944.

Overley, Fred Kuszmaul, Fred Gerard and Earl Hathaway.

The size of the hatchery was increased in 1946 to a capacity of 82,000 eggs. This made it possible to hatch 14,000 chickens each week. The hatchery at Delphi was discontinued in 1960 because many farmers no longer raised chickens. Beginning in January 1961, the FB Co-op hatchery at Frankfort hatched chickens for five counties, including Carroll.

Chickens were also available from the FB Co-op hatchery at Indianapolis. The new modern fireproof hatchery with a capacity of 500,000 eggs was built in 1959 to replace the hatchery which burned on April 21, 1959.

Egg Marketing

In June 1947 the IFBCA began operating an egg grading and marketing station at Indianapolis and another at Warsaw, Indiana.

Eggs were picked up at the farms each week by County Cooperative Associations and taken to the egg grading stations where they were graded and sold.

Farmers were urged to produce clean eggs and high

Fred Kuszmaul, employee at the CCFBCA at Delphi from 1947 to 1952.

Fred Gerard, manager of the Farm Bureau Co-op Hatchery at Delphi in 1953 and 1954.

Agnes Reed, bookkeeper for the Co-op Association, served for 29½ years from April 5, 1943 to November 3, 1972. Picture taken in 1954.

Ralph Hanna, office manager of the Carroll County Farm Bureau Cooperative Association from September 1948 until 1956.

quality eggs by gathering them often and keeping them cool.

It was necessary to have an average of one case of eggs per mile to maintain a truck route. In March 1951 arrangements were made in Carroll County for farmers to deliver their eggs to a branch of the Co-op Association, where they would be picked up twice each week and taken to the grading station.

Paint

Beginning about 1942 the CCFBCA operated a paint spraying machine to paint buildings. Keith Rider operated the machine for several years.

In 1960 a new paint spraying outfit was purchased by the association and was operated by Orton Zook and Lee Chapman. In 1969 the outfit was operated by Brian and Patrick Stevenson who were from Rhodesia in Southern Africa, and were students at Andrews College in Berrien Springs, Michigan.

For several years the Co-op Association has rented a paint spraying machine to customers who want to do their own painting.

Weed Sprayer

In 1947 the Co-op Association purchased a power sprayer to spray weeds, buildings and livestock. Purdue University had been experimenting for about two years with 2,4-D to kill weeds, and DDT to control flies in buildings and on livestock.

The sprayer was operated by Morris Skiles, Leroy Powell, and Gene Metzger.

BULK OIL PLANT

After the store in Delphi was established, directors began talking about a bulk oil plant to handle gasoline, kerosene, and lubricating oil for members. Several directors were in favor of it but others were not. Some directors did not want to jeopardize a good feed business by getting into the oil business. They were afraid that the big oil companies might put them completely out of business. A committee was appointed to investigate the possibility of a bulk oil plant. At a directors meeting held on November 2, 1929 Arthur Ritchey, chairman of the committee, reported that the committee had visited other county FB Co-op bulk oil plants and recommended that one be built in Carroll County. The directors voted to build the bulk oil plant.

E. E. Stephens, who was president of the Carroll County Farm Bureau when the association was organized, became a field man for the Indiana Farm Bureau Cooperative Association and was very active in promoting oil plants and fertilizer sales. He worked with the committee and helped establish the plant in Carroll County.

Once again the directors decided to finance the project by having people sign limited liability bonds. The project was explained to a group of interested farmers at a meeting and $6,200 was raised in 15

John DeLaCroix, manager of the Carroll County Farm Bureau Cooperative Association 1944 to 1950.

Morris Skiles, assistant manager of the Carroll County Farm Bureau Co-op Association from 1946 to 1950.

minutes. This set a record in Indiana for raising money for a bulk oil plant.

The Bulk Oil Plant was built at Camden and began operation on February 13, 1930 when the association hired four tank wagon drivers. They were: Fred Clawson, Robert Hedde, Clayton Million and Dallas Frey. On March 14, Ross Wagoner was hired as manager of the plant. During the first year of operation 40 tank carloads of petroleum products were handled.

At a directors meeting on May 20, 1930 a report of earnings since April 2, showed net earnings of $1,030.20 and accounts receivable of $1,100. According to the minutes of the meeting this resulted in a "lengthy discussion" on cash and credit. The directors voted to set a limit of $500 credit for each oil driver.

In October 1931 it was reported to the directors that the oil plant had net earnings of $6,684.52 for 10 months, while at the same time the feed department was losing money. Some of the directors who had hesitated to "jeopardize a good feed business" by getting into the oil business now wanted to continue the oil business and quit the feed business.

As more counties in Indiana got into the oil business, and as business expanded, the Indiana Farm Bureau Cooperative Association decided to build an oil compounding plant at Indianapolis to insure better quality oil for the members. In October 1931 the CCFBCA voted to buy 10 shares of stock at $100 each in the state organization to help finance this project.

During 1932 the county association sold 165 gallons of fly spray for dairy cattle. In 1933 the directors discussed the possibility of purchasing a machine to reclaim used motor oil, but after investigation decided against it.

When it was first built, the Bulk Oil Plant at Camden had two storage tanks holding 19,000 gallons each. In 1933 a tank was installed for handling anti-knock gasoline. Two 15,000 gallon tanks were added in 1947.

The first tank wagons held 380 gallons and cost about $500 each. In 1935 two of the tanks were replaced with 600 gallon tank units with four compartments. The tanks used on the trucks in 1977 held 1,850 gallons and cost about $7,500 each.

Most of the fuel delivered during the first few years was kerosene, and was measured in a five gallon can. In 1938 pumps were installed on the trucks to measure and transfer the fuel.

In 1976 the Bulk Oil Plant was moved to the Central Carroll location north of Flora. In 1979 the plant had a storage capacity of 160,000 gallons.

CCFBCA began selling gasohol at the Central Carroll location north of Flora in December 1978 and in January 1979 began delivery by tank wagon.

Oil Plant Managers

Ross Wagoner, the first manager of the oil plant, served until 1945. Roy Cornelison was manager from 1945 to July 1953; John Berkshire from July 1953 to 1965; Dale Hanna from 1965 to 1967 and Dan Baker was manager from 1967 to 1969. Richard Harriott has been manager since January 1970.

Mrs. Clara Sullivan was the first bookkeeper at the bulk plant. Others were: Harold Cook, Wilbur Richardson and Carl Raber.

OIL DRIVERS

Dallas Frey, one of the first tank wagon drivers, was replaced on March 1, 1932 by Glenn Eikenberry

Carroll County Farm Bureau Cooperative Association Bulk Oil Plant at Camden. Used from 1930 until 1976 when oil department was moved to Central Carroll location. The building is now used by Fertilizer Department.

Employees of the CCFBCA Petroleum Department in March, 1980. From left: Richard Harriott, manager and three of the tank wagon drivers, Mike Pearson, Bob Ringer and Donald Craft. Jim Hodges was on Jury Duty when picture was taken.

who had the route for 25 years. His son, Joe Eikenberry, had the route until February 1960 and since then it has been operated by Don Craft.

Fred Clawson, another of the first drivers, was replaced by his brother Russell Clawson, on January 18, 1939. Russell Clawson's son-in-law, Don Hathaway, began helping him on the route in 1948, took over the route in 1956 and operated it until November 1968. Tom Flora had the route from November 1968 until February 1973. Since then the route has been operated by Mike Pearson.

Robert Hedde operated his original route until 1943 and Chester Gardner had it until 1958. Wilmer Hodges had the route from December 1958 until December 1970, and since January 1971 it has been operated by James Hodges.

Clayton Million had his original route until 1945 when it was taken over by Wilbur and Alonzo Brady who operated it until February 1, 1949. Bobby Ringer has had the route since that time.

A fifth route was started in the county on February 1, 1942 with Eugene Titus as driver. He was drafted by the military service in April 1942, and the route was taken by Paul Gregg who operated it until November 1962. Ronald Nipple operated the route until 1965, when the fifth route was discontinued.

FERTILIZER

Fertilizer was one of the first commodities handled by the Carroll County FB Co-op Association. Farmers would pool their orders and have their fertilizer shipped in carload lots from the fertilizer plant. Farmers would either get it directly from the car, or have the association deliver it to them. Fertilizer at that time was shipped in 125 pound burlap bags.

After the IFBCA built a fertilizer plant at Indianapolis in 1939, much of the fertilizer was delivered directly to farms in trucks returning from hauling livestock to Indianapolis. Most of the fertilizer at that time was shipped in 50 pound bags.

In 1954 the IFBCA spent about a half million dollars to build an addition to the fertilizer plant at Indianapolis to make granular fertilizer. The coarser granular fertilizer could be handled with much less dust, and it did not "set", or harden, as the finer ma-

Jim Hodges one of the tank wagon drivers in 1980.

Arthur Mullin, manager of the Fertilizer Department for Indiana Farm Bureau Cooperative Association, meeting with Carroll County Farm Bureau Cooperative Association officials and employees June 24, 1949. Seated, left to right: Joseph E. Peterson, John DeLaCroix and Arthur Mullin; standing: Ralph Hanna, Morris Skiles, Merle Johnson, Robert Jenkins, B. W. "Bill" Ferguson, and Carl Johnson.

Myron Beesley, general manager of the CCFBCA from June 1950 to September 1951.

Jay L. Small, Manager of Carroll County Farm Bureau Cooperative Association, October 1951 to May 1958.

Carroll County Co-op employees in January 1980, at the Camden Plant Food left to right; Terry Maxwell, Richard Wertz and Robert Schock.

Robert Shands, manager, and Wayne Harris, employees at the FB Co-op fertilizer plant south of Bringhurst in February 1980.

terial did. Another advantage was that liquid nitrogen, a cheaper source of that element, could be used in the manufacturing process.

Fertilizer Plants at Camden and Bringhurst

In 1958 the FB Co-op Association purchased land and built a fertilizer storage and blending plant in Camden. Open house was held on April 30, 1959. In 1962, two trailer type PTO driven fertilizer spreaders were purchased and rented to farmers to apply bulk fertilizer. Additional storage bins were built in 1963 and 1964.

In 1970 the Co-op Association purchased applicators and nurse tanks for applying anhydrous am-

Carroll County Co-op Fertilizer Plant and equipment at Camden in 1980.

monia fertilizer and, the same year, purchased equipment to handle liquid fertilizer.

Kenneth Delaplane was the first manager at the Camden Fertilizer plant and Robert Schock has been manager since about 1972. Others who have served were: Herb Carter, John Moyer and Bennie Dyer.

In February 1971 the FB Co-op Association purchased a bulk fertilizer plant south of Bringhurst from the Monsanto Fertilizer Company. Robert Shands is manager of the plant. Others who served as managers were: John Moyer, Gary Overholser and Robert Adcock.

In 1971 the association purchased its first self-propelled fertilizer applicator known as the "Big A." A second one was purchased in 1974 and the third in 1976.

The Big "A", one of three used by the CCFBCA to spread fertilizer. The dry fertilizer bed is replaced with a tank when the machine is used for liquid fertilizer and spray materials.

YEOMAN LUMBER COMPANY

The directors of the CCFBCA voted to purchase the Yeoman Lumber Company on June 7, 1935. The transaction was completed in September 1935. This lumber company was owned and operated by a group of farmers in the Yeoman community, and several of them agreed to accept common stock in the CCFBCA as part of the payment for their share of the company.

Buildings included lumber storage, an office and coal sheds along the east side of the Monon Railroad, and an old school building used as a woodworking shop located west of the railroad on the south side of Main Street. A large diesel engine, used to drive the machinery in the shop was replaced with an electric motor in 1937.

In June 1945 a cement block building across the street from the lumber yard was purchased.

George Myers who had been manager when the Lumber Company was purchased continued in that capacity for a few months. Owen Downham was manager from January 1936 to August 1939. Reed Goslee was manager from October 1939 to January 1951; Edwin Burkhart from February 1951 to October 1951; Jack Goslee from October 1951 to July 1957; and Russell Sigman from July 1957 until the Lumber Company closed in 1964.

A fire believed to have been started by lightning, destroyed the Lumber Company at 12:55 A.M. on Saturday, September 19, 1964, and the branch was closed in December 1964. Employees were transferred to the Delphi branch, and continued to handle lumber and building materials. The last real estate in Yeoman owned by the Co-op Association was sold in 1968.

Lumber yard in Yeoman purchased by the Carroll County Farm Bureau Cooperative Association in 1935 and operated until it burned in 1964.

THE WAR YEARS

Shortages of material and labor during the war caused problems for the Co-op Association. During April 1942 Donald Mullin, an employee at the Delphi branch for six years; Donald Koontz, an employee at Yeoman for three years, and Eugene Titus, an oil driver for two months, were drafted into the armed services.

Orville Goslee working on a hog feeder in the old school house at Yeoman purchased in 1935 by the Co-op Association and converted into an up-to-date woodworking plant where storm windows, doors, cabinets, hog houses, hog feeders and cattle feeding racks were made.

CHAPTER VIII — FARM BUREAU COOPERATIVE ASSOCIATION • 227

Eleven from Carroll County who helped handle fertilizer at the Farm Bureau Co-op Plant at Indianapolis on September 11, 1943. Front row, left to right: Enos Berkshire, Orville Berkshire, Ernest Martz and Lloyd Metzger. Second row: Eugene Chapman, Wayne Hiatt, Bob Rohrabaugh, Keith Rider, George Jackson, Elwood Burkle and Cleo Metzger.

Rationing of tires and gasoline made it difficult to continue delivery service to farmers. A plan was worked out to make deliveries once each week. The county was divided into three areas, with deliveries made to one area on Monday, to the second area on Wednesday and the third on Friday.

Farm machinery was rationed beginning on September 17, 1942. This reduced the sales of farm machinery, and required more work to keep records and file reports. It also caused members to be dissatisfied when they could not get the machinery that they needed.

A shortage of labor reduced the amount of fertilizer that could be processed at the FB fertilizer plant at Indianapolis. The county associations helped solve the problem by sending employees and farmers to help at the plant.

CAMDEN MILL

In February 1943 the CCFBCA purchased the Snoeberger Feed Mill and Coal Yard in Camden. The Co-op spent about a year remodelling and installing equipment and the mill began operation early in 1944. A hammer mill and two feed mixers were installed, and scales and bins were added to handle grain.

Plans were made to install a soybean processing plant to furnish soybean meal for feed. A committee went to Washington, D.C. to get permission to buy the necessary equipment, but the permit was not granted.

In 1959 a 2,200 bushel grain bin with a dryer was installed at Camden. This bin was the first of its kind to be set up in Indiana.

Those who served as managers at the Camden Mill were: Ira Shaffer, Merle Johnson, Jim McFatridge,

Mill at Camden owned by the Carroll County Farm Bureau Cooperative Association from 1943 to 1970. Picture taken in 1945.

Harold Chapman, Cecil Hill, Verlin Hopp, Kelly Day and Harold Peacock.

The mill was closed on November 30, 1970 and in December 1970 was sold to Allison, Steinhart and Zook, Inc.

BRINGHURST ELEVATOR AND FEED MILL

An elevator in Bringhurst with a storage capacity of 33,000 bushels was purchased from A.B. and Rolland Cohee of Frankfort on May 1, 1945.

Russell Ayres was hired as manager and was succeeded by Merle Johnson. Wm. Ferguson was hired in April 1947. Richard Pulley has been manager since September 1, 1962.

During 1946 and 1947 an office building and warehouse were built and scales installed. The first truck for delivering bulk feed was purchased in 1957 and another in 1959. A continuous flow automatic dryer was added in 1962.

A grain storage building with a capacity of 120,000 bushels was built across the street north of the elevator in 1960. Two large storage bins with a total capacity of 109,000 bushels were added in 1977.

OCKLEY ELEVATOR

An elevator at Ockley was purchased in October 1958 from William Smock and Don Gasaway. Ralph Rohrabaugh of Camden, formerly employed at the Co-op Elevator in Camden was hired as manager.

228 • CARROLL COUNTY RURAL ORGANIZATIONS

Farm Bureau Cooperative Association elevator at Bringhurst in 1979.

Carroll County Co-op employees at the Bringhurst Elevator in January 1980. Left to right: Richard Reef, Rick Duckworth, Charles Tatman, Harold Arion and Richard Pulley.

Comet photo
K. Wayne Harris, Feed Salesman at the FB Co-op elevator at Bringhurst in February 1980.

Charles Felthoff, who had been at the elevator about 21 years was retained as millman, and Mrs. Eva Bolinger, who had been employed for about three years, was retained as bookkeeper. Others who served as managers were Laurel Larimore, Gene McCarty and Carl Scott.

In 1962 the elevator was remodeled with a feed room, a new five ton feed mixer, bulk feed bins and a new 70 foot leg for bulk feed.

The amount of business was not enough to justify a branch in that location, and it was closed in January 1969.

CO-OP ACRES

In January 1949 the CCFBCA purchased 16.27 acres of land along the east side of State Road 39, south of Delphi. Plans were made to build several buildings and move the entire operation for the county to this location. Plans did not materialize and in 1951 the

Co-op Association began selling lots for private homes. A total of 12 lots were sold. The last of Co-op Acres was sold to the Lutheran Church in 1960 for a new church building. The Lutherans purchased 5.7 acres and later sold part of it for the Delphi Nursing Home.

CENTRAL CARROLL

In November 1967 the CCFBCA purchased 19.8 acres, one half mile north of Flora and one fourth mile east of State Road 75 along the Pennsylvania Railroad.

Tanks and equipment for anhydrous and liquid plant food were installed and ready for use in the spring of 1968. Additional tanks were installed in 1975.

In June 1968 construction was started on an 80x96 foot building for a main office, farm supply store and general warehouse. The main office was moved from Delphi to the new building, and open house was held on April 18 and 19, 1969. Another building was constructed at the same time for lumber and building material.

In April 1969 construction was started on a new Co-op Elevator which was completed and ready for use that fall. Built entirely of cement, the elevator was 176 feet high. Two more cement silos and another unloading pit were added in 1974. This made a total storage capacity of 525,000 bushels.

In 1978 an area was paved, and conveyors installed to provide temporary storage for an additional 200,000 bushels of grain.

New tanks were installed and the petroleum department was moved from Camden in 1976.

Richard L. Denhart, manager of the Carroll County Farm Bureau Cooperative Association from October 1970 until November 1979.

Brookbank photo

Aerial view of the Central Carroll elevator and main office of the Carroll County Farm Bureau Co-op Association north of Flora in October 1977.

David Gingerich, manager of the Carroll County Farm Bureau Cooperative Association since December 1979. He was manager of the Dearborn County Farm Bureau Co-op for four years before coming to Carroll County.

CO-OP TOURS

The CCFBCA has sponsored many trips in order for directors and stockholders to learn more about their organization. Many groups have gone to Indianapolis to visit Co-op Association facilities there.

Employees at the Central Carroll Elevator and Store in January 1980. Left to right standing: Vernon Sutton, Dennis Wilson and Jerry Fisher; seated Doris Gascho.

Employees at the Central Carroll office in January 1980. Left to right: Laura Spitznagle, Louise Morrow, Sharon Titus and Gordon Groninger.

One of the largest of these groups was in April 1934, when 248 farmers from Carroll County went in 50 cars to Indianapolis.

Canada

One of the longest trips sponsored by the CCFBCA was a four-day bus tour to Canada starting on August 30, 1948. The Co-op Association furnished the transportation and the 37 people who went on the trip paid other expenses.

The group visited the Cockshutt Plow Company in Brantford, Canada, which for two years had been manufacturing tractors, combines, mowers, plows, rakes and hay loaders for the Co-op Association. The concern was 100 years old, and was the largest farm machinery manufacturer in Canada. The Cockshutt Company manufactured machinery for farmers all over the world. One plow being built for export was designed to be pulled by oxen.

A new and modern assembly line for building Co-op tractors was in its second day of operation. The farm cooperatives in the United States sold more than half the tractors manufactured by the company.

The tour included a visit to Niagara Falls and a stop in North Collins, New York, to see a store operated by the Grange League Federation. GLF, a Co-op sponsored by the Grange, Dairymens League and the Farm Bureau Federation, operated a large chain of GLF farm supply stores in New York and other Eastern states.

The tour also included a visit to the Ohio Cultivator Division of the National Farm Machinery Co-op at Bellevue, Ohio, where corn planters, drills, spreaders, harrows, garden tractors, and lime sowers were manufactured. People on the tour saw experimental models of several kinds of machinery, and

Pictured above are the Carroll County Farm Bureau and Co-op Directors and S & E Leaders who went on the tour of the Farm Bureau enterprises in Indianapolis on August 20, 1946. Front row, left to right: Mrs. John C. Peterson, Mrs. John DeLaCroix, Mrs. Gale Crowell, Mrs. Enos Berkshire, Mrs. Joseph E. Peterson, Mrs. Lloyd Beard, Mrs. Miles T. Martin, Mrs. Ren Fetterhoff, Mrs. Ralph Reagon, Mrs. John McCormick, Mrs. Harold Frey, Mrs. John Witter, Miss Pauline Robeson, Mrs. Reed Goslee, and Mrs. Ira Shafer. Back row, left to right: Miles T. Martin, Ira Shafer, John DeLaCroix, Gale Crowell, Levi Furst, Enos Berkshire, Joseph E. Peterson, Ren Fetterhoff, John McCormick, John C. Peterson, C. R. Clawson, John Witter, Ralph Reagon, Reed Goslee, Harold Frey, Lloyd Beard, Leroy Robeson, Sr., Lee Flora and Oren Eikenberry.

learned that the National Farm Machinery Co-op was owned by the IFBCA and 11 other state and regional farm Co-ops.

Those who went on the trip were: Mr. and Mrs. Clayton Million, Mr. and Mrs. Raymond Nicoll, Mr. and Mrs. Fred Rodkey, S. A. Wickard, Mr. and Mrs. Harold Frey, Mr. and Mrs. Joseph E. Peterson, Mr. and Mrs. John C. Peterson, Mr. and Mrs. Ralph Reagon, Mr. and Mrs. Artus Rodenharger, Mr. and Mrs. Charles Thompson, Forrest Redding, Mr. and Mrs. Charles Hanna, Mr. and Mrs. Perry Million, Mr. and Mrs. John B. McCormick, Carl Johnson, Floyd Chapman, Mr. and Mrs. Warren Woods, Levi Furst, Edgar Fountain, Mr. and Mrs. Wilmer Downham, Leroy Robeson, Sr., Pauline Robeson and J. T. Downham.

When a gang like that gets together, anything can happen. On this trip the bus ran low on fuel and the engine died several miles from the nearest filling station. Ralph Reagon got out to take pictures of the bus. The driver got the engine started and left Ralph standing in the middle of the road with his camera. A native came along on his way to market with a car full of chickens. He moved some of the chickens and made room for Ralph and they trailed the bus for several miles until it stopped at a filling station.

Chicago Tour

Starting on August 22, 1949 about the same gang left for a three day bus trip to Chicago. On the way they visited the Jasper County FBCA, a large muck crop farm, the Co-op Fertilizer Plant at Schererville and the FB Milling Co-op at Hammond.

While in Chicago the group visited the Board of Trade, Swift and Company, the Illinois Farm Supply Company, the offices of the AFBF, the Museum of Science and Industry and other points of interest.

Those on the tour were: Mr. and Mrs. Clayton Million, Mr. and Mrs. Raymond Nicoll, Mr. and Mrs. Fred Rodkey, Mr. and Mrs. S. A. Wickard, Mr. and Mrs. Harold Frey, Mr. and Mrs. Claude Remaly, Mr. and Mrs. Joseph E. Peterson, Mr. and Mrs. John C. Peterson, Mr. and Mrs. Ralph Reagon, Artus Rodenbarger, Mrs. Miles T. Martin, Mr. and Mrs. Charles Hanna, Mr. and Mrs. John McCormick, Mr. and Mrs. Lowell Ward, Mr. and Mrs. Carl Johnson, Mr. and Mrs. Floyd Chapman, Mr. and Mrs. Levi Furst, Leroy Robeson, Sr., Miss Pauline Robeson, Mr. and Mrs. Wilmer Downham and John DeLaCroix.

Co-op Refinery Tour

On August 26, 1947 twenty six from Carroll County took a trip to visit the FB Co-op Refinery at Mt. Vernon. On the way the group visited the Co-op petroleum service station and seed plant at Crawfordsville, and the new facilities of the Vanderburg County FB Co-op at Evansville and the Posey County FB Co-op at Mt. Vernon. After a tour through the modern refinery they went in the rain and mud to visit some oil wells. After a shoe shine and a night in Evansville they returned home. On the way home the group visited the Washington-Scott County FBCA at Salem, the Jackson County FBCA at Seymour, and the Decatur County FBCA in Greensburg. Here one of the P & G Family Food stores was visited.

The last stop was at the National Farm Machinery Co-op branch at Shelbyville where corn pickers were made.

Those who made the trip were: Leroy Robeson, Sr., Levi Furst, John McCormick, Homer Wilson, Charles Hanna, Raymond Nicoll, Cleo Metzger, Turpie Martin, Ira Shafer, J. T. Downham, Carl Johnson, Orville Ward, Clark Metsger, Gale Crowell, Fred Rodkey, John C. Peterson, Morris Skiles, C. R. Clawson, David Wise, Joseph E. Peterson, Bill Ferguson, Bob McCarty, Harold Frey, Enos Berkshire, Artus Rodenbarger and John DeLaCroix.

Other Co-op Tours

In the fall of 1962 Dale Cleaver and Harold Greer went with Co-op manager Charles Hoover on a three day tour of Co-op facilities. They visited the Poultry Research Farm at Lafayette, the Co-op Seed Plant at Crawfordsville, the Nitrogen Plant at Terre Haute, and the Grain Terminal, Fertilizer Plant and Oil Blending Plant at Indianapolis.

Early in the spring of 1963 the IFBCA sponsored a tour of state facilities owned by the IFBCA. There were 64 from Districts 1, 3 and 5. On the trip from Carroll County were Mr. and Mrs. Lowell Spesard, Mr. and Mrs. Ray Ralston, Mr. and Mrs. James Riley, Jr., and Mr. and Mrs. Wayne Zinn.

Co-op Research Farm

On August 20, 1964 a group of Carroll County farmers made a one day tour of the Co-op Research Farm at Lexington, Illinois. They learned about the many experiments that are run each year on various feeding programs for swine and beef cattle. The Research Farm is owned and operated by about 30 state or regional Co-op Associations, including the IFBCA. The same group owns five other research farms where research is conducted on feeds for other kinds of livestock. This is the largest feed research group in the U.S.

Those who went on the tour were Robert Overholser, Richard Pulley, Charles V. Snider, Fritz Schnepf, Sr., Charles Dillman, Rex Hinkle, Jay Pearson, Carl Scott and Fred Luper.

On August 25, 1966 another group visiting the farm included John McCormick, George McIlrath, Sam Overholt, Emmett Frey, Junior Snider, Ned Long, Joe Myers, Dean Yoder, Wayne Langston, Bob Smith, Carl Scott, Dean Peterson and Jerry Myers.

Young Farmers Tour

Carroll County Young Farmers and their wives left by bus the morning of January 25, 1977 for a two-day tour of Chicago, Illinois. The tour was sponsored by the Carroll County Farm Bureau Cooperative Association and the Indiana Farm Bureau Cooperative Association.

Highlights of the tour were the Chicago Regional Port District, IFBCA Gateway Elevator, Hyde Park Cooperative Society, Inc., Chicago Mercantile Exchange and Chicago Board of Trade Building.

The group was stranded in South Bend Wednesday evening due to the blinding and drifting snow. They continued home the following day.

Attending were: Mr. and Mrs. Jerry Sibbitt, Mr. and Mrs. Joe Scott and Mr. and Mrs. Lynn Peters of Rt. 1, Bringhurst; Mr. and Mrs. Dick Pulley of Bringhurst; Mr. and Mrs. Larry Johnson and Mr. and Mrs. Jerry Hendress of Rt. 1, Camden; Mr. and Mrs. Bill Appleton, Mike Scott, Paul Marcellino and Jerry Sparks of Rt. 2, Camden; Mr. and Mrs. Robert Schock and John Reese of Camden; Mr. and Mrs. David Nickelsburg of Flora; Mr. and Mrs. Craig Martin, Mr. and Mrs. David Minich and Mr. and Mrs. Ed Johnson of Rt. 3, Logansport; Mr. and Mrs. Robert Hicks of Rt. 1, Flora; Larry Trapp of Rt. 2, Flora; Mr. and Mrs. Ed Wagoner and Mr. and Mrs. Charles Bordner of Rt. 1, Cutler; Mr. and Mrs. Gary Cleaver and Mr. and Mrs. Larry Davies of Rt. 4, Delphi; Mr. and Mrs. Blaine Brubaker, David Fassnacht, Louis Fassnacht and Richard Denhart, FB General Manager, of Rt. 3, Delphi. Ora Callahan was tour guide.

YOUTH ACTIVITIES

In April 1933 the CCFBCA paid the expenses of two young people as delegates from the county to attend a cooperative school at McCormick's Creek State Park at Spencer, Indiana. The manager of the association paid the expenses of a third delegate. The three delegates organized a discussion club which later became the Carroll County Rural Youth organization, the subject of Chapter IX.

For several years the County Cooperative Association helped pay expenses of delegates to cooperative schools. If a Township FB would pay the expenses of a delegate from their township the County FB and FBCA would each pay half the expenses of another delegate from the township. The association has helped pay expenses for special events, such as the RY Chorus trip to Seattle in 1952 to compete in a national contest at the American Farm Bureau Federation Convention.

The Co-op Association has supported 4-H Club work in many ways, including furnishing part of the food for the 4-H members at the annual CCFB picnic at the fair. The CCFBCA has purchased 4-H animals each year at the auction held at the 4-H Fair, and has helped pay expenses of delegates to the 4-H Club Roundup at Purdue and to other events.

Carroll County FBCA is also responsible for furnishing exhibit cards for 4-H members to use in identifying their exhibits at the County 4-H Fair. This is a state wide project, with the County Farm Bureau Co-op Associations throughout the state furnishing more than 25,000 exhibit cards each year for 4-H Club members.

American Institute of Cooperation

The American Institute of Cooperation is a non profit organization sponsored by the national farm organizations, the agricultural cooperatives, and the various educational groups. It is financed by voluntary contributions of the agricultural cooperatives.

Objectives of the Institute are to stimulate research and seek facts on cooperative activities, problems and purposes and to provide an opportunity for these to become generally available. Its only commodities are education and information.

The Institute was first chartered under the cooperative laws of the District of Columbia on January 22, 1925. In March 1945 it was rechartered under the laws of Pennsylvania and new headquarters were established on Independence Square in Philadelphia. The program was enlarged with a full-time staff and a year-round program. The Institute sponsors cooperative conferences or clinics. These meetings of state or regional scope usually last one or two days and give members, directors, managers and other cooperative personnel an opportunity to discuss their problems.

The Institute's program essentially is to assist cooperatives with their general administrative and educational problems through consultation with cooperatives executives, educators, and leaders in contingent fields of thought and to encourage research programs in the sociological, economic, and legal phases of cooperation.

The annual session of the Institute, usually held on the campus of a Land Grant College, has come to be an outstanding event in the cooperative world. The first session was held at the University of Pennsylvania in 1925. Sessions were held at Purdue University in 1955 and 1967.

Many state and local cooperatives send delegates to these meetings.

For several years the CCFBCA has helped pay the expenses of delegates to the American Institute of Cooperation.

Among those from Carroll County who have attended are:

1953 Carol Flora, Dwaine Ward

1955 Janet and Jalene Joyce, Murray Langston, Martin Rinehart

1956 Jim Riley

1961 James Scott

1962 Terry Snider, Charlotte Hanna

1963 Robert Nance

1964 David Minich

1965 Ivan Burkle

1966 Sally Pickart

1967 Frank Hodge, Jr.

1971 Debbie Trapp, Eddie Hanna

1972 Dottie Mears, Rick Ayres

1973 Mr. and Mrs. Atlee Oyler (Doris)

1974 Mr. and Mrs. Gary Penn (Jane)

1976 Mr. and Mrs. David Minich (Marilyn)

1977 Mr. and Mrs. Ron Slavens (Carmen)

1978 Mr. and Mrs. Mark Martin (Gayle)

ANNUAL MEETINGS

An Annual Meeting of the CCFBCA has been held during each winter for stockholders to elect directors and hear a report of business and activities for the past year. The program at the meeting usually has included entertainment and a speaker or some report of interest to stockholders.

For the last several years the meetings have been held in the evening at the Carroll High School, with a meal served in the school cafetorium. Members who attend have paid for part of the cost of the meal, and the balance has been paid by the association.

For a few years, all-day meetings were held at the old Armory, now the City Building, in Delphi, and a meal was furnished at noon. The records show that 200 meals were served in 1948 at a cost of $134.86 for food; in 1949, 500 were served at a cost of $204.65; and in 1950 the cost was $266.43 for 650 people. At that time coffee cost 50 cents per gallon, hot dogs

234 • CARROLL COUNTY RURAL ORGANIZATIONS

Directors of the Carroll County Farm Cooperative Association, Inc., are shown at the 52nd Annual Stockholders Meeting held on January 9, 1980 at Carroll Consolidated High School Cafetorium, listed by township and position on board. From left, seated: Roy Slavens, Jefferson, vice president; Robert Ayres, Democrat, secretary; Atlee Oyler, Monroe; Jack Moss, Burlington. Standing: Hershel Trapp, Jackson; Jerry Hendress, Carrollton; Arthur Fassnacht, Rock Creek-Liberty; Gary Hufford, Clay; Gary Cleaver, Deer Creek; Ernest Minich, Washington, president; Robert Ross, Madison; Ronald Slavens, Adams; Carl Mays, director at large. James White, Tippecanoe was not present.

40 cents per pound, ham 90 cents per pound, doughnuts 35 cents per dozen, buns from 18 to 25 cents per dozen, milk four and one half cents per half pint and ice cream sandwiches were nine cents each. One year 18 dill pickles cost 75 cents.

Reports presented at annual meetings show that total sales of about $103 million have ranged from a low of about $80,000 per year in 1933 and 1934 to a high of $10,600,478 in 1976. Total net savings of about $2 million varied from a high of $225,051 in 1976 to a loss of $81,915 in 1979. Stockholders own more than $1 million in common stock which has been issued as patronage dividends. A total of more than $700,000 has been given to stockholders in cash for patronage dividends, interest on stock and redemption of common stock.

Net worth has increased from the original $70 invested by the County and Township FB organizations to $1,294,865 in 1979. Total assets were $3,462,905 in 1979. This included an investment of more than $1 million in other cooperatives, more than $1 million in land, buildings and equipment in the county and $1.3 million in inventories and other current assets.

CARROLL COUNTY FARM BUREAU CO-OPERATIVE ASSOCIATION

OFFICERS

President:

Wm. Lee Henderson	1927
Claude R. Wickard	28-33
Lloyd Beard	34
Artus Rodenbarger	35
S. A. Wickard	36-42
Joseph E. Peterson	43-51
John B. McCormick	52-57
Gardner Martin	58-61
Charles T. Black	62-63
Estal Mullin	64-65
Charles Hanna	66-67
Eldon D. Robeson	68

Captain Stubby and the Buccaneers at the Annual Meeting of the Carroll County Farm Bureau Cooperative Association at Delphi, February 16, 1950.

CHAPTER VIII — FARM BUREAU COOPERATIVE ASSOCIATION

Charles Von Snider	69-70	
Leo Bowman	71-76	
J. Ernest Minich	77	

Secretary:

Mary Kerlin	1927-34
John C. Peterson	35-36
Burton D. Honan	37
Clarence Frey	38
Oren Eikenberry	39-40
Walter Barnhart	41-42
Miles T. Martin	43-44
John B. McCormick	45-51
Russell E. Craig	52-56
Earl Powell	57-60
Robert E. Ayres	61

Vice President:

Obe Campbell	1928-30
J. W. Eikenberry	31-32
Lloyd Beard	33
Arthur Hildebrand	34
Oren Eikenberry	35-37
Miles T. Martin	38
Jake F. Harness	39-40
Oren Eikenberry	41-42
S. A. Wickard	43-53
Clayton Million	54-55
Earl Powell	56
Gardner Martin	57
Mark Garrison	58
James L. White	59
Rex Hinkle	60-61
Estal Mullin	62-63
Charles Hanna	64
J. T. Downham	65
Rex Hinkle	66
Eldon D. Robeson	67
Charles Von Snider	68
Leo Bowman	69-70
J. Ernest Minich	71-76
Roy Slavens	77

Manager:

Wm. Lee Henderson	1928-Jan. 43
Wayne Hiatt	Feb. 43-Sept. 44
John DeLaCroix	Oct. 44-June 50
Myron Beesley	June 50-Sept. 51
Jay L. Small	Oct. 51-May 58
Charles Hoover	May 58-Mar. 66
James Keller	Mar. 66-Oct. 70
Richard L. Denhart	Oct. 70-Nov. 79
David Gingerich	Dec. 79

DIRECTORS

Adams Township:

George W. Peterson	1927-31
A. D. Moore	32-37
Asa Cree	38-39
Charles Tansey	40-47
Clayton Million	48-54
Gale Crowell	55-63
Douglas Million	64-66
Raymond Nicoll	67-78
Ronald Slavens	79-

Burlington Township:

Clarence Stout	1927-31
Clyde Langston	32-33
Jake F. Harness	34-41
Joe Snyder	42-43
Fred Rodkey	44-57
Rex Hinkle	58-66
Marion Langston	67-69
Jack Moss	70

Carrollton Township:

Jesse McCain	1927
Monroe Meade	28-29
Wm. Wingard	30-31
Bert McCain	32-33
S. A. Wickard	34-53
John Billings	54-55
Robert McCain	56-63
Charles Dillman	64-66
Leo Bowman	67-78
Jerry Hendress	79

Clay Township:

Frank Redenbacher	1927-30
Lloyd Beard	31-34
Clarence Frey	35-38
Walter Barnhart	39-42
Harold Frey	43-56
Walter Barnhart	57-58
Kenneth Frey	59-64
John Burkle	65-73
Marion Ward	74-76
Gary Hufford	77

Deer Creek Township:

Andrew Gerbens	1927-31
Miles T. Martin	32-41
Joseph E. Peterson	42-51
Earl Newell	52-53
Earl Powell	54-60
Charles T. Black	61-78
Gary Cleaver	79

Democrat Township:

Artus Rodenbarger	1927-35
Hal R. Shafer	36-37

Charles Thompson	38-47
Artus Rodenbarger	48-49
Dennis Porter	50-51
Claude Zook	52
Truman Plank	53-59
Robert Ayres	60

Jackson Township:

Arthur Ritchey	1927-30
Earl Chapman	31-34
Ira Robeson	35-36
Coy C. Shanks	37-40
S.S. Yost	41-44
John L. Witter	45-48
Charles Sanderson	49-52
Gardner Martin	53-61
Charles Nance	62-67
Harold Johnson	68-70
Lee Reppert	71-72
Herschel Trapp	73

Jefferson Township:

C. B. Million	1927-28
Lawrence Landis	29-31
Charles Crook	32-33
Herbert Million	34-35
Frank Hawn	36
W. G. Million	37-39
Leon Kasten	40-41
W. G. Million	42-45
Lawrence Fry	46-47
Dean Mills	48-49
Ralph Goslee	50-51
John Burke	52-57
Charles Hanna	58-68
Roy Slavens	69

Madison Township:

Obe Campbell	1927-30
Mat Hanrahan	31-32
Harry Maxwell	33-34
Burton D. Honan	35 38
Fred Hannell	39-42
John B. McCormick	43-58
Mark Porter	59-62
Thomas Elston	63-70
Mark Porter	71-72
Robert Ross	73

Monroe Township:

Elmer Kuns	1927
J. W. Eikenberry	28-32
Oren Eikenberry	33-42
Carl Johnson	43-50
Mark Garrison	51-58
Delbert Eikenberry	59-61
Charles Von Snider	62-70

Terry L. Myer	71-73
Atlee Oyler	74

Rock Creek Township:

Leon Kasten	1927-28
S. A. Wasson	29
Arthur Hildebrand	30-34
Fred C. Martin	35-37
Walter Ringer	38-41
Paul Gregg	42
Enos Berkshire	43-55
Estal Mullin	56-65
Harold Allread	66-71
Arthur E. Fassnacht	72

Tippecanoe Township:

Wm. Lee Henderson	1927-28
Charles Ginn	29-30
C. R. Clawson	31-48
Russell E. Craig	49-56
James L. White	57-59
James Riley	60-62
Robert Scott	63-68
Raymond Zink	69-71
James L. White	72

Washington Township:

Earl A. Downham	1927
Charles O'Donnell	28-30
A. A. Newer	31-38
Leroy Robeson Sr.	39-54
John T. Downham	55-65
Eldon D. Robeson	66-68
J. Ernest Minich	69

Director at Large:

Claude R. Wickard	1928-34
Arthur R. Mullin	35-36
Loyd E. Zook	37-38
Monroe Meade	39-42
Miles T. Martin	43-44
John C. Peterson	45-51
Clarence L. Cleaver	52-54
Clayton Million	55-58
Carl Johnson	59-61
Junior F. Snider	62
Marion Langston	63-64
Junior F. Snider	65-68
Charles Hanna	69-71
Meredith Ayres	72-77
Gene Jennings	78-79
Carl Mays	80

When the Carroll County Farm Bureau Co-op Association was Incorporated June 6, 1927, the Carroll County Farm Bureau and each of the 13 township organizations purchased a $5 share of common stock, making a total of $70 capital for the new organiza-

CHAPTER VIII — FARM BUREAU COOPERATIVE ASSOCIATION • 237

tion. Additional operating capital was provided by borrowing money from the local banks using as security, limited liability bonds signed by farmers in the county. 305 signed for $100 or more and each was issued a $5 share of common stock. 34 others signed for less than $100, making a total of 339 in the following list:

Deane Adams
A. R. Aiken
B. W. Aiken
Guy Aiken
Chas. Albaugh
Willard Albaugh
John F. Allen
Chas. E. Armstrong
Frank Armstrong
Lanty E. Armstrong
Vern D. Avery
F. C. Ayres
Jos. Balkema
Ockle Barber
Frank Barnhart
M. A. Barnhart
J. Ren Bates
Jesse Beard
John Beard
Lloyd Beard
Jesse Benner
W. E. Blackwell
E. W. Bowen & Son
Walter E. Bowen
Roy Bowman
John O. Brown
Olaf K. Brown
Carl J. Buck
Obe Campbell
W. M. Campbell
I. Caughell
Earl L. Chapman
Wm. S. Clauser
Port Chissom
C. R. Clawson
Fred Clawson
Glae Clawson
Harry Clawson
O. E. Clawson
Clarence Cleaver
L. R. Coble
Roy E. Coble
Allen Cornell
Newell Cox
C. C. Cook
Eli Craig
Jesse C. Craig
Russell Craig

Albert Cree
Claude Cripe
Daniel Cripe
O. D. Cripe
Chas. E. Crook
Elliot Crowell
Lewis G. Crowel
Wilbur Crowell
Jesse Daniels
Thurman Davis
W. E. Davis
L. D. Dellinger
L. D. Dickinson
Raymond L. Dillman
Wilbur Doolittle
Earl Douglas
Wm. M. Douglas
Earl A. Downham
Lloyd O. Duff
G. E. Eaton
Chas. A. Eikenberry
J. W. Eikenberry
Oren Eikenberry
Albert Ellis
Chas. R. Fellows
O. D. Ferguson
H. C. Fincher
Joe Fincher
Floyd E. Fisher
Geo. D. Fisher
Melvin Fisher
Arvel Flora
Carl F. Flora
Clarence Forgey
Noah Fouts & Son
Taylor Fouts
W. C. Fouts
Daniel Fox
Clarence Frey
Harold Frey
Russell Frye
Frank E. Galloway
Omer Gangloff
Charles Gard
Roy Garrison
Andrew Gerbens
Nelson Giles
G. W. Gillam

John H. Gingrich
Lawrence Gingrich
Charles G. Ginn
Wm. H. Ginn
F. S. Girard
B. A. Goslee
Bert Goslee
Ralph Goslee
Wm. M. Goslee
C. T. Graham
L. C. Grimm
Parks D. Groninger
Geo. T. Guard
Larry Gruber
Guckien Bros.
Emmitt Guckien
Wm. H. Guckien
Carl Hanna
R. V. Hanna
Chas. Hannell
Fred Hannell
Mat Hanrahan
Jake F. Harness
J. M. Harrison
R. M. Harter
Bert Hayes
Robert L. Hedde
Offa C. Hendrix
Wm. Lee Henderson
Fred Hershberger
John Hicks
Arthur Hildebrand
Earl Hildebrand
A. L. Hiner
Doctor O. Hill
Thaddeus Hinkle
Albert Holloway
R. H. Holmes
Burton D. Honan
C. V. Hoover
Wilford Hufty
J. C. Humes
Z. J. Humrickhouse
Geo. A. Hunt
John V. Hurley
Frank Imler
W. B. Ireland
Martin H. Irmeger
Reed Jackson
D. C. Jenkins
Carl B. Jones
Charles W. Jones
Howard L. Jones
Ralph Jones
Floyd M. Johns
Harry Johns
Carl Johnson

Clarence Johnson
Clyde R. Johnson
Edgar Johnson
Leon H. Kasten
John L. Kennard
Almon Kingery
Carl Kingery
Irvin Kingery
Albert Kuhns
Raymond L. Kuns
Ellis Kuzmaul
E. P. Landes
Isaac N. Landes
Lawrence Landes
H. W. Lane
W. H. Lane
Ardis Landis
Chas E. Landis
Clyde Langston
Frank O. Lantz
Oscar Leatherman
A. L. Lesh
Ira Leslie
W. E. Logan
Fred Luper
Frank Lybrook
Ralph Maggart
Chas. F. Martin
Fred C. Martin
Miles T. Martin
Roy P. Martin
Turpie E. Martin
Walter Martin
Chester Maxwell
Harry Maxwell
H. R. Maxwell
Moore H. Maxwell
Sam M. Maxwell
Burt McCain
Jesse McCain
Roll McCain
John R. McCouch
Chas. A. McCracken
Wm. McVay
Monroe Meade
Ben Metzger
E. A. Metzger
Henry M. Metzger
Herschel Metzger
Bruce Milburn
Bert F. Million
C. B. Million
Herbert Million
Paul Million
Robert H. Million
W. G. Million

Wm. A. Million
John H. Mourer
Arthur R. Mullin
C. R. Mullin
Herman C. Mullin
Wm. O. Mullin
Harley A. Mummert
Glen I. Musselman
Royce Myer
Earl B. Newell
A. A. Newer
Earl Newman
John Nichter
Chas. O'Donnell
Henry Otten
D. I. Payton
Henry R. Peter
John A. Pearson
Geo. W. Peterson
Jas. V. Peterson
T. O. Peterson
Wm. F. Peterson
Chas. J. Phillips
Rhoda M. Piatt
Percy Plank
Otto Platt
Bert Pullen
C. V. Quinn
Frank Redenbacher
Elmer G. Reiff
B. M. Rice
Roy R. Richter
W. F. Riley

C. R. Rinehart
Walter Ringer
Arthur Ritchey
Eli C. Ritchey
Roberson Bros.
Webb Robeson
Leroy Robeson
Artus Rodenbarger
Frank Roskuski
Harrison D. Roth
Perry Rule
B. F. Rush
Ray Rush
C. M. Sanderson
Evan Sanderson
Glen M. Schock
Orvil Schock
W. T. Schockley
Everett Scott
Ollie C. Seward
Fred Shaefer
Hal R. Shafer
Albert Shaffer
R. L. Shankland
John U. Shanks
N. B. Sharp
J. M. Sheets
John Sheetz
Ora F. Shirar
J. A. Shirk
Clarence Shultheis
Marvin Shultheis
Guy Sibbitt

A. Simons
Ed Simons
Virgil L. Sink
Geo. E. Sites
Sam G. Sites
Addison E. Smith
A. W. Smith
Fred C. Smith
Glen L. Smith
Howard L. Smith
Lyman Smith
Milo Smith
S. D. Smith
Earl Snider
F. S. Snoeberger
Tony Snoeberger
Truman Snoeberger
Henry A. Snyder
Amel Spring
Glen H. Stair
Floyd L. Stephen
Frank Stephen
Riley Stephen
E. E. Stephens
O. E. Stewart
Clarence Stout
Erny Swan
Harry A. Temple
John Thurston
Geo. Todd
W. H. Todd
Edward P. Troxel

James Tyner
R. N. VanNatta
Roy Vanscoy
Fred Voorhees
John Wagner
Ross F. Wagoner
Walter Wagoner
W. E. Wakeland
J. E. Walker
J. A. Warden
S. A. Wasson
R. W. Whetzel
G. L. Whistler
Claude R. Wickard
S. A. Wickard
Roy Wilburn
Orville Wilson
Wm. M. Wingard
L. N. White
Andrew Wise
Carl Wise
Chas. A. Wise
Marvin Wise
Bert Wolf
I. L. Wolf
B. F. Wray
J. E. Yarian
Roy Yeakley
Samuel Yeakley
Cloyd Yerkes
Silas S. Yost
Frank Zook

CCFB CO-OP ASSOCIATION, INC.

Year	Sales	Net Savings	Net Worth
1929	$ 90,275	$ 2,301	$ 2,301
*1930	121,046	6,752	8,953
1931	102,832	6,806	15,036
1932	81,261	4,481	17,117
1933	80,861	6,467	22,365
1934	104,736	7,809	28,369
1935	155,617	6,719	35,931
1936	196,625	9,577	42,787
1937	253,708	11,864	57,939
1938	230,132	15,595	71,059
1939	208,632	10,207	72,005
1940	210,234	10,436	79,179
1941	241,186	13,228	91,568
1942	263,057	24,720	107,580
1943	336,889	24,497	124,481
1944	390,992	28,794	144,095
1945	485,915	34,209	186,443
1946	932,940	71,357	248,916
1947	1,236,132	53,546	288,346
1948	1,382,737	72,566	342,137
1949	1,427,908	50,519	410,276
1950	1,284,450	4,673	397,956
1951	1,449,308	30,401	428,943
1952	1,560,331	69,982	486,401
1953	1,528,781	67,149	549,266
1954	1,674,663	88,371	639,283
1955	1,620,830	91,517	719,360
1956	1,548,657	67,774	770,930
1957	1,705,472	58,106	811,324
1958	1,972,050	42,503	865,657
1959	1,945,756	44,683	892,805
1960	2,059,918	9,310	883,898
1961	2,218,185	40,860	910,382
1962	2,434,758	11,826	897,697
1963	2,505,077	− 3,246	878,367
1964	2,238,820	41,158	897,809
1965	1,982,376	−14,458	853,068
1966	2,360,849	12,206	850,956
*1967	1,561,077	23,621	868,022
1968	2,196,157	4,844	850,453
1969	2,365,800	−91,136	758,755
1970	3,021,393	−23,524	734,700
1971	3,177,229	−10,715	723,988
1972	3,137,115	16,109	740,097
1973	3,823,952	68,325	808,421
1974	6,143,951	260,141	1,040,851
1975	8,041,114	225,051	1,171,021
1976	10,660,478	275,970	1,396,905
1977	9,089,260	185,285	1,445,334
1978	9,065,056	−53,322	1,380,327
1979	10,137,825	−81,915	1,294,865
Total	103,450,403	1,933,999	

*Because of changes in the Fiscal Year the figures for 1930 were 11 months and for 1967 nine months.

CHAPTER IX

RURAL YOUTH

FIRST TRAINING SCHOOL

In the summer of 1933, the Indiana Farm Bureau Cooperative Association and the Central States Cooperative League sponsored eight training schools in Indiana, and asked the County Farm Bureau Cooperative Associations to send students. The Carroll County Farm Bureau Cooperative Association responded by sending three young people: Vivian Henderson, Helen Plank and John C. Peterson to the school, held at McCormick's Creek State Park from June 4 to 10. There were ten students from District Three, nine from District Five, and two from the state office, making a total of 21 students.

Instructors were Anthony Lehner from the Indiana Farm Bureau Cooperative Association, and Edwin C. Palmer and A. W. Warinner from the Central States Cooperative League. Guest speakers from the IFBCA included I. H. Hull, general manager; V. S. Everson, manager of the Co-op Oil Plant and C. H. LaSelle. Other speakers were Mrs. Lillie Scott, S & E Director for the IFB; Mrs. Austin Cochran, S & E Director from District Three FB and C. S. Masterson representing the Indiana Farm Bureau.

Martha Ritchhart, one of the students from the Indiana Farm Bureau Cooperative Association office, was in charge of recreation. She became known by many people in Indiana as "Susie," a nickname given to her at the camp.

The program for the week was a study of the Cooperative Movement and how it affected business and the lives of people. Much time was spent in studying the History of Cooperatives, and the principles which led to their success or failure. Students who attended the school gained a much better understanding of how cooperatives could help people help themselves, and some students spent the rest of their lives working for and promoting cooperatives.

COUNTY STUDY CLUB

The three from Carroll County who attended the Training School gave reports in every township at Farm Bureau and other meetings, and in the fall of 1933, working with officers of the Farm Bureau and Farm Bureau Co-op Association, organized a Young

Vivian Henderson, Martha "Susie" Ritchhart, and Helen Plank at the Co-op School at McCormicks Creek State Park in June 1933.

Peoples Cooperative Study Club in Carroll County. A meeting to make plans to organize the club was held at Camden on November 6. Farm Bureau chairmen and Co-op directors from each township were asked to bring young people from their township who might be interested in being members of the Study Club. About 50 people were present, including 26 young people. The program was explained, and anyone interested in helping organize the group was invited to come back for a meeting, which was held at Camden on November 27, 1933. The club was organized at that meeting and officers elected were: Charles T. Black, president; Lee O. Seward, vice president and Margaret Mabbitt, secretary treasurer.

Members of the nominating committee were: Fred Clawson, Edna Gerbens and Helen Caldwell. The constitution and by-laws were adopted as presented by a committee of Thomas Witter, Lee O. Seward and Loda McVay. The next regular meeting was held on December 21, 1933 at the library at Delphi with representatives from other county Study Clubs in the district.

Membership was open to anyone between the ages of 14 and 30 who was interested in learning more about cooperatives and willing to attend the regular meetings. There was no membership fee, and anyone who attended one of the early meetings and signed the constitution and by laws and pledged their support to the club was considered a charter member.

Those listed as charter members were: Robert Reiff, Loda McVay, Loris P. Stout, Raymond Huffer, Margaret Mabbitt, John McCain, Florence Allbaugh, Pauline Fouts, John Harvey Todd, Fred L. McCain, Dwight Beard, Irene DeWinton, Joseph E. Peterson, John C. Peterson, Earl Powell, George Martin, Gardner Martin, Charles T. Black, Edna Gerbens, Mr. and Mrs. Freeman Redding, Luella Simmons, Paul Snipes, Lionel Roll, Paul Miller, William Loman, Robert Bell, Charles M. Flora, Thomas Witter, Margaret Hunt, Myra Witter, Clara Belle Witter, Wilma Mae Sullivan, Everett Bowman, Leslie W. Chapman, Richard Hawn, Ruth Jenkins, Agatha Jenkins, Fred Clawson, Robert Eikenberry, Robert Ayres, Love Groninger, Hiram Martin, Truman Plank, Helen Plank, Vivian Henderson, Lee O. Seward, Helen Caldwell, Lawrence Johnson, Everett Chapman, Eva Chapman, Urban Newer, Virgil McFatridge, Lavon Johnson, Floyd Martin, J. T. Downham, Pauline Robeson, Elizabeth Hardy and Leonard Seward.

Educational material used at the meetings was primarily a study and discussion of the Farm Bureau Co-op Marketing and Purchasing program, and how it might be developed to better meet the needs of the rural community. The FBCA people believed that it was possible to have economic security in a land of plenty, and were convinced that the cooperative program was the most logical solution to many economic problems.

The club had regular meetings on the fourth Monday night of each month with an average attendance of about 50. The educational part of the program was a talk, usually by a member of the club, and sometimes by a prominent citizen of the county, or an employee of one of the cooperatives. Members in each township took their turn in providing entertainment, which included local talent programs and musical numbers, readings, plays, stunts and other features.

Recreation included folk games, and other forms of creative recreation which had been good enough to live through the years. An article written in 1935 stated: "This type of recreation fills the social and recreational needs of the young people of the community, without bringing them in contact with the degrading influences which accompany the highly commercialized forms of entertainment which have been prevalent in the community as a result of the fact that recreation and entertainment has been exploited for profit."

The members of the club were active in Farm Bureau and Extension projects. Several members were officers in township organizations, and some were 4-H leaders, and helped in many community projects.

District Study Clubs

Several counties organized Study Clubs and the Indiana Farm Bureau Cooperative Association prepared lesson material to use in the meetings. Representatives from the county clubs met on a district basis to study the material, and then gave the lesson at the county meeting. This made it possible to study in much more detail about cooperatives, and their problems and possibilities. A most interesting series of lessons concerned the modern cooperatives which had their beginning on Toad Lane in Rochdale, England.

The Rochdale Pioneers

The basic principle of people working together to help themselves and each other is as old as civilization. However, most activities were on a small scale, and usually for a short period of time. The first venture, which resulted in a permanent and successful business, took place in Rochdale, England, in 1844. A group of poor weavers, 27 men and one woman, decided to own their own store in order to supply themselves with quality products at a fair price. Many such attempts had failed during the past 200 years. In fact, two attempts to start a store in Rochdale had recently failed.

The weavers spent a year studying the problem and saving their money, and on October 24, 1844 registered under the title of "Rochdale Society of Equitable Pioneers." The members had accumulated $5 each, making a total of $140 and spent half of it to rent a room and buy fixtures. With the remaining $70 they bought a small supply of necessities, such as flour, butter, sugar, oatmeal and candles. The store was opened on December 21, 1844 on a street named Toad Lane. At the end of the first year membership had increased to 74 members, with a total of $3,500 in sales and a savings of $160 for the year.

At the end of 1857 the 13th year, there were 1,850 members with a total sales for the year of $400,000 and a savings of $27,000. Total sales for the 13 years was $1,500,000 with a savings of $100,000 of which $75,000 had been reinvested in the business.

By 1863 the Society was operating nine stores, and 426 similar societies had been organized. Forty-five of the societies joined together and organized the Cooperative Wholesale Society (CWS) which, ten years later, started buying and building factories to supply products for the stores. CWS grew and became one of the largest businesses in England. The idea spread, and cooperatives now do a large share of the business in many countries throughout the world.

Rochdale Principles

A record of success like that must have a reason, and that reason can be found in the principles used by the 28 weavers when they organized their new business. By spending a year studying the causes of failure in previous attempts of this kind, the weavers arrived at a set of principles which, with only minor changes, have been used by most successful cooperatives.

Open Membership

Membership was open to anyone, regardless of sex, race, creed or color. This was a new idea, since in most previous and some later attempts membership was limited to those who were members of another group.

Membership was also voluntary. No one was forced to join the society, nor were members required to use it for all purchases after they did join. Many other attempts to organize cooperatives have failed because the organizers depended on a contract with members for business.

Democratic Control

Each member had one vote, regardless of the number of shares of stock he held. This made the organization controlled by everyone, and not by just a few who might acquire a majority of the stock. It placed more emphasis on the value of a person, and less on the value of money.

Limited Interest on Capital

The going rate of interest was paid on capital invested by members. Thus capital was paid a fair wage the same as labor.

Distribution of Savings

At the end of each year savings were distributed to each member on the basis of the amount of business he had done with the Society. That was the first time the principle had been used. In most previous attempts, savings had been distributed to stockholders, according to the amount of stock each owned. This new principle of giving savings to patrons on the basis of patronage has been a fundamental principle for nearly all successful cooperatives. One variation developed in Denmark, known as the Danish Plan, used savings for some community project which would be of benefit to everyone.

Market Price

Merchandise was sold at the going market price. Many Co-ops have failed because they have cut price, either to get more business, or to more quickly get the benefit of savings. This has led to price wars and often to the failure of a co-op.

Cash Sales

All sales were for cash. Many co-ops have failed because sales on credit reduced their operating capital, and made it necessary to borrow so much money that the lending agency eventually told them how to run their business.

Records and Audits

The co-op kept accurate and complete records, and had them audited each year. The need for records in a co-op was greater than in an ordinary business. Since a person could become a stockholder either by buying a $5 share of stock, or by allowing his earnings to accumulate until he earned a share, it was necessary to keep accurate records for every customer in order to determine his share of earnings at the end of the year.

Depreciation and Reserves

As in any other business, the equipment depreciated, and part of the cost had to be charged to each years business in order to provide accurate records. There was no guarantee that there would be earnings every year, so it was necessary to keep a reserve for bad years.

Education

A primary reason for the success of these societies was the program of education of members and the general public. Members needed to know that competitors would sell some things at a lower price to keep the new store from doing business. They needed to know about the long-term benefits of dealing with their own store. The public needed to be informed about the program so that new members could be added to the list. All members were kept well informed about their business by giving them financial reports, and by holding regular meetings for members. At first the members met every week. Later this was changed to a meeting every three months, a practice still followed by many of the Societies. There was more emphasis on training for employees as the number of employees increased.

Neutrality

By making membership available to anyone, it was necessary for the Society to remain neutral on questions not related to the business that might be of concern to special groups. The Societies did not get involved in political discussions or other matters on which there would be a difference of opinion among the members.

CO-OP SUMMER SCHOOLS

Camp Tecumseh 1934

In the summer of 1934 the Indiana Farm Bureau Cooperative Association conducted about 25 schools in Indiana for young people interested in learning more about cooperatives. One was held at Camp Tecumseh from September 9 to 15, with students from the following counties: Carroll, 29; Clinton, 12; Howard, 12 and Cass, 3. There were several instructors including: Anthony Lehner, C. S. Masterson, Glenn Thompson, Darwin Bryan, Mary Wible, Martha Ritchhart and several other officials from the Indiana Farm Bureau Cooperative Association. Sunday School was taught by Dr. Hutchinson from the Christian Theological Seminary, Chicago.

Subjects discussed at the school included: "Organization and Administration of Cooperatives," "Why Cooperative Education," "Cooperative Marketing," "Credit Unions," "Fundamentals of Taxation," "Aids for Agriculture in Its Present Crisis," and "The Economic Depression, Its Cause and Remedy."

Students attending from Carroll County were: Robert Reiff, Maxine Hanna, Wayne Langston, Loris Stout, Esther Huffer, Florence Allbaugh, Ruth Beard, Frances Barnhart, Earl Powell, Gardner Martin, Mary Studebaker, Irene DeWinton, Joseph E. Peterson, John C. Peterson, Paul Miller, Gwendolyn Unger, Myra Witter, Doris Wagoner, Harold Newman, Richard Hawn, Martha Duff Henderson, Ruth Jenkins, Keith Sink, Love Groninger, Helen Plank, Vivian Henderson, Lavon Johnson, Lee O. Seward and Mrs. Lloyd Beard.

Bethany Park 1935

About 21 schools were conducted in Indiana in the summer of 1935. These were sponsored by the Indiana Farm Bureau and affiliated organizations, including the Indiana Farm Bureau Cooperative Association, Indiana Wool Growers, Indiana Grain Producers, Co-op Creameries and Co-op Livestock Marketing organizations.

There were 29 from Carroll and three from Jasper County who attended a school at Bethany Park from August 4 to 10, 1935. Each Township Farm Bureau organization paid the expenses of one student from the township and the County Farm Bureau and Farm Bureau Cooperative Association each paid one half the expenses for a second student.

Those from Carroll County who attended were: Ethel Leslie, Wm. Martin, Charles Nance, Opal Smith, Rosella Shanklin, Cora Belle Pearson, Emma Metzger, Dwight Beard, Margaret Lucy Martin, Raymond Leatherman, John C. Peterson, Fay Humes, Barbara Rodenbarger, Lester Yost, Ellen Louise Robeson, Jane Witter, Doris Wagoner, Mrs. John Witter, Harold

Carroll County delegates and instructors at the Co-op School at Bethany Park, August 4 to 10, 1935.

Kasten, Richard Hawn, Helen Zook, Lucille Clawson, Edith Myer, Lucyle Jenkins, Donald Mullin, Isabell Blickenstaff, Vivian Henderson, Irene Downham, and Lavon Johnson.

Bethany Park was located 25 miles southwest of Indianapolis, so arrangements had to be made for transportation. The CCFBCA furnished a truck to haul equipment, clothing and bedding. Individuals who furnished cars were: Clayton Million, John Witter, Ross Wagoner, Gardner Martin, Myron Jenkins, Leon Kasten, Robert Hedde, Frank Hedderick, Wm. Lee Henderson and Fred Clawson. A letter sent to students before the school gave this information: "Students will need to bring their necessary toilet articles, blankets, sheets and pillows, everyday clothing, notebook and pencil, and any musical instrument (except piano) they might play. There is also a small lake for boating and swimming, so a swimming suit might come in handy." Those who attended the camp reported that one student lost his bathing suit while swimming in the afternoon, and had to stay in the lake until after dark.

EXTENSION AND FARM BUREAU

During 1933, Older Youth Clubs were organized by the Extension Service in Blackford and Tipton counties for education and recreation. Young Peoples Cooperative Study Clubs sponsored by FB and FBCA similar to the one in Carroll County were also organized in several other counties.

In the fall of 1935, the State 4-H Club office at Purdue University inaugurated a service for out-of-school young people, 18 to 28 years of age, and several "Older Rural Youth" and "Young Adult" clubs were organized throughout the state.

Soon after this service was announced by the State 4-H Club office, the Department of Education of the Indiana Farm Bureau offered to cooperate in sponsoring clubs. The offer was accepted, and County Agents and Farm Bureau leaders worked with rural young people in organizing clubs all over Indiana.

Summer Camps and Schools

In 1936 an Older Youth Camp was held in each of the ten Farm Bureau districts, sponsored by the State 4-H Club office, and the Department of Education of the Indiana Farm Bureau. In 1937 five camps were held, one camp for each two Farm Bureau districts. On June 22 and 23, 1938 a state school for Older Youth was held at Purdue as a substitute for the District Camp. This was held at the same time as the Tenth Annual Rural Leadership School for Adults.

At the Second Annual Rural Leadership School for Youth at Purdue from June 19 to 23, 1939 there were 272 Rural Youth members who attended from 64 counties. Members attending from Carroll County were: Ray Robertson, Eldon Robeson, David Mullin, Cora Belle Pearson, Joan Rodenbarger and Margaret Lucy Martin.

The school at Purdue was held each year until 1952, when a State Rural Youth Camp was substituted for the school.

Battle Ground 1936

The camp for District Three was held at Battle Ground on August 9 to 15, 1936. There were 86 students from the following counties: Jasper, 12; Benton, 10; Clinton, 14; White, 11; Carroll, 14; Cass, 12, Newton, 11; and Tippecanoe, 2. Each student paid $7 for a room and meals for the six days.

Those who attended from Carroll County were: Billy Peterson, Opal Smith, Florence Allbaugh, Paul Ward, Betty Bell, Joseph E. Peterson, John C. Peterson, Ellen Louise Robeson, Richard Hawn, Lee Stair, Lucyle Jenkins, Opal Mullin, Mrs. Cleon Smith, Mabel Snoeberger and Pauline Robeson.

One student attending from Benton County was Roy Slavens, who later moved to Carroll County, and has been active in many organizations in the county.

The program was under the direction of M. K. "Si" Derrick, Director of the Department of Education for the Indiana Farm Bureau. He was assisted by Albert Avery, Audra Swift, and Lymon Caton, as well as several officials from the various organizations affiliated with the Indiana Farm Bureau. F. L. McReynolds of Purdue was in charge of recreation.

District Organization

During 1937 and 1938 the county clubs in each of the 10 Farm Bureau districts organized a District Club. The Third District Club was organized at a meeting held at Delphi on December 17, 1937. Officers elected were: John C. Peterson of Carroll County, president; Joe Strole of Newton County, vice president and Odetta Blake of Jasper County, secretary treasurer. District meetings were held four times each year. Five of the eight counties in District Three had active clubs.

First State Meeting

The first state meeting for members of Older Youth Clubs was held at Purdue University as a part of the Annual Agricultural Conference in January 1937. In a few years it became the largest state event for Rural Youth with an average attendance of about 500. Beginning in 1938, and for several years, a feature of the meeting was the Prairie Farmer-WLS Dinnerbell radio program which was broadcast directly from the university. During the program, awards to Rural Youth Clubs were announced.

Older Youth Council

Officers of the 10 Farm Bureau District Youth Clubs were called the Older Youth Council. During 1938 the Council met two times at Purdue and four times at Indianapolis. Plans were made for delegates from the ten district and seventy county clubs to meet at Indianapolis at the same time as the Indiana Farm Bureau Convention to organize a state club.

INDIANA RURAL YOUTH

Two delegates from each county club met at Indianapolis on November 16, 1938 and decided to start a state organization. Officers elected were: George Doup, president; Vera Boys, vice president; Crystal Pritchett, secretary and Beverly Berninger, now of Delphi, treasurer. After some discussion, the delegates voted to name the new youth organization Indiana Rural Youth, and recommended that the counties use the name Rural Youth for their clubs. After the vote, someone noticed that the badges they were wearing read Indiana Rural Youth.

Cyrus L. "Rusty" Dyer, representing the Department of Education of the Indiana Farm Bureau, proudly admitted that he was so sure that the new organization would be named Indiana Rural Youth, that he had it printed on the badges.

Delegates voted to use the Department of Education of the Indiana Farm Bureau and the Agricultural Extension Service of Purdue as co-sponsors.

At the second annual meeting held at Indianapolis November 15, 1939 a constitution and by-laws were adopted. George Doup was re-elected president, and the number of state officers was increased to include a second vice president who would also be program chairman. State dues were set at 10 cents per member for 1940. The state officers and the ten district presidents made up the Board of Directors which has continued to have regular meetings about six times each year.

Indiana was the third state to organize a State Club for Rural Youth and was the first state organization with a Board of Directors.

There has been a Rural Youth Club in every county in Indiana. Some have been continuous while others have disbanded and reorganized at a later date.

The business meeting of the Indiana Rural Youth is held each year at the same time and place as the annual Indiana Farm Bureau Convention. The Rural Youth business meeting, banquet and recreation has been separate from the general session of the IFB Convention.

Other regular annual events for the state organization are: State Day at Purdue in January, an Educational Tour in early spring, All Sports Day in June, and State Camp in July at the Hoosier 4-H Leadership Center at Lafayette.

Objectives

The following Objectives of Indiana Rural Youth were adopted during State Day at Purdue in January 1951:

1. To offer opportunities for mental, spiritual, social, and physical development.

2. To train young people for family, community, county, state, national, and international leadership and responsibility.

3. To analyze vocational fields so that a selection may be made to support a worthwhile and enjoyable life.

4. To develop a better understanding of social, economic and political affairs.

5. To develop self-expression and cooperation.

6. To develop habits of safe, healthful living, intelligent use of leisure time, and the desire to continue to learn.

7. To develop and maintain an interest in rural life.

Aims

The broad aims of Rural Youth are: Education, Recreation and Community Service. The more successful clubs are those who place equal emphasis on all three, and have a balanced program with something of interest for all members.

Education

Educational features includes talks by outside speakers or members on a wide variety of subjects including the many problems of government and of the individual in his business and social life. Educational tours include visits to businesses, historic sites or scenic areas.

Recreation

Recreational activities include parties, picnics, dinners, folk games, dancing and many kinds of sports. Many clubs have teams to compete with other clubs in baseball, basketball, volleyball, bowling and other sports.

Community Service

There is no limit to the community service activities of a Rural Youth Club. Members work on all kinds of projects with other organizations such as church, school, Farm Bureau, 4-H, FFA and FHA. Members help at county fairs and other activities in the county. Often they help raise money for a worthy cause by having a paper drive, bake sale, food stand or other activity.

In many counties the chairman of the Rural Youth was made a non-voting member of the Board of Directors of the County Farm Bureau, and the County Extension Committee.

Contests

Contests were established by the State Rural Youth Board of Directors as an incentive for County Rural Youth officers to use in building better county programs. Most of the contests have attractive awards sponsored by various interested organizations.

Contests for the clubs are as follows:

CITIZENSHIP, including many community service projects;

SAFETY, with emphasis on traffic safety;

NEWSLETTER, to each member;

SCRAPBOOK, a useful history of the club's activities;

TALENT FIND, to uncover talent in the club;

PUBLIC SPEAKING, to develop self-expression;

SPORTS, including bowling, volleyball, basketball and softball; and

MEMBERSHIP AND PUBLICITY.

Any Rural Youth member is eligible to enter the Exhibits Contest held each year at the State Day at Purdue in January. Ribbons are awarded to winners in several classes, including Hobby, Crafts, Home Art, Baking, Candy and Sewing exhibits.

A Barbecue Contest is also held each year during State Camp in July at the 4-H Leadership Center.

CARROLL COUNTY RURAL YOUTH ACTIVITIES

Following is a report of just a few of the activities of the Carroll County Rural Youth Club. It is not a complete report of all activities, but is a representative sample.

1945

There were 173 members in the CCRY in 1945, making it the largest club in Indiana.

On June 23, the County Rural Youth Club held a square dance at the Evan Sanderson farm. In August a square dance was held in the new barn built by Emerson Johns. There were 125 Rural Youth members present from Carroll and other counties, including Cass, Clinton, White and Hamilton.

For the meeting on September 24 members had a "Back to School" party at Delphi High School. Members dressed and acted like small children. They enjoyed Nursery Rhymes, a Spelling Bee, a Ciphering Match, a History Quiz, and threw paper wads. There was an abundant supply of licorice candy, chewing gum and bean shooting. Lois Martin, the teacher, paddled one of the larger boys. During recess they played "Drop the Hankie" and "Ring Around the Rosie."

Wayne Zinn and Kathleen Clawson sang songs, and Maxine Clawson recited a poem entitled "Patience."

Captains for the Spelling Bee were Dortha Wray and Ren C. Groninger. The champion speller was Deloris Rinehart.

Captains for the Ciphering Match were David Smith and Alice Grassmyer. The winner was Eileen Clawson.

1946

David Smith whistled and Gaylord Archibald sang at the Amateur Contest held at the Indiana State Fair in 1946. They were a part of the group representing the Third District which won first place in the State Contest.

Norma Deitz was selected by the County Rural Youth to be the Carroll County Farm Bureau Queen for 1946.

Rural Youth members helped conduct a Safety Lane on August 5, 6, and 7, sponsored by the FB Insurance Company.

1949

At the Rural Youth meeting in March 1949 members took part in a debate: "Should a young married couple live with their parents?" Those in the debate were: Elizabeth Mears, Eileen Zinn, Richard Mears, Eldon Robeson, Wilma Haslet and Jim Sharp. County Agent Howard McCarty was moderator.

Also, in 1949, the County Rural Youth purchased a new public address system with a 30 watt amplifier, two speakers, microphone and stand, and a two speed phonograph.

CHAPTER IX — RURAL YOUTH • 247

County Rural Youth who attended were: Elizabeth Mears, Eileen Zinn, Julie Smith, Kathleen Fife, Kenneth Yeakley, Kenneth Dietrick, Charles Dillman and Bobby Caldwell.

Rural Youth officers for 1950 who met at the home of president Glenn Brown to make plans for the year. Front row, left to right: Rosella Kerlin, assistant recreation leader; Sue Starkey, song leader; Elizabeth Mears, secretary and Kathleen Fife, reporter. Back row: George Downham, recreation; Kenneth Mears, treasurer; Richard Mears, recreation; Glenn Brown, president and Paul Seward, vice president.

1950

The Carroll County Rural Youth had a float in the Farmers Day Parade at the Indiana State Fair on September 7. They placed 14th in the contest.

On December 28, 1950 the club won second place in a contest sponsored by Radio Station WLS and was presented a silver award at the Dinnerbell Program at the Agricultural Conference at Purdue.

1951

The club had a food stand at Old Settlers at Delphi.

The first Square Dance Festival for Indiana was held at the Coliseum at the State Fair Grounds in Indianapolis on September 29, 1951. Those from Carroll

Rural Youth float at parade at Delphi, July 4, 1950.

Part of the Rural Youth group that entertained Tippecanoe, Jefferson and Adams Township Farm Bureaus at Pittsburg July 9, 1951. Front row, left to right: Helen Cleaver, Eileen Zinn, Julie Smith and Kathleen Fife. Back row: Charles Dillman, James Sharp, Kenneth Yeakley, Kenneth Dietrick, Robert Caldwell and Glenn Brown.

Levi Furst of Tippecanoe Township getting a lesson on how to stand correctly. The "Schoolmarm" is Bob Caldwell of Washington Township. This was part of a program by the county Rural Youth Club for a joint meeting at the Grange Hall in Pittsburg of the Tippecanoe, Adams and Jefferson Township Farm Bureaus on July 9, 1951.

The County RY Club furnished entertainment at several Township Farm Bureau meetings, including a joint meeting of Tippecanoe, Jefferson, and Adams Township Farm Bureaus held in the Tipwa Grange Hall at Pittsburg on July 9, 1951.

At the meeting of District Three Rural Youth on October 12, 1951 Elizabeth Mears from Carroll County was elected secretary treasurer of the district organization.

1952

Members of the club helped serve a Fish Fry at the County Soil Conservation District Annual Meeting.

Rural Youth officers elected to serve in 1952 were first row left to right: Geraldine Mullin, assistant secretary; Elizabeth Mears, assistant song leader; Kathleen Fife, secretary and Mrs. Miles Martin, adult leader. Back row: Charles Dillman, recreation leader; Bobby Caldwell, assistant recreation leader; Kenneth Yeakley, president; Bill Kuszmaul, treasurer and Kenneth Pyle, song leader. Officers not pictured were Mary Ellen Kempf, reporter and Jim Sharp, vice president.

Rural Youth members who helped at the Fish Fry at the Annual Carroll County Soil and Water Conservation District meeting at Flora January 24, 1952. Girls, left to right: Kathleen Fife, Helen Cleaver and Mary Louise Yeakley. Boys, left to right: Kenneth Yeakley, Bob Caldwell, Eldon Robeson, Kenneth Dietrich and Clyde Hanawalt.

Recently married Rural Youth couples, who attended the supper furnished by the Carroll County Farm Bureau at the REMC Auditorium in Delphi on January 28, 1952. Left to right: Mr. and Mrs. Clyde Hanawalt, Mr. and Mrs. Keith Mears, Mr. and Mrs. Glenn Brown, Mr. and Mrs. Joe Starkey.

On February 2, 1952 the club held a Square Dance as a part of their campaign which raised over $400 for the March of Dimes.

The big event for 1952 was the County Rural Youth Chorus and their trip to Seattle, reported later in this chapter.

The club also operated a food stand at Old Settlers in August.

1953

The County Rural Youth Club won first place in the 1952 Scrap Book Contest and the award was made at the Social and Educational Conference at Indianapolis.

Members of the Carroll County Rural Youth Club served coffee to some of the 114 people who visited a Dairy Caravan at the REMC Auditorium in Delphi, sponsored by the dairies in Carroll County, on February 6.

Other activities of the club included helping with the Rural Life Sunday program at the Methodist Church in Delphi on May 31; helping park cars at the State Farm Management Tour at the Ralph Sullivan farm on July 27; and going with others from District Three on a two-day bus tour to Detroit in July.

The Three J's, Janet, Jalene and Joetta Joyce, won first place in a contest at the County Entertainment Festival at the 4-H Fair. Several members participated in the Pageant at Old Settlers for the Centennial Celebration at Delphi. Paul Laprad won a WCTU Speech Contest.

CHAPTER IX — RURAL YOUTH 249

Kenneth Yeakley from Carroll County was elected president of the District Three Rural Youth at a District Meeting held in October.

1954

At a District Three Rural Youth meeting in Logansport on October 14, 1954 Shirley Eis won the District Talk Fest with her speech "Is Democracy Free?" She won the State Talk Fest at State Rural Youth Day at Indianapolis on November 10. In December, she gave the talk at the National Rural Youth Talk Fest

Members of the Carroll County Rural Youth who attended the State Rural Youth Day at Purdue on January 7, 1954. Left to right they are: Eldon Robeson, Jim Sharp, Kenneth Yeakley, Mary Ellen Kempf, Bobby Caldwell, Eileen Zinn, Robert McCain, Patsy Pullen, Charles Dillman and Connie Heffley.

Shirley Eis giving her talk on "Is Democracy Free", at the Indiana Farm Bureau Convention at Indianapolis on November 10, 1954 where she won first place in the State Rural Youth Talk Fest. She represented Indiana at the National Contest at the American Farm Bureau Federation convention in New York in December where she was one of the four finalists in the contest.

Harold Berry, County Agent, giving a pep talk to the Carroll County Rural Youth officers for 1955 after they were installed at a meeting on November 20, 1954. Left to right: Harold Berry, James Sharp, Robert McCain, Patricia Pullen, Delbert Shriver, Charles Dillman, Bobby Caldwell and Eldon Robeson.

held during the National Rural Youth meeting in New York City. She was one of the four finalists in the contest, and had the distinction of being the only contestant at the contest that year who was still in High School.

1955

The club was awarded second place in the District Scrap Book Contest at the State Rural Youth Day during the Agricultural Conference at Purdue in January.

The Rural Youth Chorus presented several programs, including one at the Flora Methodist Church on January 16. Other numbers on the program included a vocal duet by Marilyn Porter and Sharon Fisher, accompanied by Marta Porter on the piano. Marilyn Porter gave a tap dance, and Virginia Fisher played the piano for a musical number by Marta Porter and Glenda Fisher.

In May a Treasure Hunt was held at the home of Jim Sharp, president.

Carroll and Clinton Counties held a picnic at Shakamak State Park on June 26.

1958

Carroll County Rural Youth entertained 103 ladies in a Women's Ward at Longcliff State Hospital with a Christmas Party on December 22, 1958. Virginia and Glenda Fisher played on the piano and glockenspiel. The group sang Christmas carols and hymns. Refreshments included 25 pounds of popcorn, a bushel of apples, 40 pounds of hard candy, 120 ice cream sandwiches, and dozens of home made cookies.

250 • CARROLL COUNTY RURAL ORGANIZATIONS

Rural Youth members who helped were: Kim Black, Dwaine Ward, Kenneth Yeakley, Joe Spitznagle, Bob McCain, Eldon Robeson, Bill Redmon, Paul Laprad, Mr. and Mrs. Jim Flora, Sandra Bell, Glenda Fisher, Virginia Fisher, Nan Beck, Lucille Million and Harold Berry, County Agent.

1959

The Rural Youth Club purchased a Sno-Kone machine for $190, and used it at the County 4-H Fair and at other events. In later years it was rented to

Rural Youth Club officers for 1956 who were installed at the Rural Youth installation banquet and dance Saturday evening, November 12, 1955 at the Tipwa Grange Hall. First row, left to right: Joan Henderson, JoEtta Henderson, Doris Shultheis, Paul Laprad and Robert McCain. Second row: Lee Cree, Eldon Robeson, Kenneth Yeakley and Charles Dillman.

Quartet singing at the Rural Youth Senior night program on March 27, 1956. Left to right: Bob Caldwell, JoEtta Henderson, Doris Shultheis and Bob McCain.

Kim Black selling a Sno-Kone to Becky Bordner, while Alan Stout is looking for another customer at the County Fair at Flora in August, 1959. Sno-Kones were 10 cents each, with a choice of cherry, orange or root beer flavor.

the Jr. Leaders for their stand at the fair, and to the Delphi Lions Club for their stand at Old Settlers at Delphi.

1971

After several years of inactivity, the Carroll County Rural Youth Club was reorganized in the spring of 1971.

On June 6 the club participated in the regular church service at the Radnor United Methodist Church by providing the ushers, a choir, and special music led by Marta Trapp. After the service members went to Turkey Run for a picnic.

On June 9, a party was held in cooperation with the Cass County Rural Youth at the Burrows Community Center.

On June 12, the club had a Car Wash at Delphi, which earned $51.56.

In July members had a March for Development in which they walked from Delphi to Flora with proceeds going to the Carroll County Association for Retarded Children.

A Hay Ride Party at Pyrmont in cooperation with Tippecanoe County Rural Youth was held on July 17.

A Halloween Party was held October 30 at Riley Park in Delphi, and on November 27 the first of several annual Spaghetti Thanksgiving Suppers was served at the Tipwa Grange Hall.

1972

On August 13, a Bike Ride with 17 people participating raised $360 for the Association for Retarded Children.

On October 12, Charles Viney won the Speaking Contest held at the District Rural Youth meeting at the Cass County Fairgrounds and represented the District at the State Contest in November.

On November 25, the second Italian Thanksgiving Supper was held at the Tipwa Grange Hall.

In addition to these special activities, regular meetings were held at the REMC Auditorium in Delphi on the third Monday night of each month. Dues were $3 per year and membership was available to any single person at least 17 years old or a senior in High School.

1973

Beginning in March 1973 the regular meetings were changed to the third Wednesday night each month and dues were raised to $5 per year. The County Rural Youth had a booth at the County Fair to hand out information about Rural Youth. Two prizes were given at a drawing in which Geoffrey Burton of Flora won an AmFm Stereo with 8-Track Tape Deck and Dale Cleaver of Delphi won a portable radio.

A Bike Ride raised $800 for the Association for Retarded Children.

Marilyn Shultheis, Carroll County Rural Youth secretary, won the Bakers Dozen award at the Annual Rural Youth meeting at Purdue in January. This award was a brief case presented by the Department of Education of the IFB to each of the 13 top RY secretaries in the state.

1974

Sharon Shultheis won the Bakers Dozen award in 1974 and Teresa Clawson won in 1975.

Members of the Rural Youth Clubs in Carroll and nearby counties helped clean up several farms near Monticello after the tornado in April 1974.

Other projects during 1974 included cutting and selling firewood and collecting paper and glass for recycling. The club gave a trophy for the Grand Champion Lamb at the County 4-H Fair, and gave a Man of the Year Award to Gary Quinn. Other activities included basketball, swimming, roller skating, bowling, track meet, family night, canoe trip, and a tour through the Pioneer Seed Plant in Flora.

Members entered contests sponsored by the State Rural Youth in Baking, Sewing, Hobby and Home Art classes.

1976

The Carroll County Rural Youth won second place in the State Rural Youth Scrap Book Contest, and took top honors in state competition in a special Publicity Contest. An award of $10 was presented to the county club at the Indiana State Fair for making window displays showing the many different areas in which Rural Youth is involved. Windows used for the displays were the Public Service Company of Indiana in Delphi, the Ockley Grocery in Ockley and the Towne Pastry in Flora. Sharon Shultheis again won the Bakers Dozen Award.

The club conducted the church service at the Bringhurst United Methodist Church on July 18.

A Paper Drive conducted by the Third District Rural Youth in the spring of 1976 resulted in the collection of more than 22,000 pounds of paper.

RECORD BOOKS

Purdue University furnished a Secretary's Record Book, similar to one used by 4-H Club Secretaries, for each club to keep a record of their membership and activities for the year. The completed Record Books were given to the County Agent in each county, and sent to Purdue for summary and analysis.

Carroll County Rural Youth officers for 1977, left to right: Rose Sheldon, second vice president; Marilyn Shultheis, first vice president; Marsha Long, president and Brian Hahn, secretary treasurer.

Summary reports were made for 25 books in 1937, and for 51 in 1938. The 1938 summary showed that the 51 clubs reporting had an average membership of 71, and an average attendance of 39 at meetings. The clubs averaged 11 meetings per year with an outside speaker at 33% of the meetings, group singing at 70%, an educational project at 13% and a recreational period at 86% of the meetings. The club membership was evenly divided between young men and young women. About half the clubs charged membership dues, with 25¢ per year being the most common amount. About half the clubs planned their program for the entire year, and most of these clubs had a program booklet for members.

Each year a statistical report was prepared for all clubs in the state. The report for 1955 showed 78 clubs with a total of 4,354 members or an average of 55.8 members per club. The average club held about 18 meetings per year with 55% of the members attending regular meetings.

About 20% of the members were in high school or college, about one fourth were farming, and more than one half were from Farm Bureau families.

About one fourth were active in some extension program or contest. About half the clubs were represented by having a member on the Board of Directors of the County Farm Bureau and on the County Extension Committee.

There were 35 members in Carroll County Rural Youth in 1955.

EDUCATIONAL TOURS

For several years the State Rural Youth Club sponsored educational tours to many points of interest in the United States, Canada, Mexico, Cuba and Spain. Tours have been conducted for members to attend the Young Peoples Conference held in connection with the American Farm Bureau Federation Convention.

Rural Youth Trip To Florida

From February 20 to March 5, 1946, 32 Indiana Rural Youth members, including Mabel and Irene Vaughan from Carroll County, went to Florida on a chartered bus. The cost for transportation and lodging for the two-week trip was less than $100 per person. Pat O'Hara, Director of the Indiana Farm Bureau Education Department, was in charge of the tour. Others on the bus were Mr. Miller, the guide, and Marian Pease, a photographer for Successful Farming Magazine. Crafton Neeley, the bus driver was the same driver who took a FB Co-op group from Carroll County to Canada and Niagara Falls in August 1948.

The first stop was at a Co-op Fertilizer Plant in Ohio. Stops were made to see "Man O'War", the world famous race horse in Kentucky, and the Norris Dam in Tennessee. The group saw orange groves, and visited the Florida Citrus Canning Co-op, the largest in the world. The Co-op operated 6,000 acres with 26 varieties of fruit. One of their products was "Donald Duck" orange juice. Everyone took a drink from the "Fountain of Youth" at St. Augustine, Florida.

Most of the group went by plane to Havana, Cuba for a brief visit and reported that there was only one traffic light in Havana. At other intersections it seemed that the first driver to blow his horn had the right of way.

Many other points of interest were visited on the way home. One of the highlights of the trip was a stop at a Reptile Farm near Silver Springs, Florida, where Irene Vaughn tried on a snake necklace.

Third District Rural Youth Tours

Rural Youth members in District Three sponsored a tour to Mammoth Cave, Kentucky on September 13 and 14, 1952. Members from Carroll County who went on the trip were: Kenneth Yeakley, Kenneth Dietrick, Charles L. Dillman, Robert McCain and Eldon Robeson.

Irene Vaughan with a live snake necklace at the reptile farm near Silver Springs, Florida.

District Three Rural Youthers took a tour of historical points in Southern Indiana, September 12 and 13, 1953. The first stop was at Turkey Run for breakfast, then on to Vincennes, where the group visited the Tip Top Dairy, George Rogers Clark Memorial, Lincoln Trail, the Old Cathedral, William Henry Harrison Home, and the First Territorial Capitol. The tour included a stop at Spring Mill State Park for over night. Square Dancing was held in the evening, and religious services in the morning were conducted by members of the group. Robert McCain of Carroll County sang a solo. After religious services the group took a tour of Spring Mill Park.

After dinner at Spring Mill Inn all took a boat ride and then went to Bloomington for a tour of Indiana University, then to Martinsville for a visit at the Gold Fish Hatcheries, and then to Indianapolis for supper.

A total of 36 Rural Youth members from Clinton, Cass, Jasper, Newton, Tippecanoe, and Carroll Counties made the trip. Kenneth Yeakley, Bobby Caldwell, Charles Dillman, Eldon Robeson, Robert McCain, Lee Cree, Mary Ellen Kempf, and Eileen Zinn went from Carroll County.

Other Rural Youth Tours

Loran Lantz and Jon Rockwood from Carroll County went on a RY sponsored trip to Mexico from June 15 to 22, 1974.

In June 1976 Kevin Fossnock, and Marilyn and Sharon Shultheis were among the 174 from Indiana who went on a tour to Hawaii.

In August 1976 a meeting for Rural Youth members in the United States and Canada was held in Granby, Colorado. Members from the Carroll County club who attended were: Rose Sheldon, Teresa Clawson, Ivan Scott, Harry DuVall, Brad Woodhouse and Keith Lantz.

RURAL YOUTH CHORUS

The first meeting to organize a Rural Youth Chorus in Carroll County was held on February 4, 1952. A group of about 20 young people with Kenneth Pyle as director, made several appearances at Township and County Farm Bureau meetings. The chorus won second place in the Group Act at the Carroll County Rural Entertainment Festival held at the 4-H Fair.

The chorus won first place in the Rural Youth Amateur Contest at the State Fair on September 1. This gave them the right to compete in the National Rural Youth Talent Find at the National Rural Youth and Farm Bureau Conventions in Seattle, Washington, in December. The cost was estimated at $250 per person, and 25 planned to go. Members of the club

Ken and Julie Pyle, director of the Carroll County Rural Youth Chorus.

spent all available time that fall in projects to raise money for the trip.

Projects to raise money included a Square Dance, Cake Walk, Magazine Sales, a Scrap Drive, and a Donkey Basketball Game, at the Flora Gym on November 8, with Jim Sharp as chairman. Elizabeth Mears was chairman of the Bake Sale held at the Public Service Company office in Delphi on November 22, and a Chili Supper was held at the Methodist Church in Delphi on November 25.

The biggest project for raising money was a Variety Show in charge of Julie Pyle at the Flora Community Building on November 20, and at the Delphi High School Auditorium on Saturday night November 22.

Acts in the show included: a Barbershop Quartet from the Sharon Baptist Church, a Reading by Jane Ann Jones, a Tap Dance act by the Myers Trio of Deer Creek Township, a Comedy Skit by Eldon Robeson of Washington Township, a Musical Trio by the Three J's of Washington Township, a Novelty Number by the Delphi High School Football Team, a Vocal Duet by Jerry Daniels and Sandra Cassell, a Comedy Skit by Bob Caldwell, the Meadowlarks Vocal Trio, a Piano Duet by Sue Keys and Laura Tesh of Camden, a Madison Township Square Dance Set, a Romantic Duet by Gaylord Archibald and Mary Helen Mears and the Grand Finale by the County Rural Youth Chorus.

The County Rural Youth Chorus sang at the Indiana FB Convention at Indianapolis, on November

254 • CARROLL COUNTY RURAL ORGANIZATIONS

A quartet from the Sharon Baptist Church, from left: Robert McCain, Robert Rodgers, Richard McCain and George Flora, sang at the Rural Youth Variety Show on November 20 and 22, 1952.

Bill, Pat and Bob Myers tap dancing at the Variety Show on November 20 and 22, 1952.

The Three J's at the Rural Youth Variety Show November 20 and 22, 1952. Left to right: Joetta, Janet and Jalene Joyce.

Jane Ann Jones giving a reading at the Rural Youth Variety Show, November 20 and 22, 1952.

"Moppets" entertaining at a meeting of the Carroll County Rural Youth on November 14, 1952. Members of the Delphi High School football team, they entertained at the Rural Youth Variety Show on November 20 and 22, and called their act "The Island Sweethearts." Left to right: Joe Weaver, Dale Crowder, Rod Rodkey, Wayne Knitter, Ron Richardson and Joe Hildebrandt.

CHAPTER IX — RURAL YOUTH • 255

The Meadowlarks from Cass, Carroll and White Counties from left: Sue Keys, Nina McCombs and Sharon McCombs, singing at the Rural Youth Variety Show, November 20, and 22, 1952.

Gaylord Archibald and Mary Helen Mears at the Variety Show held in November 1952.

Vocal duet by Sandra Cassell and Jerry Daniels at the Rural Youth Variety Show on November 20, and 22, 1952.

12, and on December 4, 1952 twenty one members boarded the Hoosier Farmer "All American Special" train at Delphi for a ten-day trip to the Northwest and to attend the National Farm Bureau and Rural Youth Conventions in Seattle, Washington.

Members of the Chorus arrived in Seattle on Sunday afternoon, December 7, took a tour of the city and in the evening participated in the National Rural Youth Talent Find, held in the Olympic Bowl of the Olympic Hotel. On Monday night at the Rural Youth Banquet, held in the Chamber of Commerce Building, the Chorus was awarded a Certificate of Recognition for participation in the Talent Find.

On Tuesday afternoon the Chorus was one of the two Rural Youth Contest winners in the nation to appear before the National Farm Bureau Convention.

Other highlights of the trip were a boat trip across

Members of the Carroll County Rural Youth Chorus who boarded the special train at Delphi on December 4, 1952 for a trip to the National Rural Youth and Farm Bureau Convention at Seattle, Washington. First row from left: Roselyn Zook, Sue Keys, Patsy Pullen, Frances Redmon, Mary Helen Mears and Jim Sharp; second row: Connie Spitler, Judy Henderson, Kathryn Deitz, JoEtta Henderson, Julie Pyle, Connie Heffley, Eileen Zinn and Mary Ellen Kempf; third row: Kenneth Pyle, Phillip Campbell, Robert McCain, Eldon Robeson, Bill Kuszmaul, John Ward and Charles Dillman.

Puget Sound to Victoria, British Columbia; a ride up to the top of Mt. Hood at Portland, Oregon; and a visit to Boys Town at Omaha, Nebraska.

The names of those who went on the trip are listed under the picture.

On September 7, 1953, 22 members of the Carroll County Rural Youth Chorus sang at the State Rural Youth Contest at the Indiana State Fair. The Chorus again won the contest and the right to go to the American Farm Bureau Federation Convention at Chicago, to sing at the National Rural Youth Amateur Talent Find.

Members held a Bake Sale on November 28 to help raise money for the trip to Chicago. Money was also raised with singing engagements at Valparaiso, Columbia City, Indianapolis and other places. Contributions were made by the County Farm Bureau and Insurance Service, and the Rural Youth Club.

Twenty members of the Carroll County Rural Youth Chorus sang at the National Rural Youth Talent Find at Chicago on December 8, 1953. The Chorus was selected as the only one of the 16 acts participating to appear before the National Farm Bureau Convention in Chicago. While in Chicago the group visited Don McNeil's Breakfast Club, the Chicago Board of Trade, and the Federal Reserve Bank.

Members in the Chorus who went to Chicago were: JoEtta Henderson, Judy Henderson, Frances Redmon, Connie Heffley, Mary Ellen Kempf, Eileen Zinn, Rosalyn Zook, Mary Helen Mears, Patricia Maggart, Pasty Pullen, Connie Spitler, Bobby Caldwell, Charles Dillman, Bob McCain, Eldon Robeson, Jim Sharp, Lee Cree, Mr. and Mrs. John Ward and Mr. and Mrs. Kenneth Pyle. Mrs. Miles T. Martin, Rural Youth Advisor, accompanied them on the trip to Chicago.

REUNIONS

The first reunion for former officers of the Indiana Rural Youth was held in 1950 and has been held bi-ennially on even years since then. The first Statewide Reunion for former members of Indiana Rural Youth was held at the Indiana State Fairgrounds on September 14, 1975. Those from Carroll County who attended were: Mr. and Mrs. Charles T. Black and Mr. and Mrs. John C. Peterson.

The County Rural Youth Club sponsored the first reunion for former members in the county on November 26, 1951.

The next Carroll County Rural Youth Alumni Re-

CHAPTER IX — RURAL YOUTH   257

Kay and Charles T. Black at the Rural Youth reunion at Delphi on November 26, 1951. Charles was the first president of the club when it was organized 18 years before, but missed the first regular meeting on December 21, 1933, because that was the day his daughter Kay was born.

union, 25 years later, was held at the Camden Community Center on August 1, 1976.

Eight present who were members before 1940 were: John C. Peterson, Irene DeWinton, Truman Plank, Vivian Henderson Hoover, Charles T. and Elizabeth Black, Love Groninger Fitzgerald and Pauline Robeson.

There were 22 in attendance who were members in the 1940's and 1950's, and 13 who were members from 1950 to 1970. Also attending were 10 present members and several guests, making a total of 74 at the reunion.

Charles T. Black was recognized as the first Carroll County president of Rural Youth when it was organized. Other former presidents present were: Jim Sharp, Ren C. Groninger, Eldon Robeson, Glenn Brown, Kenneth Yeakley, Wayne Zinn, Charles Viney, Keith Lantz and Marilyn Shultheis.

Mike Jones of North Vernon, who was the state president in 1965-66, conducted the recreation for the evening after the program.

The next reunion was planned for 1981.

Mr. and Mrs. Ren Groninger of Rock Creek Township and their four children Gaye held by Mrs. Groninger, Craig and Sandra in front of Ren and Renda. They had the largest family present at the Rural Youth meeting held at Delphi on November 26, 1951, planned by present Rural Youth members as a reunion for all past members. Ren was a former president of the club, and had a record of perfect attendance for several years. Mrs. Groninger is the former Mary Alice Brown and was also an active member for several years.

COUNTY RURAL YOUTH OFFICERS

YEAR	PRESIDENT	VICE PRESIDENT	SECRETARY	TREASURER
1934	Charles T. Black	Lee Seward		Margaret Mabbitt
1935	Earl Powell	Robert Reiff		Mary Studebaker
1936	Richard Hawn	Charles Nance		Ellen Louise Robeson
1937	Charles Nance	Barbara Rodenbarger		Opal Mullin
1938	George Seward	Ray Robertson		Opal Smith
1939	Eldon D. Robeson	Robert Neuenschwander		Cora Belle Pearson
1940	Ray Robertson	Paul Johnson		Eva Seward
1941	John Harness	Dana Myer		Marjorie Shonk
1942	Ren C. Groninger			
1943	John Allbaugh	Norma McCarty		Ren C. Groninger
1944	Wayne Zinn	Robert Rodkey	Carl Martin	Ren C. Groninger
1945	Wayne Zinn	Fred Kuszmaul Edgar Fountain Robert Robbins	Ina Allbaugh	John Allbaugh
1946	Ray Robertson	David R. Smith	Dortha Wray	John Allbaugh
1947	David R. Smith	Lewis Wakeland	Eileen Zinn	Paul Ward
1948	Paul Seward	Eldon D. Robeson	Eileen Zinn	Keith Mears
1949	Paul Seward	Kenneth Yeakley Gerald Hanawalt	Joyce Zook	Keith Mears
1950	Glenn Brown	Paul Seward	Elizabeth Mears	Kenneth Mears
1951	Glenn Brown	Kenneth Yeakley	Kathryn Sines	Bill Kuszmaul
1952	Kenneth Yeakley	Jim Sharp	Kathleen Fife	Bill Kuszmaul
1953	Charles Dillman	Bobby Caldwell	Mary Ellen Kempf	Elizabeth Mears
1954	Bobby Caldwell	Charles Dillman	Kathleen Fife	Patsy Pullen
1955	Jim Sharp	Robert McCain	Patsy Pullen	Delbert Shriver Paul Laprad
1956	Robert McCain	Paul Laprad	Patsy Pullen	Doris Shultheis
1957	James Flora		Brenda McKinley	Joan Dillman
1958	Dwaine Ward	Kim Black	Nan Beck	Glenda Fisher
1959	Kim Black	Dwaine Ward	Lois Downham	Glenda Fisher
1960	James Thompson	Kim Black	Dwaine Ward	Glenda Fisher
1961	Ray Gish	Richard Long	Darilee Peter	
1962-1970	Inactive			
1971	Gayle Stout	Julie Beard	Marta Trapp	Judy Mays
1972	Charles Viney	Marta Trapp	Marilyn Shultheis	
1973	Charles Viney	Judy Mays	Marilyn Shultheis	Charles Viney
1974	Keith Lantz	Evy Sheldon	Sharon Shultheis	Marilyn Shultheis
1975	Arthur Hook	Stu Sullivan Gary Quinn		Teresa Clawson
1976	Marilyn Shultheis	Mike Gerrish Kevin Fossnock		Sharon Shultheis
1977	Marsha Long	Marilyn Shultheis Rose Sheldon		Brian Hahn
1978	Bruce Fieleke	Kevin Fossnock Brian Fieleke		Judy Taylor
1979	Rose Sheldon	Kevin Fossnock	Rose Sheldon	Kevin Fossnock
1980	Marsha Long	Rose Sheldon Kevin Fossnock		Kevin Fossnock

CHAPTER X

REMC

LET THERE BE LIGHT

"And God said, 'Let there be light,' and there was light. And God saw that the light was good, and God separated the light from the darkness. God called light Day, and the darkness He called Night.'"

That was a long time ago, and it has been that way ever since. Man is engaged in an eternal struggle to conquer the darkness with light. For centuries his primary weapon was the bonfire, either outdoors or in a fireplace in his house.

The tallow candle and the oil lamp provided better light, but did not solve the problem.

Thomas A. Edison gave man a big boost when he developed the first successful incandescent lamp in October 1879. However, it took several years to get the electric lamp perfected and in general use.

FIRST ELECTRIC LIGHTS

Wabash, Indiana, was the first city in the world to use electricity for public lighting. On March 31, 1880 four large brush carbon lamps were used to light the Courthouse Tower. A large dynamo was set up in the Courthouse yard, and Owen Riggle, a native of Adams Township in Carroll County, fired the boiler to provide the steam for power to generate the electricity. He reported that the light was used for a few hours each evening to create a light spot in the darkness in the main part of town. It was considered more of a novelty than something of practical value, and people came from a great distance to see the unusual sight. The lights were used until September 1888.

One of the carbon lamps is on display in the Courthouse in Wabash, and the dynamo is on display at a museum in northern Indiana.

In 1882 Thomas A. Edison opened the first power station serving 59 customers in Lower Manhattan. That year, for the first time, electric lights were used to decorate a Christmas tree. On July 4, 1883 Sudbury, Pennsylvania, became the first town to light their streets with incandescent lamps.

During the next few years several local groups built power plants to provide electric service for homes, trolley cars, motors and factories. These all operated on direct current, and the area that could be served was limited. In 1886 William Stanley built a generator for alternating current which could be transmitted over great distances. After a few years of debating the merits of AC and DC, the power companies in the United States nearly all now operate on 60 cycle AC, and most of them are interconnected so they can exchange electric power with other companies when necessary.

Delphi

In December 1887 a group of citizens in and near Delphi, organized the Delphi Electric Light Company. The company officials met several times with the City Council, and on January 12, 1888 signed a contract to furnish 20 carbon arc lamps of 2,000 candle power each, to be operated on a "moon schedule" until midnight each night, at a cost of $90 per lamp per year. The company also planned to furnish lights for businesses and residents of the city.

The company was incorporated on January 14, 1888 and the directors met on January 26 to put on the finishing touches, but according to an article in the local paper "a difference of opinion developed" and the corporation was dissolved.

Some of those involved in this company, along with others in the community, organized the Carroll County Electric Light Company on February 13, 1888 "for the purpose of carrying on the business of producing and manufacturing electric light, furnishing the motive power therefore, and of supplying the city of Delphi and the residents thereof and also the other cities, towns and villages and the residents thereof of said county with electric lights." The capital stock was $10,000 and the five directors were: Wm. Haugh, Wickliffe Smith, John H. Burr, Nathaniel Mohr and James C. Blythe.

On February 16, the directors made a contract with the city of Delphi to furnish 20 lights at $115 each per year and operate them until 3 A.M. Charles Barley and Nathaniel Mohr went to Columbus, Indiana, to look at two kinds of lamps being used there.

The company selected and installed Thomson-

Houston arc lamps. The streets of Delphi were lit with electric lights for the first time on Saturday night, April 21, 1888. Traveling men said that Delphi was the best illuminated city in the state.

The Delphi Times for February 1, 1889 had the following article: "A gentleman presumably from Monticello came over Saturday and hearing that his burg was about to be lit by electricity, repaired to the Electric Light Company's Building on a tour of inspection. He looked long and wild at the dynamos and other machinery, and finally picked up a piece of the wire used for connecting purposes between the street and store jets. He examined the ends closely and then was heard to remark: 'Well doggoned, if I see the hole the light goes through!'"

Electricity was provided for Delphi businesses to replace the oil and gas lamps being used. Later, electricity was available for residences, and by 1896, the lines were extended to South Delphi.

An article in the Delphi Journal for November 30, 1896 stated: "Howard Smith is kept busy now fitting out Delphi residences with electric light fixtures. As the cold and dreary winter comes in sight, people shudder when they think of filling coal oil lamps, cleaning chimneys and trimming wicks, and they escape from the nightmare by ordering electric light fixtures. Delphi's service in this respect is superior to other cities. The light goes on early in the afternoon and remains until long after daylight."

In the summer of 1898 the electric company built a brick building on the south side of Monroe Street west of the Wabash Railroad for the power plant. The company installed two 250 horsepower steam engines and, in 1902 added another 200 horsepower engine.

The Delphi Journal for August 1, 1901 reported that the Courtroom in the Courthouse was wired for electric lights. There were three 10 light chandeliers and three student lamps. The Judge's room had a four light chandelier. The other rooms in the Courthouse were already wired and lighted.

In 1910 the light plant was sold to the Fort Wayne and Northern Indiana Traction Company. Meters were installed for each customer. By 1913 there were 41 street lamps in Delphi.

In 1922 the electric power was changed from 25 cycle to 60 cycle current.

OTHER TOWNS

The first electric lights were turned on in Flora on Thursday evening, June 17, 1909. Flora purchased the electric utility from the Public Service Company on July 2, 1946 and has operated it since then.

In 1912 Camden gave a franchise to the Koheo Light and Power Company to provide 34 tungsten street lamps at $30 each per year, and current for homes and businesses at 10 cents per KWH. Records at the town office show that seven street lights were installed that year.

The Interurban Line built through Carroll County in 1907 by the Fort Wayne and Northern Indiana Traction Company provided electricity to small towns along the way. By 1916 the company was supplying Flora and Camden with electric power.

Two hydro-electric power plants in dams in the Tippecanoe River provided electric power, but most of it was used for larger cities in northern Indiana. The dam at Oakdale, creating Lake Freeman in Carroll County, was completed in 1925.

The town of Yeoman incorporated in 1925 so that the Northern Indiana Public Service Company would put in electricity.

RURAL ELECTRIFICATION

Getting electricity for a farm in Carroll County was expensive and often impossible. Only on a few farms near the towns, or along power lines between towns was it practical.

Many farmers did have private power plants with gasoline engines, generators and storage batteries to provide 32 volt electricity for lighting and small power use. These were expensive and not too satisfactory.

Wolever Photo
Building located west of the Wabash Railroad, on the south side of Monroe Street, built in the summer of 1898 by the Carroll County Electric Light Company for three steam engines and generators to supply electricity for Delphi. This building was still standing in 1980.

getting a lot of valuable experience that could be of help to other counties. Upon recommendation by the Statewide REMC, work in Carroll County was delayed until Statewide could have time to prepare a more complete plan for the counties, based on the experience in Boone County.

For the next three months there was a lot of talk about Rural Electrification, with much information and even more misinformation. No one knew exactly how the program would work, but hopes were high that something would be done soon. Little did the people involved realize that it would be two long years and a lot of hard work before any lines were energized.

MEMBERSHIP CAMPAIGN

On January 21, 1936 the directors met again, and Arthur Mullin, secretary of the Statewide REMC, explained the program and plans for a membership campaign. He reported that Mr. Wilson Taylor from the State REMC office would be in Camden for a meeting at 10:00 A.M. on February 7, and would bring and distribute the forms for the membership campaign.

Each township director was asked to bring about 10 people from his township who would be willing to help on the membership campaign. There were about 120 people at the meeting on February 7, and Mr. Taylor explained the campaign in detail. Solicitors in each township were given a map of the township cut into small sections showing the area for each solicitor. The solicitor's job was to mark on the map the location of each house and contact the owner to see if he was willing to pay a membership fee of $5 and agree to pay a minimum of $2.50 per month for electricity if and when it became available.

Arthur Mullin signed application No. one for his home in Adams Township.

Ralph Maggart, County Agent, who had been very active in organizing the REMC, wrote the following letter to the directors on February 19, 1936:

"In spite of the intense cold a good many of the townships are reporting a very favorable sign-up for the REMC membership.

"I was talking to Arthur Mullin and he says there are fifteen or twenty counties working on membership campaigns at the present time and to date there is sufficient money appropriated for approximately ten counties. If we are to be one of the ten and come within the first group, remember we are in direct competition with other counties. The sooner we can get our membership cards in and the accuracy of the cards may determine whether we can get into this first group. Why wait until the next?

"I might suggest that you make announcement of the REMC campaign at any group meetings so it will give these people time to be thinking about it and save you time while you are soliciting."

On February 27, the directors met again and learned that 110 solicitors had collected about 500 applications for membership. A summary of reports from the townships indicated that there were about 1,525 eligible homes in the county, and it was estimated that 975 would make applications for membership. Plans were made to hold meetings in each township and write articles for the local papers in order to get information to more people. Larry Gruber and Charles Davis Vaughan were appointed to work in Tippecanoe Township, since that township had no incorporator or director.

COUNTY MAP

The original campaign for members ended on the afternoon of March 14, 1936 with a meeting for members in the Assembly Room of the Courthouse. There were 1,100 applications for membership, and it was now time to make a map showing the location of all members so that the engineers could determine where it was practical to build lines. It was necessary to design the lines with an average of three members per mile of line.

Up to this time the only expenses of the County REMC was for membership in the Indiana Statewide REMC, and for a bond on the treasurer. All officers, directors and solicitors had worked without pay. Since the secretary treasurer was also secretary treasurer of the CCFBCA, the Co-op Association had furnished office space, secretarial service, postage and telephone without charge to the REMC.

At a directors meeting following the membership meeting on March 14, 1936 the board authorized the first local expenses. They were $2 to the Delphi Journal for a county map about four feet square, and $.96 to the Co-op Association for a fiber board for mounting the map. The REMC directors, at a previous meeting held on February 27, had agreed to pay the Co-op Association for office help needed to prepare the map.

Extra help hired to prepare the map included: Vivian Henderson, 32 days; Mary Cohee, 14 days; Myra Witter, 8 days and Lois Ruth Snoeberger, 8 days. They were each paid $1.34 per day. Charles M. Flora worked one and one half days at $2 per day.

The REMC paid the Co-op Association $60 for regular employees who helped make the map. This made a total labor cost of $145.80 for the map which showed the location of every home in the county. Those who had applied for membership were marked with a red dot, and others with a small circle. The houses in each section were numbered, and were then identified by a number which included the range, township, section and house number. That identification number is still used by the REMC.

Each township director checked the map and the list of names for his township. The map was completed and taken to Indianapolis on April 2, 1936.

CORPORATION APPROVED

The Public Service Commission held a hearing on May 11, 1936, and, on May 22, approved the Articles of Incorporation and issued a Certificate of Convenience and Necessity for the Carroll County REMC. The preliminary work was finished, and the Carroll County REMC was incorporated and ready to do business.

In the meantime Boone County had set their first pole on January 9, 1936 and energized their first lines on May 31, 1936. Since this was one of the first REA lines in the U.S. to be energized, Morris L. Cooke, Administrator of the REA attended the ceremony.

At a directors meeting on June 2, Mr. Yarling and Mr. Young, Engineers for the Indiana Statewide REMC presented maps showing the proposed line, and explained that more members were needed to provide enough miles of line with three members per mile to make a satisfactory project. Each director was given a map showing the proposed lines in his township. The maps were taken to the townships and shown to people along the proposed lines, and by June 13, there were 150 more applications for membership.

COUNTY FARM

With the membership campaign completed and the engineering department working on proposed lines, there was not much activity, but there were some periods of excitement. For instance, the engine on the power plant at the County Farm broke down and the commissioners did not want to spend money to replace it. Neither did they want to operate the County Farm without electricity. The commissioners considered the possibility of building a power line from Delphi to the County Farm and were making some progress when local REMC officials heard about it.

A committee from the REMC met with the commissioners and explained that the REMC had a franchise on the territory, and that it would be illegal for anyone else to build a line. The committee also pointed out that they could make no promises when a line could be built, and that the REMC had no money to enforce their legal rights. The committee explained to the commissioners that an electric line to the County Farm would also serve several farms along the way, and would make it difficult or maybe impossible for the REMC to design lines with the required three or more customers per mile to serve other farms in the area.

The commissioners agreed to wait and see if the electric plant at the County Farm could be repaired. The County Farm Bureau Co-op Association came to the rescue by hiring Hobart Wolfe to install a used Fordson Tractor engine to run the generator at the County Farm. The engine was still working when REMC electricity was available about one and one half years later.

The REMC had no money to repay the Co-op Association for this service. The Co-op Association neither asked for nor expected to receive any pay. This is just one example of the many ways in which people in Carroll County help each other in time of need.

REA ALLOTMENT

On September 29, 1936 the directors and incorporators met with Mr. Harvey B. Hartsock, attorney for the Indiana Statewide REMC, and adopted new by-laws and signed an engineering and legal contract with the Statewide REMC.

On September 9, 1936 the Rural Electrification Administration announced an allotment of $150,000, and on November 6, another $210,000 for Carroll County.

On November 6, the directors applied for a loan from REA for $360,000 to build 365 miles of line to serve 1,296 members. The interest rate was 2.77% and the loan was for a period of 20 years.

On November 14, 1936 REA approved the construction loan contract for Carroll County.

USE GOOD MATERIAL

The County REMC held a meeting for members in the Assembly Room of the Courthouse on Friday evening, December 4, with 150 people present. The main speaker for the program was to be Mr. J. J. Scherer, Chief Electrical Inspector for the State Fire Marshal, who was scheduled to talk on the proper and safe methods of house wiring, and use of electrical appliances. Mr. Scherer was an interesting speaker and was well qualified to talk on this subject, but for some reason he could not come to the meeting, and sent someone else from the office who knew very little about electrical wiring or appliances. About the only thing he said about wiring was that a person should be sure he used good material. That was good advice, but then he went on and said: "Buy it from a reliable dealer instead of at the ten cent store or Sears Roebuck."

No one thought much about that except a representative of Sears Roebuck who was in the meeting. He called Mr. Sherer, who then wrote a letter of apology stating that Sears Roebuck did handle high quality wiring material, and sent the letter to the secretary of the Carroll County REMC. Mr. Scherer made an error on the address, and the letter was delivered to someone who knew nothing about the incident. When he saw the name Sears Roebuck in the letter, he took it to their store in Logansport. The manager of the store then put the letter in a glass frame and hung it over the wiring counter for everyone to see.

WIRING THE BUILDINGS

For the protection of members, the REMC directors voted to not turn on the electricity for a member until the wiring in his buildings had been inspected to see that it met the requirements of the National Electric Code. The REMC needed someone to inspect the wiring. Seven applicants for the job went to Indianapolis and took an examination at the State Fire Marshal's office.

On December 15, 1936 the directors hired Hobart Wolfe from Madison Township as inspector at $125 per month. The officers and Mr. Wolfe spent several days visiting other counties to learn what they could about how to proceed with the program.

During the three days, December 21, 22 and 23, five meetings for REMC members were held in different parts of the county, and Mr. S. A. Anderson from Purdue discussed the approved method for wiring buildings.

When members who had signed up for electric service began to wire their homes and farm buildings, it was obvious that there were not enough professional wiremen available to do the job. Many farmers wanted to wire their own buildings, but needed help in learning how to do it properly.

The REMC directors considered the problem, and made plans to conduct a wiring school. Some professional wiremen strongly objected to the school because they did not want more people in the wiring business. The wiremen failed to visualize the size of the job, and did not realize that there would be work for anyone who was interested in working.

The first meeting of the wiring school was held at Camden on January 30, 1937 and it continued during February and March with about 150 people attending one or more sessions. Hobert Wolfe gave detailed instructions on how to wire buildings. Plywood walls were set up in the Community Building in Camden, so that those attending the school could get experience in installing switches and light fixtures and in connecting wires.

Many who attended the school wired their own buildings and helped their neighbors wire theirs. Several spent the rest of the year wiring buildings and a few continued wiring as a business. Albert Burkle got his start in wiring at this school. He later was a successful Delphi business man and a plumbing and electrical contractor for many years.

Some who had been wiring buildings before they attended the school, soon learned that their methods of wiring did not meet the requirements of the National Electric Code, and they had to change their methods. Others who did not attend the school learned the hard way when the inspector made them change a wiring job so that it would meet the requirements of the Code.

Cecil Manis of Adams Township, was hired as wiring inspector on May 15, 1937 when Hobert Wolfe resigned to take a job with the Indiana Statewide REMC.

Among others who helped inspect wiring were Paul White, Russell L. Griffith, Donald Koontz and Russell Williams.

An inspection fee of $1 was charged for each set of buildings. The inspector used a small portable electric power plant to check the wiring in buildings. The plant was also used to provide light for meetings and other special events, until someone stole it.

When the wiring school was being completed, the students were full of enthusiasm, so the directors decided to have a drawing in each township at the regular Township Farm Bureau meeting and give a labor-free wiring job for one house and one barn. A special meeting was held in Cass County, adjoining Washington Township, and one labor-free house wiring job was given. The students were to donate their time and get more training and experience in wiring. This worked fine for part of the buildings, but soon the students were so busy wiring their own buildings that it was necessary for the REMC to hire some of them to finish the last labor-free wiring jobs.

At the drawing for the labor-free wiring job held in Washington Township, the first name drawn out of the hat was Oral A. Caldwell. Since Mr. Caldwell was chairman of the Township Farm Bureau and director of the REMC he did not want to accept the award. The committee in charge of the drawing pointed out that the rules did not disqualify any member from receiving the award. The second name was also Oral A. Caldwell. The committee reported that this was possible because Mr. Caldwell had memberships for two farms. When the third name was also Oral A. Caldwell, the committee members could think of no logical explanation, so they investigated and found that every card in the hat had the same name. The correct hat with the proper cards was soon located, and the drawing was properly conducted.

The winners of labor-free wiring jobs are listed at the end of the chapter.

OFFICE ESTABLISHED

In December 1936 a committee representing the REMC made arrangements with the CCFBCA to pay $15 per month for office space, lights and heat in a part of the room used by the CCFBCA for an office.

On January 4, 1937 the directors paid $55 to John C. Peterson, secretary, for mileage driven in 1936 and appointed him as manager of the REMC at a salary of $10 per week and three cents per mile. The title was later changed to "Project Superintendent" during the period of construction of the lines. The salary increased as the amount of work increased, and was $125 per month and four cents per mile when the first project was completed in 1938.

On February 6, 1937 Kathryn Swartz was hired as the first bookkeeper at $12 per week.

MEETING OF INCORPORATORS

At the Annual Meeting of Incorporators held on March 2, 1937 it was announced that Oscar Leatherman had resigned as incorporator and director in December, since he was moving from the county. The directors had elected Lewis H. Funkhouser to replace him as director. The incorporators then elected Robert C. Wingard, Fred Voorhees and Coy C. Shanks as directors to replace S. A. Wickard, J. W. Eikenberry and Webb Robeson. The directors met after the Annual Meeting and elected officers: Oral A. Caldwell, president; Elmer G. Reiff, vice president and John C. Peterson, secretary treasurer. Clarence Frey and the three officers were elected as members of the Executive Board. At the next directors meeting held on March 10, J. W. Eikenberry was paid $20 for mileage driven in 1936 while he was president.

SLOW PROGRESS

Everyone concerned with the REMC project was anxious to start building lines. While it seemed slow at the time, several important things happened in the spring of 1937.

On April 12, 1937 bids were approved for the projects in Carroll and Hendricks Counties. Other county projects already approved were: Boone, Whitley, Shelby, Huntington, Henry and Johnson. On April 29, a contract was signed with the Ulen Construction Company of Lebanon to build the lines in Carroll County.

On May 3, 1937 the county commissioners signed a permit authorizing the REMC to construct, maintain and operate an electrical distribution system in Carroll County and to trim trees located on the county roads so that they would not interfere with the system.

It was necessary for the County REMC to get a written easement from everyone who owned property where poles or anchors would be set, or where wires crossed private property. On May 17, Oral A. Caldwell resigned as president and director in order to spend full time getting easements. Jesse L. Yeager was elected to replace him as director; Elmer G. Reiff was elected president and Coy C. Shanks was elected vice president.

In May the Statewide REMC Engineering Department started staking the lines. Hobart Wolfe who had been wiring inspector for the REMC was hired as engineer in charge of designing the lines in Carroll County. A new design for lines, developed by engineers for REA, made it possible to build the lines at about one-half the cost of lines built by other utilities at that time.

Employees of the engineering department set a stake where each pole and anchor would be located, and made a mark on each house or set a stake for a pole where a meter would be located. Detailed specifications were made showing the size and length of each pole, the size of each transformer, and the number of feet of each kind of wire to be used. Robert Duff was one member of a crew that set stakes for the lines.

The engineering office was located with the REMC office for a short time until more room was needed, and then it was moved to 111 E. Main Street. Among those who helped in the office were Helen Zook and Edith Hemmig.

The activity of the engineering department driving stakes for the lines created interest and excitement, but for people who were waiting on electricity, progress seemed to be slow. No one had any way of knowing when construction would start so most questions about when something would happen were answered with the statement: "about a week or ten days."

The story was told that someone called the office and asked, "When the lights are turned on, how long will it take the electricity to get to my house?" The standard answer "about a week or ten days" was given.

REA officials in Washington heard this story and used it in the news bulletin which was sent to all projects. However, the answer was changed to "about .00037 seconds." This answer was more nearly correct, but it missed the point of the strange combination of hope and frustration felt by the local leaders. Someone suggested that it might also be a good example of how stories (and people) change when they go to Washington and return.

CONSTRUCTION

On July 19, the Ulen Construction Company opened a local office in Delphi in the stone building on North Washington Street near the Canal. The date of July 31, 1937 was set as the official date to begin construction on the Carroll County project.

The engineering department of the Indiana Statewide REMC had been working all summer setting a stake for each pole and anchor. By this time weeds had grown along the road until the contractor had trouble finding the stakes. Edwin Ruffing and other local people were hired to cut weeds around the stakes so that the hole digging and pole setting crews could find them. The first poles arrived on August 26, when three carloads were delivered. The first holes for poles were dug on August 31, and 68 holes were dug that day. Nearly all holes were dug by hand at an average labor cost of about $1 per hole.

The first pole was set at 8:35 A.M. on September 1, 1937. It was pole No. 15 on Circuit "A" which started in Pittsburg and went north on the Range Line Road. A total of 49 poles were set the first day.

There was a brief ceremony by James C. Ashby, Chief Engineer of the Statewide REMC for the setting of the first pole. Someone suggested that it would be appropriate to break a kerosene lamp on the pole, but members were still using their kerosene lamps. Among those who watched the setting of the first pole were: Wayne Hiatt, manager of the Farm Bureau Co-op Hatchery, who took several pictures; Elmer G. Reiff, president and Oral A. Caldwell, former president of the REMC; Hobart Wolfe, engineer for the Statewide REMC; Charles Jones, director from Jefferson Township, and his grandson, Robert Mills, who became president of the REMC in 1975.

During the month of September there were 2,336 holes dug, 2,330 poles set, 2,758 poles delivered, 2,494 poles assembled with hardware, 310 anchors set, and 350 miles of 6A wire delivered.

Hiatt Photo

The first pole set by the Carroll County REMC on September 1, 1937. From left: Elmer G. Reiff, president; Oral A. Caldwell, former president of the Carroll County REMC, and Hobart Wolfe, engineer for Statewide REMC.

LOCAL ACTIVITIES

While the Statewide REMC engineers were designing and the Ulen Construction Company was building the lines, the County REMC directors and officers were busy keeping up with their work.

At a meeting on June 7, the directors voted to require each member to pay $10 for a Certificate of Indebtedness before they received electric service.

On June 26, 1937 the first check was received from REA for $5,600.

The directors met on July 6, and hired Samuel R. Dyer of Cutler to help get easements.

Four sections in Tippecanoe Township were released to the Northern Indiana Public Service Company, to build lines to serve some cottages along the Tippecanoe River. This area was not included on the proposed REMC lines, and it could easily be served by the other utility.

When construction started on the lines, many people who had been doubters and some who had been working against the project, suddenly realized that they were about to be left in the dark. Several applied for membership as the lines were built along their road. Since they had not been members when the lines were designed, there was no provision for transformers and service lines for them. This delayed the project when the engineering department had to change specifications, and the contractor had to install extra wire and transformers. This meant that other members would have to wait longer for service, and some might even be left out if too much money was used for new customers.

The directors met on September 7, 1937 and after discussing the problem passed the following resolution: "All members applying for membership since November 14, 1936 be required to wait until the proposed lines are completed before they are provided with service." Immediately word was received from REA that this action was not legal, and three days later the directors held a special meeting to rescind this motion. The directors learned the same bitter lesson that each generation of community leaders has learned the hard way—that progress is for everyone, even those who fight it.

On September 20, the directors authorized the officers to sign a contract with the Indiana Service Corporation for electric energy.

The directors voted to furnish the names of all REMC members to dealers in the community who handled electrical appliances and supplies.

The directors also voted to pay themselves five cents per mile for attending meetings since July 1, 1937. This was the first pay that the directors received, and totaled only $93.10 from July 1, to November 1.

Several homes along the lines were located some distance from the road. This created a problem since REA rules required that the REMC furnish the first span of wire, the last pole and not more than 150 feet of service line from the transformer to the members meter. It was necessary for the member to pay for any additional wire and poles. The Project Superintendent drove 1,500 miles checking these private extensions and the bookkeeper spent a lot of time figuring all the bills and collecting from the members. Later REA changed the rules and 12 years later in June 1949 all the money paid for private extensions was refunded to the members who had paid.

On December 8, 1937 the first meter was set and an interesting discovery was made. The contractor building the lines installed the wires from the transformer to the house or meter pole and it was the job of the person who wired the house to connect the wires from the meter to the wires coming from the transformer. On houses that had been wired before the lines were built, the wires from the meter were not connected to the wires from the transformer. The wireman had completed his job, and in many cases the owner had no way of connecting the wires. The REMC came to the rescue and furnished connectors and the person who installed the meter made the connections.

This was one of the first services provided beyond the call of duty, a policy which has been continued, and has helped keep members happy.

On December 21, the REMC received the second check from REA for $97,670.15.

On December 22, Clarence Darragh began working in charge of operation and maintenance of the project. A panel truck was purchased for Clarence to use for hauling tools and supplies for maintaining the lines.

LINES ENERGIZED

At 12:50 P.M. on December 23, 1937 the Indiana Service Corporation energized the two lines from the substation in Delphi, on Washington Street by Deer Creek, to the REMC lines. One main REMC line, Circuit "A" which served the area north of the Wabash River began in Pittsburg, and Circuits "B" and "C" which served the rest of the area began on State Road 421 south of Delphi, a short distance north of the intersection with County Road 300 North.

A short but impressive ceremony was held by representatives of the Indiana Service Corporation, officials of the Ulen Construction Corporation, the local REMC officials and representatives of the Indiana Statewide REMC when the current was turned on. E. F. Hauser, assistant manager and James C. Ashby, chief engineer of the Indiana Statewide REMC were present for the ceremony.

Carroll County, which was the 24th county to be approved for membership in the Statewide REMC, was the sixth county to energize lines. The first seven counties, and the dates the lines were energized were: Boone on May 21, 1936; Shelby on July 7, 1937; Huntington on July 10, 1937; Whitley on August 12, 1937; Johnson on September 19, 1937; Carroll on December 23, 1937 and Wabash on December 24, 1937.

On December 24, 1937 at 1:29 P.M. about 60 miles of REMC line on Circuit "A" was energized. This was the line beginning at Pittsburg and serving the three townships north of the Wabash River. As a safety measure, the main fuse had been removed at each house when the meter was set. It was now necessary for someone to visit each house, check the voltage, and install the fuse, then check and see if the meter, lights, and appliances were working properly. At some homes it was necessary to set the meter, and in a few places to climb the pole and turn on the transformer. Crews worked all afternoon, and some worked Christmas Day and turned electricity on for about 100 members. Only two members thanked the employees for working on Christmas Day, while many had the attitude "Why didn't you get here day before yesterday?" Many members later admitted that it was the nicest Christmas present they had ever received.

It took several days to connect everyone who was ready. By the end of the year about 150 miles of line had been energized and about 150 members connected. One crew was working New Year's Day, and late in the evening one kind lady gave them each a glass of milk and a piece of cake. The milk was sour, and the cake was made with rancid butter. That may have been a message of some kind.

On January 2, 1938 the directors met at the home of president Elmer G. Reiff who lived on Circuit "A", and was one of the first directors to have electricity. Circuit "C" in the southern part of the county was energized on January 22, and Circuit "B" in the central and northeastern part of the county was energized on February 15. By March 1938 all lines in the first project were energized, and 850 members along the lines who had their buildings wired had electric service.

FIRST ANNUAL MEETING OF MEMBERS

The annual meeting held on March 1, 1938 was the first for regular members. Previous annual meetings were for incorporators. J. Dale Maxwell was elected as the first director from Tippecanoe Township. He replaced Lewis H. Funkhouser of Deer Creek Township who had been elected to serve until someone from Tippecanoe Township was eligible; Artus Rodenbarger, Ben Metzger, and Obe Campbell were elected to replace Hal Shafer, Clarence Frey and Loyd Zook. Coy C. Shanks was elected president; Elmer G. Reiff, vice president and John C. Peterson, secretary treasurer.

PROJECT COMPLETED

In May 1938 REA inspected the lines and the first project was completed. There were 907 members receiving electrical service and an average of one new member was being connected each day. During the month of May, the average member used 33.8 KWH of electricity. Only 24% of the members were using more than 35 KWH per month.

CREDIT TO DONATED HELP

Much credit for the success of the project was due the many people who donated their time and work to get the project organized, and who had the courage and faith to keep on working even when it seemed hopeless. Directors served without pay, and more than 100 people volunteered to solicit their neighbors for membership.

Only those who helped do it can realize the problems encountered by the solicitors for membership in REMC. Farmers were recovering from the Great Depression, and $5 was a lot of money. Average prices received by farmers in Indiana for the year 1936 were: corn, 71¢ per bushel; wheat, 97¢ per bushel; soybeans, 92¢ per bushel; hogs $9.94 per hundred and eggs 22¢ per dozen. Many farmers felt that they could not afford to pay $2.50 per month for electricity. Some were afraid they might lose their farm if they signed up for membership. It was generally known that the electric utilities had investigated and decided that it was not good business to build lines in rural areas, and many felt that if the lines were built, the project would fail, and be sold to the utilities at a low price. One engineer for a utility company told the tenant on his farm who was helping organize the REMC: "Go ahead and build your lines. When the project fails we will buy it at 10 cents on the dollar."

The success of the project is a tribute to the spirit of cooperation and self help by the people in Carroll County. That the spirit is contagious was demonstrated when someone overheard one employee of the engineering department tell another: "Whenever you see a dxxx farmer, wave at him. Someday we might want him to sign an easement."

The success of the project organized and operated by farmers is even more impressive since the farmer at that time was considered to be on the low end of the economic and social totem pole. This is well illustrated by a story making the rounds at that time.

A city slicker was hired to help take the Agricultural Census. His job was to visit farms and list all the livestock and its value. He got along fine until one day he saw a goat on a farm. He didn't know what it was, and could find nothing like it in his instruction book, so he sent a telegram to Washington—"Have found animal with a forlorn face, a long beard, a skinny body and bare rump. What is its name and what valuation should I set upon it?"

The answer came back: "The animal you describe is a farmer and has no value."

LETTER TO REA ADMINISTRATION

Several interesting things that happened in the early days of REMC are in a letter written on May 14, 1938 by the Project Superintendent to Mr. John M. Carmody, administrator of REA. Following are quotations from that letter:

"We have your letter of April 20th, requesting a report on any unusual stories. We have had many of the experiences mentioned in your letter and in the 1937 annual report, but can think of no particular stories that might be called unusual, because in a program of this kind we expect anything to happen.

"It has been interesting throughout the entire program to observe the various attitudes that people have had toward the project. When we first started our program in Carroll County at a meeting held August 14, 1935 many people were skeptical, some were so enthusiastic that they thought it could all be accomplished in a few weeks and others applied for membership merely to help the program and never expected anything to be done.

"I was interested in a comment by Mr. Harry Reed, a local real estate man, a few days ago. He stated that when the program first started he was very careful to always mention to the prospective buyer that electricity would be available at the farm he was trying to sell them. Since nobody seemed to be particularly interested, he neglected to mention it any more and nearly forgot about the program. He says that it isn't necessary for him to say anything about it now because the first question the prospective buyer asks him is 'Does the farm have electricity available?'

"It is also interesting to notice that many of those who were skeptical about the program at first are now very much concerned to find that the lines have been built and do not go past their farm.

"During the campaign for membership in the spring of 1936, more than 100 farmers each donated ten or more days of time and furnished their own transportation to carry the story to their neighbors and get enough people interested to make the project practical.

"This fine spirit of cooperation has been evident throughout the program. In June 1936, when we thought everything was ready to go, we were informed that we did not have enough signed for membership. The directors and members immediately went to work and at the end of two weeks had an additional 150 applications for membership.

"After the allotments were made in September and October, 1936, and the construction loan contract was approved, November 14, 1936, we thought the work was nearly complete and that we would soon have electric lights and power.

"Very little progress seemed to be made during the next few months, and several became discouraged and a few lines were built by other power companies.

"In one particular case, a line was built by a power company to serve two farmers who were working against our program. This, they thought would prevent some of the neighbors from getting the REA line. However, the neighbors got together and furnished a private right of way so we could build the line across the field and gave them service with less cost than going around by the road. One of the farmers who had helped build the 'spite line' was township trustee and refused to make application for lights at the township school. Realizing the need for lights, the township Farm Bureau paid the membership fee, and the school now has light and power from the REA lines. When the construction contract was approved, April 29, 1937, we urged the members to wire their buildings. Several of them wired immediately but many were still doubtful about the whole program and since no poles were set until the 1st of September, 1937, only a small percent of the members wired their buildings last summer. By the first of December, construction and house wiring had progressed far enough that it seemed certain that the first line could be energized December 20th. Bad weather and other unexpected delays made it necessary for us to wait until December 24th to energize the first lines.

"During these few days, many who had lived for years without electricity, thought they could not stand it another day unless we energized the lines. For the protection of the members we checked the voltage at each home as the transformer was connected and it was necessary for us to work all day Christmas to connect approximately 100 customers on this circuit. There were two people among those we visited who expressed their appreciation of the fact that we were working Christmas day. Many others reminded us that they had expected lights several days sooner, but most of them were too excited to make any particular comment.

"It was, nevertheless, a real pleasure to have the privilege of bringing these people their first electric lights, and after the excitement was over, many admitted that it was the best Christmas present they had ever had. That evening, as well as the following evenings, many homes were well lighted and Christmas trees were really decorated for the first time.

"The problem of using electric energy was entirely new to many of the members and many peculiar things occurred. Many forgot to turn off their lights and we have several reports of cases where farmers carried their lanterns to the barn in the morning, as they had long been used to doing, and completely forgot about the lights until they went back to the house for breakfast and noticed the bright lights in the kitchen.

"The coming of electricity brought the usual number of problems. For instance, one member reported to us that he could not listen to his radio when his neighbor was using his electric razor. We investigated the matter and found that he also had an electric razor which interfered with his neighbor's radio. After some time they worked out an agreement whereby they would either both shave at the same time, or at least not while certain programs were on the radio.

"We had one case where a wireman had made the wrong connection in the wiring at the barn and a cow was electrocuted. In another case the contractor had made improper connections at the transformer and as soon as it was turned on, 6,900 volts was on the wires to the house. We had taken the precaution of having all main entrance fuses removed before the lines were energized, and no damage was done to the wiring. We were also fortunate in that the service man checking the voltage was not too near the wires at the time. At least one 32 volt radio and several 32 volt bulbs were damaged when the current was turned on before the customer had thought to remove them.

"So many members waited until the last minute to complete their wiring, that we could not install all the meters as soon as they were ready. About 8:00 P.M. Christmas day we were making final checkup for the day to see if all transformers were connected where meters had been installed and were surprised to see lights at one home where we knew the meter had not yet been installed. We stopped to investigate and had the honor of finding the first person stealing current— and only one day after the line was energized. He was connected to the same transformer with another member and so the transformer had been turned on. After seeing his neighbor had lights, he could not resist the temptation and connected two short wires across his meter base. While there, we installed his meter and brought the wires back to the office with us and are carefully preserving them as the first evidence of how human nature reacted to electricity.

"Mr. Jesse Yeager, an incorporator and director, completely remodeled his house last summer and installed a modern circulating hot water heating system, depending on an electric motor for operation. Cold weather arrived before the lines were completed, so he belted the gasoline engine on his washing machine to the system instead of the electric motor, and proceeded to use it for several months until electricity was available.

"Our office is located in the same building with the Carroll County Farm Bureau Cooperative Association and they are operating a hatchery under the efficient management of Mr. Wayne Hiatt. About a year ago we employed a very charming young lady, Miss Kathryn Swartz, as bookkeeper for our project. After becoming very efficient as bookkeeper, she developed an unusual interest in chickens. On March 15 this year she resigned her position as bookkeeper and since that time has been living on a farm along the REA line and is now known as Mrs. Hiatt. They are raising chickens with electric brooders and their electric bill last month was $8.93. We lost a good bookkeeper but have added one more to our list of satisfied patrons.

"During the big sleet storm, April 6th, our lines were given a very severe test and very little trouble developed. However, there was some trouble and our linemen worked nearly all night. About 9 o'clock that evening, one of the members called his director and told him that his lights were out. The directors lights were also out, and after discussing the matter they agreed it was time to go to bed anyway, and did not report the outage to us. However, it had already been reported and before morning service was restored.

"Now that construction has been completed, it is a pleasure and a lot of satisfaction to realize that it has all been accomplished through the cooperative effort of the REA and members of the local farm organizations interested in the improvement of living conditions in farm homes.

"As we pass from the period of construction to that of operation, it is our hope that this unselfish spirit of cooperation will still prevail and that the whole program will progress and be successful.

"There are those who seem to feel that the greater part of the work has been completed but the fact is that the real work has just started. There are numerous problems, among them, the more important one being the problem of increasing the number of customers and the use of electrcity to the extent that the organization will be able to meet its obligation promptly.

"The success of the project will depend upon efficient, energetic and unselfish leadership and work by well qualified officials and employees. There will be no place for those who have only personal selfish ambitions.

"In only a short time, electric light and power in rural homes will be taken for granted and the only time it will be given consideration will be when the lights don't work or when a person is moving from one farm to another. It has already developed that the better and more progressive farmers will not consider a farm without electric power available."

That letter summarized the three years of hard work in building the lines in the first project, and set the stage for the coming years of even harder work necessary to make the project successful. During the next 40 years the number of miles of line more than doubled and in 1979 there were more than five times as many customers with each using about 20 times as much electricity. The average monthly bill increased by 16 times during the 40 years. For more than 30 years the cost per KWH to members decreased each year, but in recent years the cost has been increasing. This information is shown for each year in a table at the end of this chapter.

MANAGERS

Clarence Darragh was named manager of the CCREMC on August 1, 1938 and served until he resigned in June 1947 to operate an appliance store.

On June 20, 1947 R. E. Thomson was hired as manager. He resigned as manager effective February 1, 1956 to accept a position as manager of the Decatur County REMC at Greensburg, Indiana.

Clarence Darragh began working for the CCREMC before the lines were energized in December 1937, and served as manager from August 1938 until June 1947.

R. E. Thomson, manager of the Carroll County REMC from June 20, 1947 to February 1, 1956.

Robert Clawson, began working for REMC on August 6, 1940 and was manager from February 1956 until March 1971.

Robert Clawson, who had been an employee of the REMC since August 6, 1940 was hired as manager. He resigned early in 1971, and was replaced by Richard T. Mills who served from March 1971 until May 5, 1972 when he resigned to accept a position as manager of a 25,000 member rural electric system in Louisiana.

Herb Isaacs, who began working for the REMC on April 13, 1945 has been manager since June 1972.

LOCAL ATTORNEYS

During the period of organizing the REMC and building the first lines, most county REMC's used Harvey B. Hartsock at Indianapolis, as their attorney.

Lewis N. Mullin, attorney for Carroll County REMC since 1956.

The problems in all counties were similar, and it was easier for one attorney to advise several counties than to have a local attorney in each county.

When local problems developed, the directors hired Floyd Julien in May 1939 as the first local attorney for the corporation. His fees were $2 for each consultation or $5 when law research was required.

Lewis Mullin has been attorney since 1956.

OFFICE EMPLOYEES

On March 15, 1938 Kathryn Swartz Hiatt resigned as bookkeeper and was replaced by Margaret Bowman who had been assistant bookkeeper since February 1. Opal Shultheis was employed on March 15.

Some of the many others who worked in the REMC office were: Freda Wolf, Thelma Quinn, Naomi Johnson, Virginia Ratcliff, Mary Shaffer, Delores Larimore, Mary Austin, Almeda Brubaker, Joan Ward, Beverly Ann Purdue, Shirley Hughes, Kathleen Clifford, Kathy Hawn, Joyce Sheets, Joyce Norris, Marjorie Rex, Marilyn O'Farrell, Sandra Jones, Evelyn Brown, Sandra Cook Roth, Joyce Logan, Sondra Jester, Annette Black, Sondra Zook, Sandra Harrison, Roberta Popejoy, Judith Schock, Bonnie Everett, Carmen Lawson Slavens, Loretta Woolridge, Cleo Logan, Nina Hatter, Jean Fisher, Connie J. Brown,

Garnette Smith, office manager of the REMC from September 10, 1948 until May 1970.

REMC employees in February 1980. Seated from left: Marjorie M. Draper, Carolyn A. Dillman, Dorothy O. Myers and Connie J. Brown. Standing from left: Lee R. Crowel, Harold W. Sprague, William Lyons and Herbert Isaacs. Jean Fisher was not present when picture was taken.

Dorothy O. Myers, Carolyn A. Dillman, Marjorie M. Draper, Marsha Floyd Stoner and Maxine Bryant.

Employees in the office in February 1980 are named under the picture.

Garnette Smith was employed as the first office manager on September 10, 1948 and served until May 1970. He was replaced by Lee Crowel who had been working for REMC since January 16, 1963.

OPERATION AND MAINTENANCE PERSONNEL

Clarence Darragh was hired a few days before the lines were energized to be in charge of operation and maintenance. Soon after the lines were energized, John Cohee and Reed C. Brackenridge were hired as linemen. Among others who helped were: Dorval A. Allen, John R. Thompson, Doyle E. Jervis, Lawrence Allen, Harold Barnes, Leo Price, Max Wilson, Ed Wingard, Herb Isaacs, Robert Clawson, William Lyons, Luther Hunt, Russell Brummett, Harry Robbins, John Sacha, Ralph Nulf, Donald Welker, Robert Welker, John Bowman, Kenneth Britton, Lee Wayne Snipes, Don Roth, Richard Dillman, William L. Blythe, Douglas Roskuski, Michael L. Chapman, Stanley R. Quinn, Robert W. Burton, Kenneth W. Boone, Jr., Lynn A. Brown, Steven R. Isley, John R. Toole and Keith Kesterson.

Employees in February 1980 are listed under the picture.

MEMBER SERVICE DIRECTOR

When Robert Clawson was hired on August 6, 1940 part of his job was to advise members on wiring

Robert Clawson, manager of the REMC presenting a gift to Reed C. Brackenridge at a meeting of directors and employees held on December 12, 1966 in honor of Mr. Brackenridge who was retiring as line superintendent after working for the REMC 29 years.

REMC employees in February 1980 from left: John Bowman, Michael L. Chapman, Steven R. Isley, Lynn A. Brown, Robert W. Burton, John R. Toole, Stanley R. Quinn, William L. Blythe, and Kenneth W. Boone.

The Sieber Building in Delphi when it was purchased in 1950 by the REMC.

and other electrical problems and to encourage the use of more electricity.

Herb Isaacs was hired on April 13, 1947 and one of his many duties was to help members with their problems.

Wayne Landes was hired on June 1, 1964 as the first full time member service director. In addition to advising members on power use, he was in charge of publishing "Kilowatt Ours" a monthly paper. He also helped with 4-H electric projects. In October 1970 Wayne left the REMC to go into the hardware business.

Jim Perdue served as member service director from April 1971 until May 15, 1974 when he left to operate an electrical wiring service.

Harold Sprague has been member service director since July 1, 1974.

OFFICE MOVED

In February 1943 the REMC directors made the decision to move from the Farm Bureau Co-op office at 120 East Franklin Street, to the Manson Campbell building across the street at 111 East Franklin Street. Both organizations were growing, and more office space was needed. Also, for five years REA had insisted that the REMC have an office of its own. In a bulletin issued October 31, 1938 regarding allotments for new lines, it stated: "Before the funds in this allotment can be released to the project, the cooperative must meet certain conditions. It will be necessary for the cooperative to establish and maintain its office separate and distinct from that of any other office or organization."

The office was expanded in April 1948 to include more room, but remained in the Campbell building until December 1950 when it was moved to the Sieber

The Sieber Building remodeled and used as the main office by the REMC beginning in 1951.

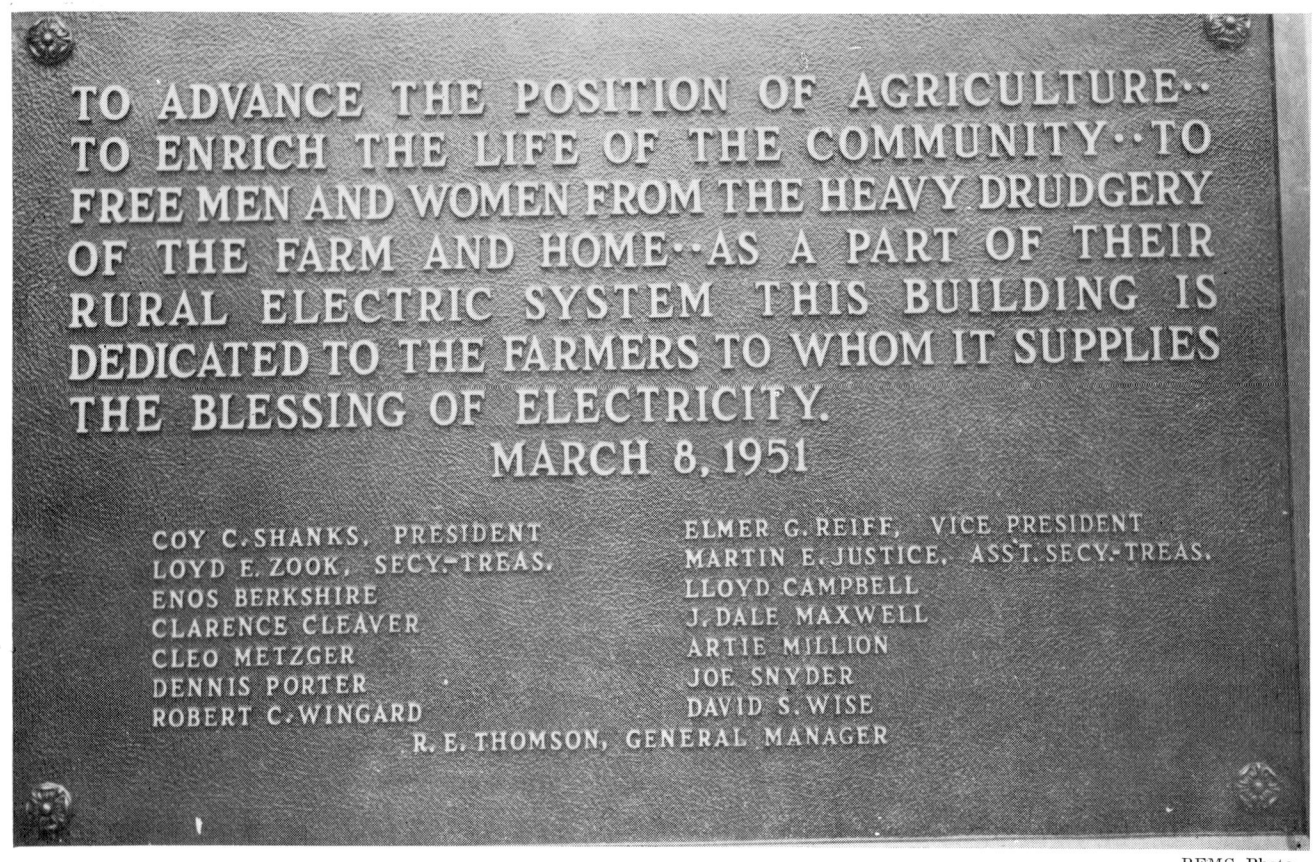

Plaque in REMC building dedicated at the Annual Meeting on March 8, 1951.

building at 119 West Franklin Street, on the corner of Franklin and Market Streets in Delphi, where it is still located. This building was purchased by the REMC on March 27, 1950 and was completely remodeled to provide office space and room for trucks and other equipment. Open house was held on January 20, 1951. The new building was dedicated at the Annual Meeting held at the Delphi Armory on March 8, 1951 with A. D. Muller, Manager of Indiana Statewide REC as the speaker.

REMC AUDITORIUM

A room upstairs was remodeled to provide an auditorium about 60 feet square with a complete kitchen to be used for demonstrations or luncheons. The room was large enough for about 500 people, and was made available for free use by the public in 1951. About 150 meetings have been held in the auditorium each year.

STORAGE BUILDING

In 1967 the REMC contracted with the CCFBCA to build a 40'x80' pole building on North Market Street in Delphi to provide garage and warehouse space for trucks, transformers and other equipment needed to build and maintain the power lines. An addition to the building was built in 1978.

CHANGES IN OPERATION

When the lines were first energized the meters were read each month by an REMC employee. This took a lot of time and many miles of driving. In October 1938 the directors decided to let part of the members read their own meters. The first experiment was not successful, but was tried again in 1941, and proved to be satisfactory. Since then members have read their own meters each month and have saved money for the organization.

Many other changes took place during the period. For the first few years arrangements were made for members to pay their electric bill at several different places in the county. One of these, beginning in April 1938 was Lanes Store at Bringhurst, where people could pay at the store or at any of the several huckster routes operated by the store. On May 1, 1942 this practice was discontinued, and all bills were paid at the main office in Delphi.

In December 1946 the first mechanical billing machine was installed in the office. In January 1949 a postage meter was used instead of licking stamps for 2,600 meter reading cards. The use of a postage meter saved about nine hours work each month, and a lot of wear and tear on tongues.

Storage building on North Market Street in Delphi, used by CCREMC for garage and warehouse. The building on the left was built in 1967 and the one on the right in 1978.

In January 1948 the first mechanical post hole digger was purchased.

In 1950 chemicals were first used to spray the roadsides under the lines to control weeds and brush. This practice was continued for several years.

When the Carroll Telephone Company changed to dial telephone service in January 1960, it created a problem for the REMC. Prior to that time the telephone operator kept a list of REMC employees who were on call for service, and any calls to the office number after hours was transferred to one of the employees. The dial system eliminated the operator, and this plan no longer worked. The problem was solved by listing the names and telephone numbers of employees along with the office number in the directory. Also, each issue of Kilowatt Ours listed the name and telephone number of each employee, and the dates that they were on call.

BUILDING LINES

In November 1938 a contract was signed with Statewide REMC for engineering on more line, and a loan contract and note for $145,000 was signed with REA. This note was for a period of 25 years at 2.73% interest. Donald Chapman, John Kennard and Earl Stewart were hired to get easements for the new project.

In March 1939, REA approved a contract with the A. A. Electric Company, Cicero, Indiana, for building 121 miles of line to serve some 354 farms in Carroll, Cass, Clinton, Howard, White and Tippecanoe Counties.

THE WAR YEARS

In 1941 REA approved a loan of $63,000 to build 63 miles of line to serve 185 members. Before the lines could be built, World War II started. The Office of Production Management issued an order providing that no material could be used for construction of new lines to serve new users unless the construction of such lines was for the sole purpose of defense. This stopped construction of lines for several years, and created some hard feelings toward the REMC as well as problems for management.

In December 1941 Mr. Darragh received the following telegram: "War makes it necessary for volunteer antisabotage armed guards for your substation, twenty four hour basis. If volunteers are not available arrange to hire men with advice of American Legion. Have Sheriff deputize guards."

With an increase in revenue, and a shortage of material for expansion, it was possible to make a substantial advance payment on the loans. This brought letters of congratulations from REA which were greatly appreciated by the board members. Those involved in management in later years agreed that it would have been much better if part of this money could have been used to expand the distribution system.

War Production Board Orders

The War Production Board issued orders regarding the construction of short electric lines to farmers having five or more animal units on their farm. An animal unit is a cow or a horse, or a specified number of other livestock that will eat about the same amount of feed as a cow or a horse.

According to the orders issued, the REMC could build no more than 100 feet of line for each animal unit on the farm served by the extension.

If the War Board granted a permit to the REMC to build the line, it was necessary for the farmer to get a permit to wire his buildings. An article written by the REMC Manager in the April 1943 issue of

Farm News stated: "If a farmer receives a certificate he is automatically assigned an AA3 rating with which to purchase material. It will be necessary for him to pick up the necessary order forms at the REMC office. These are a special form which have the certification of the USDA county war board and also the certification of purchaser attached. On these particular forms, the farmer is allowed to purchase not to exceed 75 pounds of non-ferrous metal for the purpose of wiring the out buildings and only the kitchen of the house. It is not permissible to wire any other room in the house with material secured under this order.

"The only reason wiring material is being released for the kitchen is because the Office of Defense Transportation will stop all rural ice deliveries this summer, and that some 400,000 mechanical refrigerators will be released to farmers. In wiring the kitchen you will be allowed to install one wall receptacle and one light on a drop cord. The light must be turned on and off at the light. You will not be allowed to install a wall switch for the light. You may also install one wall receptacle in the kitchen from which you may operate the refrigerator or washing machine. In case the water pump is located in the basement it will not be permissible to run the wiring to the pump in the basement.

"The above ruling is rather strict and must be adhered to before the cooperative can build an electric extension to serve the farm even though it has been granted a certificate for construction by the war board."

THE PACE ACT

On September 21, 1944 President F. D. Roosevelt signed the Department of Agriculture Organization Act of 1944. This act, introduced in the House of Representatives by Congressman Stephen Pace of Georgia, provided for several changes in the various agencies in the Department of Agriculture.

A chief feature of the act as it affected REA activities was the reduction of interest rates on all REA loans to two percent. Previous interest rates ranged from about two and one half to three percent. The act also removed the time limit on the REA loan program, which had been set to expire on June 30, 1946 by the original REA Act. Also, maximum amortization schedule for present and future loans was changed from 25 to 35 years.

This reduction in interest rates and extension of time for repayment was to encourage the building of electric lines to consumers in less densely populated areas. No longer was it necessary to have an average of three users per mile of line, and REMCs were required to build lines to anyone in the area who wanted electric service.

NEW LINES BUILT

In 1944 REA approved another loan of $58,000, which with the $63,000 approved in 1941 made a total of $121,000, to build 106 miles of line to serve 275 members, but still no material was available. In June 1945 the REMC applied for more territory in adjoining counties.

Staking lines was started on September 18, 1945 but construction did not start until Otober 7, 1946. Shortages of material and labor delayed construction. The first of the new lines were energized in July 1947, and the project was completed in November 1947.

By May 1948 plenty of material was available. The REMC built from three to five miles of line each month, and connected 20 to 40 members per month. REA approved another loan of $156,000 to finance this expansion.

MORE POWER PROVIDED

As the load on the lines increased, it became necessary to install larger transformers at the station in Delphi. One Sunday afternoon in June 1945 the entire system was turned off from 1:00 to 5:00 P.M. while the transformers were changed. The 1781 members were notified, and only one called to report that the lights were out. This might indicate that people read their notice, or maybe people had some other form of entertainment besides watching television on Sunday afternoon.

The first substation built by the REMC was north of Camden, near Rockfield and was put in use at 3:03 P.M. on December 23, 1948. It supplied power to about one third of the customers, and carried about the same load as the whole system had in 1944. In 1950 the substation at Camden was sold to Public Service Company.

In 1949 Public Service Company built a substation along State Road 29 about three miles south of Deer Creek to supply power for the southeast section of the county.

In 1953 Public Service Company built a substation along State Road 75 south of Bringhurst and Northern Indiana Public Service Company built a substation in Burnettsville and provided a metering point at Patton. In 1979 NIPSCO furnished about 20% of the REMC power at two stations, and PSC provided about 80% at five substations including one built in 1975 by REMC northeast of Delphi to supply The Andersons and about 1,000 other members.

BUILDING THE LOAD

The first electrical rate established by the CCREMC provided for a minimum payment of $2.50 per month which included 35 KWH. All too many members were trying to get by on the minimum rate, and this did not provide enough revenue for the REMC, so one of the first jobs for the directors and employees was to get people to use more electricity. About the same amount of electricity is required to energize the lines and the transformer regardless of the amount being used. This "line loss", the difference between KWH purchased and KWH sold, was as high as 40% during the first few years. More recently, it has been only about 9%.

In November 1938 a letter was sent to a random sample of the members asking them to report the appliances they were using. Reports returned by 48 members showed the following: 48 electric irons, 43 radios, 40 washing machines, 30 sweepers, 18 water pumps, 17 refrigerators, but only three electric brooders, three hot plates, two ranges and one milking machine. There were no television sets.

Early in 1939 a committee including the executive board, Clarence Darragh, manager: and Ralph Maggart, County Agent, was appointed to get more people to use electric brooders for chickens.

A brooder sales campaign was conducted during March, and 122 brooders were sold. During the next two months there was a campaign to sell other electrical appliances. Sales reported included 52 ranges, 38 refrigerators and 73 floor lamps. During the 90-day sales period appliance dealers in Carroll County reported sales of $14,700 to REMC members.

APPLIANCE SALES CAMPAIGN

During the 1940's there were several campaigns to sell electrical appliances, such as electric water systems, water heaters, ranges, poultry brooders, and electric motors to operate grain elevators and fans to dry hay in the mow.

In April 1945 the Carroll County Farm Bureau and the Carroll County REMC held a series of three joint meetings for members of both organizations.

On Tuesday evening, April 24 a meeting was held at the Pittsburg School for Adams, Jefferson, Tippecanoe and Deer Creek Townships with 185 present. Special features on the program were: Community Singing led by Rosella Zinn with Dorothy Newell at the piano, flag salute by Joy Lybrook, devotions by Maxine Henderson, clarinet solo from Deer Creek Township, and a whistling solo by David Smith accompanied by Pearl Crowell at the piano.

The next evening 225 people attended a meeting at the Flora Community Building for Burlington, Carrollton, Monroe, Democrat, Clay and Madison Townships. The program began with Community Singing led by Loyd Zook, with Mrs. Zook at the piano, devotions by Ralph Reagon, reading by Joan Booth, and singing by a girls trio from Burlington Township.

Thursday evening a meeting was held at the Burrows Community Building for Rock Creek, Liberty, Jackson and Washington Townships with 160 present. Community Singing was led by Mrs. Ross Downham, devotions by Fred C. Martin, solo by Basil Gardner, and a solo by Mrs. Charles Starkey accompanied by Mrs. Ty Welch at the piano.

At each of the three meetings the REMC had an interesting display of electrical appliances furnished by the General Electric Company of Indianapolis, the Baker Specialty Company of Logansport, and the Carroll County Farm Bureau Co-op Association. A motion picture showing uses of electrical appliances was shown by the General Electric Company.

Clarence Darragh, manager of the REMC discussed the progress since the lines had been energized seven years ago. He showed that the average member was using more than 100 KWH per month as compared to 35 KWH per month when the project first started.

A survey in the spring of 1954 indicated that nearly all members had electric refrigerators and a great majority had pressure water systems. More than half had home freezers, while less than half had electric ranges, water heaters, and television sets. About five percent had electric welders.

Security Lights

One project to sell more electricity was to encourage people to install security lights which were controlled by an automatic switch which turned them on in the evening and turned them off at daylight in the morning.

The first security light on the REMC lines was installed in May 1957 at the Miles T. Martin farm east of Camden. Thirty three security lights were installed the first year and by December 31, 1979 there were 1,884 security lights.

The cost to the member was $3 per month which included all power consumed, bulb replacement and maintenance on the fixture furnished by the REMC. The cost remained the same until 1977 when it was raised to $3.19 per month.

MAINTAINING THE LINES

The cutting and trimming of trees along the lines accounts for the largest item of expense in maintaining the lines. This is a continuing process and keeps the crews busy whenever time is available. Several special tree trimming crews have been hired to keep up with this work.

Damage caused by storms can also result in extra work. Two of the main storms have been a wind storm in 1953 and an ice storm in 1967.

1953 Wind Storm

On Friday morning, May 22, 1953 a severe wind storm hit Carroll County and caused extensive damage to the REMC lines. While only about a dozen poles were so severely damaged that they had to be replaced, there was so much damage to wire and transformers that about 2,000 of the 2,856 members were without service.

Extra crews were called in from Boone, Marshall, Parke, Tipmont and Whitley County REMCs. Seven crews, with a total of 17 men were sent in. This made a total of 14 vehicles working to repair the damage. By 2:00 A.M. Saturday all the lines that did not require replacement of poles were in service. There were still about 300 homes without electric service. By Saturday evening the number was reduced to about 50, and by 6:00 P.M. Sunday only two places, the Reuben Smith and Dean Yoder farms, were without service. Both of those required the building of new lines.

It took about 30 days to finish repairing the damage caused by the storm.

Ice Storm

A severe ice storm in February 1967 resulted in more members being without power for a longer time than at any time during the first 30 years of operation.

Five trucks and 11 men from three other REMCs helped make the repairs. Some of them helped for an entire week. Local crews worked for about two months to complete the repairs.

Radio Equipment

A radio station in the main office and a unit in each auto and truck has provided communication needed to maintain the lines.

On July 14, 1947 the REMC received the license from the Federal Communications Commission to use their new two-way radio, and had a chance to try it out the first day. At 1:41 P.M. a customer reported that he had no electricity. A few minutes later Mrs. Joe Henderson called and reported a tree limb on the line near their home. The manager used the new radio to report the information to a crew in that area, and the service was restored at 2:10 P.M. making a total of 29 minutes from the time the trouble was reported until service was restored.

The two-way radio equipment was replaced in 1959 with new and better equipment. The base station antenna was moved from the roof of the REMC building to a 60 foot tower on the hill south of Delphi near the Lutheran Church. This increased the height of the antenna about 80 feet. In 1974 the antenna was moved across the road to a 100 foot tower.

Trucks and Equipment

The first REMC truck was a panel truck purchased in December 1937 at a cost of $695.25. The second truck was a three quarter ton pickup purchased in September 1939 at a cost of $593.90 with heater and spotlight.

New trucks with modern equipment are expensive, but are necessary to provide good service for members.

In 1979 the REMC owned two cars and nine trucks which cost a total of $167,000. The newest truck was purchased at a cost of $48,000.

Replacing Poles

REMC poles seem to have a habit of getting in the way of automobiles, especially if the auto is operated by a careless driver. In the early years a pole could be replaced at a total cost of about $50. Recently the cost of replacing a pole has increased to $200 or more. A pole was replaced in 1979 at the following cost: pole and hardwear $60.85; labor $154.86; and mileage on truck $16.80 making a total of $232.52. When a transformer is on the pole, the cost can be increased from $50 to $200 depending on the size of the transformer.

CAPITAL CREDITS

In the early years not many people were concerned about who owned the REMC. Since each member paid an initial membership fee of $5 and the rest of the money was borrowed from REA for building the lines, there was not much equity for anyone to own. As the association earned money and paid off part of the loan, members began to get concerned about the problem. On December 31, 1938 the Carroll County REMC had an equity of $26,592.27. In the "Rural Electrification News" issued by the Rural Electrification Administration dated September 1938, it was stated: "Such electric power systems must, at least during the amortization period, be considered the joint property of the users and that no member shall acquire a separate financial equity in such a system. The issuance of evidences of equity, such as shares of stock or credit entries in the books, which

Picture taken in March, 1941, shows Lee Henderson, manager of the CCFBCA putting gasoline in the first truck owned by Carroll County REMC. Robert Clawson is checking the oil, while John Cohee is waiting to get the second truck filled with gasoline.

is properly recommended for other types of cooperatives, therefore does not apply in the case of rural electric cooperatives."

When Claude R. Wickard of Carroll County became Administrator of REA in June 1945, he was concerned about the problem of who owned the equity being accumulated in local projects. Along with other officials from REA he attended several meetings of directors of local rural electric associations to discuss the problem.

A meeting was held at Indianapolis on January 3, 1947 with Mr. Wickard and other REA officials, representatives from county REMCs, Hassil E. Schenck, president of the IFB; Harvey Hull, president and Marvin J. Briggs, general manager of the IFBCA, and others interested in the problem.

It was soon brought out in the meeting that a few officials of REA felt that the lines should belong to REA, while everyone else at the meeting agreed that the lines should belong to the members, just as the facilities of other co-ops in Indiana belonged to members.

As recommended at this meeting, REA proposed that the lines be owned by member users, and that "Capital Credits" be issued to each member each year in an amount equal to his share of net earnings.

Claude Wickard attended the Annual Meeting of members of the Carroll County REMC held on March 4, 1947 and explained the capital credits plan. It was approved by the members, and is still being used.

The CCREMC began in 1941 to accumulate some capital over and above the cost of operation. This money was allocated to each member in proportion to the amount of his bill for the year, and each member was notified of the amount of capital credit allocated to him. The first statement was sent to members in 1953, and reported the amount of each member's capital credit for the years 1941 through 1952. The allocation of capital credits continued each year, and the money was used to repay the loan from REA. In 1960 the directors felt that enough money had been accumulated that some money should be returned in cash to members. Checks totaling $55,690 were mailed to members in September 1960 for capital credit allocated to them for the years 1941, 1942, 1943 and 1944. In April 1962, more than $60,000 was returned to members for the years 1945 and 1946. In 1964 more than $70,000 was returned for 1947 and

1948, and in 1969 more than $98,000 was returned for 1949 through 1952. A total of $2,755,558 has been issued in capital credit, and $284,662 has been returned in cash to members, leaving a balance of $2,470,896 outstanding.

This $2.47 million in capital credits which belongs to members plus $676,872 borrowed from REA and CFC equals about $3 million, the current value of the lines and equipment used by CCREMC.

MEETINGS OF MEMBERS

Annual meetings for REMC members are held each year to elect directors and conduct any other business for the organization. Special meetings are held whenever necessary to take care of business that needs to be done before the next regular meeting. Following is a brief report of some meetings of members:

On January 20, 1939 a special meeting of members was held to amend the Articles of Incorporation to increase the territory in which the corporation was authorized to conduct its operation by including certain portions of Cass, Clinton, Howard, Tippecanoe and White Counties and to provide for more members on the Board of Directors. Only 51 of the 929 members were present. This was barely more than five percent of all members which was required for a quorum. Many people felt that since the lights were turned on there was no need to attend the meeting.

The regular Annual Meeting was scheduled for March 7, 1939 at the Armory in Delphi. Less than five percent of the members attended so another meeting was held at the Courthouse on March 18, with 156 of 955 members present. Door prizes of popcorn poppers and toasters were won by Mrs. Fannie E. Ruffing, Mrs. May Sibbitt, Joe Wise, Charles H. Leazenby and Mrs. Raymond Dillman. As recommended by the directors at their meeting held on March 6, the number of directors was changed from 13 to 14 to include a director from Liberty Township. Walter Ringer was elected as the first director from that township. Miles T. Martin was elected to replace John C. Peterson as director for Deer Creek Township.

In 1943 there was a shortage of gasoline and tires, so it was suggested that the Annual Membership Meeting be cancelled. A letter was sent to the members to get their opinion, and 97% voted to cancel the meeting.

At the Annual Meeting on March 2, 1948 a change was made so that one-third of the directors would be elected each year for a three year term, instead of all directors being elected each year for a one year term.

About 1,000 people attended the REMC Annual Meeting at the Delphi Armory on March 1, 1949. Each member who attended was given a 100 watt light bulb, and seven received special awards. S. V. Skees won an electric coffee grinder, John Kennard an electric iron, Roland Shanks an electric clock, Paul Kirkpatrick an electric iron, Herman Weiland an electric popper, Bert Hayes an electric comforter and W. P. Gates an electric range. Special music was provided by the AGR Quartet from Purdue.

An Annual Meeting was scheduled for March 14, 1950 at the Delphi Armory, but because of a shortage of fuel for heat, it was postponed until August 17, and was held at the Flora Community Park. Dr. Tennyson Guyer was the speaker, and entertainment was furnished by the Melody Men. Mr. and Mrs. Verne Wise won an electric range given at the meeting.

An unusual feature at the Annual Meeting held at the Delphi Armory on March 5, 1953 was a speech contest. Four speakers were chosen from the audience, and without any time for preparation were asked to speak on: "What My REMC Means To Me", "How Electric Power Makes Me Money", and "How the REMC Benefits the Entire Community as Well as Its Members".

The winner, Mrs. Carl Felix was given an electric blanket. The others who were each given an automatic electric toaster were: Mrs. John Scott, Mr. Fred Rodkey and Mr. Carl McCain.

A report presented by Ed Thomson, manager, reminded the members that the REMC had completed the development and construction stages, and was beginning the operating stage. Emphasis in the future would be on operating the system and building

REMC Photo
One of Carroll County's most popular quartets, the Melody Men, sang at the Annual REMC meeting on August 17, 1950. From left: Orville Hathaway, Dr. Charles N. Erbaugh, Bill Roach and Don Hathaway.

Directors of the Carroll County REMC in 1954 seated from left: Cleo Metzger, Artie Million, Clarence Cleaver, Enos Berkshire, Coy C. Shanks, Joe Snyder and Mark Garrison. Standing: Loyd Zook, Dennis Porter, Orville Campbell, J. Dale Maxwell, Robert Wingard, Martin Justice, and Russell Pearson.

heavier lines as needed to meet the demands for more electricity.

An Annual Meeting was held at the Armory in Delphi, Thursday afternoon March 3, 1955. Entertainment was provided by Captain Stubby and the Buccaneers. About 800 people were present and at least 429 were members.

An Annual Meeting was held on March 29, 1956 at the Flora Community Building. This was the first Annual Meeting to be held in the evening, and the attendance was only about 425. This attendance was much smaller than usual, and was partly due to the fact that the meeting was held during the time that many churches were having Pre-Easter services. Entertainment was furnished by the "Musical Notes" managed by Elmer Hinkle of Oxford, Ohio.

An Annual Meeting was held at the Camden Gymnasium at 7:30 P.M. on March 21, 1957. About 700 attended and were again entertained by Elmer Hinkle and his "Musical Notes".

Captain Stubby and the Buccaneers provided entertainment at the Annual Meeting at the Delphi Armory on the evening of March 6, 1958. Mr. Dave Mueller, General Manager of Indiana Statewide REMC was the speaker. There were about 1,200 people present, including about 420 members.

About 500 people attended the Annual Meeting at the Flora Community Building on March 18, 1959. Entertainment was provided by Jack Kurkowski and his Xylophone Band from Richmond, Indiana.

It was reported that Mr. Coy Shanks had been elected president of Indiana Statewide REC.

An Annual Meeting was held at the Camden Gymnasium at 7:30 P.M. on March 29, 1960 with about 500 people present. Entertainment was furnished by the Delphi High School "Top Twenty" directed by Dick Laughlin.

The Annual Meetings for 1961, 1962, 1963 and 1965 were held in the High School at Camden. Programs included the Elmer Hinkle show, and the Purdue Glee Club. Attendance averaged about 600 people.

In 1964, 1966 and every year since then the Annual Meetings have been held at the Carroll Consolidated High School with an attendance of 550 to 1,600 people. Programs have included special numbers by the musical organizations in the county schools, Purdue Glee Club and Purduettes, Sam Hunter from Tulsa, Oklahoma, the Elmer Hinkle Show, The Musical Wades, Wabash College Glee Club, Jim Pickens, Red Blanchard and the Sage Riders, Captain Stubby and the Buccaneers, and the Singing Sheriff. Programs have also included safety demonstrations and the latest information on development in Rural Electrification.

Attendance awards have included electric clocks, lamps, mixers, scissors, knives and silver dollars.

PUBLICITY

The CCREMC has used several methods to inform its members about activities of the corporation. Letters have been sent to members. News articles have been written for local papers, and many meetings have been held. Information has been given on radio and TV programs and several special publications have been used.

The Farm News

In 1941 the agricultural organizations in Carroll County including Farm Bureau, Farm Bureau Cooperative Association, REMC, Production Credit Association, County Agent and AAA joined together in sponsoring the Farm News of Carroll County which was sent to everyone who belonged to any of the organizations. The REMC used the back page for its information and news. This provided REMC news to all members as well as to many other people in the county.

This was a satisfactory arrangement and many people referred to the Farm News as the REMC paper. One feature was the "REMC Honor Roll", a list of the people using the most KWH each month. During 1941 a list of about 200 people using 100 KWH or more each month was published. At that time there were 516 miles of line with 1,527 customers using an average of 73.9 KWH per month. The average monthly bill was $3.94. The last list was published in May 1948 and there were nearly 200 using 550 KWH or more.

In June 1948 there were 657 miles of line with 2,460 members using an average of 189 KWH per month. The average monthly bil lwas $6.23. The KWH used per member per month had reached a high of 206 in April 1948.

REMC News Letter

With the increase in the number of members, with several living outside the county, it became increasingly difficult to keep the Farm News mailing list up to date so that all members received each issue. The shortage of gasoline and labor during the war gave more reason to let members read their own meters, and by this time a card was being sent to each member for them to return with their meter reading. In August 1948 the Carroll County REMC sent to each member the first issue of the official News Letter with a stamped meter reading card on part of the back page. This combined the News Letter, and the meter reading project and not only saved money, but kept new members better informed.

The first issue was called: "What's My Name"? It announced a contest for a name for the paper, and offered the award for first prize of two month's free electric service, and for second prize of one month's free electric service.

The first issue listed the names used for REMC publications in a few other counties. They were: Marco Flash for Marshall County, The Circuit Breaker for Morgan County, Current Comments for Parke County, Rural Transmitter for Decatur County, and TIPS of the MONTH for Tipmont, which includes Tippecanoe and Montgomery Counties.

Ed Thomson, manager, used a picture of his new son on the front of the first issue. The second issue, September 1948 reported that more than 100 names had been received, but that some were names for a boy instead of a publication. The second issue also reported that there were at least two television sets in homes of REMC members in Carroll County.

Kilowatt Ours

The third issue, October 1948, reported that Mr. Ed Griffith of Frankfort won the contest by suggesting the name KILOWATT OURS. Second prize went to David Crook of Galveston who suggested the name REMC JOURNAL. Honorable mentions went to John C. Crichfield, KILOWATT COURIER; Paul Snipes, WATTS NEWS; Jesse McCain, THE CURRENT NEWS, and Charles L. Mourer, RURAL HIGHLIGHTS.

This issue also reported that Miss Deloris Larimore, who had been an employee for the REMC for four and a half years, had resigned as bookkeeper to marry Charles Eberle of Lafayette. Garnette Smith was employed on September 6 as the new bookkeeper. He was a graduate of International Business College of Ft. Wayne, and lived in Delphi with his wife, the former Marilyn Holloway, and their small son Jeffrey.

Each issue listed the top 25 using the most kilowatts during the previous month. Everyone on the list used more than 800. New members for the month averaging from 10 to 30 were also listed in each issue. A list of the first ten to pay each month helped encourage members to pay early.

One little gem included was: "There isn't much to see in a small town, but what you hear makes up for it."

The First 25 Years

Each issue of Kilowatt Ours has an article written by the manager. The issue for June 1960 had the following article written by Robert L. Clawson, manager:

Dear Members:

"REMCs over the entire United States are celebrating the silver anniversary of rural electrification this year. This is the 25th year since the program began. The actual date of the beginning was May 11, 1935. On that date an executive order by the President of the United States launched the Rural Electrification Program. This order created REA as a lending agency through which groups of people could borrow money to build electric distribution lines in rural or unserved areas of our country.

"Although this is a twenty-five year celebration there are probably no REMCs which have been in actual operation for twenty-five years. Your own Carroll County REMC is only twenty-two and one-half years old. The first lines were energized on December 24, 1937. The first REMC in Indiana to get into operation was Boone County on the 31st day of May 1936. They are just over twenty-four years of age. Generally speaking, however, we can say that rural electrification is now twenty-five years of age. It has been an almost unbelievable story when all problems, technicalities and phases of the program are considered. Even the original and most staunch supporters of the idea could not have visualized the fantastic future of the program.

"So twenty-five years have passed and have proven that rural electrification is a success. Young folks who have never seen the time when their homes did not have electricity cannot appreciate the importance of this past development. To them it is just history. Those of us who have had a part in this great undertaking certainly do realize its importance to all citizens of our nation. The availability of electricity everywhere has no doubt been one of the greatest, if not the greatest motivating factor in the advancement of our economy. Some would say this would have been true regardless of who promoted the distribution of electricity or how it was done. Undoubtedly they are right, however, since REMC's did do the job why not give them credit?

"Now back to your own REMC which is one of about nine hundred and eighty-seven in the U.S.A. The total membership of your organization has grown from about 950 in 1938 to about 3,300 at the present time. Those original 950 members used an average of 50 KWH in December of 1938, the first full year of operation. In December of 1959 our members used an average of 500 KWH. The average cost per KWH to the member in 1938 was about 6½¢. The average cost has dropped to about 2½¢ per KWH today.

"The fact that ten times as much electricity is used today as was used during the first year of operation has created the need for great expansion of the distribution system. Originally one sub-station served our entire area. Now five sub-stations are required to serve the system which is of course much larger than it was originally. Practically every individual transformer that was originally installed has been replaced by a larger one. Many other improvements have been made to keep pace with the ever-increasing demand for electric service.

"What do we anticipate for the next quarter century? Without question the continued expansion of distribution facilities will be required. This will mean that more and more power must be available for delivery to our members. Our engineering forecast indicates a need for about four additional sub-stations from which to supply this power.

"This and many other problems will be encountered in the future. We are inclined to believe that the next twenty-five years will be even more difficult for REMC management than the past years have been. Great responsibility will be carried by the Directors of your REMC to maintain a continued sound member service organization".

Grandma's Receet

The following article was in the September, 1963 issue of Kilowatt Ours:

"Years ago a Kentucky grandmother gave a new bride the following "Receet" for washing clothes. It appears below just as it was written and despite the spelling, has a bit of philosophy:

1. bilt fire in backyard to heet kettle of rain water.

2. set tubs so smoke won't blow in eyes if wind is pert.

3. shave one hold cake lie soap in biling water.

4. sort things, make three piles, 1 pile white, 1 pile cullors, 1 pile work britches and rags.

5. stir flour in cold water to smooth then thin down with billin water.

6. rub dirty spots on board scrub hard, then bile. Rub cullord, don't bile, just rench in starch.

7. take white things out of kettle with broomstick handle, then rench, blew and starch.

8. spread tee towels on grass.

9. hang old rags on fence.

10. pore rench water in flower bed.

11. scrub porch with hot soapy water.

12. turn tubs upside down.

13. go put on clean dress, smooth hair with side combs, brew cup of tee, set and rest and rock a spell and count blessins.

Hang this up above your automatic washer and when things look bleak read it again".

What Is An American

This is taken from the November, 1963 Kilowatt Ours:

"He yells for the government to balance the budget and then takes the last dime he has to make the down payment on his car.

"He whips the enemy nations and then gives them the shirt off his back.

He yells for speed laws that will stop fast driving and then won't buy a car if it won't make 100 miles and hour.

"An American gets scared to death if we vote a billion dollars for education but he's cool as a cucumber when he finds out we're spending three billion dollars a year for smoking tobacco.

"He gripes about the high prices of things he has to buy but he gripes still more about the low prices of things he has to sell.

"He knows the line-up of every baseball team in the American and National leagues but doesn't know half the words in the Star Spangled Banner.

"An American will get mad at his wife for not running their home with the efficiency of a hotel and then he'll get mad at the hotel for not operating like home.

"He'll spend half a day looking for vitamin pills to make him live longer, then drives 90 miles an hour on slick pavements to make up for time he has lost.

"An American is a man who will fall out with his wife over her cooking and then go on a fishing trip and swallow half-fried potatoes, burnt fish, and gritty creek-water coffee made in a rusty gallon can and think it is good.

"An American will work hard on a farm so he can move into town where he can make more money so he can move back to the farm.

"He is the only fellow in the world who will pay 50 cents to park his car while he eats a 25-cent sandwich.

"When an American is in the office he talks about baseball, football, or fishing and when he is out at the games or on the lake he talks about business.

"An American likes to cuss his government but he gets fighting mad when a foreigner does it.

"We're in the country that has more food to eat than any other country in the world and more diets to keep us from eating it.

"We're the most ambitious people on earth and we run from morning until night to keep our earning power up with our yearning power.

"We're supposed to be the most civilized nation on earth but still can't deliver a payroll without an armored car.

"In America we have more experts on marriage than any other country in the world and more divorces.

"But we're still pretty nice people. Calling a person a "real American" is the best compliment you can pay him. Most of the world is itching for what we have but they'll never have it until they start scratching for it the way we did. That's us . . . Americans."

"Battle Over The Electric Bill" by I. M. Hep

The September, 1953 issue of Kilowatt Ours had the following article:

"I've always considered myself somewhat of an orator and a pretty good arguer. I got plenty of practice sitting around the stove in the old cross-roads store, but my little woman sure told me off the other day.

"I picked up the electric bill from the mail box, took one look at it and beat it for home to give my wife the dickens. I stomped into the kitchen, slammed the bill down on the table, squinted my eyes, threw out my jaw, deepened my voice and bellered: 'Woman, what's the meaning of this electric bill?'

"My wife was busy baking bread, roasting chicken and getting some pies ready for the oven. That part was fine with me, but I got a little peeved when she just ignored me and kept on with her work.

"'Hep', she said, (she always calls me Hep 'cause I don't like my first name), 'shut up, I'm getting a little tired of this monthly habit of your barging into my kitchen with that electric bill.'

"I didn't have much to say about that, didn't get much of a chance to say anything 'cause she had a lot to tell me and she tells it kind of fast when she gets going.

" 'Hep,' she said, 'I'll tell you what we're going to do. You're going down to the REMC office and tell them to unhook the power—then you're coming back here and take the old wood stove out of the basement and bring it up here in the kitchen—then you're going out and put the old pump handle in order and pump me about 80 gallons of water to wash dishes tonight and for some clothes washing—then you're going to heat that water on that wood stove and wring out those clothes with the old hand wringer—then you're going to get the old kerosene lamps down out of the attic and sell that new radio of ours—then you're going to get that old coal stove out of the shed and set it up in the living room again, and fill the coal box—then, Hep, you'd better make arrangements to eat in town from now on 'cause I'm never going to cook on that old wood stove again—then—

"Right about here she took a breath and I retreated with great speed out the kitchen door. She was still talking when I left the yard in the old flivver, and I was glad I couldn't hear her anymore.

"You know, until she put it the way she put it to me, I just thought of that electric bill as something else that had to be paid every month. Today you are listening to a converted man, a man who really knows when he's well off and a man who isn't about to start doing all those chores over again—those things that had to be done by hand before we got electricity.

"Well, when I left the yard in the flivver that day, I went in to the REMC office and paid the electric bill. And you know, for the first time I actually smiled at that sweet young girl who takes my money from me every month."

Indiana Rural News

In February, 1952 the County REMC directors voted to give to each member a subscription to the Indiana Rural News, published by the Indiana Statewide Rural Electric Cooperative organization. Members have continued to receive this publication which keeps them informed on activities in Indiana concerning Rural Electrification.

RFD 4

In 1956 the Carroll County REMC joined with 15 or 20 other REMCs in sponsoring a popular television farm program RFD 4, seen Monday through Friday over WTTV, Channel 4. This program provided an opportunity for REMCs to inform the public of their activities and bring to them the story of REMC as well as showing new developments and uses of electricity. The program featured Bill Anderson with the latest market news and agricultural information. The thirty minute program, 12:30 P.M. to 1:00 P.M. also included world news and weather reports.

A survey at that time indicated that nearly three-fourths of the REMC members had television sets, so a large number of people could watch the program.

Carroll County News

In 1958 the Carroll County REMC sponsored the Carroll County News presented by Arthur McDowell over radio WSAL, Logansport. It was presented each Monday, Wednesday, and Friday at 11:35 A.M.

REMC SCHOLARSHIPS

In 1970 the Carroll County REMC began a program of offering 13 scholarships of $100 each to high school seniors from families served with electricity by the Carroll County REMC. Two scholarships were offered to students in each of the three main schools: Carroll, Twin Lakes and Delphi. One scholarship was offered to students in each of the seven other schools serving the REMC area: Pioneer, Rossville, Harrison, Logansport, Lewis Cass, Northwestern and Frontier. Winners are selected by a committee appointed by the REMC directors.

Scholarships awarded to students from the various schools are listed by years. 1970: Robert Pullen, Cathy Hodge, Carroll; Mary Fassnacht, Belinda Dickinson, Delphi; Samuel G. Crawn, David C. Arthur, Twin Lakes; Jeffrey L. Miller, Rossville; Connie Beecher, Pioneer; Deborah E. Meyers, Frontier and Stephen L. Wilson, Lewis Cass.

1971: Patricia Achor, Dawn Martin, Carroll; Kathy Beale, George Mears, Delphi; Teresa Burke, John McAninch, Twin Lakes; Pamela Meyers, Frontier; Allen Gastineau, Harrison; Susan King, Logansport; Jan Schmaltz, Pioneer and Rebecca Barnhart, Rossville.

1972: Susan Marie Shepherd, Ricky Bill Mummert, Carroll; Elaine Campbell, Debra K. Trapp, Delphi; Bonnie Bernfield, Deborah Ann Mills, Twin Lakes; Lucinda Marie Page, Frontier; Sandy Spitznagle, Harrison; Lynne Ann Tribbett, Pioneer and Rebecca Ann Redding, Northwestern.

1973: Joanna Scott, Joy Ellen Duff, Carroll; Chris Barnard, Harold Ray Zink, Delphi; Marsha Lou Mills, Randy Jay Ward, Twin Lakes; Debra Schroeder, Harrison; Emily Jane Moore, Lewis Cass; Charlotte Hale, Northwestern; Sandra Rae Berkshire, Pioneer and Thomas Gene Fetterhoff, Rossville.

1974: Kim Douglas Groninger, Ann Cecelia Minnicus, Delphi; Rex Overholser, Patricia Scott, Carroll;

Cindy Dellinger, Dorothy Anita Lind, Twin Lakes; Darla Kay Reed, Rossville; Helen J. Bush, Frontier; Patti Hartman, Northwestern; Ruth A. Norris, Harrison; Debra Jean Bebee, Pioneer and Thomas D. Grandstaff, Logansport.

1975: Douglas Reed, Rossville; Georganne Martin, Harrison; Rose T. Sheldon, Kenneth Walton, Delphi; Susan E. Duff, Dale Orem, Carroll; John Scott, Pioneer; Zelpha Graham, Northwestern; Lois Denise Mills, Randy L. Lane, Twin Lakes.

1976: Barbara Carbaugh, Logansport; Terry Weiderhaft, Frontier; Larry Young, Northwestern; Kimberly Hathaway, Dean Draper, Delphi; Joy Shoff, Sherman Ward, Carroll; Robert Weller, Rossville; Larry Bohm, Pioneer; Melinda Peter, Lewis Cass; Drindy Brown and Michael Crutchen, Twin Lakes.

1977: Laverne E. Smith, Janice Elaine Coddington, Delphi; Patricia Kay Caldwell, Catharine Marie Wingard, Carroll; Debra K. Wise, Kathleen A. O'Farrell, Twin Lakes; Richard D. Butler, Rossville; LeNora Taylor, Pioneer and Teresa Jenkins, Northwestern.

1978: Joseph K. Leinberger, Ronald Dean Appleton, Delphi; Teri Diane Reiff, Gregory DuVall, Twin Lakes; Linda Hendrix, Philip L. Seward, Carroll; Deborah Patty, Pioneer; George Bryan Alexander, Northwestern; Michele Ann Sharp, Rossville; Karla Caldwell, Lewis Cass; Lindy Lee Slusser, Logansport.

1979: Loretta Ann Kremer, William John Leinberger, Delphi; Curt McVay, Rhonda Long, Twin Lakes; Sabrina Kay Britton, Dee Renea Wingard, Carroll; Brenda Lee Bowman, Northwestern; David Alan Lewellen, Pioneer; Jackie Weller, Rossville; Susan Kay Plank, Lewis Class.

1980: Teresa Patty, Pioneer; Selma Dawn Al-Abbas, Harrison; Mark Evan Weiderhaft, Frontier; William Hoyt Alexander, Northwestern; Joseph Dewayne Butler, Rossville; Marsha Morgan, Lewis Cass; Calisse Renee Miller and Denise Renee Clevenger, Twin Lakes; Teresa L. Elston and Caron Patricia Appleton, Delphi; Cynthia Sue Sparks and Doug Sibbitt, Carroll.

ESSAY CONTEST 1960

In 1960 the Carroll County REMC sponsored an essay contest open to all members of the junior classes in the high schools in the area served by the local REMC. The subject was "What Rural Electrification Means to My Community", and the award was a chartered bus trip to Washington D.C. along with winners in other counties in Indiana.

The award winning essay in Carroll County was written by Carolyn Sue Verrill of R. 2, Box 219, Delphi. Following is her essay:

"Rural Electrification has meant great, wide-spread progress in my home, my community, and my country. Many people don't realize what the benefits of rural electrification means to them but let's stop and think!

"Let us just think a few moments about the electrical situation. When the pioneers first settled here, what did they have to work with? As you think about all the things discussed in history class you realize that there were few conveniences as we know today. These pioneer women didn't have electric washers. They washed in old wooden tubs. There was no running water, pumped by electricity, instead they carried water by buckets from the nearby streams or from rain barrels. Since they also had no electric dryers, it made no difference what the weather was—rain, sun, sleet or snow—the clothes had to be hung outside to dry.

"The pioneers had no electrical lighting, therefore, they had to do all of their chores during the day. Rising early in the morning, they had to do their chores before nightfall, again, with no electrical aid.

"Besides lacking these two main conveniences of today there were many other things which they didn't have such as: an electric stove, an electric iron, a radio, a television, an electric shaver and an electric water softener.

"Let's leave the pioneers now and come up through the ages. Let's compare the inconveniences of grandmother's day with the conveniences of today brought about by electricity.

"In grandmother's day the artificial lighting was from candles, then kerosene lights and acetylene lights were used. These three different types of lighting were all sort of dangerous because they were so easy to put something on fire. Also the kerosene lamps took a lot of extra time to clean. Their chimneys had to be washed and their wicks had to be trimmed quite often.

"In the present day our lighting is very fantastic and wonderful. On the farm, lights go beyond the doors of the home out into the barn lot, chicken houses, pig houses, and feed sheds. The huge flood lights enable the farmer to do more work, beginning in the early morning hours and lasting until the later evening hours. In the farm house there are fluorescent lights, television lights, bed lights, and the regular reading lights—all of them having a special job which aids the homemaker in many ways.

"On the farm there are many other things used that take electricity. Not too long ago farmers were milking all of their cows by hand which took several hours, but now, in this modern age of machines, they have a milker that saves a lot of time and energy in the barn. In chicken houses, electricity is used for brooders, heat lamps and as a source of heating water. Heat lamps are also used for other baby animals on the farm.

"Another use of electricity that is found in several barns as well as homes is the radio. Many farmers have the radio on while the cows are being milked because it is supposed to calm the cows when they hear soft music. The radio is about always found in the farm house along with two other important pieces of equipment in this present day of age—the television set and a record player.

"A piece of electrical household equipment which is used by most homemakers is the iron. In grandmother's day their irons were very heavy pieces of flat iron which had to be heated on a coal or wood range. She had thick pads of cloth to hold on to the hot handles. A few years later, irons with detachable handles were used. One handle was adequate but two or three irons were still necessary in order to keep them hot enough to do the family ironing. What a contrast to our wonderful present day dry and steam irons, and our fast operating mangles!

"About twenty-five years ago and before, people could hardly store food and therefore could not get food much ahead of the time it was going to be used. Today foods may be stored for a year or more with the aid of the freezer. The refrigerators and freezers save people a lot of running back and forth from the home to store. It also saves all the work of canning things.

"Another electrical convenience of today is the telephone. This is a great help to the rural people in giving them an easy way of communicating with their friends.

"Besides the electrical equipment that aids in our jobs there is electrical equipment that adds to our pleasures. Previously, I mentioned the television set, which has become almost a necessity in every household. The record player is a near necessity when a teenager is around. Also two things that make summer life around the house more pleasant are air conditioners and electric fans. Here is something else that probably no one has considered. Today one of the modern trends is to own your own swimming pool. The filtration system, which is necessary for swimming pools uses electricity in the movement of the water through it. However, the most important thing that electricity does for us is to make our jobs easier and quicker so that we may have more pleasure time.

"As I have explained, rural electrification has meant great progress in my community, so keep in mind that you can "Live Better Electrically".

Following is Miss Verrill's report on her trip to Washington, D.C.:

"On the beautiful Sunday afternoon of June 19, 1960, twenty-eight high school juniors, their families and some REMC managers, met at the state REMC building in Indianapolis. Everyone was filled in on last minute details of the trip and also filled up with box lunches. At 6:00 P.M. the twenty-eight juniors and five chaperones boarded an air-conditioned Greyhound bus and left for Washington, D.C.

"During the night we made some bus stops but our first major stop was at Gettysburg, Pa., on Monday morning. A guide pointed out all of the main parts of the battlefield and the town. We saw such places as the Eisenhower home, the hotel where Lincoln stayed, and the site of Lincoln's Gettysburg Address.

"At noon we ate lunch in Thurmont, Maryland. We then journeyed on, arriving at our destination—Washington, D.C., at 2:00 P.M.

"We were privileged to have the beautiful Marriott Motor Hotel as our home for the week. A swimming pool, gift shop, restaurant, room air conditioning and televisions in our rooms were just a few of the wonderful accommodations offered to us.

"During the week, we enjoyed seeing many interesting places such as the NRECA building, Arlington National Cemetery, Mt. Vernon, the Capitol Building, Smithsonian Institute, the Pan American Union building, Bureau of Printing and Engraving, the White House, and the FBI headquarters. Several of us wore ourselves out by climbing up and down the Washington Monument. We also enjoyed one evening of fun at the Glendale Amusement Park and one noon banquet with Senator Vance Hartke.

"On Friday evening, June 24, at 7:00 P.M. we said goodbye to Washington, D.C. and on Saturday morning, June 25 at 11:00 A.M. we found ourselves back at Indianapolis, Indiana saying goodbye to each other. Although our wonderful trip is now in the past, I'm sure we will all cherish its precious memories forever."

ESSAY CONTEST 1961

In 1961 the REMC again sponsored an essay contest for high school juniors. Mary Jane Fisher won the county contest for which she was awarded a chartered bus trip to Washington, D.C. Her essay also won the state contest. Following is her essay: "WHAT RURAL ELECTRIFICATION MEANS TO MY COMMUNITY".

"Rural Electrification to my family and my community means almost the same as advancing a whole generation without aging. It has opened the door to a new world of higher living standards, health, comfort, and convenience to farm families. Before Rural Electrification, farm people were considered too poor to afford such luxury.

"To a farm girl who has been brought up with many electrical conveniences it is like listening to a fairy tale to be told that once rural homes did not have electricity—that there were no electric stoves, refrigerators, washers, radios, bathrooms or running water—that on an average sized farm it was necessary to keep hired help to care for only a small amount of livestock and to farm a few acres.

"My father tells that when he was a boy he spent many tiresome hours pumping water for hogs and cattle and that on hot summer days he thought they would never get enough to drink. Today, with electricity pumping the water, this hard work is a thing of the past. Rural Electrification means much more than pumping water; it means hundreds of ways to use electrical equipment to lighten and speed farm work such as milking machines, milk coolers, grinders, hay and grain dryers, feed carriers, brooders, heated water fountains and many other uses. Many farmers in the community have security lights which act as a beacon for farms and serves as a protection against thievery.

"Numerous electrical appliances, which are used in the home, make work faster and easier, giving the homemaker more free time for her family and community affairs. The use of radio and television offers opportunities for cultural advancement as well as entertainment. Rural Electrification brings added joy at Christmas time when children and grown-ups alike can enjoy the beauty of a gaily lighted tree.

"New all electric schools with good lighting and heating, complete electric kitchens where food can be prepared with utmost sanitation, provide safety and comfort for teachers and pupils.

"A farmer who raises 100,000 broilers a year, depends largely upon electricity to do the work. An electric auger conveys chicken feed to bins at the top of the brooder houses and from there it is carried to the feeders automatically. Automatic electric water fountains provide a continuous supply of water at all times. Large electric fans are used to force ventilation into the houses and during very hot weather sprinklers are used to spray water over the flocks to keep them cool. A time clock controls the feeding apparatus and turns lights on and off so the chicken houses are never dark.

"Another farmer who operates a dairy, milks a herd of fifty-two cows with the aid of electricity, milking on an average of a cow a minute with milking machines. As the milk flows, it passes through sanitary pipes to a bulk tank for cooling. A dial shows the quantity of milk given by each cow in pounds. After the milking is done, electricity is again put to work. A special cleaning solution is pumped through the pipes to cleanse them and the other milking equipment is also cleaned automatically. The milk house is equipped with an electric water heater to help with the cleaning operations. A pressure water system pumps water to drinking cups so the cows can drink often which results in more milk production. Feed is carried from the silo to feeding troughs by electric conveyors. The farmer manages all these operations himself and he is able to sell Grade A milk at top prices.

"A nearby neighbor has heated his home with electricity for the last four years. It has proved economical and is clean and safe. There is no smoke or soot and no danger of an explosion to destroy his home or family. Besides the comforts of warm, even heat, he does not have to worry about having a supply of fuel on hand.

"Many changes are taking place in the poultry and egg business as well as hog and cattle raising due to mechanization which has helped to increase profits the farmer could never before achieve. A small motor can do as much work in an hour as an average man can do in a day, saving the farmer hired help expenses.

"Since farming methods are becoming more and more mechanized, it is a recognized fact that rural areas need other job opportunities for young people. According to Indiana Rural News, REMCs are now working to attract new industry to rural communities. By moving to rural areas, industry would benefit from lower tax rates, more space operations and improved economic conditions for themselves as well as for people in the community.

"REMC members are kept informed of new developments and advantages of good power use through letters and the state newspaper. As indicated in these papers, farmers will soon be able to throw away the fly-swatter, insect bomb and garden spray. Electric light traps will make the garden free of bugs through the use of small black light bulbs. This alone might be one of the greatest uses of electricity there-by preserving the nation's health since this would eliminate many uses of dangerous sprays and insecticides. Feed piped like water to livestock at any point on the farm would provide a complete automatic feeding system. These, and many other things are yet to come.

"We are grateful to those men who pioneered this

wonderful project and to those who are constantly striving to better electric service so that rural people can 'Live Better Electrically' ".

Here is Mary Jane's report of the trip to Washington, D.C.:

"On Sunday, June 11, I boarded the bus at Indianapolis for Washington, D.C. There were fourteen of us from Indiana and twenty-two from Nebraska besides two chaperones from each state. From the minute we started I knew I was going to have a wonderful time; everyone was friendly and excited about the trip.

"We visited Gettysburg enroute and arrived at the Marriott Motor Hotel in Washington late Monday afternoon. This is where we were to stay—a beautiful place with cool, comfortable rooms and a nice swimming pool. However, we were so busy going we spent very little time in our rooms, didn't even have time for a dip in the pool.

"When we visited the Washington Monument, a group of us decided to walk up all 898 steps and back down again. We were hot and tired, but it was a thrilling sight to look out over Washington from the monument.

"Each day was filled with interesting places to go, Annapolis, Mt. Vernon, Bureau of Printing and Engraving, Smithsonian Institute, Washington Cathedral, Federal Bureau of Investigation and many others. Some of the highlights of our trip were visits to the REA headquarters for a tour and luncheon, NRECA for a tour and luncheon, the Department of Agriculture where we met and talked with Secretary of Agriculture, Orville Freeman, a tour of the White House, Supreme Court Building, Senate, House of Representatives and U.S. Capitol and finally, a delightful visit and luncheon with Senators and Representatives in the new Senate Office Building.

"It was a memorable trip—new friendships, wonderful food, a week packed with knowledge and fun. It was well worth the time I spent in writing the essay and I hope more high school juniors will take advantage of the opportunity next year."

SPECIAL EVENTS AND ACTIVITIES

The following is a report on a few of the many events and activities in which the CCREMC has been involved:

Award of Merit

In 1941 the Carroll County REMC was one of four in Indiana to be granted an award of merit by the U.S. Department of Agriculture. The award was based on several operating factors, including the number of members per mile, and the average KWH used per member. Carroll County ranked second in the state for revenue received per $1,000 invested. Credit for the award was given to the whole hearted co-operation between REA, the local manager, board of directors and all REMC members.

Corn Borers

In the summer of 1942 an interesting experiment was conducted on the farm owned by Mrs. George Julien and operated by Miles T. Martin, one mile east of the County Farm.

In cooperation with Purdue University and several business concerns, the REMC installed twelve 20 foot poles in a corn field. On each pole was one of several different kinds of lights. The lights were designed to attract insects to an electric grid which would kill them. Several traps were used to catch insects so that they could be marked and turned loose to see if they would return to the same place.

This was one of the first experiments of this kind and provided valuable information for use in control of the corn borer.

Welding Schools

In November 1952 the County REMC held the first of several schools to teach people how to use electric welders. Students who attended the first school are listed under the picture.

A second welding school was held in April 1953 with the following students: Dale Sharp, Fritz Schnepf, Frank Hedderick, Don Roach, Don God-

REMC Photo
Students of the Welding School held at the REMC in November, 1952. Front row from left: Lee Borden, Dick Metzger, C. L. Foss, instructor, John Ward, Clyde Peterson and Ezra Wise. Standing: Charles Davis Vaughan, Jack Ratcliff, C. L. Reedy, Chauncey Bridge, John Roth, John Burke, Dayton Neff, Bob Ward, Raymond Nicoll, Kenneth Yeakley, Bob Dittman, Roger Neff, Bob McCain, Daniel Lavy, Gene Yost and Homer Hackett. Those taking the course but not shown in the picture were: Harold Johnson, Charles Moore, Gene Maxwell, Casey Jones and George Revington.

love, Raymond Dimmitt, Richard Hansel, Harold Dimmitt, Dick Roach, Jerry Lilly, Charles Dillman, Wayne Downham, Walter Downham, Robert Hansel, Arthur Shonk. C. L. Foss was instructor.

Another welding school was conducted in October 1953 with the following students; Homer Wilson, Evan Lantz, Eddie Brubaker, Kenneth Berkshire, Glen Calloway, Clifford Long, Melvin Million, Leonard Maxwell, A. Ray Myers, Leroy Hicks, Don Long, Chauncey Bridge, Bobby Johnson, Eddie Angle, Carl Johnson, Amos Flora, Thomas Page, Lowell Switzer, Joe Garrison, Donald Robertson and Orville Berkshire.

Farm Progress Show

The REMC provided electric power for the Prairie Farmer-WLS Farm Progress Show held on the Miles T. Martin farm east of Camden in 1954. Lines were built to provide 350 KVA of capacity, which was about equal to the total capacity needed by the entire REMC in 1940, or for about 200 farm homes in 1954. It cost approximately $2,000 to install and remove the poles, wire and equipment to provide the power.

4-H Fair

Beginning in 1959 and for the next several years the CCREMC had an exhibit at the 4-H Fair at Flora. The exhibit usually included a game or contest for people attending the fair, as well as information about REMC activities.

The REMC and the Indiana Electric Association sponsor awards for members of the 4-H electric project. Some of the winners in this project are listed in Chapter VI.

American Legion Award

The Carroll County REMC was chosen by the Harry Bohannon Post No. 75 of the American Legion as the outstanding business firm for 1967 at the Annual American Legion Awards Banquet held on April 24 in Delphi.

Indiana Statewide REC

In August 1941 the Carroll County REMC became a member of Indiana Statewide Rural Electric Cooperative, Inc., an organization of county REMCs in Indiana which replaced Indiana Statewide REMC. The membership fee of two cents per member per month was raised to three cents in 1943.

The new state organization helped county member organizations by keeping them informed about activities in the state and by representing them at sessions of the state legislature.

Beginning about 1950 Statewide REC began publishing a magazine called "Indiana Rural News" to keep members informed about problems and accomplishments in the field of rural electrification. Since February 1952 this publication has been sent to each member of the CCREMC.

Coy Shanks represented Carroll County on the board of directors of Statewide REC for about 35 years and served as president from 1959 to 1977.

Mark Garrison has served as director since April 1977.

AIC

For several years the Carroll County REMC has helped send delegates from Carroll County to the meeting of the American Institute of Cooperation reported in Chapter VIII.

NRECA

Carroll County REMC has been a member of the National Rural Electric Cooperative Association since it was organized in Washington, D.C. on March 9, 1942. It is a non-profit organization owned and controlled by about 1,000 rural electric cooperatives in 46 states. Each member association elects a delegate and alternate to represent the association at a regional meeting held each fall and a national meeting held each spring. The president and vice president of the CCREMC have usually been the delegates to the meetings.

In February 1949, the manager and five directors attended a four day meeting of the NRECA in New York. They traveled by plane from Indianapolis, and this was the first flying experience for some of the directors. Those who attended were: Ed Thomson, manager; Clarence Cleaver, Elmer G. Reiff, Joe Snyder, David Wise and Martin Justice. At that time there were about 900 local rural electric cooperatives in the U.S.

Since that time most of the directors have attended both regional and national meetings.

Others may attend the meetings, and attendance at the national meeting has been more than 8,000.

About 125 business firms have exhibits at the national meeting, and this gives managers and directors an opportunity to see what is new in material and equipment used in line construction and system operations.

NRECA provides help in legislation affecting rural electric co-ops in national and state legislatures. Low cost group insurance is made available to local associations, and a publicity program helps keep members and the general public better informed. Training programs are offered for directors, managers, attorneys and employees. The association offers a group purchasing program for equipment and supplies which gives member associations the advantage of volume buying.

Since 1961 NRECA has helped organize rural electric cooperatives in many countries throughout the world.

Beginning in 1964, NRECA has worked with statewide associations of rural electric systems to sponsor a Youth Tour to Washington, D.C. each June. Several state associations, including Indiana, had sponsored tours in previous years.

Miss Rural Electrification

Every year at the NRECA annual meeting Miss Rural Electrification is chosen to serve as a goodwill representative.

The national contest is open to single girls from 16 to 21 years of age whose families receive electric service from a rural electric system financed by REA.

In March 1952, Miss Mary McCarty, daughter of Mr. and Mrs. Garland McCarty of R. 4, Delphi, was selected as Miss Rural Electrification for the state of Indiana. The award was presented at a banquet at Indianapolis on March 11. She represented Indiana at the national contest held during the NRECA convention at Chicago in March.

Willie Wiredhand

Willie Wiredhand a registered trademark, was chosen in 1950 by NRECA members to serve as their national symbol of rural electrification.

Willie was attacked by Reddy Kilowatt, the symbol used by commercial power companies. After a long and costly legal battle, Willie won a decision by the U.S. Court of Appeals on January 7, 1957.

Today Willie serves hundreds of member systems across the nation and around the world. He appears in headquarters buildings, substations, billboards, signs, letter heads, pencils, jewelry, coffee cups, neckties, and a wide variety of other items used by rural electric members and employees in their offices and homes and for promotional purposes.

Willie is the property of every NRECA member system.

CFC

At a meeting on March 20, 1969 at Atlantic City, New Jersey, delegates to the National Rural Electric Co-op Association authorized creation of the National Rural Utilities Cooperative Finance Corporation as

Willie Wiredhand

a private lending agency to supplement federal loans to rural electric cooperatives. The new organization was incorporated on April 10, and soon became known as "CFC". In a short time a majority of the rural electric cooperatives were members of CFC.

The first funds for CFC were from membership fees and member subscriptions to capital term certificates. Additional money was raised by the sale of long-term obligations to private investors. At first, CFC was able to raise three dollars in open market capital for every dollar of member capital invested. This ratio increased as CFC became an established and recognized member of the financial community.

At the end of 1969 there were applications from rural electric cooperatives for loans of more than $424 million, and REA did not have enough money available to meet the needs.

Applications for loans from rural electric cooperatives were processed by REA to determine eligibility for available funds under the REA two percent loan program. Loan applications considered eligible for more financing were forwarded by REA to CFC with an indication of REA willingness to accommodate its liens to provide equal loan security for CFC. In most cases REA made part of the loan and CFC the balance. Interest rate charged by CFC was determined by the cost of money in the open market.

On July 2, 1976 CCREMC borrowed $139,000 from CFC to use for building heavier lines.

HOOSIER ENERGY

The Hoosier Energy Division of the Indiana Statewide Rural Electric Cooperative, Inc. was organized by 17 REMCs serving about 100,000 members in 47 counties in southern Indiana.

On June 15, 1961 REA approved a loan of $60.2 million, the largest loan approved by REA up to that time, to build a generating plant on the White River near Petersburg, Indiana.

A groundbreaking ceremony was held on May 14, 1962 but a lawsuit filed by the utilities stopped construction. On January 11, 1965 the court authorized Hoosier Energy to proceed with construction.

When the 230,000 kilowatt generating plant with 1,500 miles of distribution line was completed at a cost of $80 million, a suit by the utilities prevented Hoosier Energy from operating it.

REA took over ownership of the plant and hired Hoosier Energy to operate it beginning in April 1970. Part of the electricity generated was used by seven of the member co-ops and the surplus power was sold to the TVA electric system in Kentucky.

On March 9, 1971 an agreement was signed with the Public Service of Indiana and the Southern Indiana Gas and Electric Company which called for an end to all pending lawsuits, and provides for interconnecting Hoosier Energy with the two investor owned utilities for the exchange of surplus and emergency power. This interconnection increased the reliability of electric service to consumers of both parties. Hoosier Energy was given the total responsibility of supplying power to its 17 member REMCs.

REA transferred the title of the generating plant and distribution system back to Hoosier Energy which continued to operate the plant.

After several years of extensive analysis Hoosier Energy announced in July 1975, that plans were being made to build a power plant in Sullivan County near Merom, Indiana, to generate power for members. Two years were spent in obtaining more than 20 permits and approvals from various state and federal agencies, and in November 1977 construction began on the power plant.

The coal fired generating plant was designed to burn local high sulphur coal. The first part of the plant will generate 490,000 kilowatts and is scheduled to be in production in 1981. The second unit of the same size is planned to start production in 1982. This plant will generate about four times as much electricity as the plant at Petersburg, and will be used to supply the growing needs of the 17 member REMCs. About 1,400 people were employed during 1979 and about 130 people will be required to operate the plant.

The total cost of the plant will be about $650 million, of which $120 million will be spent for pollution control equipment.

POWER GENERATION

In 1970 nearly 1,000 rural electric cooperatives operated 44 percent of the electric distribution lines in the U.S. to serve eight percent of the nation's consumers in 2,578 out of the 3,072 counties in the continental United States. The cooperatives generated only one percent of the electric power supply. These figures showed the need, and inspired rural electric directors to make a greater effort to build power generating plants in order to insure an adequate supply of electricity at a fair price.

WABASH VALLEY POWER ASSOCIATION

The Carroll County REMC is a member of the Wabash Valley Power Association which was organized in December 1963 by 22 REMCs in northern Indiana. Robert Clawson and Richard Mills, while managers of the REMC served as directors of WVPA. Joe Scott has been a director since 1971.

The purpose of the association is to carry on the general business of the manufacture, transmission, distribution and purchase and sale at wholesale rates of electric energy to members of the corporation.

The WVPA buys electricity from as many sources as necessary to meet needs of member associations, and sells it to the associations at a price based on the average cost of all power purchased. WVPA owns a 17% interest in a nuclear plant being built at Marble Hill, and plans to build other plants when needed.

Marble Hill Nuclear Power Station

On April 17, 1973, Public Service Indiana announced plans to build a nuclear generating plant in southern Indiana. The site selected was a 987 acre tract located along the Ohio River in Jefferson County about 10 miles southwest of Madison, Indiana. The name, Marble Hill, came from the fact that the area was a marble mining quarry in the 1850's.

The plant will have a capacity of 2.26 million kilowatts, and will cost more than one and one-half billion dollars. This is the largest construction project in the history of Indiana, and will supply the electrical energy needs of more than four million Hoosiers. Public Service Indiana will own 83% of the plant and Wabash Valley Power Association will own 17%.

Limited work began in August 1977, and the final permit for construction was issued on April 4, 1978.

The plant is being built in two units, with the first

scheduled for completion in 1983 and the second in 1985.

A LOOK AT THE FUTURE

Drastic changes are coming in the use of energy in the future, and no one knows for sure what they will be.

For the first 33 years the cost of electricity to members in the Carroll County REMC declined from 7.29 cents per KWH in 1938 to 2.08 cents per KWH in 1971. Since then it has increased to 4.33 cents per KWH in 1979. With higher costs for wholesale power, labor, equipment and supplies, this upward trend in cost will probably continue.

In the past the amount of electricity used on the system has doubled each nine years. This trend will continue, and may be at a faster rate, depending on how the energy problem is solved. This will result in a need for heavier distribution lines and more sources of electric power. This will require additional capital.

Investor owned utilities will continue their efforts to get control of the REMC system. For several years the utilities have been taking over the more profitable areas annexed by cities and towns. Recent action of the Indiana State Legislature may help solve this problem.

Government regulations will increase, and make life more miserable for directors and employees, and will result in higher costs for electricity.

Another problem will be the continued apathy of members who take it all for granted. All too many members have the attitude "I'VE GOT ELECTRICITY SO WHY SHOULD I WORRY."

In order to continue the progress made by the REMC, directors and management will have to work harder than ever.

As we look at the past and see the many problems that have been solved, we look at the future confident that directors, employees and members will continue to solve the many problems as they come, and that the rural electric companies will continue to supply members with an adequate amount of electricity at a reasonable price.

INCORPORATORS

Twenty one incorporators who signed the Articles of Incorporation for the Carroll County REMC on August 14, 1935 were: Elmer G. Reiff and Clayton Million, Adams; Joe Snyder, Burlington; S. A. Wickard and Robert C. Wingard, Carrollton; Clarence Frey, Clay; L. H. Funkhouser, Clarence L. Cleaver, John C. Peterson and Oscar Leatherman, Deer Creek;

There were 21 incorporators of the Carroll County REMC in 1935 and five were living in 1979. Seated, left to right: Coy C. Shanks, Clarence L. Cleaver and Robert C. Wingard. Standing, Lewis H. Funkhouser and John C. Peterson who is also the only surviving member of the first Board of Directors.

Hal R. Shafer and Artus Rodenbarger, Democrat; Webb Robeson and Coy C. Shanks, Jackson; Chas. W. Jones, Jefferson; Loyd E. Zook, Madison; J. W. Eikenberry and Fred Voorhees, Monroe; J. Dewey Zinn, Rock Creek; Oral A. Caldwell and Jesse L. Yeager, Washington.

On December 15, 1936 Oscar Leatherman of Deer Creek township resigned as an incorporator because he was moving from the county.

DIRECTORS OF THE CCREMC AND THE DISTRICT THEY REPRESENT

District 1, Tippecanoe Township and part of White and Tippecanoe Counties: J. Dale Maxwell, March 1, 1938 to March 20, 1968; James L. White since March 20, 1968.

District 2, Jefferson Township and part of White County: Charles W. Jones, September 9, 1935 to March 1, 1938; Walter Atkinson March 1, 1938 to March 4, 1941; Raymond V. Hanna March 4, 1941 to March 7, 1944; Artie Million, March 7, 1944 to March 18, 1965; Robert D. Mills since March 18, 1965.

District 3, Adams Township and part of White and Cass Counties: Elmer G. Reiff, September 9, 1935 to March 4, 1954; Russell E. Pearson, March 4, 1954 to June 25, 1963; Clayton Million, June 25, 1963 to March 16, 1966; Charles Pearson since March 16, 1966.

District 4, Liberty Township and part of Cass County: Walter Ringer, March 18, 1939 to March 7, 1945; Martin E. Justice, March 7, 1945 to March 13, 1969; Herman Benner, March 13, 1969 to March 16, 1972; William Mullin since March 16, 1972.

District 5, Washington Township and part of Cass

Directors of Carroll County REMC at a meeting on April 23, 1979. Seated, from left: Robert C. Wingard, Clarence L. Cleaver, Coy C. Shanks and Mark Garrison. Standing: William Mullin, Tom Flora, Charles Pearson, Robert D. Mills, James L. White, Robert Barnhart, Arthur E. Fassnacht, Joe Scott and Orville Campbell. Not present when picture was taken was Dennis Porter.

County: Oral A. Caldwell, September 9, 1935 to May 17, 1937; Jesse L. Yeager, May 17, 1937 to March 2, 1948; Lloyd Campbell, March 2, 1948 to November 24, 1952; Orville Campbell since November 24, 1952.

District 6, Carrollton Township and part of Cass and Howard Counties: S. A. Wickard, September 9, 1935 to March 2, 1937; Robert C. Wingard March 2, 1937 to March 19, 1980; Jerry L. Blue since March 19, 1980.

District 7, Burlington Township and part of Howard County: Joe Snyder, September 9, 1935 to April 1963; Joe Scott since April 1963.

District 8, Democrat Township and part of Clinton County: Hal R. Shafer, September 9, 1935 to March 1, 1938; Artus Rodenbarger, March 1, 1938 to March 7, 1945; Ralph Reagon, March 7, 1945 to March 5, 1946; Artus Rodenbarger, March 5, 1946 to March 4, 1947; Dennis Porter, March 4, 1947 to March 19, 1980; Carol Bordner since March 19, 1980.

District 9, Clay Township and part of Clinton and Tippecanoe Counties: Clarence Frey, September 9, 1935 to March 1, 1938; Ben Metzger, March 1, 1938 to March 7, 1945; Cleo Metzger, March 7, 1945 to March 20, 1975; Kenneth Frey, March 20, 1975 to August 1977; Robert Barnhart since August 1977.

District 10, Madison Township and part of Tippecanoe County: Loyd E. Zook, September 9, 1935 to March 1, 1938; Obe Campbell, March 1, 1938 to March 4, 1941; Loyd E. Zook, March 4, 1941 to March 6, 1958; William Dickinson, March 6, 1958 to March 18, 1970; Charles Campbell, March 18, 1970 to March 11, 1976; Tom Flora since March 11, 1976.

District 11, Monroe Township: J. W. Eikenberry, September 9, 1935 to March 2, 1937; Fred Voorhees, March 2, 1937 to March 1, 1938; Ross Shoff, March 1, 1938 to March 4, 1941; Oren Eikenberry March 4, 1941 to March 7, 1945; J. C. Yunker, March 7, 1945 to March 5, 1946; David Wise, March 5, 1946 to March 4, 1954; Mark Garrison since March 4, 1954.

District 12, Deer Creek Township: John C. Peterson, September 9, 1935 to March 18, 1939; Miles T. Martin, March 18, 1939 to March 7, 1944; Clarence Cleaver since March 7, 1944. Until 1938 the following people from Deer Creek Township represented Tip-

New directors elected at the Annual Meeting of the CCREMC on March 19, 1980 from left: Carol Bordner, District 8; Jerry L. Blue, District 6; and Robert Dittman, District 13. Retiring directors in picture were Robert Wingard, director from District 6 since 1937 and Dennis Porter from District 8 since 1947. Coy C. Shanks, director from District 13, since 1937 was unable to attend the meeting.

pecanoe Township: Oscar Leatherman from September 9, 1935 until December 15, 1936; L. H. Funkhouser from December 15, 1936 until March 1, 1938 when a director was elected for Tippecanoe Township.

District 13, Jackson Township: Webb Robeson, September 9, 1935 to March 2, 1937; Coy C. Shanks, March 2, 1937 to March 19, 1980; Robert Dittman since March 19, 1980.

District 14, Rock Creek Township: J. Dewey Zinn from September 9, 1935 to March 4, 1941; Enos Berkshire March 4, 1941 to March 6, 1958; J. Dewey Zinn, March 6, 1958 to December, 1958; Gordon Flora, December 1958 to March 22, 1973; Arthur Fassnacht since March 22, 1973.

CARROLL COUNTY REMC OFFICERS

President: J. W. Eikenberry, September 9, 1935 to March 2, 1937; Oral A. Caldwell, March 2, 1937 to May 17, 1937; Elmer G. Reiff, May 17, 1937 to March 1, 1938; Coy C. Shanks, March 1, 1938 to 1960; Martin E. Justice, 1960 to 1965; Cleo Metzger, 1965 to 1975; Robert D. Mills, since 1975.

Vice President: Elmer G. Reiff, September 9, 1935 to May 17, 1937 and 1938 to 1954; Coy C. Shanks, May 17, 1937 to March 1, 1938; Martin E. Justice, 1954 to 1960; Joe Snyder, 1960 to 1963; J. Dale Maxwell, 1963 to 1968; Robert D. Mills, 1968 to 1975; Mark Garrison, since 1975.

Secretary Treasurer: John C. Peterson, September 9, 1935 to 1939; J. Dewey Zinn, 1939 to 1941; J. Dale Maxwell, 1941 to 1948; Loyd E. Zook, 1948 to 1954; Cleo Metzger, 1954 to 1965; William Dickinson, 1965 to 1969; Mark Garrison, 1969 to 1975; Charles Pearson, since 1975.

Manager: John C. Peterson, January 4, 1937 to July 31, 1938; Clarence Darragh, August 1, 1938 to May 23, 1947; R. E. Thomson, June 20, 1947 to February 1, 1956; Robert L. Clawson, February 1, 1956 to March 1971; Richard T. Mills Jr., March 1971 to May 5, 1972; Herbert L. Isaacs, since June 1972.

Winners and alternates for labor-free wiring jobs awarded at drawings
held at Township Farm Bureau meetings in the spring of 1937.

TOWNSHIP	HOUSE	ALTERNATES	BARN	ALTERNATES
Adams	Asa Cree	Wilbur Crowell Hopewell Store	George Peterson	Elmer G. Reiff Mary E. Hoover
Burlington	John D. Brown	Harry F. Maxwell Marion Thomas	Joe Snyder	C. H. Calton Ralph Rinehart
Carrollton	A. A. Gillam	Judson Sterrett George E. Hood	Fred C. Flora	James Sink Laurel Beck
Clay	Clarence Frey	H. A. Ward John Beard	Eli Ritchey	Frank Barnhart Mary Wagoner
Deer Creek	Orville Fife	John Ramey Mrs. Kate Trawin	Hansel McHardie	Charles G. Black Lenna Powell
Democrat	Julia A. Lohrman	Martha T. Smith Mrs. John Clem	Minnie L. Wilson	Wm. B. Sibbitt Chalmer R. Trobaugh

TOWNSHIP	HOUSE	ALTERNATES	BARN	ALTERNATES
Jackson	Floyd Sterrett	Melvin Fisher George Hunt	Arvel Flora	Ira E. Robeson Lower D.C. Church
Jefferson	Leam Metz	John L. Kennard Charles E. Armstrong	Forrest Redding	Curtis McCain John Thurston
Madison	Marvin Shultheis	Joe & Lee Vaughn Howard Cleaver	Charles Schnepp	Mrs. Perry Rule Joe Henderson
Monroe	Ezra Flora	John H. Flora Earl E. Brown	Eva E. Sheets	Ralph Johns Ross Shoff
Rock Creek	C. T. Amick	Leah Brechbeil J. C. Kennedy	Wilson Sterrett	Roscoe Mullin Lulu J. Sanderson
Tippecanoe	Ed Grimm	Edgar Fountain Claude E. Zook	Ed Stephens	George Brewer
Washington	Wm. R. Caldwell	Roy Yeakley Leonard Shanks	Leonard Chapman	Vincent German Delbert McCloskey

CARROLL COUNTY REMC LONG TERM OBLIGATIONS

REA Note	Date	Original Amount of Note Including Deferred Interest	Payment Made to December 31, 1979	Balance Due as of December 31, 1979
Note A	2-1-37	$ 360,000.00	$360,000.00	$ .00
Note B	11-14-38	145,000.00	145,000.00	.00
Note C	10-5-39	20,000.00	20,000.00	.00
Note D1	11-15-41	63,000.00	63,000.00	.00
Note D2	4-10-45	58,022.39	57,200.26	822.13
Note H	12-18-46	25,028.97	23,061.38	1,967.59
Note K	5-6-48	156,424.87	136,995.22	19,429.65
Note L	12-15-48	155,621.63	129,073.55	26,548.08
Note P6	7-2-76	324,000.00	2,752.74	321,247.26
Note R6	6-17-77	170,000.00	.00	170,000.00
Totals		$1,477,097.86	$937,083.15	$540,014.71
CFC Loan	7-2-76	$ 139,000.00	$ 2,142.73	$136,857.27

The above table shows that nearly two thirds of the money borrowed from REA was repaid by December 31, 1979.

The last two loans from REA, and the loan from CFC provided money to build a new substation and to make improvements on the lines to provide for heavier loads.

CARROLL COUNTY REMC

Statistics for December 31st

Year	Number of Connected Customers	Miles of Line Energized	Average Monthly Bill	Avg. KWH per mem. per Mo.	Avg. KWH cost to mem. in cents
1938	856	362.00	$ 2.95	37	7.29
1939	1135	486.50	3.20	49	6.54
1940	1412	516.00	3.45	58	5.96
1941	1505	516.00	3.82	69	5.52
1942	1585	521.00	4.07	79	5.13
1943	1592	523.00	4.48	94	4.79
1944	1596	532.00	4.89	105	4.68
1945	1792	537.00	4.99	114	4.38
1946	1909	542.00	5.35	128	4.19
1947	2022	634.24	6.08	164	3.71
1948	2421	687.23	6.41	192	3.34
1949	2621	708.50	7.02	224	3.13
1950	2720	723.20	7.67	251	3.06
1951	2791	729.68	8.15	283	2.88
1952	2807	736.71	8.79	310	2.84
1953	2875	745.90	9.11	331	2.75
1954	2961	753.62	9.59	359	2.67
1955	3032	758.84	10.08	381	2.65
1956	3103	764.07	10.36	398	2.60
1957	3153	767.79	10.75	423	2.54
1958	3206	770.90	11.12	450	2.47
1959	3243	774.53	11.48	460	2.49
1960	3290	778.15	11.72	479	2.44
1961	3336	783.18	12.16	502	2.42
1962	3386	787.22	12.89	540	2.39
1963	3438	792.84	13.37	566	2.36
1964	3490	797.67	13.65	588	2.32
1965	3562	802.72	13.92	615	2.26
1966	3659	807.48	14.59	656	2.22
1967	3752	814.14	14.86	683	2.18
1968	3831	821.07	15.95	740	2.16
1969	3939	827.19	16.69	785	2.13
1970	4057	835.34	17.42	827	2.11
1971	4188	841.74	17.95	864	2.08
1972	4351	845.46	20.16	869	2.32
1973	4516	856.91	22.12	925	2.39
1974	4658	862.23	22.96	1002	2.29
1975	4790	862.56	27.42	1100	2.49
1976	4880	872.32	36.11	1199	3.01
1977	4962	879.	45.00	1328	3.38
1978	5061	886.	49.44	1320	3.74
1979	5127	895.	58.00	1339	4.33

CHAPTER XI

OTHER ORGANIZATIONS AND EVENTS

ROCKFIELD POLAND CHINA BREEDERS ASSOCIATION

The Rockfield Poland China Breeders Association was organized in 1915. William F. Kerlin was president, and P. M. Byrum secretary treasurer. Other members were: John W. Kerlin, Roy Snoeberger, W. H. Funkhouser and Son, George Lowery, Everett Flora, Orville Flora, and Parks and John Groninger.

The association purchased a Poland China boar named "Long Chief" in the spring of 1916 and he won grand champion at the Indiana State Fair that fall. The Association took 24 head of hogs to the State Fair and won 26 premiums amounting to $350.

In the fall of 1918 one member of the association paid $300 for a boar named "Evolution", and eleven days later sold the boar for $2,500. The next spring the same boar sold again for $25,000, a record price for a boar at that time. A litter of seven sired by "Evolution" sold for $9,500 at the age of four months. These prices focused attention of breeders throughout the U.S. for Rockfield, and gave great local impetus to other cooperatives in the area.

By the spring of 1920, prices of livestock fell so much that many breeders who paid high prices for livestock went bankrupt.

CARROLL COUNTY COOPERATIVE DUROC BREEDERS ASSOCIATION

The Carroll County Cooperative Duroc Breeders Association was organized at a meeting in Delphi on January 10, 1920. Officers elected were Dr. A. J. Cook of Flora, president; Fred Baum, vice president; Harvey E. Studebaker, secretary treasurer. Directors were: Harry F. Maxwell, Russell Craig and Elmer E. Sheets.

Meetings were held each month for several months. Auction sales were scheduled to be held at Delphi on October 16, and at Flora on November 9, 1920, but those sales were called off. Another proposed project was to sponsor a 4-H Duroc Pig Club in the county, and several individuals helped sponsor clubs.

Hog prices declined, and members lost interest in attending meetings. The association was inactive for a few years, except for activities at the County Fair. With the assistance of County Agent Harry Ackerson, a group got together at the County Fair on October 8, 1924, and reorganized the association with Harry Maxwell, president, and Leo C. Craig, secretary treasurer. Others who attended the meeting were: A. A. Newer, Lee Sink, Marshall Wagoner and Col. Enyart.

The annual meeting was held at the County Agent's office in Delphi on December 13, 1924. The speaker was Dr. James R. Wiley of Purdue who was the founder of the Hoosier Ton Litter Club. He stressed the value of the Ton Litter work from the breeders standpoint, and several members signed up for the Ton Litter Club. The members also agreed to sponsor a Fat Barrow Club for boys in 4-H.

A letter of December 15, 1924 from Robert J. Evans, secretary of the American Duroc Jersey Association, Chicago, reported that the National Association had voted to discontinue offering prizes for local shows. He reported that receipts for recording had dropped from $44,800 in 1922 to $12,808 in 1924. The letter also stated: "There never has been a time in 30 years when good breeding hogs could be bought so cheaply and the hog man who neglects to build up his herd this winter with some real brood sows will pass up a big opportunity."

A motto at the bottom of the letterhead stated: "PIGS IS PIGS, BUT IT TAKES A DUROC TO MAKE A REAL HOG".

Maxwell, Enyert and the Craigs combined for a sale on October 31, 1925 at the Maxwell farm east of Bringhurst. Some of the individual members remained active for many years, selling privately, consigning to State Association Sales, combining with others for public auctions or having their own public sales, so the association may have provided an incentive, although it finally ceased to function as an organization.

DELPHI DUROC ASSOCIATION

The Delphi Duroc Association held its first annual sale at the Flora Fair Grounds on August 26, 1939.

Committee members were: Charles Shultheis, Kenneth Vaughan, James Pierce and Wm. Schoff. Twenty three boars were sold at an average price of $41 with a top price of $127.50. Gilts averaged $26 and bred sows averaged $60 with a top of $165.

At the annual meeting in November 1939 the following officers were elected: Charles Shultheis, president; John Snoeberger, vice president; Robert Maxwell, secretary; and Kenneth Vaughan, treasurer. Others who served as directors were: Leo C. Craig, Ed Kite, Robert Martin, Fred Newman, James Pierce, and C. O. Eyer.

ARTIFICIAL BREEDERS ASSOCIATION

More than 100 dairymen and other interested people met in April 1947 and organized the Carroll County Artificial Breeders Association. Officers elected were: Clyde Cooke, president; Jay Rothenbarger, vice president; Melvin Fisher, secretary; and Homer Hanna, treasurer. W. A. Crist served with these officers on the executive board.

Township directors were: Glenn Smith, Burlington; Clyde Cooke, Carrollton; Jay Rothenbarger, Clay; Charles Nance, Deer Creek; Robert Smith, Democrat; Melvin Fisher, Jackson; Frank Lybrook, Jefferson; Mack Snyder, Liberty; W. A. Crist, Madison; Homer Hanna, Monroe; Larry Gruber, Tippecanoe; E. E. Flora, Rock Creek; John L. Bowman, Washington; and S. A. Wickard, director-at-large.

F. Michael Guckien of Burrows was engaged as technician.

There were 160 members in 1948, and officers were:

Berry Photo
Artificial Breeders Association Directors in 1953 were left to right seated: Everett Flora, treasurer, Rock Creek Township; Charles Nance, secretary, Deer Creek; Mack Snyder, president, Liberty; John McCormick, Madison; Frank DeLaCroix, American Breeders Service; Dr. P. H. Wagaman, veterinarian of Flora; and Ed Gannon, Purdue Extension Dairyman; standing: Ray Peterson, Democrat; Melvin Fisher, Jackson; Clyde Cooke, Carrollton; Glenn Smith, Burlington and Homer Hanna, Monroe Township.

Berry Photo
Jack Frost and Bill Anderson of Purdue on left met in 1954 with officers of the Carroll County Livestock Breeders Association left to right: Roy Richter, Harold Thompson, Charles Meade Sr., Lawrence Douglas and Robert Landis.

Clyde Cooke, president; Mack Snyder, vice president; Melvin Fisher, secretary and Everett Flora, treasurer.

Officers for 1949 were: S. A. Wickard, president; Mack Snyder, vice president; Loren McCormick, secretary; Everett Flora, treasurer and Homer Hanna, member of executive board.

In 1950 there were more than 200 members with 1,200 cows. Officers were the same as for 1949 except Charles Nance was secretary.

At the annual meeting January 10, 1951 it was decided to discontinue the membership fee of $10 and to return the 281 membership fees as soon as money was available. The breeding fee for each cow was continued at $7 and approximately 1,000 cows were bred during 1950.

Breeding service included Holstein, Guernsey, Jersey and Brown Swiss for dairy herds and Angus for beef cattle.

Officers for 1953 were: Mack Snyder, president, Liberty Township; Charles Nance, secretary, Jackson; Everett Flora, treasurer, Rock Creek. Directors were: John McCormick, Madison; Ray Peterson, Democrat; Melvin Fisher, Jackson; Clyde Cooke, Carrollton; Glenn Smith, Burlington; and Homer Hanna, Monroe.

Officers for 1959 were: Melvin Fisher, president; and Homer Hanna, treasurer.

In 1960 the organization was dissolved, and Mr. Guckien continued to provide service for farmers in Carroll County until he retired on January 19, 1977.

The organization was sponsored by Purdue University and the Indiana Artificial Breeders Association with headquarters at Carmel, Indiana.

LIVESTOCK BREEDERS ASSOCIATION

Purebred Livestock Breeders in Carroll County met in the County Extension office on January 12, 1953 and adopted a constitution and by-laws for the Carroll County Purebred Livestock Breeders Association.

Officers elected for the association were: Charles Meade Sr., Camden, president; Harold Thompson, Flora, vice president; Robert E. Landis, Delphi, secretary treasurer. Mark Garrison, Bringhurst, was named to represent beef; Roy Richter, Flora, swine; J. C. Lowery, Flora, sheep; Fritz G. Schnepf Sr., Bringhurst, dual purpose; and J. V. Pickart, Camden, dairy cattle.

The membership committee included Joe Loy, J. C. Lowery, William Dickinson, Eldon Robeson, Roy Richter, Lawrence Douglas and Lewis Funkhouser.

The association sponsored the Carroll County Beef and Swine School held at the REMC auditorium, all day on February 24, with W. T. Anderson and Eddie C. Miller of Purdue as speakers. Members of the panel discussion group for the school were: William Dickinson, Madison Township; Solomon Wickard, Carrollton; Roy Richter, Monroe; Lee Flora, Madison and Eddie C. Miller, Purdue swine specialist. Mr. Miller and the panel members all emphasized the importance of sanitation and a good sound feeding program of balanced rations supported by a good mineral, rather than dependence on antibiotics and other wonder drugs in having a healthy swine herd.

Seed producers in the county asked to join the association and the name was changed to Livestock Breeders and Seed Producers Association.

The association held regular Annual Meetings with a supper at various churches in the county with a variety of programs. In 1961 J. R. Rinehart reported on his trip to South America with a plane load of livestock. In 1965 Kay Aylor gave a report on two years she spent in the Peace Corps.

Hassil E. Schenck, president of the IFB was the speaker at the Annual Meeting in 1966.

On February 27, 1968 a joint meeting was held with the newly organized County Pork Producers Council. The program included a report on "The New Era in Agriculture" by Wm. Rothenberger, the first president of the National Pork Producers Council.

In 1969 another joint meeting was held with the Pork Producers Council with a report on a trip to Africa by John C. Peterson.

The last regular Annual Meeting of the association was held in 1971 with a talk by Ed Thum of the National Live Stock and Meat Board.

Others who served as president of the County Livestock and Seed Producers Association were: Fritz G. Schnepf Sr., Eldon Robeson, Kenneth Frey, Marion Langston, James Riley, Sr., Leo C. Craig and Keith Sink. Others who served as secretary treasurer were: Lawrence Douglas, Robert Crume, Clifford Joyce, Mrs. Fritz G. Schnepf Sr., Dean Todd and Mrs. Charles Childers.

CARROLL COUNTY PORK PRODUCERS

At a meeting of hog farmers at the Suburban Restaurant in Flora on January 5, 1968 the Carroll County Pork Producers Council was organized as a branch of the Carroll County Livestock Breeders and Seed Producers Association.

Officers elected for the new organization were: Robert Lamb, president; James R. Kremer, vice president; Kenneth Yeakley, secretary; Ernest Wyant, treasurer; and a 14 member board of directors with one representative from each township. Directors for 1970 were: Robert Peterson, Adams Township; Ernest Wyant, Burlington; Bill Pickart, Carrollton; Kenneth Frey, Clay; Robert Sullivan, Deer Creek; Ray Funkhouser, Democrat; Charles Yeager, Jackson; John Crowell, Jefferson; Harold Allread, Liberty; Richard McCain, Madison; Bill Kearns, Monroe; Arthur Fassnacht, Rock Creek; Dale Craig, Tippecanoe and Kenneth Yeakley, Washington.

For four years the new organization met with the Carroll County Livestock Breeders and Seed Producers Association at their regular Annual Meetings.

Officers for 1980 were: Jerry Hendress, president; Nelson Sines, vice president; Mark Martin, secretary and Ernest Wyant, treasurer. Township Directors were: Bob Lamb, Adams Township; Dean Scott, Burlington; Robert Hicks, Carrollton; Laverne Crumpacker, Clay; Gary Cleaver, Deer Creek; Ed Spraker, Democrat; Dave Barnard, Jackson; Tim Burke, Jefferson; Myron Sink, Liberty; Richard McCain, Madison; Atlee Oyler, Monroe; Steve Nichols, Tippecanoe and Ed Johnson, Washington.

Others who served as president were: J. R. Rinehart, Bill Kearns, Kenneth Yeakley, Bill Pickart, Craig Martin, Dan Snell and Ed Johnson. Other secretaries were: Bill Pickart, Byron Gilbert, John Cox and Ed Oyler.

Those who have served as directors of the state organization have been: Robert Lamb, J. R. Rinehart, Bill Kearns, Kenneth Yeakley, Ron Allread, John Cox and Steve Nichols.

CARROLL COUNTY PORK FESTIVALS
by Steve Nichols

With Carroll County being the leading pork producing county in Indiana, a group of people got together

Mrs. Bill (Susan) Mann, chairman of the committee and Dr. Earl Butz, speaker, at the Carroll County Pork Festival held at Flora on June 16, 1979. Susan is holding the plaque which she was awarded for winning the Husband Calling Contest.

and felt it appropriate to honor these producers and the total county by holding a "Carroll Pork Festival."

The first festival in Carroll County was held June 3-4 in 1978 and included several continuous activities which ran from Saturday morning until 9:00 P.M. on Sunday evening. Several ideas and suggestions were obtained through our neighbors at Tipton County who have been conducting a "Tipton County Pork Festival" for quite a few years. The featured speaker for the first Carroll County Festival was Paul Udell, anchorman for Channel 13 Eyewitness News in Indianapolis. All events and activities were free to the public with the only money-making project being the pork chop and sausage dinners served during the festival.

Susan Mann who served as General Chairman and spent many long hard hours in organizing the Festival deserves the credit for making the Pork Festival a reality in Carroll County.

The 1978 Pork Festival proved to be very successful and $800 was presented to the Carroll County 4-H Exhibit Association to be applied to the note on the new swine facility at the fairgrounds, and $800 was given to the Flora Park Recreation Board.

For 1979, a few changes were made to strengthen the Pork Festival. The date was changed to June 16-17, in order to avoid competition with the Camden Fish Fry and to allow a couple more weeks for the farmers to complete their field work. One new event that gained popularity was the "Hog Jog" which enticed 408 runners from throughout Indiana and from Florida, Illinois and Ohio. About 20% of the runners were from Carroll County. Runners had a choice of a 1.8 mile or a 5.93 mile course. All but two who started finished the race.

Another change for the better was having the Carroll County Pork Producers cook the pork chops and sausages and thus involved more participation from the community.

The featured speaker for the 1979 Pork Festival was Dr. Earl L. Butz, Dean Emeritus of Agriculture at Purdue University, and former U.S. Secretary of Agriculture. His topic was "Pigs, Profits and Politicians." Dr. Butz also helped judge a Hog Calling and

Kenneth Moore Photo

J. R. Rinehart, winner of the Hog Calling Contest at the Carroll County Pork Festival at Flora on June 16, 1979. He later won second place in the state Hog Calling Contest.

a Husband Calling Contest. Susan Mann won the Husband Calling Contest. J. R. Rinehart won the Hog Calling Contest, and later won second place in the State Fair Hog Calling Contest.

A large crowd filled the fairgrounds at Flora for the 1979 Festival and it was very successful. The Pork Festival Committee presented the 4-H Exhibit Association with a check for $1,500 to be used for the new proposed Community Building. The Flora Park Recreation Board was also given $1,500.

The dates for the 1980 Pork Festival were set for June 13-14. This is a Friday Night-Saturday format unlike the Saturday-Sunday format which had been utilized the previous two years.

If the Pork Festival continues to grow and be as prosperous in the future as has been experienced the past two years, Carroll County has a lot to look forward to.

FEDERAL FARM LOAN ASSOCIATION

The Federal Farm Loan Act of 1916 created the Federal Farm Loan Board and 12 Federal Land Bank Districts with a bank in each district to provide money for long term loans on farm real estate. The loans were handled through National Farm Loan Associations which were organized, owned and controlled by farmers.

Each person who borrows money through the Federal Land Bank Association is required to buy stock in the association equal to five percent of the amount of the loan. The association in turn buys a similar amount of stock in the Federal Land Bank, such stock is held for the repayment of association members loans. A stockholder is entitled to one vote.

Capital was required to start the system and most of the initial capital stock was subscribed by the Government. The system has been completely farmer-owned since 1947 the year in which all capital subscribed by the Government was repaid to the Treasury.

Present authority for the activities of the Farm Credit Banks and Associations, their Fiscal Agency, and the Farm Credit Administration is vested in the Farm Credit Act of 1971, PL 92-181. It supersedes all previous legislation governing the System.

CAMDEN NFLA

The Camden National Farm Loan Association was organized in September 1919. The first Annual Meeting was held at the home of Isaac Wolfe in January 1920. Officers elected were: J. C. Sink, president; Isaac Wolfe, vice president and Frank Stansell, secretary treasurer. During the first four months the association had loaned $58,000 and the appraiser had recently approved five more loans amounting to $27,400. Loans were being made at a low rate of interest with payments which would pay interest and retire the loan in 34½ years.

In September 1936 the office was moved to Delphi and Charles M. Flora was elected secretary treasurer.

At the Annual Meeting held at Camden on January 11, 1938 there were 125, including 78 stockholders present. The annual report showed that there were 219 farm loans representing over $1,500,000, and only five were delinquent.

Officers elected were: Ira Kleckner, president; J. W. Kerlin, vice president and Charles M. Flora, secretary treasurer. W. H. Lane, John W. Kerlin, Floyd M. Gish and O. E. Stewart were elected directors.

At the Annual Meeting held at the Camden Opera House on January 28, 1941 it was reported that 266 members had loans amounting to $1,363,400.

In July, 1944 the Camden NFLA was merged with the Federal Land Bank Association of Frankfort and the office was moved to Frankfort. A part time office was established in the PCA office in Delphi with a representative from the Frankfort office at the Delphi office two days each week.

In 1979 the FLBA of Frankfort built a branch office on State Road 75 south of Flora. Open House was held on August 29, 1979. Don Elliott was manager

Don Elliott, manager, and Kris McGili, office secretary at the new Federal Land Bank building at Flora.

and Kris McGill office secretary at the new office. Mark Kingen, field assistant, became branch manager in 1980.

The Frankfort Association, which includes Carroll, Clinton and Boone Counties had over $50 million in outstanding loans with over 700 borrowers.

PRODUCTION CREDIT ASSOCIATION

The Great Depression following the Stock Market Crash in 1929 created a demand by farmers for more credit than could be supplied by local banks.

The Farm Credit Act of 1933 created a Production Credit Corporation and a Bank for Cooperatives in each of the 12 Federal Land Bank Districts which had been created by the Farm Credit Act of 1916. On December 31, 1956 the duties of the Production Credit Corporation were taken over by the Federal Intermediate Credit Bank which had been created by the Farm Credit Act of 1923. The first Production Credit Association was organized in Champaign, Illinois, on September 11, 1933 and the last in Colorado on March 20, 1934.

In the spring of 1934 the Production Credit Corporation at Louisville organized 10 Production Credit Associations in Indiana.

LAFAYETTE PRODUCTION CREDIT ASSOCIATION

The organization meeting for the Lafayette Production Credit Association was held on February 13, 1934 at the Federal Building in Lafayette. The association territory included eight counties: Benton, Carroll, Clinton, Jasper, Newton, Tippecanoe, Warren and White.

Lloyd D. Beard, Arthur R. Mullin, Loyd E. Zook and Jesse McCarty from Carroll County were among the 32 incorporators who elected nine directors. The directors met February 28, 1934 to elect officers. Two directors from Carroll County were Arthur R. Mullin who served until 1936 and Lloyd D. Beard who served until 1935 and was president of the association during that time. Raymond Zink is the director representing Carroll County since 1974. Others have been Robert Hedde, Sr. 1952-67, Artus Rodenbarger 1944-51 and Hal R. Shafer 1936-37.

The first action of the board was to elect John G. McKee, one of the incorporators, as secretary treasurer. The board rented office space in the Farmer and Traders Bank Building, located on the southwest corner of the Courthouse Square where they opened for business on March 12, and remained until 1937. After being in several other locations in Lafayette, they moved in 1960 to a newly constructed Farm Credit Building at 2111 Teal Road, where it is now located along with the office of the Federal Land Bank Association, the Extension Service, Soil Conservation Service, Farmers Home Administration and ASCS.

In 1938, Mr. McKee resigned as secretary treasurer and was replaced by O. I. Richolson who served from September 1, 1938 until he died in 1954. Glenn Heitz served as secretary treasurer four years and then left to join the Farm Credit Administration in Washington, D.C., where he soon became head of the Cooperative Bank Division and later became president of the Federal Land Bank at St. Louis.

John P. Reagan who had been in charge of the office at Delphi was named secretary treasurer in 1958, and became president of the association in 1972. Under his leadership the Lafayette PCA has been one of the largest in the District, and in 1978 was the second largest in Indiana in the amount of loans outstanding. The association serves about 2,000 farmers, and in 1978 they had more than $100 million in loans outstanding and had 31 employees.

Most loans are for a year or less, and are for production needs such as feed, seed, fertilizer, insurance and other needs of the farm family. Some loans are for up to seven years for capital needs such as buildings, machinery, trucks, feeding facilities, grain handling facilities and other capital needs fitting in the Intermediate-Term Loan category.

Money is secured by selling bonds to the investing public at the current interest rate. No government funds or money from taxes are involved. The sale of bonds is handled by a Farm Credit Fiscal Agency in New York City. The rate of interest charged to members is determined by the rate that must be paid on bonds to secure money. In 1935 the rate was 5% and in 1979 it was 10¾%.

Each person who borrows money from the PCA must buy common stock in the association. This money is used as operating capital, and as security for bonds sold.

On December 28, 1950 the Lafayette Association repaid to the Bank at Louisville all the money borrowed to start the association, and became completely owned by members. By December 31, 1968 all Production Credit Associations had returned all government capital in the Federal Intermediate Credit Bank, and since then the entire Farm Credit system has been owned by farmers.

CARROLL COUNTY PRODUCTION CREDIT ASSOCIATION

When the Lafayette PCA was organized in 1934 they appointed a representative in each of the eight counties to help secure and supervise loans. Elmer G. Reiff was appointed March 19, 1934 as the first such representative in Carroll County and served until March 1, 1939. Applications for loans were made at the Carroll County Farm Bureau Cooperative Association office in Delphi and the Oil Plant in Camden. On October 16, 1936 Charles M. Flora, secretary treasurer of Camden Farm Loan Association was appointed as a representative to write applications for loans.

On February 17, 1939 Lloyd D. Beard opened the first PCA office in Carroll County with Fay Humes as secretary. The office was located upstairs in the Julius Building at 107½ South Washington Street in Delphi.

In May 1942 the office was moved to the Campbell Building at 109 East Franklin Street. New furniture for the office was purchased at a cost of $208.75. This included a desk at $72, another at $60, and four chrome chairs at $34 each.

Miles T. Martin replaced Lloyd D. Beard in 1943, and served until April 1948 when J. Dewey Zinn was appointed as the representative. The office was moved to the Masonic Temple at 215 South Washington Street. John P. Reagan served as representative from June 1953 until September 1957 when he moved to the Lafayette office. Robert F. Sprunger served for one year and was replaced by Ted L. Brown on September 1, 1958. The office was moved to 121 East Main Street, and then to the present location at 1001 South Washington in Delphi. Dan Gottschalk has been manager since Ted Brown died on January 6, 1978.

The Delphi office serves about 220 farmers in the area, and loans about $30 million per year.

Others in the Delphi office in addition to Dan Gottschalk, manager, are Susan Couk and Clara Crawford. Doug Ketterer has been assistant manager since December 1979.

FARMERS HOME ADMINISTRATION

In 1935 the Resettlement Administration was established to make loans and to give supervision to depression stricken farm families.

In 1938 the Farm Security Administration was created as a branch of the USDA, and took over the work of the Resettlement Administration. At that time supervised farm ownership loans payable over a period of 40 years were being made to farmers who were unable to get loans from other sources. Loans were also being made for water systems in drought and water shortage areas.

In 1946 the Farm Security Administration was reorganized and the name changed to Farmers Home Administration. Many programs for credit, grants and emergency loans have been added. In 1980 FmHA had some 26 different programs to administer, including supervised loans for farm ownership and operation, soil and water, housing, emergency community water and sewer, community development, rural rented housing, and business and industry loans.

Carroll County was serviced by an office located in Monticello until 1970. Raymond Bell was supervisor for the Farm Security Administration, and later for FmHA. Other administrators for FmHA at the Monticello office have been Roy Smith, Charles Sheetz, Herbert Million and David Shook who served from

Dan Gottschalk, manager and Clara Crawford, secretary in the Production Credit Association office in Delphi.

Employees at the Farmers Home Administration office at Delphi, from left: Helen Skinner, Bob Williams and Denise Syphers.

1955 until 1973. Ruth Loy was clerk in the Monticello office from 1941 to 1979.

In 1970 a full time office was established in Delphi with Robert Eugene Williams as supervisor. Helen R. Skinner has been office clerk since 1970. Sue Holloway was assistant clerk from 1973 until 1978. Denise Syphers has been assistant clerk since 1979.

ASCS

The Agricultural Stabilization and Conservation Service had its beginning in the Agricultural Adjustment Act (AAA) in 1933, which was designed to help farmers recover from the Great Depression. The act provided for a processing tax to be paid by meat packers and other processors of agricultural products. The money was used to pay farmers for reducing production, in order to help raise prices for agricultural products.

On January 6, 1936 the U.S. Supreme Court declared that the processing tax was unconstitutional. Congress appropriated money to pay for the program. Later acts by Congress changed the name to ASCS, and changed the emphasis of the program to encourage farmers to use practices which would conserve the soil.

The Agricultural Stabilization and Conservation Service known as ASCS is the arm of the U. S. Department of Agriculture which uses an office in each of the 92 counties in Indiana to administer federal farm programs pertaining to production adjustment, price support, and conservation. County and State ASCS offices each have a committee of three which serve as governing bodies. Both levels have areas for making determinations within mandatory regulations and policies of higher authority.

The State Committee (ASC) is appointed by the Secretary of Agriculture.

The County ASC Committee, which acts as a governing body for each county operation, is farmer elected. Under the County ASC Committee is a County Executive Director responsible for the day-to-day operation of the county office. He is assisted by a staff of clerks and part time field employees.

County ASC Committee members are usually elected in December to serve three years and terms are staggered to provide for one termination each year. County committee members are chosen at a county convention by Community ASC Committeemen who have been elected by farmers in an election conducted by mail. In Indiana a community normally consists of two or more townships for ASCS election purposes. In Carroll County there are four communities with a total of 12 committeemen who are provided farm program information for the purpose of keeping farmers at the local level informed. Community committee members are also utilized as part time ASCS employees, performing such jobs as commodity inspectors, grain maintenance personnel and compliance reporters.

One of the duties of the County ASCS office is to check farms for compliance with the various voluntary Federal Farm Programs. Aerial photographs of the farms are used for measuring acreage in fields. When there is a question about the acreage of a field or crop a representative of the committee visits the farm and makes the necessary measurements.

Another duty of the county committee is to administer price support programs created by the Agricultural Act of 1949 and amended by the Food and Agricultural Act of 1965. This program covers several commodities and is closely tied to efforts to keep food production in balance with needs in America. Prices are supported or supplemented through loans, purchases and payments at announced levels.

Loans to farmers are available through the county committee for storage facilities and drying equipment for grain. These loans are at a low rate of interest and may be up to 85% of the cost.

The county committee makes payments to wool growers as provided in the National Wool Act of 1954 which was designed to encourage farmers in the U. S. to produce more high quality wool.

For many years the AAA and the ASCS paid part of the cost for farmers to spread limestone on their farms. This program was a part of the Agricultural Conservation Program (ACP) which was replaced in 1971 by the Rural Environmental Assistance Program (REAP). This was used as the principal channel through which the Federal Government, in the national interest and for the public good, shared with farmers the cost of carrying out approved soil, water, woodland and wildlife conservation and pollution abatement practices on their farms. Farmers paid about one half the cost of carrying out the practice.

These practices include grass and legume crops and sod waterways to reduce erosion, planting of windbreaks and improvement of existing stands of trees, waste storage facilities, water storage reservoirs, and water development projects, such as wells, springs and pipelines in rotational pastures.

The ASCS committee uses the services of the SWCD for technical engineering work for farmers.

Robert E. Burke of Carroll County retired on December 27, 1974 as District Director of ASCS. He had been directly connected with the supervising of the program for 30 years.

Claude R. Wickard served in the Corn-Hog Division of AAA in Washington, D.C. from 1933 until 1940 and as Secretary of Agriculture from 1940 to 1945.

CARROLL COUNTY ASCS

A Wheat Production Association was organized in Carroll County in 1933. Officers elected at a meeting held on September 13, 1933 were: J. Frank Shoff, president; Turpie E. Martin, vice president; Obe Campbell, secretary and Earl B. Newell, treasurer. Members of the executive committee were: Coy C. Shanks and Burt McCain.

The records show that in 1935 the Wheat Association paid $18,000 to wheat producers in Carroll County. Officers that year were: Coy C. Shanks, president; Turpie E. Martin, vice president and Earl B. Newell, secretary treasurer. The Wheat Production Association later became a part of the AAA Committee.

The Corn-Hog Division of the AAA in Carroll County was organized in January 1934. Meetings of interested farmers were held in each township, and a committee was elected to represent the township on the county committee.

The chairmen of each township committee were: Elmer G. Reiff, Jacob Huffer, John Reeder, Clarence Frey, Walter V. Ayres, Larry Strong, Frank Hedderich, Artie Million, Burton D. Honan, Rush McCarty, J. Dewey Zinn, Robert N. VanNatta and Oral A. Caldwell.

Officers of the county committee elected in March 1934 were: Burton D. Honan, president; Oral A. Caldwell, vice president; Charles M. Flora, secretary and Frank Hedderich, treasurer. Larry Strong had served as secretary for a short time and resigned. Members elected on the Allotment Committee were Robert N. VanNatta and J. Dewey Zinn.

The Corn-Hog Program in Carroll County resulted

ASCS Employees at the Delphi Office. Left to right: Terry A. Weigle, Ethel Benner, Louise Smith, Dee Appleton.

Members of the Carroll County ASCS Committee for 1980 from left: James R. Kremer, Joe Scott, chairman and Carl Mays, vice chairman.

in a reduction of 24% in corn production and 25% in hog production in 1934. This was a reduction of 12,616 acres of corn and 26,557 hogs in the county. A total of $218,700 was paid to corn and hog producers in Carroll County in 1935.

County officers in 1935 were: J. Dewey Zinn, president; Robert N. VanNatta, vice president; Charles M. Flora, secretary and Frank Hedderich, treasurer.

Frank Hedderich was elected secretary treasurer in September 1936 when Charles M. Flora resigned to become secretary of the National Farm Loan Association. These officers served for several years.

Others who have served as chairmen of the county committee have been: Walter V. Ayres, Ross F. Wagoner, Lawrence Metzger, Fred C. Martin, Charles Pearson, Lloyd Mikesell, Ren C. Groninger, Thomas Elston, Ralph Maggart, Christopher A. Brummett, Robert Reiff, John T. Johnson, John E. Snoeberger and Joe Scott.

For several years the chairman of the county committee and the secretary were in charge of the county office. In 1956 Ralph E. Tyler was hired as office manager and served until he passed away in February 1975. Terry A. Weigle has been office manager since March 30, 1975.

Some of the secretaries in the office since 1952 have been: Joan McCain, Shirley Allen, Ruth Crowel, Esther Blocher, Julie Popejoy, Beulah Glover, Eileen Guthrie, Ruth Smith, Dee Recher Appleton, Ethel Benner, Louise Smith, Diane Duff, Joyce Goslee, Joan Benner, Gwen Benner, Marjie Guthrie, Phyllis Crowel, and Norma Sickler.

Community Committee members of the ASCS who met in December 1979 to elect a county committee for 1980 were from left seated: Ron Felz, Jefferson Township, Gary Cleaver, Madison; John T. Johnson, Burlington; Loyal Cripe, Madison; Francis Humbarger, Madison. Standing from left: Brice Crowel, Jefferson; Gary Penn, Jackson; John Reiff, Adams; Charles Bordner, Democrat; William Kearns, Monroe; and James Flora, Carrollton.

SOIL AND WATER CONSERVATION DISTRICT

At the Annual Meeting of the Carroll County Extension Committee on January 13, 1949, R. O. Cole, Extension Soil Conservationist, discussed the advantages of and the steps necessary to establish a Soil Conservation District in Carroll County.

The Extension Committee voted in favor of establishing a district, and made plans to have a county wide meeting of agricultural leaders to discuss the matter. The meeting was held at the Delphi Library at 1:00 P.M. on February 11, 1949 with about 50 farmers present.

Howard McCarty, County Agent, explained that the purpose of the meeting was to give farmers and farm leaders an opportunity to express their desires concerning the organization of a district.

R. O. Cole discussed the advantage of organizing a district, and explained the procedure necessary to establish the service. The first step was for land owners in the county to sign a petition requesting the service, and present it to the State Soil Conservation Committee. A member of the State Committee would then come to the county and hold a public hearing, giving anyone who was interested a chance to express his views. If approved at the hearing, the next step was to have a referendum in which at least 60% of the landowners in the county must cast a ballot. Of the landowners voting, 60% must vote in favor of establishing a district. Those attending the meeting voted in favor of proceeding with plans to organize a district in the county.

COMMITTEES APPOINTED

John C. Peterson, chairman of the Extension Committee appointed a Soil Conservation Committee. Members were: Miles T. Martin, Jackson Township, chairman; Levi Furst, Tippecanoe; Raymond Nicoll, Adams; Loyd Zook, Madison; Charles Thompson, Democrat and Taylor Fouts, Carrollton.

The committee appointed a representative in each township to get at least 25 people in the township to sign a petition requesting that a district be established. The township representatives were to get at least 10 from the township to attend the hearing, and were then to be in charge of an election in each township. The township representatives were: Raymond Nicoll, Adams; Clark Metsger, Burlington; Robert Simmons, Carrollton; Lawrence Metzger, Clay; Roscoe Quick, Deer Creek; Robert McCarty, Democrat; Coy C. Shanks, Jackson; Ray Hankins, Jefferson; Frank Mullin, Liberty; Fred Hannell, Madison; Carl Johnson, Monroe; Enos Berkshire, Rock Creek; Levi Furst, Tippecanoe and Samuel O. Sinn, Washington.

PETITION SIGNERS

Forty-one landowners present at the meeting who

signed the original petition were: Taylor Fouts, Roy E. Snoeberger, George Treida, John Galloway, Ray Hankins, Earl B. Newell, Melvin Fisher, Ross Wagoner, E. L. Heckathorn, Miles T. Martin, Gardner Martin, Levi Furst, W. H. Ginn, Marvin Jervis, Zelpha Quick, L. D. Dickinson, Edgar Fountain, Sr., Loyd Zook, Russell Pearson, Burton Honan, Earl Powell, Raymond Nicoll, Ward Holloway, Charles Thompson, Mildred Thompson, John C. Peterson, Charles Harter, Enos Berkshire, Coy C. Shanks, Wayne Langston, Charles Albaugh, Earl Dunk, Roy Fry, Jesse Lowery, R. F. Patty, Elmer G. Reiff, Frank Mullin, John McManus, Fred Harshberger and William Yoder.

The petition was taken to Township FB meetings and other public meetings where farmers were present, and when enough people had signed, it was presented to the State Soil Conservation Committee.

PUBLIC HEARING

L. E. Hoffman represented the State Soil Conservation Committee at a hearing held on Tuesday evening, April 12, 1949 at the Presbyterian Church in Delphi with about 150 farmers present. Every township was represented at the meeting, and farmers from each township expressed their interest in having a district organized.

At the next meeting of the State Soil Conservation Committee, the request was approved and the date of October 14, 1949 was set as the final date for the referendum in the county.

EDUCATIONAL PROGRAM

A moving picture "In Common Cause" and another "Building Back" were used in several Township Farm Bureau meetings. Information was given and questions answered about the project at all Township FB meetings.

On June 29 the township chairmen of the Soil Conservation Committee and a group of interested farmers went to Montgomery County to see how a Soil Conservation District worked and what it had accomplished.

FIELD DAYS

The next day several farmers from Carroll County attended the Soil Conservation Field Day at the Throckmorton farm eight miles south of Lafayette. There were several exhibits and demonstrations, and a program with a speech by Dr. H. H. Bennett, Chief of the Soil Conservation Service. He was recognized as the country's foremost crusader for soil conservation and was largely responsible for the establishment of the Soil Conservation Service.

On July 22, a Soil Conservation demonstration was held on the Kite farm operated by Raymond Todd, located one and one half miles south of Delphi on the Pyrmont Blacktop. The field used for demonstrations was typical of land on many Carroll County farms. Demonstrations included contoured diversion terraces, control of gullies, and establishment of sod waterways, as well as discussion of cropping and other practices necessary to renovate the field.

REFERENDUM

The referendum was conducted by a committee in each township who made an effort to visit every landowner in the county and give them a chance to vote. It was completed on October 14, and votes were cast by 1965 or 66.2% of the 2,965 eligible to vote. Of those voting, 88.9% voted for and 11.1% voted against. Polling officials were: Miles T. Martin, Coy C. Shanks, Fred Hannell and Enos Berkshire. Voting by townships ranged from a high of 81% of the landowners in Adams Township to a low of 42% in Washington Township.

DISTRICT ESTABLISHED

Carroll County was the 47th county in Indiana to organize a District. It took several months to complete the organization of the District, elect supervisors, locate and equip an office, and be ready to accept applications for service.

The CCSCD was set up as a political subdivision of the State of Indiana, but has no authority to levy taxes, and no power to enforce any rules or regulations. Its job is to provide the assistance of farm planners and engineers to help plan, lay out and carry through soil conservation practices and improved drainage on farms.

SUPERVISORS

The District is governored by a board of five supervisors, all farmers, who develop their own program and see that it is carried out. Two of the five supervisors, Miles T. Martin and Charles Thompson, were appointed by the State Soil Conservation Committee, and the other three: Levi Furst, Taylor Fouts and Enos Berkshire were elected by farmers in the county. The supervisors elected Miles T. Martin, chairman; Levi Furst, vice chairman; and Taylor Fouts secretary treasurer. Supervisors do not receive any pay for their services. The District is financed by a combination of appropriations by federal, state and local governmental units, money earned by district activities, and contributions from private sources.

OFFICE ESTABLISHED

On May 5, 1950 the Soil Conservation supervisors met with Howard McCarty, County Agent, Don

CHAPTER XI — OTHER ORGANIZATIONS AND EVENTS   311

Carroll County Soil Conservation District supervisors met May 5, 1950 in their new office in the Court House. Seated, left to right: Don Klaus, Enos Berkshire, Taylor Fouts, Miles Martin, and Charles Thompson. Standing: Ken Pyle, Howard McCarty, and Levi Furst.

Klauss, district conservator and Ken Pyle recently transferred from Fulton County as the new technician for Carroll County.

The Soil Conservation office was located just inside the east door of the Courthouse, and beginning on Tuesday, June 13, 1950 was open during Courthouse hours. In the meantime Ken Pyle attended four weeks of specialized training at the Soil Conservation Service training school near Coshocton, Ohio. The office was later moved to the Campbell Building, and is now located in another part of the building at 111 East Franklin Street.

NEIGHBORHOOD GROUPS

In the summer and fall of 1950 Ken Pyle organized several neighborhood groups to discuss soil conservation. The first group was organized in Adams Township with ten farm families. The first meeting was held on the Raymond Nicoll farm where the group analyzed the soil resources available and suggested the best land use for different areas of the farm. The second meeting was held on August 15, on the William Yoder farm. The group studied the importance of organic matter in the soil, and discussed rotations which will maintain or increase the organic matter in the soil. The third meeting was a study of erosion control methods, such as contouring and terracing.

After these series of meetings Ken Pyle helped each of the farmers lay out a land use program to fit his farm. The land use program, termed a farm conservation plan, is a long range plan designed to enable a farm to produce at maximum capacity the crops best adapted to each acre while eliminating the erosion hazard.

AIRLIFT

The Soil Conservation District and Virgil Joyce, local representative of the Flying Farmers organization, conducted an air lift on Thursday, August 2, 1951 during the 4-H Fair at Flora. A fee of $1 was charged to take an owner or operator to see his farm from the air. This made it easy for farmers to see erosion and other land use problems.

ESSAY CONTEST

In 1951 the SCD sponsored an essay contest on the subject "Soil Conservation and the Nation's Future," for all Carroll County school students between grades five and twelve. They were divided into four groups with two grades in each group. A wrist watch was given to the winner and a fountain pen to the second place in each division. Implement dealers in the county donated the money for the awards.

Each of the 225 students who entered the contest was presented a ticket by Mr. and Mrs. Joseph St. Amand to see the movie "Texas Cavalcade" at the Flora Theater which they owned and operated.

ANNUAL MEETINGS

The first Annual Meeting of the CCSCD was held at the Flora Community Building on January 25, 1951. About 450 people were present for the fish fry and program. Lawrence McKinney gave a talk on "Two Blades of Grass." Local talent entertainment was furnished by the Clay Township orchestra, Bobby Peterson of Adams Township and the Three J's of Camden.

Fish frys were held at the Flora Community Building for the Annual Meetings in 1952 and 1953. In 1954 the Annual Meeting was held at the REMC auditorium in Delphi on Monday afternoon, January 25.

Awards to winners in an essay contest being presented by Taylor Fouts, secretary treasurer of the Carroll County Soil Conservation District at the Annual Meeting in 1952. Left to right, front row: Jean Kite, New Hope, second, grades 7-8; Virginia Fisher, New Hope, first, grades 5-6; and Joyce Gushwa, Delphi, second, grades 5-6. Back row: Sharon Garrison, Flora, first, grades 7-8; Patsy Pullen, Delphi, first, grades 9-10; John Furst, Delphi, second, grades 9-10 and Richard Quinn, Delphi, first, grades 11-12.

Dr. J. B. Peterson, head of the Agronomy Department at Purdue, was the speaker.

The fifth Annual Meeting was held at the Camden Community Building on Friday afternoon, January 28, 1955. The guest speaker was Helmut Kohnke, Agronomist from Purdue University, who talked on "Water Conservation." Raymond Nicoll, chairman, reported that accomplishments by district cooperators for 1954 included 352 acres of newly established contour farming, 101 acres of strip cropping, 700 acres of cover cropping, 170 acres of pasture seeding, 1.3 miles of open ditch, and 116,146 feet of tile installed. A total of 60 farmers became cooperators during 1954, bringing the total number in the county to 299. The district employees mapped 10,841 acres of land and 25 farmers received complete soil and water conservation plans.

District supervisors conducted a Drainage School in March, two Area Pasture Tours in August, and helped with a Land Judging Contest in October.

At the annual meeting held at the Presbyterian Church in Delphi on January 26, 1956 a certificate was presented to Luke Meador of Bringhurst who retired after 30 years in the ditching business. During that time he installed over two and one-half million feet of tile for farmers in Carroll County.

In addition to the regular activities in 1955 the district helped two 4-H Club members attend the Conservation Camp at Versailles in July, had a display at the county 4-H Fair, sponsored the Tri-County Land Judging Contest in October in which 280 Vocational Agriculture students participated, and conducted a Crop Residues Field Day in November, the first of its kind in this area of Indiana.

During 1955 the supervisors also purchased a stalk shredder for rental to farmers.

The SCD continued to hold annual meetings in January or February at the REMC Auditorium every year except 1962, when it was held at the Methodist Church in Flora, and in 1963 at the Presbyterian Church in Delphi. Beginning with the 25th Annual Meeting in 1975, the meetings have been held at Honan Hall in Delphi.

For the meetings in 1957 and 1958 the fertilizer dealers in the area furnished donuts and coffee. Beginning in 1959 the annual meetings were all day meetings with the noon meal furnished by the fertilizer companies. For several years meals were furnished by the CCFBCA, Green Acres Soil Service and D. A. Garrison Trucking Company.

In 1967 other companies began helping with the meal, and in 1980 the meal was sponsored by 29 business firms including: The Andersons, Bright National Bank, Burlington State Bank, Camden State Bank, Carroll County Farm Bureau Co-op, Cohee Construction, Culligan of Delphi, Inc., Delphi Products Co., Flora Concrete Tile Co., Francesville Drain Tile Corp., Fred J. Stewart Seed Sales & Service, Jackson-Lee-Pearson, Inc., Kerlin Elevator, Inc., Kerlin Feed Mill, Massey-Ferguson, Inc., Morning Star Corp. Mount & Son Ace Hardware, Oracle Press, Pickering Seed Co., Pioneer Hi-Bred, Inc., Pro-Ag Equipment Co., Skiles & Sons Excavating, Select Seed Hybrids, Inc., Star Roller Mills Corp., Todd Hybrid Corn Co., Inc., Triangle Feeds, Inc., Union Bank & Trust Co., Wilson Farm Service, Yeager & Sullivan, Inc., and Pearson Farm Service.

Among the many who have been speakers at the annual meetings were: W. J. Mumm of Milford, Illinois; Harold Scholl, U.S. SCS; George Gettinger Executive Vice President, Wabash Valley Association; George N. Hoffer, a consultant with the Mathieson Chemical Corp.; and the following from Purdue University: Harry Galloway, Bill Farris, J. B. Peterson, Don Sisson, Marvin Phillips, Richard Kohls, Lester Smith, Jerry Mannering and Maurice Williamson.

Many local people have been on the program for annual meetings. In 1964 there was a panel discussion on grain handling by B. Jesse Zook, Bill Duff and John Allbaugh with Bill Farris from Purdue.

The new drainage law in 1966 was discussed by a panel including Lee Flora, Larry Welborn, and Charles Ritzler with Don Sisson from Purdue.

The program for the meeting on January 25, 1980 included a report on "Agriculture in China" by John B. McCormick.

EARTHMOVER

In August 1966 the CCSWCD purchased a 2½ yard earthmover to rent to farmers in the county. It was

Mauri Williamson, Executive Secretary of the Purdue Agricultural Alumni Association, who was speaker at the 1979 meeting of the Carroll County Soil and Water Conservation District.

designed to be used with a three or four plow tractor and was used to construct waterways, surface drains, diversion terraces, and do minor land smoothing and other earthmoving jobs. The rental fee was set at $3 per hour and later raised to $10 per hour.

GOODYEAR AWARDS

In 1946 a high ranking executive of the Goodyear Tire and Rubber Company of Akron, Ohio, acquired a worn-out farm in Michigan. He hired a young man to operate the farm who turned to the local conservation district for help in improving and returning the farm to profitable productivity.

The work so impressed the Goodyear executive that he personally led a movement to get the company involved with soil conservation. The company developed a program of making awards each year to outstanding Soil Conservation Districts, and awards of plaques to outstanding farmers in each district. The CCSCD was awarded second place in Indiana at the 16th Annual Meeting of the State Association of Soil Conservation Districts at Purdue in the fall of 1958.

In 1962 the county district was awarded first place in Indiana, and the Goodyear Company paid the expenses of two from the district to take a four day trip in December to visit their 14,000 acre farm near Phoenix, Arizona. There were 104 on the trip representing top districts throughout the United States. Russell Wagoner and Raymond Nicoll were selected to represent Carroll County on the trip, and they gave a report at the next annual meeting in February, 1963.

Awards to districts are determined by the state committee, and individual winners in each district are selected by the supervisors and employees in the district.

Outstanding Conservation Farmers in Carroll County who have been selected for awards in the Goodyear Contest were: Robert H. Pullen, 1954; John Ward, 1955; Carl Jester, 1956; Gilbert Gray, 1957; Robert Coble, 1958; Frank Lybrook, 1959-60; Russell Wagoner, 1960-61; Dale Cleaver, 1962-63; Herb, Dave and Don Knop, 1964; Evan Flora, 1965; John B. McCormick, 1966; John G. Allbaugh, 1967; Paul Hedderich, 1968; Alfred Burton, 1969; Keith Rider, 1970; Evan Flora, 1971; Ray Hankins, 1972; Roy Woodhouse, 1973; Roy Fry, 1974 and John G. Allbaugh, 1975.

GREEN PASTURE CONTEST

For several years the SCD sponsored a Quality Forage Program known as the "Green Pasture Contest."

The first contest was held in 1957 with 10 awards given by the Delphi Limestone Company. The first five place winners received crushed limestone, and the sixth to tenth place winners received soil probes. Winners in order were: Howard Cox, Carl Jester, Richard Metsger, Douglas Million, Charles Snow, Marion Langston, Walter Barnhart, Melvin Fisher, Ralph Replogle and Joe Cook.

Winners in 1958 in order were: Jim Haller, John McManus, Carl Jester, Don Hankins, Richard Metsger, Roger Neff, George Martin, Clayton Million, Marion Langston and Paul E. Smith.

The Delphi Limestone Company furnished driveway stone for the first and second place and soil probes to the next three in the contest for 1959. Winners in order were: Robert Ayres, Carl Jester, John Ward, Richard Sheldon and Roger Neff.

This project was continued until 1960, when the name was changed to "Quality Forage Contest" and was sponsored by the Agriculture Extension Service.

WATER CONSERVATION

When first organized, the SCD was primarily concerned with the conservation of soil. In about 10 years interest increased in water conservation and the name was changed to Soil and Water Conservation District.

The district helped organize the Bachelor Run Conservancy District and the Rock Creek Conservancy District.

Pictured with their awards were Ray Garrison, left, of near Rockfield, and Roy Fry, right, of near Camden, winners of the 1950-51 Goodyear County Soil Conservation Award. In the center is Miles T. Martin, chairman of the Carroll County Soil Conservation District board of supervisors. These winners were selected for their achievements in soil and water conservation in cooperation with the Carroll County Soil Conservation District.

BACHELOR RUN WATERSHED

The Bachelor Run Conservancy District was established in 1965, and construction began on Saturday, October 7, 1967. A ground breaking ceremony was held on the Jim Mitchell farm near the junction of Bachelor Run and Deer Creek. About 70 people attended the ceremony which included an address by County Judge William B. Smith.

The first unit of work on the project included 3.9 miles at a cost of $78,542. The entire project included 22.6 miles at an estimated cost of $747,910.

Directors of the District were: Walter Allbaugh, chairman; Royce Myer, vice chairman; Robert A. Jones, financial clerk; Harold Jones, contracting official; Clarence Watson and Milton Bowman. William Briggs was attorney and recording secretary.

Directors since 1978 were: Milton Bowman, Earl McIlrath, Clarence Watson, Keith Sink and Max Langston.

Work on the main channel was completed in 1979. Some work on tributaries remains to be done.

ROCK CREEK CONSERVANCY DISTRICT

The Rock Creek Conservancy District organized on September 22, 1967 began work in 1971 on 1.2 miles of channel between County Road 400 E. and 500 E. in Carroll County at a cost of about $100,000. Work on the second part of the project began in 1978 and was completed in 1979. This project began at County Road 500 E in Carroll County and ended at U.S. Road 35 north of Walton in Cass County. The project which cost over $1 million provided better drainage for 88 square miles of farmland in southern Cass County and northeastern Carroll County. Other work on the project, including planting trees is scheduled for 1981.

Directors of the District are: Carl B. Jones, Don Fitzer and Patrick J. O'Donnell. Lewis Mullin is the attorney.

EMPLOYEES

Ken Pyle, the first District Conservationist, continued with the job until August 1968 when he was transferred to the Hamilton County District at Noblesville. He was replaced by Larry Welborn who had been in charge of the Cass County District for about 2½ years. For 2½ years before that he had been an assistant in the Carroll County District.

Other employees in 1979 were: Joe Henderson, Wayne Mullin, David Lamm and Tod Herrli.

One of the first employees was Roy Fry who resigned as supervisor to begin part time work in 1953. He began full time work in 1956, and retired on October 12, 1975. Others who have had that job are Robert Gray, Grover West and Joe Henderson. Many others have worked for the District for a short time as a part of the program to train them for other jobs. Many specialists for USSCS have helped on special projects.

The first part time office secretary was Mary Hildebran who worked from February 1963 to October 31, 1965. Em Campbell was secretary until 1977. Marjorie Summers, the present secretary, began working in 1977.

SUPERVISORS

Two supervisors are appointed by the State Soil Conservation Committee. Those appointed and the years they served were:

Miles T. Martin	1950-64
Fred W. Martin	1965-70
David A. Minich	1971-73
Pat Powlen since	1974
Charles Thompson	1950-51
Roy Fry	1952
Raymond Nicoll since	1953

Three supervisors are elected by farmers cooperating with the District. One is elected each year for a three year term. Those elected and the years they served were:

Taylor Fouts	1950-52
Robert McCarty	1953-61
Vern Myer	1962-67
John Allbaugh	1968-73
Benny J. Redding since	1974
Levi Furst	1950-51
Walter Barnhart	1952-54
Russell Jones	1955-63

Carroll County Soil and Water Conservation District employees 1978. Left to right Joe Henderson, Harry Pierce, Mrs. Marjorie Summers, and Larry Welborn.

Past and present Soil and Water Conservation District Supervisors 1978. Left to right Gary Cleaver, Pat Powlen, Benny Redding, Raymond Nicoll, Roger Frey, James Kremer, John Allbaugh, Miles Martin, John McCormick.

James R. Kremer	1964-69
Merrill Hughes	1970-75
Gary Cleaver since	1976
Enos Berkshire	1950-53
Charles Harter	1954-56
John B. McCormick	1957-65
Herschel Smith	1966-71
Charles Campbell	1972-74
Roger Frey	1975-77
Jerry Frey since	1978

The following information was reported at the 30th Annual Meeting held at Honan Hall in Delphi on January 25, 1980:

In 1979 there were 698 farmers in Carroll County cooperating with the SCWD. Services were provided for 301 farmers and eight units of government during the year.

The following table shows the activities for 1979, and the total for the thirty years since the SCD was organized in 1949.

Practices Applied

	1979	1949-79
Contour farming	—	7,054 Ac.
Critical Area Planting	6 Ac.	469 Ac.
Erosion Control Structures	10	346
Farm Waste Systems	4	78
Grass Waterways	3 Ac.	283 Ac.
Land Adequately Treated	1,004 Ac.	129,951 Ac.
Open Drains and Channels	—	360,069 Ft.
Pasture Management	—	4,170 Ac.
Ponds	1	111
Streambank Protection	—	19,717 Ft.
Surface Drains	—	110,080 Ft.
Tile Drains	91,442 Ft.	3,945,207 Ft.
Wildlife Area Development	31 Ac.	1,894 Ac.
Woodland Management	131 Ac.	1,315 Ac.
PTO (Parallel Tile Outlet) Terraces	3,975 Ft.	6,600 Ft.

Resource Planning

	1979	1949-79
Conservation Plans and Replans	25	666
Group Projects	8	101
Inventories and Evaluations	16	87

FARMERS UNION

The Farmers Educational and Cooperative Union of America was founded in 1902 under the leadership of Mr. Newt Gresham of Emory, Texas. The organization grew rapidly, and by 1914 was established in twenty states mostly in the South and West.

The constitution stated its purposes to be:

"To secure equity, establish justice and apply the Golden Rule.

"To discourage the credit mortgage system.

"To assist our members in buying and selling.

"To educate the agricultural classes in scientific farming.

"To teach farmers the classification of crops, domestic economy, and marketing methods.

"To systematize methods of production and distribution.

"To eliminate gambling in farm products by Boards of Trade, cotton exchanges, and other speculators.

"To bring farming up to the standard of other industries and businesses.

"To secure and maintain profitable and uniform prices for cotton, grain, livestock, and other products of the farm.

"To strive for harmony and good will among all mankind and brotherly love among ourselves.

"To garner the tears of the distressed, the blood of the martyrs, the laughter of innocent childhood, the sweat of honest labor, and the virtue of a happy home as the brightest jewels known."

The Union started many cooperative enterprises, and for several years offered $1,000 to anyone who could name a cooperative enterprise in the field of agriculture that they had not tried. In 1920 the Union in Nebraska did a total business of more than $100 million.

While membership numbers were not officially reported, reliable estimates indicate that they reached a membership of about 300,000. The Farmers Union is active in several western states, and sponsors many local state and regional cooperatives. The Farmers Union Central Exchange, Inc., St. Paul, Minnesota is the third largest Regional Farm Cooperative in the United States.

The Farmers Union was organized in August 1933 in Carroll and 10 other counties in Indiana. Regular monthly meetings were held in Carroll County for about five years. Earl Monnett was president and Marvin Wise secretary in 1934, and several prominent speakers were secured for the meetings. Glen Miller, president of The Farmers Union of Iowa spoke at Flora on January 9; John A. Simpson, national president spoke at Frankfort on February 10; and E. E. Kennedy, national secretary spoke at Pittsburg School on July 31, 1934.

A capacity crowd filled the Assembly Room in the Courthouse in Delphi, for a county meeting Old Settlers night, August 11, 1934. Speakers were: Robert Spencer, president of White County Farmers Union; Samuel Moher, president of Clinton County Farmers Union; Edward A. Stinson from the State Office, and Mary Punche from the National Office.

The next year, E. V. Everson, national president, spoke at a meeting in the Courthouse on Sunday afternoon, August 4, 1935.

The 4th Annual State Convention was held at the Delphi Armory, October 26-27, 1937. At that time Marvin Wise was president and Deane Adams, secretary of the county organization. Andrew Wise was a director of the state organization, and Walter Bowen served on the tax committee.

At the next State Convention, held at Monticello in December 1938, the State Farmers Union voted to quit supporting the National Farmers Union, and most county units became inactive.

The Indiana Farmers Union was reorganized in 1954, and celebrated its Silver Anniversary in September 1979.

The Carroll County Farmers Union was reorganized and received a charter on August 25, 1954 with 101 charter members. It was active until about 1965. Roscoe Bryant was president, Joan McCain, secretary and Robert Wise, treasurer.

NFO

The National Farmers Organization was organized in 1955 in Corning, Iowa. The primary purpose of the organization was to raise farm prices by marketing agreements and contracts between producers and processors of agricultural products. The NFO has supported "holding actions" in which members refuse to sell products for less than a price set by the organization. The NFO has active organizations in several states, but figures on membership are not released by the organization.

The NFO was organized in Carroll County in 1962. Officers elected at the first Annual Meeting in January 1963 were: Carl Buschman, president; Russell Pearson, vice president; Robert Mills, secretary and Joe Ellis, treasurer. Harry Bernfield, Enos Berkshire and Fred Rodkey were elected as trustees.

One of the first activities of the organization was to have members withhold corn and soybeans from the market until contracts could be signed with processors that would assure members a price equal to the cost of production plus a reasonable profit. On March 12, 1963 the NFO had a Whole Hog Sausage Supper at the Community Building in Flora.

At the next Annual Meeting on January 6, 1964 Carl Buschman was elected president; William Dickinson, vice president; Robert Mills, secretary and Leonard Brummett, treasurer. Enos Berkshire was elected trustee and Harry Bernfield was elected board member for the district organization. Members of the Grain Board were: Michael Dwyer, Robert Reiff, John T. Johnson, James Maxwell and Fred Clem. Meat Board members were: Carol Flora, Lawrence Johnson, Vernon Payne, Ned Long and Fred Rodkey. Another Whole Hog Sausage Supper was held with Mr. E. Pfingsten, vice president of the National Organization as the speaker.

Officers in 1965 were: Carl Buschman, president; William Dickinson, vice president; Wayne Loman, secretary and John T. Johnson, treasurer. Fred Rodkey was elected trustee for three years. Leonard Brummett was chairman of the Grain Board with Robert Reiff, John T. Johnson, Harry Bernfield and Carol Flora as board members. Lawrence Johnson was elected chairman of the Meat Board with Vernon Payne, Robert Mills, William Dickinson and Robert Bordner as board members. Fred Wagoner was elected as member of the board in the second Congressional District.

On January 11, 1966 Carl Buschman was elected for his fifth term as president of the Carroll County NFO at a meeting in the REMC auditorium. Harry Bernfield was elected vice president; Fred Wagoner, secretary; Michael Dwyer, treasurer; Milton D. Bowman trustee for a three year term and William Dickinson, Carroll County Board member for the second district. Meat Board members were: Enos Berkshire, chairman; B. O. Billiard, Robert Mills, Robert Peterson and William Dickinson.

At the Annual Meeting of the Carroll County NFO held in January 1967 the following officers were elected: Carl Buschman, president; Harry Bernfield, vice president; Fred Wagoner, secretary; Michael Dwyer, treasurer, Enos Berkshire, trustee and Robert Mills, District Board member.

At the Annual Meeting in January 1968, Carl Buschman resigned as president of the county organization as he had taken a full time job working for the Meat Department of the national organization. County officers elected were: Michael Dwyer, president; Harry Bernfield, vice president; Fred Wagoner, secretary and Robert Mills, treasurer. Wayne Loman was supervisor of a Super Bargaining Structure set up to better serve the members during holding actions.

QUESTERS CLUB

On the evening of March 27, 1953 a group of invited guests met at the home of Mr. and Mrs. Charles Harter for the purpose of organizing a hobby and antique club. After some discussion the name "Questers of Carroll County" was adopted.

The club adopted a theme: "It is fun to search and a joy to find," and an aim: "To restore and preserve the beautiful and historic of today and yesterday."

The club flower selected was the columbine, later changed to daffodil.

The following officers were elected: Mrs. Charles Harter, president; Mrs. Faye B. Wise, vice president; Mrs. Orpha Meade, secretary and John Oaks, treasurer.

During the years many hobbies and antiques were used in the programs including art, poetry, music, antiques and travelogues.

The club helped save the covered bridge east of Cutler and the sycamores at Deer Creek.

The club placed a sign at the Adams Mill, east of Cutler with the following inscription:

ADAMS MILL

In 1831 John Adams, Pennsylvania, built a sawmill here. In 1832 he entered land, in 1835-36 added a flouring mill. The present building was erected in 1845, restored by Mr. & Mrs. Claude Sheets in 1940. Bolivar Village was platted around the mill in 1837 and Wild Cat P. O. 1850-1894 was in the mill. Warren Adams ran the mill after 1861. Masonic Lodge organized at the mill 1864. The covered bridge built 1872.

On Sunday evening, August 7, 1966 the club held a picnic at the covered bridge park near Cutler. On display were paintings of the covered bridge made by local artists: Mrs. Paul Crundwell, Mrs. Georgia Quinn, Mrs. Cleo McPherson and W. E. Gardner. A drawing was held and the pictures were awarded to Robert Stephan of Flora, Irene Mason and Ruth Ayres of Delphi, and Paul E. Smith of Idaville.

Those who served as presidents were: Mrs. Charles Harter, Mrs. Carlyle Kirkpatrick, Mrs. Marion Gibson, Mrs. Lewis Wise, Mrs. Paul Crundwell, Mrs. Roy Gregg, Mrs. Fred McPherson, Mrs. David Wise, Lewis Funkhouser and Mrs. Charles Loy.

The club disbanded in 1974 and money in the treasury was given to the Flora and Delphi libraries for the purchase of books.

CARROLL COUNTY WABASH AND ERIE CANAL, INC.

A section of the old Wabash and Erie Canal in Delphi extends from the Monon Railroad about 4,000 feet North to the flood control levee North of Delphi. The canal is filled with stagnant water and for a century has been a catch all for miscellaneous trash and junk that people wanted to hide from sight.

The canal provides drainage for about 200 acres of land in the North part of the city.

There has been a difference of opinion about the canal by citizens for many years. Some want to fill in the canal, while others want to preserve this section of the canal as a reminder of its importance in the development of the Wabash Valley.

A study by Larry Welborn, from the Soil and Water Conservation District, revealed that it would cost much more to fill in the canal and provide other drainage for the area than it would to restore the canal so that it might be used for a historical and recreational area.

On February 19, 1971 a group of interested citizens met at the home of Mr. and Mrs. Tom McCain and organized an association to restore and preserve a section of the canal. The meeting was sponsored by the Carroll County Historical Society. Robert G. Bradshaw served as temporary chairman and Dennis McCouch served as temporary secretary. Officers elected at a later meeting were: Mrs. Tom McCain, president; Robert G. Bradshaw and Joseph E. Peterson, vice presidents; and Faye Wood, secretary treasurer.

Charter members were: Robert G. Bradshaw, Robert Brookbank, Louis Brubaker, Audria Clements, Hope Coomey, Michael G. Griffey, Ernest L. Goff, Myron Johnson, John F. Klepinger, Bill Kirchoff, Clarence Kite, Don Moore, Phyllis Moore, Alfred Moss, Elsie G. Myers, Dale MaCurdy, Roseland McCain, Dennis McCouch, Dean Overholser, George Obear, Joseph E. Peterson, Elizabeth Peterson, John C. Peterson, Bill G. Payne, Wayne Van Sickle, Larry Welborn, Donald B. Willy, Arthur Weddell and Jerry D. Young.

In 1972 students from the local schools helped pick up trash along the canal bank. Dr. Carl F. Gerlach and a group of students from the Department of Horticulture at Purdue made a report with suggestions for restoring the canal. This information was exhibited in the Courthouse and at the county 4-H Fair.

On June 15, 1973 Articles of Incorporation were filed for the formation of the Carroll County Wabash and Erie Canal, Inc., a not for profit corporation. The purpose of the new corporation was to acquire, restore and develop portions of the canal for public recreational, educational and historical uses. Incorporators were: Roseland McCain, Hope Coomey and Dean Overholser. The first board of directors were: John F. Klepinger, Bill Kirchoff, Jerry D. Young, Roseland McCain, Wayne Van Sickle, Darilee Robbins, Hope Coomey, Charles A. Wood, Alfred Moss, Dean Overholser, Louis Brubaker and Joseph E. Peterson. The first officers were: Dean Overholser, president; Bill Kirchoff, vice president; Hope Coomey, secretary and Joseph E. Peterson, treasurer.

Several methods have been used to raise money for the project. Contributions have been made by a number of individuals and organizations. In 1972 more than $700 was raised by the sale of facsimilies of stock issued in 1846. In 1978 and 1979 a boat trip on the Madam Carroll on Lake Freeman was sponsored by the association. In 1978 the boat took an imaginary trip down the canal to Covington and return, and in 1979 the trip was to Huntington and return. Also in 1978 and 1979 the association had a stand at Old Settlers where members sold sandwiches and chances on a TV set and other merchandise.

In 1975 the city of Delphi received a grant from the Federal Government and used some of the money to clean part of the canal and provide an area for a park along the canal. Part of the money was used to buy and restore the old stone building near the canal, and to install playground equipment near the building.

In 1975 Kathy Bakes, a senior in Landscape Architecture at Purdue, made recommendations for the landscaping of the project. Dennis McCouch and some volunteers set out flowers along the banks of the canal. Part of the flowers were donated by Roseland McCain, Jerry Hurley and Judge Wm. B. Smith.

In 1976 Mohasco, owner of the Peters-Revington factory in Delphi, donated two acres of land along the canal. Scott Shaffer donated the use of his bulldozer to help clear up part of the land. Jerry Boone furnished equipment and labor for several projects.

Officers of the Canal Association in 1979 were: Dennis McCouch, president; Jerry Boone, vice president; David Hanna, secretary and Joseph E. Peterson, treasurer. Directors in addition to the officers were: Scott Shaffer, Donald Horn, Grover West, Dean Overholser, Tod Herrli, Neda Bushman, Harold Matthews and Roseland McCain.

Others who have served as directors were: Robert Brookbank, Myron Johnson, Michael Griffey, Phyllis Moore and Jim Huffer. Other officers have been: Joseph E. Peterson and Robert Brookbank, vice presidents; Jim Huffer secretary and Ed Waymire treasurer.

FLORA COMMUNITY CLUB

An article in the Hoosier Democrat on October 19, 1901 reported that a number of businessmen and others who were interested in the welfare of the town of Flora met at Linton & Son's Music Store Tuesday evening, and organized the Flora Commercial Club. Officers elected were: W. E. Callane, president; M. W. Eaton, secretary; J. V. Bright, treasurer; and C. R. Brewer, H. H. Flora, E. L. Peter, R. D. Voorhees, W. H. Linton and F. C. Horner, directors.

The Flora Commercial Club was reorganized in 1919 by a group of civic minded businessmen and professional people who saw the need of an organization to promote the growth and welfare of the community. E. E. Landis and Everett Cochran were the officers in 1920 and their first project was the establishment of a park. The land for the park was donated by Charles Reist, a leading merchant of the community. The park was dedicated on Sunday, July 21, 1920.

In 1923 the name of the club was changed to the Flora Community Club, Inc. Officers in 1923 were: L. V. Myer, president; Fred Wheeler, secretary; and Wm. Niewerth, treasurer. Directors were: Dr. Schermerhorn, George Northcutt, Wm. Leiter, John Oaks, John Roblyer, Willis Jackson, Harry Spitler, Amos Clingenpeel and Everett Cochran.

The next big project by the club was to build the Flora Community Building for use by the school system and for community activities. The estimated cost was $40,000 and of this $33,699 was subscribed. Several thousand dollars were saved by donated labor. Noah Edmonson and Charles Houser were in charge of the carpenter work. The trusses were placed under the supervision of O. F. Campbell, using block and tackle and manpower on the ropes. When the last truss was put in place it was discovered that the rope was almost severed, and if it had broken, possibly several men would have been killed or injured.

The building was dedicated on January 3, 1924 with a basketball game between Delphi and Flora which Delphi won with a score of 26-15. It was a cold night and after the game several autos had frozen radiators.

The building was leased to the school for $6,000 for six years and to finish paying off the debt on the building the committee sponsored roller skating, silent movies and used the building for many promotional shows.

Others serving the club during this period were: Warren Knapp, Wm. Weckerle, D. Elmer Cripe, Elmer Metzger, L. V. Myer, E. E. Landis, Tony Beckner, G. E. Voorhees, C. E. Budrow, J. W. Clark, Charles Burton, E. F. Krauss, Paul Kirk, Steve R. Long, Lynn Ledman, Charles Minnix, A. L. Moss, Charles Northcutt, Clarence Payne, J. Stanley Jones, J. B. Miller, Charles Thomson and A. D. Bishop.

Many projects and improvements to the town were made. In 1934 the club used WPA labor to haul dirt from behind the stores downtown and filled low places at the park. The downtown area was covered with stone and used as a parking lot. Improvements were made at the park, and a formal opening ceremony was held on June 2, 1935. The ceremony included music by the Flora High School Band directed by Wm. Marocco, and an address by Robert Ross, superintendent of schools at Monticello. The Scout Cabin at the park was originally a log cabin structure built by the WPA.

In 1937 the club activated the Flora Chapter of the American Red Cross and hired Marie Burns for several years to do the work. In 1939, through the efforts of the club, State Road 18 was extended from Road 39 to 29. It was claimed that the road would make it easier for people to get into Flora. Opponents argued it would make it just as easy for Flora residents to get out of town to do their shopping.

In the spring of 1941, the officers of the club decided to build a furniture factory for V. D. Rider. The committee of Wm. Leiter, Everett Cochran, A. D. Bishop, Ora Shirar, G. H. Haines, Ora Trent and Wayne Crook contracted with Fred Frye to build the structure which is now used by the Essex Wire Corporation.

In 1946 the Community Club built the Sayco Factory building and in 1947 added the plating room. In 1948 the club didn't have enough money to build the buffing room so they put in the footing and floor and Sayco finished the building. In 1950 the club bought the Curtis farm and Ralph Pearson was the farm manager. This area has been used for the city's expansion including: Industrial Cab Company, Flora Water Tower and Substation, Flora Iron and Steel, Allegiance Wire, John Deere Farm Implements, Robo Car Wash and Patchett Sales & Service. In 1961 it was decided to build a factory building to have one ready for future prospects. It was occupied by Allegiance Wire. In 1961 the club paid $500 to help Earl Replogle fix up the old telephone building so that he could move there, enabling a new Post Office to be built on his old location. In 1967 through the efforts of club members, Dr. Carlos Amaya was brought to Flora and the club purchased the office building of Dr. M. R. Adams and its contents and also purchased the Amanda Hill house as a future site to expand the medical building. Through the years many other projects were completed by the club which also holds one-half of the shares in Maple Lawn Cemetery.

The County 4-H Fair has been another area where many members have donated a lot of time and talent and have supervised the construction of several buildings on the fairgrounds. The club furnished most of the money to finance the first County 4-H Fair at Flora in 1932, and has helped finance fairs since then.

The Community Club was represented at the launching of the battleship USS Indiana at Newport News, Virginia in 1941 by Mr. and Mrs. Ora Shirar who went with six hundred others on the Governor's special train to the ceremonies.

The Flora Community Club has been responsible for the major portion of progress in the community. It has sponsored or cooperated wholeheartedly in every effort designed to better or improve the welfare and growth of the town of Flora.

Officers in 1979 were: Dick Oilar, president; Cullan Eikenberry, vice president; Dick T. Bishop, attorney and secretary; Joe Redmon, treasurer; Pete Jackson, Alan Ayres, John Ayres, Robert Baker, and Mrs. Bob (Sandy) Johnson, Board of Directors.

CAMDEN COMMUNITY CLUB

By B. Jesse Zook

The Camden Community Club was organized on February 8, 1950 by five couples: Thomas and Martha Sanderson, Gene and Mary Willy, B. Jesse and Anna Myrle Zook, Dean and Adriene McCain and Wilmer and Margaret Schock.

Officers elected were: Gene Willy, president; Tom Sanderson, 1st vice president; Wilmer (Bill) Schock, 2nd vice president; Adriene McCain, secretary; Anna Myrle Zook, assistant secretary; Dean McCain, treasurer; Martha Sanderson, entertainment chairman and B. Jesse Zook, chairman of By-laws committee.

The new officers went to work, and under the direction of a hard working president, Gene Willy, they had 145 members in a very few weeks. The first item of business was to order membership cards and plan regular entertainments such as card parties, dances, etc. One of the Club's first projects was to raise money through activities, such as pancake and sausage suppers, dances, and fish frys to help pay for uniforms for the new High School Band directed by Clarence Marocco. The Club gave the Band Boosters one half of the money they made and the uniforms were soon paid for.

The town of Camden had previously purchased the old cement block building located across the street north of the bank. This building had been used as a garage and later as a furniture factory. It was the concern of several citizens that much of the empty space in the building could be used for some good purpose to help promote entertainment and useful projects around Camden.

The idea of having a fish fry came from an event that had taken place sometime previously. Jess Kendall, Gene Willy, Wilmer Schock and several others decided to go down to Deer Creek and gig some suckers and have a fish fry. Everyone liked the idea and they soon had a couple of tubs of suckers. Bill Schock brought his lard kettle, Claude Patty donated five gallons of lard and others brought a covered dish of food and their own table service. A great time was had by all.

The first public fish fry sponsored by the club was in August 1950 and they engaged the Chalmers Civic Club to bring the equipment and fry the fish. It also was quite successful. Another fish fry was held in February 1951, then again in August 1951, both being done with the help of the Chalmers Club. In 1952 the Camden Community Club purchased material and made their own cooking equipment and since then they have become well known for taking care of crowds from 1,000 to 2,000 without any trouble.

The Camden Community Club remained extremely active during its first 30 years and contributed much toward the Park, Little Leagues, school programs and many other things that helped Camden's civic life.

The officers for 1979 were: Herb Yerkes, president; Bob Schock, vice president; Bob Yerkes, secretary treasurer; and directors were Jim Hodges and Gary Penn. There were about 130 members in 1979.

FLYING FARMERS

By Virgil Joyce

World War II provided a tremendous impetus to private aviation in Carroll County as well as in the whole country. This, along with the ensuing prosperity, enabled many people, including several Carroll County farmers, to start flying.

One of the first persons to visualize the importance of this new mode of transportation for farmers was Bill Renshaw, Indiana Editor of Prairie Farmer magazine. Prairie Farmer also saw the social value of an organization of farmers that flew, and the promotional value to the magazine by having the magazine associated with Flying Farmers.

Accordingly, in early 1946 the magazine issued an invitation to all subscribers who owned planes, to meet in Chicago for the purpose of organizing a Flying Farmer organization.

Farmers owning planes were there from Illinois, Wisconsin, Michigan and Indiana. Robert Barnhart, R. 4, Delphi, was among those from Indiana who attended and thus became a charter member of the Flying Farmers of Prairie Farmer Land. Prairie Farmer continued to support and to subsidize this flying organization for a number of years.

One of the first activities of this new flying organization was to hold a field day at the Purdue Airport in early August 1946. Robert Barnhart helped plan this event in which over 600 planes with more than 1,200 people flew in. This was the largest fly-in of civilian airplanes ever assembled on one airport anywhere up to that time. Thousands more drove in to see the extravaganza, including many from Carroll County.

About the same time that Prairie Farmer was organizing Flying Farmers in Illinois, Indiana, Wisconsin and Michigan, Oklahoma A & M University was doing a similar thing in the western states. The scope of their plans was larger than those of Prairie Farmer, hence their efforts later evolved into a national organization and subsequently into an International Flying Farmer organization. The Flying Farmers of Prairie Farmer Land eventually merged with the national group.

There now are state chapters in virtually all 50 states of the U.S. plus chapters in all the Canadian provinces and in one state in Mexico. The chapters from these three countries are affiliated into the International Flying Farmers with more than 10,000 members.

Very early plane owners in Carroll County were Ben Been of Burrows and Abner Bowen of Delphi, although both quit flying before the advent of "Flying Farmers."

Lee Eikenberry of Flora was probably the first "commercial" flyer in the county. He was one of the early Barnstormers following World War I and worked many years as a plane salesman for the Piper distributor.

John McCormick and Bill Dickinson were early plane owners following World War II but subsequently sold out and quit flying.

Shortly after Robert Barnhart became active in the Flying Farmers, Virgil Joyce of Washington Township, likewise took an active part in the movement and later became president of the Indiana chapter and served a term as president of the Prairie Farmer Land group. Robert and Virgil have remained plane owners continuously since 1946. Ruth Barnhart, Robert's wife, was selected Indiana Flying Farmer Queen in 1974. Elaine Smith of Flora enjoyed the same honor in 1975 and served as hostess for the International Convention held in August that year at Purdue. Eva Sisson of Flora is serving as the current Indiana Queen for 1978.

Current plane owners in the county include, Dean Sanderson, Burlington Township; Charles Shanks, Judge Don Myers, Larry Pownell, Bill Pearson and Wayne Pearson of Delphi; Charles Arthur Martin, Jackson Township; Charles Avery, Walter Squier and Phillip Duncan of Democrat Township; Bill Calhoun, John Herndon, Keith Sisson, Jean Smith and Pete Jackson, Monroe Township; Robert Barnhart, Clay Township; John Martin and Virgil Joyce, Washington Township.

There have been numerous other plane owners who have owned one for awhile and then decided to sell out. Among the reasons given for the in and outers are high cost, oppressive government regulations and a lack of landing strips at many places where people want to go.

There are several more pilots in the county who have earned a license to fly but do not own a plane. Their reasons are usually the same as above for not owning a plane. Seldom does one give up flying because he no longer enjoys it. Rather, the exhilaration of flying and the advantage of saving time is almost universally appreciated.

CORN HUSKING CONTESTS

Henry A. Wallace of Wallace's Farmer in Iowa sponsored corn husking contests, beginning in 1922, by having people send in a notarized statement telling how much corn they had shucked and the time spent.

This was not too satisfactory, so on November 24, 1924 at Alleman, Iowa, the first Midwest Corn Husking Contest was held. Only three states were represented and about 200 people were present to watch the contest which lasted 90 minutes. Each husker was penalized two pounds for each pound of corn he missed, and was penalized if he left too many husks on the ears. The winner had a net of 24.35 bushels.

In later contests the time was 80 minutes, and heavier penalties were added for leaving corn or husks.

In 1927 the official name was changed to National Corn Husking Contest, but was also known as the "Nubbin Derby" or the "Battle of the Bangboards". Interest in the contest increased, and farmers from eleven states entered the National Contest sponsored by nine farm papers including Prairie Farmer.

The 12th Annual National Corn Husking Contest was held on November 8, 1935 on the Leslie Mitchell farm near Newtown in Fountain County, Indiana. Nearly 150,000 people, including U.S. Secretary of Agriculture Henry Wallace, were there and NBC radio carried a shuck by shuck description of the contest.

This was the first year that hybrid corn was used in a National Contest. The record of 41.5 bushels in 80 minutes broke all previous records, and was topped only twice in later years. The contest was won by Elmer Carlson of Iowa. Irvin Bauman of Illinois was second and Lawrence Pitzer of Indiana was third. Mr. Pitzer would have done better, but he had such a large crowd watching him that they knocked down the corn and interfered with his work. There were two from Carroll County who claim that they came in close behind the man who won second place. They were gleaners picking up the corn that he missed.

The field was muddy and the remaining corn was broken down by the crowd and had to be picked by hand. Many people lost their overshoes in the mud. Pickpockets helped themselves to people's money and left the empty wallets on the ground. The farm owner reported that for several years he found many overshoes and wallets in the field as he plowed and worked the ground.

In 1940 the attendance at the contest near Davenport, Iowa, was estimated at 160,000 people. The winner had a net of 46.53 bushels, which set a new national record that has never been broken.

The final contest was held at Tonica, Illinois, on November 3, 1941. There was so much mud that no records were broken that day. The contest was cancelled in 1942 because of the war.

Corn husking contests were revived on a smaller scale beginning in 1970 with a local contest near Des Moines, Iowa. National contests were held every fall in later years, with the location for the contest rotating throughout 11 midwestern states. The contestants husk for only 20 minutes, and in recent years there has been a special class for women huskers as well as a class for men over 65. Old-timers from past competition are also honored and receive an All American Cornhusking Certificate.

The 1979 National Contest was held on Sunday, October 21, at the Carriage Hill Farm near Dayton, Ohio. The Ohio State Contest was held on Saturday, October 20 at the same place.

STATE CONTESTS

The first State Contest in Indiana was held on the Pullen farm near Flora on November 9, 1926 with about 2,500 people present. Hot soup was provided by the Church of the Brethren. Seventy five business and professional men of Flora and about 25 farmers helped with the contest.

Winners in the contest were: first, Charles Budd, Jasper County; second, Wm. Cole, Vermillion County; and third, Thurlow Mullendore, Carroll County.

Others from Carroll County who have been in State Contests were: Wm. Pearson, 1928, 1930; R. Kuns, 1929; Harold Trapp, 1934, 1935, 1936, 1937 and Roscoe Sheets, 1939. No one from Carroll County has been in a National Contest. After several years with no State Contest, the Indiana State Cornhusking Contest was held October 13 and 14, 1979 on the Virgil Brown farm in Henry County.

CARROLL COUNTY CORN HUSKING CONTESTS

1928

A County Corn Husking Contest was held in October 1928 on the farm of James Roth near Delphi. William Pearson won the contest, which lasted one hour and 20 minutes, by husking a net of 28 bushels after deductions were made. He was one of the 10 in the state selected by Prairie Farmer to compete in the State Contest held near Lebanon where he took sixth place, with only one bushel less than the winner.

1929

Raymond Kuns of Flora won the Carroll County Corn Husking Contest in 1929, and took part in the State Contest at Shelbyville on November 6, 1929.

1930

A Corn Husking Contest was held on the Raymond Kuns farm near Bringhurst in November 1930. William Pearson of Tippecanoe Township won the contest and represented the county at the State Contest near Elwood. Other winners in the County Contest were Raymond Kuns, second place and Joe High, third.

1931

Raymond Kuns won the County Contest held on October 31, 1931 in Monroe Township.

1932

A contest was held on October 29, 1932 on the Harve Lynch farm. Harold Trapp won the contest by husking 1,874 pounds of corn in 80 minutes. John Mohler of Delphi was second with 1,730 pounds, Harold Price of Camden was third with 1,384 pounds and Clarence Davis of Delphi was fourth with 951 pounds. Others entered in the contest were: George Hayden, Harold Frey, Raymond Kuns and Elton Stover.

1933

The contest in 1933 was held on October 28, and winners were: Harold Trapp, 1,930 pounds; Wilson, 1,790 pounds; Chapman, 1,790 pounds and Cain 1,590 pounds.

1934

Harold Trapp won the County Contest in 1934 and placed fifth in the State Contest.

1935

A Corn Husking Contest was held on the Melvin Fisher farm on November 1, 1935. Harold Trapp won with 30.24 bushels, Harold Lambertson was second with 28 bushels and Fred McCoy third with 25 bushels.

1936

Harold Trapp again won the Corn Husking Contest held on October 30, 1936 on the Miles T. Martin farm. He brought in a total of 2,380 pounds, but after deductions, had a net of 2,164 pounds. Three pounds were deducted for every pound of corn left in the field. Contestants were allowed five ounces of husks for each 100 pounds of corn, and were penalized one percent for each ounce between five and nine. After nine ounces, the penalty was three percent for each ounce.

Others in the contest and the net amounts were: Harold Lambertson 1,900 pounds, Carey Oyler 1,868 pounds and G. Oyler 1,828 pounds.

1937

The County Corn Husking Contest in 1937 was held on October 23, on the Evan Sanderson farm three miles east and one mile north of Flora with about 300 people present.

Harold Thompson was in charge of a contest for members of Vocational Agriculture classes in the county held at 9:00 A.M. The contest lasted 40 minutes and winners were: first, Melvin Swartz, Camden; second, D. Catron, Burlington and third, Ed Kite, Delphi. Others who entered in the Vo-Ag Contest were: John Harness, Burlington; Paul Johnson and Charles Dillman, Flora and Bill Myer, Camden.

The regular contest held at 11:00 A.M. was won by Harold Trapp, second was Carrie Oyler and third Roscoe Sheets.

Prizes in the regular Corn Husking Contest were $12.50, $10.00, $7.50, $5.00, $2.00 and a pair of overalls. Harold Trapp won the County Contest for the sixth time, and the County Farm Bureau paid his expenses to the State Contest in Davies County on October 29, where he placed 11th.

The committee in charge of the County Contest in 1937 was: Evan Sanderson, John H. Todd, Charles Yeager, Glenn Eikenberry, Harold Frey, Harold Thompson, Joseph E. Peterson, Phil Jones, and Joe Flora.

Jim Smith was in charge of a Fodder Cutting Contest at 1:00 P.M. Prizes of $3.00, $2.00 and $1.00 were offered to contestants taking the least time to cut three shocks of fodder.

Tractors to pull the wagons were furnished by International Harvester, Case, Allis Chalmers, Co-op, John Deere and Oliver.

Charles Eikenberry and other auctioneers in the county auctioned seed corn donated by Edw. J. Funk & Sons and DeKalb Seed Company.

1938

The contest was held Friday, October 21, at the Walter Ayres farm beginning at 11:30 A.M.

The following committees were selected:

Official timekeeper, Harry Foster, Flora.

Judges: Jesse Zook, Hugh McCorkle, Ora Platt, C. A. Davis, Charles Kerlin, Woodrow Whiteman, Wm. Smock and Milt Fross.

Gleanings and marketable corn committee: Roy Caldwell, Miles T. Martin, John McGill and Wm. Eckerle.

Calculations: Robert Maier, H. H. Thompson, Erving Olson and Stuart Guthrie.

Finance committee: John Harvey Todd, Miles T. Martin, Jesse Zook, Evan Sanderson and Glenn Eikenberry.

Scales were in charge of Charles T. Black.

Harold Price of Camden laid out the lands and Evan Sanderson arranged for the tractors, while the wagons were arranged for by each individual shucker. It was necessary to have the wagons on the grounds for the vocational boys at 8:30 A.M.

Harry Angle arranged to have the field opened up and John Harvey Todd arranged for the scales to be placed on the grounds.

Gleaners who followed the shuckers were: L. M. Pletcher, Haughey Mount, E. E. Landis, Fred Wheeler, Lewis Mummert, Jay Penn, C. I. Briggs, Lote Haslet, Lloyd Beard, Ross Wagoner, Charles Patterson, Robert Hedde, Fred Clawson, Orman Zinn, Victor J. Porter, Paul Million, Clay Landis, Gene Willy and Ed Viney.

Harold Trapp won the County Contest for the seventh time. He husked 31.26 bushels but lacked one fourth bushel of being one of the twelve to enter the State Contest.

Others in the contest in order of placing were: Dwight Platt, Roscoe Sheets, Carrie Oyler and Mark Trapp.

Lloyd Cripe won the Vo-Ag Contest with 10.68 bushels. Others in order of placing were: Ed Kite, Raymond Jones, Roger Wagoner, Charles Hufford, Charles Dillman, Bill Wertz and Harry Foreman.

1939

A County Corn Husking Contest was held on October 20, 1939 at the David Chapman farm.

Winners were: first, Roscoe Sheets; second, Carey Oyler and third, Harold Trapp. Others in the contest were: James Rodgers, C. Switzer, Lloyd Cripe, James Wilson, Harold Cox, Harry Angle, Wayne Angle and Bruce Garrison.

1940

Harold Trapp won the County Corn Husking Contest for the eighth time at the J. W. Eikenberry farm near Bringhurst in October 1940. He husked 33.35 bushels in 80 minutes but did not qualify as one of the 16 in Indiana who competed in the State Contest. Roscoe Sheets of Clay Township won second place with 32.35 bushels. Others in the contest were: Millard Robinson, 32.21 bushels; Lloyd Cripe 27.92 bushels; Harry Angle, 26.34 bushels; Virgil Trapp, 25.54 bushels and Mart Trapp 23.98 bushels.

While the corn was being weighed, an orchestra from Gettingsville furnished music. The ladies of the Bringhurst Church furnished lunch. About 500 people attended. Robert VanNatta was general chairman in charge of the contest.

1941

The Carroll County Contest was held in October 1941 on the Joe Shirar farm northeast of Flora. Harold Trapp again won the contest with 27.72 bushels in 80 minutes. Others were: Howard Cox, 27.06 bushels; Carey Oyler, 26.41 bushels; Joe Wagoner, 24.37 bushels; Harry Angle, 24.29 bushels and John Downham, 20.91 bushels.

Judges were: Willard McCloskey, E. E. Landis and Lee Dillon. Harry Foster was timekeeper and Evan Sanderson score board operator. Calculators were: B. Jesse Zook, Harry Hatton and Elmer Cripe. Pearl Johnson was official weigher. Members of the Finance Committee were: Glenn Eikenberry, Wm. Leiter, Ralph Rinehart, Ross Wagoner, Charles Bryan, Charles Kerlin and Wm. Lee Henderson. Ora Trent and Fred Holmes were in charge of tractors.

In this age of mechanization, it is hard for a person to realize the amount of hard work and skill required to husk corn by hand. Only the better huskers could average 100 bushels per day, so it was a real accomplishment to husk from 25 to 40 bushels in 80 minutes. Contestants were penalized for leaving ears in the field, and for leaving husks on the ears.

It was an art to grab an ear of corn, remove the husks and silks and throw it in the wagon while other ears were still on their way to the wagon. A good corn husker would keep three ears in the air on the way to the wagon. Like any other sport, many stories were told, and sometimes grew each time they were told. One man claimed that he lost a contest because the mules pulling his wagon got excited when they heard the gun fired to end the contest, and pulled the wagon so fast that the 25 ears of corn that he had in the air missed the wagon.

MECHANICAL CORN PICKING CONTESTS

After the war, State and National Corn Picking Contests were held for several years. Each contestant picked one-half acre of corn. Separate awards were given for one-row and two-row pickers. Awards were given on the basis of a score card which included time required for picking, amount of corn left in the field, amount of husks left on the ear and other factors. Tests at that time showed that the average corn picker left 13 bushels of shelled and ear corn per acre in the field. The contests helped encourage farmers to adjust and operate their pickers in order to reduce these losses.

The greatest number of points was based on how well the contestants observed rules for safety. Mechanical pickers were dangerous, and many farmers were injured each year while picking their corn.

STATE AND NATIONAL CORN PICKING CONTESTS

The State and National Mechanical Corn Picking Contests were held in Rush County near Rushville on October 17 and 18, 1952. The State Contest was held on the first day, and the National on the next day. More than $3,000 in prizes were awarded. Exhibits of farm machinery included picker shellers, stalk cutters, dryers, wagon unloading devices and other farm machinery.

A special feature that year was that all farmers who had lost a finger, a hand, or some other part of the body in a corn picker accident were introduced to the crowd as special guests of the contest managers.

ELMO REDDING

The most active participant in Mechanical Corn Picking Contests in this area was Elmo Redding who lived in Ervin Township in Howard County. His 480 acre farm was located on the county line, and about half of it was in Carroll County. He entered four Husking Contests in Howard County in the late 1930's and won two contests. In 1953 he won second place in the Indiana Corn Picking Contest.

In 1954 he won first in the State Contest and won the two-row championship at the National Contest held at Janesville, Wisconsin on October 16, 1954. It took 12 minutes and 20 seconds to pick his plot of corn. His score was 93.302 out of 100 points on the score card. The prizes he won included a clock trophy, 20 hole grain drill, stock tank and fountain pen.

As a winner in the National Contest he was eligible to enter the next National Contest without competing in a State Contest. He won the National Contest at St. Joseph, Missouri in 1955 with a score of 71.6. His awards included a medal and trophy, an outfit of work clothes, a 12 foot home freezer, a wagon and three bushels of seed corn.

He placed fifth in the National Contest at Columbus, Nebraska on October 11-13, 1956.

In 1957 he won second place in the State Contest near Cambridge City. His score was 95.49 compared to 95.88 for the winner. Both were eligible to enter the National Contest held at Sioux Falls, South Dakota. For the third time Elmo won the National Contest and a prize of $500. A crowd estimated at 75,000 people attended the contest.

He did not win in the National Contest at Cedar Falls, Iowa in 1958 but did meet President Eisenhower and Senator John Kennedy who were speakers at the event.

In all the contests he used a self-propelled Minneapolis-Moline Uni-picker which he hauled to the first two contests on a truck. Later he hauled it on a special trailer behind his family automobile.

FARM PROGRESS SHOW

The largest one-day gathering in the history of Carroll County, and the biggest midwest farm event of the year, was on October 7, 1954 when more than 85,000 people visited the Miles T. Martin farm, two miles east of Camden on State Road 218, for the second annual Farm Progress Show sponsored by Prairie Farmer and Radio Station WLS.

Starting at dawn, cars began streaming into the county from every direction, from 15 or 20 states. By 6:00 A.M. State Road 218 was clogged with bumper-to bumper traffic. Civil defense workers, state police, county officers and others allowed a double lane of cars on the road, and directed the estimated 25,000 cars to seven parking fields with a minimum of difficulty. There was an unconfirmed report that a stranger who knew nothing about the show was driving down the road minding his own business, and was herded into the parking lot with the other cars.

Virgil Joyce, president of the Indiana Flying Farmers, directed activities at an airstrip about a mile from the show. He reported that 975 people came in 265 airplanes. Free taxi service was provided from the airstrip to the exhibit field.

All schools in the county were dismissed for the day so that school children and teachers might see the show. Many of them helped in the food tents, in the exhibits, and with the car parking crews.

The show covered an area of nearly 900 acres on the farms of Miles T. Martin and six other nearby farms. Owners and tenants of farms involved were: Mr. and Mrs. Gardner Martin, George Martin, Mr.

Prairie Farmer Photo
Mr. and Mrs. Miles T. Martin, hosts for the Farm Progress Show.

and Mrs. Charles Jones, Mrs. Etta Jones, Mr. and Mrs. Junior Maxwell, Mrs. Daisy Kennedy, Mr. and Mrs. Guy Coplen, Mr. and Mrs. John Miller, Mr. and Mrs. Joe Fouts, Jesse Wallace, Mrs. Carrie Gardner, Charles Leazenby and Goodwin Dillon.

There were 450 acres of corn, using the latest recommended fertilizer and hybrid corn varieties, and plots demonstrating uses of chemicals and irrigation. Exhibits and demonstrations covered 165 acres while other areas were used for the Soil Judging Contest and Tractor Driving Contest. Two hundred forty acres of hay and pasture land were used for parking autos and 50 acres were used for the Flying Farmers.

More than one and one half miles of machinery, farm equipment, and educational exhibits surrounded the main exhibit field. There were more than 160 commercial exhibits and nearly 100 educational demonstrations.

Harold Berry, County Agent, reported that if a person spent two minutes at each exhibit it would take him five hours and 20 minutes to make the rounds, and he would still have all the field demonstrations, contests and shows to see. Many people visited the commercial exhibits. One exhibitor reported that he handed out more than 20,000 small bags of candy. Another said: "I've handed out 1,500 match books, and I only started an hour ago."

COOPERATING AGENCIES

Many agencies cooperated with Prairie Farmer and WLS in this event. Among them were: Purdue University, the University of Illinois, USDA, US Soil

Conservation Service, Michigan State College, University of Missouri, Indiana and Illinois Departments of Conservation and many other state and local agencies.

Carroll County Agencies cooperating included Health Council, Medical Association, Agricultural Extension Service, Civil Defense, G. I. classes, FFA, 4-H, High School Bands, Sheriff's office, Police Department, Fire Departments and County Commissioners. In addition there were many individuals and business concerns.

To show their appreciation for the many people who helped, Prairie Farmer and WLS held a chicken barbecue on Friday night, October 1, for more than 650 people who would be helping with the show.

HEALTH AND SAFETY

Every effort was made to prevent accidents, and to provide for any that might happen. No serious accidents or personal injuries were reported. Fire Fighting equipment and ambulances were available, but were not needed. A first aid tent was provided and was operated by 19 registered nurses living in the county who each volunteered their services to help for a part of the day. A doctor was present at all times. A total of 35 people were treated at the first aid tent for headaches, heel blisters, heart attack, exhaustion, tooth ache, car sickness, etc.

PICKPOCKETS

The following is a report from the Main Street column of the Delphi Citizen, October 14: "When a crowd as big as the one which visited the Farm Progress Show is expected, law enforcement officers always know that they should be on the lookout for pickpockets. Seems these unsavory individuals make a very good living by watching the papers, going to the major attractions and having a field day on unsuspecting souls who are out for a good time.

"Fortunately for Carroll County, our own very capable police officers last Thursday were augmented by a staff of especially trained pickpocket detectives hired by WLS and Prairie Farmer to police the grounds and to be sure that pickpocketing was held to a minimum. These detectives are so trained and visit so many gatherings that their practiced eye can spot known pickpockets immediately.

"Hardly had the show gotten underway at the Martin farms last Thursday when the special crew of detectives spotted two known pickpockets. They accosted one and immediately he had a 'spell', complaining of a heart attack. Now we are in no position to say that the man did or did not have a heart attack but we will say that he had it at a most convenient time. At any rate he was taken to the first aid tent where he was ministered to by a doctor and nurses, and allowed to rest. Then in not so polite language, he was told to get out and stay out. No charges were preferred because the detectives had nabbed the crew before they had a chance to operate."

PROGRAM

Events of the day started at 8:00 A.M. with a flag raising ceremony by the National Guard and Boy Scouts from Delphi and the Camden High School Band. At 9:00 A.M. a concert was presented by a 250 piece band representing all the high schools in the county.

Entertainment was provided by WLS National Barn Dance stars including: Captain Stubby and the Buccaneers, Lulabelle and Scotty, Homer and Jethro, the Beaver Valley Sweethearts, Woody Mercer and the Arkansas Woodchopper. A program was presented by Dr. John W. Holland, pastor of the Little Brown Church of the Air, heard every Sunday on station WLS. The regular WLS Dinnerbell Program conducted by Maynard Bertsch was broadcast direct from the grounds. Two Style Shows were conducted by Martha Crane of WLS. Local girls modeled more than 40 modern fashions made from cotton feed bags.

DEMONSTRATIONS

Demonstrations throughout the day included irrigation, pond building, high fertility legume grass plots, wide row corn, metal roof renovation, pole machinery shed construction, corn drying, fence building and a tractor upsetting demonstration. Machinery demonstrations included corn pickers, picker shellers, corn harvesters, stock shredders, plow adjustments, plowing, pasture renovation, tillage tools, sub-soilers and stump pulling.

The two plots that were irrigated yielded 129 and 143 bushels per acre compared to 81 and 87 for the plots not irrigated.

A fire fighting demonstration was given by the fire departments from Camden, Flora, Rockfield, Burlington, Delphi, Burrows and Logansport.

CONTESTS

There were four contests conducted during the day.

The tenth annual 4-H Tractor Handling Contest was held with six boys from six states—Indiana, Illinois, Kansas, Missouri, Wisconsin and Michigan. The winner was Terry Moses of Clinton County, Indiana. The Interstate Contest is the climax of the tractor driving and maintenance program sponsored by a major oil company in cooperation with 4-H departments in the various states.

The Land Judging Contest was won by Jack Rumbley of Palmyra, Indiana. The top team was from Decatur, Indiana. There were 60 teams from Indiana, Wisconsin, Michigan and Illinois.

A 37 year old man, Clarence Arnold, from Hammond, Indiana, won the Old Fiddlers Contest. A. P. Crowder of Chicago was second, and Garland Gardner of Idaville was third.

The heaviest Pumpkin Contest was in charge of Roscoe Fraser of the Purdue University Horticulture Department and the weighing was done at the Indiana muck crop show tent. The winning 73½ pound pumpkin was entered by Crystal DeBaillie from near Fort Wayne. She was in school, and not present for the contest, so her mother, Mrs. Charles DeBaillie was crowned as "Mother of the Champion Pumpkin Grower in the State", by Lt. Governor Harold Handley. There were 10 pumpkins entered in the contest. Five were from Carroll County and were shown by Bill Maxwell, 50½ pounds; Joe Maxwell, 49½ pounds; Carolyn Peterson, 45 pounds; David Peterson, 35 pounds; and Stephen Peterson, 25 pounds.

TADPOLE, THIRD CLASS

Lt. Governor Harold Handley was the top dignitary to attend the event. While on the program, Roscoe Fraser presented him with membership in the famous Akron Jonah Club and crowned him as "Tadpole, Third Class". The Jonah Club was well known in the area for the fish dinners they served. Their primary purpose was to avenge Jonah by eating fish.

ELECTRICAL POWER

The Carroll County REMC installed lines, equivalent to that needed for 200 farm homes to provide power for the show. It cost about $2,000 to install and remove the lines. A crew was available for any necessary repair, but none was needed during the day.

HAM RADIO

Tom McCain of Delphi was in charge of a crew of Ham Radio operators who used their mobile transmitters to keep the headquarters tent in constant contact with all phases of the operation. They also helped in the control of traffic and were available for any emergency that might develop.

WEATHER

Plans for the Farm Progress Show were made about a year before the show, and after the date was set, a primary concern was "what will the weather be like on that day?" Plans were made to have the show the next day if the weather was too bad on the day scheduled, but as the time approached it was decided to go on with the show regardless of the weather. Rain on Tuesday night before the show on Thursday caused some concern, but by Thursday the weather cleared and was a beautiful day, except it was cold and windy. Clothing merchants in Delphi and other towns along the way reported large sales of caps, boots, and jackets that morning.

HOUSING

All hotels and motels for several miles around were sold out for the event. Many people involved in the show stayed in private homes in nearby towns. Mr. and Mrs. Robert Ratcliff were in charge of housing in Delphi, and more than enough rooms were made available.

FOOD

A policy of Prairie Farmer WLS was to have nothing for sale at the Farm Progress Show except food, and that all food stands be operated by local organizations. At a meeting in March 1954, representatives of 22 churches and several other groups met and decided that all food stands would be operated by churches, and the county Rural Youth would have a stand where they would work with the Akron Jonah Club and sell fish.

The committee met ten times to make plans for the show, and had a final meeting the next March to make recommendations for plans for future shows.

Ten churches had food stands. Each was operated by a committee from the church, and many of them had co-chairmen. Several churches changed committee chairmen during the summer. The official list of the 10 churches and chairmen, as reported by Prairie Farmer was: Deer Creek Presbyterian, Kenneth Delaplane; Camden Lutheran, Mrs. Walter Sprinkle; Delphi Christian, Mrs. Meredith Treichel; Rockfield Christian, Clifford Winter; Delphi Methodist, Robert Pullen; Rock Creek Lutheran, Mrs. Raymond Shriver; Pittsburg Church of the Brethren, Mrs. Earl Eis; Pyrmont Church of the Brethren, Everett Barnhart; Ball Hill Methodist, Richard Funkhouser; Delphi Presbyterian, Mrs. John C. Peterson.

The Rural Youth stand was in charge of Bobby Caldwell. A portable pop stand, operated by one representative of each food stand was in charge of Vance Fincher. This stand moved around the grounds and followed the crowds from one demonstration to another.

A stand at the airport to provide coffee and pop was operated by Virgil Joyce.

John C. Peterson was chairman of the county food stands committee and Mrs. John C. Peterson was secretary.

The food stands all served the same menu and all purchased their supplies from the same distributors. This helped prevent a traffic problem that would result if each stand had different suppliers. Each supplier kept a truckload of supplies on the ground for the day.

The menu included hamburger, ham, and barbecue sandwiches at 25¢ each; hot dog sandwiches and pie were 15¢ each; coffee, milk, dairy orange pop were 10¢ and ice cream was 15¢. Spudnuts were two for 15¢. The Rural Youth sold fish sandwiches at 25¢ and a fish dinner at $1.25. Some sandwiches were made with whale meat from a 12 ton whale.

Total sales for the day for the 11 food tents were $18,734 with a net of $6,805. Gross sales for individual stands varied from $1,007 to $2,223 and net varied from $317 to $1,025. A major reason for differences in sales was the location of the stand, which was determined by drawing lots. All food stands were located close together, and those on the outside had more business. This problem was corrected in later shows by having food stands distributed among the exhibits.

The portable pop stand had a net of $87 and the Flying Farmers stand at the airstrip had a total sale of $34 with a net of $13.

The Camden Lutheran Church operated their stand for three days before the show and sold a total of $620 with a net of $242.

The change to cold weather slowed down the sales of pop and ice cream, but helped the coffee sales.

Total sales reported by the 11 stands included 4,185 dozen buns, 224 loaves of bread, one ton of fish, 2,515 pounds of hamburger, 860 pounds of hot dogs, 1,256 pounds of ham, 540 pounds of barbecue, 427 gallons of milk, 88 gallons of orange drink, 7,494 bottles of pop, 16,388 pieces of pie, 387 dozen spudnuts, 57 gallons of pickles, 15 gallons of relish, 288 bottles of catsup, nine gallons of mustard, 43,860 cups of coffee, 32 gallons of half and half, and 1,140 dixie cups of ice cream and 4,850 pounds of ice were used to cool the pop.

A milk company furnished two tank trucks to haul water for the food stands. Each stand furnished four barrels for paper and trash, and Joseph E. Peterson spent the day hauling and dumping the barrels.

The Union Bank and Trust Company of Delphi opened a "branch" in an automobile parked near the food tents, and John F. Klepinger spent the day supplying change for them. A total of $1,980 in change included $260 in nickels, $450 in dimes, $640 in quarters, $400 in halves and $230 in dollar bills. The bank also accepted deposits of money from the food stands.

FINANCE

All expenses for the Farm Progress Show were paid by Prairie Farmer and WLS. No admission or parking fees were charged, and the only expense for those who attended was for food sold by local churches and Carroll County Rural Youth. Each food stand and exhibitor paid for their own tent and for their share of the electric bill.

An article in Chaff and Chatter in the Delphi Journal for October 14, 1954 stated: "Many stories have been circulated as to 'what Miles Martin got' for playing host to the big event. Some have been fabulous reports. Yes, Martin will have some benefits for his trouble—extra fertilization on some of his acres, some special work done here and there, perhaps some fences which were taken down will be replaced in places where he might rather have them, and he doubtless has had a million dollars worth of free publicity.

"However, he is receiving nothing of huge remuneration.

"When Prairie Farmer and WLS first came to Carroll County, looking for a possible site for the 1954 show, that was one of the factors of chief importance in selecting a farm. Many would like to have been host on a cash rental basis.

"Martin was willing to be host as part of a huge project of cooperation, and it could probably be said that the Farm Progress Show would not have been in Carroll County had there not been a Miles Martin.

"Here and now is a fine time to pay tribute to a fine young man who first came to Carroll County last winter and began planning and working toward the big show. He is Ralph Yohe, who came a stranger as Prairie Farmer representative, and leaves within a few weeks after the final cleanup program with hundreds of friends and a reputation for fine, high-class dealing.

"His company can be proud of him as its personal representative, as a gentleman and as a wonderful administrator. There is another side to the man which few saw—he is a scholar, traveler, and student." Another article in the same issue of the Delphi Journal says: "Staging of the show was a tremendous effort, headed by Ralph Yohe, Prairie Farmer on-the-scenes representative, and County Agent Harold Berry. Planning had been done and situations anticipated until there were few emergencies to be handled on Thursday.

"The affair was another of a long series of the wonderful cooperative enterprises for which Carroll County is becoming famous. Many, many people participated in the big show and did a part. When the many parts were added into a whole, the project was staggering in its size and impact upon the community.

"Although those at the head of the planning knew that given a fair day the crowds would be huge, there were few people who probably realized the full magnitude of the undertaking."

OLD SETTLERS ASSOCIATION

The Carroll County Old Settlers Association was organized at a meeting of old settlers held at the Courthouse in Delphi on June 9, 1855. A meeting was held each year except during the war years of 1863, 1864 and 1865. Since 1871 the second Saturday in August has been the date for regular annual meetings. A few meetings were held in a grove near Delphi and for many years meetings were held at the General Samuel Milroy farm east of town. In later years meetings were held at the Courthouse, Armory or at one of the parks in Delphi. For several years the annual meetings have been held at the Delphi Community High School. For many years the Old Settlers Meeting has been held in conjunction with a carnival held for several days around the Courthouse in Delphi, including free attractions, rides, food stands and games of skill and chance (mostly chance).

Details of early Old Settlers Meetings are reported in books by James Hervey Stewart, T. B. Helm, J. C. Odell, Ben F. Stuart and Dora Thomas Mayhill. All of these books are listed in the bibliography and reprints of most of them are available in the Historical Society Museum in the Courthouse.

Those who served as presidents of the association since 1917 were: Charles Buckley, Mrs. Elizabeth Fisher Murphy, Ben F. Stuart, Wm. C. Smith, Walter G. Million, George Julien, Fraser Thomas, Reed Schermerhorn, James Odell, John K. Todd, Mrs. Catherine Brackenridge, Mrs. Auda Gee Studebaker, Mrs. Julia Gros Cowdin, Robert G. Bradshaw, Mrs. Kate Robinson Weil, Mrs. Julia Hardy Irelan, Mrs. Marie Swickard, Mrs. Mary Sims Clauser, Mrs. Lewis Wise, Miss Nellie Haughey, David Baum, George McCain, Jesse Wise, Thomas McCormick, Wm. B. Smith, Wilbur Lane, Wilbur Grantham, George Obear, Ben Jackson, Mrs. B. B. Mayhill, Mrs. Frieda Been, Mrs. Grace Clawson, Mrs. Robert Sieber, Arthur McDowell, Mrs. Dorothy Mills, Richard Grantham, Mrs. Hazel Kirkpatrick, Charles A. Wood, Mrs. Mary Pastor, Arthur Bradshaw, Mrs. Mary Smock Clawson, Lewis Mullin, Mrs. Robert Wood, Thomas Ives, Mrs. John T. Johnson, James Sullivan, John Temple, Miss Elizabeth Best, Cleon Carter, Miss Pauline Robeson, Paul E. Smith, Ren C. Groninger, Wayne Landes, Byron A. Jervis, James Guthrie, Delmar Bailey, Fred Anderson, Myron Beesley and Mark Porter.

Those who served as secretary were: John C. Odell, who served for 40 years, Mrs. Jennie Buckley, Mrs. Carrie Cox, Mrs. W. H. Bradshaw, James H. Stewart, Mrs. Elizabeth Murphy, Mrs. Mindwell Crampton Wilson, Miss Hilda Bowen, Mrs. Mary Sims Clauser, Wm. C. Smith, Mrs. Faye Buckley Wise, Mrs. Theodore Baum, Mrs. John Carney, Miss Naomi Johnson, Mrs. Jason Been, Mrs. W. L. Cowdin, Mrs. G. A. Shaffer, Mrs. Edith Farr, Miss Ruth Ayres, Mrs. Roy Coble and Mrs. Clara Sims who has served since 1953.

Research directors have been Mrs. Dora Thomas Mayhill, Charles A. Wood and Robert G. Bradshaw.

Officers for 1980 were: Mark Porter, president; Dan Clawson, vice president; Clara Sims, secretary and Robert G. Bradshaw, research director. The association had nine directors with three elected each year for a three year term. Those who served as directors since 1948 were: Wilbur Lane, Miles T. Martin, Mrs. Walter Neff, Miss Effie Guckien, John C. Peterson, Miss Ruth Ayres, Dr. H. G. Mullin, Mrs. Dora Thomas Mayhill, Jesse McCain, Arthur Ritchey, Mrs. Mary Browning, Miss Laura Temple, Fred Perry, Earl Fouts, Noah Flora, Robert G. Bradshaw, Mrs. Ben (Frieda) Been, Lewis Mullin, Mrs. Clara Sims, Mrs. Earl Newell, David Baum, Maurice Clifford, Mrs. Blanche Balser, Mrs. Jack Grimm, Dean Overholser, Mrs. Keith Mears, Robert Brookbank, Mrs. George Wason, Mrs. Fren Musselman, Mrs. John McCormick, Robert Million, Mrs. Ruth Bowman, Miss Pauline Robeson, Miss Mabel Wharton, Mrs. Woodrow Whiteman, Mrs. Robert Wood, Mrs. Clarence Cleaver, Mrs. Josephine Brown, Wm. Kerlin, Paul E. Smith, B. Jesse Zook, Mrs. Nellie MaCurdy, John Temple, Miss

Garrison Photo
The Hathaway Family singers seated from left: Orville Hathaway, Frances Hathaway, Kevin Hathaway; standing Jennifer Best, Tara Garrison, Gail Marshall, Jeffrey Marshall, Carole Thomsen, Douglas Latia and Elaine Latia. Eric Thomsen was not present for this picture.
The Hathaways provided entertainment for the Old Settlers meeting in 1977.

Elizabeth Best, Mrs. Fannie Blue, Miss Reba Shanks, Estal Mullin, Cleon Carter, Jerry Boone, Miss Margaret Mabbitt, Fred Anderson, James Neptune, Mrs. Mabel Gibson, Mrs. Jean Guyer, Myron Beesley, Carl Yeakley, Mrs. Betty McCormick, Marion Ward, Earl Rodkey, Jack Burkhalter, John Burkle, Dan Clawson, Herb Isaacs and Dan Lybrook.

Awards are usually given at annual meetings each year for the oldest and youngest people present, one who came the greatest distance and the largest family present. In August 1933 A. H. Brewer was recognized for attending 51 consecutive meetings of the association. For many years Mrs. Maggie Kirkpatrick had the largest family present.

At the meeting in 1979 Leroy Robeson Sr. 93, was the oldest man and Mrs. Mabel Mullin, 97, was the oldest woman present. The youngest person present was Daryl Brower, age four, from St. Joseph, Illinois. Mrs. Dominica Oliver (formerly Mary Farner) from Spain came the farthest. Mr. and Mrs. John C. Peterson had the largest family present.

BURLINGTON OLD SETTLERS

The town of Burlington was laid out in 1828 and named for Chief Burlington of the Wyandotte Indians who lived in that area.

In the summer of 1874 about one hundred settlers met in Robinson's Grove for a picnic dinner and decided to organize an Old Settlers Association. The first meeting was held on August 29, 1874 with more than 600 in attendance. William Runyan was elected the first president and Samuel O. Rodkey the first secretary.

Large numbers of people attended every year, and most of them came in wagons. Often two families would come together, with one furnishing the wagon and the other the team. Some came in old fashioned carriages, which were called "Summer Kitchens." The records show that 8,000 people attended the meeting in 1900.

Entertainment was provided by having sack races, potato races, greased pole climbing and other contests. Awards were given to the biggest person, the oldest person, and others. One year there was a contest for the best looking man, and five married women were appointed to find him. The report showed that their husbands each received one vote.

As groves of trees around Burlington were cut, it became difficult to find a grove large enough for the meeting, and in 1916 the meetings were discontinued after being held for 43 years.

The Association was reorganized in 1936 and meetings were held for a few years.

ANNIVERSARY CELEBRATIONS

People celebrate birthdays and other anniversaries, so it is altogether fitting and proper for a town, county, state or nation to have a celebration for an anniversary. People in Carroll County have been involved in many such celebrations. The following reports give a few of the details about some of the celebrations.

1916 Indiana Centennial

Indiana became the 19th state in the U.S. on December 11, 1816, so 1916 was the year for the celebration of its Hundredth Birthday. Mrs. Charles Buckley was in charge of the committee in Carroll County. The big event was a three day program held at Delphi on Thursday, Friday and Saturday, August 10, 11 and 12, with a parade and program each day.

The program on Thursday was in charge of Prof. J. C. Trent of Flora, with a program furnished by Washington, Carrollton, Burlington, Rock Creek, Jackson, and Monroe Townships.

The parade was led by members of the Red Men's Lodge in Indian costumes. A flag was given to David Chapman, trustee of Washington Township for having the best display in the parade. Entries from Washington Township included Indian and Pioneer scenes, and an ox-team driven by A. A. Newer. The committee from Washington Township was D. B. Chapman, A. A. Newer, Thomas Porter and Wm. Guckien.

Walter Pearson, trustee was in charge of the Monroe Township delegation which included the Boys Band of Bringhurst, a float with Campfire Girls, scenes representing life of Indian children, and several decorated autos.

Charles McCloskey headed the delegation from Carrollton Township which had two floats. One was loaded with children from Wheeling School, and the other had 18 young ladies dressed to represent the 18 states which had been admitted to the Union before 1816. Ten autos and a mule team completed the entries from Carrollton Township.

The parade included a band from Rockfield, and a variety of farm implements from Jackson Township.

So many people went to Delphi for the parade that all threshing rings in Washington Township stopped for the day, and even one ring in Cass County had to stop for want of helpers.

A prize of $5.00 in gold for the best glee club was won by Carrollton Township Glee Club.

Charles Mullikan of Camden and Miss Agnes Porter of Burrows won $2.00 as the best dressed Pioneer

Couple, and Alfred Dale of Camden won $2.00 for the best Pioneer Outfit.

A prize of $2.00 was offered for the couple bringing the largest family. Mr. and Mrs. David Chapman of Washington Township and Mr. and Mrs. David Price of Carrollton Township each brought eight children. The prize was divided between them.

A program was held after the parade with an address by Pat O'Donnell of Chicago, formerly of Washington Township. John Rice played an accordion, Henry Landis gave an old County School Declamation, Miss Adeline Rinehart of Clymers sang a solo and Mrs. Mary Hardy reported on the Settlement of her Township.

The program on Friday was put on by Democrat, Clay, Madison, Tippecanoe, Jefferson and Adams Townships, with George Sites as chairman.

An award of $5.00 for the best glee club was given to Jefferson Township Glee Club.

An award of $2.00 for the Best Dressed Couple was given to Mrs. James Obear and Mrs. J. H. Allen.

A flag was awarded to George Sites, trustee of Jefferson Township for having the best display in the parade.

Others in the parade were: Modern Woodmen, Boy Scouts, Montique Bondie Campfire Girls, and a clown riding a mule. Mrs. Perry Rule and her triplets, James Perry, Whitcomb Golden and Riley Paul, represented a Pioneer Mother and Her Family. Rev. E. P. Day of the Delphi Presbyterian Church was an old fashioned Recruit Rider in the parade each day.

The program on Saturday with about 15,000 people attending was in charge of C. F. Bradshaw, and was put on by Delphi and Deer Creek Township. The big event of the day was the unveiling and dedication of the Milroy Memorial located at the east edge of Delphi on the old Camden Road. Civic and fraternal societies of Delphi and Deer Creek Township, the Delphi Band, and soldiers from Boothroyd Post assembled for the ceremony. Speakers were Charles E. Milroy of Chicago and attorney George W. Julien of Delphi. Stories were told by Matthew Sterling, and a recitation "Your Flag and My Flag" was given by Mrs. Yantis Wells.

The celebration for the week ended on Sunday evening with a Vesper Service led by Rev. Chester W. Wharton and a solo by his sister Miss Flora Wharton.

The grand climax of the Centennial Celebration was a program at Indianapolis from October 2 to 15. In preparation for the event each county conducted a contest to select someone to represent the county in the Miss Indiana Contest. In the county contest which closed on August 28, winners were selected by selling votes at ten cents each. The money was to be used to pay for a float to be used in the state parade. Material ordered for the Carroll County float did not arrive in time for the parade, so the money was divided among the county contestants.

The winner in the Miss Indiana Contest in Carroll County was Miss Minnie Snoeberger. Others in the contest were Miss Blossom Browne and Miss Beatrice Gardner.

At the State Contest at Indianapolis the winner from each county rode on horseback in a parade.

The 14 day celebration at Indianapolis included six pageants at Riverside Park and several parades and concerts including three by the Boston Grand Opera Company. One of the speakers was W. H. Taft, former president of the U.S.

Articles furnished by Carroll County for the state pageant included a yoke of Hereford Oxen, and a chair owned by Alex Spring that had been used by every president of the U.S. except Woodrow Wilson. A band of 25 from Delphi in charge of John Lathrope was in one of the parades.

1955 Old Settlers Centennial

One of the larger events sponsored by the Old Settlers Association was a week of celebration including the 100th Annual Old Settlers Meeting held on Saturday, August 13, 1955.

The Centennial Celebration started with a Centennial Ball and Miss Centennial Contest held on Saturday night, August 6, at the Delphi Armory. Former Governor Henry F. Schricker was present to crown Virginia Sanderson as queen. Others in the contest were: Faye Hitchcock Underhill, Jane Ann Kirkendall, Betty Jane Sanderson, Doris Shultheis, Beverly Richardson, Miriam Parks, Barbara Dillman, Beverly Bitler, Nancy Bowen, Kaye McMurray and Lois Young.

Sunday evening a Vesper Service was held at Riley Park with a sermon by Rev. John Laprad of the Pittsburg Church of the Brethren. Music was furnished by a Centennial Choir directed by Mrs. Harold Dick and accompanied by Edith Farr and LaVaune Million.

Mrs. George Wagoner was general chairman of the Old Fashioned Style Show staged on Tuesday at the Delphi City Park by Mrs. L. H. Smith, president of the Delphi Women's Club.

A Pet Parade was held on Wednesday afternoon at Riley Park with classes for cats, dogs, pigs, chickens, ducks, ponies, pony carts, tricycles, decorated bicycles and many others.

An Antique and Hobby Show sponsored by the Questers Club, at the Armory was opened by Mayor Charles A. Wood on Thursday and continued through Saturday. Merchants in town also had displays in their windows for the week.

Thursday was also Farmers Day at Riley Park. There were contests for fiddlers, liars, hog callers, husband callers, and whittlers. There was a bread baking contest for women. After the program there was a balloon ascension at Riley Park Annex.

Winners in the Liar's Contest in order were: Joseph E. Peterson, John C. Peterson, Mrs. Grace Bruce of Pine Village, Glen Criswell and Carol Louthain. The winning story was about a barrel with both ends out laying on the ground with a two inch hole in the top side. It rained so hard that the water went into the hole so much faster than it could run out both ends of the barrel that it busted the barrel.

Winners in the Hog Calling Contest were: Ren C. Groninger, Jesse Wise, Homer Wilson, Don Pullen and Jasper Fouts.

Winners in the Husband Calling Contest were: Mrs. Walter Greider, Mrs. Thomas Elston, Mrs. Roger Neff, Mrs. Virgil Maxwell and Mrs. Raymond Penn.

The Old Fiddlers Contest was won by Charles Gard of Pyrmont and second place went to Grover Reed of Lafayette.

The Bread Baking Contest was won by Mrs. Floyd Gardner of Camden, Mrs. Loyd Zook, Madison Township and Mrs. Walter Greider, R. 3, Delphi.

The Rolling Pin Throwing Contest for Women was won by Mrs. Alma Houser, R. R. Delphi; Mrs. John Phillips, Delphi and Donnabelle Plank, Cutler.

The Rolling Pin Throwing Contest for Men was won by Donald Butler, Roger Neff, Charles Anderson, Jack Grimm and Melvin Kurtz.

Louis Shaffer won the grand prize for the best growth which started before June 4 in the Full Beard Growing Contest, and Bud Knitter and John Robinson were second and third. Other Beard Contest winners were: Best Chin Whiskers, Side Burns and Mustache: Marvin Brehmer, Dale Cleaver and Jerry Boone; Most Unusual Beard: Wm. Coffey, Mark Porter and Arthur Hayden; Best Full Beard started after June 4: Dale Houser, Dave Hayden and Jasper Fouts; Best Chin Whiskers, Side Burns and Mustache: John Rhine, Robert Michael and Norman Ebrite; Most Unusual Beards started after June 4: Bill Penn, Everett Rider and Charles Smith; Most Distinguished Beard, Wayne Replogle; Blackest Beard, Charles Moore; Red Beard, Bob Simons; Oldest Beard Grower, John Waymire; Feeblest Attempt, Orville Hathaway. In the Shaving Contest, Wilbur Miller and W. S. Weaver were judged the Best Shavers as they clipped the Centennial Grown Beards.

Wayne Guthrie of Indianapolis and Virgil McClintic of Monticello were judges.

A Centennial Pageant, called "Carroll County Holiday", was presented for six evenings beginning on Sunday, August 7, 1955. It was presented in Riley Park, using a 250 foot panoramic stage with trees in the hillside serving as a backdrop. Special lighting and spectacular costumes were used to show colorful and interesting episodes in the history of Carroll County.

Beginning with days of Indian campfires and councils in this area the pageant brought to life such things as the coming of the first pioneers, building of the canal, coming of the railroad, early school days, religious meetings, recreations, amusements and entertainment of long ago and many other phases of life. Included in the pageant were: high spirited horses, tandem and high wheeled bicycles, buggies and carts, a horseless carriage, covered wagon, antique auto, a "paddy" wagon and various other means of transportation through the years, right down to streamlined cars of the day, baseball game, schooldays, Charleston and Can Can Dancing, bathing beauty contest, train scene and many others. Other scenes were Civil War, departure of Indians, planting of the flag on Iwo Jima and playing of the Star Spangled Banner for the finale in each show.

Mrs. Raymond (Cecile) Nicoll and Mrs. Charles (Mina) Tansey at Old Settlers at Delphi, August 13, 1955.

At the Old Settlers meeting on Saturday, George McDowell, 92, was the oldest man present and Neva Rothenberger, 94, was the oldest woman.

Robert Fitzgerald won the prize for the most unusual entry in the parade on Saturday when he rode an old time high wheel bicycle.

1966 Indiana Sesquicentennial

The Indiana Sesquicentennial Commission made up of prominent citizens in Indiana, spent several years preparing for the celebration of Indiana's 150th Birthday on December 11, 1966. Leo C. Craig of Carroll County was a member of the State Commission and served as chairman of the Committee on Publicity and Public Information. Several meetings and special events were held, and each county was encouraged to have committees arrange programs on a county basis.

The Sesquicentennial Committee in Carroll County was organized at a meeting at the Delphi Library on October 19, 1965. Officers elected were: John C. Peterson, president; Robert G. Bradshaw, vice president; Dorothy Mills, secretary and Robert Stephan, treasurer.

The first event sponsored by the county committee was a Queen Contest won by Patricia Ann Wagner,

Pat Wagner, Carroll County Queen for the Sesquicentennial celebration during 1966.

daughter of Mr. and Mrs. Ralph Wagner of Madison Township. Pat was crowned Queen at a county meeting held on February 8, 1966 and represented Carroll County at several events during the year.

The Carroll County Sesquicentennial Committee arranged for a banquet at the Delphi Methodist Church on Tuesday evening, April 19, 1966 with 129 present. Tables were decorated with old oil lamps and old flags of the U.S. and Indiana. Mrs. Beth Barnard provided dinner music on the piano. Mrs. Kenneth Newell had a display of old sheet music.

Entertainment included special music by the Top Twenty of Delphi High School, directed by David Gocher. Raymond Romein, accompanied by Mrs. Reuben Smith, played his musical saw.

Mrs. Faye B. Wise was the speaker for the evening. Wearing a dress belonging to her grandmother McCain, she told many interesting things about the history of Carroll County, and reported that her

Beth Barnard playing the piano at the Carroll County Sesquicentennial meeting, April 17, 1966.

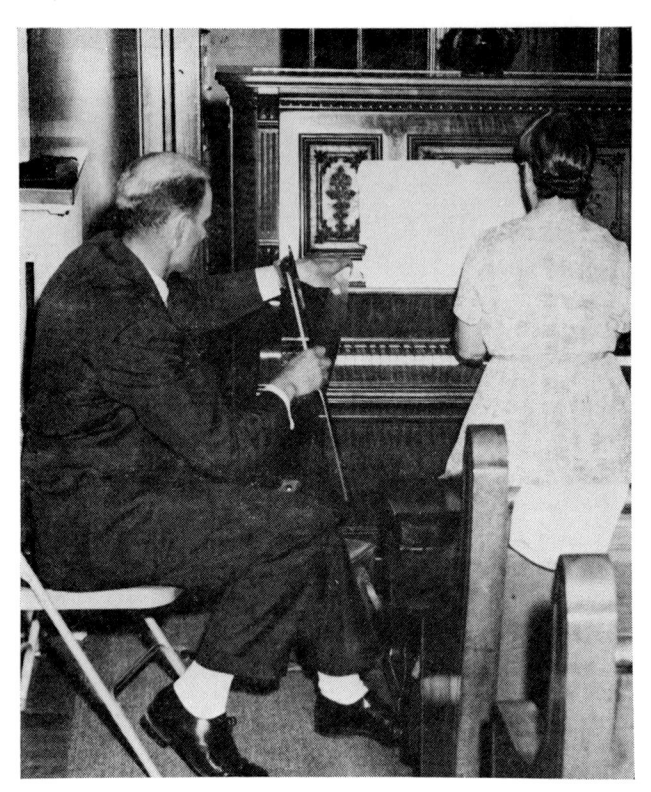

Raymond Romein playing his musical saw accompanied by Mrs. Reuben (Dorothy) Smith at the Carroll County Sesquicentennial meeting April 17, 1966.

mother, Mrs. Charles Buckley, had been chairman of the Centennial Celebration in 1916. She ended her talk with a poem which she had recently written in Hoosier dialect entitled "What is Indiana?"

Leo C. Craig reported that he had recently attended a meeting at Indianapolis where Governor Brannigan signed a proclamation officially opening an eight month celebration which would end on December 11, the 150th anniversary for Indiana.

An Indiana flag purchased by the committee was on display, and was later donated to the REMC for use in their auditorium.

About 200 license plates "Indiana 1816-1966" were sold during the year.

Robert G. Bradshaw, vice president prepared a map of Carroll County showing the location of 35 points of historic interest. Seven hundred of these maps were distributed to people throughout the county.

The Sesquicentennial HISTORYMOBILE, a large truck with historical displays was in Flora on June 7, and in Delphi on Friday, August 12, during Old Settlers week.

Mrs. Robert Wood presented her illustrated talk on "Historic Homes in Carroll County" in the REMC auditorium in Delphi on Saturday evening, August 13 during Old Settlers.

In November 1966 the county committee distributed to High School students in the county 2,500 copies each of four historic booklets published by the State Sesquicentennial Commission.

On December 4, 1966 the Civic Theater of Greater Lafayette presented a show "Spotlight 150" at the High School Auditorium in Delphi.

On June 28, 1967 a banquet was held at Indianapolis for all county committees in Indiana. Carroll County was presented a plaque which is on display in the Museum in the Courthouse at Delphi.

In July 1967 a Historical Marker furnished by the Indiana Commission was placed along State Road 421 at the east end of the bridge across the Wabash River at Pittsburg. The marker says:

NEW PURCHASE BOUNDARY

(Treaty of St. Mary's)

In October 1818, Purchasing Commissioners, Lewis Cass, Benjamin Parke and Governor Jonathan Jennings acquired Indian claims on the land shown on this marker. About one-third of modern Indiana was involved in this transaction.

Many people helped with the Sesquicentennial Celebration. Dennis McCouch wrote several poems, and organized a clean-up campaign by the Camden Boys Club in which they picked up several truck

Mrs. Faye Wise giving a report on local history at the Carroll County Sesquicentennial meeting on April 17, 1966 at the Methodist Church at Delphi.

loads of trash along the roads. Carl Snipes of Camden helped the Boys Club with several other projects.

Both local papers, the Journal-Citizen at Delphi and the Hoosier Democrat at Flora gave the program a lot of publicity during the year.

About 30 organizations and individuals were given certificates of recognition by the county committee for their contribution. The program in Carroll County was financed by donations by individuals and businesses, and by the sale of souvenirs.

When the County Celebration ended, the county committee had a balance of $256.35 which was given to the newly organized Carroll County Historical Society.

1972 Flora Centennial

During the week of July 2 to 8, 1972 Flora celebrated the Hundredth Anniversary of the founding of the town. Richard Leiter and DeVere Hoffman served as co-chairmen; Geneva Harmon, secretary; and Adolph Haines, treasurer of the event which started with a parade on Sunday afternoon, July 2. There were 137 units in the parade which lasted two hours. Special guests in the parade were: Mrs. Jean Dixon who was famous for her predictions; Tom Fouts, better known as Captain Stubby, a local boy who made good in the field of entertainment and Pat Kelly, the son of the famous clown, Emmett Kelly. Bill and Susan Mann served as co-chairmen of the Parade Committee. Carrol Stout was chairman of the Reception Committee for Jean Dixon, and Dick Ayres was in charge of the staging area.

First place winner of a trophy and $100 was a float by Delta Theta Chi sorority. Second place winner of a trophy and $75 went to the Flora Rotary Club. Third place and $50 was won by Grace Brethren Church of Flora. Twenty five dollars each for fourth and fifth places went to Flora Lions Club and Flora Rainbow Assembly.

First place for animal drawn floats went to an old hearse belonging to Allen Funeral Home at Bunker Hill, sponsored by Leiter Reinke Funeral Home of Flora. Second place went to a stage coach furnished by Benker Realty of Lafayette. Third place was a horse drawn buckboard driven by Jack Wallace of Flora.

A Queen Contest Monday evening with Connie and Fred Collins Jr. as co-chairmen, was won by Lucille Smith, with Helen Howard and Susan Mann as members of her court.

On Tuesday, July 4, there were games, contests, airplane rides, an antique show with Charles and Goldie Harter as co-chairmen; a square dance exhibition with Laurel Maxwell and Lola Mae Harmon co-chairmen, a program by Captain Stubby and fireworks in charge of a committee with Walter Allen as chairman.

An award for the oldest lady present was given to Amanda Roth, age 96 of Camden. John H. Flora, age 90, was the oldest man present. He was the great grandson of the founder of the town of Flora. Mr. and Mrs. John H. Flora received the award for the oldest married couple. They had been married 64½ years. An award for the best dressed family was given to the C. R. Powell family. Mr. and Mrs. J. R. Rinehart were awarded a prize as the best dressed couple. Robert Douglass of Seattle, Washington came the farthest for the event.

A horseshoe pitching contest with Gerald Harmon, chairman, and 42 pitchers was won by Charles Ogle of Sheridan. Second place went to Gerald Harmon and third to Byron Jervis.

During the next three days there were historical and factory tours arranged by Gerald Clingenpeel and Marie Clark; flea markets, sidewalk days with Tom and Beverly Ayres, co-chairmen; dances and a Historical Pageant with Robert and Karen Reiffel, co-chairmen.

Saturday afternoon there was an antique car parade with a total of 42 old cars. A 1925 Locomobile owned by Harlan Skaggs of Monticello was voted the best of the show. Barry Wheeler was chairman of the antique car committee.

A 1926 Chevrolet owned by Gene Lyon of Big Bear Lake, California and formerly of Flora, received the award for coming the farthest and also received the trophy given by Mann Chevrolet as the best Chevrolet in the parade.

A 1930 Model A Ford Sport Coupe owned by Fred Smith of Frankfort won the James F. Wheeler trophy for the best Ford. A 1925 Star owned by Ed and Bill Waymire of Delphi was selected as the winner in the non-Ford, non-classic division.

After the parade a ceremony was held to dig up the razor which had been buried at the beginning of the Centennial Celebration. A time capsule to be opened in 2022 was buried at the southwest corner of the Flora Public Library.

There was a display of steam engines, old tractors and other old farm machinery in charge of Bill Kearns. Among those with old machinery on exhibit were: Harold Beckom of Kokomo, R. E. Rocky of Galveston and Scott Campbell of Elwood.

At a Medicine Show held uptown, The Three Blanks, Mary Jane Chapman, Dena Kesling and JoAnn Miller sang "I Didn't Know the Gun was Loaded."

Don Craft and Emerson McKinley were co-chairmen of the beard contest in which the following awards were given: Best Beard, Don Lowery; Goatee, DeVere Hoffman; Plain Mustache, Martin Rinehart; Handlebar Mustache, Ed Oyler; Black, Don Craft; White, Cliff Bosworth; Brown, Steve Mills; Red, Jerry Sibbitt; Mixed, Howard McGill and He Tried, Roger Gibson and Chuck Stiles. Judges were: Kenny Cree of Rossville, Rodney Lowry of Delphi and Frank Hood of Flora.

Historical Marker

Members of the Carroll County Historical Society have presented a marker commemorating the history of Flora to the Centennial Historical Committee and the town of Flora. On hand for the presentation were: John H. Flora; Richard Leiter (behind Flora), co-chairman of the centennial; John Witter; Gerald Clingenpeel; and DeVere Hoffman, second centennial co-chairman.

Historical Marker at Flora presented by the Carroll County Historical Society to the Centennial Committee for the town of Flora in 1972. From left: Richard Leiter, John H. Flora, John Witter, Gerald Clingenpeel and DeVere Hoffman.

The award for bringing the largest family went to Vernon Flora and Loren Landis, both of California. The award for living at the same residence the greatest number of years was given to Lula Studebaker who had lived in the same home for 85 years.

Frank and Opal Loudon published a Historical and Pictorial Souvenir Booklet containing much information about Flora's First Hundred Years. Al Moss and Jennifer Archibald were co-chairmen of the Publicity Committee.

Richard Curts used his amateur radio equipment to advertise the centennial and exchanged messages with many other amateur radio operators.

Bill Adams was chairman of the committee for the 4th of July program and Webb and JoAnn Miller were co-chairmen for Old Timer Days. Carrol and Mary Lee Stout were co-chairmen for the Vesper Service at the Saturday night Gospel Sing.

Keith Sisson was chairman of the Airport committee, Orville Howard was in charge of the shuttle bus service, Tom Adams was chairman of the committee for concessions and rides, Don Clingenpeel was chairman of the committee for traffic, parking and Guard duty, and Norman Beck was in charge of loud speaking equipment.

Tom Gibson was chairman of the committee for kids games and contests, Dale Zinn was in charge of the croquet contest, and James Keyes directed the black powder shoot.

Blanche Loy was chairman of the old exhibits and Nettie Lou Phillipy was in charge of the quilt committee. The Historical Society of Carroll County presented a marker with a brief history of Flora to the Centennial Committee. The marker was installed in the corner of the parking lot on the north side of Main Street.

Merritt Hardt organized a Pony Express mail delivery from the State House at Indianapolis to Flora with 23 riders and horses. They picked up messages from towns along the Michigan Road and delivered them to the Centennial Headquarters in Flora. This was the first Pony Express in Indiana in many years.

1976 U.S. Bicentennial

A County Bicentennial Commission to help celebrate the 200th Birthday for the U.S. was organized at a meeting held at Flora, Indiana, on January 8, 1975. Officers elected were: Dennis McCouch, president; Mrs. Dorothy Mills, vice president; Mrs. Hazel Schenck, secretary and Cleon Carter, treasurer.

Members of the Commission and their townships were: Mr. and Mrs. Charles Pearson and Mr. and Mrs. Richard Grantham, Adams; Mr. and Mrs. William Schenck, Burlington; Mr. and Mrs. Fred McCain, Carrollton; Mr. and Mrs. Marion Ward, Clay; Mr. and Mrs. Robert Brookbank, Deer Creek; Mr. and Mrs. Cleon Carter, Democrat; Mr. and Mrs. B. Jesse Zook, Jackson; Mr. and Mrs. Robert D. Mills, Jefferson; Mr. and Mrs. Lewis Mullin, Liberty, Mr. and Mrs. Lee Flora and Mr. and Mrs. Richard McCain, Madison; Gerald Clingenpeel, Ladonna Allen and Marsha Grotrian, Monroe; Mr. and Mrs. Lawrence Zuercher, Rock Creek; Mr. and Mrs. James White, Tippecanoe and Mr. and Mrs. Patrick Powlen, Washington.

The slogan chosen for the county was "Yesterday's Heritage-Tomorrow's Horizon" and the theme for the celebration was "Preserve the Past; Prepare for the Future."

Several events in the county were held during the year. Flora held a parade on July 3 with a fish fry and fireworks at the fairgrounds. A Crafts Fair was held on September 18 and 19 in the Merchants Building at the fairgrounds with LaDonna Allen, Bicentennial Commission member from Flora in charge.

Commemorative pure silver coins were available from the Union Bank and Trust Company at Delphi.

The Carroll County ASCS office and the Indiana State ASCS office of the USDA sponsored an essay contest open to all students in the seventh grade on the subject "What Agriculture Means to Me." First place winner in Carroll County was awarded a $25 Savings Bond and the school was given an American flag which had flown over the U.S. Capitol Building. Second through fifth place winners were each given a Bicentennial silver dollar. Winners in order were: Sheryl Lynn Duff, Delphi Middle School; Janelle Lynn Ward, Delphi Middle School; Alice Hoffman,

Carroll Jr. High School; Kara Wolf, Delphi Middle School and Marla K. Stewart, Delphi Middle School.

The following is the winning essay written by Sheryl Lynn Duff:

"To me agriculture means the difference between life and death. Without agriculture survival would be almost impossible. There would be nothing to look forward to. There would be nothing to eat, nothing to wear, just nothing at all. That is one reason why agriculture is so important to me.

"I have lived on the same farm all my life. I've grown up around pigs and cattle. Agriculture is my whole life. By living on a farm I have always had everything I need. I have even learned to appreciate the smell of a pig barn.

"Agriculture is not just a field of corn and a cow or two. It's also beauty. Some city people don't realize it but without agriculture there would be no flowers for their tables, no trees to shade their homes, and their menus would be very limited. There would be no beautiful clothes to wear, which seems to be some peoples only concern. Without agriculture life indeed would be very short and drab.

"We depend on agriculture both directly and indirectly. We depend on agriculture for food, clothing, and shelter, but there is one more very important thing, life. Most people are not aware of this but it is true. I learned this when I was younger and will always remember it.

"Just seeing our cows have their calves and watching them grow is another thing I love about agriculture. Watching the calves run in the pasture until they are old enough to train for 4-H and then to sell or eat is a thrill. The meat from our cattle is so much better tasting to me because we have had a part in raising it. Another thing I love is seeing my father and my brothers working in the fields together growing beautiful corn, beans, and wheat. Helping Mom in the garden is one of my involvements with agriculture.

"Living in a rural community and being the daughter of a farmer gives me a special closeness to God. Along with the excitement of seeing a newborn calf grow into a profitable beef steer, I see tiny little seeds grow into beautiful flowers and food for our freezer. As it was centuries ago in the beginning, we on the farm, God willing, will experience many beginnings.

"This is what agriculture means to me and why I love it so much. I am very proud to be a part of it."

Delphi Community High School presented "Musical 1976" at the Little Theater in March. The Camden Elementary School had a festival "Happy Birthday, America" in April and on April 9 and 10, the Flora Psi Iota Xi sorority presented a variety show, "Trot Through Time 1776-1976" at the Flora High School auditorium.

The Carroll County Extension Homemakers Council presented a talent show at Delphi Community High School in April. On July 4, the Burlington Bicentennial Commission presented a musical "I Love America." A large parade was staged with many floats, followed by the Burlington traditional fish fry and fireworks.

A covered wagon visited the county on April 1, and made stops at the schools in Delphi and Carroll Consolidated.

Space was donated in the Mellon-Pearson building for a Bicentennial Commission office which was open five days per week. Mrs. Wilma Robinson was in the office to sell license plates, decals, jewelry, plates, and other items with the Bicentennial symbol. Income from these sales helped pay expenses. The main sources of income were from donations by businesses and individuals.

When the Bicentennial Commission dissolved, the remaining balance in the treasury was given to the Carroll County Historical Society. The remaining mementos were placed in the Carroll County Museum to be sold.

1978 Burlington Sesquicentennial

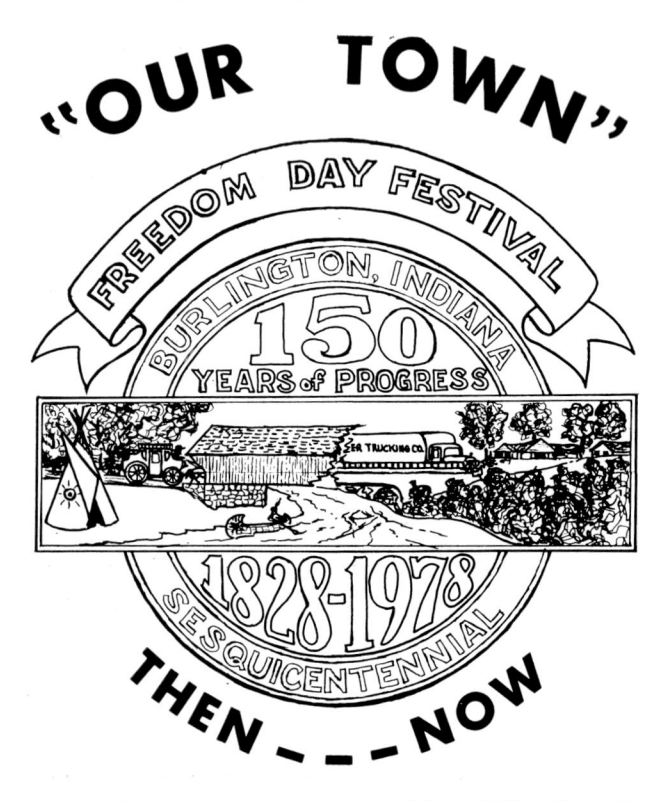

Carroll County was 150 years old in 1978. The only

community to have a big celebration for the event was the town of Burlington with a four-day celebration on July 1 to 4, 1978. They published a book entitled "Our Town, Then—Now." The following is a part of the History of Burlington in that book:

"A few hardy settlers: Mahlon Shinn, George Harness and David Ewing had moved into the Burlington area with their families as early as 1827. But it was in 1828 that David Stipp, an employee in the Government Land Office at Crawfordsville, laid out the Town of Burlington in 92 lots running South from Wildcat Creek. Stipp, who was apparently a stingy man with a cold and forbidding nature, moved onto a quarter section of land near the town plat in 1830. Not known to ever do anything for the Town of Burlington other than donate a small plot of ground for a school house, Stipp died in the area in 1848.

"In 1830-1831, Philip Rinker constructed a crude grist mill of undressed logs with two boulders from the creek bed as burrs just northwest of the town plat. He operated the mill until 1837 when it was sold to John Cromwell, who erected a frame building on the site and continued in business at that location until sometime after 1862.

"Also in 1830-31, Samuel Gwinn, William F. Gerhart, Jacob Brown, William Smith and Edmund Moss entered land near Burlington: however, it wasn't until 1833 that the first dense timber was cleared in the town plat by John Kelly and Robert Ewing.

"Andrew Watts and William Henry purchased a house erected by David Stipp and kept a tavern in about 1834. William Stockton also opened a tavern about the same time and kept the relay house for the stage horses on the Michigan Road. The Michigan Road, which ran through the middle of the town of Burlington, was to become the great thoroughfare between Madison on the Ohio River and Michigan City on the North. Work on the road was done in the Burlington area in 1830 and 1831 at an average cost of $102.00 per mile. The road was to be 100 feet in width being grubbed clean 30 feet in the center of the road and with no stumps more than a foot high. This project was financed by the sale of sections of land along the right-of-way at a fixed price of not less than $1.25 per acre. It was the opening of the road as well as the sale of the land that provided a means for travel and settlement throughout the middle of Indiana.

"David Foster, who later laid out the Town of Kokomo, settled in Burlington in 1834 and engaged in trade with the Indians (mainly alcohol) before moving into what is now Howard County. After 1835, the arrival of new families began to be regular occurrence and the Town of Burlington grew as new businesses were opened and the surrounding countryside was cleared for farming.

"Henry Bolles moved to town in 1837 and opened the first general merchandise trading center and expanded to take in a partner, E. P. Stone, in 1846.

"In the fall of 1838, Dr. Samuel Anderson became the Town's first doctor. Many family names that still remain first came to the Burlington area about this time: Garrison, Robertson, Barnard, Everman, Hendrix, and Beck just to name a few. In 1848, James Harmon constructed a brick kiln and in 1856 or 1857, Mahlon Shinn erected a saw mill on his farm northeast of the town plat. Shinn was noted for being odd, but straight forward and was connected with several substantial enterprises. He was proprietor of one of the first hotels, was the first Justice of the Peace and perhaps the first postmaster. He operated the mill for several years after which it passed to various parties among whom were Grimes and Viney, who remodeled and converted the building into a flour mill. About 1872, the mill was destroyed by fire and in 1874 Robertson and Stone erected a new flour mill with a Leffel patent turbine wheel and two runs of burrs. A saw and planing mill was erected in the south part of town in 1873 by Joseph W. Gwinn and Leroy Barnard, which regularly sawed 7,000 feet of timber per day and employed six men.

"In 1871, H. A. Lovell began to manufacture buggies in connection with his blacksmith trade. His shop, a two-story frame building in the center of town produced 10 top buggies, 2 carriages, one phaeton and 5 spring wagons in 1881.

By 1882, the town had a hotel kept by William Stombough; three general merchandise stores run by W. H. Everman, J. J. Stone and Tapp and Everman, respectively; one drug store, by J. A. Fennell, one meat market by William Taylor. Dr. Samuel Anderson, Dr. Charles Chittick, Dr. B. F. Landes and Dr. Doane were practicing physicians. William Beck and George Ewick were the town carpenters; George Hickman, the town barber and jeweler; Fullwider and Viney, saddlers and harness markers; John K. Garrison, furniture dealer and undertaker; George Appenzeller tinner and dealer in hardware, tinware and and stoves; H. A. Lovell and B. F. Landes, blacksmiths; Benjamin Bryant, wagon maker; W. H. Reagon and M. Appenzeller, boot and shoe makers.

"The Town of Burlington from the beginning has been an active, prosperous and good place to live. The individuals who carved our community from the wilderness set the example and many of their descendants still remain and take pride in our town."

BURLINGTON SESQUICENTENNIAL COMMISSION

Members of the Sesquicentennial Commission were J. R. Rinehart, Nadine Eller and Hazel Schenck.

They were appointed in 1977 by the Directors of the Burlington Community Club who were: Hazel Schenck, Marda Gene Catron, Nadine Eller, Ed Brewster, Bob Zook, Lance Alter and John Harrell.

The Directors of the Burlington Community Club for 1978 had the job of overseeing the culmination of the Sesquicentennial activities. They were: Lance Alter, Ed Brewster, Nadine Eller, Dick Crume, Kathy Revils, Marda Gene Catron and John Cox.

HISTORY OF BURLINGTON

Members of the committee in charge of the History of Burlington in the book were: Vera Gilbert, Alan Brubaker, Jessie Harness, Ennis Davis and Irene Bieghler.

Another committee collected pictures and stories about present day activities of families, businesses and organizations. Committee members were: Martha Sink, Wanda Dinger, Marda Catron, Edith Rodkey, Margaret Mabbitt, Ancel Bowley, Jane Ann Heaton, Earl Oyler, Esther Braden, Verlin Long, Jan Neptune, Bernice Anderson, Rosemary Austin, Maryanna Scott, Loris and Esther Stout, Richard and Gloria Hendrix, Carol Johnson, John (Bud) Anderson, Lottie Bray, Mary Rhine, Jan Sanderson, Diane Stout, Joyce Stout and Donna Ekstein.

In early 1977 contests were held to name the slogan for the 4th of July festivities and to design a Sesquicentennial Logo. The winning slogan, "Freedom Day Festival," was submitted by Mrs. Gayle (Diane) Stout.

The winning logo idea was submitted by Mrs. George (Iva) Melton. It depicts "Burlington Then and Now," with the stage coach entering the covered bridge across Wildcat Creek on the Old Michigan Road. Representing early history is the Indian teepee and canoe. Many area residents recall their parents talking of the Indian encampments in that very spot. At that time Burlington was a main trading post. Emerging from the new concrete bridge is a modern semi-truck. State Road 29, known as the Old Michigan Road, has been a main trucking route from Lake Michigan to the Ohio River for many years. The modern brick home to the right, owned by Mr. and Mrs. Joe Bousum, depicts the growth of modern day Burlington.

Earl Rodkey did the art work, combining the logo and slogan into a beautiful, colorful work of art.

Wolever Photo

Tourists on the Carrollton Bridge who went on a tour from Delphi to Logansport on June 1, 1921. Some can be identified in the photo. Standing along the railing are Dr. Frank Robinson, Mrs. Wolf and John H. Mourer. Standing in the center are Benjamin F. Stuart and Hoover Jones. The eight people standing along the cars are left to right: James Shirk, Mrs. N. J. Howell, Mrs. Dr. Robinson, Matthew Sterling, Joseph Grantham, Harlow Lindley, Dr. Newcomes, and John Odell. Information about this tour is presented in "History of the Wabash and Valley" by Benj. F. Stuart.

CARROLL COUNTY HISTORICAL SOCIETY

As early as 1898 a movement was started to organize a Historical Society in Carroll County. The primary purpose was to provide a place to collect and preserve some of the relics belonging to the older residents of the county.

The first Historical Society was organized on November 19, 1921 with 62 Charter Members, listed at the end of the chapter. Officers elected at the first meeting were: Wm. C. Smith, president; John C. Odell, vice president; Harry Arnold, secretary treasurer and the following directors: Benjamin F. Stuart, John Bowman, Wilson Sterrett, Mrs. Charles Buckley and Mrs. Mindwell Crampton Wilson. Dues were 50¢ per year and membership was open to anyone interested in preserving the History of Carroll County.

At the first regular meeting of the Historical Society on December 31, 1921 the following officers were elected for the next year: Wm. C. Smith, president; John C. Odell, vice president and Mrs. Charles Buckley, secretary treasurer. Directors elected were: Benjamin F. Stuart, Mrs. W. A. Breining, Mrs. Mindwell Crampton Wilson, Will Gros and Mrs. Thaddeus Guthrie.

Regular meetings of the society were held with programs on Carroll County History. Mrs. Frank Girard gave a complete History of County Fairs held prior to 1880. John C. Odell told about building the Wabash and Erie Canal. Harry Milroy drew chalk drawings of two former residents of Delphi, Dr. Stewart and James B. Scott. Benjamin F. Stuart and F. F. Stewart gave talks on local history.

The first Historical Society was active for about 15 years.

CARROLL COUNTY HISTORICAL SOCIETY REORGANIZED

Burnett's Creek Arch

Four members of the Rossville History Club sponsored by William H. Baugh, teacher of social studies in the Rossville High School, called a meeting in Delphi on September 11, 1967 for people interested in reorganizing the Carroll County Historical Society. Carroll County was one of the few counties in Indiana without a Historical Society. The boys involved were: Keith Wolf, Carl Chezem, Jon Rockwood and Leonard Meador. The latter two were residents of Clay Township. The boys presented a proposed constitution, by-laws and resolutions for establishment of the society. A nominating committee comprised of Mrs. Don Moore, Mrs. B. Jesse Zook, Mr. and Mrs. Ron Lauster and John C. Peterson was named.

About thirty Carroll County residents attended the organization meeting held at the REMC auditorium in Delphi on September 21, 1967. The constitution and by-laws were adopted and the following officers elected: Dennis McCouch, president, Cleon Carter, vice president and Mrs. Buford Pearson, secretary treasurer. Directors elected were: Robert G. Bradshaw, Charles A. Wood, Mrs. John C. Peterson, Mrs. Don Moore, Mrs. B. Jesse Zook, Ronald Lauster, Mrs. Blanche Balser, Mrs. Mabel Gibson, Lewis Funkhouser and Mrs. Roy Gregg.

Leonard Meador, a member of the Rossville History Club, who served as temporary chairman during the organizational procedure, presented the new president with a beautiful birdseye maple gavel as a gift to the new society.

Dr. W. M. Sholty, former president of the Tippecanoe County Society showed items of historical interest such as arrowheads, beads and other Indian artifacts which he had found near his home.

Mr. Ted Reser, president of the Tippecanoe County Society gave a short history of Indian tribes in the Wabash Valley of Carroll and Tippecanoe Counties.

A campaign for membership in the new society was conducted and resulted in 152 Charter Members listed at the end of the chapter.

Membership fees in the Historical Society ranged from $2 for a single annual membership to $100 for a lifetime membership. In 1980 there were a total of 107 members including eight life members. Those with life membership were: Robert G. Bradshaw, Irene DeWinton, Viola Emrick, Mrs. Jeanne Stuntz, Laura Temple, Mrs. Charles Yeager, Mrs. Irene Garrison and Camden Public Library.

The Board of Directors meet each month and about three public meetings have been held in the county each year with a special program of historic interest to members.

Historical tours sponsored by the society each year have included trips to: Parke County and Crawfordsville; Conner Prairie Settlement at Noblesville; Indianapolis, the Museum at Eagle Creek Park, Morris Butler Mansion and Indianapolis Museum of Art; Piqua, Ohio to visit the Johnston Farm and a restored section of the Miami and Erie Canal; New Harmony restored settlement; King Tut Exhibit at Chicago; Old Fort at Ft. Wayne and Cord Duesenberg Museum at Auburn; Historic Madison and Squire Boone's Cabins and Marengo Cave in southern Indiana.

The Burnetts Creek Arch sketched by Mrs. Ruben McQueen and a relic of the Wabash and Erie Canal days was adopted as the symbol. In addition to the Historical Museum the society established an Archives section to collect and preserve records and documents.

Several books pertaining to Carroll County History have been sold by the Historical Society.

A booklet has been published giving the location of cemeteries in the county and another lists the marriages in the county from 1828-1850.

Birth Records from 1921-1978 and Death Records from 1921-1979 have been compiled and a limited number of copies made available for public use.

Officers for 1980 were: Robert Brookbank, president; Charles P. McCain, first vice president; Dennis McCouch, second vice president; Mrs. Ruth White, secretary and Mrs. Doris Peterson, treasurer. Other directors were: Robert G. Bradshaw, Lewis Funkhouser, Lawrence VanDerVolgen, Miss Irene DeWinton, Mrs. Orpha Goslee, Mrs. Clara Sims, Mrs. Don (Phyllis) Moore, Curator; Mrs. B. Jesse Zook, Mrs. Cleon Carter and Mrs. Margaret Draper.

Brookbank Photo
Robert Bradshaw and Anna Myrle Zook, directors of the Carroll County Historical Society.

Others who have served as president were: Cleon Carter and Lawrence VanDerVolgen.

Special demonstrations are arranged for Old Settlers and other special occasions.

The Jr. Historical Society sponsored by Glen Dillman of Flora Jr. High School has helped on several programs and at the Museum when it was open for Old Settlers and other special events.

Many people have helped by showing how to do various old time crafts at the Museum including: Mrs. Robert Scheffee and helpers on spinning; Mrs. Lois Underhill, Mrs. Ruby Sigman and others on

Brookbank Photo
Directors of the Carroll County Historical Society who met at the REMC auditorium November 12, 1979. Left to right: Mrs. Ruth White, Dennis McCouch, Mrs. Clara Sims, Mrs. Phyllis Moore, Mrs. Doris Peterson, Mrs. Orpha Goslee, Lawrence VanDerVolgen, Mrs. Leona Carter, Charles P. McCain, Miss Irene DeWinton and Robert Brookbank. Directors not present were: Robert Bradshaw, Lewis Funkhouser, Mrs. Margaret Draper and Mrs. Anna Myrle Zook.

Lewis Funkhouser, director of the Carroll County Historical Society.

CHAPTER XI — OTHER ORGANIZATIONS AND EVENTS 343

Brookbank Photo
Mrs. Lavonne Scheffee of Tippecanoe County demonstrating a spinning wheel and Toni Cook of Flora demonstrating a drop spindle at the Open House in the Carroll County Historical Museum on November 10, 1974.

the rug loom; the Americus Quilting Club; Lewis Mullin and others splitting rails; Charles P. McCain making shingles; Mrs. Harry Latshaw tatting; Clifford Kurtz and Chief Ken Red Elk, Indians living in Carroll County; Carolyn Pearson and Jane Van Sickle, corn husk dolls; Mrs. Herbert Blohm and Debbie Kingery, chair caning and Claude Remaly with his gasoline engines.

Members of Civil Defense were on duty in the Museum and on the grounds during Old Settlers.

The Carroll County Historical Society installed eight historical markers in the county during the years 1971 to 1978. The first four had the same wording on both sides and the last four had a different legend on each side. All markers were similar to the one at Camden shown in the picture. The inscriptions on all the markers, listed at the end of the chapter, were written by Robert G. Bradshaw.

MUSEUM

In September 1922 the County Fair Association appointed Benjamin F. Stuart, Mrs. Charles Murphy and Mrs. Charles Buckley to work with the Historical Society to arrange a display of relics for the fair. A display was arranged in the County Assessors office in the Courthouse.

Brookbank Photo

Clifford Kurtz, one fourth Cherokee Indian, at the Historical Museum in Delphi in 1976 during Open House, wearing a native Indian costume which he made. His grandmother was a full blooded Cherokee Indian from Carolina and Virginia. Clifford was born in 1906 on Wea Prairie in Indiana and moved to Delphi in 1933. His Indian name is Wah-Nah-Taw.

In August 1924 the east room on the third floor of the Courthouse was turned over to the Historical Society by the County Commissioners for a Museum. Each township was assigned a part of the room, and asked to help pay for display cases. A uniform design for cases was decided upon and several were donated by townships and individuals. The first money for display cases was given by Mrs. W. C. Smith who donated the prize check she had won as a horseback rider in the Old Time Costume contest at Old Settlers. Miss Goldie Scott donated the prize money awarded for her buggy used by the W. F. Peterson family in the Old Settlers Parade.

In July 1925, John C. Odell, vice president of the Historical Society, died at the age of 86. He was the author of the History of Carroll County published in 1916.

In February 1929, the heirs of George H. C. Best presented to the Historical Society the large glass cases in the building formerly owned by Mr. Best. The cases were moved to the Museum in the Courthouse and are still being used. Mrs. Buckley arranged to have the room open for Old Settlers that year.

When the Historical Society became inactive, the Museum became a responsibility of the County Commissioners and was closed most of the time.

In 1937 the Historical Room in the Courthouse was cleaned by people hired by WPA. In 1938 the WPA did more work in the room and Lawrence Taylor arranged articles in the cases.

Mrs. Dora Thomas Mayhill took charge of the Museum, and for many years arranged to have it open for Old Settlers and other special occasions. She also arranged to have classes from school visit the Museum.

In 1960 members of the Gamma Gamma Nu sorority cleaned and organized the Museum, and arranged to have it open on special occasions.

In November 1967 the newly organized Carroll County Historical Society took charge of the Museum and has operated it since then. Displays were cleaned, organized and items recorded and the Museum was open part time. Mrs. Don (Phyllis) Moore, a member of the Gamma Gamma Nu sorority and a member of the Executive Board of the Historical Society was appointed Curator and under her guidance the Museum has continued to grow.

The County Commissioners installed a new floor and made other improvements in the Assembly Room in the Courthouse, and authorized the Historical Society to use it for the Museum. In 1973 the Museum was moved to the old Assembly Room on the ground floor of the Courthouse, and many more items have been added for display. It is open two half days each week and for special occasions.

CHARTER MEMBERS OF THE FIRST CARROLL COUNTY HISTORICAL SOCIETY ORGANIZED ON NOVEMBER 19, 1921

A. L. Akers, Mrs. A. L. Akers, Mrs. J. H. Allen, Harry Arnold, Mrs. Harry Arnold, Mrs. M. E. Ballard, Jason Been, Miss Lillian Blythe, Miss Lou Bonnell, Mrs. E. W. Bowen, Miss Hilda Bowen, Mrs. N. W. Bowen, Mrs. L. D. Boyd, Robert G. Bradshaw, Mrs. W. H. Breining, Harry S. Brewer, Frank Broadlick, Charles Buckley, Mrs. Charles Buckley, John Carney MD, Mrs. John Carney, Mrs. Dora Corbett, Mrs.

CHAPTER XI — OTHER ORGANIZATIONS AND EVENTS • 345

Brookbank Photo

Employees and some members of the Board of the Camden Library on June 22, 1977 when the Historical Marker was erected by the Carroll County Historical Society on the Library lawn. From left: Shirley Schock, librarian; Jane Penn, board member; Richard Recher, vice president of the board; Shirley Kistler and June Thomas, assistant librarians and Evelyn Sharp, member of board.

Lenora Corns, Mrs. Julia Cowdin, Mrs. Carrie Cox, Miss Florence Cox, Mrs. E. H. Dame, Miss Susie Dasher, Geneva Davidson, R. C. Davidson, Mrs. Eva Dooley, Miss Effie Dyer, John E. Ferrier, Mrs. Belle Gardner, Mrs. Lauretta Gardner, Roy E. Gardner, Frank S. Girard, Mrs. Lizzie Girard, Mrs. G. M. Gregg, Mrs. Charles Gros, Mrs. Fannie R. Gros, Mrs. Harriet Gros, Wm. Gros, J. W. Hanna, John L. Hanna, A. L. Hodgson, W. E. Holmes, Burton Honan, Mrs. Newberry Howe, Mrs. Ida M. Jackson, George Julien, Mrs. T. E. Julien, Mrs. C. M. Kerlin, Mrs. Della C. Kerlin, John W. Kerlin, Mrs. John W. Kerlin, Grover D. Kite, Mrs. Jennie F. Kite, Frank B. Lyon, Agnes J. Margowski, Mary Mason, J. A. Metsker, Charles E. Milroy, Harry C. Milroy, Mrs. John Mount, John H. Mourer, J. Reed McCain, Mrs. Laura V. McCain, Gertrude Mummert, W. F. Mummert, Mrs. Elizabeth Murphy, Jas. A. Neff, John C. Odell, Mrs. John C. Odell, Josephine Odell, C. Clay Pearson, Mrs. Levina Roach, F. H. Robinson, Mrs. F. H. Robinson, W. H. Robinson, Mrs. W. H. Robinson, Miss Florence Scott, Miss Goldie Scott, Mrs. Mae Sibbitt, James A. Shirk, Ora M. Shirk, Mrs. Jennie Silver, Geo. W. Smith, L. H. Smith, Mrs. L. H. Smith, William C. Smith, Mrs. William C. Smith, George Smock, Mrs. James C. Smock, Matthew Sterling, Benj. F. Stuart, W. P. Thompson, Miss Anna F. Trobaugh, Mary Walker, Henry B. Wilson, Mrs. Mindwell Crampton Wilson, Faye Buckley Wise, A. W. Wolever, Armina Wolfe and Mrs. Jennie Wolfe.

CHARTER MEMBERS OF THE CARROLL COUNTY HISTORICAL SOCIETY REORGANIZED ON SEPTEMBER 28, 1967

Neil Alter, Miss Ruth Ayres, Mrs. Blanche Balser, Mrs. Ruth Barnhart, Wm. H. Baugh, Mr. and Mrs. Ben Been, Miss Elizabeth Best, Dick Bishop, Mrs. Irene Bixler, Miss Josephine Blanchard, Mrs. Fannie Blue, Mrs. Wm. H. Bordner, Miss Hilda Bowen, Mrs. Ruth Draper Bowman, Robert G. Bradshaw, Mrs. Lewis Brewer, Mrs. Lynn Brookbank, Daniel M. Brown, Mrs. Josephine M. Brown, Mrs. Albert Burkle, Mr. and Mrs. Cleon Carter, Mrs. Edna Carter, Carl Chezem, Mrs. Earl Clem, Mr. and Mrs. Morris Clem, Mrs. Mable Cole, Mr. and Mrs. Leo Craig, Mr. and Mrs. Loyal Cripe, Mr. and Mrs. Roger Daugherty, Mrs. Melvin Dawson, Mr. and Mrs. Lester Dickinson, Mrs. Reva M. Disinger, Mrs. Margaret Draper, Miss Viola Emrick, Jon David Fletcher, Mr. and Mrs. Lewis Funkhouser, Mrs. Dan Farner, Mrs. Glenn Fisher, Dale Fossnock, Mrs. Mable Gibson, Jeffrey Goodwin, Mrs. Mary Margaret Goodwin, Mrs. Roberta Scott Gick, Mrs. Orpha Goslee, Mr. and Mrs. Roy Gregg, Mr. and Mrs. Reed Gushwa, Mr. and Mrs. Charles E. Harter, Mr. and Mrs. Loren D. Herrli, Clarence Hyman, Mr. and Mrs. Melvin Jackson, Mrs. Georgianna Julius, Mrs. Martha Justice, Dale Kasten, Mrs. Pollard Kelleher, Miss Mable C. Kemp, John L. Kennard, Mrs. R. D. Landis, Mr. and Mrs. Ronald Lauster, Wayne Loman, David L. Matthew, Charles Maxwell, David Maxwell, Mr. and Mrs. Junior E. Maxwell, Charles P. McCain, Mr. and Mrs. John McCain, Dennis McCouch, Tom MaCurdy, Kenneth M. McGill, Mrs. Virginia McKnight, Mr. and Mrs. Ruben McQueen, Leonard Meador, Miss Esther P. Miller, Mr. and Mrs. Don R. Moore, Gary Gene Moore, Robert D. Morrow, Mrs. Marion Moyer, Mr. and Mrs. Charles J. Mummert, Mrs. Betty M. Montage, Billy D. Murphy, Mrs. Fren Musselman, Mr. and Mrs. Homer Myers, George W. Obear, Mrs. Julia Omaht, Mrs. Buford Pearson, Mr. and Mrs. Wayne Pearson, Mr. and Mrs. John C. Peterson, Mr. and Mrs. Joseph E. Peterson, Mrs. Betty Powell, Mrs. Jack A. Pritchard, Kenneth Pyle, Mrs. Georgia Loy Quinn, Jon Rockwood, Mr. and Mrs. Lee E. Reppert, Lenard Robison, Fred E. Rodkey, Mr. and Mrs. Oscar Rohrabaugh, Eric Ross, Kevin Ross, Mr. and Mrs. Cledith Scott, Paul H. Seward, Mr. and Mrs. Charles Shanks, Mr. and Mrs. James S. Shideler, Mrs. Clara Sims, Mrs. Alice Sledge, Mrs. Irene Smith, Mrs. Mable W. Smith, Wm. B. Smith, Mrs. Jeanne Stangle, Mrs. Jeanne Stuntz, Miss Rosemary Sutton, Mrs. Don Swinford, Mrs. James A. Thomson, Mrs. Robert VanNatta, Mr. and Mrs. Verl Wagoner, Mr. and Mrs. Marion Ward, W. S. Weaver, Mrs. Ruth White, Mrs. Virginia Wilson, Keith Wolf, Mr. and Mrs. Charles A. Wood, Mr. and Mrs. Robert W. Wood and Mr. and Mrs. B. Jesse Zook.

HISTORICAL MARKERS

An article in the Delphi Journal of April 16, 1936 reported that Ross F. Lockridge distributed 1,000 historical markers in Indiana. The markers were made of metal and measured 24x36 inches with up to 50 words on each marker. Eleven were made for Carroll County and the information on them was written by a committee including Ross E. Allen, Fannie R. Carney and William C. Smith. The wording on the markers is reported in the article in the Delphi Journal.

In addition to the eleven markers, five more were put up by clubs and individuals. None of the 16 markers remained in 1979.

The first Historical marker erected by the Carroll County Historical Society was placed at the North end of the Carrollton Bridge in 1971. The marker was damaged and the post destroyed early in 1977 and was moved to the foot of the Carrollton Hill on the Mrs. Vern Stoffer property.

CARROLLTON ON THE WABASH

90 lots platted in 1836 on both sides of Wabash-Erie Canal lock. A Post Office in 1838-39. The lock passed canal boats into the river on the pool of the Great Dam at Pittsburg five miles below. The mules carried the towline across the covered bridge to the towpath on the south bank and rehitched. The Mentzer Tavern stood here until 1915. Speece Bros. Warehouse and the Fort Dearborn Trail were ½ mile east.

The Flora sign in the Flora City Parking Lot was erected in 1972 as a part of the Flora Centennial program.

FLORA

The Garden Spot of Indiana. Flora's Station, on the Logansport, Crawfordsville and Southwestern Ry., was platted in 1872 for John Flora on land entered by him in 1829. Ino Post Office established 1872, changed to Flora in 1873. Also called Fountain City from flowing wells. Pikes Peak, ½ mile South and East had sawmill and shops until 1889. Near here was located a log cabin school, and in 1876 the first church, St. Paul's Lutheran, was built.

The Delphi sign was erected on the south side of the Courthouse in 1973 by the Delphi Lions Club and the Historical Society.

DELPHI

Named and platted in 1828 by Gen. Samuel Milroy, on 100 acres donated by Wm. Wilson for the seat of Carroll Co., named for Charles Carroll, last surviving signer of the Declaration of Independence. Henry Robinson was the first settler. Transportation provided by Wabash & Erie Canal in 1840, Wabash RR in 1856, Monon in 1882. City first chartered in 1866. Products now include furniture, lime, plumbing fixtures and truck bodies.

The Burlington sign was erected in Burlington at the junction of State Roads 29 and 22 in 1973.

BURLINGTON

Laid out in 1828 by David Stipp. Promoted for seat of a new county to be made partly from the Great Miami Reserve, which began two miles east. The Lafayette & Muncie Road crossed the Great Michigan Road here. It was an important stage stop, mill village and trading center for both whites and Indians from the Reservation. Among early families were Ewing, Foster, Gwinn, Harness, Landrum, Rinker, Shinn and Stockton. Incorporated as town in 1967.

A sign was erected at the entrance to The Anderson's General Store East of Delphi in 1975, giving a brief history of Gen. Samuel Milroy and the Milroy family.

GEN. SAMUEL MILROY 1780-1845

Born in Penn. From Ky. to Ind. 1815. Constitutional Convention 1816. After nine years in Legislature removed to Carroll County, which he was instrumental in organizing. Named and helped lay out Delphi, West of his cabin home near here. Major, Colonel & Gen. of Militia. Friend of Pres. Andrew Jackson. Pioneer politician and lawmaker. Supt. of Land Office-Indian Agent.

THE MILROY FAMILY

John McElroy, last Earl of Annandale, and a lineal descendant of Robert Bruce, fled after Cullodan, to Ireland, as John Milroy. Later in Pennsylvania, he and his eldest son were killed by Indians. His second son served in the Revolution and was the father of Samuel, who removed to Kentucky where he married Martha Huston. They moved to Washington Co. Indiana in 1815 and to Carroll County in 1826. Bruce was our 1st Sheriff. Margaret m. John Adams, the miller. Frances m. Dr. Beck, Elmira m. Dr. Samuel Grimes.

Maj. Gen. Robert Huston Milroy, 1816-1890. "The Gray Eagle" Mexican & Civil Wars. Indian Agent, Washington Terr. 1875-

The Pittsburgh sign was erected at the corner of Sam's Fish House parking lot in 1976.

PITTSBURG

Platted by Merkle, Kendall & Co. in 1838 for side cut canal traffic and cheap water power from the summit level dam. Pittsburg had grain warehouses, flouring mills, oil and saw mills, wool carding and fulling, foundry and machine shops, taverns, cooper, cabinet, chair, blacksmith and shoe shops. General stores were busy until the Wabash RR came to Delphi 1856. Blowing-up the dam 1881 ended it.

PITTSBURG

The side cut from the West end of the great canal dam admitted canal boats and the cheap water power was used to capacity. It bisected a row of Blocks between this street and the river. The mill and warehouse sites and the riverbank street and wharfs have all been washed out. "The Brick Store" was Garrett A. "Doc" Depew's. Other merchants were Bolles & Colton, Spears and Bros., Timothy Donovan, Davis and Mudge. Later— Vandervolgen and Smith. From 1847 until 1856 Pittsburg probably did more in business than Delphi, separated by a ferry and plank-road. There was a Post Office from 1838 until 1915. Many flat boats were built in this area. Steamboats sometimes unloaded here when the water was high enough. When the dam was dynamited in 1881 by farmers living upstream the canal and the water-power were destroyed.

The Jackson Township and Camden Sign was erected at the Camden Library in 1977.

JACKSON TOWNSHIP

John Odell entered the first land in 1825. The twp. was laid out in 1830, extending East and South to the county line. About 1827 Moses Aldridge, Elisha Brown, Adam Porter, John & Jeremiah Ballard settled on Bachelor's Run. Other settlers were Wm. Hance, 1828, Wm. Armstrong, John Lenon 1829, Philip Hewitt, Peter Replogle, Thos. Sterling, Saml. Wise, Peter Iman, John Musselman, Levi Cline, Jas. & Wm. Martin, Jacob Humrickhouse and David Zook. Lower Deer Creek Church of Brethren was organized in 1828 by Peter Replogle, Samuel Wise and Peter Iman, first minister. Other ministers were H. Vredenburg, Nebo Methodist; John P. Hay, Cumberland Presbyterian 1830.

CAMDEN

When the School Section, No. 16, was sold in 1832 Wm. Crooks, School Commissioner, reserved 16 acres and had a town site laid out by John Armstrong, Co. Surveyor. Col. Crooks (1787-1861) (War of 1812) kept the first cabin store about 40 yds. South. John E. Snoeberger was the first Post Master 1833. Dr. F. G. Armstrong (1822-1903) was pioneer physician and legislator. Jonathan Martin gave land for a church, cemetery and school, 1835. A. J. Thomas, E. C. Rice and Philip Ray were merchants and bankers; Royal Grosvenor and Geo. C. Sanderson area teachers. Musselman, McFarland, Robeson, McCain, Replogle, Porter area millers. The railroad came in 1872.

The Pyrmont and Hopkins Expedition sign was erected in the town of Pyrmont in 1978.

PYRMONT

John Wagner built a dam, race and saw mill about a mile South in 1833 and added a grist mill. He sold to John Fisher who sold to John Fetterhoff who built a large frame mill. Joel Wagoner, James Allen, Elias Morkert, J. J. Cripe, Wm. Gardner, Bert Smoker were later operators. It burned December 7, 1929. Fetterhoff's Mill Post Office established 1851, was changed to Pyrmont in 1866.

1812 HOPKINS' EXPEDITION

On November 22nd 60 mounted scouts were ambushed and 18 killed about a mile West. This skirmish was called Spurs Defeat. Benoit Bezallion was captured and died at the stake that night in large Indian camp about a mile South. The next day a larger force under Capt. Zachary Taylor burned the empty camp in the big bend of Wildcat Creek North of the church. The army returned to Vincennes.

INDEX OF NAMES

*Indicates Picture

A

ABEL, Dave 16
ABBOTT, Connie 141*
   Dirk 134
   Gayle 184
   Mark 134, 146
   Susan 140*
ACHOR, Patricia 287
ACKERMAN, Scott 132
ACKERSON, Harry E. 45, 73, 76, 77, 79, 93, 103, 300
ADAMS, Barbara 128, 131
   Bill 337
   Dean 48, 237, 316
   John 37, 317, 347
   Linda 128
   Max R. M.D. 22, 319
   Tom 337
   Warren 37, 317
ADCOCK, Robert 225
AIKEN, A. R. 237
   B. W. 237
   Guy 237
   Ray 67
AINSWORTH, Harry F. 112
AIRHART, LaVonne 116
AITKENHEAD, Professor 89
AKERS, A. L. 344
   Mrs. A. L. 344
AL-ABBAS, Selma Dawn 288
ALBAUGH, Chas. 237, 310
ALBERTS, Marcia 170*
ALDERFER, Monte 81, 93, 130, 133, 185, 188
   Mrs. Monte 130
ALDRICH, Edith viii
ALDRIDGE, Moses 348
ALEXANDER, George Bryan 288
   William Hoyt 288
ALLBAUGH, Florence 241, 243, 244
   Ina 258
   Mrs. Jim 105
   John 188, 258, 312, 313, 314, 315*
   Walter 314
   Willard 117, 177, 237
   Mrs. Willard 198
ALLEN, Mrs. Bryan 198
   Dorval A. 274
   Harold A. 67, 69, 70*
   Mrs. Harold A. (Dorothy) 67, 69, 70*, 104
   Mrs. J. H. 331, 344
   James 348
   John F. 67, 237
   LaDonna 27, 337
   Lawrence 274
   Lenore McCarty viii, 82, 193*, 194, 195
   Mildred 95
   Pearl E. 46, 67
   Rev. 174
   Ross E. 346
   Shirley 308
   Tom 146
   Walter 335
ALLREAD, Harold 236, 302
   Mary 198
   Ron 302
ALTER, Lance 340
   Neil 346
ALTMAN, Dan 122
ALVAREZ, Abe 24
AMAYA, Dr. Carlos 319
AMICK, C. T. 67, 298
AMSTUTZ, Leroy 144
ANDERSON, Dr. A. A. 124
   Mrs. Alfred 84
   Bernice 340
   Bill 87, 287, 301*
   Charles L. 192, 332
   Mrs. Charles A. (Helen) 103, 183
   Daniel 50*
   Fred 329, 330
   Helen Robinson 109, 110
   John "Bud" 340
   Lloyd 187
   Norman 134, 146
   S. A. 265
   Dr. Samuel 339
   Stanley 187
   Wm. 184
   W. T. 302
ANGLE, Beverly 109
   Eddie 292
   Harry 323, 324
   Mrs. John 107
   Wayne 323
   Mrs. Will 108
ANLIKER, Margaret 100
APPENZELLER, George 339
   M. 339
APPLEGATE, Jonathan C. 26
APPLETON, Bill 232
   Mrs. Bill 232
   Caron Patricia 288
   Charles 47
   David Dean 184
   Mrs. Dean 95
   Dee Recher 308*
   Forrest 57
   Gene 129
   Hanna viii, 57, 58
   Perrietta 104
   Ronald Dean 288
ARBORSAL, Jimmy 170*
ARCHER, Cathy 134
   Phil 131, 136
ARCHIBALD, Gaylord 177, 178, 246, 253, 255*
   Jennifer 337
   Mrs. Wayne 198
ARIHOOD, Fred 16
ARION, Harold 228*
ARKANSAS WOODCHOPPER 326
ARMICK, F. G. 57
ARMSTRONG, Mrs. Almer 177*
   Charles E. 213, 237, 298
   Ellis 47
   Dr. F. G. 348
   Frank 237
   Grace 57
   John 348
   Lanty E. 237
   T. W. 76
   Tom 146
   Mrs. Tom 106
   Wm. 348
ARNOLD, Clarence 327
   Harry 341, 344
   Mrs. Harry 344
ARNOTT, Arthur E. 151*, 188
ARTHUR, David C. 287
ASHBA, Paul 144
   William 45, 47
ASHBY, Ivan 143
   James C. 267, 268
   John W. 164*
   Mrs. Steven 101
ATKINSON, Albert 165
   Walter 295
AUSTIN, Imogene 95
   Mary 273
   Mrs. 75
   Robert 143
   Rosemary 340
AVERY, Albert 244
   Charles 321
   Mrs. Jim 102
   Verne D. 196, 237
AYLER, Kay Ellen 82, 93, 107, 302
AYRES, Alan 319
   Carrie 184
   Clayton 15
   Dick 335
   F. C. 75, 237
   John 319
   Joni 123
   Kari 132

Loren viii, 113
Maude 24
Meredith viii, 119, 127, 128, 130, 131, 137*, 138*, 147, 148, 185, 196, 197, 199, 236
Mrs. Meredith (Sharon) 185
Richard 120
Rick 127, 131, 138, 147, 185, 199, 233
Mrs. Rick (Vickie) 105, 185
Robert E. 91, 133, 234*, 235, 236, 241, 313
Russell 227
Ruth 317, 329, 346
Tom 335
Mrs. Tom (Beverly) 335
Walter V. 163, 197, 308, 323

B

BAILEY, Allen 26
  Colleen 126*
  Delmar 329
  Gilbert 26
  Janet 130
  Wendy 140*
BAKER, C. E. 47, 57
  Carl 187
  Carol 122
  Dan 222
  Mrs. Dan (Laura) viii
  F. A. 27
  Florence 24
  Mrs. Harold 24
  Robert 319
BAKES, Kathy 318
BALDWIN, Cliff 16
BALKEMA, Jos. 237
BALL, James D. 60
BALLARD, Jeremiah 348
  John 348
  Mrs. M. E. 344
BALSER, Blanche 45, 329, 341, 346
  Burr, 174, 177
  Dean 174, 176, 177
  Dick 144
  Frank 174
BARBER, Edith 102
  Ockle 237
BARBOUR, R. T. 67
  Mrs. R. T. 67
BARD, J. B. 67
  Mrs. J. B. 67
  James 67
  Mary 67
  Taylor 67
BARLEY, Charles 259
BARNARD, Beth 333*
  Charles E. 75
  Chris 287
  Dave 302
  Douglas 184
  E. E. 43
  Mrs. 75
  Mrs. Joe Jr. 198
  Leroy 339

Mike 147
Peggy Lou 180, 182
Walter 117
BARNER, Elias 50*
BARNES, Barbara 128
  Harold 274
  John A. 37
  Lena Ireland 109
  Thomas 75
  Mrs. Thomas 75
BARNETT, James 153
  Jacquoline R. N. 22
BARNHART, Everett 327
  Frances 243
  Frank 87, 176, 237, 297
  M. A. 237
  Rebecca 287
  Robert 296*, 320, 321
  Ruth 100, 321, 346
  Walter H. 86*, 121, 196, 235, 313, 314
  Mrs. Walter H. 198
BATES, J. Ren 41, 197, 237
BAUGH, John 183
  William H. 341, 346
BAUM, Daniel Sr. 35
  David 17, 329
  Fred 300
  George W. 19
  Harry 24, 39*, 76
  Hilda viii
  Martin 56
  Ralph 143
  Theodore W. 162*
  Mrs. Theodore W. 329
BAUMAN, Irvin 321
BEADLE, Parke 26
  Mrs. Parke 26
BEALE, Charles 89, 120, 170*
  David 170*
  John 124*, 170*
  Kathy 287
  Sheryl 170*
  Susie 170*
BEAMER, Otis 113
BEARD, Clayton 143
  Dwight 241 243
  Mrs. Dwight 138
  Jesse 237
  John 237, 297
  Julie 258
  Lloyd D. 44, 165, 175, 176, 184, 190, 191, 219, 231*, 234, 235, 237, 305, 306, 323
  Mrs. Lloyd D. (Ruth) 86, 95, 98, 167, 168, 174, 195, 198, 231*, 243
  Ruth 243
  Mrs. Ward 44
BEBEE, Debra Jean 288
BECK, D. F. 48
  Dr. 347
  Laurel 177*, 297
  Nan 128, 250, 258
  Norman 337
  William 339
BECKNER, Beryl 166*, 196, 197
  Mrs. Beryl 198

Dean 170*
Mark 170*
Nathan 140*
Roger 170*
Tony 319
Wayne 170*
BECKOM, Harold 336
BEECHER, Connie 287
BEECHY, Lincoln 14
BEEN, Ben 321, 346
  Mrs. Ben (Frieda) 329, 346
  Mrs. Herbert (Mildred) 83, 107
  Jason 117, 344
  Mrs. Jason 329
  Jeff 184
  Mrs. Ward 198
BEERY, Ron 147
BEESLEY, Myron viii, 98, 124, 141*, 224*, 235, 329, 330
  Mrs. Myron (Lois) 98, 124
BEESON, Prof. K. E. 74
BELL, A. R. 26
  Alexander Graham 52
  Betty 104, 244
  Edith 102
  Raymond 306
  Robert 241
  Sandra 180, 250
  William 47
BENJAMIN, Mary 103, 110
BENNER, Ethel viii, 308*
  Fred 58
  Mrs. Fred 198
  Grace 95
  Gwen 308
  Herman 295
  Jessee 75, 237
  Mrs. Jessee 198
  Joan 129, 308
  John 58, 114
BENNETT, Dr. H. H. 310
BENTUM, Bench 46
BERKEY, Velma 115
BERKSHIRE, Bertis 146
  Enos viii, 29, 197, 227*, 231*, 232, 236, 283*, 297, 309, 310, 311*, 315, 316, 317
  Mrs. Enos 231*
  Jerry 192
  John 176*, 197, 222
  Kenneth 292
  Orville 227*, 292
  Sandra Rae 287
BERNFIELD, Mrs. Arylis 198
  Bonnie 287
  Harry 316, 317
BERNINGER, Beverly 245
BERRY, Dean 140*
  Harold R. viii, 80*, 87, 89, 93, 120, 129, 130, 249*, 250, 325, 328
  Mrs. Harold R. 129, 130
BERTO, Tony viii
BERTSCH, Maynard 326
BEST, Coy 76
  Mrs. Coy 76
  Elizabeth 42, 329, 330, 346
  George H. C. 344

Jennifer 329*
Roy 75
BEZALLION, Benoit 348
BICKETT, Mrs. David (Mary) 107
BIDDLE, Chester 88*
　Eleanor 100
BIEDERWOLF, Nancy 105
BIEGHLER, Donna 194
　Irene 340
BIERY, Gordon 147
BILLIARD, B. O. 316
　Beth 174
　Burton 91, 120
　Jim 120
　Myrna 128
BILLINGS, Charles 67
　Donald 128, 130
　John T. 176, 235
　Tom 128
BINGAMAN, Frank 14
　Kathleen 114
BISHOP, A. D. 319
　Dick 185
　Mrs. Dick N. (Jane) 24
　Dick T. 319, 346
BITLER, Beverly 331
　Clifford 68, 69
　Pearl Robinson 68, 109, 110
　Wilbur viii, 89
BIXLER, Irene 346
BLACK, Charles G. 175*, 176, 297
　Charles T. viii, 83*, 87*, 113, 118, 120, 145*, 196, 203, 234, 235, 241 243, 256, 257*, 258 323
　Mrs. Charles T. (Elizabeth) viii, 169, 170*, 171*, 256, 257
　Charmion 170*
　Jack 136*
　Kay 257*
　Kim viii, 130, 146, 250*, 258
　Mrs. Kim (Annette) 273
　Olive 116
　Vera 116
BLACKWELL, Janice 197
　Richard 192
　W. E. 237
BLAKE, Odetta 244
BLANCHARD, Josephine 346
　Louise S. 109
　Red 283
BLICKENSTAFF, Isabell 244
　Mrs. Levi 101
BLOCHER, Esther 308
　Marsha 82
BLOHM, Mrs. Herbert 343
BLOYD, Jack 137
BLUE, Fannie viii, 185, 186*, 195, 196, 198, 330, 346
　Fred D. 131*
　Jerry L. 83, 297*
　Mary Lou 22
　Roy K. 162, 177*
　Mrs. Roy K. 162
　U. M. 47
　Van C. 13, 47, 49, 55
BLYTHE, Mrs. Ed. (Minnie) 45, 95, 101, 109

James C. 259
Lillian 344
William L. 274*
BOHANNON, Harry 109, 292
　Kenneth 176
BOHM, Larry 288
BOL, Arni 148
　Mrs. Arni (Jan) 148
BOLINGER, Mrs. Earl 103
　Eva 228
BOLLER, Mel 122
BOLLES, Henry 339
BONDIE, Antoine 2, 3
　Monique 2
BONEBRAKE Clyde 51
BONNELL, Lou 344
BOONE, Blanche 114
　Jerry 318, 330, 332
　Kenneth W. 274*
　Larry 117
BOOTH, Glenn 196
　Joan 279
BOOZE, George 31
BORDEN, Lee 291*
BORDNER, Becky 250*
　Bill 163, 164*
　Bob 123*
　Carol 83, 296, 297*
　Charles 232, 309*
　Mrs. Charles 232
　John Seremis 72
　Robert 316
　Mrs. William H. (Ruth) viii, 99*, 100, 103, 346
BOSWORTH, Cliff 336
　Mrs. Cliff (Rosie) 169, 172*, 173*, 198
BOTTOM, J. C. viii, 86
BOUSUM, Joe 340
　Mrs. Joe 340
BOWEN, Abner 321
　E. W. 41, 53, 59, 174, 237
　Mrs. E. W. 344
　Mrs. Harold (Alberta) 104
　Hilda viii, 114, 174, 329, 344, 346
　Mrs. N. W. 344
　Nancy 331
　Gov. Otis 89
　Walter E. 75, 197, 237, 316
BOWERMAN, Harve 41, 54
BOWLEY, Ancil 185, 187, 340
BOWMAN, Alyne 82
　Brenda Lee 288
　Dave 147
　Donald 87, 88, 143
　Earl 219
　Evelyn 178
　Everett 241
　Hubert 147
　Jack 143
　Jean 131*
　Joaquin 181
　John 341
　John 143, 274*
　John L. 301
　Leo viii, 235
　Mrs. Leo (Mary Margaret) viii

Mara 132
Margaret viii, 109, 218*, 273
Milton D. 188, 197, 314, 316
Mrs. Milton D. (Gertrude) 198
Rosemary 75
Roy 85, 237
Mrs. Roy (Ruth Draper) 96*, 99*, 198, 329, 346
Mrs. Veaux 198
W. H. & Son 86
BOYD, Mrs. L. D. 344
BOYLES, Stanley 146
BOYS, Vera 245
BRACKENRIDGE, Catharine 45, 329
　Reed C. 274*
BRADEN, Esther 102, 340
BRADSHAW, Arthur 329
　C. F. 331
　Robert G. viii, 187, 318, 329, 333, 334, 341, 342*, 343, 344, 346
　Mrs. Robert G. (Mary) viii
　W. H. 51
　Mrs. W. H. 329
　William H. viii
　Wm. 18, 53
BRADY, Alonzo 223
　Wilbur 223
BRANBLETT, Mr. 56
BRANDON, Larry 118, 174
BRANIGAN, Governor 334
BRAY, Lottie 340
BRECHBEIL, Leah 98, 298
BREEZE, George 56
BREHMER, Marvin 332
BREINER, Janice viii
BREINING, Mrs. W. A. 341, 344
BREWER, A. H. 330
　C. R. 318
　Dale 144
　Dick 144
　George 145, 298
　Harry S. 45, 344
　Mrs. Lewis 346
　Pattie 181
BREWSTER, Carol 100
　Ed 340
BRICKEY, Dan 105
BRIDGE, Chauncey 291*, 292
BRIGGS, C. I. 323
　Mrs. Clay (Marion) viii
　Connie 128
　Mrs. Dean (Betty) 55
　Marvin J. 201, 202, 213, 214, 281
　Reba J. S. 81, 93, 104, 106
　Mrs. Ross 104
　William 314
　Mrs. William (Anne) 107, 109
BRIGHT, Jesse V. 47, 318
　R. R. 55
BRITTON, Kenneth 274
　Sabrina Kay 288
BROADHURST, Jim 38
BROADLICK, Frank 344
BROOKBANK, Agnes Arnott 109
　Mrs. Lynn (Margaret Lybrook)

109, 199, 346
Robert viii, 62, 318, 329, 337, 342°
Mrs. Robert (Virginia) viii, 337
BROOKS, James 9
Tom 192
Mrs. Tom 198
BROSMAN, Don 16
BROTHERS, Jesse 187
BROWER, Daniel 126
Daryl 330
David 134
J. W. 24
Lisa 134
Ross D. viii
Mrs. Ross D. (Carolyn) viii
BROWN, Amy 134
Bob 146
Connie J. 273°
Daniel M. 346
Mrs. Daniel M. (Lucille) viii, 98, 99
Drindy 288
Earl E. 298
Ed 144
Elisha 348
Evelyn 273
Everett 197
Mrs. Everett 198
Fern 114
George V. 47
Glenn 247°, 248°, 257, 258
Mrs. Glenn (Sue) 248°
Jacob 339
John 14, 139°
John D. 297
John G. 151, 152
John O. 237
Josephine M. viii, 329, 346
Lynn Allan 128, 274°
Mary Alice 257°
Mrs. Melvin (Donnabelle) viii, 57, 137°, 138
Olaf K. 237
P. T. 85
Richard 144
Robert 144
Robert L. 138
Rosetta 198
Ted L. viii, 81, 89, 93, 120, 130, 185, 306
Mrs. Ted L. 130
Virgil 322
Will E. 44
William 59, 113
BROWNE, Blossom 331
BROWNING, Mary 329
BRUBAKER, Alan 340
Almeda 273
Amos 47
Blaine 232
Mrs. Blaine 232
Donald 16
Eddie 292
Jim 16
Louis viii, 15, 16, 318
Roy A. 38
Steve 16

BRUCE, Grace 232
Robert 347
BRUMMETT, Christopher A. 67, 69, 308
Leonard 144, 316
Pearl 67
Russell 274
Steve 149
Mrs. Steve (Terri) 149
BRUNER, Carmen 131, 136
BRYAN, Charles 324
Darwin 243
BRYANT, Benjamin 339
Maxine 274
Roscoe 316
Mrs. Vena 56
BUCK, Carl J. 237
Donald 143
Mrs. Milton (Mabel) viii, 61
BUCKLEY, Charles S. 43, 329, 344
Mrs. Charles S. (Jennie) 44, 329, 330, 334, 341, 343, 344
BUDD, Charles 322
BUDROW, C. E. 319
BUPP, Mrs. Harvey 152
BURGE, Pam 131
BURGITT, Frieda 82, 83°, 84, 95, 96°, 108
Lloyd 83°
BURKE, Cecilia 134
Chris 130
Mrs. Herbert 198
John 87, 197, 236, 291°
Robert E. 197, 307
Teresa 184, 287
Tim 131, 134, 138, 161, 302
BURKEBILE, Del 54
BURKHALTER, Jack 330
Mrs. Jack (Augusta) 108
Mary Ruth 170°
BURKHART, Edwin 225
BURKHOLDER, A. L. 44, 45
BURKLE, Albert viii, 91, 265
Mrs. Albert (Margaret viii, 108°, 346
Chris 126
Elwood viii, 186, 188, 227°
Mrs. Elwood (Betty) viii, 95, 98, 172°, 198
Ivan 172°, 233
John viii, 119, 235, 330
Mrs. John (Carolyn) viii, 100, 103, 123, 173°, 180, 196, 198, 199
Phillip D. 132, 184
Susan 134
BURLESON, A. S. 51
BURLINGTON, Chief 330
BURNETT, Abraham 3
BURNS Frank 26
Lena 108, 109
Marie 319
Mrs. Paul 104
BURNWORTH, Mrs. Dale (Meg) 137°, 138
Lisa 134, 141°
BURR, John H. 259

Mrs. John H. 23
BURT, Mabel 69, 70°, 110, 183
Roy 56
BURTON Alfred viii, 313
Mrs. Alfred viii
Brad 131, 132, 137°, 138, 185
Mrs. Brad (Gail) 185
Brian 134
Charles L. viii, 21, 22, 187, 319
Dean 146
Don 144
Geoffrey 251
Robert W. 274°
BUSCHE, L. M. 138
BUSCHMAN, Carl 316, 317
BUSH, Gov. Edgar D. 115
Helen J. 288
Jay 123, 131
John A. D. V. M. 22, 119°, 147
Mrs. John A. (Virginia) 83
BUSHMAN, Neda 318
BUSSELL, Harold 143
BUTCHER, Mrs. Meredith (Naomi) 24
BUTLER, Donald 332
Joseph Dewayne 288
Marilyn 169°
Morris 342
Richard D. 288
BUTZ, Dean Earl L. 87, 88, 303°
BYERS, Linda 134
BYRUM, Perry M. 57, 59, 300

C

CABLE, Russell "Russ" 16, 192
CAIN, Isaac 58
Lura 108°
Mary 70
Roger 145
CALDWELL, Albert 75
Bobby 247°, 248°, 249°, 250°, 253, 256, 258, 327
Danny 176°
Helen 241
Inah 106
Joyce 131°
Karla 288
Oral A. 197, 262, 265, 266, 267°, 295, 296, 297, 308
Patricia Kay 288
Roy 45, 47, 75, 79, 323
Wayne 176°
Wm. R. 298
CALHOUN, Bill 321
Irvin 15
CALLAHAN, Estel 185
Ora 232
CALLANE, Russell D. 22
Dr. W. E. 54, 55, 318
CALLOWAY, Glen 292
CALTON, C. H. 297
Charles 172°
Mrs. Charles 172°
CALVERT, Don 138
Glenn 144

INDEX OF NAMES • 353

L. A. 50*
Raymond 113
CAMPBELL, Charles 296, 315
　Elaine 184, 287
　Em 314
　Freida 199
　Lloyd 296
　Lulu 67
　Manson 22, 275
　Dr. O. F. 47, 319
　Obe 67, 118, 175*, 176, 195,
　　197, 215 217, 235, 236,
　　269, 296, 308
　Opal 108*
　Mrs. Orvel 99*
　Orville 283*, 296*
　Phillip 131*, 256*
　Richard 20
　Scott 336
　W. M. 237
CANADA, T. L. 61
CANTER, W. G. 51
CAPPER, Bradley 144
"CAPTAIN STUBBY" Tom Fouts
　180, 234*, 283, 326, 335
CARBAUGH, Barbara 288
CAREY, Joe 175
　S. E. 48
CARLEY, Judy viii
CARLSON, Elmer 321
CARMAN, Renita Draper 123
CARMICHAEL, Nancy 132
CARMODY, John M. 269
CARNEGIE, Andrew 23
CARNELL, Bennie 53
CARNEY, Fanny R. 346
　James 37
　John, MD 344
　Mrs. John 329, 344
CARPENTER, Ed 174
CARR, Clark 144
　Eddie 145
　Olive 129
CARRIGAN, Leland 46, 116
CARROLL, Charles 35, 347
CARTER, Cleon viii, 180, 197, 329,
　　330, 337, 341, 346
　Mrs. Cleon (Leona) viii, 172*,
　　180, 198 337, 342*, 346
　D. H. 55
　Dr. 26
　Edna 346
　Herb 225
　Mrs. Jack (Eleanor) 24
　Mrs. Mark (Mary Catherine)
　　99, 106
　Martha 128
　Meredith 129, 136*
　Myra 128
CARTWRIGHT, J. A. 26
　John 49
　Mary Angel 114
CASAD, Lucille 198
　Walter H. 47
　Mrs. W. H. 198
CASE, Mrs. Fred 198
　Reed 59
CASS, General Lewis 11, 334

CASSELL, Sandra 179*, 253, 255*
CASTLE, Irene 14
　Vernon 14
CATON, Lymon 244
CATRON, D. 323
　Marda Gene 340
CAUGHELL, L. 237
CECIL, Mrs. Clarence 75
CEDARQUIST, Edna 108
CHAD, Glenn 117
CHANDLER, Fred 185
CHANEY, Catherine DuVall 135*
CHAPMAN, Darrell 169*
　David B. 197, 323, 330, 331
　Mrs. David B. 331
　Donald 277
　Earl 197, 236, 237
　Edwin 169*
　Eugene 227*
　Eva 116, 241
　Everett 116, 241
　Floyd 197, 231
　Mrs. Floyd 169*, 231
　Harold 227
　Lee 221
　Leonard 298
　Leslie W. 241
　Mary Jane 336
　Michael L. 274*
　Nancy 128
　Mrs. Voris 198
CHENOWETH, Ida 151, 167
CHEZEM, Carl 341, 346
CHILDERS, Mrs. Charles
　　(Margaret) 96*, 302
　Ellen 130
　John W. 43
　Teresa 128
CHISSOM, Jean 114
　Port 237
CHITTICK, Dr. Charles 339
　Loren 44
CHITTY, Ralph 72
CHRISTIE, Prof. George I. 71, 73,
　　79, 111, 163
CICOTT, Baptiste 3
　Emelie 3
　Sophia 3
　Zachariah 3
CLARK, Connie 138
　Delmar 176
　J. W. 319
　Marie 335
CLAUER, Marjorie Shonk viii
CLAUSER Mrs. Guy 98
　Mary Sims 329
　Samuel 57
　Wm. S. 237
CLAWSON, Courtney R. 67, 69,
　　175*, 176, 197, 231*,
　　232, 236, 237
　Mrs. Courtney R. (Maude) 67
　Dan 329, 330
　Eileen 246
　Flossie Hornbeck 109, 110
　Fred 222, 223, 237, 241, 244,
　　323
　Mrs. Fred 198

G. L. 68
Gearold 113
Glae 237
Grace 329
Harry 237
James 181
Kathleen 246
Leonard 175
Mrs. Leonard 198
Lucille 244
Mahlon viii
Mrs. Mahlon viii
Mary Smock 329
Maxine 246
Mike 16
O. E. 237
Robert L. viii, 84, 116, 185,
　186*, 188, 272*, 274*,
　281*, 284, 294, 297
Russell 166*, 175, 223
Teresa 251, 253, 258
Wayne 197
CLEAR, Chris 27
CLEAVER, Clarence L. viii, 162,
　166*, 172*, 173*, 195,
　196, 199, 236, 237, 262,
　283*, 292, 295*, 296*
　Mrs. Clarence L. (Lola) viii,
　　171*, 172*, 198, 329
　Clifford E. 85, 176
　Dale 232, 251, 313, 332
　Mrs. Dale (Kathleen) 198
　Gary 148, 232, 234*, 235, 302,
　　309*, 315*
　Mrs. Gary (Sue) 148, 232
　Helen 247*, 248*
　Howard 197, 298
　S. S. 47
CLEM, Carl 196
　David 148
　Mrs. Earl 198, 346
　Fred 316
　Mrs. Fred 81*
　Mrs. John 297
　Morris 126*, 346
　Mrs. Morris 346
　Quentin 144
　Stanley 130
　Wm. 68
CLEMENTS, Audria 24, 318
CLEVELAND, Grover 26
CLEVENGER, Denise Renee 134,
　　184, 288
CLICK, Mrs. Tom 106
CLIFFORD, Kathleen 273
　Maurice 329
CLINE, Levi 348
　Raymond 120
CLINGENPEEL, Amos 319
　Don 337
　Gerald 335, 336*, 337
CLORE, Leonard B. 72, 200
CLYMER, Mr. 25
CLYNE Brothers 14
COBLE, Dr. Albert H. 52, 53, 54
　Darlene Allen 122
　Dick 143
　Etta Gibson 109

Hazel 98, 198
Mrs. John D. 105
L. R. 237
Raymond 174
Robert 313
Roy E. 237
Mrs. Roy E. 329
COCHRAN, Mrs. Austin (Effie) 151, 168, 240
Everett 318, 319
COCHRANE, Mary 24
COCKRANE, Charles 55
Mrs. Charles 55
CODDINGTON, Janice Elaine 288
COFFEY, Annabelle 108
Wm. 332
COGHILL. Orliff 85
COHEE, A. B. 55, 227
Mrs. Asa (Laurene) 54, 198
George 163, 197
Jack 16
John 274, 281*
Mary 263
Rolland 227
COLE, Mable 346
R. O. 309
Wm. 322
COLEMAN, Prof. Thomas A. 72, 73, 113, 151, 174
COLLINS, Fred A. 54
Fred Jr. 54
Mrs. Fred Jr. (Connie) 109, 335
George W. viii, 20
Mrs. George W. viii
Louann Milner 122
Marlene 54, 193*, 194
Omer 175, 181*
COLVIN, Mrs. Edward 104
COMBS, Elizabeth 82, 93
Mrs. W. B. 152
CONGRAM, Lois 181
CONLEY, L. M. 117
CONNAWAY, Janet 126, 132, 136
JoAnne 132, 184
CONNELLY, Claude 214
Don 192
CONNER, Henry 3
James 3
William 3
COOK, A. A. 56
Dr. A. J. 49, 54, 73, 74, 300
C. C. 237
Clyde 84, 301*
Harold 222
Mrs. Harold (Phyllis) 100, 104
Joe 313
L. N. 75
Mrs. Ray 55
Tamara Jo 184
Terri 184
Toni 343*
COOKE, Clyde 196
Kenneth 146, 185
Morris L. 264
COOLEY, Oscar 29
COOMEY, Hope 318
COOPER, Edith 110

COPLEN, Guy 75, 325
Mrs. Guy 106, 325
J. H. 54, 55
COPPOCK, Mrs. Bill 106, 176
CORBETT, Dora 344
CORN, Amm 177
CORNELISON, Roy 175*, 176, 196, 222
CORNELL, Allen 237
Effie 56
Flora 110
CORNS, Lenora 345
CORY, Barbara 99
Kathy 128
COTTRELL, Mrs. Ron 102
COUK, Susan 306
COUSIN SUSIE 30
COWDEN, T. K. 61
Julia Gros 329, 345
Mrs. W. L. 329
COWELL, Thomas 197
Mrs. Tom 106
COX, Mrs. Carrie 45, 329, 345
Edwin 127, 128, 134
Florence 345
Harold 323
Howard 313, 324
Inga 125*
John 302, 340
Mary Ratcliff 95
Newell 196, 237
Mrs. Newell (Flossie) 98, 198
COY, Wayne 26
Mrs. Wayne 26
CRABB, J. A. 123*
CRAFT, Donald 223*, 336
Donelle 139*
Harold 128, 130, 131, 146
Lowell 121*
CRAIG, Caryn 128
Dale 144, 302
Mrs. Dale (Della) viii, 67, 108
Eli 67, 237
Jesse C. 237
Leo C. viii, 25, 26, 84, 114, 120, 166, 185, 300, 301, 302, 333, 334, 336
Mrs. Leo C. (Mabel) viii, 26, 346
Mildred 114
Rev. Milton 15
Phyllis Jean 181
Russell 29, 68, 69, 165, 195, 197, 235, 236, 237, 300
CRAIN, Barbara 170*
Marilyn 130, 170*
Ronnie 170*
CRAMPTON, Adelbert B. 26
Dr. C. C. 22*
Mrs. C. C. 22*
CRANE, Martha 326
Richard 130
CRAWFORD, Clara 306*
CRAWN, Mrs. Cloid (Ruth) 105
Doris 105
Ruthie 105
Samuel G. 287
CREE, Albert 197, 237

Asa 235, 297
Kenny 336
Lee 250*, 253, 256
Nellie 103
Richard 120
CRICHFIELD, John C. 284
CRIPE, Claude 237
D. Elmer 319, 324
Daniel 237
Dean 128, 132, 138
Flora 25
Gordon 147
Prof. Isaac W. 25
J. J. 348
Mrs. James 107
Jo Ann 128, 130
Mrs. Kenneth 99*, 100*
Kevin 146
Lloyd 144, 323, 324
Loyal 75, 143, 309*, 346
Mrs. Loyal 346
O. D. 237
Robert 143
CRIST, W. A. 301
CRISWELL, Glen 332
Vicki 105
CROMER, Mrs. Dan 24
James R. 54
CROMWELL, John 339
CRONK, Nick 123
CROOK, Charles 197, 236, 237
David 284
Wayne 319
CROOKS, Col. 348
Paul viii
Wm. 348
CROSBY, Byram viii
Mrs. Byram (Irma) viii, 24
CROSS, Richard B. viii
CROSSWHITE, Rev. A. G. 54, 55
CROW, Patricia Maggart viii
CROWDER, A. P. 327
Dale 254*
CROWEL, Brice 309*
Elliott 163, 164*, 237
Evelyn 182
Julie 123
Lee R. viii, 273*, 274
Lewis G. 237
Lucile viii
Phyllis 308
Ruth 308
CROWELL, Emery 114
Evelyn 101
Gale 196, 231*, 232, 235
Mrs. Gale (Pearl) 175, 178, 191, 197, 231*, 279
John 56, 188, 302
Mabel Jakes 67, 68
Wilbur 165, 176, 196, 237, 297
CRUM, Brad 147
Ruel 147
CRUME, Dick 340
Gary 127, 128, 130
Justine 105
Mary 181
Robert 119*, 120, 126, 128*, 129, 134, 302

CRUMPACKER, Laverne 302
CRUNDWELL, Mrs. Paul 317
CRUSSEL, Howard viii
CRUTCHEN, Michael 288
CRUTCHFIELD, Dave 120
CULLER, William 50, 51
CULLUM, Emma 219
CUMMINS, Richard 158
CUNNINGHAM, Bruce 146
CUNNINGHAM, Mrs. Charles 95, 98
CURTISS, Glen 14
CURTS, Richard 123, 337
CUSHMAN, Mrs. Russell (Ethel) 152, 168, 170

D

DALE, Alfred 331
DAME, E. H. 115
    Mrs. E. H. 345
DANIELS, Jerry 179*, 253, 255*
    Jesse 237
    Josephine 58
DANT, Caroline Sue 128
DARLING, Clifford 197
    Mrs. Clifford 198
DARRAGH, Clarence 268, 272*, 274, 277, 279, 297
    Mrs. Clarence (Ruth) viii
DASHER, Susie 345
DAUBY, Bernard viii, 159
DAUGHERTY, Max 137
    Roger 346
    Mrs. Roger 346
DAVIDSON, Geneva 345
    Joseph H. 47
    R. Clark 47, 76, 345
DAVIES, Mr. 148
    Hugh 117
    Larry 148, 232
    Mrs. Larry (Connie) 148, 232
DAVIS, C. A. 323
    Clarence 56, 322
    Edna 67
    Ennis 340
    Jacqueline R. N. 22
    John 47
    Kathy Graf 122
    Thurman 237
    W. E. 237
    Wm. Glenn 56, 57, 67, 69
DAWSON, Mrs. Melvin (Betty June) 92, 346
    Miss 24
DAY, Rev. E. P. 331
    Kelly 227
    Mrs. Rex 99*
DAYE, Laddie 16
DEARDORFF, Lewis viii, 165, 180
DeBAILLIE, Mrs. Charles 327
    Crystal 327
DEBOY, Gary 123*, 148
DEEL, Mabel 99, 100
    Mrs. Robert (Grace) viii, 98, 109
DEETER, Mrs. Melvin 45

DEITZ, Kathryn 256*
    Norma 182, 246
DeLaCROIX, Frank 301*
    John viii, 121, 221*, 223*, 231*, 232, 235
    Mrs. John (Jane) 231*
DELANEY, Elsie 21
    Owen W. 54
    Mrs. Owen (Thelma) 54
DELAPLANE, Kenneth 225, 327
DELLINGER, Cindy 288
    L. D. 237
DELZEL, Frank E. 47
DEMPSEY, John E. viii, 67, 69
DENHART, Richard L. viii, 83, 173*, 229*, 232, 235
DENK, Roberta viii
DENMAN, F. M. 46
DENNEY, Vance L. 153
DENNY, Chris 27
DEPEW, Garrett A. "Doc" 347
DERRICK, M. K. "Si" 75, 244
DETWILER, Wayne 87
DeVINNEY, Mrs. Raymond 14
DEWEY, Aaron 36
DeWINTON, Irene viii, 103, 198, 241, 243, 257, 341, 342*
DIAL, Thomas 24
    Mrs. Thomas (Meredith Carney) 24
DICE, F. M. 49
DICK, Mrs. Harold 331
DICKINSON, Belinda 287
    Edith 98
    J. B. 50*
    James 121, 122*
    Irene 67
    Lester D. 41, 67, 162, 175*, 176, 237, 310, 346
    Mrs. Lester D. 162, 346
    Ronald 127, 128, 130
    William 86*, 87, 296, 297, 302, 316, 321
DIESLIN, Dr. Howard G. viii, 73
DIETRICK, Kenneth 247*, 248*, 252
DILL, Donald L. 196
    Mrs. Donald L. 198
DILLING, Clarence 85
    Fay 58
    Harve 48
DILLMAN, Barbara 331
    Bob 119*
    Carolyn A. 273*, 274
    Charles 146, 196, 232, 235, 247*, 248*, 249*, 250*, 252, 253, 256*, 258, 292, 323
    Glen 24, 342
    Joan 258
    Laura 106
    Raymond L. 67, 68, 166*, 177*, 188, 196, 197, 238
    Mrs. Raymond L. (Ester) 67, 108, 198, 282
    Richard 274
DILLON, Charles E. viii, 67
    Goodwin 325

    James 114
    Lee 324
    M. W. 38
    Robert 114
DIMITT, Steve 125
DIMMITT, Francis 197
    Harold 292
    Raymond 292
DIN, John A. 50*
DINGER, Wanda 340
DISINGER, Earl 179*
    John 116
    Reva M. 346
DITTMAN, Mrs. Bill 96*, 107
    Carl 90, 91
    Jennifer 163
    Mary 106
    Robert 199, 291*, 297*
DIXON, J. E. 58
    Jean 335
DOANE, Dr. 339
DOBBINS, Walter 165
DOBLER, Helen 104
DOCTOR, Charles 163, 164*, 195
    Mrs. Charles 45, 95
DODGE, Mary Alice 23
DONOVAN, Timothy 347
DOOLEY, Eva 345
    Reuben 187
DOOLITTLE, Cecil 67
    Wilber 67, 184, 238
DOTY, Sell S. 76
DOUGLAS, Anita 129
    Earl 237
    Lawrence 84, 138, 301*, 302
    Maurice 189
    Max 129*, 146
    Raymond 198
    William M. 175*, 176, 196, 237
    Mrs. Wm. M. 198
DOUGLASS, Robert 335
DOUP, George 152, 245
DOWNEN, Earl F. 81, 93
DOWNHAM, Clarice 199
    Earl A. 75, 197, 215, 236, 237
    George 147, 247*
    Mrs. George (Elizabeth) 104
    Irene 244
    Iva 110
    Joe 134, 147
    John 324
    John T. viii, 119*, 121, 133*, 138, 197, 231, 232, 235, 236, 241
    Mrs. John T. (Elizabeth) viii, 104, 199
    Lois 128, 258
    Merila 104
    Owen 225
    Mrs. Owen 198
    Mrs. Ross 99*, 199, 279
    Walter 292
    Wayne 292
    Wilmer 231
    Mrs. Wilmer 199, 231
DOWNHOUR, David 140*
    Mrs. Richard (Mona) 137*, 138

DOYLE, Dr. L. P. 210
DRAPER, Brenda 70
   Bruce 67
   Mrs. Bruce (Mary) 67
   Mrs. Carl 100*
   Dean 288
   Mrs. Donald 198
   Freddie 170*
   Hazel viii, 103
   Janet 132
   Judy 170*
   Margaret 342, 346
   Marjorie, M. 273*, 274
   Peggy 194
   William N. 58
DUCKWORTH, Rick 228*
DUDDY, Wayne 27
DUFF, Curt 146
   Diane 308
   Donald 69, 144, 191
   Doug 149
   Mrs. Doug (Chris) 149
   Gary 184
   Joy Ellen 287
   Lloyd O. 237
   Robert 69, 266
   Robert "Bob" viii, 131*, 138*
   Mrs. Robert "Bob" (Pat) viii
   Sheryl Lynn "Sherri" 131, 141*, 337, 338
   Susan E. 184, 288
   William "Bill" viii, 16, 69, 70*, 130, 144, 312
   Mrs. William "Bill" (Wanda) viii, 69, 130
DUGAN, James P. 59
DUGGLEBY, John 184
DUKE, Betty Ann 92
   Mr. 36
DUNCAN, Phillip 321
DUNHAM, Mrs. Ernest (Mabel) 55
DUNK, Earl 310
DUNKLE, Henderson 25
DUNN, John R. 148
   Louis 146
   Opal 67
DUNWOODY, Charles 214
DuVALL, Betty 128, 130, 131, 135*
   Catherine L. 128, 135*, 161
   Clyde "Ike" 135*
   Mrs. Clyde "Ike" (Mary) viii, 135*, 138
   Clyde 128, 131, 135*, 136
   Gregory 135*, 136, 288
   Harry 135*, 136, 185, 253
   Jeffery 135*, 136
   Jim 135*, 136
   John 135*
   Larry 135*, 136, 185
   Linda 131, 135*, 136
   Mary Ann 128, 130, 131, 135*
   Nancy 128, 130, 135*, 136, 161, 184
   Richard 128, 135*
DWYER, Michael 316, 317
DYER, Bennie 225
   Bill 16
   Cyrus L. "Rusty" 245
   Effie 345
   Samuel R. 267
   Sheryl 54
DYKE, Ralph 56
   Mrs. Bill 104

E

EASTWOOD, Bernadine 108*
EASTMAN, H. J. 196
EATON, G. E. 237
   M. V. 24
   M. W. 318
EBBINGHAUS, Hubert T. 45, 138
EBERLE, Charles 284
EBRITE, Norman viii, 332
ECKERLE, Wm. 39, 122, 323
ECKERT, E. A. 66, 67
   Mrs. Lee 105
EDGING, Mrs. Jay (Faye) 54*, 55
   Monty 139*
   Ruth 25, 98
EDISON, Thomas A. 259
EDMONSON, Noah 319
EGELHOFF, Mrs. Howard 105
EIKENBERRY, Charles A. 113, 237, 323
   Cullan 128, 130
   Mrs. Cullan (Becky) 105
   Delbert 86*, 197, 236
   Mrs. Delbert 198
   E. E. 55, 113
   Glenn viii, 222, 323, 324
   Mrs. Glenn (Lena) 198
   Mrs. Glenn (Naomi) viii, 99, 100
   J. W. 74, 86*, 175*, 176, 195, 197, 217, 235, 236, 237, 262, 266, 295, 296, 297, 324
   Mrs. J. W. 108
   Jeris 128, 129, 136*, 180
   Joe 223
   Lee O. 14, 15, 321
   Oren 86*, 118, 166*, 195, 197, 231*, 235, 236, 237, 296
   Robert 241
   Mrs. Ross 99*
   Wayne viii, 113
EIS, Mrs. Earl 199, 327
   Shirley 249*
EISENHOWER, President 325
EKSTEIN, Donna 340
ELDRIDGE, Ed 75
ELLER, Mrs. Allan (Linda) 104
   Dick 148
   Madonna 128
   Mrs. Maurice 103
   Nadine 340
   Mrs. Roy 108
ELLIOTT, Don viii, 304*
   Edward C. Pres. PU 89
ELLIS, Albert 237
   Joe 316
   John B. 49
   Nancy 76, 77, 93
ELMER 179
ELSTON, John 128
   Teresa L. 288
   Thomas 236, 308
   Mrs. Thomas 332
EMERSON, Edward S., D.V.M. 22
EMERY, Ann Miller 122
EMRICK, Viola viii, 341, 346
ENGLE, Fred H. 60
ENNIS, Kathi 132
ENYART, Col. 300
EPPERS, Marcia Abbott 122
ERBAUGH, Dr. Charles N. 282*
ERWIN, Barbara 102
EVANS, Cleve 27
   Robert J. 300
EVERETT, Bonnie 273
EVERMAN, W. H. 339
EVERSON, E. V. 316
   V. S. 240
EWICK, George 339
EWING, David 339
   Dr. John M. 35
   Robert 339
EYER, Clarence O. 69, 144, 146, 301
EYMAN, B. F. 58

F

FABIARSKE, Miriam 98
FAIR, Henry 117
FARMER, Robert 143
FARNER, Mrs. Dan 346
FARR, Edith 329, 331
   Wade W. 26, 27
FARRIS, Bill 312
FARTHING, Carrie 67
   Rev. Homer 67
FASSNACHT, Arthur E. 234*, 236, 296*, 297, 302
   David 232
   Louis 232
   Mary 184, 287
FAWCETT, Henry 14
FELIX, Mrs. Carl 282
FELLOWS, Charles R. 197, 237
   Larry 123*, 148
FELTHOFF, Charles 228
   Kathryn 130, 131
FELZ, Ron 309*
FENNELL, J. A. 339
FENSTERMACHER, Ed 196
FERGUSON, B. Wm. "Bill" 223*, 227, 232
   Francis 75
   O. D. 237
FERLING, Fred 76
FERRIER, Daniel 44
   Jean Pruitt 82
   John E. 345
   Myrtle 44
FERRIS, T. I. 213
FESSLER, John 57
FETTERHOFF, Ira E. 67
   John 348
   Mrs. Lee 104

Ren 231*
Mrs. Ren 198, 231*
Thomas Gene 287
FIDNER, Mrs. Odin 198
FIELEKE, Brian 258
    Bruce 258
    Calvin 185
    Mrs. Calvin 185
FIFE, Kathleen 247*, 248*, 258
    Michael 192*
    Orville 297
    Paul 121
    Rosanna 92, 105
FINCHER, H. C. 237
    Joe 237
    Vance 327
FINE, June 82
FISCHER, Peggy 179*
    Pete 179
    Mrs. Pete 169, 170*, 171*, 173*, 179
    Virginia 170*
FISHER, Bert 76
    Floyd E. 237
    Glenda 70, 128, 130, 249, 250, 258
    Mrs. Glenn 346
    Geo. D. 237
    Mrs. Ira (Clara) 96*
    Jack 22
    Jean 273
    Jerry 230*
    John 348
    Mary Jane 289, 291
    Melvin F. viii, 84*, 86, 197, 237, 298, 301*, 310, 313, 322
    Mrs. Melvin F. viii, 178*, 198
    Mrs. Robert 198
    Sharon 249
    Virginia 128, 130, 249, 250, 311*
FITCH, W. Q. 71
FITZER, Don 314
FITZGERALD, Love Groninger 257
    Robert 333
FLANANGHAM, Nellie 103
FLEDDERJOHN, Herb 261
FLETCHER, Jon David 346
FLINN, Mrs. Paul (Nellie) 152
FLOOD, Emanuel 37
FLORA, Mrs. A. A. 104
    Amos 292
    Arvel 237, 298
    Carl F. 237
    Carol 123*, 129, 131*, 136, 146, 233, 316
    Mrs. Carol (JoEtta) 198
    Charles 38
    Charles M. viii, 241, 263, 304, 306, 308
    Dawn 180*
    Emory 59
    Esther 174
    Evan 313
    Everett 176, 300, 301*
    Ezra 298
    Fred C. 297

    George 254*
    Mrs. George 102
    Gero 113
    Gordon 297
    H. H. 318
    Irvin 48
    Jacob H. 54
    Jim 120, 138, 250, 258, 309*
    Mrs. Jim 250
    Joe 197, 323
    John 346
    Dr. John 15
    John H. 298, 335, 336*
    Mrs. John H. 335
    Kenneth 16
    Lee F. viii, 16, 87*, 90, 119, 120, 172*, 187, 197, 231*, 302, 312, 337
    Mrs. Lee F. (Helen) viii, 198, 337
    Marie 108
    Noah 197, 329
    Orville 300
    Paul 115
    Richard 146
    Ron 148
    Mrs. Rufus 108
    Russell 180
    Mrs. Russell 180
    Sherri 126, 128, 131
    Susan 132, 134
    Thomas E. 16, 128, 130, 223, 296*
    Vernon 337
FLOYD, Becky 132
    Bob 132, 134
    Marsha 125
    Mike 134
FLYNN, Brenda 128
FOLEY, John 83*
FORD, Henry 13, 33
    Jack 58
FOREMAN, Bill 163, 164*
    Harry 323
    Wm. 44
    Wm. R. 197
FORGEY, Carl 148
    Christina 128
    Clarence 237
    Dianne 127, 128
    Gary 185
    Mrs. Gary (Ruth) 185
    Joe 130, 131
    Mrs. Thomas (Ruthina) 110
    Mrs. Wayne (Helen) viii, 95, 98, 104, 119
FOSBRINK, Raleigh viii 137*
FOSS, C. L. 291*, 292
FOSSNOCK, Dale 346
    Mrs. Dale 198
    Dora 81*, 98
    Edward 196
    Mrs. Edward 198
    Kevin 253, 258
    Mabel 81*, 98, 179*
    Pam 128
FOSTER, David 339
    Harry 119, 323, 324

FOUNTAIN, Edgar Jr. 16, 143, 144, 258
    Mrs. Edgar Jr. (Jean) 108
    Edgar Sr. 197, 231, 298, 310
    Mrs. Edgar Sr. (Louisa) 99*
    Joe 16, 185
    Robert 144
    Tom 16
FOUTS, Bill 179
    Castyle 113
    Mrs. Castyle (Mildred) 106, 168, 177, 195, 198
    J. Earl 162, 329
    Mrs. J. Earl 162
    Jasper 332
    Joe 325
    Mrs. Joe 198, 325
    Noah 74, 237
    Pauline 177, 41
    Taylor 44, 74, 77, 79, 85, 88*, 116, 162, 163, 173*, 174, 175*, 176, 177*, 180, 181, 182, 195, 196, 237, 309, 310, 311*, 314
    Mrs. Taylor 95, 162, 180, 198
    Tom "Captain Stubby" viii, 180, 234*, 283, 326, 335
    W. C. 197, 237
FOWLER, Lindy Ayres 123
FOX, Daniel 237
    George 147
FRAIN, Mrs. Wm. 198
FRANEK, Rene 140*
FRANKLIN, Phyllis 82
FRANTZ, Charles 67
    Elizabeth 67
    Mae 99*
FRASER, Laura 67
    Mabel 67
    Roscoe 117, 327
    Taylor B. 67
FREEMAN, Orville 291
    Tom 137*
    Mrs. Tom (Susan) 137*
    Dean V. C. 88
FREITAG, Anna 99
FRENCH, Mrs. Ray 101
FREY, Carol 169*
    Clarence 45, 118, 166*, 172*, 174, 175*, 176, 191, 196, 235, 237, 262, 266, 269, 295, 296, 297, 308
    Mrs. Clarence (Opal) viii
    Dallas 222
    Mrs. Dallas 198
    Debbie 163
    Emmett 123*, 196, 199, 232
    Mrs. Emmett (Pat) 100, 104, 123, 173*, 180, 198, 199
    Gerald 146
    Harold 29, 231*, 232, 235, 237, 322, 323
    Mrs. Harold 231*
    Jerry W. viii, 184, 185, 199, 315
    Mrs. Jerry W. (Janice) 185
    Julie 163
    Kenneth 91, 120, 188, 196, 235,

358 • CARROLL COUNTY RURAL ORGANIZATIONS

296, 302
Mrs. Kenneth 198
Larry 163
Louann 123, 140*
Roger 128, 147, 169*, 315*
Mrs. Roger 180
Ward 128, 169*
FRICKEY, Dr. E. L. 112
FRIDAY, George 6
FRIST, Dr. R. J. 112, 113
FROELICH, John 33
FROSS, Alan 144
  Milt 323
FROST, Jack 301*
FRY, Gerald 131*
  Hazel 24
  Lawrence 197, 236
  Mrs. Lawrence 198
  Roy 310, 313*, 314
FRYE, Dorothy 105
  Fred 319
  Russell 237
FULTZ, Leonard E. 184
FUNKHOUSER, Dennis 123, 184
  Julie 134, 136
  Kay 130
  Lewis H. viii, 262, 266, 269,
    295*, 297, 302, 317, 341,
    342*, 346
  Mrs. Lewis (Rova) 346
  Ray 302
  Richard 327
  Richard "Dick" viii
  W. H. 300
FURNAS, Eugene 13
FURNHAM, John 180
FURR, Ralph 16
FURST, John 145, 146, 311*
  Levi 172*, 197, 231*, 232,
    247*, 309, 310, 311*,
    314
  Mrs. Levi 99*, 231
  Mary 131*

G

GADDIS, Lella 101
GALBREATH, Delmar 187
  W. H. 57
GALLOWAY, Frank E. 237
  Harry 312
  John 310
  Sylvia 114, 115
GAMBLE, R. G. 69
GANGLOFF, Omer 237
  Mrs. Omer 118
GANGWER, Bob 147
  Carla 139*
  Dan 147
GANNON, Prof. E. A. 74, 115, 301*
GARD, Charles 174, 179*, 180*,
  237, 332
GARDINER, Rudy 192*
GARDNER, Basil 279
  Beatrice 331
  Belle 345
  Carrie 325

Chester 223
Mrs. Floyd 332
Garland 327
Lauretta 345
Murray 44
Myra 25
Mrs. Raymond 107
Roy E. 172*, 345
W. E. 317
William 36, 348
GARRISON, Mrs. Billy (Wilma) 55
  Bruce 323
  Erin 132
  Jim 146
  Joe 292
  John K. 38, 339
  Irene 341
  Mark viii, 235, 236, 283*, 292,
    296*, 297, 302
  Pearl 102
  Phyllis viii
  Ray 313*
  Ross 75, 196
  Mrs. Ross 198
  Roy 237
  Sharon 311*
  Tara 329*
GASAWAY, Don 227
  S. H. 73
  Stanley 174
GASCHO, Doris 230*
GASTINEAU, Allen 287
GATES, W. P. 282
GAUMER, Fred 56
GAYLORD, Fay C. 89
GEHEB, Charles viii, 138*
  Mary K. 128
GENTRY, Norwood 185
GEORGE, Barbara Jo 128
  Mrs. Dean 101
GERARD, Bob 144
  C. E. viii
  Frank 164*
  Fred 197, 220*
  Mrs. Fred (Mildred) viii, 199
  Margaret 53*
GERBENS, Andrew 196, 215, 235,
  237
  Edna 241
  Ralph 143
GERHART, William F. 339
GERLACH, Dr. Carl F. 318
GERMAN, Vincent 298
GERRISH, Mike 258
GETTINGER, George 312
GIBSON, Mrs. Charles 106, 107
  Mabel 330, 341, 346
  Marion 106, 317
  Roger 336
  Tom 337
  Virginia 106
GICK, Roberta Scott 346
GILBERT, Byron 128, 302
  Vera 340
GILES, Loe 109
  Nelson 176, 237
GILL, Olive 56
GILLIAM, A. A. 297

Elmer 113
G. W. 237
Mrs. Jack (Roberta) 55
GILLEFORD, George 67
GINGERICH, David 230*, 235
GINGRICH, John H. 68, 237
  Johnny 170*
  Lawrence 237
  Murray 148
  Mrs. Murray (Christina) 148
GINN, Charles G. 56, 77, 163, 197,
  236, 237
  Geneva 114
  Howard 114
  Kenneth 113
  Martha 99*
  Ralph 113
  Wm. H. 88, 237, 310
GIRARD, Frank S. 44, 77, 163, 174,
  196, 237, 345
  Mrs. Frank S. 341
  Mrs. John A. 75, 76
  Lizzie 345
  Paul 163, 196
  Mrs. Paul 174
GISH, Floyd M. 304
  Ray 126, 129, 258
GIVLER, William 117
GLASSCOCK, O. N. 58
GLICK, Cecil 91
  Mary viii
GLOVER, Beulah 308
GOCHENOUR, John 169*
GOCHER, David 333
GODLOVE, Don 291
GOFF, Ernest L. 318
GOODWIN, Jeffrey 346
  Larry 192
  Mary Margaret 346
GOLTZ, Mrs. Tom 96*
GORBUSKY, Jenny 66
GOSLEE, B. A. 237
  Bert 175, 237
  Dale 114
  Dean 57
  Ethel 24
  Jack 120, 225
  Joyce 308
  Orpha viii, 81*, 103, 173*, 198,
    342*, 346
  Orville 226*
  Ralph 162, 236, 237
  Mrs. Ralph 162
  Reed 120, 225, 231*
  Mrs. Reed 231*
  William M. 56, 237
GOSNEY, Charles viii
GOSS, Albert S. 70
GOTTSCHALK, Dan viii, 146, 148,
  149, 306*
  Mrs. Dan (Cindy) 104, 148,
    149
  Joe 147
GRAHAM, A. B. 111
  C. T. 237
  Gordon 88*
  John 57, 58
  Milton R. 26

Mrs. Patrick 198
Zelpha 288
GRANDSTAFF, Thomas D. 288
GRANT, Mrs. Lillian 58
GRANTHAM, Joseph 340*
   Mrs. Luther (Grace) 98
   Richard viii, 6, 175, 329, 337
   Mrs. Richard (Polly) viii, 337
   Wilbur 329
   Mrs. Wilbur (Lorene) 95, 98
GRASSMYER, Alice 246
GRAVES, Mrs. William (Linda) 104
GRAY, Bob 16
   Finley 160
   Gilbert 313
   Robert 314
GREEN, Bernard 185
   Mrs. Bernard 185
   R. C. 25
GREENLEE, Joy Carol 125*
GREENUP, Lou 98
GREENWALT, John 115
GREENWOOD, Ermal 196
   Mrs. Meredith 103
GREER, Harold 232
   Mrs. Harold 199
GREGG, Mrs. G. M. 345
   Paul 223, 236
   Mrs. Paul (Josephine) 198
   Roy 38, 346
   Mrs. Roy (Esther) viii, 21, 22*, 44, 106, 114, 317, 341, 346
GREIDER, Mattie 118
   Mrs. Walter 332
GRESHAM, E. H. 26
   Newt 315
   Samuel Davis 18
GRIFFEY, Mrs. Dale (Cecilia) viii, 105
   Harold 144
   Michael G. viii, 318
GRIFFITH, Connie 123
   Ed 284
   Harry 67, 163, 164*
   Mrs. Harry (Elva) 67
   Isaac 35
   Paul 118
   Russell L. 265
GRIMES, Dr. Samuel 347
GRIMM, E. O. 44, 67, 298
   Jack 332
   Mrs. Jack 329
   L. C. 237
GRITTEN, Don 192, 193*
GRONINGER, Craig 257*
   Debbie Miller 123
   Gaye 257*
   Gordon viii, 230*
   John 300, 308, 329, 332
   Kim Douglas 184, 287
   Love 241, 243
   Mike 148
   Parks D. 237, 300
   Ren C. viii, 90, 120, 186, 187, 188, 197, 246, 257*, 258
   Mrs. Ren C. 257*
   Renda 257*
   Sandra 257*

GROS, Mrs. Charles 345
   Fannie R. 345
   Harriet 345
   Wm. "Will" 44, 341, 345
GROSS, Frances 99, 100
   Mrs. Guy E. (Lois) 152
GROSVENOR, Royal 348
GROTRIAN, Marsha 337
GRUBB, R. E. 177
GRUBER, Larry E. 67, 69, 197, 237, 263, 301
   Mrs. Larry (Nellie) 67, 69, 199
GUARD, George 174, 237
GUCKIEN Bros. 237
   Charles 114
   Effie 329
   Emmitt 237
   F. Michael viii, 301
   Mrs. John 104
   Madonna 162*
   Marilyn 104
   Michael 144
   Ron 83
   William 162*, 237, 330
   Mrs. William 162*
GUGE, Bethan 126*
   Janella 126*
GUILD, M. D. 208
GUSHWA, Henry 50*
   Joyce 311*
   Reed 346
   Mrs. Reed 346
GUTHRIE, Eileen 308
   James 188, 329
   Marjie 308
   Nelson 197
   Mrs. Thaddeus 341
   Stuart F. 143, 144, 146, 323
   Wayne 332
GUY, Delbert 76
   Mrs. Delbert 76
GUYER, Jean 330
   Dr. Tennyson 282
GWINN, Joseph W. 339
   Rolla 45
   Samuel 339

H

HAAN, J. P. 67
HACKETT, Homer 291*
HADLEY, William A. viii, 153
HAGGARD, Dr. J. Marcus 69, 185, 186
   Mrs. J. Marcus (Rachel) 108*
HAHN, Brian 251*, 258
HAINES, Adolph 121*, 335
   Clark A. 162
   Mrs. Clark A. 162
   G. H. 319
   J. F. 117
   John 111
HALE, Charlotte 287
HALL, Okel F. 75
HALLER, Jim 313
HAMLING, John 45
HAMMER, Mrs. Robert 198

HANAWALT, Clyde 248*
   Mrs. Clyde 248*
   Doris 178*
   Gerald 178*, 258
   W. R. 197
   Mrs. W. R. 198
HANAWAY, Charles B. 38
   Frank 143
   George 146
   Mrs. George Jr. (Janice) 105
   Hobart 143, 144
   W. T. 74
HANCE, Wm. 348
HANDLEY, Lt. Gov. Harold 327
HANKINS, Bob 145
   Don 144, 197, 313
   Mrs. Don 105
   Martha 105
   Mary 114
   Ralph 146
   Ray 309, 310, 313
HANNA, Barbara 24
   Carl 237
   Charles R. viii, 123, 125*, 173*, 185, 186, 188, 196, 197, 199, 203, 231, 232, 234, 235, 236
   Mrs. Charles R. (Helen) viii, 114, 198, 231
   Charlotte 233
   Dale 222
   David 318
   Delores 128
   Eddie A. 184, 233
   Gerald 185
   Mrs. Gerald 185
   Harry 27
   Homer 301*
   J. W. 345
   Joe 50
   John L. 345
   Maxine 243
   Palestine 47
   Ralph 181, 220*, 223*
   Mrs. Ralph (Annabel) 82, 105
   Raymond V. 237, 295
HANNELL, Charles 237
   Mrs. Charles (Lena) 44, 98, 107
   Fred 41, 83*, 84, 236, 237, 309, 310
   Joan 168
   Wm. 114
HANRAHAN, Marie viii, 95, 186, 198
   Matt 117, 236, 237
HANSEL, Richard 292
   Robert 292
HANSEN, Arthur G. Pres. PU 89
HARAMY, John 176
HARDT, Merritt 125, 337
   Mrs. Merritt 125
HARDY, Elizabeth 241
   Mrs. Leroy 199
   Mary 331
HARGRAVES, Charles 44
HARLEY, Charles 23
HARLOW, Richard 138, 148
HARMON, Geneva 335

Gerald 335
James 339
Lola Mae 335
HARNER, Elias 47
Glenn 91
HARNESS, George 339
Jake F. 196, 235, 237
Jessie 340
John 258, 323
John R. 46, 75, 196
Spud 196
HARPER, Claude 89
Neal 184
HARRELL, John 340
HARRINGTON, Paul 138
HARRIOTT, Richard 222, 223*
HARRIS, K. Wayne 228*
Wayne 224*
HARRISON, Fedora 106
J. M. 237
Sandra 273
HARSHBERGER, Fred 310
HART, Charles 33
HARTER, Charles E. viii, 310, 315, 317, 335, 346
Mrs. Charles (Goldie) viii, 83*, 131*, 168, 169, 171*, 172*, 173*, 177*, 180, 195, 198, 317, 335, 346
Russell 118
R. M. 237
HARTKE, Senator Vance 289
HARTMAN, Patti 288
HARTSOCK, Harvey B. 262, 264, 272
HARVEY, George R. 75, 153, 164, 171*
HASKELL, William 24
HASKINS, Perry 192
HASLET, Harry 174
Lote 323
Samuel H. 50*
W. S. 50*
Wilma 131*, 246
Wm. 45, 114
HASLEY, Mr. 35
HASSELBRING, Bertha 116
HATCH, Mrs. Ed (Verna) 152, 167
HATFIELD, Shirley 109
HATHAWAY, Cindy 184
Donald 197, 223, 282*
Mrs. Donald (Maxine) 103
Earl 220
Kevin 329*
Kimberly 184, 288
Orville 282*, 329*, 332
Mrs. Orville (Frances) viii, 103, 329*
Stanley 184
HATKE, Brad 146
HATTER, Nina 273
HATTON, Harry 324
HAUGH, Wm. 259
HAUGHEY, Nellie 329
HAUN, Earl 38
J. P. 58
Martin G. 38
HAUSENFLUCK, Lesta 180

O. L. 174, 176, 180, 197
Mrs. Vernon (Mildred) 105
HAUSER, E. F. 268
HAWKINS, Ann 185
Jack 122
HAWLEY, William 117
HAWN, Frank 197, 236
Kathy 273
Richard 190, 241, 243, 244, 258
HAY, John P. 348
HAYDEN, Arthur 332
Dave 332
George 322
HAYES, Bert 237, 282
Mrs. Bert 199
Lorene 178
HAYNES, Elwood 13
HAZLET, William S. 58
HEATON, Jane Ann 340
HECKARD, Mrs. Robert 107
HECKATHORN, E. L. 310
HEDDE, Robert Sr. 83*, 84, 121, 162, 165, 186, 197, 219, 222, 223, 237, 244, 305, 323
Mrs. Robert Sr. 162
HEDDERICH, Carolyn 126
Edward 14
Frank 119, 197, 244, 291, 308
Mrs. Frank 198
Frank & Son 86
Fred 176*
Lee 14
Margaret 82, 126, 175
Paul 313
HEDDRICK, Mrs. Ed 102
Maude 162*
HEFFLEY, Connie 249*, 256*
HEFNER, Earl 41
Mark 67
Mrs. Mark (Zola) 67
HEILAND, Charles 175
HEINRICH, Rev. William 148
HEITZ, Glenn 305
HELFER, Albert 19
HELLMAN, Greg 138
HELM, Thomas B. 17, 25, 329
HEMMIG, Edith 266
HENDERSHOT, Pat Long 123
HENDERSON, Bessie 109
Donald E. viii, 165, 185, 188
Florence Dunkard 109
Joan 250*
Joe viii, 197, 298, 314*
Mrs. Joe (Martha Duff) viii, 138, 198, 243, 280
JoEtta 124*, 126, 127, 131*, 136*, 250*, 256*
Judith "Judy" 129, 256*
Marvin 197
Mrs. Marvin (Maxine) 199, 279
N. C. 47
Vivian 151, 162, 168, 195, 198, 240*, 241, 243, 244, 263
Wm. Lee 165, 168, 197, 215, 217*, 218*, 219, 234, 235, 236, 237, 244, 281*, 324
Mrs. Wm. Lee (Hattie) 176

HENDRESS, Jerry 83, 147, 149, 232, 234*, 235, 302
Mrs. Jerry (Mara) 149, 232
HENDRICKS, Tom 166, 219
HENDRIX, Mrs. Charles 99*
J. M. 54
Linda 288
Offa C. 44, 237
Richard 340
Mrs. Richard (Gloria) 340
Robert Lee 128*, 129
HENRY, Victor 56
William 339
HEP, I. M. 286
HERNDON, Diane 130
John 321
Mrs. John 198
HERR, Emmett 128
Harold 148
HERRLI, Loren D. 346
Mrs. Loren D. 346
Tod 314, 318
HERRON, Frank 146
HERSHBERGER, Blanche 101
Fred 86, 117, 237
HERTENSTEIN, Teresa 134
HESS, L. H. 175
HESSLER, Alfred 75
HEWITT, Philip 348
HIATT, Wayne viii, 166, 196, 219*, 227*, 235, 267, 271
Mrs. Wayne (Kathryn Swartz) viii, 271, 273
HICKMAN, C. W. 151
George 339
HICKS, Jane 184
John 237
Leroy 292
Robert 232, 302
Mrs. Robert 96*, 232
Mrs. Russell 106
Mrs. Weldon 107
HIGH, Joe 322
HILDEBRAN, George 144
Mary viii, 192*, 194, 314
HILDEBRAND, Arthur 197, 235, 236, 237
Earl 237
Julie 109
HILDERBRANDT, Joe 254*
Mrs. Joe 105
HILE, Marilyn 104
Paul Dean 20
HILL, Amanda 319
Cecil 227
Doctor O. 237
Mrs. Doctor O. 198
HINDER, Ward B. 13
HINDMAN, William T. 58
HINER, A. L. 237
HINKLE, Blanche 99*, 198
Dan "Danny" 119, 120, 133
Elmer 283
Mrs. Frank 198
J. H. (Hank) 58
John P. 176
Michael 187
Nelson 197

Nora 44
Rex 91, 120, 196, 232, 235
Thaddeus 237
Vernon 161
Mrs. Vernon 161
HODGE, Cathy 287
Frank Jr. 233
Wilmer 197, 223
HODGES, Donna 128
Jim viii, 148, 223*, 320
Judith 126
Melodie 105
HODGSON, A. L. viii, 44, 77, 93, 106, 114, 115, 164*, 345
Mrs. A. L. 77, 176
HODSON, Ronnie 148
HOFFER, George N. 312
HOFFMAN, Alice 337
DeVere 187, 335, 336*
Mrs. DeVere (Martha) viii, 24
Leroy E. 73, 129*, 310
Roscoe 196
Mrs. Roscoe (Gladys) 98, 123
HOLLAND, Dr. John W. 326
HOLLIS, Karen 27
HOLLOWAY, Albert 237
Buddy 69
Lawrence 151
Marilyn 284
Pat 68
Sue 307
Ward 310
HOLLOWELL, Mrs. Keith 96*, 106
HOLMES, Edith 103
Fred 324
Harry 165, 196
Max 116
R. H. 237
Vera 116
W. E. 345
HOLTMAN, Mrs. Walter (Alice) viii
HONAN, Burton D. viii, 45, 47, 151, 163, 164*, 173*, 174, 176, 195, 235, 236, 237, 308, 310, 345
Mrs. Burton D. (Helen) viii, 95, 96
HOOD, Carol Jane 180
Debbie 105
Frank 336
Fred 177, 196
George E. 297
HOOK, Arthur 258
HOOPINGARNER, Tim 121*
HOOVER, C. V. 45, 47, 76, 237
Mrs. C. V. (Mary) 101
Charles 58, 185, 186*, 203, 232, 235
Mrs. Charles (Vera) viii
Herbert 52, 174
Jesse viii, 194*
Mrs. Jesse (Vivian Henderson) viii, 194*, 257
Mary E. 297
Sue Ellen 194*
HOPP, Verlin 227
HORN, Donald 318

Mrs. Donald (Shirley) 22
HORNBECK, Mrs. Emma 56
O. F. 47
Mrs. C. W. 94
HORNER, F. C. 318
HORSLEY, Joseph R. 26
HORTON, Catherine viii
HOSHAW, David 123*
Loyal 67, 165, 176
HOUSER, Charles 319
Mrs. Alma 332
Dale 332
HOVDE, F. L. Pres. PU 88
HOWARD, Bonnie 132, 179
Helen 335
J. R. 150
Millie 134
Orville 337
Ted viii, 147, 149
HOWE, Carolyn 123
Mrs. Newberry (Mary C.) 23, 24
HOWELL, Mrs. N. J. 340*
Ruth 194
HUDDLESON, H. L. 47
HUDSON, Dana 148
Eddie 15
HUFF, Donald E. viii, 144, 148, 178*
Melody 131
HUFFER, Charles 143
Mrs. Dale 105
Esther 243
Jacob 172*, 308
Jim 318
Raymond 241
HUFFMAN, Mrs. Don (Betty) 108
HUFFORD, Charles 323
Dennis 179*
Ed 143
Gary 234*, 235
Mary E. 98, 103
HUFTY, C. J. 48
J. J. 46
Wilford 48, 237
HUGHES, Allen 137*, 138, 149
Mrs. Allen (Barbara) 122, 137*, 138, 149
Arlie 68
Mrs. Charles 169*, 171*
Charlotte 169*
Judy 169*
Max 144
Merrill 144, 315
Ralph 119*, 145, 146
Shirley 129*, 273
Warda 129*
HULL, J. Harvey 118, 153, 160, 200, 201, 206, 215, 240, 261, 281
HUMBARGER, Dale 170*
Francis 123*, 173*, 196, 199, 309*
Mrs. Francis (Maxine) viii, 108*, 198, 199
Gene 128
Marjorie 170*
Pauline 108*

HUMES, Carlisle 85
Fay 198, 243, 306
J. C. 86, 197, 237
HUMMEL, Denise 127
Prof. 113
HUMRICKHOUSE, Jacob 348
Z. J. 237
HUNDLEY, Neva 104
HUNT, G. A. 197, 237
George 174, 298
Mrs. George 198
John E. 3
Luther 274
Margaret 241
Paul 117
Zopher 26
HUNTER, Sam 283
HUNTLEY, Martha E. 67
HUNTSINGER, Allen 26
HURLEY, Jerry 318
John V. 237
HURT, Bob 76
Ray 146
HUSE, Joseph 128
Raymond 177*, 187, 196
Mrs. Raymond 198
HUSTON, Martha 347
HUTCHINSON, Dr. 243
HYMAN, Clarence 346
Mrs. Clarence 175

I

IMAN, Peter 348
IMLER, Frank 68, 165, 176, 237
INGERSOLL, Charles L. 71
IRELAN, Julia Hardy 329
IRELAND, Leonard 91
W. B. 237
IRMEGER, Edward 184
Martin H. 237
Virgil H. 196
Mrs. Virgil 198
Walter 196
ISAACS, Herbert L. viii, 91, 120, 272, 273*, 274, 275, 297, 330
ISHERWOOD, R. M. 26
ISLEY, Steven R. 274*
Vernon 143
IVES, George R. 43
Joseph T. Jr. (Thomas) 187, 329
Mary 24

J

JACKS, Merrill 148
JACKSON, Pres. Andrew 347
Ben 329
Charles 67
Mrs. Charley 108
Governor Ed 6, 153
George 227*
Ida M. 345
Laura 67

Melvin "Doomsday" 29, 30, 346
Mrs. Melvin (Mary) 199, 346
Orpha 67
Pete 121*, 319, 321
Reed 237
Willis 319
JACOBS, Charles 121
JAMES, John 114
JEFFRIES, Jerry 146
Paul 146
Mrs. Paul 198
JENKINS, Agatha 241
D. C. 197, 237
Mrs. D. C. 198
Mrs. David 108
Rev. Howard 75
Jerry 140*
Lucyle 244
Myron 197, 244
Robert 223*
Ruth 241, 243
Teresa 288
JENNINGS, Brad 163
Diana 131*
Gene viii, 123*, 170, 173*, 196, 197, 199, 236
Mrs. Gene (Patsy Pullen) viii, 82, 95, 96, 173*, 198, 199
Gov. Jonathan 334
Scott 131, 134, 136, 139*, 146, 163
JERVIS, Byron A. 88, 329, 335
Mrs. Byron A. (Evelyn) viii
Doyle E. 274
Mrs. Doyle E. (Juanita) 104
Mrs. Herbert (Grace) 99*, 104
J. F. 74
John T. 76
Madonna 82, 126, 127, 128, 130, 131, 161
Marvin V. 87, 310
Mrs. Marvin 198
JESTER, Carl 89, 313
Charles 115
Glenn 114
Sondra 273
JIMMY 308*
JOHNS, Carol 92
Charles 76
Emerson 246
Floyd M. 76, 237
Harry 237
Joetta 127, 128, 131
Karen 125*
Leanna 82, 130
Phil 134
Ralph 298
JOHNSON, Barbara 128, 130
Bernice 114
Bobby 169*, 292
Mrs. Bob (Sandy) 319
Carl C. viii, 29, 117, 166*, 185, 186*, 195, 197, 223*, 231, 232, 236, 237, 292, 309
Mrs. Carl C. viii, 198, 231
Carol 340
Charlene 100*

Clarence 196, 237
Mrs. Clarence 102
Clyde R. 237
E. E. 58
Ed 149, 232, 302
Mrs. Ed (Caren) 109, 137*, 138, 149, 232
Edgar 237
Eric 126*, 130
Gentry L. 184
Gus 51
Harold 236, 291
Inez 53*
Jesse 37
John T. viii, 37, 38, 91, 308, 309*, 316
Mrs. John T. 329
Larry 149, 232
Mrs. Larry (Kathi) 24, 109, 149, 232
Lavon 178, 199, 241, 243, 244
Lawrence 241, 316
Mrs. Lawrence (Mary Ellen) 98, 110
Mrs. Lowell 106, 107
Merle 223*, 227
Merritt E. 86
Myra Sue 128
Myron 26, 318
Naomi 273, 329
Paul 146, 176, 258, 323
Pearl 324
Perry 56
Mrs. Richard 107
Robert F. 37
Mrs. Robert F. 198
Ruth 22
Vicki Sue 128
JONES, Aaron 70
Bob 179*
Carl B. 237, 314
Carolyn 129
Casey 291
Charles 325
Mrs. Charles 95, 325
Charles W. 176, 237, 262, 267, 295
Debbie Mann 122
Etta 325
Fred 120
Geneva 98
Gordon 129*
Harold 314
Mrs. Harold 198
Harry, D.D.S. 22, 122
Hoover 340*
Howard L. 237
J. Stanley 319
Jane Ann 128, 180, 253, 254*
Jim 179
Marsha 127, 128, 130
Mike 257
Mildred 114
Pauline Fouts viii
Phil 323
Ralph 237
Raymond 323
Robert A. 143, 314

Russell 314
Sandra 273
Suanne 105
JORDON, Mrs. Robert 99*
Seve 192
JOYCE, Chester 79, 116
Clifford 302
Jalene 133, 179, 233, 248, 253, 254*, 311
Janet Lou 128, 130, 133, 179, 233, 248, 253, 254*, 311
Joetta 125*, 128, 131, 133, 179, 248, 253, 254*, 311
Lloyd 116
Virgil viii, 115, 116, 311, 320, 321, 325, 327
Mrs. Virgil (Gladys) viii, 110
Will 116
JULIEN, Evan 47
Floyd 273
George W. 76, 329, 331, 345
Mrs. George 176, 291
Dr. Ren C. 59, 77, 113, 163, 164*, 173, 174, 175
Mrs. T. E. 345
JULIUS, C. O. 45
Georgianna 346
JUSTICE, Jerome 58
M. F. 46
Martha 346
Martin E. 283*, 292, 295, 297
Martin Jr. 120
R. O. 58
William F. viii, 214*
Mrs. William F. (Paulita) 214*
Wilson 165

K

KAHLER, Karen 130
KAMSTRA, Mrs. Garrott 198
KARASYNSKI, Antoni 38
KASTEN, Dale R. viii, 80*, 90, 91, 93, 123, 185, 186*, 187, 346
Harold 182, 243
Leon 118, 197, 215, 236, 237, 244
KEARNS, Bill viii, 123*, 127, 128, 129, 130, 132, 302, 309*, 336
Mrs. Bill (Jane Williams) viii, 100, 102, 122
Lisa 134, 136
W. B. 24, 176
KEEN, Sandy 105
KELLEHER, Mrs. Pollard 346
KELLER, James 235
KELLEY, Oliver Hudson 63, 66
KELLY, Emmett 335
Jack 54
John 339
Mrs. Kenneth (Ann Louise) 95, 104
Pat 335
KELSEY, Manford 67
Mrs. Manford (Etta) 67

KEMPF, Mable C. 346
   Mary Ellen 173*, 195, 248, 249*, 253, 256*, 258
KENDALL, Jess 320
   Mrs. Richard 101
KENNARD, Glenn 75
   Mrs. Glenn 198
   John L. viii, 45, 48, 68, 117, 191, 197, 237, 277, 282, 298, 346
   Mrs. John L. 45
KENNEDY, Daisy 325
   E. E. 316
   Dr. Eva 24
   Frank 58
   J. C. 298
   Jerilyn Jones 122
   Senator John 325
KENRICK, Mrs. Wilbert 104
KENZLOR, George 167*
KERBER, Charles 214
KERKHOVE, Dr. B. C. 9
KERLIN, Charles 68, 323, 324
   C. M. 59, 76
   Mrs. C. M. 345
   Della C. 345
   H. G. 53, 165
   Hiram 45
   John W. 43, 44, 45, 57, 76, 300, 304, 345
   Mrs. John W. 345
   Mary 235
   Rosella 247*
   Wm. 329
   William F. 300
KESLER, Ross 48
KESLING, Dena 336
KESNER, Frank 176*
   Mrs. Frank (Madeline) 25
KESTERSON, Keith 274
KETTERER, Doug 306
KEYES, Burr R. 26, 27
   Chester A. 26
   Dora 58
   Jasper 26
   James 337
KEYS, Mrs. Everett (Ida) 180, 198
   Sue 256*, 253, 255*
KILLINSWORTH, Carmen Blocher 82
KILMER, Dave 140*
   Mary 106
   Ray 192
KILOWATT, Reddy 293
KIME, Mr. 74
KINCAID, Meredith M. 153
KING, Edna 106
   Mrs. Junior 107
   Susan 287
KINGEN, Mark 305
KINGERY, Almon 237
   Carl 237
   Debbie 343
   Irvin 237
   Robert 146
KINNEAR, Herb viii
KINTNER, Franklin 178
KINZER, Mrs. Terry 107

KIRCHOFF, Bill 318
KIRK, Paul 319
KIRKENDALL, Jane Ann 331
KIRKPATRICK, Mrs. Carlyle 317
   Edna 114
   Mrs. Frank 75
   Hazel 22, 329
   Mrs. John 186
   Maggie 330
   Owen 48
   Paul 282
   Mrs. W. E. 174
KISTLER, Shirley 345*
KITE, Arthur 68
   Bruce 143, 144
   Clarence 318
   Ed Jr. 144, 323
   Ed L. 144, 301
   Grover D. 67, 117, 177, 345
   Mrs. Grover D. (Jennie) 345
   Jean 311*
KITZMILLER, E. G. 13, 24, 74
KLAUSS, Don 310, 311*
KLECKNER, Ira 304
   Nancy 25
KLEIN, Venus 94
KLEPINGER, John F. 318, 328
   Will G. 59, 76, 163, 165, 197
   Mrs. Will G. (Martha) 10, 45, 47
KLOPFEINSTEIN, Diana 194
KNAPP, Warren M. 55, 162, 319
   Mrs. Warren M. 55, 162
KNITTER, Bud 332
   Wayne 254*
KNOP, Dave 313
   Don 313
   Herb 313
KOHLS, Richard L. 87, 312
KOHNKE, Helmut 312
KOONTZ, Donald 226, 265
KRAMER, Jean 116
KRAUSS, E. F. 319
   Edgar Jr. 24
KREMER, James R. viii, 18, 302, 308*, 315*
   Mrs. James (Betty) viii
   Karen 184
   Kevin 179
   Linda 184
   Loretta Ann "Lori" 128, 130, 132, 136, 140*, 141*, 179, 184, 288
   Madonna 184
KRIEG, Reneé 82, 83*, 93, 119*, 136, 137*
KUHNS, Albert 237
   Gary 147
KULL, Elaine 185
KUNS, Elmer 197, 215, 236
   Merle 146
   Raymond L. 237, 322
KURKOWSKI, Jack 283
KURTZ, Clifford 343, 344*
   Melvin 332
KUSZMAUL, Bill 248*, 256*, 258
   Ellis 166*, 237
   Mrs. Ellis (Lydia) 198

Fred 197, 220*, 258
Mrs. Fred (Betty) 198

L

LAKE, Birdie 105
   Mrs. William 105
LAMB, Mrs. Mary 24
   Monica 123
   Robert 302
LAMBERT, Loretta 102
   Robert 134
LAMBERTSON, Harold 322, 323
LAMM, David 314
LANDES, Dr. B. F. 339
   E. P. 237
   Ethel 102
   Goldie Smith 108
   Isaac N. 237
   Susie 102
   Wayne viii, 138, 275, 329
   Winifred 105
LANDIS, Annette 116
   Ardis 75, 237
   Mrs. Ardis 75
   Charles B. 25
   Chas E. 237
   Clay 323
   Dan 49
   E. E. 122, 184, 318, 319, 323, 324
   Henry 331
   I. N. 75
   Jasper 49
   Katherine 116
   Larry 177*
   Mrs. Larry 198
   Lawrence 197, 236, 237
   Loren 337
   Margaret 181
   Noah 59, 66
   Mrs. R. D. 346
   Robert E. 301*, 302
   Mrs. Robert M. (Gladys) 108*
   Roy 56
   Sonia 126
   Sue 129*
   W. J. 74
   William 192
LANE, B. W. 45
   Bert 44
   Burton D. 165, 196
   Darryl 149
   Mrs. Darryl (Sue) 109, 149
   H. W. 237
   Lois viii
   Mary 100
   Randy L. 288
   Roy 75
   Dr. W. H. 47, 118, 119, 237, 304
   Wilbur 329
LANGSTON, Cindy 123
   Clyde 235, 237
   Mrs. Clyde 198
   Marcia 128
   Marion 185, 186*, 187, 195,

196, 235, 236, 302, 313
Mrs. Marion 198
Max 131, 314
Murray 128, 130, 233
Mrs. Stanley 107
Wayne 232, 243, 310
Mrs. Wayne (Freida) 95, 108
LANTZ, Evan 292
Frank O. 237
Fred 56
Keith 253, 257, 258
Loran 243
LAPRAD, Rev. John 331
Paul 248, 250*, 258
LARGEN, Pauline 198
LARIMORE, Delores 273, 284
Laurel 228
LARSON, Ron 147
Shirley 56, 57
LaSELLE, C. H. 240
LATHAM, Billy Joe 147
LATHROPE, John 331
LATIA, Douglas 329*
Elaine 329*
LATSHAW, Mrs. Harry (Modena) 343
LATTA, Prof. William C. 71, 151
LAUGHLIN, Dick 283
LAUSTER, Ronald 130, 341, 346
Mrs. Ronald 130, 341, 346
LAVY, Daniel 291*
LAWRENCE, Marshall viii 214
LAWSON, Dr. Dianella 9
LAYMAN, Cheryl Gooding 123
LEAHY, Matt 140*
LEATHERMAN, Oscar 76, 165, 237, 262, 266, 295, 297
Raymond 118, 243
LEAZENBY, Charles H. 282, 325
LEDMAN, Lynn 15, 119, 319
LEHNER, Anthony 240, 243
LEINBERGER, Bernie 140*
Betty 82
Bill 130, 132, 136
Joseph K. 288
Rita 132, 134
William John 288
LEITER, Richard viii, 120, 335, 336*
Wm. 319, 324
LENNON, Clara 24
LENON, Harve 56
John 348
LESH, A. L. 237
Fredona 100*
James 57
LESLIE, Ethel 243
Gov. Harry 89
Ira 187, 237
LEWELLEN, David Alan 288
LEWIS, Betty DuVall 135*
John L. 162
LILEY, Peter 130
Mrs. Peter (Elaine Kull) viii, 81, 82*, 93, 130, 186
LILLY, Jerry 56, 119, 292
LIMP, Louella 108
LINCOLN, Abraham 71

Murray D. 201
LIND, Dorothy Anita 288
John 124
Mrs. John 124
LINDLEY, Harlow 340*
LINTON, W. H. 47, 318
LITTMAN, Mrs. Ed 108
LLOYD, James 16
LOCKRIDGE, Ross F. 346
LOGAN, Ben 217
Cleo 273
Edgar 163, 164*, 196
Ellis 58
Gordan 192
Jake 74
Joyce 273
Noble 214
Mrs. Nona 168, 181, 195, 198
W. E. 237
LOGSDON, Pam 92
LOHRMAN, Mrs. Floyd 198
Julia A. 297
Pat viii
Wayne 166*, 197
Mrs. Wayne 173*, 198
LOMAN, Brett 139*
Chalmer 117
Mrs. Chalmer 99*
Wayne 316, 317, 346
William 241
LONG, Clifford 292
Don 292
James D. 58
Jane Ann 130
Margaret 114
Marsha 251*, 258
Ned 232, 316
Mrs. Ned (Lucy) viii
Rhonda 101, 288
Richard 258
Steve R. 319
Verlin 340
LOOKER, Josiah 67
Mrs. Josiah (Lydia E.) 67
LOSER, Mary 99, 100
LOUDON, Frank 337
Mrs. Frank (Opal) 337
LOUTHAIN, Carol 332
LOVELACE, Robert & Family 125
LOVELAND, George 115
Kate 53*
LOVELL, H. A. 339
LOWDEN, Frank 161
LOWE, Isey 102
Joseph F. 47
Paul S. 77, 93, 163
S. D. 58
Stephen 58
LOWERY, Mrs. Ben 198
Don 336
George 300
J. C. 67, 122, 302
Jesse 310
Lana 139*
Ruth 67
LOWRY, Rodney 336
LOWTHER, Everett 47
James 47

June H. 81, 82*, 93
LOY, Mrs. Charles (Blanche) 99, 100, 104, 198, 317, 337
Joe 302
Ruth 307
LUCAS, George 68
Larry 184
LUHMAN, William E. 99
LUPER, Fred 232, 237
LYBROOK, Dan 69, 83, 91, 131*, 145, 146, 161, 330
David 140*
Frank 69, 197, 237, 301, 313
Mrs. Frank (Ethel Hornbeck) viii, 109, 110, 198, 199
Joy 279
Neal 139*
LYNCH, Eva Overholser 109
Harve 322
LYON, Dorothy 116
Frank B. 345
Gene 335
LYONS, Dr. F. P. 55
Frank 51
Virginia viii, 193*, 194
William 273*, 274
LYTLE, Areline 115
W. T. 24

M

MABBITT, Margaret viii, 95, 102, 177, 241, 258, 330, 340
Pearl 162, 176
MaCURDY, Dale 318
Mrs. Dale (Nellie) viii, 329
Tom 346
MADISON, James 103
MAGGART, Patricia 129, 256
Ralph J. 29, 79*, 80*, 85, 86, 87*, 93, 116, 175, 185, 186*, 237, 262, 263, 279, 308
MAIER, Robert 323
MAIO, Delma P. 95
MANGES, Marvin 192
MANIS, Cecil 265
MANKER, O. P. 177
MANN, Bill 335
Mrs. Bill (Susan) 303*, 304, 335
MANNERING, Jerry 312
MANSFIELD, O. W. 71
MARCELLINO, Mrs. George 104
Mrs. 81*
Paul 232
Terri 109
Virginia 104
MARGOWSKI, Agnes J. 345
William S. 43, 44, 117
MARION, L. D. 50*
MARKLEY, Kathy 132
Sue 128, 131
MAROCCO, Clarence 320
Wm. 319
MARSH, Richard G. viii, 23
MARSHALL, Gail 329*

Jeffrey 329*
MARTIN, Charles Arthur 321
　Barbara 82, 126, 128, 131
　Bill 188
　Blanche Carmichael 109
　Carl 258
　Catherine 107
　Chas. F. 237
　Craig 147, 149, 185, 232, 302
　Mrs. Craig (Jeannie) 102, 137*, 138, 149, 185, 232
　David 126, 130
　Dawn 287
　Floyd 241
　Fred C. 175, 236, 237, 279, 308
　Mrs. Fred C. 198
　Fred W. 91, 133, 186, 188, 314
　Gardner 87, 176*, 186, 197, 234, 235, 236, 241, 243, 244, 310, 325
　Mrs. Gardner 198, 325
　Georganne 288
　George 241, 313, 325
　Hiram 241
　Dr. J. Holmes 211
　Jas. 348
　Jesse 57
　Jim 138
　Mrs. Jim (Mary) 138
　John 56, 321
　Jonathan 348
　Lois 246
　Margaret Lucy 243, 244
　Mark 233, 302
　Mrs. Mark (Gayle) 233
　Max 144
　Meta 97
　Miles T. ix, 84, 85, 88*, 89, 124, 131*, 162, 166*, 172*, 173*, 175*, 176, 189, 195, 197, 219, 231*, 235, 236, 237, 279, 282, 291, 292, 296, 306, 309, 310, 311*, 313*, 314, 315*, 322, 323, 325*, 328, 329
　Mrs. Miles T. (Ruby) ix, 95, 98, 99*, 103, 124, 162, 167, 168, 173*, 180, 195, 198, 231*, 248*, 256, 325*
　N. G. 58
　Nancy DuVall 135*
　Nellie Foust 108
　Paul 176
　Phil 125*, 130
　Robert 143, 144, 301
　Roy P. 77, 163, 165, 175, 197, 237
　Shawn 140*
　Thomas V. 62
　Turpie E. 118, 232, 237, 308
　Walter 197, 237
　Mrs. William (Peggy) 98, 99, 107
　Wm. 243, 348
MARTZ, Ernest 227*
MARVEL, William F. 153
MASON, Irene 317
　Jim 200

Mary 77, 82, 193, 195, 215, 345
MASTERSON, C. S. 240, 243
MATSON, Mrs. Leroy 106
MATTHEW, David L. 346
MATTHEWS, Harold 318
MAXWELL, Adelia 109, 110
　Bernadine 98
　Bill 327
　Charles 346
　Chester 237
　Mrs. Chester 198
　Cindy 82
　Clay 143
　David 128, 346
　Debra 123, 126, 128, 139*, 140*
　Florence Goslee 109
　Gene 143, 144, 291
　Mrs. Gene 138
　Harry F. 297, 300
　Harry R. 41, 45, 175, 197, 236, 237
　J. Dale 269, 283*, 295, 297
　Mrs. J. Dale (Anna) 199
　James 316
　Joe 327
　Mrs. John (Anna) 107
　Junior E. 325, 346
　Mrs. Junior E. (Betty) 55, 325, 346
　Laurel 335
　Leonard 292
　Moore H. 237
　Phil 148
　Mrs. Phil (Teresa) viii, 122, 148
　Robert 301
　Sam M. 75, 197, 237
　Sandy 83
　Terry 224*
　Mrs. Virgil 332
　W. F. 48
　William 138
　Zelda 107
MAYHILL, Bert B. 25, 26
　Mrs. B. B. (Dora Thomas) 3, 25, 47, 329, 344
　Noah E. 25, 26
　Mrs. Noah 44
　Roger ix, 25
　Thomas ix, 25, 26
MAYO, Henry 144
MAYS, Carl 133, 197, 199, 234*, 236, 308*
　Mrs. Carl (Joan) ix, 103, 138
　Janet 128
　Judy, 128, 258
　Mrs. Lawrence, Pearl 103
　Linda Jeanne 128, 130, 163, 184
　Mary Jo 128
　Roger 134
MEADE, Charles Jr. 119, 128, 130, 138
　Charles Sr. ix, 84, 102, 119, 120, 121, 138, 166*, 301*, 302
　Mrs. Charles Sr. ix
　Chris 134
　Monroe 181*, 191, 195, 196, 235, 236, 237
　Mrs. Monroe (Orpha) 106, 162, 175*, 176, 198, 317
　Patricia Ann 123*, 127, 128, 136*, 146
MEADOR, Leonard 341, 346
　Luke 312
MEARS, Dottie 233
　Elizabeth Ann 161, 168, 246, 247*, 248*, 253, 258
　George 184, 287
　Keith 248*, 258
　Mrs. Keith 248*, 329
　Kenneth 247*, 258
　Martin 170*
　Mary Helen 129, 131*, 253, 255*, 256*
　Richard 131*, 144, 246, 247*
　Mrs. Richard (Magdalene O'Farrell) ix, 82
MECHLING, E. J. 48
MEEK, Jill 83*
　Joyce 131*
　Thomas viii
MEEKER, Ivan 75
MEIKS, Scott 158, 165, 174
MELIN, Ralph 124*
MELLINGER, Gene 192
MELLON, Dennis 137*
MELTON, Mrs. George (Iva) 340
MENAUGH, Edna 103
MENTZER, Ignatious 6
MERCER, Lucille 58
　Woody 326
MEREDITH, Edwin T. 134
　Virginia C. 94
MERILLEE 30
MERSON, Linda 128
METSGER, Clark 232, 309
　Mrs. Clark 75, 99*, 181, 198
　Richard 313
　Treva 181
METSKER, J. A. 345
　Junior 113
METZ, Leam 298
METZGER, Agnes 98
　Ben 86, 195, 196, 237, 269, 296
　Mrs. Ben (Harriet) 175*, 176, 179*, 198
　Brian 138
　Cleo ix, 86*, 196, 227*, 232, 283*, 296, 297
　Dick 291*
　E. A. 237
　Edith 169*
　Elmer 319
　Emma 243
　G. E. 174
　Gene 219, 221
　Henry M. 237
　Herschel 237
　Lawrence 29, 196, 308, 309
　Linda 169*
　Lloyd 175*, 176, 191, 196, 227*
　Ruth 103
MEYER, W. R. 74
MEYERS, Deborah E. 287

Pamela 287
MICHAEL, Addison 54
　　Greg 122
　　Nancy 122
　　Robert 332
MIKESELL, Lloyd 308
　　Mrs. Paul (Joan) 105
MILBURN, Bruce 237
　　Mrs. Carl (Ina) 102
　　Henry 128
MILES, Tom 123
MILEY, Harry B. 197
MILLER, Beth 101
　　Calisse Renee 288
　　Dave E. 54
　　Mrs. Doyle (Marjorie) 95, 101, 105
　　Eddie C. 302
　　Esther P. 346
　　Flora 97
　　Glen 316
　　J. B. 122, 319
　　Jeffrey L. 287
　　John 325
　　Mrs. John 325
　　Judith 128, 169*
　　Kathy D. 184
　　Mrs. Kenneth 169*
　　Mrs. Lon 118
　　Marie 114
　　Paul 119*, 187, 241, 243
　　Phyllis 102
　　Stanley 169*
　　Webb 337
　　Mrs. Webb (JoAnn) 336, 337
　　Wilbur 332
MILLIKAN, Charles 330
MILLION, Artie 283*, 295, 308
　　Bert F. 237
　　C. B. 197, 215, 236, 237
　　C. L. 47, 57
　　Cecil S. 176
　　Clayton 29, 195, 196, 222, 223, 231, 235, 236, 244, 262, 295, 313
　　Mrs. Clayton (Esther) ix, 28, 123, 173*, 183, 185, 186*, 188, 195, 196, 197, 231
　　Douglas 181, 196, 235, 313
　　Herbert ix, 197, 236, 237, 306
　　John 56, 116
　　Lucille 134, 183, 250
　　Melvin 292
　　Pat 57
　　Mrs. Pat (June) ix, 83
　　Paul 237, 323
　　Perry 116, 166*, 231
　　Mrs. Perry 231
　　Robert H. 237
　　Mrs. R. H. (Dene) 98, 101
　　Robert R. 56, 329
　　Mrs. Robert R. (LaVaune) ix, 331
　　W. G. 59, 163, 164*, 175*, 176, 197, 236, 237, 329
　　Mrs. W. G. 106
　　Wm. A. 238
MILLS, Dean ix, 29, 236

Mrs. Dean (Ruth) ix
Deborah Ann 184, 287
Lois Denise 288
Marsha Lou 287
Richard T. Jr. 272, 294, 297
Robert D. ix, 187, 267, 295, 296*, 297, 316, 317, 337
Mrs. Robert D. (Dorothy Newell) ix, 88, 329, 333, 337
Steve ix, 147, 336
W. O. "Brick" 87
MILNER, Mrs. Richard 138
MILROY, Charles E. 331, 345
　　Elmira 347
　　Frances 347
　　Harry C. 19, 26, 44, 45, 46, 341, 345
　　Henry B. 25
　　John 347
　　Margaret 347
　　Mollie 19
　　Maj. Gen. Robert Huston 347
　　Gen. Samuel 50*, 329, 347
MINICH, David A. 149, 232, 233, 314
　　Mrs. David (Marilyn) 149, 232, 233
　　J. Ernest 188, 234*, 235, 236
　　Mrs. J. Ernest 102
　　Mrs. James E. 101
MINNEMAN, Dianne 127
MINNICUS, Ann Cecelia 287
MINNIX, Charles 319
　　Kathryn 55
MITCHELL, Alonzo 51
　　Florence 104
　　Goldie 99
　　Jim 314
　　Leslie 321
　　Samuel 55, 56
　　Mrs. Walter 104
MITTY, Jacob 3
MOCHERMAN, Carl 148
　　Mrs. Lloyd 104
　　Mrs. Russell (Pearl) 54*, 55
MODLIN, Mrs. Harry (Gertrude C.) 152, 161
MOHER, Samuel 316
MOHLER, Bobby 147
　　John 322
MOHR, Nathaniel 259
MOLTER, Sam 214
MONNETT, Earl 316
MONROE, James 2
MONTAGE, Betty M. 346
MONTGOMERY, C. W. 76
　　Charles 197
　　Edward 50
　　Joe 51
　　Mrs. Kent (Sharon) 125, 138
MOON, Hollys 153, 165
MOORE, A. D. 196, 235
　　Mrs. Albert 197
　　C. S. 151
　　Charles 291, 332
　　Charles W. 44
　　Don R. 318, 346

Mrs. Don R. (Phyllis) ix, 318, 341, 342*, 344, 346
Doyle 54
Emily Jane 287
Gary Gene 346
Ira 45, 165
Jerri 141*
Robert 20
T. W. 57
MOREHOUSE, Dave 192, 197
MORGAN, Doit 214
　　Lowell 179
　　Marsha 288
MORKERT, Elias 348
MORRICAL, Eva 114
MORRIS, Rev. E. E. 120
　　Peter 124
　　Rachel 129
MORRISON, Lewis 184
　　Rose 108
　　W. K. 50*
　　Wm. 146
MORROW, Louise ix, 230*
　　Robert D. 346
MOSES, Terry 326
MOSS, Alfred L. viii, ix, 26, 27, 185, 318, 337
　　Mrs. Alfred L. (Joan) 26, 27
　　Ashwell Lynn 27, 319
　　Barbara 126, 127, 128, 131, 163
　　Beaulah 114
　　C. I. 196
　　Edmund 339
　　F. A. 26, 27
　　Frank 47
　　J. J. 75
　　Jack ix, 119*, 147, 234*, 235
　　James J. 47, 54
　　Jeffrey 126, 127, 128, 130, 131, 184
　　Jerry 125*, 126, 127, 128, 130, 132
　　John 126, 127, 128, 131, 132, 134, 163, 184
　　Walter 113
MOUNT, Haughey D. 45, 119, 323
　　John H. 44, 118
　　Mrs. John 345
MOURER, Charles L. 75, 126, 284
　　John H. 60, 238, 340*, 345
　　Marion 182
MOYER, Betty 180
　　Jeanne Bailey 26
　　John 225
　　Marion 346
MUEHL, Miss 74
MUELLER, Dave 283
MULLENDORE, Bernice 108
　　John 37
　　Nelson 47
　　Thurlow 322
MULLER, A. D. 276
　　Jeanne 81*, 93, 96*, 129, 131
MULLIN, Arthur R. ix, 86, 174, 195, 214*, 223*, 236, 238, 262, 263, 305
　　Mrs. Arthur (Mary) 98, 197, 198

INDEX OF NAMES

Bill 56
C. R. 238
Clayton 143, 148
David 244
Diane 130, 131
Donald 183, 191, 197, 226, 244
Estal ix, 195, 234, 235, 236, 330
Mrs. Estal (Mabel) ix, 169, 198
Frank 56, 58, 120, 309, 310
Geraldine 248°
Herman C. 238
Dr. H. G. 329
John 143
Lewis N. ix, 91, 186, 187, 188, 272°, 273, 314, 329, 337, 343
Mrs. Lewis N. (Hazel) ix, 95, 96, 109, 183, 337
Mabel Jayne 176, 330
Merlin 187, 197
Opal 198, 244, 258
Roscoe 298
Wayne 314
William 58, 295, 296°
Wm. O. 238
MUMM, W. J. 312
MUMMERT, Mrs. Charles ix, 106, 198
Charles J. 346
Mrs. Charles J. 346
Gertrude 345
Harley A. 238
James 146
Lewis 323
Ricky Bill 287
W. F. 345
MUNDELL, Richard 148
MUNSON, Robert 115
MURDOCK, William 33
MURPHY, Billy D. 346
Mrs. Charles 45, 343, 344
Elizabeth Fisher 329, 345
M. M. 19, 20
Mrs. M. M. 19, 20
MURRAY, Dorothy 92
Ken 122
Kenneth viii, 159
MUSSELMAN, David L. 41, 60
Mrs. Fren 329, 346
Glen I. 238
John 348
MYER, Bill 323
Dana 258
Donnabell 105
Dorothy 55
Edith 244
Helen 114
Kenneth H. 197
Mrs. Kenneth H. 198
L. V. 318, 319
Mrs. Otis 104
Ronald 128
Royce 238, 314
Terry L. 236
Vern 20, 314
MYERS, A. Ray 91, 292
Bill 254°
Bob 254°

Mrs. Charles 108
Don 321
Dorothy O. 108°, 273°, 274
Elsie G. Overley ix, 82, 318
Emma 23, 24
Fred 75
George 225
Homer 114, 346
Mrs. Homer 346
Jerry 232
Joe 232
Mrs. John 198
Marion 108
Pat 254°
Shelia 122
McALHANEY, Betsy 24
McANINCH, John 287
McCAFFERTY, Ed 214
McCAIN, Adriene 320
Bert 196, 235, 237, 308
Bob 120, 177°, 291°
Carl 282
Charles P. 342°, 343, 346
Curtis 298
Daniel 36, 124°
David 125°
Dean 197, 320
Don 119, 169°
Mrs. D. J. 102
Fred L. ix, 98, 124, 185, 241, 337
Mrs. Fred L. (Iris) ix, 95, 98, 102, 124, 183, 185, 337
George 329
Iona 23, 24
J. Reed 345
Jesse 196, 215, 235, 237, 284, 329
Joe 128, 130
John ix, 57, 178, 241, 346
Mrs. John 346
Laura V. 345
Magdalena 36
Marilyn 128, 130, 161, 169°
Richard ix, 254°, 302, 337
Mrs. Richard (Joan) ix, 308, 316, 337
Richard Leslie 169°
Robert 235, 249°, 250°, 252, 253, 254°, 256°, 258
Roll 237
Susan 169°
Tom 317, 327
Mrs. Tom 317, 318
McCARTY, Bob 232
Carl K. 75
Donna ix, 100
Garland 85, 196, 293
Mrs. Garland 180, 293
Gary 132
Gene 138, 228
Harry 85
Howard 80°, 93, 128°, 129°, 131°, 138, 246, 309, 310, 311°
Mrs. Howard (Nadine) 108°, 128°, 129°
J. M. 26, 48

Jack 148
Jesse 305
Lenore 180, 195
Mary 293
Norma 258
Robert 197, 309, 314
Rush 197, 308
Mrs. Rush 198
McCLEAN, James 144
McCLINTIC, Virgil 332
McCLOSKEY, Charles V. 56, 330
Mrs. Charles 102
Daniel M. 56
Delbert 298
D. V. 74
John J. 178°
Willard 324
McCOMBS, Nina 255°
Sharon 255°
McCORKLE, Hugh 323
McCORMICK, Belle 109
Betty 330
Eric 16, 170°
George 19
Harold 25, 192
John B. ix, 16, 29, 86°, 87, 91, 173°, 175, 197, 231°, 232, 234, 235, 236, 301°, 312, 313, 315°, 321
Mrs. John B. (Mary) ix, 231, 329
Loren 301
Maggie 140°
Susan 170°
Thomas 329
McCOUCH, Agnes C. 67
Dennis ix, 67, 69, 70, 318, 334, 337, 341, 342°, 346
John R. 237
Mrs. John 68, 198
Ray 41
McCOY, Charles 80°, 93
Fred 322
McCRACKEN, Charles A. 51, 237
Mark ix, 55°
McCRAY, Gov. Warren T. 153
McDANIELS, J. 148
McDOWELL, Arthur ix, 26, 185, 186, 188, 287, 329
George 333
McELROY, John 347
McFARLAND, E. A. 57
John Wm. 76, 93, 113
McFATRIDGE, Carol 194, 195
Jim 227
Lewis 119
Virgil 197, 241
McGAUGHEY, Leon 147
McGILL, Howard 336
John 119, 323
Kenneth M. 24, 346
Kris Shriver 123, 304°, 305
McGREEVEY, C. J. 19
M. J. 58
McGRUFF, Charles 47
McHARDIE, Hansel 297
McILRATH, Dewey 148
Doyal 136°, 148

Earl 314
George 232
Jane Ann 130, 131
Randy 147
Wilma 131°
McKAIN, A. A. 19
McKAY, Hilda 198
McKEE, Mrs. Jim (Reneé Krieg) ix, 83, 136
John G. 305
McKINLEY, Brenda 136°, 258
Emerson 336
Helen 97
Mrs. Mills (Vella) 55
McKINNEY, Barb 109
Flora Bell 104
Harold 147
Mrs. Harold 81°
Lawrence 311
McKNIGHT, Virginia 346
McLELAND, Mrs. James 199
McMAHAN, Bertia 67
McMANUS Family 122
John 310, 313
Mrs. John (Leone) 101
McMURRAY, Kaye 331
McNEAL, Dr. 53
McPHERSON, Cleo 317
Mrs. Fred 104, 317
McQUEEN, Ruben 346
Mrs. Ruben 342, 346
McREYNOLDS, F. L. 244
McVAY, Curt 288
Del 75
Mrs. Del 75
Leda 241
Sam 76
Wm. 237
McMULLIN, Guy 151
McNUTT, Paul V. 176

N

NAGELE, Mrs. Gray (Alta) 99, 100
NANCE, Charles 190, 236, 243, 258, 301°
Marilyn 119
Robert 233
NAYLOR, Charles A. 25
NEED, David 147
Jim 147
NEEDLER, J. F. 19
NEELEY, Crafton 252
NEFF, Dayton 291°
James A. 47, 345
James L. 47
Roger 291°, 313, 332
Mrs. Roger 332
Mrs. Walter 329
NEIBEL, Joseph 75
NELSON, Alfred P. 80, 93
Ed 119°
Mrs. Ed 96°, 102
Ira 56
NEPTUNE, James 330
Jan 340
NEUENSCHWANDER, Donna 169°

Lucille 81°
Robert 258
NEWBY, Marilyn 129°
NEWCOMES, Dr. 340°
NEWELL, Dorothy 194, 279
Earl B. 78, 86°, 87, 88°, 144, 162°, 165, 176, 196, 235, 238, 308, 310
Mrs. Earl (Maude) 107, 108, 162°, 198, 329
H. E. 76
H. E. & Son 86
Kenneth 87, 144
Mrs. Kenneth (Marjorie) 108°, 194, 198, 333
Mary Ann 82, 170°
Richard 170°
NEWER, A. A. 44, 56, 74, 165, 174, 176, 184, 197, 236, 238, 300, 330
Urban 241
NEWHOUSER, Frances 100
Mrs. Roy 180
NEWMAN, Earl 238
Fred 143, 144, 301
Harold 243
John 37
NICEWANDER, Florence 56
NICHOLS, Steve ix, 20, 80, 81°, 83°, 93, 119°, 302
NICHTER, A. M. 86°
John 238
Hilary 115
NICKELSBURG, David 232
Mrs. David 232
NICOLL, Raymond ix, 291°, 309, 310, 311, 312, 313, 314, 315°
Mrs. Raymond (Cecile) ix, 76, 99°, 138, 173°, 196, 198, 231, 232, 235, 332°
NIEWERTH, Louis 13
Wm. 318
NIMMINS, W. J. 55, 67
Mrs. W. J. (Laura) 67
Wm. 75
NIMMIUR, Richard M. 48
NIPPLE, John 50°
Ronald 223
NOBES, Charles E. 27, 54
NOBLE, Dennis ix
NOONKESTER, Dale 194
NORRIS, Joyce 273
Ruth A. 288
Mrs. Wayne 56
NORTHCUTT, Mrs. Bill 102
Charles 47, 319
George 319
NORTON, Catherine 114
NULF, Ralph 274

O

OAKS, Mrs. Dave 108
Harold 113
John 317, 319
OBEAR, George W. 318, 329, 346

James O. 23
Mrs. James 331
OBERKROM, Floyd W. 56, 57
O'BRIAN, Patrick H. 26
ODELL, James C. 17, 26, 42, 329
John 348
John C. 329, 340°, 341, 344, 348
Mrs. John C. 345
Josephine 345
Otto 75
O'DELL, Pauline 198
O'DONNELL, Charles 236, 238
Mary 104
Pat 331
Patrick J. 314
O'FARRELL, Kathleen A. 288
Marilyn 273
Mark 130, 140
Mike 161
Paul 140°
Mrs. Paul (Carol) 140°
Rita 131, 136, 140°
Tara 139°, 141°
OGG, Mrs. R. A. 108
OGLE, Charles 335
O'HARA, Pat 146, 252
OHLER, P. C. 158
OILAR, Dick 319
Ed 149
Mrs. Ed (Marsha) 149
Glenda 109
Michelle 134, 139°
Richard 119°, 139°
OLIVER, Ed 31
Mary Farner 330
OLSON, Erving 323
Pete 117
OMAHT, Julia 346
O'NEAL, Edward A. 168, 174, 201, 261
ONYMOUS, A. N. 30
OREM, Dale 147, 288
Kenneth 83, 128, 130, 136°, 148
Mrs. Kenneth 130
ORR, Forrest 45
Jack 219
Ray ix
OSCAR the Office Boy 29°
OTTEN, Henry 238
OUSLEY, Mrs. Roy L. 102
OVERHOLSER, Carl 196
Dean ix, 27, 318, 329
Mrs. Dean (Donna) ix, 27
Gary 225
Joel 49
Mrs. Ralph 198
Rex 121°, 287
Robert 232
Terry 130
OVERHOLT, Sam 232
OVERLEY, Bob 219
OYLER, Atlee 233, 234°, 236, 302
Mrs. Atlee (Doris) 233
Carey 113, 323
Earl 340
Ed 302, 336

G. 323
Glenda 100
John H. 47
Mrs. Paul 99*, 100*
Russell 113
Mrs. Russell 99*, 100*

P

PACE, Stephen 278
PAGE, Lucinda Marie 287
    T. E. 76
    Thomas 292
PALMER, Edwin C. 240
PAPET, Phil 207
PARKE, Benjamin 334
PARKER, Elsie 99*
    Mrs. Wilma 99*
PARKS, Miriam 331
PARR, Charles 33
PARRETT, Mrs. Walter 171*, 198
PASTOR, Mary 329
PATCHETT, Mr. 147
PATRICK, Dr. 31
PATTERSON, Charles 323
PATTON, Grace Latshaw 109
PATTY, Claude 320
    Deborah 288
    Edith 106
    Jody 105
    Martha 54*
    R. F. 310
    Mrs. Robert 55
    Teresa 288
PAULEY, Mary Ellen Kempf 194*, 195
PAYNE, Bill G. 318
    Clarence 319
    Mrs. Clarence 104
    Vernon 316
PAYTON, D. I. 238
PEACOCK, Chester 146
    Harold 227
PEARSON, Bill 16, 121*, 321
    Buford 341, 346
    C. Clay 44, 45, 345
    Carolyn 343
    Charles 100*, 295, 296*, 297, 308, 337
    Mrs. Charles (Marjorie) 337
    Cora Belle 243, 244, 258
    Eva Lu 182
    J. S. 67
    Jay 232
    John 49
    John A. 238
    Lou Ann 128, 131
    Mike 223*
    Ralph 319
    Robert ix, 67, 69
    Mrs. Robert (Ethel) 67, 103
    Russell E. 166*, 196, 283*, 295, 310, 316
    Mrs. Russell E. (Margaret) 105, 198
    Sanford 170*
    W. V. 24
    Walter 330
    Wayne 15, 16, 321, 346
    Mrs. Wayne 346
    Wm. 322
PEASE, Marion 252
PEEK, Bill 137*
    Charles E. ix, 54
PENN, Bill 332
    Gary 148, 233, 309*, 320
    Mrs. Gary (Jane) 105, 233, 345*
    Jay 323
    Larry 148
    Mrs. Raymond 332
    Roselyn 55
    Ross R. II 14
PENNINGTON, Vonda 193*, 194
PERDUE, Jim 275
    Linda, 24, 194
PERIGO, Lon 117
PERRY, Fred 329
PETER, Berdena 187
    Darilee 128, 258
    Dr. E. L. 55, 318
    Henry R. 238
    Melinda 288
PETERS, Carl 146
    Edith 98
    Jack 144, 145
    Lynn 232
    Mrs. Lynn 232
    Orton 56
PETERSON, Albert E. 31, 47
    Bill 146, 244
    Carolyn 127, 128, 130, 131, 170*, 327
    Cindy 137*
    Clyde 291*
    David L. ix, 125*, 126*, 127, 128, 130, 170*, 327
    Dean 232
    Donald 170*
    George W. 177, 196, 215, 217, 235, 238, 297
    Mrs. George W. (Norma) ix, 16, 96*, 101, 180, 197
    Dr. J. B. 312
    Jas. V. 238
    John C. 83*, 84, 86*, 91, 116, 117, 119, 172*, 173*, 178, 185, 186, 188, 190, 195, 196, 218*, 219, 231*, 232, 235, 236, 240, 241, 243, 244, 256, 257, 262, 266, 269, 282, 295*, 296, 297, 302, 309, 310, 318, 327, 329, 330, 332, 333, 341, 346
    Mrs. John C. (Doris) 108, 119*, 137*, 138*, 172*, 199, 231*, 256, 327, 330, 341, 342*, 346
    Joseph E. ix, 29, 86*, 87, 88*, 116, 172*, 178, 184, 196, 199, 219*, 225*, 231*, 232, 234, 235, 241, 243, 244, 318, 323, 328, 332, 346
    Mrs. Joseph E. (Elizabeth) ix, 95, 103, 107, 198, 219*, 231*, 318, 346
    Lois 124*
    Mark 134
    Mrs. Norman Jr. (Marjorie) 54*, 55*
    Ray 301*
    Robert 128, 302, 311, 316
    Stephen 124*, 125*, 130, 170*, 327
    T. O. 238
    Mrs. T. O. 197
    Virginia 126, 127, 128, 130, 131, 170*
    Wm. F. 219, 238, 344
    Wm. F. & Sons 86
PETRIE, Pat Todd 122
PETRY, T. Neal, M.D. 21, 22
    Tom 184
PETTINER, W. O. ix, 57, 58, 119
PFENDLER, Dean D. C. 88
PFINGSTEN, E. 316
PHILLIPS, Charles J. 67, 238
    George 58
    Mrs. John 332
    Marvin 312
    Saide 67
    W. H. 47
PHILLIPY, Nettie Lou 337
PIATT, Rhonda M. 238
PICKART, Bill 122, 149, 302
    Mrs. Bill (Jodi) 149
    J. V. 302
    Sally 233
PICKENS, Jim 283
PICKETT, Bob 123
PIERCE, Alma 98
    Harry 314*
    James 75, 143, 144, 301
PINKERTON, Von O. 28
PITMAN, W. W. 67
PITTENGER, L. A. 152
PITZER, Lawrence 321
PIXEY, Vic 15
PLANK, Donnabelle 125*, 128, 332
    Harry 56
    Helen 240*, 241, 243
    Jesse 57
    Noah 58
    Olive 98
    Percy 238
    Mrs. Robert L. ix
    Susan Kay 288
    Truman 84*, 86*, 87*, 133, 180, 236, 241, 257
    Mrs. Truman (Genevieve) ix, 99*, 180, 186
PLATT, Dwight 323
    Moses E. 36
    Mr. 36
    Ora 75, 323
    Otto 176, 238
PLETCHER, L. M. 46, 323
POLK, W. V. 74
POLLARD, C. R. 26
    John A. 47
    Kathleen 82
    Robert C. 43

POPE, Alice 103
POPEJOY, George 31, 46
    Jack 31
    Julie 308
    Roberta 273
PORTER, Adam 348
    Agnes 330
    David 170*
    Dennis 236, 283*, 296, 297*
    Emma 58
    Florence 103
    Joe 170*
    Marilyn 170*, 249
    Mark ix, 195, 197, 236, 329, 332
    Mrs. Mark (Charlene) ix, 170*, 198
    Marta 128, 249
    Pat Toole 82
    Phyllis 69
    Richard 129
    Thomas 330
    Mrs. Tom 198
    Victor J. 323
FOWELL, Betty 346
    C. R. 335
    Earl T. ix, 235, 241, 243, 258, 310
    Lenna 297
    Leroy 221
    Lois 131*
POWERS, Mary M. Thompson ix, 81, 93
POWLEN, Jim 119
    Patrick 314, 315*, 337
    Mrs. Patrick 337
POWNELL, Frank 75
    Mrs. Frank 75
    Larry 321
PRAFKA, Shirley 21
PRATT, Hon. D.D. 12
PRICE, David 331
    Mrs. David 331
    Harold 322, 323
    John 192
    Leo 274
    Walter 174
PRINCESS Silver Heels 116
PRITCHARD, Mrs. Jack A. (Evelyn) 198, 346
PRITCHETT, Crystal 245
PROCTOR, Robert G. viii
PRUITT, E. E. 45
PRYOR, Horace 138
PULLEN, Bert 238
    Mrs. Bert 75
    Don 332
    Duane 128
    Dwight 128
    Mrs. Elver 198
    Frances 105
    Mrs. Harold (Eileen) 102
    Joyce 122
    Maxine 170*
    Patsy 161, 249*, 256*, 258, 311*
    Robert H. 197, 287, 313, 327
    Mrs. Robert (Mary) 198

Rose 105
PULLEY, Richard ix, 147, 227, 228*, 232
    Mrs. Richard 232
PUNCHE, Mary 316
PURDUE, Beverly Ann 273
    Calvin 75
    John 71
PURKHIZER, Don 148
PURNELL, Hon. Fred 174
PYLE, Kenneth 89, 248*, 253*, 256*, 311*, 314, 346
    Mrs. Kenneth (Julie) 253*, 256*

Q

QUICK, Paul 45, 117
    Roscoe 67, 145*, 197, 309
    Mrs. Roscoe (Zelpha) 67, 310
QUINN, Mrs. C. V. (Mary) 95, 167, 195, 238
    Gary 251
    Georgia Loy 317, 346
    Mrs. Harry 108
    Mrs. Jasper 102
    Kenneth 115
    Nell 24, 25
    Rebecca Jane 131*
    Richard 311*
    Mrs. Robert (Lucile) ix, 95, 96*, 108*
    Stanley R. 274*
    Thelma 273

R

RABER, Carl 222
    Charles 57
RADABAUGH, Walter 47
RADERSTORF, Jim 146
RAGAN, Bruce ix, 82, 83*, 93, 138
RAINBOLT, Richard 25
RALSTON, J. C. 112
    Ray 232
    Mrs. Ray 232
    Wilber 45
RAMEY, John 297
RAMSEY, Don 83
    Mrs. Don (Marlene) 103
    Susan 128
RANCATORE, Jean 100
RANDLE, Aaron 67
    Mrs. Aaron (Elva) 67, 108*
    Sherrie ix
RANDOL, Rick 54
RANDOLPH, Mrs. Robert (Betty) 138*
RANKIN, A. M. 57
RATCLIFF, Jack 291*
    Robert 327
    Mrs. Robert (Mary) 96*, 108, 327
    Virginia 273
RATHBONE, Sam 51
RAY, James B. 11
    Leon 113

Philip 348
Robert 59
RAZLER, Hazel 114
REAGAN, John P. 305, 306
    Ralph 46, 162, 166*, 178*, 191*, 192, 197, 231*, 279, 296
    Mrs. Ralph (Lois) ix, 162, 231*
    W. H. 339
RECHER, Rev. Richard 25, 345*
REDDING, Benny J. ix, 147, 314, 315*
    C. S. 76
    Elmo 324, 325
    Forrest J. ix, 197, 231, 298
    Mrs. Forrest J. (Florence) ix, 106, 198
    Freeman 241
    Mrs. Freeman 241
    Mark 138
    Rebecca Ann 287
    Tim 134, 147
    Z. A. 50*
RED ELK, Ken 343
REDENBACHER, Frank 47, 118, 196, 215, 235, 238
REDMON, Bill 170*, 250
    Frances 256*
    Joe 319
REED, Agnes ix, 220*
    Darla Kay 288
    Douglas 288
    Grover 332
    Harry E. 45, 67, 270
    Harry James 72
    Mrs. James 107
REEDER, James J. 38
    John 174, 308
REEDY, C. L. 291*
REEF, Don 148
    Geneva 98
    Jerry 148
    Richard 228*
    Mrs. Robert 99*
REEL, Richard 137*
REESE, John 232
REIFF, Bill 123, 137*
    Blanche 101
    Elmer & Son 86
    Elmer G. 238, 262, 266, 267*, 269, 292, 295, 297, 306, 308, 310
    J. W. 74
    John 309*
    Robert ix, 172*, 241, 243, 258, 308, 316
    Teri Diane 184, 288
REIFFEL, Robert 335
    Mrs. Robert (Karen) 335
REIST, Charles 318
REMALY, Claude 176, 196, 231, 343
    Mrs. Claude 231
    Eddie 169*
    Wayne 169*
RENSHAW, Bill 320
REPLOGLE, Earl 319
    Peter 348

INDEX OF NAMES

Ralph 313
  Wayne 131*, 332
REPPERT, John 20
  Katheryne 114
  Lee E. ix, 236, 346
  Mrs. Lee E. ix, 346
RESER, Ted 341
REVILS, Kathy 340
RETHERFORD, C. 55
REVINGTON, George 291
REX, Marjorie 273
REYNOLDS, E. E. 151
  Mildred 99*
RHINE, John 332
  Mary 340
  May 99*
  Sam 125*
RICE, B. M. 238
  Bennie 48
  Charles 51
  E. C. 53, 348
  Geneva 116
  Hazel 116
  John 331
  Nettie 24
  Thelma 116
RICHARDSON, Barbara 169, 198
  Beverly 331
  Gordon 75
  Ron 254*
  Vicki 185
  Wilbur 222
RICHOLSON, O. I. 305
RICHTER, Bonnie 105
  Roy 175*, 176, 191, 197, 238, 301*, 302
RICKETTS, Victor L. 25
RIDER, Everett 332
  Jeff 132
  Keith 221, 227*, 313
  Mrs. Leo (Clara) 83
  Paul 134
  V. D. 319
REIFFEL, Mrs. Robert (Karen) 24
RIEGEL, Kay Shriver 122
RIGGLE, Owen 259
  K. L. 58
RILEY, Frank 47, 75, 118, 119
  James D. 44, 48
  James Jr. 232, 233
  Mrs. James Jr. 232
  James W. Sr. 120, 195, 197, 236, 302
  Mrs. James W. Sr. (Mary) ix
  W. F. 68, 238
  Mrs. W. F. 198
RINEHART, Adeline 331
  C. R. 238
  Deloris 246
  Dick 119
  Henry 55
  Isabelle 23, 24
  J. R. 122, 302, 303*, 304, 335, 340
  Mrs. J. R. 335
  Martin 122, 128, 129, 130, 233, 336
  Mrs. Murtie 99*

Ralph 75, 85, 121, 122, 166, 190, 191, 196, 197, 297, 324
Mrs. Ralph (Nina) ix, 198
Mrs. Richard 107
RINGER, Bob 223*
  Opal 25
  Raymond 197
  Mrs. Raymond 198
  Walter ix, 117, 236, 238, 282, 295
  Mrs. Walter ix
RINKER, Philip 339
RITCHEY, Arthur 197, 215, 217, 221, 236, 238, 329
  Eli 196, 236, 297
  Mrs. Joyce 140*
RITCHHART, Martha "Susie" 240*, 243
RITCHIE, Laurie 194
RITZLER, Charles ix, 91, 312
ROACH, Bill 131*, 144, 145, 282*
  Dick 292
  Don 291
  George 44
  Levina 345
  Mrs. Melvin 198
  Mr. 36
ROBBINS, Don 146
  Mrs. Don (Darilee Peter) ix, 82, 318
  Harry 274
  Robert 258
  Mrs. Robert (Pat) 196
ROBERSON Bros. 238
  Ira E. 298
  Mrs. I. E. 198
  Marjorie Shanks ix
  Myna Ruth 198
ROBERTS, Earl 165, 185
ROBERTSON, Donald 292
  Eddie 170*
  Elaine 170*
  Merle Henderson 109
  Myna 180
  Ray ix, 126, 127, 191, 192, 195, 196, 244, 258
  Mrs. Ray (Rosella) 170*, 198
  Roy 125
ROBESON, Annalea 134
  Dottye 109
  Eldon D. ix, 84, 86*, 87*, 120, 161, 168, 181, 197, 199, 234, 235, 236, 244, 246, 248*, 249*, 250*, 252, 253, 256*, 257, 258, 302
  Mrs. Eldon (Wilma) ix, 98, 104, 169, 199
  Ellen Louise 243, 244, 258
  Ira 236
  Kevin L. 132, 184
  Leroy Jr. ix
  Mrs. Leroy Jr. (Charlene) ix, 110
  Leroy Sr. ix, 29, 47, 56, 86*, 87, 119, 120, 191, 197, 231*, 232, 236, 238, 330
  Nina 56

Pauline ix, 27, 95, 110, 181, 182, 185, 188, 199, 231*, 241, 244, 257, 329
Webb 86, 88, 174, 197, 238, 262, 266, 295, 297
ROBINSON, Abner 35
  Dr. Frank H. 23, 340*, 345
  Mrs. Frank H. 340*, 345
  Henry 35, 36, 347
  Joe 146
  John 332
  Lydia Ann 35
  Millard 324
  Sarah B. 35
  Sylvester ix, 163, 164*, 197
  Mrs. Sylvester ix
  Thomas 38, 57
  W. H. 50*, 345
  Mrs. W. H. 345
  W. L. 65
  Wilma 338
ROBISON, Lenard 346
  Plato 47
ROBLYER, John 319
ROCKWOOD, Jon 253, 341, 346
ROCKY, R. E. 336
RODENBARGER, Artus 29, 162, 175*, 176, 191, 195, 197, 215, 231, 232, 234, 235, 236, 238, 262, 269, 295, 296, 305
  Mrs. Artus (Mabel) 162, 198, 231
  Barbara 243, 258
  Joan 174, 244
RODGERS, Helen 161
  James 323
  Janet 141*
  Mrs. John 101
  Milton 138
  Mrs. Milton (Pat) 98, 138
  Mrs. Pete 101
  Robert 19, 254*
RODKEY, Dale 38
  Earl 330, 340
  Edith 340
  Fred E. 29, 196, 231, 232, 235, 282, 316, 346
  Mrs. Fred E. (Beth) ix, 99*, 100, 102, 198, 231
  Ladene 181
  Robert 181, 258
  Rod 254*
  Russell 38
  Samuel O. 330
ROGERS, Joan 83*, 92
ROHRABAUGH, A. A. 50*
  Bob 227*
  Earnest 144
  H. S. 50*
  Josephine E. 68
  Oscar 346
  Mrs. Oscar 346
  Ralph 91, 227
ROHRER, Diana 82, 93
ROLL, Lionel 241
ROMEIN, Raymond 130, 179, 333, 334*

Mrs. Raymond (Donna) 123, 130, 199
ROOSEVELT, Franklin D. 261, 278
ROSENBARGER, I. A. 48
ROSKUSKI, Charles 117
    Douglas 274
    Frank 238
    Fred 122
ROSS, Mrs. Charles 198
    Eric 346
    Kevin 346
    Mrs. Kevin (Kay Walton) 137*, 138
    Mrs. Luther 108
    Robert 234*, 236, 319
ROTH, Amanda 335
    Don 120, 274
    Mrs. Don (Sandra Cook) 273
    Gladys 106
    Harrison D. 238
    James 322
    John T. 69, 291*
    Mrs. John (Helen) 100*, 108
ROTHENBARGER, Jay 301
    Neva 333
    Wm. 302
ROULS, Janalyce 98
ROWE, Mrs. John 198
ROYCE, Hal 213
ROZHON, Henry 91
RUDD, Tony 147
    Mrs. Luther 108
RUEGAMER, Dana 125*
    Gladys 131*
RUEGER, Mrs. Raymond 106
RUFFING, Edwin 267
    Fannie E. 282
    Joseph E. 43
RULE, Hubert 147
    James Perry 331
    Perry 47, 57, 68, 74, 75, 77, 114, 163, 174, 195, 238
    Mrs. Perry 298, 331
    Riley Paul 331
    Wayne 143
    Whitcomb Golden 114, 331
RUMAN, Lewis 128
RUMBLEY, Jack 327
RUNYAN, William 330
    L. K. 9
RUPE, Mrs. Nelson 151
RUSH, B. F. 47, 238
    Ray 75, 238
    Sue 124*, 136*
RUSSELL, Arden 146

S

SACHA, John 274
SALES, Donna 122
    Louise 54
SAMPLE, Glenn W. 88*, 153, 162
    T. M. 94
SANDERSON, Betty Jane 331
    Charles 29, 162, 166*, 173*, 197, 236, 238
    Mrs. Charles 162

Dean 321
Mrs. Dean (Joyce) 138
Dee 126, 128, 132, 136, 138, 141*
Evan 118, 162, 177*, 196, 238, 246, 323, 324
Mrs. Evan 162
Frances 181
Mrs. Frank 44
Geo. C. 348
Jan 340
Lisa 132
Lucile 116
Lulu J. 298
Martha 320
Robert 116
Thomas 115, 320
Virginia 331
SARGENT, Charles 188
SCAGNOLI, Loretta Leazenby 123
SCALES, O. L. 44
SCHAKEL, Wilber M. 153
SCHEFFEE, Mrs. Robert (Lavonne) 342, 343*
SCHENK, Hassil E. 152, 162, 176, 189, 213, 281, 302
    William 337
    Mrs. William (Hazel) 337, 340
SCHERER, J. J. 264, 265
SCHERMERHORN,, Dr. 318
    Reed 329
SCHIELE, Carolyn ix, 109
SCHILLING, Julia 53*
SCHMALTZ, Jan 287
SCHMITTER, Bernard 143
    Carol 170*
    Robert 144
SCHNEPF, Fritz Jr. 126, 132, 134, 146
    Fritz G. Sr. ix, 84, 86, 119, 120, 133*, 173*, 176, 195, 197, 232, 291, 302
    Mrs. Fritz G. Sr. (Esther) ix, 171*, 198, 302
    Marjorie Ann 82, 126, 128*, 129, 134, 146
    Martha 127, 128, 130, 146
    Mary Lou 128
SCHNEPP, Charles E. 45, 47, 298
    P. E. 50*
    Robert 143
    T. W. 74
    Wm. 143, 144
SCHOCK, Billy Jr. 169*
    Glen M. 238
    Judith 273
    Lorene 116
    Lucile 116
    Margaret 320
    Orvel C. 100*, 162, 177, 196, 238
    Mrs. Orvel C. 162
    Robert ix, 224*, 225, 232, 320
    Mrs. Robert (Shirley) ix, 25, 232, 345*
    Wilmer (Bill) 320
SCHOCKLEY, W. T. 238
SCHOFF, Chris 144

Wm. 301
SCHOLL, Harold 312
    Mrs. 75
    Susan 27
SCHRICKER, Gov. Henry F. 99, 168, 331
SCHROEDER, Mrs. Alden 105
    Debra 287
SCHULTZ, Dr. J. Raymond 175
    Dr. R. P. 74
SCHWAB, John 84
SCHWARZKOPF, Carol 102
    Kirk 128, 131
    Mark 131
SCIPIO, Mrs. O. A. 75
SCOTT, Aleta Marie 161
    Mrs. Benjamin (Lillie) 152, 240
    Bud 75
    Mrs. Bud 75
    Carl 228, 232
    Cledith 346
    Mrs. Cledith (Mary) 346
    David Jay 184
    Dean 302
    Elnora 106
    Ernie 143, 144
    Everett E. 176, 238
    Florence 345
    Goldie 344, 345
    Helen 102
    Ivan 253
    James B. 25, 341
    James R. 130, 233
    Janet 128
    Jeff 134
    Jim 144
    Joanna 82, 287
    Joe ix, 147, 232, 294, 296*, 308*
    Mrs. Joe 102, 232
    John 66, 288
    Mrs. John 282
    Maryanna 340
    Mary Ellen 82, 127, 128, 161, 184
    Mike 232
    Patricia 287
    Richard 125*, 131
    Robert 138, 197, 236
    Rosanne 95
SEAGRAVES, Donnabelle 181
    Willie 56
SEARCY, Glenn 211
SEGRAVES, Cindy 131
SELL, Mrs. Glen 101
SENESH, Lawrence 87
SETTLE, Wm. H. 152, 174, 188, 189
SEWARD, Bertha 199
    Eva 178, 258
    Geoorge 258
    Lee O. 178, 241, 243, 258
    Mrs. Lee O. (Nancy) 178
    Leonard 117, 241
    Ollie C. 197, 238
    Paul H. 197, 247*, 258, 346
    Philip L. 288
    Mrs. William 102

SEWELL, Mrs. Charles W. (Edna) 152, 161, 176
SHAEFER, Fred 238
SHAEFFER, Mrs. John A. 176
SHAFER, Hal R. 118, 197, 235, 238, 262, 269, 295, 296, 305
   Mrs. Hal R. 198
   Ira 227, 231*, 232
   Mrs. Ira 231*
SHAFFER, Albert 238
   C. B. 44, 45, 216
   Eleene 106
   G. A. 45
   Mrs. G. A. 329
   Geneva 182
   Mrs. George 198
   Helen Louise 114
   John 114
   Katherine 116
   Louis 332
   Mary Lou 131*, 273
   Scott 318
SHANDS, Robert 224*, 225
SHANKLAND, R. L. 238
SHANKLIN, George W. 58
   Rosella 243
SHANKS, Bill 16
   Charles 321, 346
   Mrs. Charles 346
   Clay 56
   Coy C. 197, 236, 262, 266, 269, 283*, 292, 295*, 296*, 297, 308, 309, 310
   Donald A. 161, 168
   Frank 53
   Harold 16
   Jane 139*
   Jeff 138
   John U. 38, 238
   Mrs. Junior F. (Mildred) 95, 98, 99*, 175*, 176, 180
   Leonard 298
   Lowell 114
   Mike 16
   Oris 56
   Reba 99*, 100, 138, 330
   Roland 282
SHARP, Dale 291
   Evelyn 25, 345*
   Jim 129* 246, 247, 248, 249*, 253, 256*, 257, 258
   Kenneth 146
   Michelle Ann 288
   N. B. 238
SHAVER, Gene 159
SHAW, Margaret 50*
SHEETS, Anthony 37
   Claude ix, 38, 317
   Mrs. Claude ix, 317
   Elmer E. 44, 45, 163, 164*, 197, 300
   Emma 98
   Eva 108, 298
   Flo 99*
   Gertrude 103
   J. L. 67
   J. M. 238
   Joyce 273
   Mary ix
   Randy 192*
   Roscoe 322, 323, 324
SHEETZ, Charles 306
   John 238
   Pamela Sue 184
SHELDON, Evy 128, 131, 258
   Mollie 82, 128, 130
   Richard 69, 313
   Mrs. Richard (Mary Catherine) ix, 83*, 92, 173*
   Rose T. 251*, 253, 258, 288
SHELLEY, Zena 103
SHEPARD, Elizabeth 109
   Helen L. 98
   Henry 174
   Mrs. Henry (Vera) 105
   Susan Marie 287
SHIDELER, James S. 346
   Mrs. James S. 346
SHINN, Mahlon 339
SHIPSIDES, Stanley H., D.V.M. 22
SHIRAR, Joe 324
   Ora ix, 122, 174, 178*, 180, 238, 319
   Mrs. Ora ix, 178*, 319
SHIRK, James A. 13, 76, 77, 163, 215, 238, 340*, 345
   Ora M. 345
SHOEMAKER, Debbie 82
SHOFF, Dean 131*
   J. Frank 44, 45, 47, 76, 163, 197, 308
   Mrs. Frank 108
   Joy 288
   Ross 162, 296, 298
   Mrs. Ross 162
SHOLTY, Dr. W. M. 341
SHONK, Arthur ix, 292
   Mrs. Arthur ix
   Marjorie 175, 182, 191, 258
   Wanda 99, 100
SHOOK, David 306
SHOPE, Mrs. Galen (Kathern) 24
SHORTRIDGE, Nora 103
SHRIVER, Delbert 249*, 258
   Kay Lynn 128, 169*
   Kenneth 38
   Mrs. Kenneth 171*
   Leonard 196
   Mrs. Raymond 171*, 327
SHULL, Frances 92
SHULTHEIS, Charles 143, 301
   Clarence 238
   Mrs. Clarence 198
   Doris 250*, 258, 331
   John H. 50*
   Marilyn ix, 128, 251*, 253, 257, 258
   Marvin 176, 238, 298
   Opal 273
   Orville 188
   Mrs. Orville (Ruby) 103
   Mrs. Robert 103
   Sharon 251, 253, 258
SHUTTLEWORTH, Louis F. 160
SIBBITT, C. E. 176
   Doug 147, 288
   Guy 122, 165, 238
   Jerry 232, 336
   Mrs. Jerry 232
   Mae 345
   Margaret 105
   May 282
   Wm. B. 297
SIBERT, Manson H. 47
SIBRAY, G. M. 67
   Mrs. G. M. 67
   Mrs. Robert 106, 107
SICKLER, Norma 308
SIDENBENDER, Sandra 126
   Mrs. Ted (Eva) ix, 96, 110
SIEBER, Chas. 75
   Enoch 57
   Foss 47
   Janene 184
   Mrs. Robert (Donnabelle) ix, 329
SIGMAN, Ruby 342
   Russell 225
SILVER, Jennie 345
SIMMERMAN, Frank 91
SIMMONS, Bob 125, 332
   Mrs. Bob 125
   Dickie 170*
   Eleanor 99*
   Luella 241
   Robert 129*, 196, 309
   Mrs. Robert (Donna) 172*, 173*, 198
SIMONS, A. 238
   Ed 238
   Fannie 53*
SIMPSON, John A. 316
SIMS, Mrs. Paul (Clara) ix, 103, 107, 329, 342*, 346
SINES, Kathryn 258
   Marjorie 114
   Nelson 302
   Mrs. Nelson (Pearl) 198, 199
   Thelma 108*
SINK, Ernest 174
   Frank 113
   Mrs. Grover 106
   J. C. 304
   J. W. 27
   James 297
   John 45
   Keith ix, 88, 120, 190, 196, 197, 243, 302, 314
   Mrs. Keith ix, 95
   Lee 300
   Lloyd 178
   Martha 340
   Myron 127, 131, 302
   Russell K. 48, 75
   Virgil L. 238
SINN, Samuel O. 166*, 197, 309
   Mrs. Samuel O. 138
SISSON, Don 312
   Eva 321
   Keith 15, 321, 337
SITES, Francis 114
   George E. 44, 45, 47, 75, 87*, 163, 173*, 175*, 176, 195, 197, 238, 331

Mrs. George E. 198
Mabel 174
Mary 174
Sam G. 41, 165, 196, 217, 238
Mrs. Sam G. 47, 167, 195, 198
SKAGGS, Harlan 335
SKEES, S. V. 282
SKILES, Larry 147
Morris 191, 219, 221*, 223*, 232
SKINNER, Dean J. H. 89, 151
Helen R. 306*, 307
SLAVENS, Ronald 137*, 138, 233, 234*, 235
Mrs. Ronald (Carmen Lawson) 137*, 233, 273
Roy 91, 120, 138, 192, 197, 234*, 235, 236, 244
Mrs. Roy 169
SLEDGE, Alice 180, 181, 182*, 346
SLUSSER, Lindy Lee 288
SMALL, Jay L. 224*, 235
SMELTZGER, Floyd 87
SMITH, A. W. 238
Addison E. 238
Albert ix, 177
Annabelle 106
Becky 169*
Bill "Jugaway" 48
Bob 232
C. A. 67
Charles 332
Charles A. 219
Charles H. 67, 68
Mrs. Cleon 95, 199, 244
Dan 131, 134, 136
David 175, 178, 180, 183, 246, 258, 279
Mrs. David (Betty Lou) ix, 105, 180, 183
Mrs. David (Cathy Peterson) ix, 82, 83*
Delbert 122
Doris 109
Elaine 15, 321
Fern Young 109
Fred C. 44, 45, 165, 174, 238, 336
Fred Craven ix
Mrs. Fren 68
Garnette ix, 273*, 274, 284
Geo. W. 345
Glen L. 238
Glenn 301*
Mrs. Gwinn 176
Helen 174, 181
Herb ix, 22
Herschel 143, 144, 315
Hester 67
Howard 100*, 180, 196, 238, 260
Irene 346
Mrs. Jack 106
James A. 67
Jane 108*
Jean 321
Jeffrey 284
Jim 323

Joan 99
Mrs. John T. (Cathy) 24
Johnny 169*
Josie 68
Julie 247*
L. H. 345
Mrs. L. H. 3, 25, 331, 345
Laverne E. 288
Leon 114
Lester 312
Leveda 128, 130
Lucille 335
Lucy M. 67
Lyman 114, 238
Mrs. Lyman 199
Mable W. 346
Mrs. Mark 102
Martha J. 67
Martha T. 297
Mary Harper 67
Milo 238
N. J. 67
Opal 218*, 243, 244, 258
Paul E. 313, 317, 329
Mrs. Paul E. (Louise) ix, 105, 308*
Rebecca 128, 184
Reuben ix, 100*, 197, 280
Mrs. Reuben (Dorothy) 198, 333, 334*
Mrs. Richard 95, 96*
Robert 119*, 146, 301
Roy 306
Mrs. Russell (Betty) ix
Ruth 308
Sam D. 163, 164*, 173*, 176, 195, 197, 238
Susan 131, 136
Wickliffe 259
William 339
William B. ix, 116, 118, 314, 318, 329, 346
William C. 6, 31, 58, 59, 76, 329, 341, 345, 346
Mrs. Wm. C. 344, 345
Will S. 50
Mrs. Will S. (Maude) 98
Zora Mayo 72, 112
SMOCK, A. P. 50*
Edward R. 47, 59, 76
George 345
James 165
Mrs. James C. 345
William 227, 323
SMOKER, Bert 348
SNEATHEN, Jerry 146
Mildred 116
SNELL, Dan 119*, 122, 131, 138, 302
Mrs. Dan (Bonnie) 138
Mrs. Everett 171*, 177*, 198
SNIDER, Charles 130
Charles Von 232, 235, 236
Earl 238
Junior F. ix, 120, 130, 138*, 183, 195, 196, 197, 199, 232, 236
Mrs. Junior F. (Maxine) ix, 95,

96, 98, 102, 107, 130, 183, 196, 198, 199
Max 120, 128
Terry 127, 128, 138, 161, 233
SNIPES, Carl 335
Lee Wayne 274
Paul 241, 284
Mrs. Paul (Amy) 107
Wilma 183
SNOEBERGER, Frank 38
F. S. 238
Galen 148
John E. 348
John E. ix, 85, 114, 115, 116, 301, 308
Mrs. John E. (Mabel) ix, 22, 217, 244
Joyce 126*
Linda 136*
Lois Ruth 263
Minnie 331
Richard 172*
Roy E. ix, 85, 116, 172*, 176, 300, 310
Tony 238
Truman 75, 238
W. W. 44, 45
Wiladean 109
SNOW, Charles 313
Mrs. Charles 171*, 172*, 198
SNYDER, Beverly 181
Henry A. 238
Joe 191, 196, 235, 262, 283*, 292, 295, 296, 297
Mrs. Joe 99*
L. 67
Mack 301*
Theodore 42
SOESBE, Harry E. 55
SOMMERS, Katherine 98
SORRELLS, Rita 109
SPANGLER, Vera 99, 100
SPARHAWK, Roberta 91
SPARKS, Cynthia Sue 288
Jerry 232
John 49
Naomi 103
SPEAR, Cloyd 146
SPEARS, James 59
SPENCE, Mrs. Ernest 105
Joseph 98
Kay 105
SPENCER, Maxine 56
Robert 316
SPESARD, Laura 134
Lisa 134
Lonnie 126, 131, 132, 147
Lowell 119, 121, 232
Mrs. Lowell 232
SPITLER, Bill 15
Charles 113
Connie 194, 195, 256*
Elmer 177, 196
Harry 15, 319
SPITZNAGLE, Joe 179*, 250
Laura 230*
Sandy 287
SPOONER, Mrs. Chuck (Janet) 138

INDEX OF NAMES

SPRAGUE, Forrest 137
    Harold W. 138, 273*, 275
SPRAKER, Ed 302
SPRING, Alex 331
    Amel 238
    Mrs. Amel 162
    Mary 109
SPRINKLE, Shirley 176*
    Walter 176*, 197
    Mrs. Walter 198, 327
SPRUNGER, Robert F. 306
SPRY, Gladys 67
    Wm. 67, 68
SQUIER, Walter 321
STACKHOUSE, Marion 123, 152
STAIR, Glen 197, 238
    Mrs. Glen 95
    Lee 244
ST. AMAND, Joseph 311
    Mrs. Joseph (Cora Zell) 69, 81*, 93, 99*, 100*, 106, 107, 108, 138, 311
STANGLE, Jeanne 346
    Mr. 25
STANLEY, William 259
STANSELL, Frank 304
STARKEY, Mrs. Charles 95, 279
    Joe 197, 248*
    Mrs. Joe (Louann) 83, 104, 105, 248*
    Mike 125*
    Sue 175, 247*
STAUFFER, Ben 140*
    Dr. Lawrence 83, 138
    Mrs. Lawrence 138
    Liesl 123, 139*, 140*, 141*
STAYER, Harold 54
STEINHART, John G. 39
    Robert 120
STEINMAN, Phyllis 82, 108
STEPHAN, Robert 317, 333
STEPHEN, Floyd L. 238
    Frank 238
    Riley 238
    Vernie 75
    Mrs. Vernie 95, 199
STEPHENS, Cecil 197
    Mrs. Ed 106, 107
    Edward E. 45, 165, 184, 195, 205, 214, 215, 221, 238, 298
    Mrs. Edward E. (Virginia E.) 103, 176
    Elizabeth 174
    Ernest 190*, 195
STEPHENSON, D. C. 48
    Rev. 177*
STERLING, Laura Lennon 58
    Matthew 331, 340*, 345
    S. T. 74
    Thos. 348
STERRETT, Floyd 298
    Judson 297
    Lee 16, 197
    Wilson 298, 341
STERZIK, Ray 137
STEVENS, Mrs. O. W. 151, 168
STEVENSON, Brian 221
    Patrick 221
STEWART, Albert P. 99
    Charley 51
    Mrs. Charles 67
    Donald 144
    Dr. 341
    Earl 59, 75, 77, 163, 197, 277
    Mrs. Everett 198
    F. F. 341
    Fred J. ix, 197
    Mrs. Fred J. (Irene) ix
    James 203
    James Hervey 329
    Marla K. 338
    O. E. 238, 304
    Vera 58
STILES, Chuck 336
STINSON, Edward A. 316
STIPP, David 339, 347
STOCKTON, William 339
STOFFER, Mrs. Vern 346
STOMBOUGH, William 339
STONE, E. P. 339
    J. J. 339
STONEBRAKER, Greg 146
    Pratt W. 58
STONER, Mrs. John (Marsha Floyd) 138, 274
STONG, Ruth 103
STORM, Larry 148
    Mrs. Larry (Marla) 148
STOUT, Alan 170*, 250*
    Carrol 335, 337
    Mrs. Carrol (Mary Lee) 337
    Clarence 75, 144, 196, 215, 217, 235, 238
    Mrs. Clarence 176
    Mrs. Gayle (Diane) 105, 170*, 258, 340
    Joyce 340
    Loris P. 172*, 241, 243, 340
    Mrs. Loris P. (Esther) 102
    Mabel 99*
    Richard 170*
STOVER, Elton 322
STROLE, Joe 244
STRONG, Larry 75, 308
STRYCKER, Dare 194
STUART, Benjamin F. 6, 329, 340*, 341, 343, 345
STUDEBAKER, Auda Gee 60, 329
    Harvey E. 55, 300
    Joseph E. 55
    Lula 337
    Mary 243, 258
STUNTZ, Ed 16
    Mrs. Ed (Jeanne) 341, 346
STURDIVANT, Susan 132
SULLIVAN, Clara 222
    James A. 176*
    James R. 329
    Joe 58
    Max ix
    Mrs. Max (Norma) ix, 82*, 83*, 91, 93
    Michelle 126, 128, 130, 131, 132, 139*
    Ralph ix, 6, 87, 120, 248
    Mrs. Ralph (Elizabeth) ix
    Robert 302
    Stu 258
    Wilma Mae 241
SUMMERS, H. B. 58
    Marjorie 314*
SUMNER, Claude 98, 99
SUMPTER, John P. 91
SURFACE, A. L. 57
SUTHERLIN, Paul 16
SUTTON, Kim 134
    Rosemary 346
    Vernon 230*
SWAIM, Bessie 108
SWAIN, W. 50*
SWAN, Erny 238
SWANSON, D. L. 158
SWARTZ, Isaac 196
    Kathryn 266, 271
    Melvin 323
SWATTS, Isaac 74
    Jack 114
    Wayne 144
SWAYZE, Ron 119*
SWICKARD, Dick 143
    Marie 329
SWIFT, Audra 244
SWINFORD, Mrs. Don 346
SWITZER, C. 323
    Lowell 292
SYPHERS, Denise 306*, 307

T

TABOR, S. J. 66
TAFT, W. H. 331
TAM, Joseph S. 58
TANSEY, Charles 118, 119, 235
    Mrs. Charles (Ermina) 168, 173*, 178, 181, 182*, 195, 197, 332*
TARKINGTON, James F. 128
TATMAN, Charles 228*
TAYLOR, Flora 99*
    Harold B. 112
    Judy 258
    Lawrence 344
    LeNora 288
    Lewis 152, 154, 173, 189, 190, 200
    William 339
    Wilson 263
    Capt. Zachary 348
TEACH, E. O. 56
TEDDIE 46
TEEL, Arnold 192*
TEMPLE, Harry A. 238
    John 186, 187, 329
    Laura 116, 329, 341
TESH, Laura 253
    U. E. 53, 57
THELEN, Mrs. Don (Judy) 124, 138
THOMAS, A. J. 348
    Anson 153, 171*
    Fraser 329
    Frazier 50

George A. 163, 164*, 174, 195, 197
Mrs. George 108
Dr. Guy A. 44
Mrs. Guy 109
Harvey A. 55, 73
Mrs. Harvey 108
Homer 196
Mrs. Homer 198
Jerry Arthur 128
Joe 128
June 25, 345*
Marion 47, 297
Mary Jo 170*
Mary Mason ix
THOMPSON, Charles W. 67, 68, 118, 191*, 196, 197, 231, 236, 309, 310, 311*, 314
Mrs. Charles W. (Mildred) 67, 68, 198, 231, 310
Glenn 243
Harold H. ix, 88*, 138, 146, 147, 180, 197, 301*, 302, 323
Mrs. Harold H. (Ruby) ix, 95, 96*, 180, 198
James 126, 128, 131, 258
Jane 121, 127, 130, 131
John R. 274
Larry 148
Mrs. Larry (Donna) 148
Lillian Haines 82, 193
Madie Brown 108, 109
Mary 168
Mary Jo 126, 127, 128, 130, 132, 146, 180*
Samuel L. 153
Sarah A. Anderson 38
Wade P. 60, 345
THOMSEN, Carole 329*
Eric 329
THOMSON, Charles 319
Mrs. James A. 346
R. E. "Ed" 272*, 282, 284, 292, 297
Mrs. R. E. (Mabel) 108*
THUM, Ed 302
THURSTON, John 238, 298
TIDRICK, R. S. 55
TIMMONS, Virginia 54
TINKLE, Mrs. Hiram 24
TIPTON, General John 11
TITLOW, Mead 51
TITUS, Eugene 223, 226
Jane Witter 82
Sharon 230*
TODD, Dan 115
Dean 302
Geo. 238
John 117, 174
Mrs. John 77
John Harvey 91, 119, 241, 323
John K. 77, 163, 196, 329
Marlene 130, 132
Patricia 128
Pauline 174
Raymond 67, 69, 87, 88*, 89, 310

Mrs. Raymond (Geneva) 67, 108*
Warren H. 175*, 176, 196, 238
Mrs. Warren H. 102
TOOLE, John R. 274*
TOWE, Capt. 4
Gene 75
TOWNSLEY, Robert 115
TRAPP, Debra K. "Debbie" 233, 287
Harold 322, 323, 324
Hershel 197, 234*, 236
Larry 83, 138, 232
Lori 123, 131, 136, 163
Mark 323
Mart 324
Marta 250, 258
Virgil 324
TRAWIN, George 50*
Kate 297
TREICHEL, Meredith 327
TREIDA, George 197, 310
Mrs. George 199
TRENT, J. C. 330
Ora 319, 324
Ruby 22
Thelma R.N. ix, 21, 22, 106
TREVETHICK, Richard 33
TRIBBETT, Jim 144
Lynne Ann 287
TRIPLET, M. W. 26
TROBAUGH, Anna F. 345
Chalmer R. 75, 297
George D. 67
Roy 44, 46
TROXEL, Edward P. 176, 238
John G. 19
TULLY, Harold 120
Twillie 127, 128, 130, 132
TULP, Roy 22
TURPIE, Robert 50*
TWEED, A. D. 25
TYLER, Elsie 109
Ralph E. 308
Mrs. Ralph ix

U

UDELL, Paul 303
ULERY, Kathryn 114
ULM, Buel F. 25, 26, 59
UNDERHILL, Faye Hitchcock 331
Lois 342
UNGER, Gwendolyn 243
John 197
Mrs. John 108
Lloyd 197
URBAN, Frieda 100
URICK, H. C. 197
URMSTON, LeRoy 38

V

VAN DER VOLGEN, Lawrence 342*
VANDEVENTER, Daniel F. 35
VAN GUNDY, P. W. 57

VAN METER, Barbara Sue 128*, 129
VAN NATTA, Robert N. 121, 197, 238, 308, 324
Mrs. Robert N. (Ann) 47, 199, 346
VAN NUYS, Charles 137
VANSCOY, Roy 238
VAN SICKLE, Jane 343
Wayne 318
VAN SLYKE, Robert A. 79, 93, 121
VASS, Hilda 128
Lawrence 196
VAUGHAN, Charles Davis 263, 291*
Mrs. Charles Davis (Belva Guthrie) 109, 171*, 172*, 199
Irene 252*
Kenneth 301
Mabel 252
Opal 199
VAUGHN, George 117
Joe 208
Kenneth 143, 144
Lee 298
VEACH, Chuck 146
Willard 113
VERRILL, Carolyn Sue 128, 130, 288, 289
VICTOR, Max 134
VINARD, Nancy 128
VINEY, Charles 251, 257, 258
Ed 323
Mrs. James (Blanche) 152, 173, 195, 198
Mrs. Leon (Margaret) 55
Lydia 67
Newman 67
W. S. 55
VOLLENWEIDER, Paul 176, 197
Mrs. Paul 172*, 198
VOORHEES, Edward 13, 41
Fred 165, 238, 262, 266, 295, 296
Mrs. Fred 108
G. E. 319
Gertha 13
Mrs. Jack 106
Mrs. Lee (Elva) ix, 108
R. D. 318
Terry 147
VOLPERT, J. W. 48
VORHEES, Jane 22
VRENDENBURG, H. 348
VURPILLAT, Mrs. 24, 25

W

WADE, Leroy E. 175, 196
Ruth 198
WADSWORTH, Henry A. "Hank" 90, 188
WAGAMAN, Dr. P. H. 301*
WAGNER, Clint 48
Fred 144
Jerry 16, 128

John 238, 348
Josephine 116
Patricia Ann "Pat" 127, 128, 170*, 333*
Ralph 333
Mrs. Ralph 333
Tom "Tommy" 128, 131, 170*
WAGONER, Ann 141*
Betty 170*
Dale 170*
Della 102
Mrs. Don (Esther) 108
Doris 198, 243
Douglas 131*
Ed 147, 149, 232
Mrs. Ed (Wanita) 149, 232
Fred 316, 317
George W., M.D. 22
Mrs. George W. 331
Mrs. Glen (Helen) 108
Joe 178, 324
Joel 348
JoEllen 125*
John 37, 196
Mrs. John 197
Keith 16
LaDene 136*
Linda 170*
Manford 196
Mrs. Manford 198
Marilyn, M.D. 22
Marshall 300
Martin 123*, 148
Mary 297
Mrs. Ralph 198
Roger 323
Ross F. 75, 190, 191, 222, 244, 308, 310, 323, 324
Mrs. Ross 106
Russell 313
Verl 197, 346
Mrs. Verl (Alice) 198, 346
W. F. 55
Walter 238
WAKELAND, Earl 196, 238
Lewis 258
WALGUMUTH, Charles 192
WALKER, Dr. Edward 53
J. E. 238
John ix, 54
G. P. 84*
Mary 345
Suzannah ix
WALKEY, F. L. 167*
WALLACE, Beth 141*
Charlotte 105
Henry A. 321
Jack 335
Jesse 325
Joe 148
L. Tim 188
WALTERS, Mrs. Carol (Fern) 104
Jackie 179
Jean 53*
Jerry 148
Mrs. Kenneth 152
Mary 105
WALTON, Kay Ellen 132, 184

Kenneth 288
Robert 24
WARD, Arthur 56
Bob 291*
Diane 170*
Dwaine 119, 121, 127, 128, 130, 131, 233, 250, 258
Mrs. Dwaine 130
H. A. 297
Janelle Lynn 337
Jean Ann 128
Joan 273
Mrs. Joe (Mary Catherine) 108
John 256*, 291*, 313
Mrs. John (Betty) ix, 105, 106, 192*, 194, 256
Lowell 87, 197, 231
Mrs. Lowell 173*, 198, 231
Marion 196, 235, 330, 337, 346
Mrs. Marion (Mary) 337, 346
Martha 58
Montgomery 64
Myrtle 58
Orville 197, 232
Paul 244, 258
Randy Jay 287
Robert 172*, 196
Mrs. Robert 171*, 172*, 198
Roy 146
Sherman 288
Sulie 58
WARDEN, J. A. 238
WARINNER, A. W. 240
WARNICK, Wm. W. 197
Mrs. Wm. W. 198
WARREN, Nettie 26
WASON, Mrs. George 329
James P. 23
Robert 116
WASSON, S. A. 58, 197, 236, 238
WATERMAN, Mr. 262
WATKINS, Mrs. Max (Katherine) 104
WATSON, Annette 132
Clarence 314
Lydia 103
Thomas A. 52
WATTS, Andrew 339
Harry 192
WAYMIRE, Bill 336
Ed 16, 318, 336
John 332
WEAVER, Dix 119*, 125*, 128, 130, 131, 138
Mrs. Eugene (Mabel) 108*
Herman 119
Joe 254*
Martha Kay 128
Samuel 37
W. S. ix, 87, 89, 91, 137*, 138*, 144, 145*, 146, 332, 346
WEBB, Daisy 103
WEBER, Dr. Robert 25
WECKERLE, Wm. 319
WEDDELL, Arthur O. ix, 22, 318
WEDLHUIZEN, Mrs. Paul 105
WEHLEGE, James R. 192
WEIDERHAFT, Mark Evan 288

Terry 288
WEIGLE, Terry A. ix, 308*
WEIL, Kate Robinson 98, 329
WEILAND, Herman 282
WEISS, Ellwyn 133*
WELBORN, Larry ix, 312, 314*, 317, 318
WELCH, Carole 128
Dick 131
Mrs. Ty 279
WELKER, Donald 274
Robert 274
WELLER, Jackie 131, 288
Robert 288
WELLS, Yantis 67
Mrs. Yantis 44, 331
WENTZELL, Mrs. A. E. 58
WERTZ, Bill 146, 323
Delores 102
Richard 224*
Mrs. Robert 108
WEST, Grover 314, 318
John 56
W. F. 58
WESTERN, Rev. H. H. 75
WHARTON, Rev. Chester W. 331
Flora 331
James W. 19
Mabel 329
WHEELER, Barry 335
Fred 67, 116, 318, 323
James F. 336
WHETZEL, R. W. 238
WHISTLER, G. L. 238
Mrs. G. L. 198
James H. B. 49
Mrs. Lawrence 47, 95, 101, 108
WHITE, Beatrice 53*
James L. ix, 16, 173*, 197, 234, 235, 236, 295, 296*, 337
Mrs. James L. (Maxine) ix, 173*, 199, 337
L. N. 238
Paul 265
Robert 119, 128
Ronnie 146
Ruth 100, 103, 342*, 346
Mrs. 58
WHITEMAN, Woodrow 16, 323
Mrs. Woodrow 329
WHITHAM, Herschel ix
WHITLEY, Amy Brown 109
WHORLEY, Leo 57
WIBLE, Mary 243
WICK, Rev. Joe 87
WICKARD, Claude R. 57, 79, 162, 163, 164*, 167, 173, 176, 195, 215, 217, 234, 236, 238, 261, 281, 308
S. A. 29, 172*, 175*, 176, 196, 212, 231, 234, 235, 238, 262, 266, 295, 296, 301, 302
Mrs. S. A. (Faith) 198, 231
WIDNER, Oliver 20
WIGNER, Dwaine 56
WILBURN, Roy 238
Mrs. Roy 197

WILE, C. E. 50*
WILEY, Hazel F. 13
　Dr. James R. 300
WILIMITIS, Chris 147
　Deanna 139*
WILKEN, Eleanor 194, 195
　Joan 184
　Sharon 184
WILLEY, C. V. 163, 164*, 197
WILLIAMS, Dick 192*, 193*
　Jane 128, 136*, 180
　Jerry 124*
　Jesse L. 6, 7
　Larry 176
　Lottie 56
　Mrs. Lloyd (Mary) 102
　Myrtle 58
　Robert Eugene ix, 306*, 307
　Russell 265
WILLIAMSON, Maurice L. viii, 31, 32, 89, 312*
WILLY, Donald B. ix, 123*, 185, 186*, 192*, 199, 318
　Gene 320, 323
　Mary 320
WILSEY, Richard 75
WILSON, Anne 124*
　C. A. 118
　Carol 131*
　Charles N., D.D.S. 22
　Della 67
　Dennis 230*
　Donald J. 197
　Dr. 122
　E. H. (Gene) viii, 165, 185
　Mrs. Harold 108, 138
　Harry 84, 119, 120, 133*, 172*, 345
　Mrs. Harry (Mary) ix, 95, 96*, 133*, 172*
　Mrs. Henry B. (Mindwell Crampton) 26, 329, 341, 345
　Homer ix, 87, 166*, 197, 232, 292, 332
　Mrs. Homer (Mildred) 173*, 178, 194*, 195, 198
　James 323
　Jesse 144, 178*
　John D. 50
　Linda 131*
　Margaret 67
　Max 274
　Minnie L. 297
　Nellie 198
　Omer 67
　Orville 88, 238
　Paul 67
　Mrs. Paul 198
　Pauline 56
　Ray 132
　Roger 146
　Ruth 104
　Stephen L. 287
　Tiffin 48
　Mrs. Tiffin 108
　Virginia 346
　Mrs. Wilbur J. 173*, 198

　William L. 65
　Wm. 347
　Woodrow 331
WINE, Terry 100
WINGARD, Mrs. Aaron 58
　Catharine Marie 288
　Dee Renea 288
　Mrs. Dora L. 108, 198
　E. P. 67
　Mrs. E. P. 67
　Ed 274
　Frances 114
　G. B. 57
　Robert C. ix, 86*, 87, 113, 118, 196, 262, 266, 283*, 295, 296*, 297*
　Mrs. Robert (Myrtle) ix, 102
　William M. 175*, 176, 235, 238
WINTER, Clifford 327
WIREDHAND, Willie 293*
WISE, Andrew 238, 316
　C.L., M.D. 22
　Carl 238
　Chas. A. 238
　Mrs. Claude 106
　Mrs. Dallas 101
　David 232, 292, 296
　Mrs. David 317
　Debra K. 288
　Mrs. Edwin 101
　Ezra 291*
　Fred 16
　Jesse E. 67, 69, 329, 332
　Mrs. Jesse E. (Opal) ix, 67
　Joe 282
　John 49, 197
　Mrs. John 173*, 180, 198
　Mrs. Lewis (Faye Buckley) 114, 187, 317, 329, 333, 334*, 335
　Marjorie 175
　Marvin 238, 316
　Mildred 114
　Ralph 16
　Robert 180*, 316
　Saml. 348
　Verne 196, 282
　Mrs. Verne 282
WITTER, Clara Belle 241
　Jane 193, 194, 195, 243
　John L. ix, 175*, 176, 197, 231*, 236, 244, 336*
　Mrs. John L. (Fanny) 168, 173*, 195, 198, 231*, 243
　Myra 241, 243, 263
　Pat 105
　Thomas 241
　Mrs. Tom (Chestine) 107
WOLEVER, Andrew viii, 62, 345
WOLF, Kara 338
　Bert 238
　Charles 147, 148
　Freda 273
　I. L. 238
　Isaac 47, 304
　Keith 341, 346
　Maurice 148
　Mrs. 340*

WOLFE, Armina 345
　Hobart 197, 264, 265, 266, 267*
　Jennie 345
WOOD, Carolyn 122
　Charles A. 54, 318, 329, 332, 341, 346
　Mrs. Charles A. (Opal) ix, 53*, 346
　David A. 54
　Robert W. ix, 54, 62, 346
　Mrs. Robert W. (Faye) 53*, 318, 329, 334, 346
WOODEN, George 196
WOODHOUSE, Brad 253
　Roy 313
WOODS, Frank 54
　Warren 197, 219, 231
　Mrs. Warren 231
WOOLEY, Oliver 182
WOOLRIDGE, Loretta 273
WORKINGER, Glenn 166*
WRAY, B. F. 238
　Mrs. Charles 118
　Dortha 246, 258
WRIGHT, Francis 144
WYANT, Alan 132, 134
　Anita 134, 136
　Annette 123, 128, 130, 136, 141*
　Don 125
　Ernest ix, 302
　Kym 125
WYATT, Bob 91
　Effie 24
　Harold 57
　Mrs. Harold 138
　O. W. 57
WYSONG, Richard 197
　Mrs. Richard 173*, 198

Y

YARIAN, J. E. 238
　Rev. Jack 177
YARLING, Mr. 264
YEAGER, Charlene 178, 182
　Charles L. ix, 38, 302, 323
　Mrs. Charles L. 341
　Jesse L. 262, 266, 271, 295, 296
　Mrs. Jesse 95
　Thelma 116
YEAKLEY, Carl 58, 85, 330
　Curtis 126, 130, 131, 138
　Kenneth 91, 120, 130, 179*, 247*, 248*, 249*, 250*, 252, 253, 257, 258, 291*, 302
　Mrs. Kenneth (Lona) 104, 130
　Margaret 104
　Margie 104
　Mary Louise 248*
　Roy 56, 238, 298
　Samuel 238
　Sheila 109
YEATER, Noah 113

Wilber 113
YERKES, Cloyd 238
    Herb 320
    Lloyd 57, 58,
    Robert "Bob" 320
    Mrs. Robert "Bob" 101
YERRICK, Mrs. Harry (Carrie) 99, 100
YOCUM, Ruth 99*
YODER, Dean 232, 280
    Mrs. Devon (Maxine) 108
    William 310, 311
YOHE, Ralph 328
YORK, James ix, 123*, 165, 183
YOST, Gene 291*
    Lester 243
    Silas S. 197, 236, 238
YOUNG, H. E. 71
    Jerry D. 318
    John 192
    Larry 288
    Lois 331
    Mary 67
    Mr. 264
    Wilbur 75
    Mrs. Wilbur 75
    William 67
YUNKER, J. C. 197, 296
    Mrs. J. C. 24

Z

ZARING, Miss 74
ZARTMAN, Donald 181
Glen 196
James D. 56
Mrs. Russell 102
ZAWISZA, Rita Dittman 123
ZINK, Harold Ray 127, 128, 131, 184, 287
    Jon 138
    Randa 126, 127, 128, 130, 131
    Raymond 123, 185, 196, 197, 236, 305
    Mrs. Raymond (Frances) 119, 123, 185, 196, 199
    Teresa 126, 127, 128
ZINN, Dale 337
    J. Dewey 262, 295, 297, 306, 308
    Mrs. J. Dewey (Cletus) 198
    Eileen 246, 247*, 249*, 253, 256*, 258
    Jessie 48
    Orman 323
    Rosella 194, 279
    Teresa 122
    Wayne 16, 144, 191, 232, 246, 257, 258
    Mrs. Wayne 232
ZOLPER, Kimbra 132, 134
ZOOK, B. Jesse ix, 22, 38, 39, 312, 320, 323, 324, 329, 337, 346
    Mrs. B. Jesse (Anna Myrle) 98, 320, 337, 341, 342*, 346
    Bethany E. 184
    Bob 340
    Claude E. 175, 197, 236, 298
David 348
Dennis L. 39
Frank 41, 238
Harold 124*, 146
Helen 70, 198, 244, 266
Joyce 258
Laverna 182
Loyd E. 29, 67, 68, 119, 173*, 175, 195, 197, 236, 262, 269, 279, 283*, 295, 296, 297, 305, 309, 310
Mrs. Loyd E. (Eunice) 67, 198, 279, 332
Mertha 125*, 126*, 170*
Orton ix, 197, 219, 221
Mrs. Orton (Hazel) 95, 98, 107, 180
Orton, Jr. 144
Roger 131*
Roselyn 256*
Sondra 273
Treva 170*
Truman 172*, 197
    Mrs. Truman (Evelyn) 107, 171*, 172*, 178, 198
Wayne 144
ZUERCHER, Lawrence 337
    Mrs. Lawrence 337

GENERAL INDEX

*Indicates Picture

A

A. A. Electric Company 277
ABC Inc. 16
Action Realty 125
Adam Porter Mill 38
Adams Mill 13, 37*, 187, 317
Aggressive Young Farmers 148
AGRICULTURAL Adjustment
    Program (AAA) 85, 308
    Experiment Station 65, 71
    Extension Service 65, 71-93
    Marketing Act 207
    Opportunity Day 88
    Research Building at Purdue 158
    Short Course at Purdue 161
    Stabilization and Conservation
        Service 307-309
        Committee 308*, 309*
        Employees 308*
Agri-Petco International 206
Agway Inc. 64, 208, 214
Akron Jonah Club 89, 327
Allison, Steinhart and Zook Inc. 38, 39, 227
Alloy Crafts Company 16
AMERICAN Automobile Association 70
    Auto Top Factory 44
    Cooperatives Inc. 212
    Farm Bureau Federation 150, 163, 201
        Agreement with USDA, 150
        Leadership Conference 163
    Institute of Cooperation 133, 145, 201, 233, 292
    Legion 19, 292
        Award 292
    Plant Food Council 70
    Youth Foundation 132
AMPI (Associated Milk Producers Inc.) 125
Andersons, The 2, 122, 174, 278, 312
Angle Bros. Trucking 122
Animal Science Workshop 132
Annual Extension Homemakers
    Chorus Festival 99
Area Plan Commission 91
Artificial Breeders Association 301*
Aschanhort Insurance 122
Assistant County Agents 81, 93
Associated Country Women of World 95, 160
Atlantic Richfield Foundation 132
AUTO Races 13, 14
    Show 13
AYRES Hardware 122
    Memorial Children's Room 24

B

Bachelor Run Conservancy District 314
Balser Quartet 116
Bangs Eradication Bill 155
Banker-Farmer Tour 79
Bank for Cooperatives at Louisville 216
Barn Raisings 39
Bassett and Talbert 120, 138
Battle Ground Summer School, 1936 244
"Battle of the Bangboards" 321
Battle Over the Electric Bill 286
Beaver Valley Sweethearts 326
Beckman, Swenson and Associates 91
Beesley's Department Store 138
Ben Franklin Stores 137
Berry Feeds 122
Bethany Park Summer School, 1935 243*, 244
Better Farming Better Living
    Program 81
Big "A" 225*
Binghampton Chamber of Commerce 150
Birth Records of Carroll County 22
Bishop & Lane 122
Black Lamb 121*
Blacksmith Shops 39
Blanchard, Red and Sage Riders 283
Blazers Saddle Club 124
Blue Sky Law 153
Blythe & Son 18, 184
Board of Zoning Appeals 91
Bohannon, Harry Post #75 19
Bollei Farrer Company 122
Bondie's Reserve 2
Bowen & Co., A. T. 23
Boys' and Girls' Clubs 71
Bradshaw Insurance Agency Inc. 125
Briggs Fertilizer Plant 202
Bright National Bank 121, 122, 125, 312
BRINGHURST Elevator and Feed
    Mill 227, 228*
    Poultry Association 75
    Tel. Co. 55
British Petroleum Corporation 205
Broome County Farm Bureau 150
Brosman's IGA 124, 138
Brucellosis 156
Budrow Hardware 122
Bulk Oil Plant at Camden 221, 222*
BURLINGTON FFA 148
    History 340
    Kiwanis Club 131
    Old Settlers 330
    School 16
    Sesquicentennial 1978 338-340
        Commission 340
        Emblem 338*
    State Bank 125, 312
    Tel. Co. 53, 58
Burnett's Creek Arch 5*, 6, 187, 341*
Burnettsville FFA 148
Burrows Tel. Co. 58
Business Assoc. of Greater S.W.
    Monticello 122
Butcherings 40

C

C & C Energy Inc. 124
CAMDEN Community Club 320
    Elementary School 16
    Elevator 38
    Expositor 26, 27
    Fairs 43
    FFA 148
    Flora Elevators 123, 124
    H. S. Minstrel Band 118
    Hog Market 122
    Lions Club 124, 138
    Mill 227*
    National Farm Loan Assoc. 304, 305
    Public Library 24, 341
    Record 26
    State Bank 122, 124, 312
    Tel. Co. 56, 57, 58
    Women's Literary Club 24
CAMP Miniwanca 132
    Tecumseh 22*, 23*, 78, 79, 116, 243
Captain Stubby and the Buccaneers 234*, 283, 326
Carcass Evaluation 123*
Carnegie Libraries 23, 24
Carroll Consolidated School
    Corporation 16
CARROLL COUNTY Agricultural
    Club 88
    Agricultural Extension Agents
        76, 77, 78, 79*, 80*,

81*, 82*, 83*, 93
Agricultural Extension Service 71-83
Agricultural Leaders, 1920 164*
Agricultural Society 42
Airplanes 14, 15, 320, 321
Airports 15, 16
Area Plan Commission 91
ASCS 307, 308*, 309*
Birth Records 22
Board of Education 76, 77
Canning Club 115
Changes in Agriculture 31-34, 92
Churches 17
Citizen 26
Citizen-Times 26
Comet 27
Community Development Committee 90, 188
Cooperative Duroc Breeders Assn. 300
Cooperative Tel. Assn. 58
Cooperative Tel. Co. 59
Corn Husking Contests 321, 322, 323, 324
Council 124
Courthouses 17, 18*, 19*
Court System 157
Created 35
Death Records 22
Demonstrator 76
EFNEP Program 91
Electric Light Company 259, 260*
Elevation 1
Express 25
Extension Homemakers Assn. 94-110
Fair Assn. 43, 116
Fairs 42-47, 69, 74, 116-126, 176
Farm 20, 264
Farm Bureau 117, 123, 124, 129, 130, 150-199, 215
Farm Bureau Coop Assn. 120, 121, 122, 124, 215-239, 240, 312
Farmers' Assn. 77, 163
Farmers Institutes 74, 75, 76
Farm Management Assn. 87
Farm News 27-30, 284
Fire Departments 20, 21
4-H Clubs 111-141
FFA 142-149
Gas and Oil Wells 2
Granges 67-70
Highway Garage 20
Historical Markers 331, 336*, 345, 346-348
Historical Society 341-346
Historical Society Museum 343, 344
Home 20
Hybrid Seed Producers 125
Indian Reserves 2
Indiana Sesquicentennial 333, 334

Committee 333
Historymobile 333*, 334
Programs 333*, 334*
Queen 333*
Interurbans 10*, 11
Jails 20*
Junior Leaders 130, 131*, 136*
Loan and Trust Company 184
Loan, Trust and Savings Company 184
Location 1
Map xii
Natural Resources 1
News 287
Newspapers 25-30
Old Settlers Assn. 329
Packing Plants 57-61
Parks 20, 187
Plank Toll Roads 11
Plan Commission 91
Planning and Zoning 90, 91, 188
Pork Festivals 302, 303, 304
Pork Producers 120, 121, 123, 124, 302
Pork Producers Council 302
Press 27
Production Credit Assn. 305, 306
Public Health Department 21
Public Libraries 23, 24, 25
Public Schools 16, 17, 35, 36
Purebred Livestock Breeders Assn. 302
Railroads 8-10
REMC 121, 124, 259-299
Roads and Bridges 13
Rural Free Delivery 49-52
Rural Youth 112, 120, 125, 232, 240-258
Sanitary Landfill 20
Soil & Water Conservation District 1, 125, 132, 309-315, 317
State Highways 11-13
Study Club 240
Telephones 52-59
Threshers Assn. 41
Towns 3
Townships 3
Transportation 3-16
U.S. Bicentennial Emblem 337*
Voluntary Agricultural Assn. 43
Wabash and Erie Canal Inc. 317, 318
CARROLL High School 17
Lumber Co. 122, 125
Manor 20
Telephone Company 23, 53, 277
CARROLLTON Bridge 6, 340*
Township Clown Band 118
Township Farm Bureau Meetings 177*
Township School 177
Carter Funeral Home 122
Cebeco-Handelsraad 208
CENTRAL Canada Potash Co. Ltd. 203
Carroll North of Flora 222, 229*
Farmers Industries Inc. 202, 203

Nitrogen, Inc. 203
States Cooperative League 240
States Grain Assn. 207
States Soft Wheat Growers Assn. 207
Changes in Agriculture 31-34, 92
CHARTER MEMBERS of First Carroll County Historical Society 344, 345
Carroll County Historical Society Reorganized September 28, 1967 346
Carroll County Rural Youth 241
Chicago Board of Trade 133
Chicago Grain Market 61
Chicken Barbecues 87
Chief Eagle Feather 116
Churches 17
CIMCO 44 6, 185-188
Circle F. Builders 121
Cities Service Oil Company 127
Citizens National Bank of Delphi 216
Citizenship Seminar 162, 163
Citrus World 208
Clarence Eyer Syrian Relief Project 69
Clawson, Fred Grocery 122
Clay Township Orchestra 174, 179*, 311
Clore Act 72, 112
Cockshutt Plow Company 212, 230
Cohee Construction 312
College Conference Feed Board 203
Collegiate 4-H Club 133
Comet Kohoutek 27
Commission on Domestic Animals and Poultry Diseases 156
Commodity Marketing 133
Community Development Committee 90, 188
Consumers Cooperative Assn. 212
CONTESTS Amateur 118, 169, 175, 180, 253
Beard 332, 336
Best Dressed 331, 335
Bread Baking 332
Corn Husking 19, 144, 321-324
Corn Picking 324, 325
Dinner Calling 118
Egg Carrying 118
Entertainment 118
Essay 70, 182, 288, 289, 311*, 337
From Greatest Distance 330, 335
Goodyear 313
Green Pasture 313
Heaviest Pumpkin 327
Hog Calling 118, 174, 303*, 332
Horse Pulling 118
Horseshoe Pitching 174, 335
Husband Calling 118, 303*, 332
Land Judging 327
Largest Family 330, 331
Liars 332
Miss Indiana 331
Nail Driving 118
Old Fiddlers 174, 327, 332

Oldest Person 330, 335
Poster 169
Public Speaking 181
Quartet 174, 178*
Queen 168, 182, 331, 333*, 335
Rolling Pin Throwing 332
Rural Church Improvement 161
Rural Youth 246
Rural Youth Talk Fest 249
Sack Race 174
Share the Fun 179
Stuffed Toy 70
Tractor Handling 326
Tug of War 117*
Youngest Person 330, 335
CO-OP Acres 228
   Creameries 243
   Creamery at Crawfordsville 165
   Finance Corporation 293
   Livestock Marketing 243
   Movement 240
   Oil Refinery at Mt. Vernon 205, 206, 231
   Research Farm 232
   Tours 230-232
   Tractor 211, 212, 219*
   Seeds, Inc. 209
   Wholesale Society (CWS) 242
CORN Borers 291
   Hog Division of the AAA 308
   Husking Contests 79, 321-324
   Picking Contests 324, 325
   Pig Club 113
   To Europe 174
   Yield — U.S. 31, 92
Country Women's Council 160
COURTHOUSE Bell 18, 19*
   Cannon 19
   Fence 17*, 18
   First 17
   Monument 18*, 19*
   Second 17, 18*
   Third 18*, 19*
Cow Testing Assn. 115
Crabbs, Reynolds, Taylor Company 209
Crawford Petroleum 124
Crime Prevention 183
Crime TRAP 183
Criminal Code 157
Cripe, Elmer & Co. 122
Crop Activities 78
Crop Chemicals 209
Culligan of Delphi Inc. 312
Culligan Water Conditioning 138
CUTLER Bank 184
   Bridge 13*
   FFA 147
   Grain & Feed Co. 122
   Tel. Co. 58
Cyanamid Company 123

D

Danforth Foundation 132
Danny and His Dainty Dollies 176*
Darwin Pike 49

Day Hardware 122
Death Records Carroll County 22
Deer Creek Tel. Co. 55, 56, 58
Deer Creek Township Farm Bureau Play 178*
Deere, John 33
DELPHI A & P Store 137
   Businessmen's Assn. 115
   Chamber of Commerce 15, 116, 139
   Citizen 26
   City Council 15, 23
   Commercial Club 60
   Community School Corporation 16
   Daily Herald 27
   Dollar Journal 25
   Duroc Assn. 300
   Electric Light ompany 259
   FFA 143, 144, 145*, 146
   Gang 177
   Greenhouses 125
   Herald 25
   High School 16, 23
   Historical Markers 331, 334, 347
   Journal 25, 26
   Journal-Citizen 26
   Lime Company 2
   Limestone 2, 120, 122, 124, 131
   Lumber Company 120
   Merchants 124, 138
   Middle School 16
   Municipal Airport 15
   Oracle 25
   Products Co. 312
   Public Library 23
   Times 26
   Weekly Journal 25
Delta Theta Chi Sorority 122
Department of Veterinary Science 155
Diagnostic Laboratory at Purdue 155
Dial Room 24
Dial Telephone 52, 55, 56, 58
Dimitt Registered Hampshires 125
Dinner Bell 40
Dinner Calling Contest 118
Direct Primary Law 157
Directors of Extension 73
DISTRICT FARM BUREAU Co-op Directors 213
   Directors 151, 152
   Insurance Adjusters 192
   Meetings 171
DISTRICT 4-H Adult Leader Training Conference 112
   Rural Youth Study Clubs 241
Dixie Boys Quartet 118
Doctor, First 35
Donaldsonville Fertilizer Plant 203
Dougherty Mill 37
Dried Food 40
Duplex Machine Company 211
DuVall Family Completes 147 Years of 4-H 135*
Dye Lumber Co. 122

E

EastLawn School 16
Eastern Order Buyers Inc. 159
Eastman Kodak Outstanding Leader Award 138
Eaton and Cripe Motor Sales 122
Economic Report 187
Egg Carrying Contest 118
Egg Marketing 220
ELECTRIC LIGHTS First Towns 259
   Delphi 260, 261
   Other Carroll County Towns 260
EMERGENCY Relief Appropriation Act 261
   War Agent 76
   War Food Agent 81, 93
Entertainment Contest 118
Erny's Fertilizer Service 122, 125
Essay Contests 70, 182, 288, 289, 311*, 337
Esserman Tire Service 122
"Evolution" 300
Executive Order No. 7037 261
Exhibit Trains 73
Extension Committee 83*
EXTENSION HOMEMAKERS CLUB 94-110
   Chorus 98, 99*
   Chorus Trip to Washington, D.C. 99*
   Chorus Directors and Accompanists 98
   Chorus Officers and Members 1979 99
   Clothing Project 97
   Creed 94
   Fashion Show 98
   4-H Activities 97
   Location 101*
   Officers 95, 96*
   Prayer 94
   Presidents 95
   Project Lessons 96
   Seal 94*
EXTENSION HOMEMAKERS CLUBS 100-110, 124
   Adams 101
   Aim-Hi 101
   Burlington 101, 102
   Burrows 101, 102
   Carrollton 101, 102
   Carrolltonettes 101, 102
   Classie Lassies 101, 102
   Clay Harmony 101, 102, 103
   Cutler 101, 103
   Deer Creek Township 101, 103
   Dolly Madison 101, 103, 104
   Double Dozen 101, 104
   Flora 101, 104
   Forty Niners 101, 104, 105
   Friendly Circle 101, 105
   Goal Getters 101, 105
   Happy Homebuilders 101, 105, 106
   Home Endeavor 101, 106
   Jackson, 101, 106

Jefferson 101, 106
Junior Home Endeavor 101, 106, 107
Liberty Belles 101, 107
Madison 101, 107
Modern Homemakers 101, 107, 108*
Modern Mrs. 101, 108
Monroe 101, 108
Rock Creek 101, 108, 109
Silver Belles, 101, 109
Sycamores 101, 109
Tippecanoe 101, 109, 110
Washington 101, 110
EXTENSION Office 82
    Office Secretaries 82
    Research Support Committee 91
    Staff 83*

F

FACTS 92
Fairacre Farm 122
Fairfield Processing Company 70
FAIRS AT Camden 42, 43
    Delphi 42, 47, 69, 116, 117, 118
    Flora 43, 47, 118-126, 176
    Pittsburg 42
    Poplar Grove 43
FALL Crop Show 139
    Festivals at Flora 118
    Frolic 98
Fan Dance 178
FARM BUREAU 150-199
    Amateur Contests 180
    At County Fair 176
    Band 181*
    Chorus 168, 180
    Citizenship Seminar 162, 163
    Committees for 1979 199
    County Officers 173*, 195, 196
    District Directors 151, 152
    District Meeting 172*
    District Tax School 172*
    Districts 151
    Dues 164
    Early Township Meetings 176
    Essay Contests 182
    Field Men 164
    Fire and Tornado Insurance Company 189
    Foundation Inc. 161
    4-H Achievement Trip 128*, 129*
    Insurance 188-194
    Insurance Agents 190*, 191*, 192*, 193*
    Membership 164
    Modlin Memorial Fund 161, 169
    Mutual Insurance Company 189
    Office 192, 193*
    Office Secretaries 192*, 193*, 194*
    Pet and Hobby Club Leaders 168, 169*, 170*
    Pet and Hobby Club Members 169*, 170*
    Pet and Hobby Club Motto 169
    Picnics 174, 175, 176
    Public Relations Committee 185, 186*
    Public Speaking Contests 181, 182*
    Purchasing Department 165
    Queen Contest 168, 182
    Roll Call Captains 166*
    Safety Lane 183, 246
    Scholarships 184
    Serum Corp. 213
    S & E Directors Conference 171*
    State Convention 1934 188
    Tenure Awards 130, 131
    Thirty-Year Members 1949, 175*
    Tours 161, 162*
    Township Officers 196-199
    Women's Department 152, 167-169, 197-199
FARM BUREAU CO-OP ASSN. 200-239
    AIC 223
    Annual Meetings 233, 234*
    Bringhurst Elevator and Feed Mill 227, 228*
    Camden Mill 227*
    Central Carroll 222, 229*
    Common Stock 217
    Contracts With Oil Companies 204
    Co-op Acres 228
    Co-op Tractor 211, 212, 219*
    County Directors 213, 215, 223*, 234*, 235, 236
    District Directors 213, 214*
    District Field Men 214
    Egg Marketing 220
    Employees 217*, 218*, 219*, 220*, 221*, 222, 223*, 224*, 225, 226, 227*, 228*, 229*, 230*, 235
    Farm and Building Supplies 212
    Farm Machinery 211, 212, 219
    Feed 203, 204
    Fertilizer 202, 203, 223, 224*, 225*, 227*
    Field Men 214
    Finance 201, 215, 216
    Fiscal Year 217
    Grain Handling 207, 208, 209
    Growth 214, 239
    Hatcheries 210, 219, 220
    Indiana Plan 201
    Limited Liability Bonds 216
    Limited Liability Bond Signers 237, 238
    Milling Company 203, 204
    Net Worth 239
    Officers 234*, 235, 236
    OIL 204-206, 221, 222*, 231
        Company 204
        Compounding Plant 204
        Drivers 222*
        Pipe Line 205
        Plant at Camden 221, 222*
        Plant Managers 222
        Refinery at Mt. Vernon 205, 206, 231
        Wells and Refinery 205, 206
    P & C Family Foods 213
    Paint 221
    Participating Contract 202
    Poultry 210
    Poultry Breeding and Research Farm 204, 211
    Refunds 216, 217
    Research Farm 232
    Sales 239
    Savings 239
    Seed 209, 210
    Serum Co. 213
    Services, Inc. 212
    Stores at Delphi 217-221, 218*
    Summer Schools 240, 243
    Tours 230, 231*, 232
    Transportation 206
    War Years 226
    Weed Sprayer 221
    Wool Marketing 212, 213
    Yeoman Lumber Yard 226*
    Youth Activities 232, 233
FARM Investment in U.S. 31
    Population in U.S. 31
    Management Assn. Officers 87*
    Mortgage Company 189
    News 27, 28, 29, 30, 284
    Power 32, 33
    PROGRESS SHOW, 292, 325-329
        Contests 326, 327
        Cooperating Agencies 325, 326
        Demonstrations 326
        Electric Power 327
        Farms Involved 325
        Finance 328
        Food 327, 328
        Ham Radio 327
        Health and Safety 326
        Hosts 325*
        Housing 327
        Pickpockets 326
        Program 326
        Tadpole, Third Class 327
        Weather 327
    Publications 28
    Record Assn. 86*
    Research Department at Purdue 155
    Sales 40
    Week 25
FARMERS Co-op Packing Co. of Ind. 60
    Forage Research, Inc. 209
    Grain Dealers Assn. of Ind. 164
    Grain and Supply Company 38
    Home Administration 306*, 307
    Institutes 71, 74-77
    Mutual Insurance 126
    Mutual Tel. Co. 53
    National Grain Co-op 207
    Traders Life Insurance Company 64
    World Affairs 160, 161

CARROLL COUNTY RURAL ORGANIZATIONS

Union 201, 315
Union Central Exchange Inc. 212, 214
Farmland Industries Inc. 214
Federal Farm Board 207
Federal Farm Loan Assn. 304*
Federated Stores 137
Federated Marketing Service 159, 160
Federation of Farmers Assn. 160
Fertilizer Plants at Camden and Bringhurst 224*
Fire Departments 20
FIRST Airplanes 14, 15
    Automobile 13, 14*
    Auto Races 13, 14
    Auto Show 13
    Bridge Across Wabash 6
    Carroll County Historical Society 341
    Church 17
    Corn Husking Contest 321
    Courthouse 17
    County Agents 72, 76
    Doctor 35
    Electric Lights 259, 260
        Delphi 260
        Other Carroll County Towns 260
        Sudbury, Penn. 259
        Wabash, Ind. 259
    Extension Homemakers Club in Carroll County Indiana 110
    Indiana 94
    4-H Camp at Camp Tecumseh 116
    4-H Clubs 71, 111, 113
    Home Demonstration Agents 81
    Iron Bridge in Carroll County 8*
    Jail 20
    Local Grange in Carroll County 67
        U.S. 63
    Merchant 35
    Mill 36*
    Newspaper 25
    Radio Station 52
    Railroad 8
    REMC Lines Energized 268
        Pole Set 267*
        Security Light 279
    Rural Route in Carroll County 49, 66
        U.S. 65
    Rural Youth Clubs 244
    School 35
    Telephones 52
    TV 52
    White Settlers 35
Fleet Supply Inc. 122
Flies 40
Flood Control Commission 155
FLORA Aviation Corporation 15
    Centennial 1972 335
    Centennial Emblem 335*
    Community Building 319
    Community Club 73, 79, 115, 118, 119, 120, 122, 124, 180, 318, 319
    Concrete Tile Co. 312
    Enterprise Sentinel 27
    FFA 146, 147
    FFA Judging Teams 146
    Jr. Historical Society 342
    Monroe Public Library 24
    Municipal Airport 15
    Pike 49
    Produce 122, 184
    Rotary Club 187
    School 17
    Tel. Co. 54
Flying Farmers 320, 321
Food Science Laboratory at Purdue 157
Ford Grant, Ralph Sullivan 120
Ft. Wayne and Northern Indiana Traction Co. 10, 260
Ft. Wayne and Wabash Valley Traction Company 10
Fountain City Enterprise 27
4-H 111-141
    Achievement Programs 181
    Adult Leaders Banquet 137*, 138*
    Agricultural Exhibit Assn. 118, 119*
    Assistants 82
    Awards 124-141
    Band 132
    Beef Auction 114, 121, 122
    Cattle Barn 120
    Chorus 132
    Citizenship Shortcourse 130
    Commercial Beef Feeders 123*
    Community Building 121
    Club Conference 112, 126
    Club Congress 112, 126
    Club Creed 111
    Club Emblem 111*
    Club History 111
    Club Motto 111
    Club Pledge 111
    Club Roundup 112, 133, 134
    Clubs in 1921 114
    Day 117
    Enrollment 123
    Fall Fair and Festival 116, 117, 118
    Fair Book 121
    Fair Buildings 119, 120, 121
    Fair Pictures 124*, 125*, 128*, 139*, 140*, 141*
    Fair Queen Contest 122
    IFYE 112, 133, 160
    Junior Leaders 130, 131*, 136*
    Junior Leadership Training Conference Delegates 131*
    Key Club Award 127
    Leaders 137*, 138*
    Picnic 115
    Scholarships 134
    Tenure Awards 130, 131
Francesville Drain Tile Corp. 312
Fred Wheeler Implement Company 122
French Post Park 11, 20, 187
FS Services Inc. 214
FUTURE FARMERS OF AMERICA 142-149
    Alumni Assn. 143
    Chapters Burlington 148
        Burnettsville and Twin Lakes 148
        Camden 148
        Cutler 147
        Delphi 143, 144, 145*, 146
        Flora 146, 147
        Rossville 147
    Cornhusking Contests 144
    Creed 142
    Degrees 143
    Emblem 142*
    Motto 142

G

Garrison, D.A. Trucking Company 312
Gasohol 158, 206
Georgetown Stone Quarry 5, 7
German Raiffeisen Supply Central Coop. 209
Gillam Schoolhouse 49
Gold Kist, Inc. 208, 214
Gold Medal Projects 78, 84, 85
Gold Proof Elevator 208
Golden Cross Bantam Sweet Corn 209
Golden Gate Tour 161, 162
Good Luck Flour 38
Goodyear Awards 313*
Grain Exports 208
Grain Marketing 207, 208, 209
Grain Marketing Associations 61
Grain Terminals 208
Grain Threshing Separator 41*
Grand Canal 5
Grandma's Receet 285
GRANGE 63-70
    Achievements 70
    Business Ventures 63
    Carroll County 67-70
    Ceres 63
    Degrees 63
    Emblem 63*
    First Local 63
    Float at Old Settlers 68*
    Flora 63
    Future Of 70
    Indiana 66
    Junior 66
    League Federation (GLF) 64, 230
    Legislation 64, 65, 66
    National 63
    National Bicentennial Year Cookbook 66
    Pomona 63, 67
    Purpose 63
    Star in the West #2057 67
    State Meetings at Delphi 66, 67
    Stores 64

Subordinate 63
Tipwa #2300 68
Welcome Inn #2227 68
Women 66
Granger Laws 65
Gravel Hill Schoolhouse 49
Gravel Roads 11
Green Acres Soil Service 312
Green Tree Feeds 122
Gross Income Tax Bill 154
Guernsey Calf Club 114
Gulf Central Pipe Line Company 203
Gut Creek 59

H

Halstead, W. C. and Company 23
Hanenkratt Grain Co. 122
Hargraves Motor Sales 120
Hatch Act 65, 71
Hathaway Family Singers 180, 329*
Heinold Commodities 122
Heinold Hog Market 122
Hello Girl, Last 58
Hi Grade Food Company 122
Hillbilly Musicians 118
Hillcrest Elementary School 16
HISTORICAL MARKER 6, 317, 331, 334, 336, 345-348
 Adams Mill 317
 Burlington 347
 Burnett's Creek Arch 6*
 Camden and Jackson Township 345*, 348
 Carrollton on the Wabash 346
 Delphi 331, 334, 347
 Flora 336*, 346
 Gen. Samuel Milroy and Milroy Family 331, 347
 Treaty of St. Mary's 334
 Pittsburg 347
 Pyrmont and 1812 Hopkins' Expedition 348
Historical Sites 187
HISTORICAL SOCIETY 341-346
 Charter Members 344, 345, 346
 Directors 342*
 Museum 343, 344
 Museum Demonstrations 343*, 344*
HOG Barn 120
 Calling Contest 118, 174, 303*, 332
 Jog 303
 Point 61
Holding Company Law 156
Home Demonstration Agents 81*, 82*, 93
Home Economics Club Variety Show 100*
Homemakers Exchangees 95
Homemakers Short Course at Purdue 161
Homer and Jethro 326
HOOSIER Christmas Special 162
 Democrat 26, 27, 122
 Energy 294

Farm Bureau Life Insurance Company 189
Farmer 151
Farmer Northwest Expedition 162*
4-H Leadership Center 132, 134
Gold Medal Club 84
Harvest Special 162
Travel Service 162
Hopewell Store 297
Horse Pulling Contest 118
Horse Thief Detective Assn. 47, 48
Hospitalization Insurance 194
Howe Fund 24
Huckster Routes 59
Husband Calling Contests 118, 303*, 332
Husking Bees 39
Hybrid Corn 209
Hygrade Foods, Inc. 147

I

Illinois Farm Supply Company 203
Indian Reserves 2, 3
INDIANA Agricultural Cooperative Act 153
 Agricultural Marketing Assn. 161
 Centennial 1916 330
 Chain Store Council 137, 138
 Condensed Milk Company 74, 115, 184
 Crop Improvement Assn. 132
 Electric Assn. 124
 Extension Homemakers Assn. 94
INDIANA FARM BUREAU 150-164, 190, 200
 Branch Warehouses 160
 Cooperative Assn. 200-215, 222, 232, 240, 243
 Emblem 150*
 Offices 190
 Presidents 152
 Purchasing Department 160, 200
INDIANA Farm Fresh Market 161
 Farmers Grain Dealers Assn. 160, 207
 Federation of Farmers Associations 151, 153, 164
 4-H Foundation 112, 134, 135
 FFA Chapter 143
 Grain 2, 208
 Grain Producers, Inc. 207, 208, 243
 Home Demonstration Assn. 94
 Home Economics Assn. 94, 95
 Limestone 10
 Plan for Cooperatives 201
 Probate Code 157
 REMC's 124
 Rural News 287
 Rural Youth 244-246
 Service Corporation 268
 Sesquicentennial Emblem 333*
 Soft Wheat Growers Assn. 207
 State Grange 160, 164
 State Livestock Sanitary Board 156

Statewide REC 292
Statewide REMC 261, 262, 267
Statewide REMC Act 154, 261
Swine Breeders 213
Vocational Education Act 72
Vocational Technical College 153, 156
Wool Growers Assn. 212, 213, 243
INDIANAPOLIS 500 Mile Race 14
 Motor Speedway 14
 Public Elevator 208
 Stockyards Marketing Institute 147
 Traction Terminal 10
Intangible Tax Bill 154
INTERNATIONAL Farm Youth Exchange (IFYE) 112
 4-H Youth Exchange (IFYE) 133, 160
 IFYE Caravan 133
 IFYE Representatives 133
 Fund 160
 Harvester Company 143
 Livestock, Hay and Grain Show 115, 116
 Minerals and Chemical Corporation 203
Interstate Commerce Act 65
Interstate Highway Construction Program 157
Interurbans 10*, 260
Ivy Tech 153, 156

J

Jackson-Kitchell Inc. 122
Jackson-Lee Inc. 16
Jackson-Lee-Pearson, Inc. 121, 122, 125, 312
Jackson Township Farm Bureau 125
J Bar D Quarter Horse Farm 124
Jane Award 98, 107
Jersey Calf Club 115
Julius Clothing Co. 122
Junior Leader Training Conference 112, 131*
J. P. Court System 157

K

Keener Packing Company 122
Kellogg, W. K. Foundation 92
Kerlin Elevator 120, 122, 312
Kerlin Feed Mill 120, 122, 124, 138, 312
Kilowatt Ours 28, 275, 277, 284, 285, 286
Kingan & Company 122
Kitchen Kabinet Orchestra 118
Kiwanis Club 112
Knightstown Banner 25
Koehler Bros. Nursery 105
Koheo Light and Power Company 260

386 • CARROLL COUNTY RURAL ORGANIZATIONS

Kroger Store, Delphi 137
Ku Klux Klan 48, 49
Kuhner Packing Company 122

L

Lafayette Cooperative Elevator
    Company 207
Lafayette Production Credit Assn.
    191, 305
Lake Delphi 1
Lake Freeman 1, 4
Lancaster Bridge 13
LAND Grant Act 71
    Grant Colleges 65
    Judging 89
    O'Lakes, Inc. 208, 214
    Use Planning Program 89
Landmark Co-op Assn. 203, 208,
    215
Last Street Fair in Delphi 46
Lawyer Bill 155
Leiter Funeral Home 122
Let There Be Light 259
Limited Liability Bonds of CCFBCA
    216
    Bond Signers 237, 238
Literary Club 25
LIVESTOCK and Meat Caravan 84
    Breeders Assn. 302
    Breeders and Seed Producers
        Assn. 302
    Marketing 158
    Marketing Associations 61, 165,
        216
    On Farms in Carroll County 32
    Projects 78
    Scales 120
Logansport Livestock Yards, Inc.
    122, 124
"Long Chief" 300
Lower Deer Creek Church 298
Loy Roofing Company 138
Lulabelle and Scotty 326

M

Magic Show 177
Maish Act 72
Mann Chevrolet-Buick Inc. 122
Mann Chevrolet Company 122
Marble Hill Nuclear Power Station
    294
Marblehead Lime Company 2
Marketing Farm Products 59-62
Martin Farms Inc. 122
Massey-Ferguson, Inc. 312
Massey Harris Company 219
McCall's Pattern Company 70
Meadowview York & Hamp Farm
    122
Mechanical Corn Picking Contests
    324, 325
Medical Service 21
Medusa Aggregates Company 2
Meet Your Neighbor 29

Melody Men 282*
Membership Campaigns 166, 263
Mentzer Tavern 6*
Merchant, First 35
Meredith Loan Fund 94
Methodist Church at Delphi 17
Michigan Road 3, 11, 12
Mid-Continent Tel. Co. 54
Midland Cooperative, Inc. 214
Mid States Feeder Pigs 122
Midwest Producers Creameries, Inc.
    213
Milk Dumping Bill 154
Millinery Project 97
Milroy Memorial 331
Modern Homemakers H.E. Club
    Officers 108*
Modlin Memorial Committee 161
Modlin Memorial Fund 161, 169
Monday Club 23
Monon Railroad 9
Monroe Meade Memorial Trophy 124
Monroe Township F.B. Quartet 178*
Monsanto Fertilizer Company 225
Montgomery County Farm Bureau
    204
Montgomery Ward & Company 64
Monticello Implement Company 122
Monticello School 16
Montman Mill 36
Moore Singers 116
Moorman Feeds 122
Moppets 254*
More Fun 177
Morning Star Corp. 312
Morning Star Fertilizer 122
Morrill Act 65
Mosquitoes 89
Motor Vehicle Inspection Law 156
Mount & Son Hardware 120, 312
Murphy Fountain 19
Musical Wades 283
Mutual Telephone Co. of Logansport
    52

N

Nail Driving Contest 118
NATIONAL Award Programs 134
    Cooperatives, Inc. 201
    Electric Code 265
    Farm Bureau Meetings 170
    Farm Machinery Co-operative
        212
    Farmers Organization 316
    4-H Citizenship Shortcourse 130
    4-H Club Conference 112, 126
    4-H Club Congress 112, 126
    Grange Mutual Insurance Company 64
    Home Demonstration Council
        95
    Livestock Producers Assn.,
        Chicago 159
    Poultry Tribune Trophy 211
    Rural Electric Cooperative Assn.
        292

Scholarship Funds 134
    Wool Marketing Assn. 213
Natural Resources 1, 2
Natural Resources Leadership Camp
    132
New Generation Young Farmers 149
Nichols Durocs 122
Northcutt Bros. 184
Northern Indiana Entomology Field
    Day 138
Nutrition Project 97
"Nubbin Derby" 321
Number of Farms in Carroll County
    32
    U.S. 31

O

Oakridge Farms 122
Oaks and Minix 184
Ockley Elevator 227
OHIO Cultivator Company 212
    Farm Bureau 201
    Farm Bureau Cooperative Assn.
        212
    Wool and Sheep Growers Assn.
        212
OLD SETTLERS Assn. 329, 330
    Centennial 1955 331, 332*, 333
OLDER YOUTH Camp 244
    Clubs 244
    Council 245
Oliver's Boarding Kennels 125
"One Horse" Meeting 176
Open Door Law 158
OPERATION Brainpower 88
    Citrus 183
    Traffic Count 182
Oracle Club 23
Oracle Press 312
Organized Farmer 151
Out of the Wastebasket 29
Outdoor Cookery 89

P

Pace Act 278
Pacific All West Expedition 162
Packing Plants 59, 60, 61
Paralysis in Poultry 210
Parcel Post 51, 66
Parke County 187
Parke County Covered Bridge
    Festival 187
Party Line 52
Patchett Sales & Service 122
Patrons of Husbandry 63
Payne's Stores 124
Pearson Farm Service 122, 312
Pearson, R. E. Sales & Service 122,
    138
Penn Central Railroad 9
Pennies for Friendship 160
People Fed Per Farmer in U.S. 31, 92
Perdue's Electrical Service 121

Pickering Seed Co. 312
Pickpockets 321, 326
Picture Projectors 183
Pioneer Hi-Bred, Inc. 312
Pioneer Seed Corn Co. 122
Pioneers Social Life 39
PITTSBURG 8*
    Dam 7
    Fair 42
    School 16
Plank Toll Roads 11
Planning and Zoning 90
Plant City Phosphate Complex 203
Plant Science Jamboree 132
Pleasant Run Schoolhouse 51
Poland China Pig Club 113
Population of Carroll County 1
Pork Barbecue 117
Pork Chop Barbecue 123*
Pork Demonstration 183
Pork Festival 303*
Potawatomi 2, 3, 11
Poultry Research Farm at Lafayette 204, 211
Poultry Tribune 211
Power Generation 294
Prairie Farmer WLS Farm Progress Show 84, 325-329
Premier Feeds 122
Premier Hybrids Inc. 122
Presbyterian Church 18, 23
Pro-Ag Equipment Co. 312
P & C Family Foods 213
PRODUCERS Commission Assn. 158, 184
    Commission Co. 122
    Livestock Assn. of Ohio 159
    Marketing Assn. 159, 213
        Branch Markets 159
    Marketing Assn. at Klondike 159
    Marketing Assn. at Logansport 159
Production Credit Assn. 138, 305
Product Research Laboratory 204
Public Parks 20
Public Service Company of Indiana 124, 278
Pullorum in Poultry 210
Pumpkin Contest 327
Pumpkin Seed 29
Pumpkinville Pike 13
PURDUE Ag Alumni Assn. 87, 88*
    Ag Alumni Assn. Fish Fry 89
    Glee Club 283
    University 71
    Threshing Crew 118
Purduettes 283
Pure Seed Law 153
Pure Seed Processing 122

Q

Queen Contests 168, 182, 331, 333*, 335
Questers Club 317

R

Radio Station, First 52
Radio Station WSAL 124
Railroads 8, 9, 10
Rainbow Restaurant 125
Randolph Bakery 124
Ranger Products 120
Re-codification of Animal Health Laws 156
Red Mill 36, 62
Refinery at Mt. Vernon 205, 206, 231
Regional Co-operatives 214
Rehm Grain & Nutrena Feeds 122
Ric-Mar Bassetts 125
Rinehart Auction & Real Estate 122
Ritchey Dog House 122
Roach's Mill 36
Road Numbers 187
Roads and Bridges 13
Robeson Equipment, Inc. 122
Robinson's Mill 36*
Rochdale Pioneers 241, 242
Rochdale Principles 242
Rock Creek Conservancy District 314
Rockfield Poland China Breeders Assn. 300
Rockfield Tel. Co. 57
Rodkey, Ralph R. Inc. 125
Role of Extension Service 92
ROSSVILLE Consolidated School Corporation 17
    FFA 147
    History Club 341
Rotary Club 112, 187, 136, 137
Rotary 4-H Leaders Training Conference 136, 137*
Roundup 112, 133, 134
Rural Acceptance Corporation 189
Rural Church Improvement Contest 161
REMC Carroll County 121, 124, 259-299
    Achievement Trip 127
    Act 155
    Allotment 264
    American Institute of Cooperation 292
    American Legion Award 292
    Appliance Sales Campaign 279
    Attorneys 272*, 273
    Auditorium 276
    Award of Merit 291
    Building Lines 267, 277, 278
    Building Load 279
    Capital Credits 280, 281
    Certificate of Indebtedness 267
    Changes in Operation 276
    Cooperative Finance Corporation 293
    County Farm 264
    County Map 263, 264
    Credit to Donated Help 269
    Directors 283*, 295, 296*, 297*
    Essay Contests 288-291
    Farm Progress Show 292, 327
    First Annual Meeting of Members 269
    First Pole 267*
    First Trucks 281*
    First 25 Years 284
    4-H Fair 292
    Future 295
    Honor Roll 284
    Hoosier Energy 294
    Ice Storm 1967 280
    Incorporators 262, 266, 295*
    Indiana Statewide REC 292
    Indiana Statewide REMC 261, 262, 267
    Letter to REA Administrator 269-271
    Local Activities 267
    Lines Energized 268
    Long Term Obligations 298
    Maintaining Lines 274, 276, 279
    Managers 272*
    Meetings of Members 264, 265, 266, 269, 282, 283
    Member Service Director 274
    Membership Campaign 263
    Miss Rural Electrification 293
    More Power Provided 278
    National Rural Electric Co-op Assn. 292, 293
    News Letter 284
    Office 218*, 266, 273, 275*
    Office Employees 273*
    Office Established 266
    Office Moved 275
    Operation and Maintenance Personnel 274*
    Project Completed 269
    Publicity 284-287
    Radio Equipment 280
    Replacing Poles 280
    Rural Electrification Act of 1936 261
    Rural Electrification Administration 261, 262
    Rural Electrification News 280
    RFD 4, 287
    Scholarships 287, 288
    Security Lights 279
    Special Events and Activities 291
    Statistics 299
    Storage Building 276, 277*
    Trucks and Equipment 280, 281*
    Wabash Valley Power Assn. 294, 295
    War Years 277
    Welding Schools 291*, 292
    Willie Wiredhand 293*
    Wind Storm 1953 280
    Winners of Labor Free Writing 297, 298
    Wiring Buildings 265
Rural Electrification 85, 260, 261
Rural Electrification Act 65, 154, 155, 261
Rural Free Delivery 49-62, 65, 66
RFD Mail Boxes 50*
Rural Insurance Agency 190
RURAL YOUTH 112, 120, 125, 232, 240-258

Activities 247*, 248*, 249*, 250*, 252*, 254*, 255*
Aims 245
Charter Members 241
Chorus 232, 253*-256*
Contests 246, 248, 249, 253, 255
District Organization 244
Educational Tours 252, 253
Emblem 240*
Indiana 244-246
Objectives 245
Officers 247*, 248*, 249*, 250*, 251*, 258
Reunions 256, 257*
Study Club 240-243
Training Schools 240*, 243*, 244

S

Safety Lane 183, 246
Safety Seminar 163
St. Mary's Treaty 2
Salt Pond Field 206
Sanitary Landfill 20
Schlosser Brothers Creamery 115
Schmear Kase 76
Scholarships 134, 184, 287, 288
School Enumeration Records 22
Schools 16, 17, 35, 36
Scott-Robeson-Yeager Orchestra 174
Sears Roebuck 265
Sedalia Elevator 125
Seed Staining Act 209
Seedonics Hybrid Corn Co. Inc. 122
Select Seed Hybrids, Inc. 312
Share the Fun 133
Sheep Dipping 182
Sherman Antitrust Act 65
Shirar Feed Co. Inc. 125
Short Courses 73
Show Ring 120
Singing Sheriff 283
Sisson Jewelry Store 125
Sites Trio 116
Skiles & Sons Excavating 312
Smear Family 137*
Smith Act 71
Smith Construction Company 16, 122
Smith-Hughes Act 65
Smith-Lever Act 65, 72, 76, 150
Smith Tire Service 122, 125
Smock, W. C. Company 184
Snake Heads 10
Snoeberger Feed Mill and Coal Yard 227
Social and Educational Department 152, 167-169, 197-199
Social Life of Pioneers 39
Soil Conservation Act of Indiana 155
SOIL CONSERVATION DISTRICT
    Airlift 311
    Annual Meetings 311, 312*
    Committee 309
    Established 310
    Earthmover 312

Employees 314*
Essay Contest 311*
Field Days 310
Goodyear Award Winners 313*
Green Pasture Contest 313
Neighborhood Groups 311
Petition Signers 309, 310
Referendum 310
Sponsors 312
Supervisors 310, 311*, 314, 315*
Soil and Water Conservation District 1, 125, 132, 309-315, 317
Soil Savers Young Farmers 149
Soldiers and Sailors Monument 18*, 19*
Southern States Cooperatives, Inc. 214
Sovereigns of Industry 64
Soyland Seeds, Camden (Fouts Bros.) 184
Spears and Case 59
Spears, Dugan and Company 59
Spitler's Field 15
Star Roller Mill 38, 122, 312
Stark & Wetzel Banquet 123
Stark & Wetzel Trip 127
STATE and National Mechanical Corn Picking Contests 324, 325
    Corn Husking Contest 79, 321, 322
    Excise Tax 157
    Fair Achievement Trip 127
    Fair Boys School 126
    Fair Camp 126, 152
    Fair Girls School 115, 125
    Fair School Scholarships 134
    Farm Bureau Meetings 171
    Farm Mutual Auto Insurance Company 184
    Fish and Game Laws 157
    4-H Band 132
    4-H Chorus 132
    4-H Club History 111
    4-H Scholarships 134
    Highways 11
    Junior Leaders Conference 131*
    Junior Leader Council 131
    Legislature from 1921 to 1979 153-158
    Livestock Sanitary Board 210
    YMCA 22
Statewide REMC 261
Steinhart Grain Company 39
Stephan's IGA 124
Stewart, Fred J. Seed Sales & Service 312
Stoney Pike Sale Barn 122
Stouse, Charles Service Station 122
Stranathan Threshing Ring 41
Street Fairs at Delphi 43-47
Stuffed Toy Contest 70
Stuntz Yeoman Company 2, 120
Sunset Bill 158
Superior Parts 190
Swine Breeders Pure Serum Company 213
Sycamore Row 13

T

Tax and Legislative Department of FB 152
Teays Valley 1
TELEPHONES 52-59, 187
    First 52
    Operators, Delphi 53*
        Flora 54*
Television, First 52
Tenbrook Sales 122
Tennessee Copper and Chemical Company 202
Tenure Awards 130, 131
Thompson Funeral Home 122, 138
Thompson's Drug Store 122
Three J's (Joyce Sisters) 133, 254*, 311
Threshing Rings 40
Tipwa Grange Officers 70*
Toad Lane 241, 242
TODD, Dean Seeds 122
    George & Son 120
    Hybrid Corn Co. 124, 132, 312
    McLemore Motors, Inc. 138
    Seed Company 121, 122
Toepfer, Alfred C. Export, Inc. 208
Ton-Litter Club 78
Top Twenty 283
TRAP (Total Registration of All Property) 183
Towns 3
Township Farm Bureau Officers 196
Township Farm Bureau Organizations 124
Townships 3
Towpath Walkers 7
Trash Disposal 187
Treaty of the Wabash 3
Triangle Feeds 122, 312
Tri-County Fairs 43
Tri-County Institutes 75
Tri State Trader 25
True Love and Good Oil 204
Tug of War 117*
20th Century Pioneer 206, 207
Twin Lakes FFA 148
Twin Lakes School Corporation 16
Twin Pines 95

U

Ulen Construction Company 266, 267
Union Bank & Trust Company 120, 122, 124, 138, 312
UNITED Cooperatives of Ontario, Canada 208
    Cooperatives, Inc. 204
    Farm Bureau Mutual Insurance Company 189
    Feeds, Inc. 122
    Fund 186
U.S. Bicentennial 1976 337
    Bicentennial Emblem 337*
    Census of Agriculture 32
    Department of Agriculture 65,

71, 150
Grain Growers Assn. 207
Universal Cooperatives 210
Use Good Material 264

V

Valentines 98
Value of Farm Products Sold—
    Carroll County 32
Vandalia Railroad 9
Vesicular Exanthema in Hogs 156
Veterinary Science School at Purdue 156
VOCATIONAL Agriculture Teachers
    at Carroll H.S. 147
    Agriculture Teachers at Delphi 146
    Education 65
Voorhees Lumber Company 122

W

WABASH AND ERIE CANAL 4-8
    Aqueducts and Arches 5
    Boats 7
    Bridges and Locks 5
    Burnett's Creek Arch 5*
    End 8
    Maintenance 7
    Revenue 7
Wabash and Erie Canal, Inc. 317, 318
    Charter Members 318
    Emblem 317*
    Officers and Directors 318
WABASH College Glee Club 283
    Railroad 8
    River 3, 4
    Valley Power Assn. 294
Waddell's IGA 122, 124
Wakanda (Ouibachi) 127
Wallman's Certified Foods of Delphi 124, 138
Walnut Stump Church 49
War Production Board Orders 277
Ward, Montgomery & Co. 64
Washington, D.C. Trips 127
Water Power Mills 36, 37, 38
Wertheimer Cattle Company 120
Western Banner 25
What is an American? 286
What Rural Electrification Means to
    My Community 288, 289
Wheat Pools 207
Wheat Production Assn. 308
White Settlers, First 35
Whiteman Bros. Elevator 122, 125, 138, 174
WILD CAT Masonic Lodge 37
    Post Office 37
    Utilities Company 37
WILO Radio 122
WILSON Farm Service 122, 138, 312
    Foods Corp. 122
    Packing Company 123, 159
Wiring the Buildings 265
Women in Farm Bureau 152
Women in Grange 66
Wool Marketing 212, 213
Wright Brothers 14
Wynkoop Pharmacy 138

Y

Yeager and Sullivan, Inc. 122, 125, 312
YEOMAN Lumber Company 225
    School 16
    Tel. Co. 56
Young Farmers 185
Young Farmers Tour 232
Young Peoples Cooperative Study
    Club 241, 244
Youth Agents 82, 83*, 93

Z

Zinn Kitchens Inc. 122